Personality Disorders in Modern Life

Personality Disorders in Modern Life

SECOND EDITION

THEODORE MILLON

and

Seth Grossman
Carrie Millon
Sarah Meagher
Rowena Ramnath

WILEY

JOHN WILEY & SONS, INC.

Library of Congress Cataloging-in-Publication Data:

Personality disorders in modern life.—2nd ed. / Theodore Millon . . . [et al.].
    p. cm.
  Rev. ed. of: Personality disorders in modern life / Theodore Millon and Roger D. Davis. c2000.
  Includes bibliographical references (p.).
  ISBN 0-471-23734-5
  1. Personality disorders. I. Millon, Theodore. II. Millon, Theodore. Personality disorders
in modern life.
  RC554.M537   2004
  616.85′81—dc22
                                      2004043374

Foreword

It is a pleasure to introduce the reader to the second edition of this highly acclaimed volume, *Personality Disorders in Modern Life.* The first edition, which I had the honor to review for *Contemporary Psychology: APA Review of Books,* was excellent, and the second edition by Theodore Millon and his team of coauthors—Seth Grossman, Carrie Millon, Sarah Meagher, and Rowena Ramnath—expands and updates the first. The senior author of this volume has reached the status of icon in the psychological sciences and has inspired a generation of workers in the field of personality theory, assessment, psychotherapy, and nosology. He is almost single-handedly responsible for the resurgence of a nearly moribund area in psychology—personology, the study of the human personality system, of interest to humankind since the dawn of consciousness—and the concomitant development of language, cognition, and culture—only a recent development. Personality theory nearly became extinct during the latter half of the past century, dismissed as a useless artifact of "prescientific psychology." However, the advances of clinical sciences, such as diagnosis, classification, and psychotherapy, spearheaded by Millon, beckoned leaders in the field to prevent this clinically and socially useful area of discourse and science from going the way of other prescientific precursors of our field, such as phrenology—the study of the contours of the head and their relationships to various neuropsychological functions.

As I described in my review of the original edition, published at the turn of the century, this volume represented significant advances over the first 100 years of modern psychology. Advances in the fields of psychotherapy, psychopathology, and personality theory have been substantial. Over a century ago, William James (1890) published his two-volume work, *Principles of Psychology,* which many consider a landmark in psychology and which ushered in the birth of modern psychology. Certainly, there were other groundbreaking works that had similar impact on the clinical sciences, such as Freud's (1900) *Interpretation of Dreams,* which during the same time span, gave birth to psychoanalysis and what many consider to be the beginning of modern psychotherapy. Over the course of the first century of modern psychology, many have attempted to elaborate the realm of the personality system; but few have been as comprehensive in this endeavor as Millon. This volume represents the accumulated wisdom and theoretical, clinical, and empirical findings over the past century. It affords us the opportunity to be introduced or reawakened by one of the most interesting subjects of our time: personality and its disorders. The insight offered in this volume allows all of us to understand the complexities of the plethora of converging forces that leads to alterations in personality and how they are represented, conceptualized, and treated.

The audience for this text is advanced undergraduate and graduate students, but it will serve as an introduction to all interested readers and excite even the most hesitant reader. Its broad coverage introduces undergraduate students to the fascinating world of clinical sciences with easy-to-follow case illustrations through the eyes of a student struggling to understand how these constructs and theories apply to clinical reality. For advanced students, this text serves as a consolidation of Millon's other works and introduces his conceptual system, which, for many, will lead to the reading of his other groundbreaking volumes on the topic. As a practicing clinician and personality theorist, I share Millon's view that personality is the main organizing system of humankind,

and any understanding or attempt at altering the suffering encountered in clinical practice requires a deep appreciation of the domains of human personality.

For those pursuing careers in the social or clinical sciences, this volume is one for
your library of reference books. I guarantee that you will refer to it often. The systematic theoretical modeling and self-other awareness that this volume engenders will enrich those students who are attracted to other disciplines. All of us at one time will
encounter individuals similar to those described in this volume. It is important that we
not use personality labels pejoratively or stigmatize those who suffer from personality
dysfunction but, rather, that we develop a deeper appreciation for the variety of personality types profiled in this volume. This appreciation will enable those in various
careers to be more effective when assigned a narcissistic boss or when reading about a
psychopathic individual who preys on society, such as some of the infamous figures
presented in this text. Those in the medical professions will gain a keener appreciation
for their patients and for how their psychological immune system, as Millon has
termed it, functions and dysfunctions under stressful conditions.

Millon and his team have carefully laid the groundwork for you to build a working
model of human personality functioning and dysfunction. The framework is based on
the dominant psychiatric model of diagnosing personality disorders but provides an
even richer, more textured system, pioneered by Millon and based on evolutionary
principles and clearly articulated domains of functioning. You will begin to acquire an
appreciation for how clinical syndromes such as anxiety, depression, and eating disorders emanate from the unique configuration of the personality system, which will
allow you to embark on an incomparable journey of self- and other understanding. You
will be challenged with many of the constructs and terminology, but familiarization
with Millon's system has both clinical utility and value in understanding the unique
and shared characteristics of the human race. Dr. Millon is one of the most prominent
personality theorists of contemporary times; his work will inspire successive generations, just as William James and Sigmund Freud did more than 100 years ago. Enjoy
the journey!

JEFFREY J. MAGNAVITA, PHD, ABPP
Fellow, American Psychological Association
Adjunct Professor in Clinical Psychology, University of Hartford
Director, Connecticut Center for Short-Term Dynamic Psychotherapy

References

Freud, S. (1900). The interpretation of dreams. In J. Strachey (Ed.), *The standard edition of the complete
    psychological works of Sigmund Freud* (Vols. 4 & 5, pp. 1–715). London: Hogarth Press.
James, W. (1890). *The principles of psychology* (Vols. 1 & 2). New York: Henry Holt.
Magnavita, J. J. (2001). A century of the "scientific" study of personality: How far have we come? [Book
    Review: *Personality disorders in modern life*]. *Contemporary Psychology: APA Review of Books,
    46*(5), 514–516.

Preface

The first edition of my *Disorders of Personality* text (1981) was widely regarded as the classic book in the field. Given its coordination with a theory of personality and psychopathology and with the then newly published *DSM-III,* it gained immediate acceptance among mental health professionals, the audience for which it was intended. As the years wore on, however, the readership of the book began to change. With the emergence of personality disorders as a distinct axis in the *DSM,* doctoral programs began to instruct their students on the role played by personality in creating and sustaining psychopathology. By the mid-1980s, my *Disorders of Personality* text gradually became required reading in most graduate programs, and even enjoyed some use at the undergraduate level.

With the publication of the *DSM-IV* in 1994, the *Disorders* text was ready for revision. Published in 1996, the second edition was greatly revised and expanded, its 800 pages of two-column text reflecting growing interest in personality disorders. Again, the book was an immediate success at the professional level. Unfortunately, with its increased length and complex writing style, the book was no longer appropriate for the limited background and experience of undergraduate students.

In mid-1998, a group at the Institute for Advanced Studies in Personology and Psychopathology began working in earnest on a revision for advanced undergraduate and beginning graduate students. About half of the material was simplified from the extensive *Disorders of Personality,* second edition, and about half the material was essentially new. This text was entitled *Personality Disorders in Modern Life,* published in 1999.

Students found the *Modern Life* text both informative and absorbing. Instructors found it well-organized and easy to teach. An optimal balance was struck between abstract concepts and concrete clinical case materials. Students appreciated the vivid examples that demonstrate personalities "in action." To that end, each of the clinical chapters began with a case vignette, which was then discussed in terms of the *DSM-IV.* The result was a cross-fertilization that brought the rather dry diagnostic criteria to life for the student and provided a concrete anchoring point to which student and instructor could refer again and again as the discussion of the personality was elaborated. The psychodynamic, cognitive, interpersonal, and evolutionary sections referred back to the cases as a means of providing a clearer understanding of otherwise abstract and difficult to understand concepts. This was true even where the text discussed the development of a particular personality disorder, which was then linked back to the concrete life history of the particular case. Students thus saw not only how psychological theory informs the study of the individual, but also how the individual came to his or her particular station and diagnosis in life. Each chapter included two or three cases interwoven in the body of the text.

This new second edition of *Modern Life* has added two important elements to strengthen the text. First, we added a full chapter on personality development (Chapter 3) so that the origins and course of personality pathology could be more fully and clearly articulated. And second, with the growth of empirical research in the field, considerable reference is now made throughout the book to spell out supporting data for ideas contained in the text.

While case studies provide continuity between concrete clinical phenomena and abstract concepts and theories, other sections of each chapter address continuity in different ways. Since there is no sharp division between normality and pathology, an entire section of each clinical chapter is devoted to their comparison and contrast. The introductory case receives a detailed discussion here, and it is shown exactly why he or she falls more toward the pathological end of the spectrum. Such examples help students understand that diagnostic thresholds are not discrete discontinuities, but instead are largely social conventions, and that each personality disorder has its parallels in a personality style that lies within the normal range. Each chapter invites students to find characteristics of such normal styles within themselves, thus opening up their interest for the material that follows. The hope is that students will learn something about their own personalities, and what strengths and weaknesses issue therefrom. Continuity between normality and abnormality in personality gives the text a "personal growth agenda" that most books in psychopathology lack.

In addition, the text also focuses on the continuity between the personality pathology of Axis II and the Axis I disorders, such as anxiety and depression. As practitioners have recognized, depression in a narcissist is very different from depression in an avoidant. While some sources present only comorbidity statistics for Axis II and Axis I, our contention is that the next generation of clinical scientists will be best prepared if it is understood why certain personalities experience the disorders they do. When a dependent personality becomes depressed, for example, what are the usual causes, and how do they feel to the person concerned? Once students understand how the cognitive, interpersonal, and psychodynamic workings of each personality lead them repeatedly into the same problems again and again, they are ready for the last section of each chapter, focused on psychotherapy.

We are pleased to report that an excellent 240-minute videotape entitled "*DSM-IV Personality Disorders: The Subtypes*" has been produced and is distributed by Insight Media (800-233-9910, www.Insight-Media.com), psychology's premier publisher of videos and CD-Roms. It is available for purchase by instructors and students who wish to view over 60 case vignettes that illustrate all *DSM-IV* personality prototypes and subtypes, as interviewed by psychologists and discussed by the senior author of this book.

Thanks and credit for this second edition are owed to each member of the team of young associates at the Institute, all co-authors of this text. In addition, the Institute's executive director, Donna Meagher, provided an organizing force throughout, drawing the various pieces together into a coherent whole. We would also like to thank the many hundreds of instructors and thousands of students who have offered constructive suggestions that have made this second edition even more useful and attractive than the first.

THEODORE MILLON, PhD, DSc
Institute for Advanced Studies
in Personology and Psychopathology

Coral Gables, Florida
IASPP@aol.com

Contents

ix

Personality Disorders in Modern Life

Chapter 1

Personality Disorders: Classical Foundations

Objectives

- What is *personality?*
- Distinguish among personality, character, and temperament.
- What makes a personality disordered?
- What is the *DSM?*
- Make a list of terms important in the study of personality and its disorders.
- Explain the *DSM*'s multiaxial model. What are the reasons for having a multiaxial classification system?
- Why is personality analogous to the body's immune system?
- What are the three criteria that distinguish normal from abnormal functioning?
- Why is eclecticism perforce a scientific norm in the social sciences?
- Explain how ideas progress in the social sciences.
- What are the different components of the biological perspective?
- Describe Freud's topographical and structural models of the mind.
- What is the function of defense mechanisms? How do they work?
- Describe the stages of psychosexual development.
- What are *character disorders?*
- Explain the significance of object relations theory.
- Explain Kernberg's use of the term *structural organization.*

What sort of a person are you? What do you see as distinctive about your personality? How well do you know yourself? Are there aspects of your personality of which you are unaware? Do others know you as you know yourself? What are the best and worst things about your personality? Questions such as these are easy to ask, but are often difficult to answer. Yet, they go directly to the essence of what we are as human beings. Personality is that which makes us what we are and that which makes us different from others. People who are especially different, for example, are said to have "personality" or be "quite a character." Other people have "no personality at all." Depending on how someone affects us, he or she may be viewed as having a "good personality" or a "bad personality."

In the past several decades, the study of personality and its disorders has become central to the study of abnormal psychology. In the course of clinical work, we encounter subjects with vastly different pathologies. Some are in the midst of a depressive episode, and some must cope with the lasting effects of traumas far beyond the range of normal human experience. Some are grossly out of contact with reality, and some have only minor problems in living rather than clinical disorders. Although the problems of patients vary, everyone has a personality. Personality disorders occupy a place of diagnostic prominence today and constitute a special area of scientific study. The issues involved are complex, certainly much more sophisticated than the everyday understanding of personality described in the previous questions. This chapter introduces the emergence of this new discipline by analyzing personality and personality disorders by comparing and contrasting the basic assumptions that underlie different approaches to these ideas and by presenting the fundamentals of the classical perspectives on personality, which are essential to the understanding of the clinical chapters that follow. The questions are: What is personality? How does our definition of personality inform our understanding of personality disorders? Do the assumptions underlying the concept of personality support the use of the term **disorder?** How can the content of different personality disorders best be described?

One way to investigate the definition of a term is to examine how its meanings and usage have evolved over time. The word **personality** is derived from the Latin term **persona,** originally representing the theatrical mask used by ancient dramatic players. As a mask assumed by an actor, persona suggests a pretense of appearance, that is, the possession of traits other than those that actually characterize the individual behind the mask. In time, the term persona lost its connotation of pretense and illusion and began to represent not the mask, but the real person's observable or explicit features. The third and final meaning personality has acquired delves beneath surface impression to turn the spotlight on the inner, less often revealed, and hidden psychological qualities of the individual. Thus, through history, the meaning of the term has shifted from external illusion to surface reality and finally to opaque or veiled inner traits. This last meaning comes closest to contemporary use. Today, personality is seen as a complex pattern of deeply embedded psychological characteristics that are expressed automatically in almost every area of psychological functioning. That is, personality is viewed as the patterning of characteristics across the entire matrix of the person.

Personality is often confused with two related terms, character and temperament. Although all three words have similar meanings in casual usage, **character** refers to characteristics acquired during our upbringing and connotes a degree of conformity to virtuous social standards. **Temperament,** in contrast, refers not to the forces of socialization, but to a basic biological disposition toward certain behaviors. One person may be said to be of "good character," whereas another person may have an "irritable temperament." Character thus represents the crystallized influence of nurture, and temperament represents the physically coded influence of nature.

Abnormal Behavior and Personality

The concept of personality disorders requires an understanding of their role in the study of abnormal behavior. The *Diagnostic and Statistical Manual of Mental Disorders* (*DSM*) is considered the bible of mental disorders by psychologists and psychiatrists. The first official edition, published in 1952, was heavily influenced by previous systems established by the Army and the Veterans Administration to assist in understanding the mental health problems of World War II servicemen. In time, the *DSM* evolved beyond its original military purpose, becoming the standard or compendium for all of abnormal behavior. Now in its fourth edition, the *DSM-IV* is widely considered the official classification system or taxonomy for use by mental health professionals. It describes all mental disorders widely believed to exist, as well as a variety of others provisionally put forward for further research. Twelve personality disorders are included in *DSM-IV*, 10 of which are officially accepted, and 2 of which are provisional. In addition, this text briefly discusses two others that appeared in the revised third edition of the *DSM*. Although deleted from the latest edition, their diagnostic labels remain in widespread clinical use. Table 1.1 gives brief descriptions of these 14 personality disorders, an overview to the later chapters of this book.

BASIC VOCABULARY

Abnormal psychology has its own special vocabulary, or jargon. Many terms used in the discussion of abnormal behavior appear repeatedly in this book. Learn them now, for you will see them again and again. **Diagnostic criteria** are the defining characteristics used by clinicians to classify individuals within a clinical category. Essentially, diagnostic criteria constitute a checklist of features that must be present before a diagnosis can be made. Each disorder has its own unique list. Some lists are short; others are longer. For example, seven criteria are used to diagnose the antisocial personality. One of these is "deceitfulness, as indicated by repeated lying, use of aliases, or conning others for personal profit or pleasure" (*DSM-IV*, 1994, p. 650). Eight criteria are used to diagnose the histrionic personality. One of the most interesting is "interaction with others is often characterized by inappropriate sexually seductive or provocative behavior" (p. 657).

The criteria list for each personality disorder includes either seven, eight, or nine items, each of which details some characteristic trait, attitude, or behavior strongly related to that particular disorder. In the antisocial criteria, deceitfulness is considered a **personality trait,** a long-standing pattern of behavior expressed across time and in many different situations. The histrionic criteria can also be considered as tapping the personality trait of seductiveness, because histrionics are known for inappropriately sexualizing their communications. Where many such personality traits typically occur together, they may be said to constitute a **personality disorder.** Antisocials, for example, are much more than just deceitful; they are often manipulative, reckless, aggressive, irresponsible, exploitive, and lacking in empathy and remorse. When all of these characteristics are taken together, they constitute what is called a personality

TABLE 1.1   Brief Description of the Fourteen Personality Disorders of *DSM-III*, *DSM-III-R*, and *DSM-IV*

Schizoid	Apathetic, indifferent, remote, solitary. Neither desires nor need human attachments. Minimal awareness of feelings of self or others. Few drives or ambitions, if any.
Avoidant	Hesitant, self-conscious, embarrassed, anxious. Tense in social situations due to fear of rejection. Plagued by constant performance anxiety. Sees self as inept, inferior, or unappealing. Feels alone and empty.
Depressive[1]	Somber, discouraged, pessimistic, brooding, fatalistic. Presents self as vulnerable and abandoned. Feels valueless, guilty, and impotent. Judges self as worthy only of criticism and contempt.
Dependent	Helpless, incompetent, submissive, immature. Withdraws from adult responsibilities. Sees self as weak or fragile. Seeks constant reassurance from stronger figures.
Histrionic	Dramatic, seductive, shallow, stimulus-seeking, vain. Overreacts to minor events. Exhibitionistic as a means of securing attention and favors. Sees self as attractive and charming.
Narcissistic	Egotistical, arrogant, grandiose, insouciant. Preoccupied with fantasies of success, beauty, or achievement. Sees self as admirable and superior, and therefore entitled to special treatment.
Antisocial	Impulsive, irresponsible, deviant, unruly. Acts without due consideration. Meets social obligations only when self-serving. Disrespects societal customs, rules, and standards. Sees self as free and independent.
Sadistic[2]	Explosively hostile, abrasive, cruel, dogmatic. Liable to sudden outbursts of rage. Feels self-satisfied through dominating, intimidating and humiling others. Is opinionated and close-minded.
Compulsive	Restrained, conscientious, respectful, rigid. Maintains a rule-bound lifestyle. Adheres closely to social conventions. Sees the world in terms of regulations and hierarchies. Sees self as devoted, reliable, efficient, and productive.
Negativistic[1]	Resentful, contrary, skeptical, discontented. Resist fulfilling others' expectations. Deliberately inefficient. Vents anger indirectly by undermining others' goals. Alternately moody and irritable, then sullen and withdrawn.
Masochistic[3]	Deferential, pleasure-phobic, servile, blameful, self-effacing. Encourages others to take advantage. Deliberately defeats own achievements. Seeks condemning or mistreatful partners.
Paranoid	Guarded, defensive, distrustful and suspiciousness. Hypervigilant to the motives of others to undermine or do harm. Always seeking confirmatory evidence of hidden schemes. Feels righteous, but persecuted.
Schizotypal	Eccentric, self-estranged, bizarre, absent. Exhibits peculiar mannerisms and behaviors. Thinks can read thoughts of others. Preoccupied with odd daydreams and beliefs. Blurs line between reality and fantasy.
Borderline	Unpredictable, manipulative, unstable. Frantically fears abandonment and isolation. Experiences rapidly fluctuating moods. Shifts rapidly between loving and hating. Sees self and others alternatively as all-good and all-bad.

[1] Listed as a provisional disorder in *DSM-IV.*
[2] From the Appendix of *DSM-III-R.*
[3] Called Self-Defeating in *DSM-III-R* appendix.

prototype, a psychological ideal found only rarely in nature. The disorder is the prototype, put forward in terms of its purest expression.

Real persons, however, seldom are seen as "pure types." The *DSM* does not require that subjects possess each and every characteristic of a personality disorder before a diagnosis can be made. Typically, some majority of criteria will suffice. For example, five of eight criteria are required for a diagnosis of histrionic personality disorder, and five of nine are required for a diagnosis of narcissistic personality disorder. Many different combinations of diagnostic criteria are possible, a fact that recognizes that no two people are exactly alike, even when both share the same personality disorder diagnosis. Although Charles Manson and Jeffrey Dahmer might both be considered antisocial personalities, for example, their personalities are nevertheless substantially different. Determining exactly what separates individuals such as Dahmer and Manson from the rest of us requires a great deal of biographical information. Each chapter in this text, therefore, focuses on factors important in the development of a personality disorder. For example, a chummy relationship between father and daughter is one of the major pathways in the development of an adult histrionic personality disorder.

Categorical typologies are advantageous because of their ease of use by clinicians who must make relatively rapid diagnoses with large numbers of patients whom they see briefly. Although clinical attention in these cases is drawn to only the most salient features of the patient, a broad range of traits that have not been directly observed is often strongly suggested. Categories assume the existence of discrete boundaries both between separate personality styles and between normality and abnormality, a feature felicitous to the medical model, but not so for personality functioning, which exists on a continuum. The arguments of those who favor the adoption of dimensional models enter mainly around one theme: The categorical model, because it entails discrete boundaries between the various disorders and between normality and abnormality, is simply inappropriate for the personality disorders. Although trait dimensions have a number of desirable properties, there is little agreement among their proponents concerning either the nature or number of traits necessary to represent personality adequately. Theorists may "invent" dimensions in accord with their expectations rather than "discovering" them as if they were intrinsic to nature, merely awaiting scientific detection. Apparently, the number of traits required to assess personality is not determined by the ability of our research to disclose some inherent truth but rather by our predilections for conceiving and organizing our observations. Describing personality with more than a few such trait dimensions produces schemas so complex and intricate that they require geometric or algebraic representation. Although there is nothing intrinsically wrong with such quantitative formats, they pose considerable difficulty both in comprehension and in communication among clinicians.

THE *DSM* MULTIAXIAL MODEL

The disorders in the *DSM* are grouped in terms of a multiaxial model. **Multiaxial** literally means multiple axes. Each axis represents a different kind or source of information. Later, we concentrate on exactly what these sources are; now, we just explain their purpose. The multiaxial model exists because some means is required whereby the various symptoms and personality characteristics of a given patient can be brought together to paint a picture that reflects the functioning of the whole person. For example, depression in a narcissistic personality is different from depression in a dependent personality. Because narcissists consider themselves superior to everyone else, they usually become depressed when confronted with objective evidence of failure or inadequacy too profound to ignore. Their usually puffed-up self-esteem deflates, leaving feelings of depression in its wake. In contrast, dependent personalities seek powerful others to take care of them, instrumental surrogates who confront a cruel world. Here, depression usually follows the loss of a significant caretaker. The point of the multiaxial model is that each patient is more than the sum of his or her diagnoses: Both are depressed, but for very different reasons. In each case, what differentiates them is not their surface symptoms, but rather the meaning of their symptoms in the context of their underlying personalities. By considering symptoms in relation to deeper characteristics, an understanding of the person is gained that transcends either symptoms or traits considered separately. To say that someone is a depressed narcissist, for example, conveys much more than does the label of depression or narcissism alone.

The multiaxial model is divided into five separate axes (see Figure 1.1), each of which gets at a different source or level of influence in human behavior. Axis I, *clinical syndromes,* consists of the classical mental disorders that have preoccupied clinical psychology and psychiatry for most of the history of these disciplines. Axis I is structured hierarchically. Each family of disorders branches into still finer distinctions, which compose actual diagnoses. For example, the anxiety disorders include obsessive-compulsive disorder, posttraumatic stress disorder, and generalized anxiety disorder. The mood

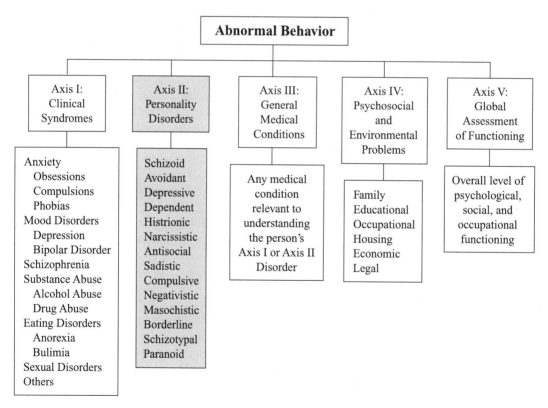

FIGURE 1.1   Abnormal Behavior and the Multiaxial Model.

disorders include depression and bipolar disorder. Other branches recognize sexual disorders, eating disorders, substance abuse disorders, and so on. Finally, each disorder is broken down into diagnostic criteria, a list of symptoms that must typically be present for the diagnosis to be given. Axis II, *personality disorders,* is the subject of this text.

Axis III consists of any *physical or medical conditions* relevant to understanding the individual patient. Some influences are dramatic, and others are more subtle. Examples of dramatic influences include head injury, the effects of drug abuse or prescribed medications, known genetic syndromes, and any other disease of the nervous, respiratory, digestive, or genitourinary system, brain structure, or other bodily system that impacts psychological functioning. Examples of subtle influence include temperament as the pattern of activity and emotionality to which an individual is genetically disposed, as well as constitutional and hormonal patterns. Essentially, Axis III recognizes that the body is not just the vessel of the soul. Instead, we are all integrated physical and psychological beings. A computer metaphor illustrates the concept: Software always requires hardware, and, depending on the hardware, different software functions may be either enhanced or disabled or just run in a different way. Some individuals have a central processing unit that keeps crunching busily, for example, whereas others run hot and have a great-looking case, but not much more. Physical factors always impact psychological functioning, if only because the body is the physical matrix from which mind emerges. Anyone who has had a lobotomy undoubtedly knows this already, but probably doesn't much care.

Axis IV consists of all *psychosocial and environmental factors* relevant to psychological functioning. Included are problems related to the family or primary support group, such as the death of a family member, marital separation or divorce, sexual or physical abuse, family conflict, or inappropriate or inadequate discipline at home. Also included are problems in the social environments outside the family. Educational problems include poor reading skills, lack of sufficient instruction, and conflict with teachers. Occupational problems include threats to employment, actual job loss, and conflict with authority figures and coworkers. Finally, Axis IV includes miscellaneous issues such as *general economic* and *legal problems,* for example, a pending criminal trial.

Axis IV recognizes that each person exists and functions in a variety of contexts and, in turn, these contexts often have profound effects on the individual. For example, if a narcissistic person is fired from employment, odds are that the firing has something to do with the person's intolerable attitude of superiority. Narcissists are above it all, to the point of not bowing to the boss. Some even view themselves as being above the law, as if the rules of ordinary living could not possibly apply to them. By putting all the pieces together—current symptoms, personality characteristics, and psychosocial stressors—a complex, but logical, picture of the total person is obtained. When considered in relation to specific biographical details, the result is an understanding that links the developmental past with the pathological present to explain how particular personality characteristics and current symptoms were formed, how they are perpetuated, and how they might be treated. This complex integration of all available information is known as the **case conceptualization.**

In contrast to the other axes, Axis V contains no specific content of its own. Once the case has been conceptualized, the next question is the level of severity: How pathological is this total picture? To make this determination, problems across all other axes are collapsed into a global rating of level of psychological, social, and occupational functioning, the **Global Assessment of Functioning (GAF)** Scale, which ranges from 0 to

100. Ratings may be made at any particular moment in time, perhaps admission to the hospital emergency room, at intake, or at discharge. Alternatively, ratings can sum up functioning across entire time periods, perhaps the past week or the past year. Limitations due to physical handicaps are excluded. In general, Axis V functions as an overall index of psychological health and pathology. Such measurements are often useful in tracking total progress over time.

Although you could memorize the five axes of the multiaxial model, it is much better to understand the purpose for which the model was constructed—why it exists as it does. The most fundamental reason is that the model increases clinical understanding by ensuring that all possible inputs to the psychopathology of the given subject receive attention. If you went to the doctor for a physical, you would want him or her to check your lungs, heart, kidneys, stomach, and all other major organs and systems. A doctor who pronounced you healthy after taking only your blood pressure would not be much of a doctor at all.

The same is true of the mental disorders. Psychopathology is much more complex, but nothing of importance should be neglected. Each of the axes in the multiaxial model corresponds to a different level of organization, so that each axis contextualizes the one immediately below it, changing its meaning and altering its significance. Axis I is the presenting problem, the reason the patient is currently being held in psychiatric emergency or sits chatting with a psychotherapist. In turn, Axis II, the personality disorders, provides both a substrate and context for understanding the symptoms of Axis I. As a substrate, personality inclines us toward the development of certain clinical disorders rather than others. For example, avoidant personalities typically shun contact with others, even though intimacy, approval, and self-esteem are what they most desperately seek. In contrast, narcissistic personalities, who are frequently indulged as children, grow up with a sense of superior self-worth that others often see as prideful and grandiose. Of the two, the avoidant is much more likely to develop a fear of public speaking, and the narcissist is much more likely to be fired from a job for being arrogant to everyone. The kinds of problems that a particular individual might develop can, in many cases, be predicted once his or her personality characteristics are known. In turn, personality rides on top of biology and rests within the psychosocial environment. We are both physical and social beings. When problems seem to be driven principally by personality factors, we speak of maladaptive personality traits or personality disorders. When difficulties concern primarily environmental or social factors, an Axis I adjustment disorder may be diagnosed or Axis IV problems in living may be noted. Personality is the level of organization in which these influences are synthesized (see Figure 1.2).

The multiaxial model draws attention to all relevant factors that feed into and perpetuate particular symptoms, and it also guides our understanding of how psychopathology develops. In most cases, the interaction of psychosocial stressors and personality characteristics leads to the expression of psychological symptoms; that is, Axis II and Axis IV interact to produce Axis I (see Figure 1.3). When personality includes many adaptive traits and relatively few maladaptive ones, the capacity to cope with psychosocial calamities such as death and divorce is increased. However, when personality includes many maladaptive traits and few adaptive ones, even minor stressors may precipitate an Axis I disorder.

In this sense, personality may be seen as the psychological equivalent of the body's immune system. Each of us lives in an environment of potentially infectious bacteria, and the strength of our defenses determines whether these microbes take hold, spread,

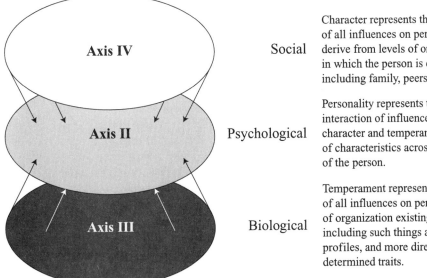

Character represents the sum total of all influences on personality that derive from levels of organization in which the person is embedded, including family, peers, and society.

Personality represents the complex interaction of influences from both character and temperament, the patterning of characteristics across the entire matrix of the person.

Temperament represents the sum total of all influences on personality from levels of organization existing below the person, including such things as neurotransmitter profiles, and more directly genetically determined traits.

FIGURE 1.2 Levels of Organization and Their Relationship to the Multiaxial Model.

and ultimately are experienced as illness. Robust immune activity easily counteracts most infectious organisms, whereas weakened immune activity leads to illness. Psychopathology should be conceived as reflecting the same interactive pattern. Here, however, it is not our immunological defenses, but our overall personality pattern—that is, coping skills and adaptive flexibilities—that determine whether we respond constructively or succumb to the psychosocial environment. Viewed this way, the structure and characteristics of personality become the foundation for the individual's capacity to function in a mentally healthy or ill way. Every personality style is thus also a coping style, and personality becomes a cardinal organizing principle through which psychopathology should be understood.

PERSONALITY AND THE MEDICAL MODEL: A MISCONCEPTION

By describing the personality disorders as distinct entities that can be diagnosed, the *DSM* encourages the view that they are discrete medical diseases. They are not. The causal assumptions underlying Axis I and Axis II are simply different. Personality is the patterning of characteristics across the entire matrix of the person. Rather than being limited to a single trait, personality regards the total configuration of the person's characteristics: interpersonal, cognitive, psychodynamic, and biological. Each trait reinforces the others in perpetuating the stability and behavioral consistency of the total personality structure (see Figure 1.4). For the personality disorders, then, causality is literally everywhere. Each domain interacts to influence the others, and together, they maintain the integrity of the whole structure. In contrast, the causes of the Axis I clinical syndromes are assumed to be localizable. The cause of an adjustment disorder, for example, lies in a recent change in life circumstances that requires considerable getting used to. Here, causes and consequences are distinguishable, with discrete distinction

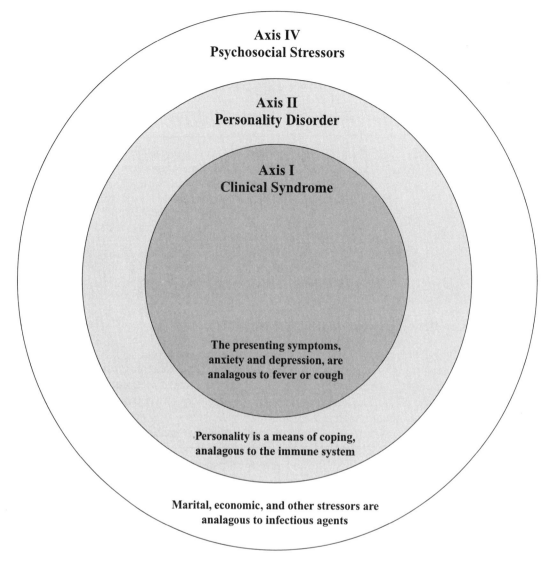

FIGURE 1.3   Axis IV and Axis II Interact to Produce Axis I.

between the underlying "disease" and its symptom expression. Difficulty making an adjustment might result in feelings of depression, for example. For the personality disorders, however, the distinction between disease and symptom is lost. Instead, causality issues from every domain of functioning. Each element in the whole structure sustains the others. This explains why personality disorders are notoriously resistant to psychotherapy.

Personality disorders are not diseases; thus, we must be very careful in our casual usage of the term. To imagine that a disorder, of any kind, could be anything other than a medical illness is very difficult. The idea that personality constitutes the immunological matrix that determines our overall psychological fitness is intended to break the

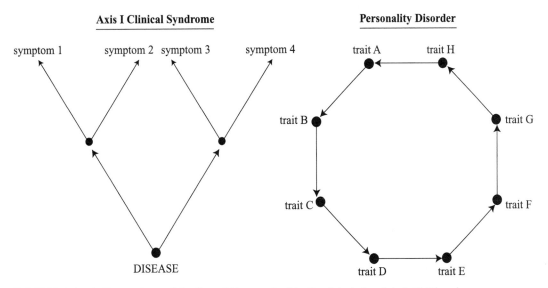

FIGURE 1.4 A Comparison of the Causal Pattern for Idealized Axis I and Axis II Disorders.

long-entrenched habit of conceiving syndromes of psychopathology as one or another variant of a disease, that is, as some "foreign" entity or lesion that intrudes insidiously within the person to undermine his or her so-called normal functions. The archaic notion that all mental disorders represent external intrusions or internal disease processes is an offshoot of prescientific ideas, such as demons or spirits that possess or hex the person. The role of infectious agents and anatomical lesions in physical medicine has reawakened this view. Demons are almost ancient history, but personality disorders are still seen as involving some external entity that invades and unsettles an otherwise healthy status. Although we are forced to use such terminology by linguistic habit, it is impossible for anyone to *have* a personality disorder. Rather, it is the total matrix of the person that constitutes the potential for psychological adaptation or illness.

NORMALITY VERSUS PATHOLOGY

Normality and abnormality cannot be differentiated objectively. All such distinctions, including the diagnostic categories of the *DSM-IV*, are in part social constructions and cultural artifacts. Although persons may be segregated into groups according to explicit criteria, ostensibly lending such classifications the respectability of science, the desire to segregate and the act of segregating persons into diagnostic groups are uniquely social. All definitions of pathology, ailment, malady, sickness, illness, or disorder are ultimately value-laden and circular (Feinstein, 1977). Disorders are what doctors treat, and what doctors treat is defined by implicit social standards. Given its social basis, **normality** is probably best defined as conformity to the behaviors and customs typical for an individual's reference group or culture. **Pathology** would then be defined by behaviors that are uncommon, irrelevant, or alien to the individual's reference group. Not surprisingly, American writers have often thought of normality as the ability to function independently and competently to obtain a personal sense of contentment and satisfaction.

Other cultures may have other standards; in Asian societies, for example, individualism is not valued as highly as respect for group norms.

Normality and pathology reside on a continuum. One slowly fades into the other. Because personality disorders are composed of maladaptive traits, there are two ways that personality pathology becomes more severe when moving along the continuum from health to pathology. First, single traits can become more intense in their expression; assertiveness can give way to aggression, for example, or deference can give way to

TABLE 1.2   The Compulsive Personality, from Adaptive to Severely Disordered

	Adaptive	Subclinical	Disordered	Severely Disordered
Perfectionistic	"I take pride in what I do."	"I feel I have to work on things until I get them right."	"I can't stop working on something until it's perfect, even if it already satisfies what I need it for."	"Because nothing is ever good enough, I never finish anything."
Hard-working	"I believe in the work ethic."	"I rarely take time off for leisure or family."	"It drives me crazy if something is unfinished. I have never taken a vacation."	"I panic if I leave the office with something left undone. I work so late that I usually end up sleeping there."
Planful	"I like to consider my choices before I act on something."	"I have to analyze all the alternatives before I make up my mind."	"I try to consider so many eventualities that it becomes very difficult to make a decision."	"I get so lost in trying to anticipate all the possibilities and details that I put things off and never commit to anything."
Morally scrupulous	"I like to do the right thing."	"I am sometimes intolerant of people whose moral standards are less than my own."	"I am disgusted by the moral laxity and indulgence I see in 99% of humanity."	"I think anyone who deviates from the straight and narrow should be punished swiftly for their sins."
Conscientious	"I like to take my time and do things right."	"Sometimes I think others will disapprove of me if they find even one small mistake."	"I find it hard to stop working until I know others will be satisfied with the job I've done."	"I check and recheck my work until I'm absolutely sure that no one can find a mistake in what I've done."
Emotionally constricted	"I rarely get excited about anything."	"I don't believe in expressing much emotion."	"There are only a few things I enjoy, and even with those, I can't let myself go."	"I have never found any use for emotion. I have never felt any enjoyment from life."

masochism. Second, the number of maladaptive traits attributed to the given subject may increase. By comparing the statements given in Table 1.2 for a subset of compulsive traits, we can easily see how normality gradually gives way to personality disorder.

Personality disorders may best be characterized by three pathological characteristics (Millon, 1969). The first follows directly from the conception that personality is the psychological analogue of the body's immune system: Personality disorders tend to exhibit a tenuous stability, or lack of resilience, under conditions of stress. The coping strategies of most individuals are diverse and flexible. When one strategy or behavior isn't working, normal persons shift to something else. Personality disorder subjects, however, tend to practice the same strategies repeatedly with only minor variations. As a result, they always seem to make matters worse. Consequently, the level of stress keeps increasing, amplifying their vulnerability, creating crisis situations, and producing increasingly distorted perceptions of social reality.

A second characteristic overlaps somewhat with the first: Personality-disordered subjects are adaptively inflexible. Normal personality functioning entails role flexibility, knowing when to take the initiative and change the environment, and knowing when to adapt to what the environment offers. Normal persons exhibit flexibility in their interactions, such that their initiatives or reactions are proportional and appropriate to circumstances. When constraints on behavior come from the situation, the behavior of normal individuals tends to converge, regardless of personality. If the boss wants something done a particular way, most people will follow directions. Such situations are highly scripted. Almost everyone knows what to do and behaves in nearly the same way.

By contrast, the alternative strategies and behaviors of personality-disordered subjects are few in number and rigidly imposed on conditions for which they are poorly suited. Personality-disordered subjects implicitly drive or control interpersonal

FOCUS ON CULTURE AND PERSONALITY

The Misunderstood Student

The Interplay of Culture

Jenna, a first-year graduate student in psychology, was required to write up her impressions of a videotaped therapy session featuring a beginning therapist and a female Asian student referred by her instructor for excessive shyness. Eventually, Jenna noticed that regardless of what the therapist said, the student always seemed to agree. At the end of the session, the therapist was interviewed and asked for his impressions. The therapist reinforced the instructor's opinion about the student's shyness and felt change would be fast because the student offered little resistance. As Jenna's instructor pointed out, this conclusion was incorrect. In fact, the much younger female student was prevented from disagreeing with the much older male therapist because of cultural norms. Once the student was empowered to disagree, it was discovered that conventions appropriate to her reference group largely accounted for her behavior with her instructor, not long-standing personality traits. Accordingly, therapy was refocused on adjustments to the expectations of American culture, not on personality change.

situations through the intensity and rigidity of their traits. In effect, the personality-disordered person provides the most powerful constraints on the course of the interaction. Because they cannot be flexible, the environment must become even more so. When the environment cannot be arranged to suit the person, a crisis ensues. Opportunities for learning new and more adaptive strategies are thereby even further reduced, and life becomes that much less enjoyable.

The third characteristic of personality-disordered subjects is a consequence of the second. Because the subjects fail to change, the pathological themes that dominate their lives tend to repeat as vicious circles. Pathological personalities are themselves pathogenic. In effect, life becomes a bad one-act play that repeats again and again. They waste opportunities for improvement, provoke new problems, and constantly create situations that replay their failures, often with only minor variations on a few related, self-defeating themes.

FOCUS ON PERSONALITY AND RELATIONSHIPS

The Compulsive Entrepreneur

How Do Personalities Interact?

Eager to learn about the characteristics of the different personality disorders, Jenna asked her clinical supervisor for materials that might bring the different personalities vividly to life. She received an audiotape of a husband-and-wife interview with consent of the subjects. During the session, the wife bitterly complained that her husband, married once previously, spent almost no time with the family. Asked why his first wife had divorced him, the man stated solemnly that she was incapable of taking life seriously and refused to help while he toiled hour after hour checking and rechecking the operational details of their new business. Further probing revealed that although both women acknowledged his ability to stay focused on task, both also complained that the marriage had no intimacy, spontaneity, or romance. As additional data came to light, the husband was diagnosed as an obsessive-compulsive personality. His rigid work ethic and unending earnestness created almost identical problems across two relationships.

Early Perspectives on the Personality Disorders

The history of every science may be said to include a prescientific "natural history" phase, where the main questions are, "What are the essential phenomena of the field?" and "How can we know them?" Ideally, as more and more data are gathered through increasingly sophisticated methodologies, common sense begins to give way to theoretical accounts that not only integrate and unify disparate observations, but also actively suggest directions for future research. The existence of black holes, for example, is predicted by the theory of relativity, and the accumulated evidence of several decades now suggests that one or more black holes exist at the center of every galaxy. No one will ever smell, taste, touch, hear, or see an actual black hole. Because even light cannot escape their gravitational power, they must remain forever hidden from observation. Instead, scientists must infer the existence of black holes from the predictions of relativity and from their observable effects on surrounding space-time. Technological advances have since allowed many other predictions of relativity to be tested.

With this brief example, the function of theory in science becomes clear. Theories represent the world to us in some way that accounts for existing observations, but nevertheless also goes beyond direct experience, a characteristic known as **surplus meaning.** Theories embrace the available evidence, but allow us to make novel predictions precisely because they exceed the evidence. Thus, the mathematics of relativity may be used to predict exactly what would happen if you fell into a black hole, though you would never return to report about it.

Theory and experimentation are given equal weight in the natural sciences. Sometimes in the history of science, as with the theory of relativity, theory outpaces the capacity of science to make observations. Black holes, for example, were a known mathematical consequence of relativity long before scientists began to figure out ways to observe their effects. Alternatively, new technologies may make possible observations that are more detailed, more precise, and more abundant than ever before, challenging existing theories to the point that entire fields are sent into chaos. The ready availability of new observations allows testing to progress unfettered, quickening the pace of theory formation in turn. Thus, the science matures. The yield of the Hubble space telescope, for example, is so vast that cosmologists cannot yet assimilate everything their new tool allows. Because there are usually multiple competing theories for any given phenomenon, determining which account is correct depends on the construction of a **paradigm experiment,** one designed to produce results consistent with one theory but inconsistent with the other. In this way, research tends to close in on the truth, whittling down the number of possible theories through experimentation over time.

The social sciences, however, are fundamentally different. Whereas investigation in the natural sciences eventually comes to closure through the interplay of theory and research, the social sciences are fundamentally open. Here, advancement occurs when some new and interesting point of view suddenly surges to the center of scientific interest. Far from overturning established paradigms, the new perspective now exists alongside its predecessors, allowing the subject matter of the field to be studied from an additional angle. A perspective is, by definition, just one way of looking at things. Accordingly, paradigm experiments are either not possible or not necessary, because it is understood that no single perspective is able to contain the whole field. Tolerance thus becomes a scientific value, and eclecticism a scientific norm. In personality, the dominant perspectives are psychodynamic, biological, interpersonal, and cognitive. Other, more marginal conceptions could also be included, perhaps existential or cultural. Some offer only a particular set of concepts or principles, and others generate entire systems of personality constructs, often far different from those of the *DSM.* Hopefully, the most important ways of looking at the field are already known, though it is always possible that alternative conceptions remain undiscovered. The chapters in this text that discuss the specific personality disorders address these different perspectives: the cognitive, the psychodynamic, the biological, and the interpersonal views of the antisocial personality, for example.

The open nature of the social sciences has further important consequences for how they are presented for study. The history of physics as a science is interesting, but only incidental to the study of its subject matter. Universal laws are universal laws. If Einstein had never been born, the equations that describe the relationship between energy and matter, space and time, would still be the same. We may disagree about politics and religion, but we all live in the same physical universe, and the mathematics describing that universe constitute one truth about its nature.

In the social sciences, however, different perspectives on the field are discovered in no necessary order. Later perspectives tend to be put forth as reactions to preceding ones. The social sciences have what philosophers might call a contingent structure: Had Freud never been born, the history and content of psychology would be very different. In fact, primacy is perhaps the single most important reason that Freud has been so influential. Freud was simply first. When psychoanalysis was becoming established, the only truly competing perspective was biological. In time, psychoanalysis became so dominant it was synonymous with the study of abnormal behavior. Because the cognitive and interpersonal perspectives had not yet been founded, it took some time to discover that psychoanalysis is really just one part of psychopathology, rather than the whole science. Later thinkers studied Freud's work to draw important contrasts with their own points of view so that today, the father of psychoanalysis is one of the most famous and most refuted figures in history. And naturally, in studying Freud, these important thinkers were also influenced by him, in effect becoming psychoanalysts, at least somewhat, in order to become something more.

In any field, perspectives seldom emerge fully formed. Instead, novel ideas coalesce slowly, so that only after a period of time does their presence as a new point of view become apparent. When this occurs, many individuals formerly seen as belonging to the old school are now seen as transitional figures, difficult to classify. Harry Stack Sullivan, about whom you will read more later, reacted so strongly against psychoanalysis that he is regarded as the father of the interpersonal perspective. Nevertheless, many of Sullivan's notions were anticipated by Alfred Adler, who also reacted against Freud. Yet, Adler is regarded as psychodynamic, and Sullivan is regarded as interpersonal. Even so, contemporary interpersonal theory has advanced so far that Sullivan sometimes looks analytic in contrast.

Understanding the open nature of social sciences and how they evolve may seem tangential, but in fact, it is fundamental to understanding personality and its disorders. Each perspective contributes different parts to personality, but personality is not just about parts. Instead, personality is the patterning of characteristics across the entire matrix of the individual. Whatever the parts may be, personality is about how they intermesh and work together. Occasionally, you may hear someone say that personality is really just biological, or really just cognitive, or really just psychodynamic. Do not believe them. The explicit purpose of a perspective is to expose different aspects of a single phenomenon for study and understanding. A single element cannot be made to stand for the whole. By definition, each perspective is but a partial view of an intrinsic totality, and personality is the integration of these perspectives, the overall pattern or gestalt. Each point of view belongs to the study of personality, but personality itself is more than the sum of its parts. In the next two sections, we trace the history and importance of two competing approaches to personality, the biological and the psychodynamic. Among other things, these perspectives have given the field important units of analysis—temperament and character, respectively—that have sometimes sought to replace personality itself as the proper focus of clinical study.

THE BIOLOGICAL PERSPECTIVE

Axis III of the *DSM* recognizes an important truth about human nature: We are all biological creatures, the result of five billion years of chemical evolution here on planet Earth. In the course of everyday life, we do not ordinarily think about the link between mind and body. Especially when we are young, our physical matrix usually hums along so smoothly that its functions are completely transparent. Subjectively, our existence seems more like that of a soul captured or held within a body, not that of a self that emerges from a complex physical organization of neurons communicating chemically across synapses. So strong is the illusion that philosophers have debated for centuries whether the universe is ultimately composed of mind or matter or both. To us, our minds seem self-contained, and our will free. Because our choices always seem to be our own, we cannot imagine that our bodies are anything more than vessels. No wonder, then, that many religions maintain that each of us has an immortal soul that escapes upon the body's demise. From the standpoint of science, however, humans are social, psychological, and biological beings. As such, our will is neither totally determined nor totally free, but constrained by influences that cut across every level of organization in nature.

Biological influences on personality may be thought of as being either proximal (nearby) or distal (far away). Distal influences originate within our genetic code and often concern inherited characteristics transmitted as part of the evolutionary history of our species. Many such characteristics are sociobiological. These exist because genetic recombination could not exist in the absence of sexuality. As a prerequisite for evolution, we are gendered beings who seek to maximize the representation of our own genes in the gene pool. For the most part, the influence is subtle, but even among human beings, males tend to be more aggressive, dominant, and territorial, and females tend to be more caring, nurturant, and social. Such tendencies are only weakly expressed among normals, but some personality disorders do caricature their sex-role stereotype, notably the antisocial and narcissistic personalities among males and the dependent and histrionic personalities among females.

Other biological influences in personality focus on proximal causes, influences that exist because we are complex biological systems. When the structures that underlie behavior differ, behavior itself is affected. Two such concepts important to personality are temperament and constitution.

Temperament

Just as everyone has a personality, everyone has characteristic patterns of living and behaving that to a great extent are imposed by biology. Each child enters the world with a distinctive pattern of dispositions and sensitivities. Mothers know that infants differ from the moment they are born, and perceptive parents notice differences between successive children. Some infants have a regular cycle of hunger, elimination, and sleep, whereas others vary unpredictably. Some twist fitfully in their sleep; others lie peacefully awake in hectic surroundings. Many of these differences persist into adulthood. Some people wake up slowly, and others are wide awake almost as soon as their eyes open.

The word **temperament** came into the English language in the Middle Ages to reflect the biological soil from which personality develops. Temperament is thus an underlying biological potential for behavior, seen most clearly in the predominant mood

---

FOCUS ON GENDER ISSUES

Gender Bias in the Diagnosis of Personality Disorders

Do Clinicians Have Gender Expectations?

Do certain personality disorders favor men and others favor women? The answer may depend on where you look. Because more women than men seek treatment for mental disorders, there are usually more women among the patients in mental health centers. Conversely, because more men than women are veterans, you would expect more male patients at Veterans Administration hospitals.

Nevertheless, certain personality disorders do seem weighted toward a particular gender. For some researchers (Kaplan, 1983; Pantony & Caplan, 1991), these discrepancies in diagnostic frequency, particularly in the larger number of females diagnosed borderline, dependent, and histrionic, are inherently sexist. However, although the *DSM-IV* agrees that these three are more frequently diagnosed in women, it also states that the paranoid, schizoid, schizotypal, antisocial, narcissistic, and obsessive-compulsive are more frequently diagnosed in men. If there is a bias, then, it would appear to go against the males.

One problem that creates bias is that certain diagnostic criteria seem to refer to both normalcy and pathology. Most people would argue that the histrionic criterion "consistently uses physical appearance to draw attention to self," for example, is exceptionally ambiguous in a society where a pleasing physical appearance is an expected part of the female gender role. Accordingly, where subjects have several traits of the histrionic personality, it is possible that clinicians might simply assume that this ambiguous criterion is met. Widiger (1998) argues that the more unstructured the interview situation, the more likely it is that clinicians will rely on sex stereotypic bias when diagnosing.

Even where diagnostic criteria are not ambiguous, it may nevertheless prove difficult to apply them equally across the sexes. The criteria for the dependent personality, for example, seems to emphasize as pathological female types of dependency, but fails to include masculine types of dependency. For example, Walker (1994, p. 36) argues that "men who rely on others to maintain their homes and take care of their children are . . . expressing personality-disordered dependency." Were this criterion added, many more men would certainly be diagnosed dependent.

Future DSMs must profit from these considerations if diagnostic criteria are to be devised that can replace implicit sex-stereotypic conceptions to be valid for both genders.

---

or emotionality of individuals and in the intensity of their activity cycles. Although A. H. Buss and Plomin (1984, p. 84) refer to it as consisting of "inherited personality traits present in early childhood," we might argue that temperament is the sum total of inherited biological influences on personality that show continuity across the life span. A case can certainly be made that temperament is more important than other domains of personality and more pervasive in its influence. Because our physical matrix exists before other domains of personality emerge, biologically built-in behavioral tendencies preempt and exclude other possible pathways of development that might take hold. Thus, although an irritable, demanding infant may mature into a diplomat famous for calmly understanding the issues on all sides, the odds are stacked against it. Similarly, a child whose personal tempo is slower than average is unlikely to develop a histrionic style, and an unusually agreeable infant is unlikely to develop an antisocial personality. Thus, biology does not determine our adult personality, but it does constrain development, channeling it down certain pathways rather than others, in interaction with social and family factors.

The doctrine of bodily humors posited by the early Greeks some 25 centuries ago was one of the first systems used to explain differences in personality. In the fourth century B.C., Hippocrates concluded that all disease stems from an excess of, or imbalance among, four bodily humors: yellow bile, black bile, blood, and phlegm. These humors were the embodiment of earth, water, fire, and air, the declared basic elements of the universe according to the philosopher Empedocles. Hippocrates identified four basic corresponding temperaments: choleric, melancholic, sanguine, and phlegmatic. Centuries later, Galen would associate each temperament with a particular personality trait; the choleric temperament was associated with irascibility, the sanguine temperament with optimism, the melancholic temperament with sadness, and the phlegmatic temperament with apathy. Although the doctrine of humors has been abandoned, giving way to the study of neurochemistry as its contemporary analogue, the old view still persists in contemporary expressions such as being sanguine or good-humored.

Constitution

Constitution refers to the total plan or philosophy on which something is constructed. The foremost early exponent of this approach was Ernst Kretschmer (1926), who developed a classification system based on three main body types—thin, muscular, and obese—each of which was associated with certain personality traits and psychopathologies. According to Kretschmer, the obese were disposed toward the development of manic-depressive illness, and the thin toward the development of schizophrenia. Kretschmer also believed that his types were associated with the expression of normal traits. Thin types were believed to be introverted, timid, and lacking in personal warmth, a less extreme version of the negative symptoms exhibited by withdrawn schizophrenics. Obese persons were conceived as gregarious, friendly, and interpersonally dependent, a less extreme version of the moody and socially excitable manic-depressive.

Kretschmer's work was continued by Sheldon (1942), who saw similarities between the three body types and the three basic layers of tissue that compose the embryo: ectoderm, mesoderm, and endoderm. The endoderm develops into the soft parts of the body, the mesoderm eventually forms the muscles and skeleton, and the ectoderm forms the nervous system. Each embryonic layer corresponds to a particular body type and is associated with the expression of certain normal-range personality characteristics. Accordingly, endomorphs, who tend toward obesity, were believed to be lovers of comfort and to be socially warm and goodwilled. Mesomorphs, who usually resemble athletes, were believed to be competitive, energetic, assertive, and bold. Ectomorphs, who tend toward thinness, were believed to be introversive and restrained but also mentally intense and restless. Although interesting, the idea of body types is no longer influential in personality theory. Rather than study the total organization of the body, researchers have begun to examine the role of individual anatomical structures in detail, many of which lie in the human brain.

Neurobiology

Research psychiatrist Cloninger (1986, 1987b) proposed an elegant theory based on hypothesized relationships of three genetic-neurobiologic trait dispositions, each of which is associated with a particular neurotransmitter system. Specifically, *novelty seeking* is associated with low basal activity in the dopaminergic system, harm avoidance with high activity in the serotonergic system, and reward dependence with low basal noradrenergic system activity. Novelty seeking is hypothesized to dispose the individual toward exhilaration or excitement in response to novel stimuli, which leads to the pursuit of potential rewards as well as an active avoidance of both monotony and punishment. *Harm avoidance* reflects a disposition to respond strongly to aversive stimuli, leading the individual to inhibit behaviors to avoid punishment, novelty, and frustrations. *Reward dependence* is seen as a tendency to respond to signals of reward, verbal signals of social approval, for example, and to resist extinction of behaviors previously associated with rewards or relief from punishment. These three dimensions form the axes of a cube whose corners represent various personality constructs (see Figure 1.5). Thus, antisocial personalities, who are often seen as fearless and sensation seeking, are seen as low in harm avoidance and high in novelty seeking, whereas the imperturbable schizoid is seen as low across all dimensions of the model. The personality disorders generated by Cloninger's model correspond only loosely to those in the *DSM-IV.* A number of personality disorders do not appear in the model at all.

A different approach, proposed by Siever and Davis (1991), is termed a **psychobiological model.** It consists of four dimensions—cognitive/perceptual organization, impulsivity/aggression, affective instability, and anxiety/inhibition—each of which has both Axis I and Axis II manifestations. Thus, *cognitive/perceptual organization* appears on Axis I in the form of schizophrenia and on Axis II especially as the schizotypal personality disorder but also the paranoid and the schizoid. All exhibit a disorganization of thought, dealt with by social isolation, social detachment, and guardedness. *Impulsivity/aggression* appears on Axis I in the form of impulse disorders and on Axis II particularly as the borderline and antisocial personalities. Borderlines are prone to sudden outbursts of anger and suicide attempts, and antisocials are unable to inhibit impulsive urges to violate social standards, for example, stealing and lying. *Affective instability,* a tendency toward rapid shifts of emotion, is manifested in the affective disorders on Axis I and in the borderline, and possibly histrionic, on Axis II. *Anxiety/inhibition,* associated with social avoidance, compulsivity, and sensitivity to the possibility of danger and punishment, is manifested in the anxiety disorders on Axis I and particularly in the avoidant personality on Axis II, but also in the compulsive and dependent.

Heredity

Genetics is a distal influence on personality. Researchers explore the influence of genes on behavior by searching for the presence of similar psychopathologies in siblings and relatives of an afflicted subject, by studying patterns of transmission across generations of the extended family, and by comparing the correlation of scores obtained on personality tests between sets of fraternal twins and identical twins reared together and apart. Other esoteric methodologies are also available, including structural equation modeling (Derlega, Winstead, & Jones, 1991) and Multiple Abstract Variance Analysis (Cattell, 1982). A comparison of correlations for identical twins reared together and apart shows that both are approximately equal, running at about 0.50 across a variety of personality

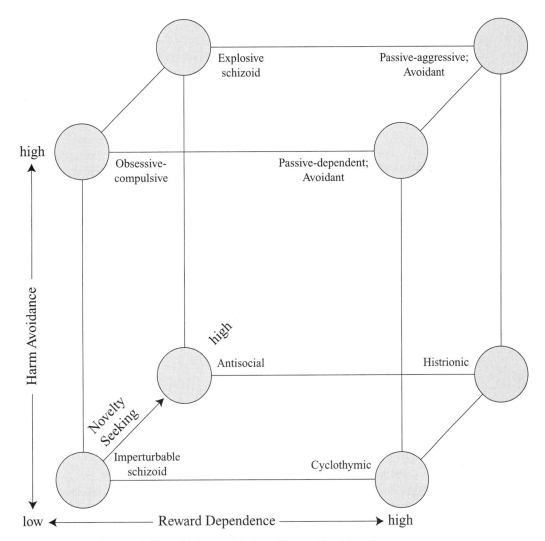

FIGURE 1.5 Cloninger's Neurobiological Model of Personality Disorders.

traits (Bouchard, Lykken, McGue, Segal, & Tellegen, 1990). Even measures of religious interests, attitudes, and values have been shown to be highly influenced by genetic factors (Waller, Kojetin, Bouchard, Lykken, & Tellegen, 1990).

Studies of the heritability of the personality disorders have been less definite. Trait researchers can avail themselves of large samples of normal subjects, but the sample sizes generated by personality disorders are comparatively small and highly pathological in comparison to normal samples, which can distort correlational statistics. Moreover, because personality disorders exist as overlapping composites of personality traits, genetic-environmental interactions are much more complex than for single traits alone. In a review of the evidence, Thapar and McGuffin (1993) argue that the evidence for heritability is most strong for antisocial and schizotypal personality disorders. In another review, Nigg and Goldsmith (1994) suggest that the paranoid and schizoid personality disorders may be linked genetically with schizophrenia. Another popular genetic hypothesis is that the wild emotional swings of the borderline personality are evidence of its association with the affective disorders, which include depression and manic-depression.

Livesley, Jang, Jackson, and Vernon (1993) sought to examine the heritability of 18 dimensions associated with personality disorder pathology, as assessed by the Dimensional Assessment of Personality Pathology (Livesley, Jackson, & Schroeder, 1992). They found that the dimensions of anxiousness, callousness, cognitive distortion, compulsivity, identity problems, oppositionality, rejection, restricted expression, social avoidance, stimulus seeking, and suspiciousness all have heritabilities of between 40% and 60%. Because these are all facets of one or more personality disorders, their study provides indirect support that at least certain problematic traits are indeed heritable to a degree. For example, callousness is often thought of in association with the antisocial, sadistic, and narcissistic personalities, and stimulus seeking is associated with the histrionic and antisocial personalities. Cognitive distortion is associated with the schizotypal; suspiciousness is obviously associated with the paranoid. Social avoidance is associated with the avoidant personality; oppositionality is likely associated with the negativistic personality. Other associations could also be drawn.

THE PSYCHODYNAMIC PERSPECTIVE

Of the several classical perspectives on personality, the psychoanalytic is perhaps the most conceptually rich and yet the most widely misunderstood. Sigmund Freud, the father of psychoanalysis, was born in 1856. As the oldest child of an adoring mother whose belief in her son's destiny never flagged, Freud knew he would be famous. Naturally attracted to science and influenced by Darwin, he settled on a medical career and spent a period of time involved in pure research. Eventually, practical necessity intervened, and Freud began a more applied course, specializing in neurology and psychiatry. In 1885, he traveled to France and witnessed Jean Charcot cure a case of hysterical paralysis using hypnosis. Because the psychiatric treatments of the times were highly ineffective, Freud was impressed and began to experiment with the technique on his own, eventually developing the foundational ideas of psychoanalysis (Gay, 1988).

The Topographic Model

By the early 1890s, Freud and his friend Josef Breuer, a respected physician and original scientist in his own right, had begun to explore the use of hypnosis together. Breuer had already discovered that when subjects with hysterical symptoms talked about their problems during a hypnotic state, they often experienced a feeling of **catharsis,** or emotional release. Eventually, the two formed the theory that hysterical symptoms resulted from early sexual molestation, leaving memories so distressing that they were intentionally forgotten and could only be fully remembered under hypnosis. Later, Freud discovered that when these memories were completely recalled to consciousness in an emotional release, the symptoms disappeared. This became Freud's first theory of neuroses, the idea that behind every neurotic conflict lies a forgotten childhood trauma. Such memories are said to be **repressed.** Motivated to forget what it knows, the mind defends against the painful experiences by actively excluding them from conscious awareness. The past cannot be rewritten, but its impact can be contained. In fact, massive repression is one of the major coping strategies used by the histrionic personality, the contemporary parallel to the turn-of-the-century hysterical syndromes through which the basic principles of psychoanalysis were discovered.

Freud elaborated his insights into what is known as the **topographic model,** the idea that the mind has an organization or architecture that overflows consciousness and can be described in terms of different levels or compartments. At the foundation lies the unconscious, a mysterious realm consisting of everything that we cannot become aware of by simple reflection alone. According to classical psychoanalytic theory, the unconscious is the only part of the mind that exists at birth. Just above the unconscious lies the preconscious, which consists of everything that can be summoned to consciousness on command, for example, your phone number. And finally, there is the part of the mind that forms our waking lives, which we call **conscious awareness.** According to Freud, the desire to bring satisfaction to our unconscious instincts continues to be the main motivator in human behavior throughout the life span. By declaring the unconscious and its drives to be the origin and center of psychological existence, Freud effected a Copernican revolution against the Enlightenment rationalism that dominated the times. Behavior was not fundamentally rational; it was irrational. Just as the earth is not the center of the universe, conscious awareness is but a backwater that conceals the main currents of mental life. For this reason, the idea of making the unconscious conscious, the goal Freud and Breuer had in mind with hypnosis, is a major goal of many contemporary psychotherapies.

The Structural Model

Despite his original enthusiasm for hypnosis, in time, Freud developed additional techniques that allowed him to map the contents of the unconscious, such as free association. In doing so, he discovered an additional organizing principle, the structural model of id, ego, and superego. The id consists of the basic survival instincts and the two dominant drives of personality: sex and aggression. At birth, infant behavior is motivated by the desire for immediate instinctual gratification, which Freud referred to as the **pleasure principle:** I want what I want, and I want it now! In a way, the id is like a dictator that knows only how to repeatedly assert its own desires, something that makes the world a very frustrating place.

To relieve this frustration and ensure greater adaptability in the organism, a second part of the personality, the ego, develops to mediate between the demands of the id and the constraints of external reality. Whereas the id is fundamentally irrational, the ego is fundamentally rational and planful, operating on the **reality principle.** To be effective, the ego must perform sophisticated intellectual activities such as risk-benefit and means-ends analysis, projecting the consequences of various courses of action into the future, judging the range of possible outcomes and their respective cost and reward, all the while modifying plans and embracing alternatives as necessary.

Not every course of action that the ego might imagine is acceptable, however. Eventually, a third part of the personality emerges that internalizes the social values of caretakers, the superego. The process by which the superego forms is called **introjection,** which literally means "a putting inside." The superego consists of two parts, the conscience and the ego ideal: what you shouldn't do and what you should do and should become. The conscience is concerned with the **morality principle,** the right and wrong of behavior. In contrast, the ego ideal pulls each of us toward the realization of our unique human potentials. Breaking moral codes results in feelings of guilt; satisfying the ego ideal results in feelings of pride and self-respect.

For Freud, personality is seen as a war of attrition fought by three generals. As the executive branch of the personality, the ego must balance and mediate between constraints on all sides. On the one hand, the id, upwelling from below, is always percolating, yearning for gratification. On the other hand, the prohibitions of the superego prevent its desires from being directly satisfied. For this reason, the psychoanalytic perspective is often regarded as intrinsically pessimistic: Human beings are said to exist in a state of perpetual conflict between the needs and constraints of various parts of the personality. We can endure, but we cannot escape.

Many of the personality disorders are in exactly this situation. Avoidant personalities, for example, deeply desire close connectedness to others, but also feel a sense of shame about themselves so profound that very few such relationships are possible. Instead, avoidants retreat into a shell where they can at least be alone with their humiliating defects and deficiencies. Compulsive and negativistic personalities wrestle with issues related to the obedience versus defiance of authority. Compulsives express this conflict passively by overconforming to internalized superego demands; on the surface, they appear normal and in control, but beneath, they are taut, anxious, and ever circumspect of their own conduct. In contrast, the negativistic personality, formerly called the passive-aggressive, expresses conflict actively by vacillating between loyalty and insubordinate sabotage. Knowing the outcomes that others seek, they work subtly within the system to bring the plans of others to ruin or at least cause them great frustration. Only a subset of the antisocial personality, the psychopath, escapes conflict. Given their stunted superego development, psychopaths have no need to evaluate their actions according to some standard of right or wrong; instead, their ego is free to select any pathway to gratification that seems realistically possible, even if it includes deceitfulness, misconduct, or irreparable damage to the lives of others. Accordingly, they pause only when self-conscious of the raw punishment society might inflict on them because of their transgressions.

Defense Mechanisms

Because the ego is constantly trying to satisfy the impulsive demands of the id while honoring the constraints of reality and the moral constraints of the superego, awareness is always vulnerable to feelings of anxiety. On the one hand, id instincts are like barbarians at the gate, always threatening to break through ego controls and saturate behavior with raw animal forces. Awareness of this possibility produces what Freud referred to as **neurotic anxiety.** On the other hand, the superego demands perfection, threatening to flood awareness with guilt whenever the satisfaction of id demands is not sufficiently disguised, which Freud referred to as **moral anxiety.** One is a sinner; the other, a saint. Finally, threats from the external world can produce **reality anxiety.** If you hear on the radio that the stock market has just crashed, your concern about your investments is realistic. Whatever the source, anxiety is a signal to ego that some form of corrective action must be taken to reinforce its controls.

But how does the ego protect itself from being overwhelmed? In time, Freud and his disciples discovered the **defense mechanisms.** Through his studies of hysteria, Freud had already been led to the existence of the unconscious and the discovery that guilt can be transformed into a symptom. He found, for example, that uncontrollable aggressive urges might lead to a hysterical paralysis in the hand that might be used to strike someone. Although the goal is always the same—to protect the sanctity of awareness by reducing the level of perceived anxiety or threat—different defense mechanisms work in

FOCUS ON HISTORY

Carl G. Jung

Jung's Contribution to Personality Theory

Although Jung is among the seminal thinkers in personality, his contributions have rarely been applied in the personality disorders. Once Freud's primary disciple, Jung broke from Freud, insisting that there is more to mental life than sex. Most students are acquainted with his distinction between extroversion and introversion. Extroverts explain events from the viewpoint of the environment. They see the focus of life as being driven by events outside themselves and fix their attention firmly on the external world. In contrast, introverts are essentially subjective, drawing from the environment that which satisfies their own inner dispositions. Because, for most of us, the external world is primarily social, extroversion is also associated with sociability, whereas introversion is associated with turning inward, away from the interpersonal world. Among the contemporary personality disorders, the histrionic is notoriously gregarious, an important facet of the larger extroversion construct. In contrast, the schizoid personality is almost completely asocial. The avoidant personality, who desires social relationships yet recoils from engaging others for fear of humiliation, can be seen as conflicted on these dimensions.

Interacting with his famous extroversion-introversion polarity, Jung proposed that thinking-feeling and sensing-intuiting form four additional psychological modes of adaptation or functioning (Jung, 1921). Thinking refers to logical and directed thought, a tendency to approach situations in a cool, detached, and rational fashion; feeling refers to a tendency to value your own subjective, emotional appraisals over any rational process. Because feelings very often have multiple contradictory aspects that are deeply felt and have to be figured out, this mode need not refer to impulsive emotionality. Sensation refers to stimuli experienced immediately by the senses. As an orientation, it refers to a tendency to be oriented to the events of the present moment, without reinterpretation or inference. Intuition is the analogue of sensation in the internal world. Like sensation, its products are given immediately to consciousness, without awareness of any intermediate process. As an orientation, it refers to a tendency to go with your hunches, global appraisals that come from within but whose source or justification is not immediately clear.

Although these additional dimensions do not translate directly into contemporary Axis II constructs, certain personality disorders nevertheless seem stuck in one of Jung's four modes. Compulsive personalities, for example, are famous for a "paralysis of analysis," a heroic effort to get all of life into a rational mode, though mainly because they fear making a mistake and being condemned for it. Histrionic and antisocial personalities are famously sensation seeking, so much so that they fail to anticipate the consequences of their actions in favor of momentary pleasures. Because Jung is now mainly a historical figure, the study of the thinking-feeling and sensing-intuiting polarities in connection with pathological personality has not yet come to fruition.

radically different ways. Some seem simple. Denial, for example, is a straightforward effort to ignore unpleasant realities. Repression is similar but is intended to keep unpleasant thoughts from ever reaching conscious awareness. If repression is successful, there is nothing to deny. Histrionics, for example, use repression to keep their world sweet and simple; they simply cannot be bothered with the deep existential riddles of human existence, nor do they wish to confront their own hypersexual manipulation of others.

In contrast to denial and repression, other defense mechanisms seem more complex or convoluted. Rationalization, for example, is often used to justify a particular action after the fact. In effect, ego looks at both its own behavior and the situation as it might be perceived by others and asks, "How can what I've done be made to seem reasonable?" This defense is a favorite of narcissists, whose self-centeredness often leads them to act without thinking through in advance the consequences for others or how their own actions might be viewed. Other defense mechanisms seem convoluted. In projection, for example, unacceptable motives are transferred from the self and attributed to others. Paranoids use projection to rid themselves of guilt about their own aggressive impulses; by attributing such threats to others, it is the paranoid who becomes the persecuted, endangered, sympathetic victim. A list of defense mechanisms is given in Table 1.3.

Although many psychodynamic ideas have withered over time—penis envy, for example—the defense mechanisms constitute an enduring heritage that continues to inform contemporary theories of the personality disorders. Early analysts were interested in what psychodynamic jargon calls the **vicissitudes of instincts,** that is, their transformation by the ego and eventual expression in behavior, often as symptoms. Gradually, however, thinkers became interested more in the various ways the ego defends itself from anxiety, as well as its own inherent capacities. Whereas Freud held that the ego developed from out of the id and, therefore, was dependent on its supply of libidinal energy, these ego psychologists asserted that the study of the id was only a first phase in the study of the total personality. They believed the ego possessed its own autonomous capacities, completely independent of the id. Naturally, the ego's method of defending itself against other agencies within the personality was a central focus of the thought.

Today, the defense mechanisms are viewed as so important that they constitute an Axis proposed for further study, to be considered for inclusion in *DSM-V,* still some years in the future. Although every individual uses a variety of defenses, each personality disorder seems to prefer a particular subset of defenses over the others (Millon, 1990). These can be used to construct a defensive profile that illustrates how that personality disorder protects itself from internal and external sources of anxiety, stress, and challenge. The compulsive personality, for example, must cope with intense aggressive urges created by parents who were excessively controlling and demanding of perfection. Using reaction formation, the compulsive transforms these urges into their opposite. By overconforming to internalized superego strictures, compulsives seem highly controlled and self-contained, though they are often boiling with rebellion underneath. Their need to stifle upwelling aggressive forces is so profound that they often make excessive use of another mechanism: isolation of affect. By stripping the emotions from ideas, the compulsive creates a mental working environment sterilized against the disorganizing influence of uncomfortable affects, while an awareness of the intellectual aspects of the ideas remains. Then the compulsive can get down to business.

TABLE 1.3 Common Defense Mechanisms

Defense	Definition	Example
Acting Out	Conflicts are translated into action, with little or no intervening reflection.	A student disrupts class because she is angry over an unfair grade.
Denial	Refusal to acknowledge some painful external or subjective reality obvious to others.	A woman refuses to acknowledge a pregnancy, despite positive test results.
Devaluation	Attributing unrealistic negative qualities to self or others, as a means of punishing the self or reducing the impact of the devalued item.	The formerly admired professor who gives you a D on your term paper is suddenly criticized as a terrible teacher.
Displacement	Conflicts are displaced from a threatening object onto a less threatening one.	A student who hates his history professor sets the textbook on fire.
Dissociation	Conflict is dealt with by disrupting the integration of consciousness, memory, or perception of the internal and external world.	After breaking up with a lover, a suicidal student is suddenly unable to recall the periods of time during which they were together.
Fantasy	Avoidance of conflict by creating imaginary situations that satisfy drives or desires.	A student from a troubled home daydreams about going to college to become a famous psychologist.
Idealization	Attributing unrealistic positive qualities to self or others.	A student worried about intellectual ability begins to idolize a tutor.
Isolation of Affect	Conflict is defused by separating ideas from affects, thus retaining an awareness of intellectual or factual aspects but losing touch with threatening emotions.	A biology student sacrifices a laboratory animal, without worrying about its right to existence, quality of life, or emotional state.
Omnipotence	An image of oneself as incredibly powerful, intelligent, or superior is created to overcome threatening eventualities or feelings.	A student facing a difficult final exam asserts that there is nothing about the material that he doesn't know.
Projection	Unacceptable emotions or personal qualities are disowned by attributing them to others.	A student attributes his own anger to the professor, and thereby comes to see himself as a persecuted victim.
Projective Identification	Unpleasant feelings and reactions are not only projected onto others, but also retained in awareness and viewed as a reaction to the recipient's behavior.	A student attributes her own anger to the professor, but sees her response as a justifiable reaction to persecution.
Rationalization	An explanation for behavior is constructed after the fact to justify one's actions in the eyes of self or others.	A professor who unknowingly creates an impossible exam asserts the necessity of shocking students back to serious study.
Reaction Formation	Unacceptable thoughts or impulses are contained by adopting a position that expresses the direct opposite.	A student who hates some group of persons writes an article protesting their unfair treatment by the university.
Repression	Forbidden thoughts and wishes are withheld from conscious awareness.	A student's jealous desire to murder a rival is denied access to conscious awareness.
Splitting	Opposite qualities of a single object are held apart, left in deliberately unintegrated opposition, resulting in cycles of idealization and devaluation as either extreme is projected onto self and others.	A student vacillates between worship and contempt for a professor, sometimes seeing her as intelligent and powerful and himself as ignorant and weak, and then switching roles, depending on their interactions.
Sublimation	Unacceptable emotions are defused by being channelled into socially acceptable behavior.	A professor who feels a secret disgust for teaching instead works ever more diligently to earn the teaching award.
Undoing	Attempts to rid oneself of guilt through behavior that compensates the injured party actually or symbolically.	A professor who designs a test that is too difficult creates an excess of easy extra-credit assignments.

Psychosexual Stages

As Freud and his associates viewed it, personality develops through a series of five psychosexual stages; four of the five involve erogenous zones that provide sexual gratification. For Freud, the term **sexual** was not limited to genital stimulation but instead referred to any pleasurable feeling. Over the course of normal maturation, each psychosexual stage naturally gives way to the next, presenting the individual with a sequence of maturational challenges. First is the oral stage, which runs from birth to about 2 years. Here, the mouth, lips, and tongue are the primary focus; pleasure is received through oral activity, such as nursing at the mother's breast, thumb sucking, and later, biting and swallowing. Next is the anal stage, which runs from about ages 2 to 3. Pleasurable stimulation occurs through defecation, the voiding of feces. Unlike the oral stage, however, the anal stage moves the child into a confrontation with caretakers, who now demand that anal activities be delayed until they can be performed in the proper place, the bathroom. Third is the phallic stage, at ages 3 to 6, during which the focus of sexual gratification moves to the penis or clitoris. Also at this point, children begin to experience libidinal desires for the opposite-sex parent and compete for attention with the same-sex parent, the famous Oedipal complex. Although Freud's idea of penis envy is now dismissed, it is nevertheless true that a special relationship with the opposite-sex parent seems important in the development of several personality disorders. The narcissistic personality, for example, is often an only or first-born male indulged by the mother for being special or gifted; similarly, the histrionic personality enjoys a special relationship with a doting father who reinforces behaviors that are cute and pretty. During ages 6 to 12, sexuality subsides in the latency stage, only to flair again in the genital stage, which begins at puberty. Whereas before, the goal was to maximize sexual pleasure from one's own body, the goal here is to invest sexual energy in relationships with others, through which mature love becomes possible.

Character Disorders

The term **character,** derived from the Greek word for "engraving," was used originally to signify distinctive features that served as the "mark" of a person. In contemporary colloquial usage, character refers to our civilized animal nature, as reflected in the adoption of the habit systems, customs, and manners of prevailing society, taught especially during early childhood.

In the psychodynamic perspective, character has a technical meaning, referring to the way in which the ego habitually satisfies the demands of id, superego, and environment (Fenichel, 1945). Because the study of personality begins with the psychodynamic study of character, many of the personality disorders have direct characterological counterparts. The oral character, for example, closely parallels the dependent personality, and the anal character closely parallels the compulsive. A list of personality disorders and their characterological antecedents is presented in Table 1.4. As later analytic writers such as Shapiro (1965) became interested in the relationship among character, defense, interpersonal conduct, and cognitive style, the relationship between character and personality has grown even stronger.

The foundations of analytic characterology were set forth by Karl Abraham (1927a, 1927b, 1927c) in accord with Freud's psychosexual stages of development, detailed previously. Freud believed that either indulgence or deprivation could result in the *fixation* of libidinal energy during a stage, thus coloring all subsequent development. For

TABLE 1.4   Character Types and Personality Disorder Parallels

Psychodynamic Character Disorder	Contemporary Personality Disorder
Oral (Abraham) ⟶	Dependent
Anal (Abraham) ⟶	Compulsive
Phallic-Narcissistic (Reich) **Narcissistic-Libidinal** (Freud) ⟶	Narcissistic
Impulsive (Reich) ⟶	Antisocial
Phobic (Fenichel) ⟶	Avoidant
Masochistic (Reich) ⟶	Self-Defeating*
Hysterical (Wittels) **Erotic** (Freud) ⟶	Histrionic
Paranoid (Ferenczi) ⟶	Paranoid

* *DSM-III-R*, not *DSM-IV.*

example, the oral period is differentiated into an oral-sucking phase and an oral-biting phase. An overly indulgent sucking stage yields an oral-dependent type, imperturbably optimistic and naïvely self-assured, happy-go-lucky, and emotionally immature. Serious matters do not affect this type. In contrast, an ungratified sucking period yields excessive dependency and gullibility, as deprived children learn to "swallow" anything just to ensure that they receive something. Frustrations at the oral-biting stage yield aggressive oral tendencies such as sarcasm and verbal hostility in adulthood. These **oral-sadistic characters** are inclined to pessimistic distrust, cantankerousness, and petulance.

In the anal stage, children learn autonomy and control. Their increasing cognitive abilities allow them to comprehend parental expectancies, with the option of either pleasing or spoiling parental desires. **Anal characters** take different attitudes toward authority depending on whether resolution occurs during the anal-expulsive or analretentive period. The anal-expulsive period is associated with tendencies toward suspiciousness, extreme conceit and ambitiousness, self-assertion, disorderliness, and negativism. Difficulties that emerge in the late anal, or anal-retentive, phase are usually associated with frugality, obstinacy, and orderliness; a hair-splitting meticulousness; and rigid devotion to societal rules and regulations. Such characteristics are obviously reminiscent of the compulsive personality.

With the writings of Wilhelm Reich in 1933, the concept of character was expanded. Reich held that the neurotic solution of psychosexual conflicts was accomplished through a total restructuring of the defensive style, ultimately crystallizing into a "total formation" called "character armor." The emergence of specific pathological symptoms now assumed secondary importance. Symptoms were thus to be understood in the context of this defensive configuration, similar to the contemporary multiaxial model, which holds that symptoms must be understood in the context of the total personality. Reich also extended Abraham's characterology to the phallic and genital stages of development. In the phallic stage, frustration may lead to a striving for leadership, a need to stand out in a group, and poor reactions to even minor defeats. Such "phallic narcissistic characters" were depicted as vain, brash, arrogant, self-confident, vigorous, cold, reserved, and defensively aggressive.

Object Relations

The development of the psychodynamic perspective can reasonably be divided into three periods. Classical psychoanalysis was almost exclusively an id psychology, emphasizing the role of instincts in creating psychological symptoms, the various psychosexual stages of development, environmental conflicts that could occur during these stages, the fixation of id energy in the concerns of a particular stage, and the id's role in the emergence of character. Freud created and perpetuated his id psychology through several key assumptions. Not only did the ego and superego develop from out of the id, they were forced to rely on basic instinctual drives as their only energy source. The ego and superego were derivative and dependent structures in the study and treatment of psychopathology, whereas the id was central. Understanding a particular mental disorder, then, meant understanding how that disorder served the expression of the basic sexual and aggressive drives in the context of the realistic constraints of the ego and the moral and idealized constraints of the superego. In contemporary terms, Freud was focused on Axis I: His interests were with psychological symptoms, their origin, and their development.

Eventually, however, opponents of Freud's "sexual psychology" shifted their interest from the id to the ego. These new thinkers discovered new forces in personality, so that the entire field began to be described as psychodynamic rather than psychoanalytic. Jung, for example, developed numerous, highly original ideas, including the collective unconscious, synchronicity, and the trait dimension of introversion-extroversion. Adler focused on social influences and on compensations against inferiority feelings. Later thinkers went so far as to assert that the ego is fundamentally an adaptational structure and, as such, is necessarily endowed with its own innate potentials prepared over the course of human evolution. Some of these are simple perceptual abilities present at birth; others are adaptive capacities, including reasoning and cognitive abilities (Hartmann, 1958). The ability to break complex tasks into subtasks, for example, may be necessary to satisfy the sexual drive, but it is difficult to understand how this capacity might derive from sexuality itself. Moreover, because the ego is concerned with coordinating psychological needs with the realities of the external world, ego psychologists naturally became more interpersonal. One important theorist was Karen Horney. Many of the constructs derived from her theory bear a surprising resemblance to the contemporary personality disorders.

The final stage in the development of the psychodynamic perspective is called **object relations.** The name seems cryptic at first, but its origin is easily understood as a throwback to the sexual reductionism of classical analysis. Every instinct has an aim and an object: The aim is always the satisfaction of instinctual desires; the object is something in the outside world through which this aim can be achieved. For Freud, the id instincts formed the basis of human nature. Other aspects of the personality, such as the ego and the superego, and persons in the outside world were valuable, or real, to the id only insofar as they brought with them satisfaction. Accordingly, id psychology cannot be a psychology of human relatedness. Others are just the furniture of mental life, objects whose presence promises instinctual satisfaction, not other beings knowable apart from their capacity for drive reduction.

In contrast, modern object relations theory is simultaneously cognitive and interpersonal, emphasizing first that the outside world is known through mental representations, or internal working models (Bowlby, 1969), and second, that the content of these models is interpersonal, being developed largely during early childhood from experiences with caretakers and significant others, prior even to the development of self-awareness. In effect, object relations are to the individual what paradigms are to scientific theories: For the most part, they exist as unconscious mental structures that organize experience but are only partially accessible to conscious reflection. As the most recent phase in the development of psychodynamic theory, object relations might be called a "superego psychology," because it is explicitly concerned with introjects, aspects, and images of others internalized in the course of development. However, it is more broadly concerned with how the mental representations of self and others influence ongoing behavior in the present, not just with condemnation and the morality principle.

The foremost object relations thinker in the personality disorders is Otto Kernberg (1967, 1984, 1996). Kernberg advocates classifying various personalities, some from the *DSM* and some from the psychoanalytic tradition, in terms of three levels of structural organization—psychotic, borderline, and neurotic—which represent degrees of organization or cohesiveness in the personality (see Figure 1.6). Normals possess a cohesive, integrated sense of self that psychoanalysts term **ego identity.** Most of us know who we are, and our sense of self remains constant over time and situation. We know our likes and dislikes, are conscious of certain core values, and know how we are similar to others and yet different from them as well. Individuals with a well-integrated ego identity are said to possess ego strength, the ability to remain integrated in the face of pressure or stress. In addition, normal persons also possess a mature and internalized social or moral value system, the superego, which includes features such as personal responsibility and appropriate self-criticism.

In contrast, the neurotic level is characterized by a well-developed ego identity, complicated by "unconscious guilt feelings reflected in specific pathological patterns of interaction in relation to sexual intimacy" (Kernberg, 1996, p. 121). Neurotic personalities are worried about sexual matters, a concern that leaks into their interpersonal relationships, creating feelings of guilt that affect behavior. The character types described by Kernberg vary somewhat from those of the *DSM-IV.* The neurotic level includes the depressive-masochistic, obsessive-compulsive, and hysterical personalities. The depressive-masochistic character, for example, derives primarily from reaction formation, that is, the tendency to do the opposite of unconscious wishes. Thus, the tendency is to deprive or sabotage oneself, rather than indulge what would otherwise be pleasurable or satisfying. In contrast, the hysterical personality is more obviously sexual, exhibiting a superficial provocativeness but with underlying sexual inhibition. Both the masochistic-depressive and hysterical reflect more integrated levels of more primitive character structures. The hysterical personality, for example, exists at the neurotic level, but is also related to the so-called infantile personality, which tends to be more demanding, impulsive, and aggressive. The two are said to exist on a *spectrum,* a term commonly used to express the relationship between higher functioning and lower functioning character types.

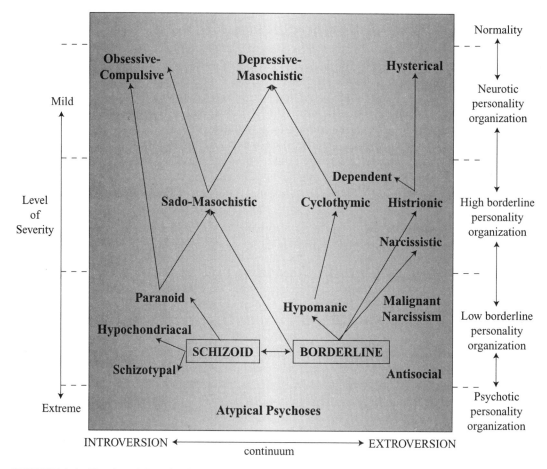

FIGURE 1.6   Kernberg's Levels of Personality Organization. (Adapted from Kernberg, 1996.)

The borderline level of personality functioning exists between the neuroses and the psychoses. Superficially, personalities at the borderline level are often similar to neurotics but are not as integrated. Like neurotics, they are in contact with reality but nevertheless sometimes dissociate or experience psychotic episodes. Moreover, they tend to rely on primitive defense mechanisms, not those of mature adults. According to Kernberg, all individuals at the borderline level exhibit what is called **split object-representation,** which accounts for much of their behavior. Normal persons realize that very few people or situations are either all good or all bad; instead, most are somewhere in the middle, with both good and bad aspects. The good and bad can be held in mind simultaneously, creating a picture that is complex but realistic. Personalities at the borderline level, however, see persons and situations as either all good or all bad; people are either angels or devils. Such persons invariably exhibit severe difficulties in their interpersonal relationships, particularly intimate relationships, and exhibit various degrees of sexual pathology. You can imagine what your friends would think of you if you suddenly switched from worshipping them to hating them and back again. All the psychoanalytic character types, according to Kernberg, derive from the basic borderline

FOCUS ON HISTORY

Whatever Happened to Behaviorism?

Are We Just a "Tabula Rasa"?

The duality between empiricism and rationalism has a long history in philosophy and psychology. Empiricism is most often identified with the English philosophers John Locke and David Hume. Locke emphasized the role of direct experience in knowledge, believing that knowledge must be built up from collections of sensations. Locke's position became known as associationism. Here, learning is seen as occurring through a small collection of processes that associate one sensation with another. Empiricism found a counterpoint in the rationalism of continental philosophers, notably the Dutch philosopher Spinoza, the French philosopher Descartes, and the German philosopher Leibniz. In contrast, the empiricists held that innate ideas could not exist. Locke, for example, maintained that the mind was a tabula rasa, or blank slate, on which experience writes. Eventually, however, the elements of learning were recast in the language of stimulus and response. The foundations of behaviorism are perhaps more associated with J. B. Watson than with any other psychologist, though Watson was preceded by other important figures in the history of learning theory, notably Thorndike and Pavlov. Although a variety of learning theories eventually developed, behaviorism as a formal dogma is most associated with the views of B. F. Skinner.

According to Skinner's strict behaviorism, it is unnecessary to posit the existence of unobservable emotional states or cognitive expectancies to account for behavior and its pathologies. Hypothetical inner states are discarded and explanations are formulated solely in terms of external sources of stimulation and reinforcement. Thus, all disorders become the simple product of environmentally based reinforcing experiences. These shape the behavioral repertoire of the individual, and differences between adaptive and maladaptive behaviors can be traced entirely to differences in the reinforcement patterns to which individuals are exposed. Inner states, such as traits or schemata, are considered throwbacks to primitive animism. Instead, the understanding of a behavior can be complete only when the contextual factors in which the event is embedded are illuminated. The logic is relatively simple: If there are no innate ideas, sensation or stimuli are by definition all that exist. Because sensation originates in the environment, the environment must ultimately control all behavior, however complex. The mind becomes an empty vessel, or tabula rasa, that contains only what the environment puts there. All behavior is said to be under stimulus control. For this reason, the relationship between personality and behaviorism has been mainly antagonistic, and understandably so, because behavioral psychology exclusively focuses on observable surface behavior rather than on inferred entities, such as personality traits, cognitive schemata, instinctual drives, or interpersonal dispositions, all essential units in the study of personality.

By the mid-1980s, a number of crucial reinterpretations of traditional assessment had been made that allowed clinically applied behavioral approaches to become successively broader and more moderate. Most notably, the diagnoses of Axis I, regarded in psychiatry

(Continued)

FOCUS ON HISTORY *(Continued)*

as substantive disease entities, were reinterpreted with the behavioral paradigm as inductive summaries, labels that bind together a body of observations for the purpose of clinical communication. For example, whereas depression refers to a genuine pathology in the person for a traditional clinician, a behavioral clinician sees only its operational criteria and their label, not a disease. As a result, behavioral assessment and traditional assessment could thus speak the same tongue, while retaining their respective identities and distinctions. This allowed behavioral therapists to rationalize their use of diagnostic concepts without being untrue to their behavioral core. Likewise, as the cognitive revolution got underway in earnest in the late 1960s and early 1970s, behavioral psychologists began seeking ways to generalize their own perspective to bring cognition under the behavioral umbrella. In time, cognitive activity was reinterpreted as covert behavior. Finally, the organism itself began to be seen a source of reinforcement and punishment, with affective mechanisms being viewed as the means through which reinforcement occurs. Contemporary behavioral assessment, then, is no longer focused merely on surface behavior. Instead, behavioral assessment is now seen as involving three "response systems," namely, the verbal-cognitive mode, the affective-physiological mode, and the overt-motor response system, a scheme originated by Lang (1968).

However, behavioral theorists have gone far toward rediscovering personality. The relationship among responses across the three response systems, for example, has been extensively studied (see Voeltz & Evans, 1982, for a review). Behavioral psychologists now talk about the organization of behavior, an idea that draws on the conception that the individual person is more than a sum of parts, even where those parts are only behavioral units. An especially seminal thinker, Staats (1986) has developed a more systematic approach to personality that broadens the behavioral tradition. In what he terms "paradigmatic behaviorism," Staats has sought a "third-generation behaviorism" that adds a developmental dimension, arguing that the learning of "basic behavioral repertoires" begins at birth and proceeds hierarchically, with each new repertoire providing the foundation for successively more complex forms of learning. Thus, some repertoires must be learned before others. For example, both fine motor movements and the alphabet must be learned before cursive writing can develop. Staats holds that repertoires are learned in the language-cognitive, emotional-motivational, and sensorimotor response systems, and these systems are interdependent and only pedagogically distinct. Personality thus becomes the total complex hierarchical structure of repertoires and reflects the individual's unique learning history. Different repertoires mediate different responses, so individual differences simply reflect different learning histories. Thus, the concept of a behavioral repertoire is simultaneously both overt and idiographic, making it acceptable from both behavioral and personality perspectives and capable of spanning both normality and abnormality.

and schizoid personalities, end points of a continuum of extroversion-introversion. The relationships are complex and technically unimportant now. Many are reviewed in subsequent chapters.

The psychotic level of personality organization need not be described in detail, for nearly everything we think of as personality is lost in this case. Rather than integration and organization, we find only broken, random pieces, with little or no sense of an integrated identity. Instead of distinction, there is often fusion between self and other or even between self and physical environment. The psychotic level is particularly characterized by an intense and inappropriate aggression. There are no personality disorders described in the *DSM-IV* that typically function at the psychotic level.

Summary

In the last two decades, the study of personality and its disorders has become central to the study of abnormal psychology. Chapter 1 introduces the emergence of this new discipline by analyzing the constructs of personality and personality disorders, by comparing and contrasting the basic assumptions that underlie approaches to these constructs, and by presenting the fundamentals of the classical perspectives on personality, which are essential to the understanding of the clinical chapters that follow. The word **personality** is derived from the Latin term *persona,* originally representing the theatrical mask used by ancient dramatic players. Today, personality is seen as a complex pattern of deeply embedded psychological characteristics that are expressed automatically in almost every area of psychological functioning. That is, personality is viewed as the patterning of characteristics across the entire matrix of the person. Personality is often confused with two related terms, **character** and **temperament.** Character refers to characteristics acquired during our upbringing and connotes a degree of conformity to virtuous social standards. Temperament, in contrast, refers not to the forces of socialization, but to a basic biological disposition toward certain behaviors.

Understanding personality disorders requires an understanding of their role in the study of abnormal behavior. **Diagnostic criteria** are the defining characteristics used by clinicians to classify individuals within a clinical category. Each disorder has its own unique list. In general, the list of criteria for the personality disorders runs either seven, eight, or nine items, each of which details some characteristic trait, attitude, or behavior strongly related to that particular disorder. A **personality trait** is a long-standing pattern of behavior expressed across time and in many different situations. Where many such personality traits typically occur together, they may be said to constitute a **personality disorder.** When all of these characteristics are taken together, they constitute a **personality prototype.**

The mental disorders in the *DSM* are grouped in terms of the **multiaxial model.** Each axis represents a different kind or source of information. The multiaxial model exists because some means is required whereby the various symptoms and personality characteristics of a given patient can be brought together to paint a picture that reflects the functioning of the whole person. The multiaxial model is divided into five separate axes, each of which gets at a different source or level of influence in human behavior. Axis II, the personality disorders, provides both a substrate and context for understanding the symptoms of Axis I. Every personality style is also a coping style, and personality is a cardinal organizing principle through which psychopathology should be understood.

Normality and abnormality cannot be distinguished on a completely objective basis. Normality and pathology usually reside on a continuum. Personality disorders do seem to be characterized by three pathological characteristics. First, personality disorders tend to exhibit a tenuous stability, or lack of resilience, under conditions of stress. Second, personality-disordered subjects are adaptively inflexible. Disordered personalities create vicious cycles by repeating their pathology again and again.

In personality, the dominant perspectives are psychodynamic, biological, interpersonal, and cognitive. Biological influences on personality may be thought of as being either proximal or distal. Distal influences originate within our genetic code and often concern inherited characteristics transmitted as part of the evolutionary history of our own species. Other biological influences in personality focus on proximal causes, influences that exist because we are complex biological systems. When the structures that underlie behavior differ, behavior itself is affected. Two such concepts important to personality are constitution and temperament.

The word **temperament** came into the English language in the Middle Ages to reflect the biological soil from which personality develops. Temperament is an underlying biological potential for behavior, seen most clearly in the predominant mood or emotionality of an individual and in the intensity of his or her activity cycles. As such, it refers to the sum total of inherited biological influences on personality that show continuity across the life span. Because our physical matrix exists before other domains of personality emerge, biologically built-in behavioral tendencies preempt and exclude other possible pathways of development that might take hold. **Constitution** refers to the total plan or philosophy on which something is constructed. The foremost early exponent of the constitutional approach was Ernst Kretschmer (1926), who developed a classification system based on three main body types—thin, muscular, and obese—each of which was associated with certain personality traits and psychopathologies.

More recently, neurobiological models have been proposed by Cloninger (1986, 1987b), as well as by Siever and Davis (1991). Cloninger's model is based on the interrelationship of three genetic-neurobiologic trait dispositions, each of which is associated with a particular neurotransmitter system: dopaminergic, serotonergic, or noradrenergic. Each is hypothesized to dispose the individual toward a different type of behavioral tendency. Siever and Davis suggest a psychobiological model consisting of four dimensions—cognitive/perceptual organization, impulsivity/aggression, affective instability, and anxiety/inhibition—each of which has both Axis I and Axis II manifestations.

The most distal influence in personality is genetics. Researchers explore the influence of genes on behavior by searching for the presence of similar psychopathologies in siblings and relatives of an afflicted subject, by studying patterns of transmission across generations of the extended family, and by comparing the correlation of scores obtained on personality tests between sets of fraternal twins and identical twins reared together and apart. The evidence for a genetic influence on personality is strongest for antisocial and schizotypal personality disorders. Other evidence suggests that the paranoid and schizoid personality disorders may be linked genetically with schizophrenia. A popular genetic hypothesis is that the wild emotional swings of the borderline personality are evidence of its association with the affective disorders, which include depression and manic-depression.

Of all the classical perspectives on personality, the psychoanalytic is perhaps the most conceptually rich. Sigmund Freud, the father of psychoanalysis, was born in 1856. Freud's first theory of neuroses emerged from his work with hypnosis and referred to the idea that behind every neurotic conflict lies a forgotten childhood trauma. The memories of that trauma are said to be **repressed.** Motivated to forget what it knows, the mind defends against the painful experiences by actively excluding them from conscious awareness. Eventually, Freud elaborated his insights into the **topographic model,** the idea that the mind has an organization or architecture that overflows consciousness and can be described in terms of different levels or compartments: the unconscious, the preconscious, and conscious awareness. Later, Freud developed a structural model of the mind constituted by the id, consisting of the basic survival instincts and drives; the ego, which develops to mediate between the demands of the id and the constraints of external reality; and the superego, which represents the internalized social values of caretakers. The id works on the basis of the **pleasure principle,** whereas the ego works on the **reality principle.** Breaking moral codes results in feelings of guilt, while satisfying the ego ideal results in feelings of pride and self-respect. For Freud, personality is seen as a war of attrition fought by three generals. As the executive branch of the personality, the ego must balance and mediate between constraints on all sides. On the one hand, the id, upwelling from below, is always percolating, yearning for gratification. On the other hand, the prohibitions of the superego prevent its desires from being directly satisfied.

The workings of the id, ego, and superego produce different types of anxiety, which is a signal to the ego that something must be done. In time, Freud and his disciples discovered the **defense mechanisms.** Although every individual uses a variety of defenses, each personality disorder seems to prefer a particular subset of defense over the others. These can be used to construct a defensive profile that illustrates how that personality disorder protects itself from internal and external sources of anxiety, stress, and challenge.

According to Freud, personality develops through a series of five psychosexual stages. Over the course of normal maturation, each psychosexual stage naturally gives way to the next, presenting the individual with a sequence of maturational challenges. In the psychodynamic perspective, character has a technical meaning, referring to the way in which the ego habitually satisfies the demands of the id, superego, and environment. Since the study of personality begins with the psychodynamic study of character, many of the personality disorders have direct characterological counterparts. As later analytic writers became interested in the relationship among character, defense, interpersonal conduct, and cognitive style, the relationship between character and personality has grown even stronger.

The final stage in the development of the psychodynamic perspective is called **object relations.** Every instinct has an aim and an object. The aim is always the satisfaction of instinctual desires. The object is something in the outside world through which this aim can be achieved. For Freud, the id instincts formed the basis of human nature. In contrast, modern object relations theory is simultaneously cognitive and interpersonal, emphasizing first, that the outside world is known through mental representations or internal working models, and second, that the contents of these models are interpersonal, being developed largely during early childhood from experiences with caretakers and significant others, prior even to the development of self-awareness. The foremost object relations thinker in the personality disorders is Kernberg, who advocates classifying various personalities, some from the *DSM* and some from the psychoanalytic tradition, in terms of three levels of structural organization—psychotic, borderline, and neurotic—which represent degrees of organization or cohesiveness in the personality.

Chapter 2

Personality Disorders: Contemporary Perspectives

Objectives

- In what important way does the interpersonal perspective differ from the psychodynamic and biological perspectives?
- Explain Sullivan's contribution to the study of personality.
- List and explain Leary's levels of personality.
- What is the *interpersonal circumplex?*
- Explain the principle of complementarity.
- Explain Benjamin's Structured Analysis of Social Behavior model.
- What are *cognitive styles?*
- What are *cognitive schemata?* How do they differ from *cognitive styles?*
- What are *cognitive distortions?*
- What is the five-factor model?
- Describe the major principles of an evolutionary theory of personality.
- What are the domains of personality?

Chapter 1 focused on classical theories and foundational issues, covering the nature of personality disorders, their relationship to abnormal behavior through the multiaxial model, and their character and temperament—the two great historical concepts of the person.

Personality study is not limited to the classical psychodynamic and biological models. As noted in Chapter 1, the history of the social sciences has a contingent structure: Given no strong experimental method by which to falsify reasonable alternatives, the most important perspectives on the field do not emerge all at once, but instead make their appearance at different points in history. In this chapter, our focus shifts from the study of those early perspectives to those that have matured more recently, namely, the interpersonal, the cognitive, the trait and factorial, and the evolutionary. At the end of the chapter, we present an integration of these perspectives. Just as personality is concerned with the patterning of characteristics across the total person and personality disorders with failures in the adaptation of these characteristics to the environment and its challenges, it is the total organism that either survives and reproduces to go forward or else succumbs to disease or predatory threat. To enhance their survival chances, organisms have developed sophisticated ways of relating and communicating with one another, as well as complex information-processing strategies that allow them to prioritize, analyze, and optimize solutions to pressing environmental problems and survival concerns.

The Interpersonal Perspective

The perspectives of Chapter 1 attempted to understand personality in isolation from the environment. Personality flows from within, either through its foundation in biological temperament or through the vicissitudes of unconscious forces, wrought by psychodynamic conflicts among the id, ego, and superego. Where others did enter the picture, with the object relations dynamic variant, the focus nevertheless remained on experiential representations internalized by the individual. With object-representations in innerplace, the person could again be understood from the inside out.

The interpersonal perspective argues that personality is best conceptualized as the social product of interactions with significant others. Very few of our needs can be satisfied, our goals reached, or our wishes and potentials fulfilled in a nonsocial world. Even when we are alone, interpersonal theorists argue, we continue to interact with others. When lying down to sleep, for example, our reflections about the important events of the day almost always involve people. We do not dream about doorknobs or the private lives of hamsters, but about others who are important in our own lives or significant in some way. According to Allen Frances, (chairperson of the committee that guided the construction of *DSM-IV*):

The essence of being a mammal is the need for, and the ability to participate in, interpersonal relationships. The interpersonal dance begins at least as early as birth and ends only with death. Virtually all of the most important events in life are interpersonal in nature and most of what we call personality is interpersonal in expression. (quoted in Benjamin, 1996, p. v)

From beginning to end, we are always transacting either with real or imagined others and their expectations. Personality cannot be understood from the inside out, because it is intrinsically immersed in context. Life itself is about relationships. Only in the context of these relationships does personality develop, and only there can it be fully understood.

A relational understanding of personality goes far toward dispelling certain cultural myths about human nature and points to the role played by cultural values in the genesis of scientific theories. As noted by Kiesler (1996), for example, the emphasis on individualism in Western culture runs counter to the basic assumptions of the relational view. For Westerners, identity is self-contained and self-determined. As individualists, we assume that we are the authors of our own being and our own destiny. Free will alone

FOCUS ON CULTURE

Culture and Personality

How Do Culture and Personality Interact?

Because societies are composed of individuals and because every individual has a personality, it follows that culture and personality are inextricably intertwined. Their relationship has been studied by anthropologists, psychologists, and other social scientists since the birth of these sciences. American anthropologists of the early 1900s saw culture as an extension of personality, expanded physically and temporally to a larger scale. Some (Benedict, 1934; Mead, 1928) argued that culture provides behavioral ideals that contextualize, and thereby influence, the natural unfolding of temperament characteristics over the course of maturation. Others (Kardiner, 1939) believed that society shaped a basic personality structure guided primarily by child-rearing practices and family organization Alarcon, Foulks, and Vakkur (in press) offer an incisive review of this literature. More recent research has examined cultural differences in the prevalence of personality disorders (Loranger et al., 1994). Although some disorders appear to be more common in certain cultures than in others, it nevertheless appears that all personality disorders have substantial cross-cultural validity, occurring in nearly every culture with at least some frequency.

Accordingly, given the universality of the *DSM* scheme of personality constructs and the interpenetration of personality and culture mentioned previously, it should be possible to generalize the constructs of a theoretical model of personality to a cultural level (Escovar, 1997). The evolutionary model (Millon, 1990) consists of three dimensions that motivate, prompt, energize, and direct human behavior, anchored to three evolutionary imperatives—survival, adaptation, and replication—that operate across all levels of organization in nature. Both viruses and government, for example, must obey evolutionary laws.

The first evolutionary imperative, survival, is expressed as a dimension of pleasure and pain. Events that we subjectively experience as pleasurable are those that contribute to the survival of the individual or species—sexuality, for example. Events experienced as painful are associated with death, injury, or disease. At a cultural level, malevolence versus benevolence refers to differences in the extent to which pain versus pleasure is used as a motivator. In some cultures, pain bestows absolution for previous transgressions, so members of the culture view pain as a penance. Other cultures take the attitude that individuals will intrinsically actualize in a productive direction if the society will only provide support for basic needs, such as food, water, and housing.

The second evolutionary imperative, adaptation, is expressed along a continuum of passive to active. Passive organisms seek to adapt themselves to their environment, whereas active organisms seek to adapt the environment to their own needs. At a cultural level, this distinction is expressed in the duality between the preference for a more leisurely and traditional lifestyle and one that is more industrious and dynamic. Societies thus differ in their rates of social change; in the rate that they adopt innovations, technical or otherwise; and in their level of relatedness to their environment.

The third evolutionary principle, replication, is expressed as a sociobiological duality between a desire to pursue one's own self-interest and a desire to nurture others. Some species produce many offspring that are left to fend for themselves, a male strategy;

other species produce only a few offspring, which they nurture to adulthood, a female strategy. This duality has its counterpart at a cultural level in the distinction between individualism and collectivism (Triandis, 1995). In the collectivist culture, personal goals are subordinated to those of the collective; in the individualistic culture, the views, needs, and goals of the self are ascendant. Because every individual implicitly adopts the values and standards of the larger culture at an unconscious level, the type of culture in which he or she lives profoundly affects many aspects of human functioning. Collectivist cultures emphasize intimacy and in-group relatedness; the self is defined socially through its relations with others. In contrast, individualist cultures emphasize independence; the self stands on its own apart from the group, and not being able to do so is a sign of weakness. When it comes to social interactions, collectivists value harmony, so much so that they suppress negative feelings and "tell others what they want to hear, rather than tell the truth and create bad feelings" (Triandis, 1994, p. 293). In contrast, individualists seek to "tell it like it is," emphasizing facts at the expense of feelings.

determines who we are and who we will become. Others cannot influence, much less change, us unless we give them permission.

According to the interpersonal perspective, individuality is an illusion wrought by the Western emphasis on objectivity and rationalism. Western understanding requires that things be analyzed, dissolved into parts, distilled into fundamental units, and, finally, isolated from the larger ecology that sustains and nurtures them and may even provide their reason for being. The Western ego ideal is strength, independence, and self-sufficiency. Although we certainly have relationships, we do not require them, for relatedness entails dependency, and dependency entails weakness. Our scientific theories have inherited this bias. Even a notion that many psychologists would take for granted—that personality is composed of smaller units, or traits—can be viewed as a cultural distortion.

ORIGINS OF THE INTERPERSONAL APPROACH

Harry Stack Sullivan is considered the father of the interpersonal perspective. Sullivan's ideas were developed largely as a reaction against the classical analytic and medical models that dominated psychiatry in the early to mid-twentieth century. Biographers universally emphasize the stormy nature of his own development, yet Sullivan probably felt that both models implicitly blame the person without properly considering the role of social factors. Classical psychoanalysis is based on the conflict between upwelling sexual and aggressive id instincts and their containment through the defensive processes of the ego. Others are only objects that satisfy or frustrate the demands of the id, not real persons with their own lives, desires, hopes, and aspirations. By voiding others of their personhood, Freud made pathology a private affair. Likewise, the medical model presents psychopathology as a disease of the person, for it is the person who is abnormal, who receives a diagnosis, and who must be treated.

Sullivan's contribution lay in realizing that some forms of mental disorder, although perhaps most dramatically and tangibly manifest through the individual, are nevertheless created and perpetuated through maladaptive patterns of social interaction and communication. According to Sullivan (1953, pp. 110–111), then, personality is "the recurrent set of interpersonal situations which characterize a person's life." Perhaps our family, boss, or spouse makes us crazy, for example. By relocating pathology as part of a transactional system, Sullivan not only put psychopathology back into its proper ecological context, but also brought greater empathy and humanism to its treatment. No longer was the individual simply a vessel for his or her symptoms; instead, pathology could be seen as being created and sustained by patterns of communication.

The discovery that the origins of pathology might be interactional rather than individual, however, was only a beginning, a possibility rather than a process. It does not explain how disordered communication develops. Fortunately, Sullivan was acquainted with the most recent advances in many adjacent fields of knowledge. In outlining the interactional basis of psychopathology, he drew particularly from the symbolic interactionism of George Mead and the work of the anthropologist Edward Sapir in culture and linguistics. The issue with which Sullivan struggled, the essential basis of the interpersonal approach, concerns the nature of the self. Implicitly, all of us regard the self as a thing, a concrete entity or substance with sharply defined boundaries, like a rock. If this were true, we should know exactly who we are all the time. As Freud had already shown, however, self-consciousness does not exhaust mentality, but instead floats atop the unconscious—inaccessible and remote. But Sullivan went even further. No essential self lies hidden beneath the veils of the unconscious. Instead, there is only a self-concept that is continually being defined and redefined by the interpersonal communications of others. Keep telling a child that he or she is bad, and the child will soon believe you.

The consequences of Sullivan's insight bridge psychology and existentialism. We are not self-contained entities. In fact, we are never exactly sure who and what we are. Instead, the self-concept is a collection of probabilistic hypotheses, some of which we seek to support and some of which we seek to deny. Existentialism argues that first we exist; then we define ourselves. The interpersonalists, however, argue that others are essential to the formation of our self-identity. The communications we experience as most validating confirm our ideal self. Confusing communications leave us stranded on uncertain existential ground. These are either inconsistent with our concept of who we really are, the actual self, or else portray the self in an undesirable way, threatening self-esteem and arousing anxiety and insecurity. This provides an important contrast between interpersonal and psychodynamic views. For Freud, the ego is essentially a diplomat skilled in repression and other defense mechanisms. Anxiety is a signal to the ego that instinctual drives are on the edge of breaking openly into conscious awareness and must be defended against. For Sullivan, however, anxiety is interpersonal and, therefore, cannot exist unless others are at least symbolically involved or otherwise present in thought.

Despite his many interesting and brilliant contributions, Sullivan is not considered to be a systematic thinker. Many of his books, in fact, represent past lecture series organized for publication by dedicated followers. Moreover, the personality constructs he proposed are not notably interpersonal, at least by contemporary standards. These constructs include, for example, the stammerer and the homosexual personality. Nevertheless, Sullivan is regarded as one of the most important theorists of the twentieth century. His ideas spawned diverse lines of research, including work that led to the famous "double-bind" theory of schizophrenia (Bateson, Jackson, Haley, & Weakland, 1956), the study of family communication patterns, and even studies of nonverbal gestural communication, called kinesics.

After Sullivan, the next important figure in the emerging interpersonal movement was Timothy Leary (1957). Whereas Sullivan was brilliant but scattered, Leary was brilliant and systematic. Like Sullivan, he borrowed much from psychoanalysis. In particular, he believed that personality should be thought of in terms of levels, not unlike the psychodynamic idea of levels of consciousness. Leary's levels, however, organize a much wider array of information. The first level, public communication, refers to what is observable and objective in interpersonal behavior. The second, conscious description, is expressed through the verbal content of statements made about self or others. Because this level regards the world of subjective experience—by definition, always somewhat of a distortion of consensual social reality—reports of an individual's experience of self and others are often especially revealing. The third level, private symbolization, is concerned with preconscious and unconscious attributions, as expressed through "projective, indirect fantasy materials" (p. 79), including projective tests, fantasies, artistic productions, wishes, dreams, and free associations. Leary's fourth level, unexpressed unconscious, refers to issues that are censored from consciousness and "systematically and compulsively avoided by the subject at all the other levels of personality . . . and are conspicuous by their inflexible absence" (p. 80). Finally, the fifth level, values, is expressed not only in the ego ideal but also in the standards through which self and others are judged.

THE CIRCUMPLEX MODEL

Leary also contributed to the development of the **interpersonal circumplex,** one of the most influential geometric models in the history of personality theory (Freedman, Leary, Ossorio, & Coffey, 1951; Leary, 1957). The circumplex is often called the interpersonal circle. Whereas the *DSM* presents the personality disorders as discrete diagnostic categories with no necessary relationship, the circumplex organizes its constructs like the segments on a circle or like the face of a clock. Each personality thus shades gently into its nearby neighbors.

The circle is formed by crossing the two content dimensions believed to define interpersonal communication: dominance and affiliation (Kiesler, 1996). Though each segment of the circle, each personality, receives a different name, each is a blend of different quantities of dominance and affiliation. Segments that are near each other are closely related, whereas those that are opposite on the circle are opposites in real life. In Leary's original circle, for example, the dependent personality was represented as consisting of about equal levels of affiliation and submission, and the compulsive personality, which Leary called the responsible-hypernormal, consisted of about equal levels of affiliation and dominance. Leary also noted relationships between the interpersonal circle and other perspectives. The four quadrants, he suggested, capture the temperaments or humors of Hippocrates, and the horizontal and vertical axes capture the two basic drives of psychoanalysis—sexuality and aggression. Figure 2.1 presents Kiesler's (1986) 1982 interpersonal circle, one of the foremost current models.

Complementarity

One of the most attractive features of the interpersonal approach is the tight linkage between the theory and its derived constructs: Interpersonal principles map directly to the

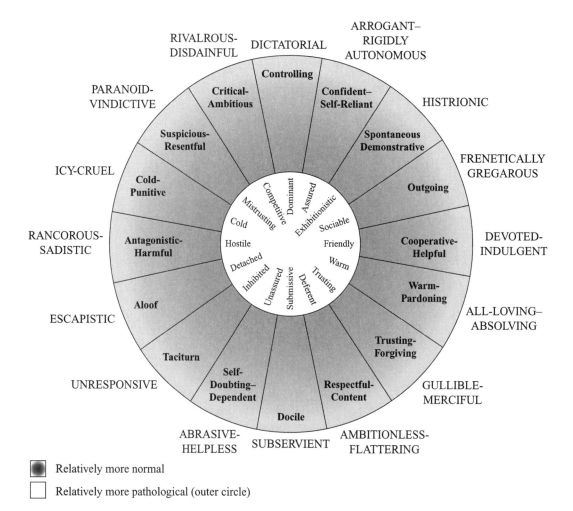

Relatively more normal

Relatively more pathological (outer circle)

FIGURE 2.1 Kiesler's 1982 Interpersonal Circle. (Adapted from Millon & Klerman, 1986.)

circle. One of the most important of these is *complementarity*. According to Kiesler (1983, p. 198), "Our interpersonal actions are designed to invite, pull, elicit, draw, entice, or evoke 'restricted classes' of reactions from persons with whom we interact, especially from significant others." Every interpersonal bid is intended to implicitly exclude invalidating responses—those incongruent with how we would like others to see us—and implicitly include only validating responses—those that confirm the self-presentation. If each party in the interpersonal process successfully controls the response class of the other, the needs of each participant are mutually satisfied. On the other hand, responses that are irrelevant or inconsistent with the self-presentation are likely to be ignored or to arouse insecurity and tension. On the interpersonal circle, behaviors are considered complementary when they are opposite on the vertical axis—control—or similar on the horizontal axis—affiliation. Translated into everyday language, dominance pulls for submission and submission pulls for dominance. However, friendliness pulls for friendliness, and hate pulls for hate (Carson, 1969; Kiesler, 1983).

Normality and Abnormality

The management of presentation always entails implicit beliefs about self and others, a particular perspective on the world. As explained by Kiesler (1996, pp. 87–88), "a person brings about the very consequences of his or her own prediction . . . simply by virtue of the effects of the prediction itself." For example, an individual who is highly competitive tends to view others as highly competitive and begins to compete even harder, producing a competitive atmosphere that draws out competition from others. As a general principle, the social reality associated with any particular interpersonal style evokes responses that confirm that reality, culminating in a self-fulfilling prophecy. In some cases, this is highly adaptive; a friendly person naturally pulls friendliness from others, brightening everyone's day.

FOCUS ON SOCIAL DYNAMICS

The Talented Antagonist

Personality and the Work Environment

In another videotape, Jenna watched a young employee, referred for problems at work, explain how he had turned his work environment into a cruel contest. Although his supervisors unanimously agreed that he did an excellent job, they also agreed that his presence in the office somehow made everyone tense. Eventually, he was reassigned to another position, where he worked mainly on his own. When his coworkers were asked for honest feedback, they replied that he seemed to turn everything into a competition—he needed to prove that he could work better, longer, and faster than anyone else. Their formerly relaxed office was thus transformed into a racetrack. In time, no one could stand him.

For the personality disorders, however, the results are most often a vicious circle. Pathologically rigid individuals possess a constricted conception of self. Only a particular kind of response from others is experienced as validating, and only this kind of response is sought from interpersonal interactions. Because their needs are strong and consistent, individuals with a constricted self-concept may be experienced as controlling or coercive. Narcissists, for example, require constant indulgence and flattery to support their sense of specialness or superiority. Kiesler (1996, p. 127) cites the compulsive personality as an example. Compulsives present as rational, logical, and controlled; in response, however, others feel bored, impatient, or evaluated. Moderately rigid persons usually find someone with whom communications can be experienced as validating; pathologically rigid persons, however, are so restrictive that others seek simply to disengage. In turn, the rigid person senses anxiety and tries even harder, making others work even harder to withdraw, producing a vicious circle. During especially stressful periods, such individuals may fall back on overlearned and automatic behaviors, restricting the scope of their responses further, thus causing them to become even more rigid, a phenomenon called "transactional escalation." In effect, the individual has become the driving force behind his or her own pathologies.

Just as personality traits are present to a greater or lesser degree, interpersonal behavior also has a dimension of intensity. Normal persons modulate their behaviors to be appropriate to what the situation requires. An emergency, for example, necessarily elicits an extreme response. Some individuals, however, are always overacting; in effect, they are intense all the time, generating behaviors highly evocative of the confirmatory response class. Although almost every narcissistic personality evinces an attitude of superiority, for example, some are more arrogant than others. The 1982 interpersonal circle shown in Figure 2.1 offers different labels for individuals within the normal range and those closer to the pathological extreme. For example, there are persons who are trusting and forgiving and those who are gullible and merciful; there are those who are outgoing and those who are frenetically gregarious. Together, rigidity and intensity constitute two important interpersonal criteria for judging abnormality. Some individuals are rigid and intense, the worst of both worlds.

FOCUS ON RELATIONSHIPS

The Case of the Cantankerous Couple

How Does Personality Affect Couples?

As part of her prepracticum class, Jenna observed an experienced psychologist interview a middle-age couple, who wanted to discuss their relationship and consider the possibility of divorce. The wife felt that she had no separate identity. She wanted to get a college degree and start her own career. Whenever she discussed it, however, she noticed that her husband became overcontrolling, long an issue in their marriage. Inevitably, any discussion of her attending school led to hostile argument, followed by long periods of uncomfortable silence, and an enduring irritability on both sides. After a stressful promotion at work that added to his duties, she noticed that her husband had become even more controlling than usual, which led to even more frequent arguments. His most frequently used interpersonal strategy was now the only one he could apply to their relationship.

STRUCTURED ANALYSIS OF SOCIAL BEHAVIOR

A creative contemporary development of interpersonal theory is Benjamin's (1974, 1996) **Structured Analysis of Social Behavior (SASB)**. The SASB seeks to integrate interpersonal conduct, object relations, and self-psychology in a single geometric model. As her point of departure, Benjamin (1974) sought to synthesize the interpersonal circle with another influential model, Shaefer's (1965) circumplex of parental behavior. As Benjamin noted, both have been influential, and both are supported by clinical theory and research. Moreover, both have affiliation as their horizontal axis.

Where the classical interpersonal circle, the "Leary circle," places submission as the opposite of control, however, Shaefer places autonomy-giving. As every parent knows, there is a fundamental tension between controlling children and eventually giving up control, thereby allowing them to develop into responsible adults, masters of their own destiny. When parents gradually grant autonomy, children mature into genuine selves free to realize their own intrinsic potentials. Otherwise, they may become resentful of lost opportunities and lack of trust or accept control and become extensions of the parental ego. In the psychodynamic perspective, this tension is expressed in the idea of separation-individuation (Mahler, Pine, & Bergman, 1975). Infants attach to their care-takers, from whom they must separate to develop an individual identity.

Benjamin (1974) combines the Leary (1957) and Shaefer (1965) circles by developing a three-circumplex model of personality, presented in a condensed form in Figure 2.2. According to Benjamin, the principle of complementarity is not confined to the Leary constructs, but instead relates corresponding points between communications focused on others and those that are focused on self. Thus, when emancipated, others tend to separate and grow in their direction. In contrast, the Leary circle does not include a differentiated space. As with the Leary circle, half of the SASB space is friendly, and half is hostile. The additional emphasis on control versus emancipation, however, allows the SASB to include loving behaviors that endorse freedom. These affirm the other person and pull for their complement: additional disclosure. The SASB also includes autonomy-giving behaviors that are implicitly attacking. These ignore others, causing them to wall off in response: the complementary position. Such combinations are impossible on the Leary circle.

In addition, the SASB attempts to describe the introjected contents of the self, the object relations of the psychodynamic perspective. The basic idea is that we tend to treat ourselves as others treat us. In early development, this leads to persistent patterns

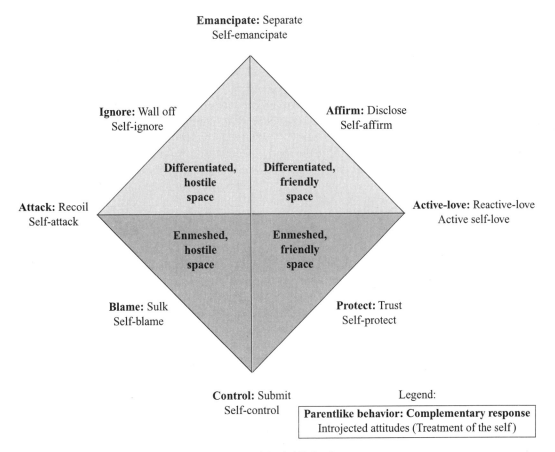

FIGURE 2.2   Benjamin's Structured Analysis of Social Behavior.

of self-regard that endure across the life span. Thus, those who are loved by their care-takers tend to love themselves, and those who are ignored by their caretakers tend to neglect their own welfare. The SASB model provides a consistent reference point throughout this text.

The Cognitive Perspective

The relevance of cognition for personality is obvious to the most casual observer. Not only do cognitive factors mediate behavior, but even common knowledge of human cognition mediates behavior. Children, for example, wait until their parents are "in the right mood" to ask permission or request a new toy. Spouses learn to avoid sensitive subjects and actions that might be misinterpreted by their significant other. Job applicants work hard to make the right first impression, hoping that the momentum of professionalism and competence exuded during a brief interview will be interpreted as a traitlike personality feature and sweep them into employment. Presenters warm up an audience with humor, hoping, "If they like me, they'll like what I have to say." Advertisers saturate ads with subliminal messages intended to motivate the audience at an unconscious level. Diplomats counsel patience, hoping that "cooler heads" will prevail. As these examples illustrate, the casual use of knowledge about human cognition—metacognitive knowledge—is routine, automatic, implicit, spontaneous, nonconscious, and, moreover, expected. For example, the applicant who is inappropriately dressed is believed to be secretly saying, "This job is not really important to me."

Although we rarely become conscious of our own mental processes, the foundations of the cognitive perspective are deep. Ultimately, they return to epistemology, that branch of philosophy concerned with the nature of knowledge, how knowledge is acquired, and its limits. The Latin origin of the term **cognitive,** cognitare, means "to have known." Questions such as, "How do we learn?," "What can we learn?," and "How are sensation and perception related?" connect the study of cognition to human development and to everyday life. Other questions, such as, "How can we best verify our judgments?," carry the relevance of cognition on into scientific methodology and the philosophy of science. In fact, because you will never think or perceive anything that does not require a mental representation of some kind, the study of cognition becomes connected to just about every field of human inquiry and every aspect of life, no matter how mundane, all the way from simple sensation to mystical experience. Although ideas are not reality, ideas are all the mind will ever know. Using ideas, we represent the world, ourselves, others, and the future. Ideas let us get things into our heads and perform operations on them, selecting some features for further analysis, discarding others, and altering the significance of still others. No wonder, then, that strong proponents of cognitive psychology have proposed that cognition be regarded as an integrative model for personality.

ORIGINS OF THE COGNITIVE APPROACH

Cognitive psychology began in the 1950s as a reaction against behaviorism. Many experimental psychologists felt that by banishing mental content from investigation, psychologists had effectively banished the study of the human mind. Moreover, problems were coming into the foreground that behaviorism would find paradigm-shattering. Each featured some complex, sequential organization of behavior nearly impossible to explain in terms of the simple stimulus-response bonds. For psychologists, the classic clash of cognitive and behavioral ideas came in connection with the question, "How is language acquired?" In his 1957 work, Skinner attempted to explain speaking through standard behavioral principles. Speech was simply a shaped response chain operating in conformity with the laws of reinforcement, all under stimulus control. Good productions were reinforced, becoming more frequent; poor productions were not reinforced and thus became extinct over time. Because the environment controls what is reinforced and what is not, true novelty, or freedom of thought, was ruled out from the very beginning.

Chomsky (1959) gave Skinner (1957) a devastating review. As a linguist, Chomsky believed that language was just too complex to be learned behaviorally. Instead, language was regarded as possessing both a surface structure, the actual words spoken, and what he called a "deep structure," a grammatical code through which ambiguities in the surface structure are untangled. Chomsky also pointed to real-world examples: During the critical period for language learning, children sometimes learn five or six new words a day, a feat that cannot be explained through reinforcement. Chomsky thus not only put mental mechanisms squarely into Skinner's black box, but also made them central to the understanding of language, presumably a uniquely human faculty.

Other developments occurred outside cognitive psychology that were essential to the emergence of computers (see Gardner, 1985, for a thorough discussion) and, therefore, to the development of cognitive science and of information processing as a metaphor for the mind. In 1936, Alan Turing showed that any problem that was in principle computable could be carried out using a series of binary operations, the ones and zeros of the modern computer. Building on Turing's work, the mathematician John von Neumann sketched out the architectural structure of modern computer systems. In the late 1930s, Claude Shannon developed information theory, which allowed information to be thought of in terms of its own fundamental units, binary digits, or bits, quite apart from the physical matrix in which it was contained. By the mid-1950s, Newell and Simon had developed a computer program that could manipulate logical symbols and derive mathematical proofs. Later, they would develop the General Problem Solver, able to break large problems down into smaller ones and then assess which approaches might move closer to the solution, or goal state. Parallels between the operation of computers and the operation of the mind were becoming obvious.

Today, cognitive science—an emerging discipline that synthesizes cognitive psychology, linguistics, neuroscience, artificial intelligence, and various branches of philosophy—is the latest in a series of revolutions instrumental in overturning our "species narcissism," the idea that humans are somehow special beings anointed to play some pivotal role in cosmic affairs. First, Copernicus proved that the earth was not the center of the universe. Cosmic events work accordingly to their own laws, revolving neither around the earth nor around the humans on it; astrology is not a science, and comets are not omens that forebode catastrophe. You could still believe, however, that humans were unique in the capacity to reason. Then came Darwin, who showed that the same processes responsible for the diversity of plant and animal life also explained the existence of human beings. The difference between human and animal was now one of degree rather than kind. Intelligence was not uniquely human, but the product of simple biological law. You could still believe, however, that humans were at least self-aware. Then came Freud, who argued that conscious awareness resembles the ripples on the surface of the ocean; the true determinative forces of behavior lay elsewhere, in the unconscious.

Cognitive science extends these earlier discoveries by arguing that the biological foundations of thought are simply a special instance of more general principles that, once decoded, might allow intelligence and self-awareness to be enabled in any physical matrix, perhaps a sophisticated computer. Each might have special biases depending on its architecture, but in principle, the difference between an artificially intelligent computer of the far future and a human being would resemble the difference between Ford and Chrysler: two different brands of the same thing. If the trend holds, we might conclude that every genuine scientific revolution must trivialize some aspect of human narcissism; otherwise, it cannot be a revolution at all.

COGNITIVE STYLES

The cognitive perspective is perhaps best appreciated by considering the deficiencies of alternative models. As an information processor, the mind actively gathers and selects information about the world, self, and others, at both conscious and nonconscious levels. Additionally, it takes into account past probabilities and future circumstances in developing plans that further its own self-generated goals and eventually takes action, judges outcomes, and profits from experience. In contrast, the commonsense view is that the mind works like a sophisticated tape recorder. If so, everything that you have ever experienced should be preserved unaltered, somewhere inside your brain. The boundary between conscious and unconscious plays a protective function: The amount of information is vast; you cannot be allowed to have complete access to all your memories, for you would easily be overwhelmed. With a good tape recorder, every internal representation would perfectly parallel objective reality. No distinction would exist among sensation, perception, and interpretation; to perceive would be simply to sense. In philosophy, this commonsense view is known as **realism.**

In contrast, the cognitive perspective emphasizes that the mind is actively and constantly developing "construals" of the world, self, others, and the future. Some of these have far-reaching implications. The belief that "I am a worthwhile person" or "Other people are out to get me," for example, is formed on the basis of repeated experiences and has long-term consequences for psychological functioning. If the mind were not a good recorder simply because its representational abilities were too limited, cognition would be irrelevant to personality. Everyone would have the same map of reality; some people would just be a little more out of focus than others. The concept of an intelligence quotient, the idea that intelligence can be assessed on a single dimension, is really a throwback to this inaccurate view.

For students of personality, it is here that matters get interesting: What does the individual select as worthy of attention? Why it is selected? How is the stimulus interpreted? Avoidant personalities, for example, believe that the self is defective and shameful; as such, they are hypersensitive to cues of disapproval and embarrassment. Anything that might be interpreted as pointing to deficiencies in the self is abstracted from the background of ongoing communications as proof of their defects, ultimately leading to recoil from almost all social engagement. Paranoid personalities transform innocent remarks into criticism. Narcissistic personalities need to believe in their superiority and, thus, are extraordinarily alert to slights about their talent or intelligence. The conclusion is that the tape recorder model fails because the mind distorts whatever it touches.

When cognitive distortions cohere as a pattern, they may be thought of as cognitive styles. Different personalities process consensual reality in different ways. The scattered style of the histrionic, for example, serves an adaptive function. Histrionics are simply not given to deep, existential reflection. Depressive personalities may ruminate about the human situation to no end, but not the histrionic. Instead, their thoughts flutter from one thing to the next. Nothing is processed to any depth, insulating the individual against anxiety, and particularly worry, where the object of concern is held constantly in mind and examined again and again from every angle. Instead, the histrionic forgets problems simply by moving on to something lovely, entertaining, and stimulating. Compulsives, whom Leary (1957) aptly regarded as the "hypernormal personality," live in constant fear of making a mistake, which might lead to condemnation from authority figures, including those internalized in their own superego. In consequence, the compulsive becomes, in the words of Piaget (1954), much more of an assimilator than an accommodator. Because compulsives cannot risk disapproval, they must do what is approved and expected; it is far better to be a mundane conformer than to be criticized for an apparently ingenious idea that somehow proves flawed in the final analysis. Compulsives thus tend to pursue a conservative course, mulling over the possibilities again and again, justifying them from all sides before acting. They make excellent critics, but not good innovators. The self-confidence of the narcissist is better suited to discovery. Each of the personality disorders has its own style of cognitive processing, discussed in detail in each of the personality chapters in this book.

COGNITIVE THERAPY

Although cognitive psychology would seem to be the natural foundation for theory and research on the role of cognitive constructs in the personality disorders, this has not been the case. Instead, theoretical speculation and research have come mostly from those involved in cognitive therapy. Ideally, every applied science should grow from some pure science foundation, just as engineering grows naturally out of physics. In contrast, cognitive therapy, much like the rest of psychotherapy, has developed almost independently of any pure science foundation. Beck is without a doubt one of the most seminal figures in the history of therapy. Almost every book about cognitive therapy written by Beck or his associates includes a paragraph stating that cognitive therapy began in the mid-1950s when Beck was seeking experimental support for the notion that depressed subjects have a masochistic need for suffering, the main psychodynamic model of depression at the time. Beck's own research showed that depressed subjects greatly desired success, however, leading him to pursue a cognitive direction. No mention is made in this tale of the broader cognitive revolution that was occurring simultaneously or that it influenced Beck's thinking. Such events often occur in the applied social sciences.

Cognitive therapists hold that behavior can be explained by examining the contents of internal mental structures called **schemata.** Historically, schemata derive from work by Bartlett (1932) and Piaget (1926). Although the term has been defined in different ways, its meaning is obviously related to scheme and schematic. Both suggest a generic plan of action that might be elaborated to suit the particulars of a given situation. Schemata are assumed to mediate cognitive processing at every level, from sensation to paradigms and on to action plans that the organism can use to affect the world. Moreover, they are always available for mental operations. They can be changed or elaborated through new learning, but their very reason for being is to produce meaning from raw input. Like a cognitive filter, they are ever ready to be applied to create an interpretable world. Everything put through the filter is automatically processed. As such, their primary advantage lies in allowing experience to be processed with great efficiency. Given a variety of schemata that code for interpersonal conduct, for example, the individual does not have to invent new hypotheses for interacting with every new acquaintance.

The information-processing economy that schemata afford, however, also comes at a cost. Because schemata necessarily exist between the raw data of sensation and the meaningful world of subjective experience, they introduce interpretive biases that preempt other construals, possibly distorting consensual reality. Like scientific paradigms, schemata have a kind of conceptual priority that dictates the construction of the world. They decrease cognitive load but also inhibit the development of other approaches and an appreciation for other perspectives. In fact, information that is highly incongruent with schematic expectations may not be perceived at all. Paranoid, antisocial, and sadistic personalities, for example, anticipate hostility and easily overlook gestures of assistance and support. All suffer from a form of social neglect. The schematic structures required to process the full range of interactions are either absent or underdeveloped, giving these disorders an irascible, callous, or hard-hearted nature. Perception, it would seem, is half presumption, and the personality disorders are very presumptuous indeed.

Aaron Beck and his associates have been particularly successful in developing cognitive therapies for a wide range of Axis I disorders, especially depression (Beck, 1976; Beck, Rush, Shaw, & Emery, 1979). Because most mental disorders have cognitive symptoms, cognitive therapy provides an important avenue for treatment. In more recent years, Beck, Freeman, and associates (1990) applied the cognitive perspective to the personality disorders, describing the schemata, or core beliefs, that shape the experience and behavior of such individuals. Like other beliefs, these schemata are always available and always working to produce order from sensation. As such, they operate at a nonconscious level and give rise to "automatic thoughts," which influence emotion and behavior. In the paranoid personality, for example, core beliefs such as, "People are malicious and deceptive" (p. 47) lead, in actual interpersonal situations, to automatic thoughts such as, "He is trying to fool me," and "I cannot afford to believe him," which naturally leads to anger and an interpersonal posture of guardedness and hostility. As paranoids categorize the situation as just another attack on their person, the level of anger increases, further biasing their perception and recall in support of the original automatic thought. The result is a cognitive-interpersonal vicious cycle.

In addition, Beck and associates (Pretzer & Beck, 1996) also emphasize the importance of cognitive distortions. These are chronic and systematic errors in reasoning that promote the misinterpretation of consensual reality. For example, one of the foremost distortions is dichotomous thinking. Here, an entire distribution of possibilities is artificially limited to two mutually exclusive categories. The compulsive personality, for example, demands perfection from the self; a minor mistake tarnishes the whole effort, leading to the conclusion, "I have failed." Because only perfection is acceptable, dichotomous thinking in the compulsive leads to another distortion, catastrophizing. Here, things are viewed as being disastrous, a catastrophe, not in realistic terms; thus, the compulsive may further conclude, "I am likely to be fired." Another example is personalization. In this case, the cause of external events is always attributed to the self. Thus, if people at a party start laughing for unknown reasons, an avoidant personality may conclude that they are laughing at his or her social awkwardness. Other, more realistic reasons that people might laugh at a party are automatically excluded in favor of an interpretation that promotes pathology.

TABLE 2.1   Primeval Strategies and Beliefs of the Personality Disorders

Strategy	Personality	Example Belief
Predatory	Antisocial	"Others are patsies."
Help-Eliciting	Dependent	"I need people to survive."
Competitive	Narcissistic	"I'm above the rules."
Exhibitionistic	Histrionic	"I can go by my feelings."
Autonomous	Schizoid	"Relationships are messy."
Defensive	Paranoid	"Goodwill hides a hidden motive."
Withdrawal	Avoidant	"People will reject the real me."
Ritualistic	Compulsive	"Details are crucial."

The cognitive therapy model of Beck et al. (1990) is anchored to evolution and links the personality disorders to certain primeval evolutionary strategies, adaptive in moderation, but exaggerated in personality pathology. For example, the dependent personality exemplifies a "help-eliciting" strategy. Although asking for help when faced with obstacles is adaptive from both a personal and an evolutionary viewpoint, dependents make this strategy the organizing principle of their entire existence. Conversely, antisocials have underdeveloped schemata for being responsible and for feeling guilt about violating social convention. They exaggerate the "predatory strategy" and, thus, are naturally victim-seeking. In contrast, compulsives are disposed to judge themselves responsible and guilt-ridden, but are underdeveloped in the inclination to interpret events spontaneously, creatively, and playfully. A list of primeval strategies and associated beliefs, condensed from Pretzer and Beck (1996), is presented in Table 2.1.

FOCUS ON PERCEPTION

The Minimizing Antisocial

Personality and Frame of Reference

Still studying the art of psychotherapy that she would begin to practice in her second year, Jenna sat in with an experienced clinician conducting therapy with a group of prisoners, most of whom had been diagnosed as antisocial personalities. Gradually, their cognitive core beliefs and distortions became evident. Defending his actions in the outside world, one convict protested, "Look, you're either a goody-goody or you're out for yourself in this world, and everyone I've ever known has been out for themselves. Taking advantage from those kind of people ain't so bad." Many of the others nodded in agreement. Jenna, however, was immediately able to recognize two self-serving cognitive distortions: dichotomous thinking and minimization. Moreover, by constructing the world so that everyone was "out for themselves," the speaker was essentially able to justify taking advantage of anyone.

Trait and Factorial Perspectives

The theoretical models presented here and in Chapter 1 are all perspectives on personality. By definition, they represent partial views of an intrinsic totality. Historically, each has attempted to outcompete the others to establish itself as a single truth, and each has had its period of dominance and enthusiasm. The cognitive view, for example, is now highly fashionable among theorists and therapists. Although the inductive perspective has yet to come into its own, it shows some promise and is included here only as an example of an approach that is currently in vogue.

Although the history of psychopathology has been guided by a succession of theories, from the trait and factorial perspectives, theory is exactly the problem. Theory must be built on principles, and these principles are assumed to organize the contents of all of personality. Other perspectives are thus cast as peripheral or derivative. Interpersonal theorists, for example, see interpersonal conduct as fundamental. In contrast, cognitive theorists argue that, because internal cognitive structures always mediate perception, interpretation, and communication, cognitive theory is the best candidate for an integrative model. And herein lies the problem with theory: its tendency to endorse certain parts of personality while rejecting others. Although some are content to tolerate an eclecticism of multiple views, those of the inductive mind-set seek to begin again by making copious observations and applying sound scientific methodology. Theory construes the world from the top down; in contrast, the trait approach seeks a solid foundation from which to build again from the bottom up. The theory emerges later, only after a long process of systematically examining the relevant phenomena and processing them through the methodological mill.

In personality, the factorial perspective is intimately tied up with the history of trait psychology. As defined in Chapter 1, traits are single dimensions of individual differences expressed consistently across time and pervasively across situations. Behavior should be consistent no matter when or where you look, though the expression of the same trait is sometimes manifest in different ways. Males, for example, are usually regarded as being aggressive; females are not. For males, aggression usually involves threats of territorial encroachment and the possibility of physical violence. Females, however, are usually socialized against such displays and, therefore, tend to express aggression relationally (Crick & Bigbee, 1998), threatening to withdraw from relationships, manipulate access to empathy or intimacy, or spread vicious rumors. Aggressiveness thus often has a different expression, depending on gender.

The return to fundamentals, however, faces two related problems as an approach to personality. First, scientific models are required to be as comprehensive as possible. In general, a model that seems to explain more with a small number of principles is preferred over a model that seems to explain less. To ensure comprehensiveness, researchers eventually turned to the dictionary in an effort to document all the traits that might be used to describe personality. Allport and Odbert (1936) were apparently the first to apply the approach in the United States, culling almost 18,000 terms that "distinguish the behavior of one human being from that of another" (p. 24) from the 400,000 words listed in the unabridged 1925 edition of *Webster's New International Dictionary*. After deleting positively and negatively evaluative terms such as *good, excellent,* and *poor,* just over 4,500 terms reflecting "generalized and personalized determining tendencies" (p. 26) remained. The idea of turning to the dictionary as a repository of traits has since become known as the lexical approach, which holds that all terms relevant to personality description have already become encoded in the language, a controversial assumption. The dictionary guaranteed comprehensiveness, but it led to a second problem: 1,000 traits are not exactly a small number of principles. How, then, can literally thousands of traits be organized or reduced to a manageable number without losing something essential to human nature in the process?

To help solve these problems, scientists turned to a statistical technique called **factor analysis.** Although the mathematics is complex, only the purpose is important here. In brief, factor analysis is a way of looking at the relationships among a large number of personality traits to determine which are most fundamental. For example, every language contains terms that mean almost the same thing, differing only in some subtle way. The words *obstinate* and *stubborn,* for example, are near synonyms; if one term is excluded, little is lost. Factor analysis provides a mathematical way of examining the overlap among such characteristics and even suggests a much smaller number of dimensions in which the original traits are best summarized. By retaining only what is most central to personality, more narrow or redundant traits can be excluded with minimal loss of descriptive power. Many hundreds of traits can thus be telescoped into a much smaller framework. A variety of factor models have been developed within both normal and abnormal personality domains, derived not just from analyses using words taken from the dictionary, but also through studies of the *DSM* personality criteria and the underlying structure of personality tests (see Table 2.2).

SOME MAJOR FACTOR MODELS

The most prominent current factor model of personality is the **Five-Factor Model** (Costa & McCrae, 1989). The five-factor model was derived from analyses of various personality inventories, not words from the dictionary. Nevertheless, the results have proven similar, with some exceptions. As the name indicates, this model consists of five broad higher order dimensions. In turn, each dimension consists of several lower order facet traits, thus lending the model a hierarchical structure. Higher order traits make broad, but somewhat imprecise, predictions about behavior; and lower order traits make predictions that are more precise but somewhat narrow. For example, individuals who are high on the first factor, *neuroticism,* are likely to feel anxious, angry and hostile, depressed, self-conscious, impulsive, and vulnerable. However, although being high in neuroticism increases the chances of impulsive behavior or feelings of depression, these are not inevitable. Likewise, many people are impulsive without being terribly anxious, angry or hostile, or depressed. Thus, saying that someone is neurotic makes a broad statement but isn't very detailed, and saying that someone is impulsive makes a detailed statement but doesn't say much more. The opposite of neuroticism is emotional stability, that is, a tendency to be free of worry, calm, and controlled.

Four other factors round out the five-factor model. Definitions of each factor and their facet traits are described in Costa and McCrae (1992) and paraphrased here. The second factor, *extroversion,* includes the facets of warmth, a tendency to be affectionate and friendly; gregariousness, a tendency to seek social stimulation; assertiveness, a tendency to be dominant and forceful; activity, a tendency toward movement and energy; excitement seeking, a tendency to crave stimulation; and positive emotions, a tendency toward joy, happiness, love, and optimism. The third factor, *openness to experience,*

TABLE 2.2   Factor Models of Normal and Abnormal Personality Domains

Normal Personality Models	*Personality Disorder Factor Models*	

Lexical "Big Five" Model	**Livesley and Associates**	**Clark and Associates**
1. Surgency (or Extroversion)	1. Compulsivity	1. Suicide proneness
2. Agreeableness	2. Conduct problems	2. Self-derogation
3. Conscientiousness	3. Diffidence	3. Anhedonia
4. Emotional stability	4. Identity problems	4. Instability
(vs. Neuroticism)	5. Insecure attachment	5. Hypersensitivity
5. Intellect (or Culture)	6. Intimacy problems	6. Anger/Aggression
	7. Narcissism	7. Pessimism
Five-Factor Model	8. Suspiciousness	8. Negative affect
1. Neuroticism	9. Affective lability	9. Suspiciousness
2. Extroversion	10. Passive oppositionality	10. Self-centered exploitation
3. Openness to experience	11. Perceptual cognitive distortion	11. Passive-aggressiveness
4. Agreeableness	12. Rejection	12. Dramatic exhibitionism
5. Conscientiousness	13. Self-harming behaviors	13. Grandiose egocentrism
	14. Restricted expression	14. Social isolation
Big Seven Model	15. Social avoidance	15. Emotional coldness
1. Positive valence	16. Stimulus seeking	16. Dependency
2. Negative valence	17. Interpersonal disesteem	17. Conventionality-rigidity
3. Positive emotionality	18. Anxiousness	18. Dependency
4. Negative emotionality		19. Impulsivity
5. Conscientiousness	**Harkness and Associates**	20. High energy
6. Agreeableness	1. Aggressiveness	21. Antisocial behavior
7. Conventionality	2. Psychoticism	22. Schizotypal thought
	3. Constraint	
	4. Negative emotionality–neuroticism	
	5. Positive emotionality–extroversion	

consists of the facets of fantasy, the use of imagination and creativity to enrich life; aesthetics, the ability to appreciate art, beauty, and poetry; feelings, a receptivity to inner feeling and deep emotional experience; actions, a preference for novelty over the routine and familiar; ideas, an intellectual curiosity and willingness to entertain unconventional ideas; and values, an openness to examining established social, political, and religious values. The fourth factor, *agreeableness,* consists of the facets of trust, a willingness to believe that others are honest and well-intentioned; straightforwardness, a tendency to be frank and sincere; and four other facets. The fifth factor, *conscientiousness,* consists of the facets of competence, a tendency to be capable and effective; order, a tendency to be neat and organized; dutifulness, a tendency to keep to ethical principles and moral obligations; achievement striving, a tendency to invest time in moving forward with ambition; self-discipline, a willingness to complete tasks in spite of distraction or boredom; and deliberation, the tendency not to act without premeditation. Each factor consists of six facets.

Whereas five-factor researchers have approached personality disorders through models derived from normal subjects, other researchers have produced factor models specifically within the domain of personality pathology. Clark (1990) factored a pool of descriptors that focused on *DSM-III* personality disorder criteria, as well as certain non-*DSM* personality-relevant concepts, including Cleckley's (1964) description of the psychopath and criteria from certain personality-related disorders on Axis I, resulting in more than 20 dimensions (see Table 2.2). In contrast, Livesley and associates (Livesley, Jackson, & Schroeder, 1989) used in-depth reviews of the personality literature in conjunction with detailed consideration of the Axis II criteria of the revised third edition of the *DSM* to suggest the basic traits of personality pathology. Seventy-nine trait dimensions were required to represent the 11 personality disorders of the *DSM-III-R*. Self-report items were then written and given to two samples from the general population, ultimately increasing the total number of scales to 100. A factor analysis then extracted 15 factors; 3 others were added on rational grounds, resulting in a total of 18 constructs (see Table 2.2). They also studied the relationship between their results and the five-factor model and concluded that although the other factors are relevant to personality pathology, openness to experience plays only a limited role.

Other researchers have sought to show the limitations of the five-factor model by gathering their information in different ways. Harkness and McNulty (1994) found five personality dimensions, but with substantial differences from the five-factor model. In particular, their model includes two factors called constraint and psychoticism, which they regard as being qualitatively different from conscientiousness or openness to experience. Finally, Tellegen and Waller (1987) reported a seven-factor model, arguing that the tradition based originally on Allport and Odbert (1936) erroneously excludes evaluative terms such as ordinary, excellent, and bad, so important to abnormal behavior and global appraisals of the self. When 400 personality traits were isolated from the 1985 *American Heritage Dictionary* and factor analyzed, the **Big Seven** model was born. To further strengthen their claim, Almagor, Tellegen, and Waller (1995) researched the cross-cultural validity of the Big Seven in Hebrew, arguing that cultural and linguistic differences between Israel and the United States would provide a strong test of its replicability. Seven factors were robust across rotation methods and number of factors extracted, with six of the seven present in the previous study. More important, the two largest factors were again positive evaluation and negative evaluation, indicating clear evidence for the replicability of these factors in a culture substantially different from that in which the Big Seven were originally found. Strangely, the remaining factors do not bear much resemblance to the five-factor model.

The variety of available factor models and the continuing contention among different groups of researchers have been important forces in moderating the widespread acceptance of any particular factor model as the final word in personality description. Accordingly, the personality disorders chapters of this book do not discuss the inductive approach alongside the biological, cognitive, psychodynamic, and interpersonal perspectives.

The Evolutionary-Neurodevelopmental Perspective

The perspectives outlined previously all appeal to organizing principles that derive from a single domain of personality. In Chapter 1, we noted that whereas the physical sciences advance mainly through attempts to falsify established models, the social sciences advance when heretofore-undiscovered domains of content move to the forefront of scientific thinking. Adherents of the latest fad believe that their perspective is the final word in personality and that soon it will outcompete its rivals and assume its rightful place as lord of the realm, the perfect scientific model, with total comprehensiveness of scope and perfect theoretical coherence. Psychology has romanced biological, psychodynamic, interpersonal, and cognitive perspectives at one point or another in the past. Each has recruited large numbers of disciples who keep the papers flowing into academic journals. Eventually, each fad runs its course, and the perspective fades somewhat as its founders pass into history. After that, it becomes an acknowledged part of psychological tradition, but the enthusiasm is largely gone. Skinner is gone. Freud is still a respected figure, but psychodynamic theory is on the decline. The rise and fall of diverse points of view is a consequence of the open nature of the social sciences, where the success of any particular model depends as much on the charisma and energy of its founders as on its real merits.

As each perspective vies for dominance, personality is kept in a state of perpetual warfare. Models go on the offensive by pressing foreign variables, those from other viewpoints, directly into taxonomic service to organize the competing constructs of other domains. The variables of the particular perspective are central; others are peripheral. Freud, for example, held that human nature could be reduced to sex and aggression operating in the context of restraining social forces. Leary (1957) was influenced by the psychodynamic idea of levels of consciousness, but nevertheless believed that interpersonal principles were central and could organize material at the level of personality he called "private symbolization," namely, unconscious and preconscious material expressed through "projective, indirect fantasy materials" (p. 79), including projective tests, fantasies, artistic productions, wishes, dreams, and free associations. Kiesler (1986), for example, translated his 1982 interpersonal circle to the level of behavioral acts. Benjamin (1986) translated her SASB model to embrace both the affective and cognitive domains. Factor researchers have sought to translate the personality disorders into profiles of their own statistically derived dimensions (Widiger & Costa, 1994). Such translations are obviously impressive, for they demonstrate the scope of the model by illustrating its organizing power within adjacent domains.

In the final analysis, however, we are left with a patchwork quilt that fails to converge on an integrated view of personality. Rather than capitulate to this uncertain eclecticism, we might ask if any theory embraces personality specifically as the patterning of variables across the entire matrix of the person. Such a theory would be explicitly developed not to become simply another perspective. Instead, it would develop a classification system of personality styles and disorders specifically as an integration of the major viewpoints. As we have stressed so often, personality is an intrinsic totality of interacting domains. Logically, a theory of personality must be constructed to be as integrative as the construct of personality itself (see Figure 2.3). The key to constructing such a theory lies in locating organizing principles that fall outside the field of personality proper (Millon, 1990). Otherwise, we could only repeat the errors of the past by asserting the importance of some new set of variables heretofore unemphasized, building yet another perspective inside personality as a total phenomenon, while missing a scientific understanding of the total phenomenon itself. Rather than go forth and conquer, such a theory would derive a set of holistic constructs that exist "above" any particular perspective, thereby allowing their integration as parts of the whole. The alternative is an uncomfortable eclecticism of unassimilated partial views.

EVOLUTIONARY FOUNDATIONS OF PERSONALITY

Evolution is the logical choice as a foundation for an integrated science of the person. Just as personality is concerned with the total patterning of variables across the entire matrix of the person, it is the total organism that survives and reproduces, carrying

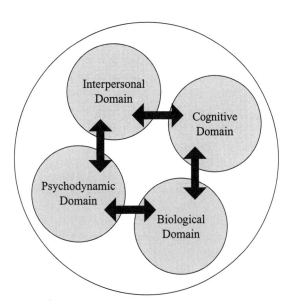

FIGURE 2.3   Personality as a Totality of Interacting Domains.

forth both its adaptive and maladaptive potentials into subsequent generations. Although lethal mutations sometimes occur, the evolutionary success of most organisms is dependent on the fit between the entire configuration of their characteristics and potentials and those of the environment. Likewise, psychological health is dependent on the fit between the entire configuration of a person's characteristics and potentials with those of the environments in which the person functions, such as family, job, school, church, and recreation.

Survival: Life Preservation and Life Enhancement (Pain-Pleasure Polarity)

The first task of any organism is its immediate survival. Organisms that fail to survive have been selected out, so to speak, and fail to contribute their genes and characteristics to subsequent generations. Whether a virus or a human being, every living thing must protect itself against simple predatory threat and homeostatic misadventure. There are literally millions of ways to die. Evolutionary mechanisms related to survival tasks are oriented toward life enhancement and life preservation. The former are concerned with improvement in the quality of life and dispose organisms toward behaviors that improve survival chances and, hopefully, lead them to thrive and multiply. The latter are geared toward orienting organisms away from actions or environments that threaten to jeopardize survival. Such mechanisms form a polarity of pleasure and pain. Behaviors experienced as pleasurable are generally repeated and generally promote survival; those experienced as painful generally have the potential to endanger life and thus are not repeated. Organisms that repeat painful experiences or fail to repeat pleasurable ones do not endure for long.

As noted, evolutionary mechanisms associated with this stage relate to the processes of *life enhancement* and *life preservation*. These two superordinate processes may be called *existential aims*. At the highest level of abstraction, such mechanisms form, phenomenologically or metaphorically, what we have termed the **pleasure-pain polarity.**

Most humans exhibit both processes, those oriented toward enhancing pleasure and avoiding pain. Some individuals, however, appear to be conflicted concerning existential aims (e.g., the sadistic), while others possess deficits in such aims (e.g., the schizoid). In terms of evolutionary-developmental stages (Millon, 1969, 1981, 1990), orientations on the pleasure-pain polarity are set during a "sensory-attachment" period, the purpose of which is to further mature and selectively refine and focus the largely innate ability to discriminate between pain and pleasure signals.

Adaptation: Ecological Accommodation and Ecological Modification (Passive-Active Polarity)

The second evolutionary task faced universally by every organism is adaptation. To exist is to exist within an environment. Organisms must either adapt to their surroundings or adapt their surroundings to conform to and support their own style of functioning. Every organism must satisfy lower order needs related, for example, to nutrition, thirst, and sleep. Mammals and human beings must also satisfy other needs, for example, those related to safety and attachment. Whether the environment is intrinsically bountiful or hostile, the choice is essentially between a passive and an active orientation, that is, a tendency to accommodate to a given ecological niche and accept what the environment offers, versus a tendency to modify or intervene in the environment, thereby adapting it to oneself. These modes of adaptation differ from the first phase of evolution, being, in that they regard how that which is endures.

Once an integrated structure exists, it must maintain its existence through exchanges of energy and information with its environment. This second evolutionary phase is framed also as a two-part polarity: a passive orientation—that is, to be *ecologically accommodating* in one's environmental niche—versus an active orientation—that is, to be *ecologically modifying* and to intervene in or to alter one's surroundings. In terms of psychological development, this polarity is ontogenetically expressed as the "sensorimotor-autonomy stage," during which the child typically progresses from an earlier, relatively passive style of accommodation to a relatively active style of modifying his or her physical and social environment.

The accommodating-modifying polarity necessarily derives from an expansion of the systems concept. Whereas in the Survival phase the system is seen as being mainly intraorganismic in character, the Adaptation phase expands the systems concept to its logical progression, from person to person-in-context. Some individuals, those of an active orientation, operate as genuine agencies, tending to modify their environments according to their desires. For these individuals, an active-organism model is appropriate. Other persons, however, seek to accommodate to whatever is offered or, rather than work to change what exists, seek out new, more hospitable venues when current ones become problematic. For these individuals, a passive-organism model is appropriate.

Replication: Reproductive Nurturance and Reproductive Propagation (Other-Self Polarity)

The third universal evolutionary task faced by every organism pertains to reproductive styles, essentially sociobiological mechanisms, that each gender uses to maximize its representation in the gene pool. All organisms must ultimately reproduce to evolve. At one extreme is what biologists have referred to as the *r*-strategy; here, the goal is to reproduce a great number of offspring, which are then left to fend for themselves against the adversities of chance or destiny. At the other extreme is the *K*-strategy, in which the relatively few offspring produced are given great care by parents. Although individual exceptions always exist, these parallel the more male *self-oriented* versus the more female *other-nurturing* strategies of sociobiology. Psychologically, the former strategy is often judged to be egotistic, insensitive, inconsiderate, and uncaring; the latter is judged to be affiliative, intimate, protective, and solicitous (Gilligan, 1981; Rushton, 1985; Wilson, 1978). Organisms that make reproductive investments in many offspring so that their resources are spread too thinly or make a long gestational investment but fail to nurture their young are strongly selected against.

Although organisms may be well adapted to their environments, the existence of any life form is time-limited. To circumvent this limitation, organisms exhibit patterns of the third polarity, **replicatory strategies,** by which they leave progeny. As noted, these strategies relate to what biologists have referred to as an *r*- or *self*-propagating strategy, at one polar extreme, and a *K*- or *other*-nurturing strategy at the second extreme. Like pleasure-pain, the self-other polarity is not unidimensional. Whereas most humans exhibit a reasonable balance between the two polar extremes, some personality disorders are conflicted on this polarity, as are the compulsive and negativistic personalities. In terms of developmental stages, an individual's orientation toward self and others evolves largely during the "intracortical-identity" stage.

As with the passive-active polarity, the self-other bipolarity necessarily derives from an expansion of the systems concept. Whereas with the adaptation phase the system was seen as existing within an environment, here the system is seen as evolving over time. As before, the goal of the organism is its survival or continuance. When expressed across time, however, survival means reproducing and strategies for doing so.

In addition to the three polarities described previously, the theory holds that many individuals experience ambivalence concerning the pleasure-pain and self-other polarities. For example, the compulsive and negativistic (passive-aggressive) personalities, to be described fully in later chapters, share an ambivalence concerning whether to put their own priorities and expectations first or to defer to others. The negativistic acts out this ambivalence, repressed in the compulsive. The two personalities are thus theoretically linked, and the theory predicts that if the submerged anger of the compulsive can be confronted consciously, the subject may tend to act out in a passive-aggressive manner until this conflict can be constructively refocused or resolved. Figure 2.4 puts this relationship into a circumplex format and relates these disorders to the "interpersonally imbalanced" personalities: antisocial, narcissistic, histrionic, and dependent. The right side of the figure shows that the negativistic and compulsive shade into each other, the negativistic shades into the antisocial and histrionic, and the compulsive shades into the narcissistic and dependent. Loosely speaking, to transform a compulsive into a narcissist, therapy should resolve the conflict between self and other toward a preoccupation with the individual's own self-concerns. To transform a compulsive into a dependent, therapy should resolve this conflict in favor of the needs of others. Table 2.3 illustrates how the constructs of the *DSM-III, DSM-III-R,* and *DSM-IV* may be derived from various combinations of the underlying polarities when the additional idea of conflict is included.

NEURODEVELOPMENTAL FOUNDATIONS OF PERSONALITY

The three stages of development described in the following sections parallel the three evolutionary phases discussed previously. Each evolutionary phase is related to a different stage of ontogenetic neurodevelopment (Millon, 1969). For example, life

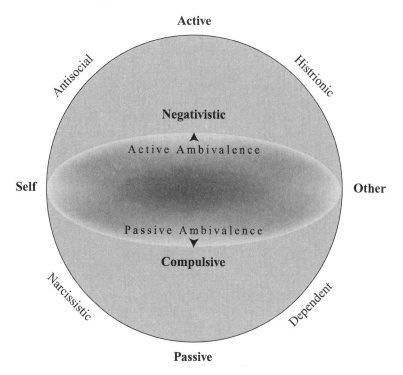

FIGURE 2.4   Interpersonally Imbalanced and Interpersonally Conflicted Personality Disorders.

enhancement-life preservation bipolarity of evolution corresponds to what is called the **sensory-attachment stage** of development in that the latter represents a period when the young child learns to discriminate between experiences that are enhancing and those that are threatening.

Stage 1: Sensory-Attachment

The first year of life is dominated by sensory processes, functions basic to subsequent development in that they enable the infant to construct some order from the initial diffusion experienced in the stimulus world, especially that based on distinguishing pleasurable from painful objects. This period has also been termed that of **attachment** because infants cannot survive on their own but must "fasten" themselves to others who will protect, nurture, and stimulate them, that is, provide them with experiences of pleasure rather than those of pain.

Such themes are readily understood through an evolutionary theory of personality development. While evolution has endowed adult humans with the cognitive ability to project future threats and difficulties as well as potential rewards, human infants are comparably impoverished, being as yet without the benefit of these abstract capacities. Evolution has, therefore, provided mechanisms or substrates that orient the child toward those activities or venues that are life-enhancing (pleasure) and away from those that are potentially life-threatening (pain). Existence during this highly vulnerable stage is literally a to-be or not-to-be matter.

The neonate cannot differentiate between objects and persons; both are experienced simply as stimuli. How does this initial indiscriminateness become progressively refined

TABLE 2.3   Polarity Model and Its Personality Style and Disorder Derivatives

	Existential Aim		Replication Strategy	
	Life Enhancement	Life Preservation	Reproductive Propagation	Reproductive Nurturance
Polarity	Pleasure–Pain		Self–Other	
Deficiency, Imbalance, or Conflict	Pleasure (low) Pain (low or high)	Pleasure Pain (Reversal)	Self (low) Other (high)	Self (high) Other (low)	Self–Other (Reversal)
Adaptation Mode	*DSM* Personality Disorders			
Passive: Accommodation	Retiring **Schizoid Depressive***	Yielding **Masochistic**	Agreeing **Dependent**	Asserting **Narcissistic**	Conforming **Compulsive**
Active: Modification	Hesitating **Avoidant**	Controlling **Sadistic**	Outgoing **Histrionic**	Dissenting **Antisocial**	Complaining **Negativistic**
Structural Pathology	**Schizotypal**	**Borderline, Paranoid**	**Borderline**	**Paranoid**	**Borderline, Paranoid**

*The schizoid is passive and low in both pleasure and pain; the depressive is low in pleasure and high on pain. "Retiring" is the normal variant of the schizoid.

into specific attachments? For all essential purposes, the infant is helpless and dependent on others to avoid pain and supply its pleasurable needs. Separated from the womb, the neonate has lost its physical attachment to the mother's body and the protection and nurturance it provided; it must turn toward other regions or sources of attachment if it is to survive and obtain nourishment and stimulation for further development.

Whether the infant's world is conceptualized as a buzz or a blank slate, it must begin to differentiate venues or objects that further its existential aims, supplying nourishment, preservation, and stimulation, from those that diminish, frustrate, or threaten them. These initial relationships, or "internal representational models" (e.g., Crittenden, 1990), apparently "prepared" by evolution, become the context through which other relationships develop.

Stage 2: Sensorimotor-Autonomy

In the sensorimotor-autonomy stage, the focus shifts from existence in itself to existence within an environment. From an evolutionary perspective, the child in this stage is learning a **mode of adaptation,** an *active* tendency to modify its ecologic niche, versus a *passive* tendency to accommodate to whatever the environment has provided. The former reflects a disposition toward taking the initiative in shaping the course of life events; the latter, a disposition to be quiescent, placid, unassertive; to react rather than act; to wait for things to happen; and to accept what is given. Whatever alternative is pursued, it is a matter of degree rather than a yes-no decision. Undoubtedly important in the child's orientation toward the environment are its attachments. Those children who possess a secure base will explore their environments without becoming fearful that their attachment figure cannot be recovered (Ainsworth, 1967). On the other hand, those without such a base tend to remain close to their caretakers, assuming the more passive mode, one likely to ultimately restrict their range of coping resources through decreased or retarded sociocognitive competence (Millon, 1969).

Stage 3: Intracortical-Reproductive Identity

Somewhere between the 11th and 15th years, a rather sweeping series of hormonal changes unsettle the psychic state that had been so carefully constructed in preceding years. These changes reflect the onset of puberty and the instantiation of sexual and gender-related characteristics, which are preparatory for the emergence of the *r-* and *K-* strategies—strong sexual impulses and adultlike features of anatomy, voice, and bearing.

These strategies are psychologically expressed, at the highest level of abstraction, in an orientation toward self and an orientation toward others. Here the male can be prototypically described as more dominant, imperial, and acquisitive, and the female more communal, nurturant, and deferent.

These representations—self and other and their coordination—are essential to the genesis of the personality system. Both attachment theory and the evolutionary model presented here recognize the importance of self and other constructs. From an attachment perspective, these constructs represent inchoate interpersonal relationships, the intricacies of which are made possible by cognitive developments.

Initially, the child must acquire abstract capacities that enable him or her to transcend the purely concrete reality of the present moment and project the self-as-object into myriad futures contingent on its own style of action or accommodation. Such capacities are both cognitive and emotional and may have wide-ranging consequences for the personality system if they fail to cohere as integrated structures, as in the more severe personality disorders, for example, borderline and schizotypal.

When the inner world of symbols is mastered, giving objective reality an order and integration, youngsters are able to create some consistency and continuity in their lives. No longer are they buffeted from one mood or action to another by the swirl of changing events; they now have an internal anchor, a nucleus of cognitions that serves as a base and imposes a sense of sameness and continuity on an otherwise fluid environment. As they grow in their capacity to organize and integrate their world, one configuration becomes increasingly differentiated and begins to predominate. Accrued from experiences with others and their reactions to the child, an image or representation of self-as-object has taken shape. This highest order of abstraction, the sense of individual identity as distinct from others, becomes the dominant source of stimuli that guides the youngster's thoughts and feelings. External events no longer have the power they once exerted; the youngster now has an ever-present and stable sphere of internal representations transformed by rational and emotional reflections, which govern his or her course of action and from which behaviors are initiated.

Just as ontogeny recapitulates phylogeny, so, too, does the developmental character and sequence parallel the core elements of evolution. This theme is more fully elaborated in other writings by the senior author (Millon, 1990; Millon & Davis, 1996). The evolution-development parallel has been described in these writings as "neuropsychological stages."

DOMAINS OF PERSONALITY

The evolutionary theory offers several polarities in developmental stages and content levels. First are the polarities and their derived personality functions, such as survival and adaptation. Second are the neurodevelopmental stages that parallel the evolutionary progression. Third is the *content of personality characteristics.* Here we draw on the distinction between function and structure made in the biological sciences. Anatomy is concerned with permanent structures, and physiology is concerned with the functions that these structures permit. The anatomy of the hand, for example, is composed of bone, muscle, and nerves, and the function of a hand is manual manipulation. Likewise, the *structural domains* of personality provide essentially permanent substrates that provide "hardware support" for the *functional domains* of personality, that is, behaviors, social conduct, cognitive processes, and unconscious mechanisms that manage, balance, and coordinate the give-and-take between inner and outer life. Figure 2.5 shows the relationship among personality, its perspectives, and their domains. The following paragraphs provide a brief exposition of the characteristic domains that we draw on in later chapters.

Expressive Acts

Whereas the concept of a trait refers to behavioral consistencies that are pervasive across time and situation, expressive acts are the discrete units of behavior in which traits are expressed. Traits are more general; acts are more particular. Moreover, there are nearly an infinite number of acts in which a particular trait might be expressed. At the extreme, acts can even refer to stimulus-response chains, hence their close connection with the formerly popular behavioral perspective of Watson and Skinner.

Interpersonal Conduct

This functional domain captures the interpersonal perspective, originating with Sullivan and continued today by notables such as Kiesler and Benjamin. Interpersonal

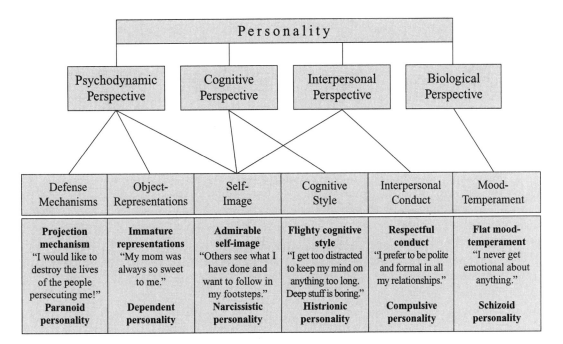

FIGURE 2.5   Personality, Its Perspectives, and a Subset of Its Domains.

FOCUS ON THERAPY

The Misunderstood Narcissist

Personality and the Therapeutic Relationship

A local university student scheduled an appointment with a psychologist in private practice, complaining that his instructors rarely understood his ideas. When asked why he did not present this to the counseling center, he explained that ordinary counselors would be unable to understand his problems. During the first session, he was confident but congenial. By the second session, however, a condescending attitude of superiority had broken through. During the third session, he appeared to regard the psychologist with contempt. When a clarifying question was asked, he responded, "I would think you would have enough information to understand everything that you need to know by now." Arrogant and exploitive interpersonal conduct is often associated with the narcissistic personality.

conduct is concerned with the person's characteristic style of relating to others, including not only the motives that underlie, prompt, and give shape to relational behavior, but also its intended and unintended impacts on others, their counterreactions, and the vicious circles created thereby.

Cognitive Styles

This functional domain captures the cognitive style tradition, perhaps most eloquently expressed by Shapiro (1965, 1981). **Cognitive style** refers not to the content of any isolated belief, but to perceptual distortions, attentional biases, appraisal mechanisms, and so on, all characteristic ways of processing information received from the psychosocial environment.

FOCUS ON SELF-AWARENESS

The Histrionic Coed

Personality and Self-Reflection

A young college student presented for therapy, saying that she wanted to "understand herself." When asked to define her issues more precisely, she was entirely diffuse and long-winded in her discourse, providing detailed minutia about the most trivial aspects of her friendships, oscillating from one notion to another in quick succession, overly dramatizing each fragment, but without going into anything too deeply. This may be described as a "scattered" cognitive style, as it covers much ground but says relatively little. This is often one of the "functional domains" of the histrionic personality pattern.

Defense Mechanisms

Although mechanisms of self-protection, need gratification, and conflict resolution are consciously recognized at times, they operate primarily on an unconscious level. The goal is always the same: to protect conscious awareness from overwhelming feelings of anxiety. Nevertheless, the defense mechanisms are rarely open to conscious reflection, at least without many sessions of psychotherapy. As such, they often contribute to vicious circles, intensifying the very problems they were intended to avoid. Some defense mechanisms are simple, others are complex, and still others, convoluted. This domain of personality is associated most closely with the psychodynamic perspective on personality.

FOCUS ON SELF-VALUES

The Compulsive English Professor

Personality and Perception of Morality

A young man described his English composition instructor as "a morally uptight, proper person" who seemed reluctant to give high grades and actually seemed to enjoy assigning lower grades. Always methodical, the instructor was particularly meticulous about the rules of grammar and punctuation. Any student who expressed a flair for individuality, or simply an air of nonchalance about his or her studies, could be ensnared on the most trivial technicality. According to rumor, when one student complained of being persecuted through the written word, the professor explained that it was he who was being persecuted, because the university required him to grade the young man's papers. A mix of reaction formation and projection is not unusual in compulsive personalities with sadistic traits.

Self-Image

This structural domain spans the interpersonal perspective, the cognitive perspective, and the psychodynamic perspective. In the course of development, the swirl of uncoordinated perceptions eventually gives way to a growing sense of order and continuity. The concept of self provides a stable anchor of continuity or sameness across time in the face of changing experiences. Although everyone has some notion of "who they are," individuals differ greatly in the clarity and accuracy of their self-perceptions.

Object-Representations

Early experiences with caretakers leave a structural imprint composed of memories, attitudes, and emotions, impressions engraved on the mind even before the dawn of self-awareness. As such, object-representations become the primary template for all later interpersonal relationships. They preempt the formative power of later experiences by serving as a basis for perceiving and reacting to ongoing events in the psychosocial world. This domain belongs to the psychodynamic perspective.

FOCUS ON SOCIAL INTERACTION

The Studious Avoidant

Personality and Social Life

An intelligent young woman, Linda, sought guidance concerning a girlfriend, Cathy, a social isolate who almost never came out of her dorm room except to attend classes and eat hurried meals at the cafeteria. Although the other girls on her floor had tried to approach her, Linda was the only one Cathy had let approach her and only then after two years of living on the same floor. If the other girls tried, Cathy would explain in a nervous voice that her classes had extensive reading requirements and that she needed complete privacy to study. In fact, Linda revealed, Cathy felt an extreme sense of inferiority and feared that if she ever became involved with the other girls, she would eventually find them making fun of her behind her back. Such fears of shame and humiliation, associated with an alienated self-image, are common in the avoidant personality.

Morphological Organization

This domain refers to the overall architecture of the mind and self. An individual's psychic interior may display weakness in its structural cohesion, exhibit deficient coordination among its components, or possess few mechanisms by which to maintain homeostatic balance and harmony, regulate internal conflict, or mediate external pressures. The "organization of the mind" is a concept derived from inferences almost exclusively made with information that might be gathered from the psychodynamic perspective.

Mood-Temperament

Although almost all people experience variations in their emotional reactions, many individuals are strongly disposed toward certain emotional reactions rather than others, a

FOCUS ON DEVELOPMENT

The Homesick Dependent

Personality and Attachment

During his first semester in college, a young man presented to the counseling center complaining that he felt inconsolably homesick. Appearing obviously naïve and childlike, he spoke warmly of his parents, especially his mother, a "sweet" person who always "watched out for me, helped me with my homework, and made sure nothing would hurt me." Even though his family lived 90 miles away, he drove home every other day to spend the evening with his mother. Such immature object-representations, continuing to regard caretakers as he did as a child, are typical of the dependent personality.

potential that reflects their prevailing mood, sometimes imposed by life events but most often disposed by biology. Temperament is closely related to mood but best refers to the sum total of biological constraints on personality. Because our physical matrix exists before other domains of personality emerge, biologically built-in behavioral tendencies preempt and exclude other possible pathways of development before they can take hold.

FOCUS ON TEMPERAMENT

The Difficult Roommate

Personality and Interpersonal Conflict

A quiet, easygoing sophomore presented to the university counseling center complaining about her roommate, who, she stated, was literally driving her crazy. She frequently came back from classes to find that her favorite dress had somehow fallen off its hanger, her phone messages had been "accidentally" erased, and even bookmarks had been pulled out and reinserted in the wrong pages. Her roommate denied everything, asserting, "You're just a paranoid, get over it." But what really disturbed her was that, despite every attempt to get along, her roommate seemed to work hard at taking offense, resented her academic success and social skills, and would sometimes sigh in annoyance whenever she made the slightest noise. Such irritable temperament is frequently associated with the negativistic (passive-aggressive) personality.

OPERATIONALIZING THE PERSONALITY DISORDERS

Simply to derive a set of personality constructs on the basis of some theoretical framework is not enough. By stopping here, we would be left only with a list of personality constructs, but no means of integrating the various perspectives inside these constructs. Stepping outside personality itself and appealing to the imperatives of evolution allow us to develop a framework that transcends any particular viewpoint. Otherwise, we would have only repeated the errors of the past, committing a part-whole fallacy by building yet another perspective on personality from some narrow set of variables and presenting it as the whole story.

The purpose of this last step, then, is to make good on the definition of personality originally put forward in this text as the patterning of variables across the entire matrix of the person. Table 2.4 presents a matrix of descriptors for all the functional and structural domains across each of the 14 personality disorders of *DSM-III-R* and *DSM-IV.* Even more specificity can be gained by paragraphs that anchor each of the descriptors, as shown for the compulsive personality in Table 2.5. Because the psychodynamic, biological, cognitive, and interpersonal are the most important perspectives through which personality has been studied in the past century, the claim is that they exhaust all of personality. As we discuss in the next chapter, the *DSM-IV* cannot say as much. In Chapter 3, we put the functional and structural domains to use by illustrating their role in the *assessment* and *therapy* of personality disorders.

Table 2.4   Personality Disorder Attributes by Personality Domain*

	Expressive Behaviors	Interpersonal Conduct	Cognitive Style	Self-Image	Object-Representations	Regulatory Mechanisms	Morphologic Organization	Mood-Temperament
Schizoid	Impassive	Unengaged	Impoverished	Complacent	Meager	Intellectualization	Undifferentiated	Apathetic
Avoidant	Fretful	Aversive	Distracted	Alienated	Vexatious	Fantasy	Fragile	Anguished
Depressive	Disconsolate	Defenseless	Pessimistic	Worthless	Forsaken	Asceticism	Depleted	Melancholic
Dependent	Incompetent	Submissive	Naïve	Inept	Immature	Introjection	Inchoate	Pacific
Histrionic	Dramatic	Attention seeking	Flighty	Gregarious	Shallow	Dissociation	Disjointed	Fickle
Narcissistic	Haughty	Exploitive	Expansive	Admirable	Contrived	Rationalization	Spurious	Insouciant
Antisocial	Impulsive	Irresponsible	Deviant	Autonomous	Debased	Acting out	Unruly	Callous
Sadistic	Precipitate	Abrasive	Dogmatic	Combative	Pernicious	Isolation	Eruptive	Hostile
Compulsive	Disciplined	Respectful	Constricted	Conscientious	Concealed	Reaction formation	Compartmentalized	Solemn
Negativistic	Resentful	Contrary	Skeptical	Discontented	Vacillating	Displacement	Divergent	Irritable
Masochistic	Abstinent	Deferential	Diffident	Undeserving	Discredited	Exaggeration	Inverted	Dysphoric
Schizotypal	Eccentric	Secretive	Autistic	Estranged	Chaotic	Undoing	Fragmented	Distraught or Insentient
Borderline	Spasmodic	Paradoxical	Capricious	Uncertain	Incompatible	Regression	Split	Labile
Paranoid	Defensive	Provocative	Suspicious	Inviolable	Unalterable	Projection	Inelastic	Irascible

*From Millon & Davis (1996).

TOWARD AN INTEGRATED SCIENCE OF PERSONOLOGY

In Chapter 1, we noted that the evolution of the physical sciences and that of the social sciences are fundamentally different. The phenomena of the natural sciences are more sharply bounded and accessible via strong mathematical formalisms. Strong constraints on theorizing are thus provided by the subject matter of the disciplines themselves. The timing and discovery of particular theories may be interesting, but the authors themselves are irrelevant: A physical law is a physical law. If Einstein had failed to discover the Theory of Relativity, someone else would have. In contrast, the phenomena of the social sciences are more loosely bounded, fundamentally open, leaving the history of the social sciences with a contingent structure. Different perspectives emerge at different times, and the gurus of these perspectives compete with one another for disciples. If Freud had never been born, for example, the study of personality would look far different today. In contrast, in the natural sciences, physical laws are drawn into formulations of ever greater generality. No longer is it believed that there are four fundamental forces of nature—gravity, electromagnetism, and the strong and weak nuclear forces—instead, these have been unified in esoteric formulations such as string theory.

In contrast, the loosely boundaried, open nature of the social sciences gives rise to an almost limitless number of perspectives on its subject matter. Most personality theories are content to assert that certain variables are fundamental, while attempting to organize the constructs of competing perspectives. Often, the theories advanced by past thinkers have amounted merely to a list of pet constructs, without any stopping rules that determine why these constructs are fundamental rather than others. The list of character disorders in the psychodynamic perspective is one example; the list of dimensions produced by the various factor models is another. Here, we must accept, as an article of faith, that these constructs exhaust what that perspective has to offer to personality.

TABLE 2.5   The Compulsive Personality: Functional and Structural Domains

Functional Domains		Structural Domains	
	Disciplined	**Self-Image**	**Conscientious**
Expressive Acts	Maintains a regulated, highly structured and strictly organized life; perfectionism interferes with decision making and task completion.		Sees self as devoted to work, industrious, reliable, meticulous, and efficient, largely to the exclusion of leisure activities; fearful of error or misjudgment, hence overvalues aspects of self that exhibit discipline, perfection, prudence, and loyalty.
	Respectful	**Object Representations**	**Concealed**
Interpersonal Conduct	Exhibits unusual adherence to social conventions and proprieties, as well as being scrupulous and overconscientious about matters of morality and ethics; prefers polite, formal, and correct personal relationships, usually insisting that subordinates adhere to personally established rules and methods.		Only those internalized representations with their associated inner affects and attitudes that can be socially approved are allowed conscious awareness or behavioral expression; as a result, actions and memories are highly regulated, forbidden impulses sequestered and tightly bound, personal and social conflicts defensively denied, kept from awareness, maintained under stringent control.
	Constricted	**Morphological Organization**	**Compartmentalized**
Cognitive Style	Constructs world in terms of rules, regulations, schedules, and hierarchies; is rigid, stubborn, and indecisive and notably upset by unfamiliar or novel ideas and customs.		Morphologic structures are rigidly organized in a tightly consolidated system that is clearly partitioned into numerous distinct and segregated constellations of drive, memory, and cognition, with few open channels to permit interplay among these components.
	Reaction Formation	**Mood/Temperament**	**Solemn**
Regulatory Mechanism	Repeatedly presents positive thoughts and socially commendable behaviors that are diametrically opposite deeper contrary and forbidden feelings; displays reasonableness and maturity when faced with circumstances that evoke anger or dismay in others.		Is unrelaxed, tense, joyless, and grim; restrains warm feelings and keeps most emotions under tight control.

Note: Shaded domains are the most salient for this personality prototype.

The evolutionary theory, however, is fundamentally different. Perspectives on personality are the product of the evolutionary history of our particular species. Life on other worlds may differ in their societies, social relationships, mechanisms of cognition, brain structures and neurotransmitters, and perhaps the very metaphysical categories used to parse the stream of sensory stimulation into a subjective experience of "reality." Unless we believe that humans are the prototype for intelligent life everywhere in the universe (surely a delusion), we must admit that there could well be no equivalency between the perspectives of their science of personality and those of our own. In contrast, pleasure-pain, active-passive, and self-other form a necessary framework applicable wherever survival, adaptation, and reproduction exist as evolutionary imperatives, whether on Earth or elsewhere (Millon, 1990). Similarly, there is much to be gained in providing an overarching schema for integrating the diverse activities of clinicians and personologists. A blueprint for such a framework has recently been provided by the senior author in his American Psychological Association's "Distinguished Professional Contribution Award Address" (Millon, 2003).

Summary

The interpersonal perspective argues that personality is best conceptualized as the social product of interactions with significant others. From beginning to end, we are always transacting either with real or imagined others and their expectations. Personality cannot be understood from the inside out, because it is intrinsically immersed in context. Harry Stack Sullivan is regarded as the father of interpersonal perspective. Sullivan's contribution lay in realizing that some forms of mental disorder, while perhaps most dramatically and tangibly manifest through the individual, are nevertheless created and perpetuated through maladaptive patterns of social interaction and communication. The issue with which Sullivan struggled, the essential basis of the interpersonal approach, concerns the nature of the self. Implicitly, all of us regard the self as a thing, a concrete entity or substance with sharply defined boundaries, like a rock. If so, we should know exactly who we are all the time. According to Sullivan, that is not the case. No essential self lies hidden beneath the veils of the unconscious. Instead, there is only a self-concept that is continually being defined and redefined by the interpersonal communications of others. After Sullivan, the next important figure in the emerging interpersonal movement was Timothy Leary, who believed that personality should be thought of in terms of levels, not unlike the psychodynamic idea of levels of consciousness: public communication, conscious description, private symbolization, attributions, unexpressed unconscious, and values. Leary also contributed to the development of the interpersonal circumplex, a figure that organizes personality constructs like the segments of a circle, which is formed by crossing the two content dimensions believed to define interpersonal communication—dominance and affiliation. Interpersonal principles map directly to the circle. According to complementarity, for example, interpersonal behavior is designed to elicit from others actions that validate the sense of who we are. Pathologically rigid individuals possess a constricted conception of self. Only a particular kind of response from others is experienced as validating, and only this kind of response is sought from interpersonal interactions. Since their needs are strong and consistent, individuals with a constricted self-concept may be experienced as controlling or coercive. The most creative contemporary development of interpersonal theory is Benjamin's (1974, 1996) SASB. The SASB seeks to integrate interpersonal conduct, object relations, and self-psychology in a single geometric model.

Cognitive psychology began in the 1950s as a reaction against behaviorism. As an information processor, the mind actively gathers and selects information about the world, self, and others at both conscious and nonconscious levels. When cognitive distortions cohere as a pattern, they may be thought of as cognitive styles. Different personalities process consensual reality in different ways. Each of the personality disorders has its own style of cognitive processing.

Cognitive therapists hold that behavior can be explained by examining the contents of internal mental structures called schemas. Schemas are assumed to mediate cognitive processing at every level, from sensation to paradigms, and on to action plans that the organism can use to affect the world. Like a cognitive filter, they are ever ready to be applied to create an interpretable world. Everything put through the filter is automatically processed. As such, their primary advantage lies in allowing experience to be processed with great efficiency. The information-processing economy that schemas afford, however, also comes at a cost. Because schemas necessarily exist between the raw data of sensation and the meaningful world of subjective experience, they introduce interpretive biases that preempt other construals, possibly distorting consensual reality. Beck et al. (1990) applied the cognitive perspective to the personality disorders, describing the schemas, or core beliefs, that shape the experience and behavior of personality-disordered individuals. In addition, they emphasize the importance of cognitive distortions. These are chronic and systematic errors in reasoning, which promote the misinterpretation of consensual reality.

In personality, the inductive perspective is intimately tied up with the history of psychology. The most influential factor model of personality is the Five-Factor Model, derived from analyses of various personality inventories, not words from the dictionary. As the name indicates, this model consists of five broad higher order factors: Neuroticism, Extroversion, Openness to Experience, Agreeableness, and Conscientiousness. In turn, each dimension consists of several lower order facet traits, thus lending the model a hierarchical structure.

The evolutionary-neurodevelopmental model believes that evolution is the logical choice as a foundation for an integrated science of the person. Psychological health is dependent on the fit between the entire configuration of a person's characteristics and potentials with those of the environments in which the person functions. The first task of any organism is its immediate survival. Organisms that fail to survive have been selected out, so to speak, and fail to contribute their genes and characteristics to subsequent generations. Evolutionary mechanisms related to survival tasks are oriented toward life enhancement and life preservation. Such mechanisms form a polarity of Pleasure and Pain. Behaviors experienced as pleasurable are generally repeated and generally promote survival, while those experienced as painful generally have the potential to endanger life and thus are not repeated. The second evolutionary task faced universally by every organism is adaptation. To exist is to exist within an environment. Organisms must either adapt to their surroundings or adapt their surroundings to conform to and support their own style of functioning. The choice is essentially between a Passive versus Active orientation, that is, a tendency to accommodate to a given ecological niche and accept what the environment offers, versus a tendency to modify or intervene in the environment, thereby adapting it to themselves. The third universal evolutionary task faced by every organism pertains to reproductive styles, essentially sociobiological mechanisms, that each gender uses to maximize its representation in the gene pool. All organisms must ultimately reproduce to evolve. A parallel framework of neurodevelopment is outlined to demonstrate the ontogenetic stages through which humans progress so as to acquire the sensitivities and competencies required to function in accord with their evolutionary origins.

According to evolutionary theory, personality is manifested in eight different domains: expressive acts, interpersonal conduct, cognitive style, defense mechanisms, self-image, object-representations, morphologic organization, and mood-temperament.

Chapter 3

Development of
Personality Disorders

Objectives

- Understand the relevance of *developmental pathogenesis* to the study of personality.
- Understand interplay of necessary, sufficient, and contributory causes for the development of personality pathology.
- Gain insight into how personality dynamics interact in relation to their environment.
- Learn about the hypothesized relationship between some personality disorder expressions and more acute pathology, such as schizophrenia.
- Explain how different temperaments at birth may contribute to vastly different life experiences and ultimate expressions of personality.
- Explain the term *pathogenic,* and list the three types of events that may contribute to pathogenesis.
- Identify parental behaviors and inconsistencies that are thought to cause difficulty in later adaptation.
- Describe the role of traumatic experiences in personality development.
- Explain the importance of early learning.
- Explain how culture, with its values, ideals, and institutions, interfaces with personality development.

Tracing the developmental history of personality and its disorders is one of the most difficult but rewarding phases in the study of medical and psychological science. This study of causation is frequently termed **etiology** in medicine and **developmental pathogenesis** in psychology. It attempts to establish the relative importance of a number of determinants of personality pathology and seeks to demonstrate how overtly unrelated determinants interconnect to produce a clinical picture. Methods such as laboratory tests, case histories, clinical observation, and experimental research are combined in an effort to unravel this intricate developmental sequence.

Most people have been conditioned to think of causality in a simple format in which a single event, known as the cause, results in a single effect. Scientists have learned, however, that particular end results usually arise from the interaction of a large number of causes. Furthermore, it is not uncommon for a single cause to play a part in a variety of end results. Each of these individual end results may set off an independent chain of events that will progress through different intricate sequences.

Thus, study of developmental etiology is complicated by the fact that a particular end result, such as a physical disease, may be produced by any one of a number of different and, on occasion, even mutually exclusive causal sequences; for example, you can get cancer from smoking or from radiation. It should be obvious that causation is not a simple matter of a single cause leading to a single effect. Disentangling the varied and intricate pathways to personality pathology is an especially difficult task indeed.

In philosophy, causes are frequently divided into three classes: necessary, sufficient, and contributory. A **necessary cause** is an event that *must* precede another event for it to occur. For example, certain theorists believe that individuals who do not possess a particular genetic defect will not become schizophrenic; they usually contend that this inherent defect must be supplemented by certain detrimental experiences before the schizophrenic pattern will emerge. In this theory, the genetic defect is viewed as a necessary but not a sufficient cause of the pathology.

A **sufficient condition** is one that is adequate *in itself* to cause pathology; no other factor need be associated with it. However, a sufficient condition is neither a necessary nor an exclusive cause of a particular disorder. For example, a neurosyphilitic infection may be sufficient in itself to produce certain forms of psychopathology, but many other causes can result in these disorders as well.

Contributory causes are factors that increase the probability that a disorder will occur, but are neither necessary nor sufficient to do so. These conditions, such as economic deprivation or racial conflict, add to a welter of other factors that, when taken together, shape the course of pathology. Contributory causes usually influence the form in which the pathology is expressed and play relatively limited roles as primary determinants.

In personality, causes are divided traditionally into predisposing and precipitating factors.

Predisposing factors are contributory conditions that usually are neither necessary nor sufficient to bring about the disorder but that serve as a foundation for its development. They exert an influence over a relatively long time span and set the stage for the emergence of the pathology. Factors such as heredity, socioeconomic status, family atmosphere, and habits learned in response to early traumatic experiences are illustrations of these predispositions.

No hard-and-fast line can be drawn between predisposing and precipitating causes, but a useful distinction may be made between them. **Precipitating factors** refer to clearly demarcated events that occur shortly before the onset of the manifest pathology. These factors either bring to the surface or hasten the emergence of a pathological disposition; that is, they evoke or trigger the expression of established, but hidden, dispositional factors. The death of a parent, a severe car accident, the sudden breakup of a romantic relationship, and so on illustrate these precipitants.

The premise that early experience plays a central role in shaping personality attributes is one shared by numerous theorists. Stating this premise, however, is not to agree as to which specific factors during these developing years are critical in generating particular attributes, nor is it to agree that known formative influences are either necessary or sufficient. Psychoanalytic theorists almost invariably direct their etiologic attentions to the realm of early childhood experience. Unfortunately, they differ vigorously among themselves as to which aspects of nascent life are crucial to development.

There is reason to ask whether etiologic analysis is even possible in personality pathology in light of the complex and variable character of developmental influences. Can this most fundamental of scientific activities be achieved given that we are dealing with an interactive and sequential chain of causes composed of inherently inexact data of a highly probabilistic nature in which even the very slightest variation in context or antecedent condition, often of a minor or random character, produces highly divergent outcomes? Because this looseness in the causal network of variables is unavoidable, are there any grounds for believing that such endeavors could prove more than illusory? Further, will the careful study of individuals reveal repetitive patterns of symptomatic congruence, no less consistency among the origins of diverse clinical attributes such as overt behavior, intrapsychic functioning, and biophysical disposition? And will etiologic commonalities and syndromal coherence prove to be valid phenomena, that is, not merely imposed on observed data by virtue of clinical expectation or theoretical bias?

Among other concerns, the hard data, the unequivocal evidence from well-designed and well-executed research, are sorely lacking. Consistent findings on causal factors for specific clinical entities would be extremely useful were such knowledge only in hand. Unfortunately, our etiologic database is both scanty and unreliable. As noted, it is likely to remain so because of the obscure, complex, and interactive nature of influences that shape psychopathologic phenomena. The yearning among theorists of all viewpoints for a neat package of etiologic attributes simply cannot be reconciled with the complex philosophical issues, methodological quandaries, and difficult-to-disentangle subtle and random influences that shape mental disorders. In the main, almost all etiologic theses today are, at best, perceptive conjectures that ultimately rest on tenuous empirical grounds, reflecting the views of divergent schools of thought positing their favorite hypotheses. These speculative notions should be conceived as questions that deserve empirical evaluation, rather than promulgated as the gospel of confirmed fact.

Inferences drawn in the clinical consulting room concerning past experiences, especially those of early childhood, are of limited, if not dubious, value by virtue of having only the patient as the primary, if not the sole, source of information. Events and relationships of the first years of life are notably unreliable because of the lack of clarity of retrospective memories. The presymbolic world of infants and young toddlers comprises fleeting and inarticulate impressions that remain embedded in perceptually amorphous and inchoate forms—forms that cannot be reproduced as the growing child's cognitions take on a more discriminative and symbolic character. What is recalled, then, draws on a highly ambiguous palette of diffuse images and affects, a source whose recaptured content is readily subject both to direct and subtle promptings from contemporary sources, for example, a theoretically oriented therapist.

Arguments pointing to thematic or logical continuities between the character of early experience and later behaviors, no matter how intuitively rational or consonant with established principles they may be, do not provide unequivocal evidence because their causal connections are different; equally convincing developmental hypotheses can be and are posited. Each contemporary explication of the origins of most personality disorders is persuasive, yet remains but one among several plausible possibilities.

Among other troublesome aspects of contemporary etiologic proposals are the diverse syndromal consequences attributed to essentially identical causes. Although it is not unreasonable to trace different outcomes to similar antecedents, there is an unusual inclination among theorists to assign the same "early conflict" or "traumatic relationship" to all varieties of psychological ailment. For example, an almost universal experiential ordeal that ostensibly undergirds varied syndromes such as narcissistic and borderline personalities, as well as a host of schizophrenic and psychosomatic conditions, is the splitting or repressing of introjected aggressive impulses engendered by parental hostility, an intrapsychic mechanism requisite to countering the dangers these impulses pose to dependency security, should they achieve consciousness or behavioral expression.

It is unlikely that singular origins would be as ubiquitous as clinicians often posit them, but, even if they were, their ultimate psychological impact would differ substantially depending on the configuration of other concurrent or later influences to which individuals were exposed. "Identical" causal factors cannot be assumed to possess the same import, nor can their consequences be traced without reference to the larger context of each individual's life experiences.

To go one step further, there is good reason, as well as evidence, to believe that the significance of early troubled relationships may inhere less in their singularity or the depth of their impact than in the fact that they are precursors of what is likely to become a recurrent pattern of subsequent parental encounters. It may be sheer recapitulation and consequent cumulative learning that ultimately fashions and deeply embeds the entrained pattern of distinctive personality attributes we observe. Although early encounters and resolutions may serve as powerful forerunners, the presence of clinical symptoms may not take firm root in early childhood but may stem from repeated reinforcement.

Despite these arguments, the authors of this text share the commonly held view that, unit for unit, the earlier the experience, the likely greater its impact and durability. For example, the presymbolic and random nature of learning in the first few years often precludes subsequent duplication and, hence, "protects" what has been learned. But, we believe it is also true that singular etiologic experiences, such as "split introjects," are often only the earliest manifestation of a recurrent pattern of parent-child relationships. Early learnings may fail to change, therefore, not because they have jelled permanently but because the same slender band of experiences that helped form them initially continues and persists to influence them for years.

On the Interactive Nature of Developmental Pathogenesis

Despite the title of this book, personality disorders are not disorders at all in the medical sense. Rather, personality disorders are theoretical constructs employed to represent varied styles or patterns in which the personality system functions *maladaptively* in relation to its environment. When the alternative strategies employed to achieve goals, relate to others, and cope with stress are few in number and rigidly practiced (**adaptive inflexibility**); when habitual perceptions, needs, and behaviors perpetuate and intensify preexisting difficulties (**vicious circles**); and when the person tends to lack resilience under conditions of stress (**tenuous stability**), we speak of a clinically maladaptive personality pattern.

For pedagogical purposes, a maladaptive personality system can be heuristically decomposed into various clinical domains. While these facilitate clinical investigation and experimental research, no such division exists in reality. Personality development represents the complex interplay of elements within and across each of these domains. Not only is there an interaction between person and environment, but also there are interactions and complex feedback loops operating within the person at levels of organization both biological and psychological.

Because all scientific theories are to some extent simplifications of reality—the map rather than the territory—all theories involve trade-offs between scope and precision. Most modern developmental theories are organismic and contextual in character. By embracing a multidomain organismic-contextual model, we aspire to *completely* explain personality disorder development as a totality. However, we must simultaneously accept the impossibility of any such explanation. Despite our aspirations, a certain amount of imprecision is built into the guiding metaphor. It posits the existence or reality of experimental error, that is, that the interaction of personality variables is often synergistic, combinatorial, and nonlinear rather than simply additive.

Certain conceptual gimmicks could be used to recover this imprecision or to present an illusion of precision. We might give an exposition of personality disorder development from a *single-domain* perspective, whether cognitive, psychodynamic, or behavioral. Such explanations might increase precision, but this feat would be accomplished only by denying essential aspects of the whole person. Such reductionism with respect to content is incommensurate with the guiding metaphor, that of the total organism. Thus, while any one personologic domain could be abstracted from the whole to give an exposition of personality disorder development from a particular and narrow perspective, this would *not* do justice to a "pathology" that "pervades" the entire fabric of the person.

Accordingly, interaction and continuity are the major themes of this chapter. The discussion stresses the fact that numerous biogenic and psychogenic determinants covary to shape personality disorders, the relative weights of each varying as a function of time and circumstance. Further, this interaction of influences persists over time. The course of later characteristics is related intrinsically to earlier events; an individual's personal history is itself a constraint on future development. Personality disorder development must be viewed, therefore, as a process in which organismic and environmental forces display not only a mutuality and circularity of influence, but also an orderly and sequential continuity throughout the life of the individual.

Pathogenic Biological Factors

That characteristics of anatomic morphology, endocrine physiology, and brain chemistry would not be instrumental in shaping the development of personality is inconceivable. Biological scientists know that the central nervous system cannot be viewed as a simple and faithful follower of what is fed into it from the environment; it not only maintains a rhythmic activity of its own but also plays an active role in regulating sensitivity and controlling the amplitude of what is picked up by peripheral organs. Unlike a machine, which passively responds to external stimulation, the brain has a directing function that determines substantially what, when, and how events will be experienced.

Each individual's nervous system selects, transforms, and registers objective events in accord with its distinctive biological characteristics.

Unusual sensitivities in this delicate orienting system can lead to marked distortions in perception and behavior. Any disturbance that produces a breakdown in the smooth integration of functions, or a failure to retrieve previously stored information, is likely to create chaos and pathology. Normal psychological functioning depends on the integrity of certain key areas of biological structure, and any impairment of this substrate will result in disturbed thought, emotion, and behavior. However, although biogenic dysfunctions or defects may produce the basic break from normality, psychological and social determinants almost invariably shape the *form* of its expression. Acceptance of the role of biogenic influences, therefore, does *not* negate the role of social experience and learning (Eysenck, 1967; Meehl, 1962, 1990b; Millon, 1981, 1990; Millon, Blaney, & Davis, 1999; Millon & Davis, 1996).

Although the exact mechanisms by which biological functions undergird personality disorders will remain obscure for some time, the belief that biogenic factors are intimately involved is not new. Scientists have been gathering data for decades, applying a wide variety of research methods across a broad spectrum of biophysical functions. The number of techniques used and the variety of variables studied are legion. These variables often are different avenues for exploring the same basic hypotheses. For example, researchers focusing on biochemical dysfunctions often assume that these dysfunctions result from genetic error. However, the methods they employ and the data they produce are different from those of researchers who approach the role of heredity through research comparing monozygotic with dizygotic twins. This chapter proceeds to subdivide the subject of development into several arbitrary (but traditional) compartments, beginning first with heredity.

HEREDITY

The role of heredity is usually inferred from evidence based on correlations among traits in members of the same family. Most psychopathologists admit that heredity must play a role in personality disorder development, but they insist that genetic dispositions are modified substantially by the operation of environmental factors. This view states that heredity operates not as a fixed constant but as a disposition that takes different forms depending on the circumstances of an individual's upbringing. Hereditary theorists may take a more inflexible position, referring to a body of data that implicate genetic factors in a wide range of psychopathologies. Although they are likely to agree that variations in these disorders may be produced by environmental conditions, they are equally likely to assert that these are merely superficial influences that cannot prevent the individual from succumbing to his or her hereditary inclination. The overall evidence seems to suggest that genetic factors serve as predispositions to certain traits, but, with few exceptions, similarly affected individuals display important differences in their symptoms and developmental histories (Livesley, Jang, & Vernon, 2003). Moreover, genetically disposed disorders can be aided by psychological therapies (Millon, 1999), and similar symptomatologies often arise without such genetic dispositions.

A number of theorists have suggested that the milder pathologies, such as personality disorders, represent undeveloped or minimally expressed defective genes; for example, the schizoid personality may possess a schizophrenic genotype, but in this case

FOCUS ON GENDER

Gender Bias in the Diagnosis of Personality Disorders

Are Some Axis II Disorders More Prevalent in One Gender than Another?

With so many varied and insidious sources of potential gender bias in the diagnosis of personality disorders that overlap and interact with each other, it is nearly impossible to untangle real differences from artifacts. Bias can enter the equation at any point from the *DSM* diagnostic criteria themselves, to the clinicians who diagnose patients, to the populations sampled in our empirical research, all generated and maintained within the context of an overarching biased and often misogynistic culture. Where do we begin an attempt at sorting out all of these potential sources?

One body of evidence to consider when pondering this question of bias in diagnosing personality disorders is the prevalence rates of different categories of disorders in both males and females. The *DSM-IV* (APA, 1994) reports that certain personality disorders—namely, antisocial personality disorder—are more frequently diagnosed in males while borderline, histrionic, and dependent personality disorders are more frequently diagnosed in females. Hartung and Widiger (1998) compiled findings from a variety of sources to determine that more males are diagnosed as paranoid, schizoid, schizotypal, antisocial, narcissistic, and compulsive; and more females are diagnosed as borderline, histrionic, and dependent. Other studies have reported roughly equal numbers of males and females diagnosed as schizotypal personality disorder. However, it seems as though males possess more eccentric/odd symptoms and females possess more ideas of reference, magical thinking, and social anxiety (Roth & Baribeau, 1997). One often-cited criticism in these prevalence figures is that we have very biased samples of patients. We take samples of convenience at hospitals, the VA, prisons, and the like and generalize the numbers to clinical populations and nonclinical populations alike. We have done a fairly poor job of seeking out representative samples to gather reliable prevalence statistics.

Surprisingly, overall, both men and women are equally as likely to receive a diagnosis of a personality disorder (Kass, Spitzer, & Williams, 1983). An equal prevalence of personality disorder diagnoses across gender as a whole does not preclude the existence of gender bias. Hartung and Widiger (1994) suggest that there is a very real possibility that either men or women may in fact have more personality pathology. Should it be a goal of psychologists to have equal numbers of women and men diagnosed as personality disordered? More specifically, should it be a goal that equal numbers of men and women be diagnosed in each category? Widiger (1998) argues that "the purpose of the *DSM-IV* is to provide an accurate classification of psychopathology, not to develop a diagnostic system that will, democratically, diagnose as many men with a personality disorder as women" (p. 98). While this may be true, it does not excuse the profession from investigating and correcting the potential sources of bias that are contributing the differences we are observing under our current system.

One consideration that adds more complexity to the issue includes the empirical evidence that has been amassed to suggest that there is a systematic failure on the part of the diagnosticians in adhering to the clinical criteria set forth in the *DSM* when making diagnoses (refer to Widiger, Corbitt, & Funtowitz, 1994, for a more comprehensive review of this literature). For example, a study by Ford and Widiger (1989) found that

FOCUS ON GENDER *(Continued)*

clinicians diagnosed females with histrionic personality disorder when they failed to meet *DSM* criteria for the histrionic personality disorder and instead met criteria for antisocial personality disorder. Further, when clinicians were asked to individually assess each of the *DSM* antisocial and histrionic criteria, the sex of the patient had no effect. Ford and Widiger assert that this is evidence to suggest that the problems lie not in the criteria themselves, but in clinicians' failure to adhere to the guidelines.

Other evidence supports this contention of a problem at the level of diagnostic labels, not necessarily in the diagnostic criteria. Sprock (2000) used a method derived from the act-frequency approach to have undergraduate students generate behavioral examples of *DSM* histrionic personality without regard to sex or sex roles. Then, she had a sample of psychologists and psychiatrists rate the representativeness of the symptoms for either histrionic criteria or histrionic personality disorder. She discovered that "feminine" behaviors were rated as more representative of histrionic personality disorder and somewhat more representative of the histrionic criteria than "masculine" behaviors, supporting the same notion that Ford and Widiger argued: The female sex-role is more related to the *label* than to the *criteria*. These same arguments can be made for dependent personality disorder, which includes many traditionally feminine qualities such as putting other people's needs above your own or relying on a husband to provide an income and home.

These differences in the prevalence rate for females are hardly a one-sided bias on the part of the *DSM*. It is just as easily arguable that there are male stereotyped behaviors to be found in criteria for personality disorders. For example, the narcissistic personality disorder contains criteria that are traditionally ascribed to healthy male functioning such as an inflated sense of self-importance, a preoccupation with fantasies of unlimited success and power, possessing a sense of entitlement, lacking empathy, and assuming an arrogant manner. Traditionally socialized male characteristics can be seen in the criteria for antisocial personality as well, such as deceitfulness, impulsivity, aggressiveness as evidenced by getting into physical fights, and irresponsibility (APA, 1994).

While neither side of the debate would likely argue that these criteria mirror sex-typed behavior, they would argue as to the significance of this fact. Many feminists would argue that labeling women as personality disordered is an act of punishing women for conforming to the very criteria we ask them to conform to (Landrine, 1989; Walker, 1994). They argue that women are actually in a double bind. If they do not act in a manner that is deferential, dependent, and sexually provocative, they risk becoming social outcasts. If they do, they are branded "mad" or "disordered." Landrine (1989) asserts:

> The purposes of masquerading gender roles as madness may be (a) to locate falsely within persons all of the ludicrous cognitive and behavioral limitations that actually reside in gender roles and stratification so that (b) to direct our attention—not to changing gender roles or to eradicating gender stratification—but to changing individuals through therapy and to eradicating their ostensible personal problems. (p. 332)

Or worse, it is a way to label victims of sexual abuse or domestic violence as "sick" rather than placing the blame on the perpetrators of these crimes. Given that a huge percentage of

(Continued)

FOCUS ON GENDER *(Continued)*

women diagnosed as personality disordered have histories of sexual and physical abuse, this argument is convincing (Brown, 1992).

Others (including Widiger, Corbitt, & Funtowitz, 1994) argue that just because these disorders are founded on a biased society that encourages some of these characteristics does not negate the fact that in these extreme forms of expression, they are pathological. If we conceptualize personality disorders as lying on a continuum rather than as categorical, it is justifiable that at these extreme ends, the behaviors, whatever their original source of motivation, are disordered.

There is empirical support for this notion that several personality disorders are exaggerations of normal socialized sex-typed behaviors. Landrine (1987, 1989) proposes what she calls a *social-role hypothesis* that posits:

> Each personality disorder represents the role/role-stereotype of the specific status group (Sex X Social Class X Marital Status Group) that tends to receive that diagnosis most often, such that the personality disorder categories as a whole represent the role/role-stereotypes of both sexes. Thus, women might receive certain diagnoses more often than men—and vice versa—because the category on question is by and large equivalent to their role.

Based on this social-role hypothesis that a personality disorder might be differentially assigned to males or females when the description is consistent with gender-role stereotypes, Rienzi and Scrams (1991) argued that clinically untrained people should be able to accurately make this distinction as well. If assigning these diagnoses to men and women is a social construction, nonclinicians should fall as victim to these biases as psychologists. In their study of university students, they asked students to assign gender to six descriptions of *DSM-III*-R personality disorders. Significant agreement was found, with paranoid, antisocial, and compulsive personality disorders being viewed as male and dependent and histrionic personality disorders viewed as female. In another study along this same vein, Rienzi, Forquera, and Hitchcock (1994) asked undergraduates to assign either a label of male or female to gender-ambiguous vignettes and found a similar bias to labeling the narcissistic vignette as a male and the dependent vignette as female.

Another line of research lends an additional slant on this argument. Some theorists have hypothesized that histrionic personality disorder and antisocial personality disorder are actually "expressions of the same latent disposition" (Hamburger, Lilienfeld, & Hogben, 1996, p. 52). What we observe superficially are only the gender-stereotyped behaviors of the same underlying pathology. As Widiger and Spitzer (1991) argue, the differences we see in the distribution of personality disorders may be due to etiological factors such as different sex hormones that influence the final expression of pathology. Histrionic and antisocial personalities may be an example of such an effect. They may both represent expressions of the same pathology, and we are misconceptualizing them as two separate entities because their superficial expressions (the symptoms they outwardly express) are different.

Yet another area of the literature to contemplate when considering gender bias in diagnosing personality disorders is the area of criminal behavior. The once hard-and-fast rule that men display more criminal and antisocial behavior is rapidly changing. Historically, female crime rates have been incredibly small and considered an aberration.

FOCUS ON GENDER *(Continued)*

In the late 1890s, Lombroso proposed what he called the "masculinity hypothesis" to explain women who committed crimes. He believed that excessive body hair, wrinkles, and an abnormally shaped head were all outward signs of the female criminal. Perhaps because of Lombroso's belief that female criminals are masculine-like and, therefore, somehow unnatural, it has been widely believed that female criminals are somehow sicker than male criminals. Lombroso even quotes an Italian proverb, "Rarely is a woman wicked, but when she is she surpasses the man," which illustrates this belief (Lombroso & Ferrero, 1916, p. 147). Clearly, the prototype for an antisocial was considered a male antisocial. A female antisocial is somehow only a poor cousin to the prototype or "real" antisocial.

Conclusions

After weighing all perspectives and sources of evidence, it is clear that there are problems on multiple levels. Our conceptualizations are fuzzy, our samples are biased, our measures are biased, and our clinicians fall prey to their own biases. The question of what to do is even more difficult to address. At the theoretical level, we have great room for improvement. A logical place to start is at the *DSM* level. However, tales of how *DSM* committees work are horrifying (see Caplan, 1991, for details on how the self-defeating personality diagnosis was retained in the *DSM)*. What we put faith in as an unbiased and scientific system for diagnosing mental disorders is often a very political and even random set of criteria. To add further fuel to the fire, the vast majority of *DSM* authors and committee members on personality disorder workgroups have been male. Eighty-nine percent of *DSM-III* personality disorder workgroup members (8 of 9) were male, 84% for *DSM-III*-R (32 of 38), and 78% for the *DSM-IV* (7 of 9; Widiger, 1998). Future revisions of the *DSM* need to draw on the resources of a far wider clinical base than the 1,000 individuals involved in the production of the *DSM-IV.* Additionally, if our clinical samples are biased, as a community, we need to make the investment in solid epidemiological research to determine real prevalence rates, even if we are using our flawed diagnostic criteria. It is difficult to obtain a clear picture of where to fix a problem if we do not know how pervasive the problem is.

The fairly convincing evidence that clinicians do not adhere to the existing criteria when making diagnoses is also troubling. How to tackle these failures is a complex issue. Perhaps raising awareness of biases is a first step. If clinicians have taken the time to introspect a little on why they assume histrionics are female and narcissists are male, they may pause to consider alternative diagnoses. The *DSM-IV* contains only one sentence about this issue buried within the general discussion of personality disorders:

> Although these differences in prevalence probably reflect real gender differences in the presence of such patterns, clinicians must be cautious not to overdiagnose or underdiagnose certain Personality Disorders in females or in males because of social stereotypes about typical gender roles and behaviors. (APA, 1994, p. 632)

(Continued)

---

the defective gene is weakened by the operation of beneficial modifying genes or favorable environmental experiences (Meehl, 1990b). An alternate explanation might be formulated in terms of polygenic action; polygenes have minute, quantitatively similar, and cumulative effects. Thus, a continuum of increasing pathological severity can be accounted for by the cumulative effects of a large number of minor genes acting on the same trait (Millon, 1969).

The idea that psychopathological syndromes comprise well-circumscribed disease entities is an attractive assumption for those who seek a Mendelian or single-gene model of inheritance. Recent thinking forces us to question the validity of this approach to nosology and to the relevance of Mendelian genetic action. Defects in the infinitely complex central nervous system can arise from innumerable genetic anomalies (Plomin, 1990). Moreover, even convinced geneticists make reference to the notion of phenocopies, a concept signifying that characteristics usually traceable to genetic action can be simulated by environmental factors; thus, overtly identical forms of pathology may arise from either genetic or environmental sources. As a consequence, the clinical picture of a disorder may give no clue to its origins since similar appearances do not necessarily signify similar etiologies. To complicate matters further, different genes vary in their responsiveness to environmental influences; some produce uniform effects under all environmental conditions, whereas others can be entirely suppressed in certain environments (Plomin, DeFries, & McClearn, 1990). Moreover, it appears that genes have their effects at particular times of maturation and their interaction with environmental conditions is minimal both before and after these periods.

Despite these ambiguities and complications, there can be little question that genetic factors do play some dispositional role in shaping the morphological and biochemical substrate of certain traits. However, these factors are by no means necessary to the development of personality pathology, nor are they likely to be sufficient in themselves to elicit pathological behaviors. They may serve, however, as a physiological base that makes the person susceptible to dysfunction under stress or inclined to learn behaviors that prove socially troublesome.

BIOPHYSICAL INDIVIDUALITY

The general role that neurological lesions and physiochemical imbalances play in producing pathology can be grasped with only a minimal understanding of the structural organization and functional character of the brain. However, it is important that naive misconceptions be avoided. Among these is the belief that psychological functions can be localized in neurohormonal depots or precise regions of the brain. Psychological processes such as thought, behavior, and emotion derive from complex and circular feedback properties of brain activity. Unless the awesomely intricate connections within the brain that subserve these psychological functions are recognized, the result will be simplistic propositions that clinical or personality traits can arise as a consequence of specific chemical imbalances or focal lesions (Purves & Lichtman, 1985). Psychological concepts such as emotion, behavior, and thought represent diverse and complex processes that are grouped together by theorists and researchers as a means of simplifying their observations. These conceptual labels must not be confused with tangible events and properties within the brain. Certain regions are more involved in particular psychological functions than others, but it is clear that higher processes are a product of brain area interactions. For example, the frontal lobes of the cortex orchestrate a dynamic pattern of impulses by selectively enhancing the sensitivity of receptors, comparing impulses arising in other brain spheres, and guiding them along myriad arrangements and sequences. In this regnant function, it facilitates or inhibits a wide range of psychological functions.

Clinical signs and symptoms cannot be conceived as localized or fixed to one or another sphere of the brain. Rather, they arise from a network of complex interactions and feedbacks (Purves & Lichtman, 1985). We might say that all stimuli, whether generated externally or internally, follow long chains of reverberating circuits that modulate a wide range of activities. Psychological traits and processes must be conceived, therefore, as the product of a widespread and self-regulating pattern of interneuronal stimulation. If we keep in mind the intricate neural interdependencies underlying these functions, we should avoid falling prey to the error of interpretive simplification.

Nevertheless, if the preceding caveats are considered, certain broad hypotheses seem tenable. Possessing more or less of the interactive neurological substrates for a particular function, for example, such as pleasure or pain, can markedly influence the character of experience and the course of learning and development. Evidently, the role of neuroanatomical structures in psychopathology is not limited to problems of tissue defect or damage. Natural interindividual differences in structural anatomy and organization can result in a wide continuum of relevant psychological effects (Davidson, 1986; R. J. Williams, 1973). If we recognize the network of neural structures that are upset by a specific lesion and add the tremendous individual differences in brain morphology, the difficulties involved in tracing the role of a neurological disturbance become apparent. If the technical skills required to assess the psychological consequences of a specific brain lesion are difficult, we can only begin to imagine the staggering task of determining the psychological correlates of natural anatomic differences.

TEMPERAMENT DISPOSITIONS

Each child enters the world with a distinctive pattern of dispositions and sensitivities. Nurses know that infants differ from the moment they are born, and perceptive parents notice distinct differences in their successive offspring. Some infants suck vigorously; others seem indifferent and hold the nipple feebly. Some infants have a regular cycle of hunger, elimination, and sleep, whereas others vary unpredictably (Michelsson, Rinne, & Paajanen, 1990). Some twist fitfully in their sleep, while others lie peacefully awake in hectic surroundings. Some are robust and energetic; others seem tense and cranky.

The question that must be posed, however, is not whether children differ temperamentally but whether a particular sequence of subsequent life experiences will result as a consequence of these differences; childhood temperament would be of little significance if it did not undergird subsequent patterns of functioning. The clinician must ask whether the child's characteristics evoke distinctive reactions from his or her parents and whether these reactions have a beneficial or a detrimental effect on the child's development (Kagan, Reznick, & Snidman, 1989; Maccoby & Martin, 1983). Rather than limit attention to the traditional question of what effect the environment has on the child, the focus might be changed to ask what effect the child has on the environment and what the consequences of these are on the child's development.

Patterns of behavior observed in the first few months of life are apparently more of biogenic than psychogenic origin. Some researchers speak of these patterns as "primary" because they are displayed before postnatal experience can fully account for them. Investigators have found that infants show a consistent pattern of autonomic system reactivity; others have reported stable differences on biological measures such as sensory threshold, quality and intensity of emotional tone, and electroencephalographic waves. Because the pertinence of psychophysiological differences to later personality is unknown, investigators have turned attention to the relationship between observable behavior and later development.

The studies of a number of research groups (Escalona, 1968; Escalona & Heider, 1959; Escalona & Leitch, 1953; Murphy, 1962; Murphy & Moriarty, 1976; Thomas & Chess, 1977; Thomas, Chess, & Birch, 1963, 1968) have been especially fruitful in this regard. Their work has contributed to not only an understanding of personality development in general but also the development of personality pathology in particular. Several behavioral dimensions were found to differentiate the temperament patterns of infants. Children differ in the regularity of their biological functions, including autonomic reactivity, gauged by initial responses to new situations; sensory alertness to stimuli and adaptability to change; characteristic moods; and intensities of response, distractibility, and persistence (Goldsmith & Gottesman, 1981). Although early patterns were modified only slightly from infancy to childhood, this continuity could not be attributed entirely to the persistence of innate endowments. Subsequent experiences served to reinforce the characteristics that were displayed in early life (Kagan, 1989). This occurred in great measure because the infant's initial behaviors transformed the environment in ways that intensified and accentuated initial behaviors.

Theorists have often viewed disorders to be the result of experiences that individuals have no part in producing themselves (Jones & Raag, 1989; Zanolli, Saudargas, & Twardosz, 1990). This is a simplification of a complex interaction (Sroufe & Waters, 1976). Each infant possesses a biologically based pattern of sensitivities and dispositions that shape the nature of his or her experiences. The interaction of biological dispositions and environmental experience is not a readily disentangled web but an intricate feedback system of crisscrossing influences. Several components of this process are elaborated because of their pertinence to development.

Adaptive Learning

The temperament dispositions of the maturing child are important because they strengthen the probability that certain traits will become prepotent (Bates, 1980, 1987; Thomas, Chess, & Korn, 1982). For example, highly active and responsive children relate to and rapidly acquire knowledge about events and persons in their environment. Their zest and energy may lead them to experience personal gratification quickly, or, conversely, their lively and exploratory behavior may result in painful frustrations if they run repetitively into insuperable barriers. Unable to fulfill their activity needs, they may strike out in erratic and maladaptive ways. Moreover, temperament also influences the expression of psychological variables such as attachment (Belsky & Rovine, 1987).

Organismic action in passive children is shaped also by their biological constitution. Ill-disposed to deal with their environment assertively and disinclined to discharge their tensions physically, they may learn to avoid conflicts and step aside when difficulties arise. They may be less likely to develop guilt feelings about misbehavior than active youngsters, who more frequently get into trouble and receive punishment and are, therefore, inclined to develop aggressive feelings toward others. Passive youngsters may also deprive themselves of rewarding experiences, feel "left out of things," and depend on others to protect them from events they feel ill-equipped to handle on their own.

Interpersonal Reciprocity

Previously, we spoke of personality as a system. However, a systems notion need not be confined to operations that take place within the organism. Interpersonal theorists often speak of dyads and triads as systems of reciprocal influence. Childhood temperament evokes counterreactions from others that confirm and accentuate initial temperamental dispositions (Papousek & Papousek, 1975). Biological moods and activity levels shape not only the child's own behaviors but also those of the child's parents. If the infant's disposition is cheerful and adaptable and care is easy, the mother quickly displays a positive reciprocal attitude (Osofsky & Danzger, 1974). Conversely, if the child is tense or if his or her care is difficult and time consuming, the mother may react with dismay, fatigue, or hostility. Through this distinctive behavioral disposition, then, the child elicits parental reactions that reinforce the initial pattern. Innate dispositions can be reversed by strong environmental pressures. A cheerful outlook can be crushed by parental contempt and ridicule. Conversely, shy and reticent children may become more self-confident in a thoroughly encouraging family atmosphere (Smith & Pederson, 1988).

There is an unfortunate tendency of clinicians and theorists to speak of parental responses to their children as if they were identical (uniformly abusive or uniformly loving, etc.). In fact, what is most likely is that parents differ in their attitudes and behaviors toward the child, often rather strikingly so. When parental consistency occurs, it may be relatively easy to trace the connection between early experiences and later behavior styles. However, when these crucial parental relationships differ appreciably, the equation of influence becomes much more complex, especially if we also consider the effects of one or more siblings, perhaps some older and others younger.

Depending on the character and mix of influences, what is learned may result in any number of behavioral and attitudinal styles on the part of the child. Some youngsters may develop conflicting or split images of self; others may find a way to synthesize these contrasting patterns; still others may shift or vacillate from circumstance to circumstance, depending on their similarity to their parents' divergent behaviors (e.g., learning to behave in a caring and affectionate manner with women because of the actions of a consistently nurturing and valuing mother; with men, however, this same person inevitably behaves in a competitive and hostile manner because of the father's rejecting and derogating attitudes).

Although the idea that biophysical aspects constrain future development is easily understood, *not* all features of an individual's constitution are activated at the moment of birth. Individuals mature at different rates. Potentials may unfold only gradually as maturation progresses. Thus, some biologically rooted influences may not emerge until the youngster is well into adolescence, and it is not inconceivable that these late-blooming patterns may supplant those displayed earlier.

A crucial determinant of whether a particular temperament will lead to personality pathology appears to be parental acceptance of the child's individuality. Parents who accept their child's temperament and modify their practices accordingly can deter what might otherwise become pathological. On the other hand, if parents experience daily feelings of failure, frustration, anger, and guilt, regardless of the child's disposition, they are likely to contribute to a progressive worsening of the child's adjustment. These comments point once more to the fact that biogenic and psychogenic factors interact in complex ways.

Pathogenic Experiential History

In the previous section, we stressed the view that biological functions play an active role in regulating what, when, and how events will be experienced; the nervous and endocrine systems do not accept passively what is fed into them. This active process means that unusual biological sensitivities or defects may result in perceptual distortions, thought disorders, and pathological behaviors.

Although behavior pathology may be triggered by biogenic abnormalities, the mere specification of a biogenic cause is not sufficient for an adequate etiological analysis. Even in cases where clear-cut biogenic factors can be identified, it is necessary to trace the developmental sequence of experiences that transform these defects into a manifest form of psychopathology; the need for this more extensive developmental analysis is evident by the fact that some individuals with biological defects function effectively, whereas other, similarly afflicted individuals succumb to maladaptation and psychopathology (Davidson, 1986). The biological defect, in itself, cannot account for such divergences in development. Pathological behaviors that are precipitated initially by biological abnormalities are not simple or direct products of these defects; rather, they emerge through a complex sequence of interactions, which include environmental experience and learning.

A major theme of this chapter is that psychopathology develops as a result of an intimate interplay of intraorganismic and environmental forces; such interactions start at the time of conception and continue throughout life. Individuals with similar biological potentials emerge with different personality patterns depending on the environmental conditions to which they were exposed. These patterns unfold and change as new biological maturations interweave within the context of new environmental encounters. In time, these patterns stabilize into a distinctive hierarchy of behaviors that remain relatively consistent through the ever-changing stream of experience.

That biological factors and environmental experiences interact is a truism; we must be more specific and ask how, exactly, these interactions take place.

Before we begin, let us discount questions about the proportionate contribution of biological factors as contrasted to environmental learning. The search to answer such questions is not only impossible from a methodological point of view but also logically misleading. We could not, given our present state of technical skill, begin to tease out the relative contribution of these two sources of variance. Furthermore, a search such as this would be based on a misconception of the nature of interaction. The character and degree of contribution of either biogenic or psychogenic factors are inextricably linked to the character and degree of the contribution of the other. For example, biological influences are not uniform from one situation to the next but vary as a function of the environmental conditions within which they arise. The position we take, then, is that both factors contribute to all behavior patterns and their respective contributions are determined by reciprocal and changing combinations of interdependence.

We return now to the question of how, exactly, biogenic and psychogenic factors interact in the development of personality and psychopathology.

In the previous section, we examined a number of ways in which biological factors shape, facilitate, or limit the nature of the individual's experiences and learning. For example, the same objective environment is perceived as different by individuals who possess different biological sensibilities; people register different stimuli at varying intensities in accord with their unique pattern of alertness and sensory acuity. From this fact, we should see that experience itself is shaped at the outset by the biological equipment of the person. Furthermore, the constitutional structure of individuals strengthens the probability that they will learn certain forms of behavior. Their body build, strength, energy, neurological makeup, and autonomic system reactivity not only influence the stimuli individuals will seek or be exposed to but also determine, in large measure, types of behaviors individuals find are successful for them in dealing with these encounters.

We must recognize further that the interaction between biological and psychological factors is *not unidirectional* such that biological determinants always precede and influence the course of learning and experience; the order of effects can be reversed, especially in the early stages of development. From recent research, we learn that biological maturation is largely dependent on favorable environmental experience; the development of the biological substrate itself, therefore, can be disrupted, even completely arrested, by depriving the maturing organism of stimulation at sensitive periods of rapid neurological growth. The profound effect of these experiences on biological capacities is a central theme in personality development; we contend that the sheer quantity as well as the quality of these early experiences is a crucial aspect in the development of several pathological patterns of personality.

Beyond the crucial role of these early experiences, we argue further that there is a circularity of interaction in which initial biological dispositions in young children evoke counterreactions from others that accentuate their disposition. The notion that the child plays an active role in creating environmental conditions, which, in turn, serve as a basis for reinforcing his or her biological tendencies, is illustrated well in this early observation by Cameron and Margaret (1951):

. . . the apathy that characterizes an unreactive infant may deprive him of many of the reactions from others which are essential to his biosocial maturation. His unresponsiveness may discourage his parents and other adults from fondling him, talking to him or providing him with new and challenging toys, so that the poverty of his social environment sustains his passivity and social isolation. If such a child develops behavior pathology, he is likely to show an exaggeration or distortion of his own characteristic reactions in the form of retardation, chronic fatigue or desocialization.

This thesis suggests, then, that the normally distributed continuum of biological dispositions that exists among young children is widened gradually because initial dispositions give rise to experiences that feed back and accentuate these dispositions. Thus, biological tendencies are not only perpetuated but also intensified as a consequence of their interaction with experience.

The argument that biogenic and psychogenic factors are intimately connected does not mean that psychogenic events cannot produce personality pathology of their own accord. Geneticists refer to the concept of **phenocopies,** that is, characteristics arising entirely from the action of environmental events that simulate those produced by genes. In a like fashion, psychogenic experiences may lead to pathological behaviors that are indistinguishable from those generated by the interplay of biological and psychological forces. Severe personal trauma, social upheaval, or other more insidious pressures can reverse an individual's normal pattern and prompt a pathological reaction. Thus, not only are there exceptions to the general rule that biological dispositions and experiences interact to shape the course of adjustment, but a promising beginning may be upset by unusual or unfortunate circumstances.

Despite the fact that there are cases in which later experience can reverse early behavior patterns, we cannot understand these cases fully without reference to the historical background of events that precede them. We assert that there is an intrinsic continuity throughout life of personality functioning; thus, this chapter follows the sequence of natural development. Furthermore, we contend that not only are childhood events more significant to personality formation than later events but also later behaviors are related in a determinant way to early experience. Despite an occasional and dramatic disjunctiveness in development, there is an orderly and sequential continuity, engendered by mechanisms of self-perpetuation and social reinforcement that link the past to the present. The format for this chapter demonstrates this theme of developmental continuity.

Sources of Pathogenic Learning

Attitudes and behaviors may be learned as a consequence of instruction or indoctrination on the part of parents, but most of what is learned accrues from a haphazard series of casual and incidental events to which the child is exposed. Not only is the administration of rewards and punishments meted out most often in a spontaneous and erratic fashion, but the everyday and ordinary activities of parents provide the child with unintended models to imitate.

These conditions *do not* activate protective or defensive behaviors as do emotionally disruptive events; they merely reinforce styles of behavior that prove deleterious when generalized to settings other than those in which they were acquired. The roots of behavior—how people think, talk, fear, love, solve problems, and relate to others; aversions; irritabilities; attitudes; anxieties; and styles of interpersonal communication—are all adopted and duplicated by children as they observe the everyday reactions of their parents and older siblings. Children mirror these complex behaviors without understanding their significance and without parental intentions of transmitting them. The old saying, "Practice what you preach," conveys the essence of this thesis. Thus, a parent who castigates the child harshly for failing to be kind may create an intrinsically ambivalent learning experience; the contrast between parental manner and their verbalized injunction teaches the child simultaneously to think kindly but to behave harshly.

The particulars and the coloration of many pathological patterns have their beginnings in the offhand behaviors and attitudes to which the child is incidentally exposed. It is important, therefore, in reviewing this chapter, to remember that children acquire less from intentional parental training methods than from casual and adventitious experience.

People simply do not learn in neatly arranged alley mazes with all confounding effects nicely controlled; the sequence is not only complicated by manifold "extraneous variables" to which learning becomes attached but also subject to highly irregular "schedules of reinforcement."

A matter that should be self-evident, but is often overlooked or simplified in presenting pathogenic influences, relates to our prior notation that most children acquire their ideas and models from *two parents,* as well as one or more siblings. Children are exposed to and frequently learn different and contrasting sets of perceptions, feelings, attitudes, behaviors, and so on, as well as a mixed set of assumptions about themselves and others. In a manner similar to **genetic recombination,** where the child's heredity-based dispositions reflect the contribution of both parents, so, too, do the child's experiences and learnings reflect the input and interweaving of what he or she has been subjected to by both parents. For example, one parent may have been cruel and rejecting, whereas the other may have been kindly and supportive. How this mix ultimately takes psychological form and which set of these differential experiences predominates will be a function of numerous other factors. However, we should expect that children will be differentially affected by each parent and that pathogenesis will reflect a complex interaction of these combined experiences. Be mindful that few experiences are singular in their impact; they are modulated by the interplay of multiple forces, but mostly by the commingling and consolidation of two sets of parental influences.

Three types of events may be described to illustrate the concept of **pathogenic:**

1. Events that provoke undue anxiety in the individual because they make demands beyond his or her capacity or because they otherwise undermine his or her feelings of security and comfort. Persistence of these emotionally disruptive events elicits coping reactions that, ultimately, may lead to the *learning* of **generalized defensive strategies.** These strategies may be successful in diminishing certain feelings of discomfort, but they may prove detrimental in the long run to healthy functioning because they may be applied to circumstances for which they are ill-suited.

2. Emotionally neutral conditions that lead to the learning of **maladaptive behaviors.** These conditions do not activate protective or defensive behaviors as do emotionally disruptive events; they merely teach or reinforce styles of behavior that prove deleterious when generalized inappropriately to settings other than those in which they were acquired. The roots of these difficulties, therefore, *do not* lie in stress, anxiety, or unconscious mechanisms of defense, but rather in the simple conditioning or imitation of maladaptive behavior patterns.

3. An *insufficiency* of experiences requisite to the learning of **adaptive behavior.** Thus, general stimulus impoverishment, or minimal social experience, may produce deficits in the acquisition of adaptive behaviors. The sheer lack of skills and competence for mastering the environment is a form of pathological *underlearning,* which may be as severe as those disorders generated either by stressful experiences or by defective or maladaptive learning.

The research and theoretical literature on pathogenic sources do not lend themselves to this threefold schema; another format must be used to present this body of work. Nevertheless, remember these distinctions while studying the ensuing pages.

The belief that early interpersonal experiences in the family play a decisive role in the development of psychopathology is well accepted among professionals, but reliable and unequivocal data supporting this conviction are difficult to find. The deficits in these data are not due to a shortage of research efforts; rather, they reflect the operation of numerous methodological and theoretical difficulties that stymies progress. For example, and as discussed in prior pages, most of these data depend on retrospective accounts of early experience; these data are notoriously unreliable. Patients interviewed during their illness are prone to give a warped and selective accounting of their relationships with others; information obtained from relatives often is distorted by feelings of guilt or by a desire to uncover some simple event to which the disorder can be attributed. In general, then, attempts to reconstruct the complex sequence of events of yesteryear that may have contributed to pathological learning are fraught with almost insurmountable methodological difficulties.

To these procedural complications may be added problems of conceptual semantics and data organization; these complications make comparisons among studies difficult and deter the systematic accumulation of a consistent body of research data. For example, what one investigator calls a "cold and distant" parent, another may refer to as "hostile or indifferent"; an "indulgent" mother in one study may be referred to as a "worrier" in another or "overprotective" in a third. Furthermore, descriptive terms such as *cold, overprotective,* and so on represent gross categories of experience; variations, timing sequences, and other subtleties of interpersonal interaction are lost or blurred when experiences are grouped together into these global categories. The precise element of these experiences, which effectively accounts for maladaptive learning, remains unclear because of the gross or nonspecific categories into which these experiences are grouped. We must know exactly what aspect of parental coldness or overprotectiveness is pathogenic. It is hoped that such specifications will be detailed more precisely in future research. Until such time, however, we must be content with the global nature of these categories of psychogenesis.

In the following sections, we differentiate the sources of pathological learning into two broad categories. The first comprises experiences that exert an influence throughout the child's entire developmental sequence—*enduring and pervasive experiences.* The second category includes adverse conditions of relatively brief duration that occur at any point in the life span, but exert a profound influence on development—*traumatic experiences.*

ENDURING AND PERVASIVE EXPERIENCES

An atmosphere, a way of handling the daily and routine activities of life, or a style and tone of interpersonal relatedness come to characterize the family setting in which the child develops. Events, feelings, and ways of communicating are repeated day in and day out. In contrast to the occasional and scattered events of the outside environment, the circumstances of daily family life have an enduring and cumulative effect on the entire fabric of the child's learning. In this setting, the child establishes a basic feeling of security, imitates the ways in which people relate interpersonally, acquires an impression of how others perceive and feel about him or her, develops a sense of self-worth, and learns how to cope with feelings and the stresses of life. The influence of the family environment is preeminent during all of the crucial growth periods in that it alone among all sources exerts a persistent effect on the child.

In what ways can these enduring experiences be differentiated?

Because the ebb and flow of everyday life consists of many inextricably interwoven elements, any subdivision that can be made must reflect some measure of arbitrariness. You will not fall prey to the errors of etiological simplification if you remember that the following features separated into five categories represent only single facets of an ongoing and complex constellation of events.

Parental Feelings and Attitudes

The most overriding, yet the most difficult to appraise, aspect of learned experience is the extent to which the child develops a feeling of acceptance or rejection by his or her parents. With the exception of cases of blatant abuse or overt deprecation, investigators have extreme difficulty in specifying, no less measuring, the signs of parental neglect, disaffiliation, and disaffection. Despite the methodological difficulties that researchers encounter, the child who is the recipient of the following three rejecting cues has no doubt but that he or she is unappreciated, scorned, or deceived:

1. To be exposed throughout a child's early years to parents who view him or her as unwanted and troublesome can only establish a deep and pervasive feeling of isolation in a hostile world. Deprived of the supports and security of home, the child may be ill-disposed to venture forth with confidence to face struggles in the outer world. Rejected by his or her parents, the child may anticipate equal devaluation by others (Emde, 1989; Maccoby & Martin, 1983). As a defense against further pain, the child may learn the strategy of avoiding others; he or she may use apathy and indifference as a protective cloak to minimize the impact of the negative reinforcements now expected from others. Different strategies may evolve, depending on other features associated with rejection; children may imitate parental scorn and ridicule and learn to handle their disturbed feelings by acting in a hostile and vindictive fashion. Rejected by parents, the child is likely to anticipate equal devaluation by others (Cicchetti & Carlson, 1989; Dodge, Murphy, & Buchsbaum, 1984; Dornbusch, Ritter, Leiderman, & Roberts, 1987; Mueller & Silverman, 1989; Steinberg, Elmen, & Mounts, 1989).

2. Parental attitudes represented by terms such as seduction, exploitation, and deception contribute their share of damage to the child's personality, although it is usually the sense of being unwanted and unloved that proves to have the most pervasive and shattering of effects (Cicchetti & Beeghly, 1987). Children can tolerate substantial punishment and buffeting from their environment if they sense a basic feeling of love and support from parents; without them, a child's resistance, even to minor stress, is tenuous (Billings & Moos, 1982; Lewinsohn, 1974).

3. More important than heretofore considered is the fact that parental feelings and attitudes need not be the same, nor uniformly conveyed by both parents. Differences in parental relationships are the norm for most children. One parent may be attentive and overprotective while the other is hostile or indifferent. In a sense, the recombinant process of hereditary transmission, in which the child receives half of his or her chromosomes from each of two parents, is duplicated at the experiential level as well. Dissimilar aspects of human thought, feeling, and behavior are conveyed by each parent through implicit modeling or direct tuition. The child incorporates these two variant models, either keeping them as separate modes of experience or fusing them in a combinatorial synthesis.

Hence, it is not uncommon for children to acquire attitudes and feelings about themselves that are divided or split, partly reflecting the relationship with their mother, and partly with their father, as well as with older siblings or relatives. As we read the typical background of one or another of several personality disorders, we may find individuals who have experienced two or more of the characteristic histories described. Exposed to a single parent, one who was consistent and whose attitudes and feelings were not subverted or countermanded by other adult models, the child may develop into a pure textbook type. However, for the most part, youngsters reflect the impact of a variety of adult models, resulting in a mixed personality configuration, for example, somewhat narcissistic and somewhat compulsive or partly dependent and partly avoidant and so on. In later chapters pertaining to personality subtypes, we discuss personality disorder mixtures that reflect different, and sometimes conflictual, combinations of parental feelings and attitudes to which the youngster was exposed.

Methods of Behavior Control

What training procedures are used to regulate the child's behavior and to control what he or she learns? As noted earlier, incidental methods used by parents may have a more profound effect than what the parent intended; that is, the child acquires a model of interpersonal behavior by example and imitation as well as by verbal precept. Five of the pathogenic methods of control are discussed in the following sections (Glidewell, 1961; Patterson, 1982; Sears, Maccoby, & Levin, 1957).

Punitive Methods.   Parents disposed to intimidate and ridicule their offspring, using punitive and repressive measures to control their behavior and thought, may set the stage for a variety of maladaptive patterns (El Sheikh, Cummings, & Goetsch, 1989; Loeber & Stouthamer-Loeber, 1986).

If the child submits to pressure and succeeds in fulfilling parental expectations (i.e., learns instrumentally to avoid the negative reinforcement of punishment), he or she is apt to become an overly obedient and circumspect person. Typically, these individuals learn not only to keep in check their impulses and contrary thoughts but also, by vicarious observation and imitation, to adopt the parental behavior model and begin to be punitive of deviant behavior on the part of others. Thus, an otherwise timid and hypertense 16-year-old boy, whose every spark of youthful zest had been squelched by harshly punitive parents, was observed to be "extremely mean" and punitive when given the responsibility of teaching a Sunday school class for 7-year-olds.

Should these youngsters fail to satisfy excessive parental demands and be subject to continued harassment and punishment, they may develop a pervasive anticipatory anxiety about personal relationships, leading to feelings of hopelessness and discouragement and resulting in instrumental strategies such as social avoidance and withdrawal. Others, faced with similar experiences, may learn to imitate parental harshness and develop hostile and aggressively rebellious behaviors. Which of these reactions or strategies evolves depends on the larger configuration of factors involved (Ferster, 1973; Lazarus, 1968; Lewinsohn, 1974; Patterson, 1977).

Contingent Reward Methods.   Some parents rarely are punitive but expect certain behaviors to be performed before giving encouragement or doling out rewards. Positive reinforcements are contingent on approved performance. Youngsters reared under these conditions tend to be socially pleasant and, by imitative learning, tend to be rewarding to others. Often, however, we observe that they seem to have acquired an insatiable and indiscriminate need for social approval. For example, a 15-year-old girl experienced brief periods of marked depression if people failed to comment favorably on her dress or appearance. In early childhood, she had learned that parental approval and affection were elicited only when she was "dressed up and looked pretty"; to her, failure on the part of others to note her attractiveness signified rejection and disapproval. It would appear, therefore, that contingent reward methods condition children to develop an excessive need for approval; they manifest not only a healthy social affability but also a dependency on social reinforcement.

Inconsistent Methods.   Parental methods of control often are irregular, contradictory, and capricious (Maccoby & Martin, 1983; Patterson, 1982). Some degree of variability is inevitable in the course of every child's life, but there are parents who display an extreme inconsistency in their standards and expectations and an extreme unpredictability in their application of rewards and punishments. Youngsters exposed to such a chaotic and capricious environment cannot learn consistently and cannot devise nonconflictive strategies for adaptive behavior; whatever behavior they display may be countermanded by an unpredictable parental reaction.

To avoid the suspense and anxiety of unpredictable reactions, some children may protectively become immobile and noncommittal. Others, imitatively adopting what they have been exposed to, may come to be characterized by their own ambivalence and their own tendency to vacillate from one action or feeling to another. We know that irregular reinforcements build difficult-to-extinguish behavior patterns; thus, the immobility or ambivalence of these youngsters may persist long after their environment has become uniform and predictable.

Protective Methods.   Some parents so narrowly restrict the experiences to which their children are exposed that these youngsters fail to learn even the basic rudiments of autonomous behaviors (Baumrind, 1967; C. C. Lewis, 1981). Overprotective mothers, worried that their children are too frail or are unable to care for themselves or make sensible judgments on their own, not only succeed in forestalling the growth of normal competencies but also, indirectly, give their children a feeling that they are inferior and frail. These children, observing their actual inadequacies, have verification of the fact that they are weak, inept, and dependent on others (Millon, 1981; Millon & Davis, 1996; Parker, 1983). Thus, these youngsters not only are trained to be deficient in adaptive and self-reliant behaviors but also learn to view themselves as inferior and become progressively fearful of leaving the protective womb.

Indulgent Methods.   Overly permissive, lax, or undisciplined parents allow children full rein to explore and assert their every whim. These parents fail to control their children and, by their own lack of discipline, provide a model to be imitated, which further strengthens their children's irresponsibility. Unconstrained by parental control and not guided by selective rewards, these youngsters grow up displaying the inconsiderate and often tyrannical characteristics of undisciplined children. Having had their way for so long, they tend to be exploitive, demanding, uncooperative, and antisocially aggressive. Unless rebuffed by external disciplinary forces, these youngsters may persist in their habits and become irresponsible members of society (Millon, 1969; Millon, Simonsen, Birkit-Smith, & Davis,1999).

Family Styles of Communication

The capacity of humans to symbolize experience enables us to communicate with one another in ways more intricate and complex than are found in lower species. Free of the simple mechanisms of instinctive behavior and capable of transcending the tangibles of our objective world, humans can draw from events of the distant past and project to those of the distant future. The symbolic units and syntax of our language provide us with a powerful instrumentality for thought and communication.

Each family constructs its own style of communication, its own pattern of listening and attending, and its own way of fashioning thoughts and conveying them to others. The styles of interpersonal communication to which the child is exposed serve as a model for attending, organizing, and reacting to the expressions, thoughts, and feelings of others. Unless this framework for learning interpersonal communication is rational and reciprocal, the child will be ill-equipped to function in an effective way with others. Thus, the very symbolic capacities that enable humans to transcend their environment so successfully may lend themselves to serious misdirections and confusions; this powerful instrument for facilitating communication with others may serve instead to undermine social relationships. Although illogical ideas, irrational reactions, and irrelevant and bizarre verbalizations often arise because of extreme stress, their roots can be traced as frequently to the simple exposure to defective styles of family communication (Campbell, 1973; Mash & Johnston, 1982; J. R. Morrison, 1980; Tizard & Hodges, 1978).

The effects of amorphous, fragmented, or confusing patterns of family communication have been explored by numerous investigators (Bateson et al., 1956; Lidz, Cornelison, Terry, & Fleck, 1958; Lu, 1962; Singer & Wynne, 1965). Not only are messages attended to in certain families in a vague, erratic, or incidental fashion, with a consequent disjunctiveness and loss of focus, but when they are attended to, they frequently convey equivocal or contradictory meanings. The transmission of ambivalent or opposing meanings and feelings produces what Bateson refers to as a **double bind.** For example, a seriously disturbed 10-year-old boy was repeatedly implored in a distinctly hostile tone by his equally ill mother: "Come here to your mother; mommy loves you and wants to hug and squeeze you, hug and squeeze you." The intrinsically contradictory nature of these double-bind messages precludes satisfactory reactions; the recipient cannot respond without running into conflict with one aspect of the message; he is "damned if he does, and damned if he doesn't." Exposed to such contradictions in communication, the youngster's foundation in reality becomes increasingly precarious (Reid, Patterson, & Loeber, 1982; Reiss, 1981). To avoid confusion, the child learns to distort and deny these conflicting signals; but in this defensive maneuver, the child succumbs even further to irrational thought. Unable to interpret the intentions and feelings of others and encumbered with a progressively maladaptive pattern of self-distortions, the child falls prey to a vicious circle of increasing interpersonal estrangement.

Content of Teachings

Parents transmit a wide range of values and attitudes to their children either through direct tuition or unintentional commentary (Dorr, 1985; Emde, 1979; M. Lewis & Saarni, 1985). The family serves as the primary socialization system for inculcating beliefs and behaviors. Through these teachings, the child learns to think about, be concerned with, and react to certain events and people in prescribed ways.

Kinds of teachings that lend themselves to the learning of pathological attitudes and behaviors include these:

• The most insidious and destructive of these teachings is training in anxiety. Parents who fret over their own health, who investigate every potential ailment in their child's functioning, and who are preoccupied with failures or the dismal turn of events teach and furnish models for anxiety proneness in their children (J. C. Coolidge & Brodie, 1974; Parker, 1983; Waldron, Shrier, Stone, & Tobin, 1975). Few incidents escape the pernicious effects of a chronically anxious and apprehensive household. Fantasies of body disease, vocational failure, loss of prized objects, and rejection by loved ones illustrate the range of items to which a generalized disposition this tendency intrudes and colors otherwise neutral events.

• Feelings of guilt and shame are generated in the teachings of many homes. A child's failure to live up to parental expectations, a feeling that he or she has caused undue sacrifices by the parents, or a feeling that he or she has transgressed rules and embarrassed the family by virtue of some shortcoming or misbehavior are events that question the individual's self-worth and produce marked feelings of shame and guilt. Furthermore, the sacrificing and guilt-laden atmosphere of these parental homes provides a model for behavioral imitation. Youngsters who are admonished and reproached repeatedly for minor digressions often develop a deep and pervasive self-image of failure. If children admit their misdeeds and adopt their parents' injunctions as their own, they will come to view themselves as unworthy, shameful, and guilty persons. To protect against feelings of marked self-condemnation, such children may learn to restrict their activities, to deny themselves the normal joys and indulgences of life, and to control their impulses far beyond that required to eschew shame and guilt. In time, even the simplest of pleasures may come to be avoided.

• Other destructive attitudes can be taught directly through narrow or biased parental outlooks; feelings of inferiority and social inadequacy are among the most frequent. Particularly damaging are teachings associated with sexual urges. Unrealistic standards that condemn common behaviors such as masturbation and petting create unnecessary fears and strong guilt feelings; sexual miseducation may have long-range deleterious effects, especially during periods of courtship and marriage.

Family Structure

The formal composition of the family often sets the stage for learning pathogenic attitudes and relationships (Clausen, 1966).

Deficient Models.   The lack of significant adult figures in the family may deprive children of the opportunity to acquire, through imitation, many of the complex patterns of behavior required in adult life (Emery, 1982; Ferri, 1976; Millon, 1987). Parents who provide undesirable models for imitation, at the very least, are supplying some guidelines for the intricate give-and-take of human relationships.

The most serious deficit usually is the unavailability of a parental model of the same sex (Hetherington, Cox, & Cox, 1982). The frequent absence of fathers in underprivileged homes or the vocational preoccupations of fathers in well-to-do homes often produce sons who lack a mature sense of masculine identity; they seem ill-equipped with goals and behaviors by which they can orient their adult lives.

Family Discord.   Children subject to persistent parental bickering and nagging not only are exposed to destructive models for imitative learning but also are faced with upsetting influences that may eventuate in pathological behaviors (Crockenberg, 1985; Cummings, Pellegrini, Notarius, & Cummings, 1989; Millon, 1987; Rutter & Giller, 1983). The stability of life, so necessary for the acquisition of a consistent pattern of behaving and thinking, is shattered when strife and marked controversy prevail. There is an ever-present apprehension that one parent may be lost through divorce; dissension often leads to the undermining of one parent by the other; an air of mistrust frequently pervades the home, creating suspicions and anxieties; a nasty and cruel competition for the loyalty and affections of children may ensue. Children often become scapegoats in these settings, subject to displaced parental hostilities (Hetherington, 1972). Constantly dragged into the arena of parental strife, the child not only loses a sense of security and stability but also may be subjected to capricious hostility and to a set of conflicting and destructive behavior models.

Sibling Rivalry. Sibling relationships often are overlooked as a major element in shaping the pattern of peer and other intimate competitions (Circirelli, 1982; Dunn & Kendrick, 1981; Wagner, Schubert, & Schubert, 1979). The presence of two or more children in a family requires that parents divide their attention and approval. When disproportionate affection is allotted to one child or when a newborn child supplants an older child as the "apple of daddy's eye," seeds of discontent and rivalry flourish. Intense hostility often is generated; since hostility fails to eliminate the intruder and gains, not the sought-for attention, but parental disapproval, the aggrieved child often reverts to regressive or infantile maneuvers, for example, baby talk or bed-wetting. If these methods succeed in winning back parental love, the youngster will have been reinforced through instrumental learning to continue these childish techniques. More often than not, however, efforts to alter parental preferences fail miserably, and the child may continue to experience deep resentments and a sense of marked insecurity. Such persons often later display a distrust of affections, fearing that those who express them will prove to be as fickle as their parents. Not unlikely also is the possibility that the intense hostility they felt toward their siblings will linger and generalize into envious and aggressive feelings toward other "competitors."

Ordinal Position. It seems plausible that the order of a child's birth in the family would be related to the kinds of problems he or she faces and the kinds of strategies he or she is likely to adopt. For example, the *oldest child*, once the center of parental attention, experiences a series of displacements as new sibs are born; this may engender a pervasive expectation that "good things don't last." However, to counteract this damaging experience, he or she may be encouraged to acquire the skills of autonomy and leadership, may be more prone to identify with adult models, and may learn, thereby, to cope with the complications of life more effectively than his or her less mature siblings. The *youngest child*, although petted, indulged, and allotted the special affections and privileges due the family baby, may fail to acquire the competencies required for autonomous behaviors. He or she may be prone to dependency and prefer to withdraw from competition; the higher incidence of mental disorder among the last-born child in families lends support to these interpretations (Dohrenwend & Dohrenwend, 1976). *Only children* appear to be especially resilient to severe emotional difficulty. This may reflect their special status as sole recipient of parental attention, approval, and affection. In his or her singular and unhampered state, the child may learn to view himself or herself as especially gifted. With this confidence in self-worth as a base, the child may venture into the larger society secure in the conviction that he or she will be as well received there as in the parental home. Despite this sound beginning, the child is ill-equipped to cope with the give-and-take of peer relationships because he or she has not experienced the sharing and competition of sibling relationships.

Numerous other features of the family environment, some relating to structural elements (e.g., sex of sibs and presence of problem sibs) and some to roles assumed by family members (e.g., domineering or seductive mothers or inadequate or effeminate fathers), can be specified and their likely effects on learning speculated about. A listing of such events and relationships, however, is too exhaustive for our purposes. A number of these elements are discussed in later chapters when we present characteristic experiential histories.

TRAUMATIC EXPERIENCES

It is a common belief, attributable in large measure to popularizations of psychology in our literature and news media, that most forms of psychopathology can be traced to a single, very severe experience, the hidden residues of which account for the manifest disorder. Freud's early writings gave impetus and support to this notion, but he reversed himself in his later work when he was made aware of the fact that patient reports of early trauma often were imaginative fabrications of their past. Current thinking in the field suggests that most pathological behaviors accrue gradually through repetitive learning experiences.

Despite the primacy that enduring and pervasive experiences play in shaping most pathological patterns, there are occasions when a particularly painful event can shatter the individual's equanimity and leave a deeply embedded attitude that is not readily extinguished. An untimely frightening experience, be it abusive or not, or an especially embarrassing and humiliating social event illustrate conditions that can result in a persistent attitude.

The impact of these events may be particularly severe with young children because they usually are ill-prepared for them and lack the perspective of prior experience that might serve as a context for moderating their effects (Field, 1985; Garmezy, 1986; Weissman & Paykel, 1974). If a traumatic event is the first exposure for a youngster to a particular class of experiences, the attitude he or she learns in reaction to that event may intrude and color all subsequent events of that kind. Thus, an adolescent whose first sexual venture resulted in devastating feelings of guilt, inadequacy, or humiliation may carry such feelings within long after the event has passed.

Traumatic events persevere in their learned effects for essentially two reasons. First, a high level of neural activation ensues in response to most situations of marked distress or anxiety. Many diverse neural associations become connected to the event; the greater the level of neural involvement, the more deeply and pervasively will be the learned reaction and the greater the difficulty will be in extinguishing what was learned. Second, during heightened stress, there often is a decrement in the ability to make accurate discriminations within the environment; as a consequence, the traumatized individual generalizes his or her emotional reaction to a variety of objects and persons who are only incidentally associated with the traumatic source. For example, a youngster injured in an auto accident may develop a fear reaction not only to cars but also to all red couch covers (the color of the seat of the car in which he was riding), to men in white jackets (the color of the uniform of the medical intern who attended to him after the accident), and so on. Because of the seemingly illogical nature of these fears (the difficulty of tracing their connection to the accident), they are not readily amenable to rational analysis and unlearning.

Despite the severity and persistence of the effects of certain traumatic events, they tend to be stimulus-specific, that is, limited to stimulus conditions that are highly similar

FOCUS ON RESEARCH

Attention Deficit-Hyperactivity Disorder (ADHD), Oppositional Defiant Disorder (ODD), Conduct Disorder (CD), and Adult Antisocial Personality Disorder (APD)

A Special Risk Factor

There seems to be an important subgroup of the childhood-onset cohort that are at special risk for developing adult problems. Although the theoretical underpinnings of why ADHD, ODD, CD in childhood, and APD in adulthood are related is yet unclear, there is substantial empirical support to suggest that they are. Lahey and Loeber (1997), drawing on 30 years of empirical literature exploring these relationships, cite several lines of research that help explicate the connections between these childhood disorders and adult antisocial behavior. The first is the well-supported finding that children with ADHD are more likely to display antisocial behavior as adolescents and adults than are children without ADHD. A second involves the relatively poor prognosis for children who have concurrent ADHD and CD. Those who meet criteria for both have higher rates of CD over time than for those with CD alone. Less is known about the ways that ODD is linked to CD and later adult antisocial behavior, but there is some preliminary evidence to suggest that it is even more strongly linked than ADHD.

However, further conclusions are much muddier. For example, Lahey and Loeber cite two studies that do not support the hypothesis that children with ADHD in the absence of CD are at risk for later developing antisocial behavior (Loeber, 1988; Magnusson & Bergman, 1990) and three studies that did (Gittelman, Mannuzza, Shenker, & Bonagura, 1985; Lambert, 1988; Mannuzza et al., 1991). Loeber, Burke, Lahey, Winters, and Zera (2000) propose that while ODD and CD appear to place adolescents at risk for several subsequent disorders, there seems to be a modal sequence; namely, ODD is often a precursor for CD, which may be a precursor to APD. To confuse matters more, ADHD is often a comorbid condition with ODD and CD but may not affect the course of CD without prior ODD.

Much of this research is plagued with methodological issues that make clear interpretations of the findings difficult. You can imagine the problems that arise in developmental research. One is an issue of longitudinal versus cross-sectional samples. If you are trying to determine the developmental nature of a disorder (i.e., Does a child with ADHD and CD develop into an adult with antisocial personality disorder?), it makes sense to follow the same people from childhood, through adolescence, and into adulthood. Research of this sort is very costly and is confounded by ever-evolving diagnostic criteria. Throughout the various incarnations of the *DSM,* criteria for all of these diagnoses have changed considerably with an accompanying change in the prevalence of each disorder. So, a child with a set of symptoms may meet criteria for ODD one year, but because criteria changed with a new edition of the *DSM,* three years later, with the same constellation of symptoms, he or she no longer meets criteria for ODD. This renders interpreting results both within and between studies a tricky business.

to those in which they were first learned. In certain cases, however, these experiences may give rise to a chain of reactions and events that establish pervasive pathological trends. In the next section, we see that the conditions of early experience, whatever their nature, may persist long after the event that prompted them has passed.

Comment: We have taken the liberty in this section of bringing together many of the diverse notions and findings that theorists have used to identify the principal psychogenic sources of personality pathology; only briefly have we commented on the adequacy of these data or the methods employed in obtaining them. Our presentation would be amiss if we failed to appraise, albeit briefly, the soundness of the evidence.

The view that the particular setting and events of early experience play a decisive part in determining personality is assumed by psychologists of all theoretical persuasions. But where, in fact, are the hard data, the unequivocal evidence derived from well-designed and well-executed research? Such data, unfortunately, are sorely lacking. Most of the research in the field can be faulted on methodological grounds, biased populations, poor assessment techniques, unreliable diagnostic categories, and, most significantly, failures to include appropriate control groups by which comparative evaluations can be made. Without controls, for example, it is impossible to determine whether the specific parental attitude, training procedure, or traumatic event under investigation can be assigned the significance attributed to it.

Disconcerting findings show us that there may be no substantial difference in deleterious childhood experiences between normal men and psychiatric patients. It is known, furthermore, that many adults who have been reared in seemingly devastating childhood environments not only survive but thrive, whereas adults raised under idealistic conditions often deteriorate into severe pathological patterns. The combination of factors and the sequence of events involved in producing pathology are awesomely complex and difficult to unravel. Unless future lines of research are based on sound premises and executed with the utmost of methodological care, investigators will continue to go around in circles, confirming only what their naive prejudices incline them to find.

The importance of well-reasoned and well-designed studies is nowhere more evident than in the investigation of psychogenic sources of personality pathology; few studies of the past have met the basic criteria of good research. We minimized reference to specific studies in this section lest we lead you to believe that there are data from well-designed research to support the notions presented. You should view these notions as propositions that will be confirmed or disconfirmed as a result of *future* research.

Continuity of Early Learnings

We contended in the preceding sections that childhood experiences are crucially involved in shaping lifelong patterns of behavior. To support this view, we elaborated several conditions of early upbringing and their consequences, noting first the impact of the sheer quantity of stimulation on maturation and, second, the effect of particular kinds of experiences on the learning of complex behaviors and attitudes. Although few theorists of psychopathology would deny the paramount role we have attributed to early experience, they may differ among themselves as to not only *why* these experiences are important but also *how* exactly they come to play their significant role in later behavior.

Early experience should be more important than later experiences. Throughout evolutionary history, early life has been a preparation for later life. Until recently, and except at times of massive environmental upheavals, all species have lived in the same basic ecological niches throughout their history. Under these conditions, the experiences of early life provide an opportunity for the young organism to acquire sensitivities and behaviors that enable it to function more adequately in its environment. It learns to become acquainted with the elements of its habitat, differentiating those components that are gratifying from those that are endangering. It learns to imitate the behavior of its parents, acquiring thereby methods and competencies that would otherwise take appreciably longer, if ever, to learn.

The importance of early learning cannot be overstated for creatures that continue to live in the same environments as had their ancestors. Until recently, this continuity was true for humans, as well. Thus, if a young boy's father was a farmer, he quickly learned how to function in an environment where farming was a primary and important occupation. If a young girl's mother tended to the children and to the home, she observed and imitated her parent's behaviors and attitudes. In these earlier times, the ambiance of an individual's neighborhood—its values, beliefs, and customs—were likely to have been the very same beliefs, values, and customs of ancestors of the past; similarly, these attitudes corresponded with those shared by the person's larger community in adulthood and, in time, with that likely to be experienced by his or her progeny, as well.

Infancy and childhood prepare children well for life in adulthood, perhaps too well. Problems have arisen in the past century since radical environmental and cultural shifts have taken place, upsetting the continuity between past and present family and societal values and customs. This sharp break between what may have been learned in childhood and what an individual may have to face in adulthood accounts in part for many of the personality difficulties we observe today. In infancy and toddlerhood, each child learns a series of thoughts, feelings, and behaviors; it is these that are retained and carried into later childhood and adulthood. This continuity served the youngster well in the past because the patterns of adulthood life were well ingrained in childhood. In recent decades, however, childhood learnings are often inapplicable and inappropriate when applied to the family, neighbors, and societies of adulthood. Children who learned to fear humiliating and disparaging parents carry what they have learned into new relationships that may be radically different from those of childhood. Their aversive behaviors may no longer be appropriate nor applicable, yet they will likely persist and generate new difficulties because of this continuity of past learnings into the present. It is this persistence of early learned behaviors into adulthood, what psychoanalysts speak of as transference, and behaviorists refer to as generalization, that underlies many of the problems we consider to be personality disorders.

We are now in a society in which few constants persevere, where values and customs are in conflict, and where the styles of human interaction today are likely to change tomorrow. We see the emergence of a new unstructured and highly fluid personality style that is commonly diagnosed today as the borderline disorder. In these adults, we find a reflection of the contradictory and changing customs and beliefs of contemporary society. This newest pattern of childhood adaptation leaves the person unable to find the "center" of himself or herself. Such persons have learned *not* to demonstrate consistency and continuity in their behaviors, thoughts, and feelings, no less in their way of relating to others. We discuss these unstable and contradictory cultural patterns more in a later section and chapter. Similarly, we discuss the impact of experiential discontinuities as a key factor in creating the borderline personality disorder.

Is the impact of early experience, as we have asserted in previous sections, a consequence of the young child's susceptibilities during sensitive maturational stages? That is, are early experiences more significant than later experiences because the developing child is more plastic and impressionable than the fully matured adult? Can other explanations be offered to account for the special status in shaping behavior assigned to early experience?

Alternate interpretations are offered. Some state that influences common both to children and adults arise more often in childhood; that is, there is nothing distinctive about childhood other than the *frequency* with which certain experiences occur. Were these events equally frequent in adulthood, there would be no reason to assume that they would affect adults less than they do children. Others state that the difference may be that children experience the impact of events more intensely than adults because they have fewer skills to handle challenges and threats. A somewhat similar hypothesis suggests that the importance of childhood experience lies in its *primacy,* that is, the fact that the first event of a set of similar effects will have a more marked impact than later ones. According to this view, an event experienced initially in adulthood will have the same effect on an adult as it does on a child. These theorists note, however, that it is more likely that the first of a series of similar experiences will occur in childhood.

There is little question that the special status of early experience can be ascribed in part to the simple facts of frequency and primacy; events that come first or more often will have a bearing on what comes later and thereby justify our assigning them special impact value. The question remains, however, as to whether frequency and primacy, in themselves, are sufficient to account for the unusual significance attributed to childhood experiences.

Acceptance of the role that these two factors play does not preclude additional hypotheses that assign unusual vulnerabilities or sensitivities to young children. There is no fundamental conflict between these views; each factor, primacy, frequency, and biological sensitivity may operate conjointly and with undiminished singular effects. A later discussion attempts to show how these varied influences weave together to give early experiences their special role.

This section concentrates on the notion of continuity in behavior because the significance of early experience lies not so much in the intensity of its impact but in its durability and persistence. Experiences in early life not only are ingrained more pervasively and forcefully but their effects tend to persist and are more difficult to modify than later experiences. For example, early events occur at a presymbolic level and cannot easily be recalled and unlearned. They are reinforced frequently as a function of the child's restricted opportunities to learn alternatives; they tend to be repeated and perpetuated by the child's own behavior. For many reasons, then, a continuity in behavior—a consistent style of feeling, thinking, and relating to the world—once embedded in early life, perseveres into adulthood.

Part of the continuity we observe between childhood and adulthood may be ascribed to the stability of biological constitutional factors, which were described earlier in this chapter. But there are numerous psychological processes that contribute as well to this longitudinal consistency (Chess & Thomas, 1984; Kagan et al., 1989; Millon, 1969; Millon & Davis, 1996; Plomin & Dunn, 1986; Robins & Rutter, 1990). Because these processes enable us to see more clearly how pathology develops, we cannot afford to take them for granted or merely enumerate them without elaboration.

The processes that coalesce to bring about continuity may be broadly grouped into three categories: resistance to extinction, social reinforcement, and self-perpetuation.

RESISTANCE TO EXTINCTION

Acquired behaviors and attitudes usually are not fixed or permanent. What has been learned can be modified or eliminated under appropriate conditions, a process referred to as **extinction.** Extinction usually entails exposure to experiences that are similar to the conditions of original learning but that provide opportunities for new learning to occur. Essentially, old habits of behavior change when new learning interferes with, and replaces, what previously had been learned; this progressive weakening of old learnings may be speeded up by special environmental conditions, the details of which are not relevant to our discussion.

What happens if the conditions of original learning cannot be duplicated easily? According to contiguity learning theory, failure to provide opportunities for interfering with old habits means that they will remain unmodified and persist over time; learnings associated with events that are difficult to reproduce are resistant to extinction.

The question we next must ask is: Are the events of early life experienced in such a manner as to make them difficult to reproduce and, therefore, resistant to extinction? An examination of the conditions of childhood suggests that the answer is yes. The reasons for asserting so have been formulated with extraordinary clarity by numerous theorists and researchers.

Presymbolic Learning

Biologically, young children are primitive organisms. Their nervous systems are incomplete, they perceive the world from momentary and changing vantage points, and they are unable to discriminate and identify many of the elements of their experiences. What they see and learn about their environment through their infantile perceptual and cognitive systems will never again be experienced in the same manner in later life.

Infants' presymbolic world of fleeting and inarticulate impressions recedes gradually as they acquire the ability to identify, discriminate, and symbolize experience. By the time they are 4 or 5, they view the world in preformed categories and group and symbolize objects and events in a stable way very different from that of infancy.

Once growing children's perceptions have taken on discriminative symbolic forms, they can no longer duplicate the perceptually amorphous, presymbolic, and diffusely inchoate experiences of earlier years. Unable to reproduce these early experiences in subsequent life, they will not be able to extinguish what they learned in response to those early experiences; no longer perceiving events as initially sensed, they cannot supplant their early reactions with new ones. These early learnings persist, therefore, as feelings, attitudes, and expectancies that crop up pervasively in a vague and diffuse way.

Random Learning

Young children lack not only the ability to form precise images of their environment but also the equipment to discern logical relationships among its elements. Their world of objects, people, and events is connected in an unclear and random fashion; they learn to associate objects and events that have no intrinsic relationship; clusters of concurrent but only incidentally connected stimuli are fused erroneously. Thus, when a young child experiences fear in response to his father's harsh voice, he may learn to fear not only that voice but also the setting, the atmosphere, the pictures, the furniture, and the odors—a whole bevy of incidental objects, which by chance were present at that time. Unable to discriminate the precise source in his environment that caused his fear, the child connects his discomfort randomly to all associated stimuli; now each of them become precipitants for these feelings.

Random associations of early life cannot be duplicated as children develop the capacity for logical thinking and perception. By the time children are 4 or 5, they can discriminate cause-and-effect relationships with considerable accuracy. Early random associations do not "make sense" to them; when they react to one of the precipitants derived from early learning, they are unable to identify what it is in the environment to which they are reacting. They cannot locate the source of their difficulty because they now think more logically than before. To advise them that they are reacting to a picture or piece of furniture simply will be rejected; they cannot fathom the true features that evoke their feelings because these sources are so foreign to their new, more rational mode of thought. Their difficulty in extinguishing the past is compounded because not only is it difficult for them to reexperience the world as it once may have been but also they will be misled in their search for these experiences if they apply their more developed reasoning powers.

Generalized Learning

Young children's discriminations of their environment are crude and gross. As they begin to differentiate the elements of their world, they group and label those elements into broad and unrefined categories. All men become "daddy"; all four-legged animals are called "doggie"; all foods are "yumyum." When children learn to fear a particular dog, for example, they learn to fear not only that dog but all strange, mobile four-legged creatures. To their primitive perception, all of these animals are one of a kind.

Generalization is inevitable in early learning. It reflects more than the failure of young children to have had sufficient experiences to acquire greater precision; children's indiscriminateness represents an intrinsic inability to discriminate events because of their undeveloped cortical capacities.

As the undifferentiated mass of early experiences becomes more finely discriminated, learning gets to be more focused, specific, and precise; a 10-year-old learns to fear bulldogs as a result of an unfortunate run-in with one but does not necessarily generalize this fear to collies or poodles, since the child knows and can discern differences among these animals.

Generalized learning is difficult to extinguish. Young children's learned reactions are attached to a broader class of objects than called for by their specific experiences. To extinguish these broadly generalized reactions in later life, when their discriminative capacities are much more precise, requires that they be exposed to many and diverse experiences. For example, assume that a 2-year-old was frightened by a cocker spaniel. Given the child's gross discriminative capacity at this age, this single experience may have conditioned him to fear dogs, cats, and other small animals. Assume further that in later life, the child is exposed repeatedly to a friendly cocker spaniel. As a consequence of this experience, we find that he has extinguished his fear, but only of cocker spaniels, not of dogs in general, cats, or other small animals. His later experience, seen through the discriminative eye of an older child, was that spaniels are friendly but not dogs in general. The extinction experience applied then to only one part of the original widely generalized complex of fears he acquired. His original learning experience incorporated a much broader range of stimuli than his later experience, even though the objective stimulus conditions were essentially the same. Because of his more precise discriminative capacity, he now must have his fear extinguished in a variety of situations to compensate for the single but widely generalized early experience.

These three interlocking conditions—presymbolic, random, and generalized learning—account in large measure for the unusual difficulty of reexperiencing the events of early life and the consequent difficulty of unlearning the feelings, behaviors, and attitudes generated by these events.

SOCIAL REINFORCEMENT

Of the many factors that contribute to the persistence of early behavior patterns, none plays a more significant role than social and interpersonal relationships. These relationships can be viewed fruitfully from the perspective usually taken by sociologists and social psychologists. To these scientists, the varied cultural and institutional forces of a society promote continuity by maintaining a stable and organized class of experiences to which most individuals of a particular group are repeatedly exposed. Reference to these broader social determinants of continuity are made occasionally in later chapters. For now, our focus is on the more direct and private side of interpersonal experience.

As pointed out in an earlier section, ingrained personality patterns develop as a consequence of enduring experiences generated in intimate and subtle relationships with members of an individual's immediate family. We described a number of events that lead to the acquisition of particular types of behaviors and attitudes. Here our attention is not on the content of what is learned but on those aspects of relationships that strengthen what has been learned and that lead to their perpetuation. Three such influences are described: repetitive experiences, reciprocal reinforcement, and social stereotyping.

Repetitive Experiences

The typical daily activities in which young children participate are restricted and repetitive; there is not much variety in the routine experience to which children are exposed. Day in and day out, they eat the same kind of food, play with the same toys, remain essentially in the same physical environment, and relate to the same people. This constricted environment—this repeated exposure to a narrow range of family attitudes and training methods—not only builds in deeply etched habits and expectations but also prevents children from having new experiences that are so essential to change. The helplessness of infants and the dependency of children keep them restricted to a crabbed and tight little world with few alternatives for learning new attitudes and responses. Early behaviors fail to change, therefore, not because they may have jelled permanently but because the same slender band of experiences that helped form them initially continue and persist as influences for many years.

Reciprocal Reinforcement

The notion that children's early behaviors may be accentuated by their parents' response to them was raised earlier in the chapter; we noted that a circular interplay often arises, which intensifies children's initial biological reactivity pattern. Thus, unusually passive, sensitive, or cranky infants frequently elicit feelings on the part of their mothers that perpetuate their original tendencies.

This model of circular or reciprocal influences may be applied not only to the perpetuation of biological dispositions but also to behavior tendencies that are acquired by learning. Whatever the initial roots may have been—constitutional or learned—certain forms of behaviors provoke or pull from others reactions that result in a repetition of these behaviors (Leary, 1957). For example, a suspicious, chip-on-the-shoulder, and defiant child eventually forces others, no matter how tolerant they may have been initially, to counter with perplexity, exasperation, and anger; the child undermines every inclination on the part of others to be nurturant, friendly, and cooperative. An ever-widening gulf of suspicion and defiance may develop as parents of such children withdraw, become punitive, or "throw up their hands in disgust"; controls or affections that might have narrowed the gulf of suspicion and hostility break down. Each participant, in feedback fashion, contributes his or her share; the original level of hostile behavior is aggravated and intensified. Whether the cause was the child or the parent, the process has gotten out of hand and will continue its vicious and inexorable course until some benign influence interferes or until it deteriorates into pathological form (Gottman & Katz, 1989).

Social Stereotypes

The dominant features of a child's early behavior form a distinct impression on others. Once this early impression is established, people expect that the child will continue to behave in his or her distinctive manner; in time, they develop a fixed and simplified image of "what kind of person the child is." The term **stereotype,** borrowed from social psychology, represents this tendency to simplify and categorize the attributes of others.

People no longer view a child passively and objectively once they have formed a stereotype of him or her; they now are sensitized to those distinctive features they have learned to expect (Farrington, 1977). The stereotype begins to take on a life of its own; it operates as a screen through which the child's behaviors are selectively perceived so as to fit the characteristics attributed to the child. Once cast in this mold, the child experiences a consistency in the way others react to him or her, one that fails to take cognizance of the varieties and complexities of his or her behaviors. No matter what the child does, he or she finds that the behavior is interpreted in the same fixed and rigid manner. Exposed time and time again to the same reactions and attitudes of others, the child may give up efforts to convince others that he or she can change. For example, if a defiant child displays the slightest degree of resentment to unfair treatment, he will be jumped on as hopelessly recalcitrant; should the child do nothing objectionable, questions will be raised as to the sincerity of his motives. Faced with repeated negative appraisals and unable to break the stereotype into which he has been cast, the youngster will relapse after every effort to change and continue to behave as he did originally and as others expect.

SELF-PERPETUATION

Significant experiences of early life may never recur again, but their effects remain and leave their mark. Physiologically, we may say they have etched a neurochemical change; psychologically, they are registered as memories, a permanent trace, and an embedded internal stimulus. In contrast to the fleeting stimuli of the external world, these memory traces become part and parcel of every stimulus complex that activates behavior. Once registered, the effects of the past are indelible, incessant, and inescapable. They now are intrinsic elements of the individual's makeup; they latch on and intrude into the current events of life, coloring, transforming, and distorting the passing scene. Although the residuals of subsequent experiences may override them, becoming more dominant internal stimuli, the presence of earlier memory traces remains in one form or another. In every thought and action, the individual cannot help but carry these remnants into the present. Every current behavior is a perpetuation, then, of the past, a continuation and intrusion of these inner stimulus traces.

The residuals of the past do more than passively contribute their share to the present. By temporal precedence, if nothing else, they guide, shape, or distort the character of current events. They are not only ever present, then, but also operate insidiously to transform new stimulus experiences in line with past. We elaborate four of these processes of perpetuation in this section: protective constriction, perceptual and cognitive distortion, behavior generalization, and repetition compulsion.

Protective Constriction

Painful memories of the past are kept out of consciousness, a process referred to as **repression.** Similarly, current experiences that may reactivate these repressed memories are judiciously avoided. The individual develops a network of conscious and unconscious protective maneuvers to decrease the likelihood that either of these distressing experiences will occur.

As a consequence of these protective efforts, however, individuals narrow or constrict their world. Repression reduces anxiety by enabling individuals to keep the inner sources of their discomfort from awareness, but it also thwarts them from unlearning these feelings or learning new and potentially more constructive ways of coping with them. Likewise, by defensively reducing their activities to situations that will not reactivate intolerable memories, individuals automatically preclude the possibility of learning to be less anxious than in the past and diminish their chances for learning new reactions to formerly stressful situations. For example, a highly intelligent and physically attractive 15-year-old boy had progressively withdrawn from school and social activities; for several years, there had been marked disharmony at home, culminating in a well-publicized scandal involving his parents. Despite the fact that his teachers and peers viewed him personally in a favorable light and made efforts to show their continued acceptance, his embarrassment and fear of social ridicule led him into increasing isolation and fantasies that he would be humiliated wherever he went.

As a result of their own protective actions, then, individuals preserve unaltered their memories; in addition, those memories persist and force them along paths that prevent resolution. Moreover, the more vigilant their protective maneuvers and the more constrictive their boundaries, the more limited are their competencies for effective functioning and the more they are deprived of the positive rewards of life.

Perceptual and Cognitive Distortion

Certain processes not only preserve the past but also transform the present in line with the past. Cameron (1947) described this process, which he referred to as **reaction-sensitivity,** with insight and clarity. Once a person acquires a system of threat expectancies, that person responds with increasing alertness to similar threatening elements in his or her life situation. For example, persons who develop bodily anxieties often become hypochondriacal, that is, hyperalert to physiological processes that most people experience but ignore.

Beck's notion of cognitive schemas (Beck et al., 1990) may be seen as an extension of the concept of reaction-sensitivity. People acquire anticipatory cognitive attitudes from not only threatening but also all forms of past experience; these schemas guide, screen, code, and evaluate the stream of new experiences to which the individual is exposed. Thus, a person who has learned to believe that "everyone hates him" tends to interpret the incidental and entirely innocuous comments of others in line with this premise.

The role of habits of language as factors shaping an individual's perceptions is of particular interest. As Whorf (1956) and others have shown, the words we use transform our experiences in line with the meaning of these words. For example, children who have been exposed to parents who respond to every minor mishap as "a shattering experience" tend to use these terms themselves in the future; consequently, they begin to feel that every setback they experience is shattering because they have labeled it as such.

The importance of expectancies, reaction-sensitivities, and language habits lies in the fact that they lead to the distortion of objective realities. Disturbed individuals may transform what most people would have perceived as a beneficent event into one that is humiliating, threatening, and punishing. Instead of interpreting events as they objectively exist, then, individuals selectively distort them to fit their expectancies and habits of thought. These expectancies may channel individuals' attention and may magnify their awareness of irrelevant and insignificant features of their environment; they intrude constantly to obscure and warp an accurate perception of reality. The following quote from Beck (1963) illustrates this process well:

A depressed patient reported the following sequence of events which occurred within a period of half an hour before he left the house: His wife was upset because the children were slow in getting dressed. He thought, "I'm a poor father because the children are not better disciplined." He then noticed a faucet was leaky and thought this showed he was also a poor husband. While driving to work, he thought, "I must be a poor driver or other cars would not be passing me." As he arrived at work he noticed some other personnel had already arrived. He thought, "I can't be very dedicated or I would have come earlier." When he noticed folders and papers piled up on his desk, he concluded, "I'm a poor organizer because I have so much work to do."

Often inexact labeling seems to contribute to this kind of distortion. The affective reaction is proportional to the descriptive labeling of the event rather than to the actual intensity of a traumatic situation.

A man reported during his therapy hour that he was very upset because he had been "clobbered" by his superior. On further reflection, he realized that he had magnified the incident and that a more adequate description was that his superior "corrected an error he had made." After re-evaluating the event, he felt better. He also realized that whenever he was corrected or criticized by a person in authority he was prone to describe this as being "clobbered."

Selective abstraction refers to the process of focusing on a detail taken out of context, ignoring other more salient features of the situation and conceptualize the whole experience on the basis of this element.

A patient, in reviewing her secretarial work with her employer, was praised about a number of aspects of her work. The employer at one point asked her to discontinue making extra carbon copies of his letters. Her immediate thought was, "He is dissatisfied with my work." This idea became paramount despite all the positive statements he had made.

This distortion process has an insidiously cumulative and spiraling effect. By misconstruing reality in such ways as to make it corroborate their expectancies, individuals, in effect, intensify their misery. Thus, ordinary, even rewarding, events may be perceived as threatening. As a result of this distortion, patients subjectively experience neutral events as if they were, in fact, threatening. In this process, they create and accumulate painful experiences for themselves where none exists in reality.

We sometimes see in patients a progressive worsening of their behavior, despite the fact that the objective conditions of their life have improved. Once the pathological process of distortion has begun, patients misinterpret experiences in terms of their outlook; they now are caught in a downward spiral in which everything, no matter how objectively good it might be, is perceived as distressing, disheartening, or threatening. Their initial distortions have led to a succession of subjectively experienced stresses; this progressive cumulation of stress drives patients further and further away from an objective appraisal of reality; all efforts to counter and reverse the pathological trend are utterly useless at this point. The process of perceptual and cognitive distortion has built up its own momentum, resulting not only in its perpetuation but also its intensification.

Behavior Generalization

We just described a number of factors that lead individuals to perceive new experiences in a subjective and frequently warped fashion; perceptual and cognitive distortions may be viewed as the defective side of a normal process in which new stimulus conditions are seen as similar to those experienced in the past. This process, though usually described in simpler types of conditions, commonly is referred to as **stimulus generalization.** In this section, we turn our attention to another closely related form of generalization—the tendency to react to new stimuli in a manner similar to the way in which an individual reacted in the past—**behavior generalization.**

Stimulus generalization and behavior generalization often are two sides of the same coin; thus, if an individual distorts an objective event so as to perceive it as identical to a past event, it would be reasonable to expect that his or her response to it would be similar to that made previously. For example, assume that a child learned to cower and withdraw from a harshly punitive mother. Should the child come into contact with a somewhat firm teacher who possesses physical features similar to those of the mother, the child may distort his perception of the teacher, making her a duplicate of the mother, and then react to her as he had learned to react to his mother.

As noted previously, this tendency to perceive and to react to present events as if they were duplicates of the past has been labeled by psychoanalytic theorists as the process of **transference.** This concept signifies the observation that patients in treatment often magnify minor objective similarities between their parents and the therapist and transfer to the therapist responses learned in the family setting.

The transference of past behaviors to novel situations is necessary to efficient functioning; we cannot approach every new circumstance of life without some prior notion of how to perceive and react to it. From the viewpoint of efficiency, then, generalization enables us to apply what we have learned, that is, to react in the same way to situations that are comparable. A problem arises, however, when we transfer responses incorrectly because we have failed to discriminate between dissimilar situations, for example, reacting to novel circumstances in the present as if they were duplicates of the past.

The tendency to generalize inappropriate behaviors has especially far-reaching consequences because it often elicits reactions from others that not only perpetuate these behaviors but also aggravate the conditions that gave rise to them. Bateson and Ruesch (1951) have noted that communications between people convey more than a statement;

they carry with them some anticipation of what the response will be. Leary (1957), Carson (1969), and Kiesler (1996), along similar lines, suggest that interpersonal behaviors often are designed unconsciously to "pull" a reaction from others. For example, a phrase such as, "I think I'm doing poorly," is not merely a message denoting an individual's personal feelings but a social statement that he or she normally expects will elicit a reciprocal reaction such as, "Of course not! You did beautifully."

How does the generalization of interpersonal behavior perpetuate conditions that give rise to these behaviors?

An example may be useful. A person whose past experiences led him to anticipate punitive reactions from his parents may be hyperalert to signs of rejection from others. As a consequence of his suspiciousness, he may distort innocuous comments, seeing them as indications of hostility. In preparing himself to ward off and counter the hostility he expects, he freezes his posture, stares coldly and rigidly, and passes a few aggressive comments himself. These actions communicate a message that quickly is sensed by others as unfriendly and antagonistic. Before long, others express open feelings of disaffection, begin to withdraw, and display real, rather than imagined, hostility. The person's generalized suspicious behavior has evoked the punitive responses he expected. He now has experienced an objective form of rejection similar to what he received in childhood; this leads him to be more suspicious and arrogant, beginning the vicious circle again.

By intruding old behaviors into new situations, individuals provoke, with unfailing regularity, reactions from others, which reinforce their old responses. Almost all forms of generalized behavior set up reciprocal reactions that intensify these behaviors. Docile, ingratiating, or fearful interpersonal actions, for example, draw domineering and manipulative responses; confident and self-assured attitudes elicit admiration and submissiveness. In short, generalization not only is a form of perpetuation itself but also creates conditions that promote perpetuation.

Repetition Compulsion

Maladaptive behaviors persist not only as a consequence of generalized learned habits. There are intrapsychic sources that drive the individual to recreate situations of the past that were frustrating or unresolved. Freud spoke of this process as **repetition compulsions;** by this, he meant the unconscious tendency to reconstruct situations in the present that parallel failures or disappointments of the past and to persist in the attempt to undo these disappointments even though these attempts repeatedly have proven unrewarding.

A contradiction may appear between **protective constriction,** noted earlier, and repetition compulsion. The inconsistency can be resolved if we think of protective constriction as a process of avoiding conditions that have no hope of resolution. Repetition compulsions, in contrast, may be viewed as a process of reinstating conditions that provided partial gratification in the past and that give promise of ultimate fulfillment. In this process, the individual arranges situations to use maneuvers that were *periodically* successful. The individual employs these partially reinforced behaviors again and again in the hope of finally achieving a full measure of the ends sought.

The derivatives of these partially fulfilled drives constitute a reservoir of strivings that persist and seek gratification. Thus, the individual repeats past patterns not only through generalization but also through active efforts to recreate and overcome what was not achieved fully. For example, a highly charged sibling rivalry between two brothers generated intense hostile and destructive feelings on the part of the older brother, a

21-year-old college student seen at his university's counseling service. These feelings were vented in a variety of malicious maneuvers, some of which were successful some of the time but never fully gratified; that is, the drive to undo, humiliate, and even destroy the younger brother remained only a partially fulfilled striving. In new interpersonal situations, the older brother recreated the sibling relationship; time and time again he made friends, only to repeat the malicious maneuvers of deprecation and humiliation he had employed with his brother in the past. These relationships only partially fulfilled his needs, however, because the real object of his hatred was his brother, and the goal he really sought, that of total destruction of his competitor, never was achieved. He repeated compulsively, in one relationship after another, the same destructive behavior patterns he learned in the past; although he never gratified his unconscious objectives fully, he obtained sufficient symbolic rewards in these peer relationships to perpetuate his behavior.

In contrast to protective constriction, then, a process limited to conditions in which failure and pain were inevitable, repetition compulsions apply to those conditions where rewards are periodically achieved and where the motivation to obtain greater fulfillment persists. Nevertheless, intolerable duplicates of the past are recreated.

Sociocultural Influences

We would be remiss in our presentation if we failed to recognize that personality pathology may be shaped by the institutions, traditions, and values that comprise the cultural context of societal living; these cultural forces serve as a common framework of formative influences that set limits and establish guidelines for members of a social group. However, we must be careful to view "society" and "culture" not as entities but as convenient abstractions that characterize the pattern of relationships and responsibilities shared among group members.

The continuity and stability of cultural groups depend largely on the success with which their young are imbued with common beliefs and customs. To retain what has been wrought through history, each group must devise ways of molding its children to "fit in," that is, to accept and perpetuate the system of prohibitions and sanctions that earlier group members have developed to meet the persistent tasks of life. All infants undergo a process of "socialization" by which they learn to progressively surrender their impulsive and naive behaviors and to regulate or supplant them with the rules and practices of their group. Despite the coerciveness of this process and the loss of personal freedom that it entails, children learn, albeit gradually, that there are many rewards for cooperative and sharing behaviors. Societal rules enable them to survive, to predict the behaviors of others, to obtain warmth and security, and to learn acceptable strategies for achieving the rich and diverse rewards of life. It is important to recognize, then, that the traditions of a culture provide its members with a shared way of living by which basic needs are fulfilled for the greater majority with minimal conflict and maximal return.

In previous sections, we noted that for many children the process of cultural training and inculcation is far from ideal; methods by which societal rules and regulations are transmitted by parents often are highly charged and erratic, entailing affection, persuasion, seduction, coercion, deception, and threat. Feelings of stress, anxiety, and resentment may be generated within the young, leaving pathological residues that are perpetuated and serve to distort their future relationships; several of these pathogenic experiences were dealt with earlier.

Attention in this sociocultural section focuses not on the more private experiences of particular children in particular families, but on those more public experiences that are shared in common among members of a societal group. In a sense, we speak of forces that characterize "society as the patient," a phrase that Lawrence K. Frank (1936) suggested close to 70 years ago. He wrote:

Instead of thinking in terms of a multiplicity of so-called social problems, each demanding special attention and a different remedy, we can view all of them as different symptoms of the same disease. That would be a real gain even if we cannot entirely agree upon the exact nature of the disease. If, for example, we could regard crime, mental disorders, family disorganization, juvenile delinquency, prostitution and sex offenses, and much that now passes as the result of pathological processes (e.g., gastric ulcer) as evidence, not of individual wickedness, incompetence, perversity or pathology, but as human reactions to cultural disintegration, a forward step would be taken.

The notion that many of the pathological patterns observed today can best be ascribed to the perverse, chaotic, or frayed conditions of our cultural life has been voiced by many commentators of the social scene (Fromm, 1955; Millon, 1987; Millon & Davis, 1996; Riesman, 1950; Wachtel, 1983; Yankelovich, 1981); these conditions have been characterized in phrases such as "the age of anxiety," "growing up absurd," and "the lonely crowd." It is not within the scope of this book to elaborate the themes implied in these slogans; a brief description of three conditions of contemporary life suffices to provide some idea of what these writers are saying. First, we note the operation of forces that compel individuals to surpass the standards to which they were exposed in early life; second, we point up the effects of changing, ambiguous, and contradictory social values; and third, we describe the consequences of the disintegration of social beliefs and goals.

ACHIEVEMENT STRIVING AND COMPETITION

Few characterizations of American life are more apt than those that portray our society as upwardly mobile. Ours has been a culture that has maximized the opportunity of its members to progress, to succeed, and to achieve material rewards once considered the province only of the aristocracy and well-to-do. With certain notable and distressing exceptions, the young of our society have been free to rise, by dint of their wits and their talents, above the socioeconomic status of their parents. Implicit in this well-publicized option to succeed, however, is the expectancy that each person will pursue opportunities and will be measured by the extent to which he or she fulfills them. Thus, our society not only promotes ambition but also expects each of its members to meet the challenge successfully. Each aspiring individual is confronted, then, with a precarious choice; along with the promising rewards of success are the devastating consequences of failure, as may be seen in the developmental background of certain narcissistic personality subtypes.

Upwardly mobile opportunities are shared by most members of our society; this can only bring forth intense competition. The struggle for achievement is geared, therefore, not only to transcend an individual's past but also to surpass the attainments of others. No better illustration can be seen of the consequences of competitive failure and inadequacy than in the constant testing and grading that children experience throughout their school years; this early form of teaching competitiveness persists and pervades every fabric of societal life. It is evident in athletics, in the desire to be accepted by prestigious colleges, in the search for pretty dates, for getting a job with a title, having the highest income, buying up to a status car, belonging to the right country club, and so on.

The competitive success struggle is insatiable and fruitless since few can reach the top, and there are no spheres of life in which invidious comparisons cannot be made. Thus, a depressed man of 47, who had risen from a poor immigrant family background to a respected and financially rewarding career as a lawyer, became despondent and considered himself a failure following his unsuccessful bid for the elective office of county judge.

Guilt for having let others down, self-devaluation for your limitations, and self-recrimination for failures—all of these pathogenic feelings well up within many members of our society. We have been well trained to compete and to seek public achievements without examining their aims, their inevitable frustrations, and their limited rewards.

UNSTABLE AND CONTRADICTORY SOCIAL STANDARDS

Achievement strivings refer to the need to surpass one's past attainments; competition describes the struggle among individuals to surpass one another in these achievements. What happens, however, if the standards by which people gauge their achievements keep changing or are ambiguous? What happens if people cannot find dependable and unequivocal standards to guide their aspirations?

It has been the historical function of cultural traditions to give meaning and order to social life, to define the tasks and responsibilities of existence, and to guide group members with a system of shared beliefs, values, and goals. These traditions, transmitted from parents to child, provide the young with a blueprint for organizing their thoughts, behaviors, and aspirations.

One of the problems we face today is the pace of social change and the increasingly contradictory standards to which members of our society are expected to subscribe (Millon, 1987). Under the cumulative impact of rapid industrialization, immigration, urbanization, mobility, technology, and mass communication, there has been a steady erosion of traditional values and standards. Instead of a simple and coherent body of customs and beliefs, we find ourselves confronted with constantly shifting and increasingly questioned standards whose durability is uncertain and precarious. No longer can we find the certainties and absolutes that guided earlier generations. The complexity and diversity of everyday experience play havoc with simple archaic beliefs and render them useless as instruments to deal with contemporary realities. Lacking a coherent view of life, we find ourselves groping and bewildered, swinging from one set of standards to another, unable to find stability and order in the flux of changing events. There have been few times in the history of man when so many have faced the tasks of life without the aid of accepted and durable traditions. As is elaborated in our discussion of the borderline personality disorder's experiential background, the factors described previously are likely to be central influences in giving shape to their internal psychic dissonance.

This profusion of divergent standards is compounded by intrinsic contradictions among the beliefs to which people are exposed; we are sermonized to "turn the other cheek" but exhorted to "compete and win" as well. The strain of making choices among conflicting values and loyalties besets us at every turn. Competing claims on our time and divergent demands to behave one way here and another there keep us in constant turmoil and prevent us from finding a stable anchor or from settling on a fixed course.

For example, an anxious and dejected 36-year-old mother of three could not resolve the problem of whether to follow her former career as a lawyer, which she had interrupted at the time of her first child's birth, or whether to remain a housewife; when first seen, she was torn between the desire to accept a position as legal counsel for a public agency engaged in humanitarian social programs and feelings of guilt that, by so doing, she would fail to fulfill her responsibilities to her husband and children. With no system of consistent values, we drift erratically from one action to another; countervailing pressures only lead us into uncertainty, confusion, conflict, and hypocrisy.

DISINTEGRATION OF REGULATORY BELIEFS AND GOALS

Large segments of our society find themselves out of the mainstream of American life; isolated by the unfortunate circumstance of social prejudice or economic deprivation, they struggle less with the problem of achieving in a changing society than with managing the bare necessities of survival. To them, the question is not which of the changing social values they should pursue but whether there are any social values that are worthy of pursuit.

Youngsters exposed to poverty and destitution, provided with inadequate schools, living in poor housing set in decaying communities, raised in chaotic and broken homes, deprived of parental models of success and attainment, and immersed in a pervasive atmosphere of hopelessness, futility, and apathy cannot help but question the validity of the "good society." Reared in these settings, individuals quickly learn that there are few worthy standards to which they can aspire successfully. Whatever efforts are made to raise themselves from these bleak surroundings run hard against the painful restrictions of poverty, the sense of a meaningless and empty existence, and an indifferent, if not hostile, world.

As is discussed in our presentation of the so-called antisocial personality disorder, many young Black people today reject outright the idea of finding a niche in contemporary society; they question whether a country that has preached equality, but has degraded their parents and deprived them of their rights and opportunities, is worth saving at all. Why make a pretense of accepting patently "false" values or seeking the unattainable goals of the larger society when reality undermines every hope and social existence is so evidently and pervasively painful and harsh?

Deteriorating and alienated communities feed on themselves; they not only perpetuate their decay by destroying the initiative and promise of their young but also attract the outcast and unstable who drift into their midst. Caught in this web of disintegration, the young and the downwardly mobile join those who already have retreated from the values of the larger society. Delinquency, prostitution, broken homes, crime, violence, and addiction increasingly characterize these communities, and the vicious circle of decay and disintegration not only persists but also is intensified.

We must remember, however, that harsh cultural and social conditions rarely *cause* personality pathology; rather, they serve as a context within which the more direct and immediate experiences of interpersonal life take place. They color and degrade personal relationships and establish maladaptive and pathogenic models for imitation.

Summary

The obstacles confronting investigators engaged either in the design, execution, or interpretation of studies of personality disorders are formidable. Numerous questions have been raised about both the methodological adequacy of earlier research and the likelihood that these studies will prove more fruitful in the future.

Since it is impossible to design an experiment in which relevant variables can systematically be controlled or manipulated, it is impossible to establish unequivocal cause-effect relationships among these variables and personality pathology. Investigators cannot arrange, no less subvert and abuse, an individual or a social group for purposes of scientific study; research in this field must, therefore, continue to be of a naturalistic and correlational nature. The problem that arises with naturalistic studies is the difficulty of inferring causality; correlations do not give us a secure base for determining which factors were cause and which were effect. For example, correlations between socioeconomic class and personality disorders may signify both that deteriorated social conditions produce mental disorders and that mental disorders result in deteriorated social conditions.

Throughout the chapter were comments indicating the lack of definitive research to support assertions about the role of pathogenic factors in personality pathology. That pathogenic factors of both a psychosocial and biologic nature are significantly involved seems axiomatic to most theorists, but science progresses not by supposition and belief but by hard facts gained through well-designed and well-executed research. This paucity of evidence does not signify neglect on the part of researchers; rather, it indicates the awesome difficulties involved in unraveling the intricate interplay of influences productive of personality pathology. Despite these apologetics, there is reason for caution in accepting the contentions of pathogenic theorists.

We have no choice but to continue to pursue the suggestive leads provided us both by plausible speculation and exploratory research; difficulties notwithstanding, we must caution against inclinations to revert to past simplifications or to abandon efforts out of dismay or cynicism. Our increasing knowledge of the multideterminant and circular character of pathogenesis, as well as the inextricable developmental sequences through which it proceeds, should prevent us from falling prey to simplifications that led early theorists to attribute personality pathology to single factors. Innumerable pathogenic roots are possible; the causal elements are so intermeshed that we must plan our research strategies to disentangle not isolated determinants but their convergencies, their interactions, and their continuities.

Chapter 4

Assessment and Therapy of the Personality Disorders

Objectives

- Is assessment a useful prelude to therapeutic planning?
- Distinguish between nomothetic and idiographic approaches.
- What different types of sources can be used to assess personality?
- List some biasing and distorting factors in the measurement of personality.
- What are the different levels of interpretation for information obtained in psychological tests?
- Describe the two major self-report inventories (MMPI and MCMI) in terms of their advantages and disadvantages.
- Describe the two widely used clinical interviews.
- Describe and evaluate contemporary trends in psychotherapy.
- Define *synergistic psychotherapy.*
- Describe *potentiated pairings* and *catalytic sequences.*

The first three chapters of this text were concerned with the nature of personality, classical and contemporary perspectives on the field, and ideas related to the development of personality characteristics and disorders. This chapter turns from theoretical to practical concerns: the process of psychological assessment and therapy. Unfortunately, theory, assessment, and intervention have developed along nearly independent pathways. Cognitive therapy, for example, has developed alongside cognitive psychology. Uncoordinated to some larger conceptual framework, the field is littered with hundreds of assessment instruments and psychotherapies. In some cases, instruments constructed decades ago remain in widespread use, their structure and content minimally revised, if at all, in the light of more recent advances. The theme of this chapter is that assessment and therapy should be continuous with personality as an integrative construct. If we were astronomers looking through telescopes designed without regard for the principles of optics, our view of the universe would be highly distorted. Similarly, assessment should be constructed and psychotherapy practiced with an appreciation for the nature of personality as the patterning of variables across the entire matrix of the person.

The Assessment of Personality

Assessment should serve as a guide to therapy. Without it, therapy cannot proceed with a logical foundation. The goal of assessment is essentially the goal of science, but applied to the whole person rather than a field of study. The clinician should gain a scientific understanding of the interaction of the patient's current symptoms, personality traits, and psychosocial factors. The components of the *DSM* multiaxial model should be separately assessed and then integrated into a single composite: the case conceptualization.

RELATIONSHIP BETWEEN PURE AND APPLIED SCIENCE

Probably the best way to understand the process of assessment and therapy is by contrasting the pure and applied sciences. Where do they come from? In chemistry and physics, the two go hand in hand, so that pure science discoveries eventually trickle down to create new technologies and new instruments. The human genome project, for example, promises to revolutionize medicine. In the social sciences, however, the pure and applied branches of science have often developed independently. We continue to use instruments constructed decades ago, and the number of psychotherapies continues to increase without end.

The Nomothetic Approach

As many have argued, there are really two sciences of psychology. One, the **nomothetic approach,** is focused on hypothetical constructs and the theoretical propositions that relate different constructs to each other, called the **nomological network.** Research questions such as, "What is the relationship of locus of control to depression?" and "How does the continuum of self-schema complexity relate to stress vulnerability?" focus purely on psychological constructs. Individuality, the focus of clinical work, is actively excluded by gathering large samples of subjects. The particular characteristics of any one person must not contaminate the results. Two narcissists with unhappy marriages could be a coincidence; 200 constitute a finding.

The nomothetic approach serves the needs of science, which thrives on universal relationships. As a science, personality cannot afford to discover laws of behavior specific to one person; the fact that you cannot wake up without your morning coffee is not publishable. Instead, the purpose of science is to develop theories applicable to realms of manifest phenomena not heretofore seen or understood. No one has ever seen, smelled, or touched a black hole, but the Theory of Relativity allows us to predict what would happen if you fell into one. In the same way, personality psychologists strive to identify universal propositions about behavior that can be demonstrated again and again over repeated experiments. Allport (1937, p. 4) compared the nomothetic approach to "finding a single thread running from individual nature to individual nature, visible only through the magical spectacles of a special, theoretic attitude."

The Idiographic Approach

The **idiographic approach** emphasizes the complexity of individuality. Each person is the unique product of a history of transactions between biological and environmental factors that has never existed before and will never exist again. Here, so-called universal laws and classification systems are of highly limited value. Instead, understanding individuals requires a knowledge of the particulars of their existence: where they were born, how they were influenced by their first-grade teacher, why they chose psychology over hamster farming as a career, and how their father's death in that awful storm in the spring of their fifth-grade year shattered their faith. According to Henry Murray (1938, p. 604), "The history of personality is the personality."

At its most extreme, the idiographic approach holds that there is something ineffable about individuality, that its complexity cannot be wholly contained within any single classification system. As such, taxonomies are only provisional explanatory systems to be modified as needed when additional evidence becomes available. Theoretical systems are only a point of departure, to be used as a self-conscious contrivance that facilitates understanding, not as an end point. Cross-sectional descriptions, such as diagnoses and personality profiles, are only the beginning. Because the most important goal is creating a rich description of each person, any concept from any theory or classification system is acceptable if it helps capture and communicate the uniqueness of the individual. Here, the eclecticism of multiple theories is not frowned on, but instead seen as offering fertile soil from which truly illuminating portrayals of individuality can be achieved.

DIAGNOSIS VERSUS ASSESSMENT

If the phenomena of psychology were as sharply boundaried as those of chemistry and physics, every person would be diagnosed into one and only one category, which would completely exhaust all his or her particular nature. Everything that you are about as a person would be telescoped into a single label, and by knowing this label, the kinds of problems to which you are vulnerable would automatically be known as well, as would the most effective therapies to treat them. In fact, everything would be predictable in advance. Sound measurement techniques would allow clinicians to isolate exactly what makes you tick, and the application of psychological laws would allow the small behaviors, feelings, and attitudes to be modified. Every fact of your being would be accountable within the context of this deterministic science. From this perspective, individuality is the enemy, a nuisance that obscures detection of the underlying pattern. By knowing a person's diagnostic label, you would know the person. If the person deviates in some way from diagnosis, this is noise, unessential information that can be discarded. Obviously, matters are not this simple; nevertheless, the search for such an idealized classification system continues.

The *DSM* personality disorders attempt to retain the best of a construct-centered approach, while allowing a measure of individuality. First, the *DSM* allows multiple personality disorder diagnoses to be assigned. Combinations of two, three, or even four personality disorders are not uncommon. Second, each personality disorder is operationalized as a prototype that consists of many characteristics, its diagnostic criteria, as noted in Chapter 1. Because only a subset of the total number of criteria is needed to achieve a diagnosis, there are literally scores of ways of being a histrionic personality, a schizoid personality, a masochistic personality, and so on. There are probably hundreds of ways of satisfying the diagnostic criteria for any two personality disorders. Such vast possibilities are intended to accommodate individuality within the diagnostic system, whereas the shorthand of diagnostic labels nevertheless recognizes that all subjects who receive the same diagnosis bear a "family resemblance." All histrionics resemble one another, though some are more needy and demonstrative and others are more seductive, for example.

FALSIFICATION OF THE CLASSIFICATION SYSTEM

In any categorical classification system, the question is which labels the subject will receive. The idiographic perspective, however, reminds us that taxonomies take us only so far, that diagnostic constructs are only reference points that facilitate understanding, against which the individual should be compared and contrasted. If the individual is characterized as narcissistic, the next question is: "How is the person different from the pure narcissistic personality?" Asking such a question redirects attention away from simple diagnostic labels and toward an understanding of the individual. Because the goal is an idiographic understanding of the person, assessment is really an endeavor to show the limitations of the diagnostic system with respect to the person at hand. A variety of self-report and projective instruments are available to help this process along. The study of personality thus begins as a science, but ends as an art.

Once the subject has been conceptualized in terms of personality prototypes of the classification system, biographical information can be added to answer the questions, "How did these personality characteristics develop?" and "Where did they come from?" Some answers come easily. For example, subjects might report, "My father was always stubborn, and I'm the same way," or "My mother was sick all the time when I was little, so I grew up to be independent." Such responses automatically lead

---

FOCUS ON CLINICAL SKILLS

Developing Clinical Acumen

What Happens When Traits from Different Diagnoses Commingle?

Jenna felt overwhelmed by all the information she had gathered during the assessment of her first client. Although her client met the *DSM-IV* diagnostic criteria for compulsive personality disorder, he also seemed to possess additional traits not easily captured by this diagnosis. When Jenna met with her supervisor, a review of her clinical interview and test results suggested pervasive dependent tendencies, though these fell short of the threshold for dependent personality disorder. Jenna felt relieved when her supervisor suggested that clinical work was both an art and a science. Rather than limit herself to the findings of her instruments, Jenna was free to draw on her total knowledge of the subject, including her own experience of the subject gained in the assessment session, when composing her first clinical report.

to additional questions. The first subject might identify strongly with his father or might regard stubbornness as a negative trait that should be eliminated from his personality, just as his father's should be eliminated. The second subject might feel neglected or might be proud that she was able to come through a difficult childhood with a capacity to stand on her own.

The developmental antecedents of personality are not always available for conscious report, however. Subjects differ in their level of insight as well as their ability to provide biographical details. Some are simply poor historians; others may have repressed large portions of their childhood. The cognitive style of certain personalities, notably the histrionic personality, permits the recall of broad impressions but few specific details. Not everything can be found out in advance; not everything can be found out during the assessment. Profound connections and insights are often made months later as therapist and subject have a chance to reflect on the origin of maladaptive patterns repeated again and again across the years. Once this additional biographical element is added, diagnostic labels begin to look very impoverished indeed.

Because different patterns of developmental pathways lead to different personality disorders, the search for developmental antecedents is often assisted by the person's personality disorder diagnosis. For example, clinical lore suggests that the narcissistic personality is often associated with being the first male or only child. Even if a narcissistic subject has many siblings, it is highly probable that he or she occupied a position of special status in the family. Future narcissists experience noncontingent love so indulging and intense that they fail to learn that others have an independent existence outside their own glow. As a result, they develop egocentricity, arrogance, insensitivity, and a sense of entitlement; they expect others to anticipate their needs and may become rageful when they feel ignored. Each personality disorder has its own characteristic early experiences. In-depth knowledge of these developmental pathways can be used to further focus the clinical interview, thereby validating the clinical diagnosis or suggesting alternatives.

THE NATURE OF MEASUREMENT

In the hard sciences, the nomothetic and idiographic approaches often refine each other as science progresses. For example, although astronomers are interested in the properties of particular classes of stars, they are also interested in understanding the behavior of one single, very important star, our own sun. By analyzing its composition and applying complex models of fluid dynamics, many characteristics of solar behavior can be predicted with surprising precision, including the intensity of the next sunspot cycle. Here, one particular entity is understood through the application of universal laws. On the other hand, a peculiar anomaly may also drive science forward. If a new particle is found following the collision of superaccelerated antiprotons, for example, the fundamental theories of nature must be revised so that its existence is an expected result of the experiment. Once the theory has been generalized, the anomaly is an anomaly no more.

Two characteristics of the physical sciences combine to make the constructive interplay between the particular and the general possible. First, instrumentation in the physical sciences is highly developed, allowing extremely precise observations. The nature of the measurement instrument does not contaminate the measurement itself. Temperature provides an example. Everyone understands what it means when the temperature is 32 degrees; whether a mercury or an alcohol thermometer was used is not important. Furthermore, two different instruments in the physical sciences can often be substituted

---

FOCUS ON CONTEXT

Finding the Historic Parallel

How Do Family Influences Affect Personality Development?

Several sessions into therapy, Justin was still complaining about his "thick-headed" creative writing instructor, who failed to recognize his superior intelligence or make special allowances for his gifted ability. Eventually, Jenna shifted the conversation to Justin's parents. As expected, his mother had always been completely devoted to his welfare, anticipating his every need. Even though he'd been gone from home over a semester, she still called every day and sent weekly care packages of his favorite snacks. He really was the center of the universe, at least for his mother. By bringing his early environment into therapy, Jenna led Justin to the very edge of insight. Unfortunately, he was not yet able to connect his arrogance and disappointment in his instructor with the expectations formed from his mother's worship.

---

for each other, with little loss of measurement precision or with losses that are at least quantifiable. An alcohol thermometer and a mercury thermometer provide just about the same reading. Second, once precise measurements have been made, they can be entered into highly developed mathematical models. Users can forget about the source of their measurements and instead concentrate on understanding the phenomena at hand. Many physical models work in this fashion.

Measurement in the social sciences, however, suffers from intrinsic imprecision. The phenomena of the social sciences are loosely bounded, with emergent properties not easily understood in terms of lower levels of organization. Chemistry builds on the physical properties of matter, biology builds on chemistry, and psychology builds on biology. But wetness is not easily understood from the properties of hydrogen and oxygen alone, and consciousness is not easily understood through biology. Moreover, social science phenomena often cannot be understood apart from the context in which they occur. At the psychological level, the variables of the science are hypothetical constructs, such as anxiety or masochism. They may have biological correlates, perhaps in certain brain structures or neurotransmitter systems, but they also have a psychological component that cannot be reduced to biology.

In contrast to the physical sciences, measurement instruments in personality and psychopathology are inherently imprecise. If the thermometer reads 50 degrees, everyone knows it's jacket weather. However, if a therapist reports that a subject obtained a score of 50 on a depression scale, the question automatically asked is, "Which scale?" The correlation between an alcohol and a mercury thermometer is extremely high, but that of personality measures is often modest and sometimes very disappointing. Even instruments designed as parallel forms do not correlate perfectly. The therapist must know the identity of the measurement instrument; otherwise, the score is meaningless. Moreover, two instruments of the same kind may be given to the same subject but disagree in their findings. Two personality disorder instruments might produce substantially different profiles, for example, or an inventory and a clinical interview might disagree. Everyone has driven in the rain; when you look at the drops on the windshield,

FOCUS ON CLINICAL PROGRESS

Appropriateness of the Measure

Measuring Psychotherapeutic Change

Toward the end of Jenna's first semester of clinical training, her supervisor suggested that she reassess Justin using tests from her original battery and compare the results. Her battery contained three different measures of depression. Two showed remarkable improvement, and the third only a little improvement. Jenna and her supervisor compared the item content of all three instruments and discovered that the dissenting measure focused mainly on the identification of long-standing difficulties and, therefore, was not a sensitive measure of psychotherapeutic change.

the world beyond goes somewhat out of focus. Measurement in personality and psychopathology is the same way: Our view of the subject matter beyond is always somewhat obscured by particularities of the measuring device and by biases inherent in the source of the information.

INFORMATION SOURCES

Information is the basis of all measurement and, therefore, the basis of all clinical assessment. Five broad sources of information are available to help describe the clinical problem; each has its own advantages and limitations. The first source is the **self-report inventory;** subjects literally report on themselves by completing a standard list of items. The second is the **rating scale and checklist;** a person familiar with the subject completes this form in order to provide an alternative perspective. The third is the **clinical interview;** the clinician asks the questions and the subject responds verbally, often in a free-form style. The clinician is free to follow any particular line of questioning desired and usually mixes standard questions with those specific to the current problem. The fourth source of information is the **projective technique,** an attempt to access unconscious structures and processes that would not ordinarily be available to the subject at the level of verbal report. These sources are discussed in the following sections. The use of intimates of the subject, perhaps a spouse, teacher, parent, or good friend, someone who can provide perspective on the problem, might also be considered a source of information. Physiological measurements, neurotransmitter or hormone levels, for example, provide a final source, though these are not available to most therapists.

Self-Report Inventories

A self-report inventory is simply a list of questions completed by the subject. Most are in paper-and-pencil form, though some are also computer administered. Self-report tests are available for almost every conceivable theoretical concept and clinical condition. Each usually consists of a minimum of about eight items to a maximum in the several hundreds. Answer formats vary from simply true versus false, to never, seldom, often, and always. The variations are endless. Short tests usually assess only a single construct;

longer tests, called self-report inventories, might assess 20 or more. On longer tests, scale scores may be plotted as a profile configuration.

Because self-reports represent the subject's own responses, they can be especially valuable in quickly identifying clinical problems. Unless the individual is violent or psychotic, a self-report inventory can be given at any point during the clinical process, often with minimal supervision. A profile obtained at the beginning of therapy, for example, can be used as a baseline to evaluate future progress. Some questions, such as, "I am too outgoing for my own good," assess personality traits. An item like this might be answered true by a histrionic personality, for example. Other questions, called critical items, are written to assess desperate situations that should receive immediate clinical attention, such as, "I intend to commit suicide." In the era of managed care, where progress must be carefully documented, brief serial assessments with self-report measures chart the clinical course with speed and convenience.

Rating Scales and Checklists

A rating scale can be completed by anyone who knows the subject well, perhaps a spouse, teacher, parent, coworker, priest, or even parole officer. Such persons are in a position to offer a unique perspective on the problem, its severity, and its causes. Rating scales and checklists may also be completed by the clinician, who makes a series of judgments on the basis of all available information, including the clinical interview. Here, rating scales and checklists often serve as a memory aid, ensuring that everything relevant to the disorder is included in developing a treatment plan. Rating scales usually have more items than the *DSM-IV* diagnostic criteria for the same syndrome and are usually held to a higher standard of scientific rigor. Because they have more items, they provide more fine-grained measurements, but they also take more time to complete. For example, the revised Psychopathy Checklist (PCL-R; Hare, 1991) consists of 20 items, whereas the *DSM-IV* offers only seven criteria for the diagnosis of antisocial personality disorder. Although the PCL-R is widely used in the study of psychopathy, few rating scales exist for use with other personality disorders.

The Clinical Interview

The clinical interview is usually thought of as the criterion standard in psychopathology, against which the validity of all other assessment instruments is judged. The development of a variety of formalized, systematic clinical interviews, beginning around 1960, remains an important milestone in the history of clinical assessment. Because interviews standardize the questions asked of patients, they greatly increase interdiagnostician reliability, defined as the extent to which different clinicians agree about the diagnosis of the same subject. This is especially true for the personality disorders, which are broad and overlapping constructs.

Two kinds of clinical interviews exist, structured and semistructured. **Structured interviews** are intended to be administered by trained nonprofessionals and are usually used in large research projects, not in normal clinical work. A fixed series of questions is asked, and the interviewer is not allowed to deviate from these questions in any way. This standardizes the assessment process across interviewers, thus compensating somewhat for their lack of professional experience. Otherwise, the interviewer might get lost in some irrelevant tangent and waste time or record unnecessary information. Many structured interviews are exclusively research instruments to be used in conjunction with governmental research funding. Subjects are often paid to participate and may answer questions for several hours.

In contrast, **semistructured interviews** draw on the experience and knowledge of the professional by allowing additional probes to be inserted as desired. Thus, if the subject makes a statement that might be relevant to any part of the assessment, the clinician is free to pursue the issue immediately, if desired. Some semistructured interviews are geared to a comprehensive assessment of Axis II. These can take up to two hours to administer and score, even with training. Other semistructured interviews focus on a single construct and take only about an hour. Given the necessary time commitment, semistructured interviews are not widely used in actual clinical practice. Nevertheless, they can be extraordinarily useful in clinical training. Because they already contain interview questions of demonstrated utility, they allow the student to quickly acquire a degree of knowledge in unfamiliar diagnostic terrain.

Projective Techniques

Some situations offer a chance for flexibility, novelty, and the expression of individual differences in behavior, and others do not. When situations are highly scripted, environmental constraints dominate and the behavior of different individuals tends to converge, regardless of their personality traits. Almost everyone stops at a red light, and almost everyone cries at a funeral or at least tries to look sad. In contrast, when the social pull for any particular behavior is weak, behavior is no longer determined by the environment but by factors inside the person. An observer is, therefore, entitled to ask, "Of all the possible ways of behaving, why these particular responses, rather than others?"

Projective techniques seek to draw out internal, and frequently unconscious, influences on behavior by presenting the subject with inherently unstructured, vague, ambiguous situations. The Rorschach Inkblot Test is the classic example. The subject is presented with a series of 10 blots in turn and asked to report what he or she sees. Although the blots are not intended to look like anything in particular, subjects almost always report seeing something, ranging from the trivial to the obviously psychotic. In the Incomplete Sentence Blank, the subject writes in a response following an item stem, such as "My mother _____." The Thematic Apperception Test uses pictures of various interpersonal situations. The subject constructs a story to explain what is happening in the picture, what led up to these events, and how matters will end. Because projective instruments are time-consuming and not widely regarded as being as scientific as self-report inventories or interviews, their use has waned in recent years, especially with the ascendancy of managed care.

BIASING AND DISTORTING FACTORS

Measurement in all sciences is limited by biasing and distorting factors. In the physical sciences, these influences can often be quantified directly to limit the loss of measurement precision. Stars twinkle because of heat and atmosphere impurities. Instruments on large earth-based telescopes, however, now sample the properties of the atmosphere and mathematically factor out the twinkle to produce sharper images. In personality and psychopathology, however, such precise control is usually not possible. Instead, information is limited in both its quantity and quality. Some subjects are poor historians, show little insight, or have limited verbal ability. Even when intellectual level and memory are good, subjects can report only what they know about themselves or what they believe they know. God may have a monopoly on truth, but human beings must work with fallible indicators. Psychodynamic critics might even argue that the most important truths are the most threatening and, therefore, the most likely to remain repressed in the unconscious, beyond the reach of either self-report instruments or clinical interviews.

Personality Style Factors

Certain distortions arise because of the personality style of the respondent or interviewer. Different personalities construe the world in different ways. Persons with an extraordinarily passive approach to life, such as the immature dependent personality, are unlikely to develop nuanced representations of self and other. With their instrumental surrogates to take charge of life and confront the world, immature dependents fail to develop functional competencies. As such, they may acquire only a thin fund of information about the world around them. Similarly, schizoids withdraw from social life, possessing little interest in anything, even their own emotional affairs. Likewise, histrionics are notoriously scattered and impressionistic. When asked detailed questions during a clinical interview, all three are vulnerable to interpretations cast in coarse cognitive categories; they fail to make distinctions where real distinctions exist. In effect, the test or interview items are often more nuanced, subtle, or complex than the subject's own understanding, leading to significant limits on validity.

Other limitations on clinical information arise from subjects' motives and their level of personality pathology. Compulsives, for example, fear condemnation from authority figures and from a punishing, sadistic superego that insists perfectionist standards be maintained. As a result, such individuals are highly motivated to appear normal; Leary (1957), in fact, referred to the compulsive as the "hypernormal personality."

Focus on Somatic Signs

Looking at Significant Stressors

What Else Can Account for Somatic Symptomatology?

One of Jenna's most challenging clients during her first semester of training was a histrionic female freshman who presented with vague somatic complaints, including headache, muscle aches, and weakness. Examination at the campus medical center failed to find any physical cause to account for the symptoms. During the standard intake interview, the student was asked to report significant recent stressors, which included leaving home to attend the university and a breakup with her boyfriend back home. When asked about her current feelings, the student responded with global impressions that obviously exaggerated her situation. "I feel so awful, like a million tons of bricks just fell on me. I'm so depressed I can't stand it," she would say, and then pause, waiting for Jenna to provide the solution. When asked what she found most attractive about her ex-boyfriend's personality, she responded, "Oh, I don't know . . . he was just so awesome." Reflecting about the inner lives of others continued to be a problem for her throughout the remainder of therapy. As she finally began to reflect on her own identity and feelings some semesters later, her somatic symptoms began to abate.

They present themselves in a socially acceptable light, maximizing impressions of health and minimizing or even omitting negative characteristics, behaviors, and symptoms that might become an important focus of treatment, if only they were known. Compulsive interviewers sometimes overestimate pathology when confronted with subjects who appear overly frivolous or grandiose, such as the histrionic and narcissistic personalities. In contrast to the compulsive, the masochistic personality is invested in bringing harsh punishment on the self; masochists may, therefore, overadmit to problems.

Sometimes, distortions of reality are corroborated by two or more individuals because of the personality dynamics of their relationship. A narcissistic member of a couple may damn his masochistic counterpart for her failings, while the masochist sits in agreement. To an interviewer focused only on verbal report, the masochist is the problem and, therefore, the proper focus of treatment. Functionally, however, the masochist is what family therapists refer to as the identified patient, the scapegoat whose symptoms help a pathological system limp along. Both subjects distort reality at a level below conscious awareness. The influence of personality style factors in limiting the validity of information, then, extends across both the patient and other informants.

Dissimulation

Some personalities consciously distort information to somehow take advantage of the system or to avoid some unpleasant consequence of their own behavior. Antisocials and histrionics, for example, sometimes fake illness if they believe there is something to gain in doing so. Perhaps the antisocial would rather spend time in a psychiatric facility than a prison, for example. Similarly, informants close to the subject, even a spouse or a family member, may have their own agenda, leading to distortions or omissions. Informants may underpathologize their report to avoid embarrassment to the family, for example. Alternatively, they may overpathologize the subject to secure some reward, perhaps continued social assistance. Most self-report instruments have indexes that can detect attempts to fake good or fake bad, though they must be interpreted cautiously in the context of other test information. Whatever the situation, clinicians are always advised to keep the principle of self-interest firmly in mind.

State versus Trait

Most patients who require psychological testing present with one or more Axis I disorders. **Traits** refer to long-standing personality characteristics that endure over time and situations. In contrast, **states** refer to potentially short-lived conditions, usually emotional in nature. Anxiety, depression, and loss of reality contact can all affect the results of personality testing. J. Reich, Noyes, Coryell, and Gorman (1986), for example, obtained personality profiles on a group of persons with panic disorder and agoraphobia. Those judged improved six weeks later showed significantly increased emotional strength and extroversion and significantly decreased interpersonal dependence. Some disorders also have a motivational or cognitive dimension that can affect the validity of test results. Depressed individuals report increased feelings of worthlessness and shame, which can lead to overendorsement of items intended to assess low self-esteem as a personality trait, for example. Research on mood-congruent memory shows that different emotional sets make different schemata more available, negatively biasing reflections on self, world, and future (Beck et al., 1990). Problems with concentration and low energy can make depressed persons more indecisive, which superficially resembles a characteristic of the dependent personality, who needs help making decisions. Some questions tap both state and trait characteristics because of their wording. An item such as, "I am a very dependent person," will be answered affirmatively by both dependent personalities and those whose Axis I disorder or physical condition forces them to rely on others, however resistant they might be. Subjects desperate for help sometimes use the assessment as a means of communicating their helplessness. By adopting a low threshold for answering any item in a pathological direction, they inflate scores almost everywhere in the inventory. Crossover effects from state to trait are an expectable part of assessment and must be considered by whoever interprets the test results.

FOCUS ON MALINGERING

The Significance of Collaborative Data

Clinical Findings without Client Compliance

Jenna's second client was referred for a psychological evaluation by the university disciplinary committee after "recklessly endangering" the welfare of others when one of his experiments in the chemistry lab exploded, producing a major fire. Very charming and personable, he denied any wrongdoing, stating that he wanted to cooperate fully. Nevertheless, psychological testing showed that he denied even minor faults to which almost everyone else would ordinarily admit. Despite his protests of innocence, a criminal record, together with consultation with family members, confirmed the presence of narcissistic and antisocial traits, ultimately contributing to his expulsion from the university.

LEVELS OF INTERPRETATION IN PSYCHOLOGICAL TESTS

Items, scales, and profiles thus form three levels of interpretation in psychological assessment. The **item** is the standard stimulus in psychological assessment. Because every subject who completes an instrument answers the same items, responses can be directly compared to those of others. A **scale** is composed of many items that tap the same psychological construct, so that a scale score reflects a summary of the particular behaviors expressed in those same item responses. Means scores constitute expectable behavior across a group, and substantial deviations from the mean are expected to have interpretive significance. The more deviant from average, the more significant the result. A set of scale scores is referred to as a **profile** or **profile configuration.** The profile stands in place of the person as a collection of scales, just as a collection of items stands in place of the construct they assess. Accordingly, for the profile to be valid, every scale composing the profile should be valid. Methods for writing items, constructing scales, and interpreting profiles are highly developed within the self-report format, with which this section is mostly concerned.

The Item Level

Most test items are so specific that they usually have little relevance to the overall assessment. For example, the item, "I like to go to parties," may or may not be indicative of a histrionic personality; not everyone who likes parties is a histrionic. Some items, however, are so dramatic that they are interpreted on their own terms. For example, if a patient responds "true" to the item, "I have been thinking strongly about killing myself," the assessing clinician has the responsibility to establish the likelihood of suicidal intent by interviewing the subject. Such critical items are literally critical to the clinical situation. These are usually built into the inventory by intent, though some may be identified through research after the test has been constructed. After the patient has completed the inventory, answers to all the items, especially the critical items, can be quickly scanned by the clinician, suggesting issues that should be explored further during the clinical interview.

The Scale Level

Because individual test items usually refer to highly specific behaviors, they do not make broad predictions about behavior. For this reason, items are usually grouped into scales. Taken together, items such as, "I like to go to parties," "I am a dramatic and emotional person," and "I like to be the center of attention," begin to point to a histrionic pattern. The scale thus makes a broader prediction about behavior but loses some specificity in the process. Not all histrionics will answer affirmatively to, "My thoughts are scattered and hard to focus."

Ideally, every scale item should tap some aspects of the construct the scale is intended to assess. When all the important aspects of a construct have been anchored to different items, the scale is said to possess **content validity.** The narcissistic personality, for example, consists largely of the traits of grandiosity, exploitiveness, and lack of empathy. As such, any scale lacking items that assess grandiosity cannot be a valid measure of the narcissistic construct, as content essential to the construct is missing. Careful consideration of the different facets of every construct is, therefore, essential to scale development. Scales that perform in accordance with the expectations of psychological theory are said to possess the additional property of **construct validity** (Cronbach & Meehl, 1955). If a new antisocial personality scale fails to correlate highly with an established measure of substance abuse, for example, this calls the validity of the antisocial scale into question.

Profiles and Codetypes

Tests are given to a large number of subjects, called the **normative sample,** to determine what is expectable and what is statistically deviant. Although any scale can be interpreted on its own, whole inventories consisting of many scales can be constructed simultaneously using the same sample. When any one person completes the inventory, his or her scores can be graphed as a profile configuration. The two or three highest scales in the profile are usually called a **codetype.** The profile stands in place of the person just as a set of items stands in place of its scale. For interpretive purposes, the profile is the person. Accordingly, the scales of an inventory should exhaust all of personality, just as the items that assess a construct tap every aspect of its content. The scales must have content validity for the person. Inventories developed according to some theoretical or methodological rationale provide some assurance that the individual has been assessed along the essential dimensions of personality and thus ultimately support the content validity of the clinical report that will eventually be written on the subject.

SELF-REPORT INSTRUMENTS

A variety of self-report instruments are available that assess the personality disorders.

Minnesota Multiphasic Personality Inventory–2nd Edition (MMPI-II)

With more than 550 items, the MMPI-2 (Butcher, Dahlstrom, Graham, Tellegen, & Kaemmer, 1989) is not so much a standardized test as a standardized item pool that belongs to psychology itself. Literally hundreds of personality scales have been derived from the MMPI throughout its long career. In fact, there are now more auxiliary scales than there are items on the MMPI (Graham, 1990). Morey, Waugh, and Blashfield (1985) constructed a set of MMPI-I scales to represent the 11 *DSM-III* personality disorders, based on the strategy used by Wiggins (1966) in the construction of the Wiggins content scales. Item selection proceeded through two stages. In the initial phase, scales were rationally derived by four experienced clinicians who culled the item pool for items representative of *DSM-III* personality disorder criteria. Those items selected by two or more clinicians formed the preliminary scales; items could be assigned to more than one scale, mirroring the diagnostic overlap of *DSM-III*. These were then subjected to empirical refinement. Nonoverlapping scales were constructed by assigning each overlapping item to the scale with which it exhibited the highest correlation. The final scales consist of from 14 to 38 items for the overlapping scales and from 13 to 20 items for the nonoverlapping scales. As should be expected, the internal consistencies of the longer, overlapping scales are appreciably higher, ranging between 0.675 (compulsive scale) and 0.859 (avoidant scale). Those of the nonoverlapping scales range from 0.619 (histrionic scale) to 0.791 (schizotypy scale). These internal consistencies are superior to those of the clinical scales and comparable to those of the Wiggins content scales. Specific item assignments are available in Morey et al. Norms for the updated MMPI-2 have been supplied by Colligan, Morey, and Offord (1994).

Millon Clinical Multiaxial Inventory (MCMI)

Now in its third edition (MCMI-III; Millon, Davis, & Millon, 1996), the MCMI is by far the most widely used personality disorders inventory. A principal goal in constructing the MCMI-III was to keep the total number of items constituting the inventory small enough to encourage use in all types of diagnostic and treatment settings, yet large enough to permit the assessment of a wide range of clinically relevant behaviors. At 175 items, the final form is much shorter than are comparable instruments, with terminology geared to an eighth-grade reading level. As a result, most subjects complete the MCMI-III in 20 to 30 minutes. The inventory is intended exclusively for subjects believed to possess a personality disorder and should not be used with normals. The MCMI is frequently used in research. More than 650 publications to date have included or focused primarily on the MCMI, with approximately 65 new references currently published annually.

The inventory itself consists of 24 clinical scales (presented as a profile in Figure 4.1) and three modifier scales—Disclosure, Desirability, and Debasement—which identify tendencies to overdisclose or underdisclose pathology, favor only socially desirable responses, or endorse only those highly suggestive of pathology, respectively. The next two sections constitute the basic personality disorder scales. The first section contains moderately severe personality pathologies, ranging from schizoid to masochistic, and the second section represents the severe personality pathologies—the schizotypal, borderline, and paranoid. The masochistic and sadistic personalities, included in the third revised edition of the *DSM,* but not in the fourth edition, have been retained in the

CONFIDENTIAL INFORMATION FOR PROFESSIONAL USE ONLY

CATEGORY		SCORE RAW	SCORE BR	PROFILE OF BR SCORES	DIAGNOSTIC SCALES
MODIFYING INDICES	X	111	68		DISCLOSURE
	Y	12	55		DESIRABILITY
	Z	22	80		DEBASEMENT
CLINICAL PERSONALITY PATTERNS	1	8	67		SCHIZOID
	2A	7	59		AVOIDANT
	2B	11	68		DEPRESSIVE
	3	11	77		DEPENDENT
	4	17	72		HISTRIONIC
	5	14	66		NARCISSISTIC
	6A	7	64		ANTISOCIAL
	6B	15	74		AGGRESSIVE (SADISTIC)
	7	7	28		COMPULSIVE
	8A	12	72		NEGATIVISTIC
	8B	7	75		MASOCHISTIC
SEVERE PERSONALITY PATHOLOGY	S	6	61		SCHIZOTYPAL
	C	18	89		BORDERLINE
	P	5	62		PARANOID
CLINICAL SYNDROMES	A	9	80		ANXIETY DISORDER
	H	13	85		SOMATOFORM DISORDER
	N	13	80		BIPOLAR: MANIC DISORDER
	D	17	85		DYSTHYMIC DISORDER
	B	3	61		ALCOHOL DEPENDENCE
	T	2	60		DRUG DEPENDENCE
	R	5	50		POSTTRAUMATIC STRESS
SEVERE SYNDROMES	SS	14	70		THOUGHT DISORDER
	CC	14	85		MAJOR DEPRESSION
	PP	1	25		DELUSIONAL DISORDER

Profile of BR Scores column markers: 0   60   75   85   115

FIGURE 4.1   Millon Clinical Multiaxial Inventory–III.

MCMI-III. The next two sections cover the Axis I disorders, ranging from the moderate clinical syndromes, such as anxiety and dysthymia, to those of greater severity, such as thought disorder and delusional disorder (Millon, 1997).

The MCMI can be used on a routine basis in outpatient clinics, community agencies, mental health centers, college counseling programs, general and mental hospitals, the courts, and private practice offices. The division between personality and clinical disorders scales parallels the multiaxial model and has important interpretive implications. The resulting profile is helpful in illuminating the interplay between long-standing characterological patterns and current clinical symptoms. Scores on the personality and clinical syndromes scales run from 0 to 115, with those above 85 suggesting pathology in the disordered range. More comprehensive and dynamic interpretations of relationships among symptomatology, coping behavior, interpersonal style, and personality structure may be derived from an examination of the configural pattern of the clinical scales. To further increase its coordination with the *DSM,* the items that assess the personality disorders have been written to reflect the diagnostic criteria of their respective constructs. For example, the first criterion for the *DSM-IV* dependent personality disorder reads: "Has difficulty making everyday decisions without an excessive amount of advice and reassurance from others," and its parallel MCMI-III item reads: "People can easily change my ideas, even if I thought my mind was made up."

Computer-generated clinical reports are available at two levels of detail. The Profile Report of scale scores is useful as a screening device to identify patients who may require more intensive evaluation or professional attention. Individual scale cutting lines on the MCMI-III can be used to make decisions concerning primary behavior disorders or syndrome diagnoses. Similarly, elevation levels among subsets of scales can furnish grounds for judgments about impairment, severity, and chronicity of pathology. More comprehensive and dynamic interpretations of relationships among symptomatology, coping behavior, interpersonal style, and personality structure may be derived from an examination of the configural pattern of all 24 clinical scales. Alternatively, the Interpretive Report provides both a profile of the scale scores and a detailed analysis of personality and symptom dynamics as well as suggestions for therapeutic management.

Other Self-Report Inventories

A number of other self-report instruments are available. Notable are two variants of the MMPI and MCMI designed for adolescents; the first, the MMPI-A (Butcher et al., 1992) is a bit briefer than the MMPI, as is the Millon Adolescent Clinical Inventory (MACI) (Millon, 1993). Another recent variant of the MCMI is the M-PACI, the Millon Preadolescent Inventory (Millon, Tringone, Millon, & Grossman, in press) for use with youngsters in the 9- to 12-year age range. The Personality Diagnostic Questionnaire (e.g., Hyler & Rieder, 1987) is now in its fourth revision. F. L. Coolidge and Merwin (1992) reported on the reliability and validity of the Coolidge Axis II Inventory. The Personality Assessment Inventory (Morey, 1992) consists of 344 items on 4 validity scales, 11 clinical scales, 5 treatment scales, and 2 interpersonal scales. Only three scales, however—Paranoia, Borderline Features, and Antisocial Features—directly assess personality pathology. The Dimensional Assessment of Personality Pathology-Basic Questionnaire was constructed by Livesley (1987) and his associates (Livesley & Schroeder, 1990; Livesley et al., 1992; Schroeder, Wormworth, & Livesley, 1992) based on an extensive literature review and a comprehensive scale development effort. The Schedule of Nonadaptive and Adaptive Personality (Clark, McEwen,

Collard, & Hickok, 1993) is a 375-item true-false instrument primarily oriented to trait dimensions derived from factor analytic research. However, diagnostic scales for the *DSM* personality disorders are also included. The Tridimensional Personality Questionnaire (Cloninger, Przybeck, & Svrakic, 1991) is based on *novelty seeking*, *harm avoidance*, and *reward dependence*, temperament dimensions proposed by Cloninger (1987b). Finally, the Wisconsin Personality Disorders Inventory (Klein et al., 1993) is a 360-item inventory developed to operationalize the interpersonal theory of Benjamin (1996). Items were developed to represent the internal experience of each personality disorder as conceived from the perspective of the SASB. The NEO-PI-R (Costa & McCrae, 1992), originally designed to assess normal personality factors, has also been employed recently to evaluate clinical personality traits.

CLINICAL INTERVIEWS

A number of clinical interviews are available for the personality disorders. Two of the more widely used are reviewed.

Structured Clinical Interview for DSM-IV Axis II Personality Disorders (SCID-II)

The SCID-II (First, Gibbon, Spitzer, Williams, & Benjamin, 1997) is a semistructured diagnostic interview assessing the 12 personality disorders included in *DSM-IV;* the sadistic and masochistic personality constructs from the third revised edition of the *DSM* are not included. According to First and colleagues, the interview has often been used in research settings to describe the personality profiles found in particular samples or to select patient groups for further study. In clinical settings, the SCID-II may be used routinely as part of a standard intake. Alternatively, a subset of the interview may be used to confirm the presence of a suspected personality disorder. Phrased to coordinate with the language employed in the *DSM* diagnostic criteria, the interview questions are grouped by personality disorder (e.g., all the avoidant personality questions are asked together) and scored absent, subthreshold, true, or inadequate information to code. All available sources of information can be used for scoring, not just the subject's own report. The SCID-II can even be administered to an informant. Specific probes are included to assist in exploring the presence of each interview item. The SCID-II also includes a 119-item self-report screening questionnaire that can greatly reduce administration time. Each self-report question corresponds to an interview item but is asked in such a way that it elicits a much greater frequency of true responses. The questionnaire thus serves as a screening inventory, for the interviewer need only scan the completed form and inquire into positive admissions.

Structured Interview for DSM-IV Personality Disorders (SIDP-IV)

The SIDP-IV (Pfohl, Blum, & Zimmerman, 1997) is a semistructured clinical interview that assesses all the personality disorders of the *DSM-IV,* plus the self-defeating personality from the revised third edition of the *DSM* (the sadistic personality is not included). Whereas the questions of the SCID-II are grouped by disorder and closely rephrase the diagnostic criteria, those of the SIDP-IV are phrased more conversationally and grouped into 10 topic areas, such as interests and activities and emotions. Using this more natural format, information elicited by previous questions is more readily applied to others with the same theme. Interviewing and scoring typically take 80 to 120 minutes. An informant may consume another 20 to 30 minutes. The authors suggest that administration time can be reduced by dropping questions from the optional personality disorders (the self-defeating, depressive, and negativistic personalities). An alternative form of the SIDP-IV is available with the questions grouped by disorder. Subjects are encouraged to respond according to "what you are like when you are your usual self." Because personality is enduring over time, interviewers are required to use the five-year rule, meaning that "behaviors, cognitions, and feelings that have predominated for most of the last five years are considered to be representative of the individual's long-term personality functioning." Items are scored *not present, subthreshold, present,* and *strongly present.* Tentative ratings may be made during the interview, but a final rating, based on all available data, is deferred until the end. The manual states that the interview has been used in more than 60 studies and translated into several languages.

Other Interviews

Other interviews have been developed specifically to research particular personality disorders, including the depressive personality (Gunderson, Phillips, Triebwasser, & Hirschfeld, 1994), the narcissistic personality (Gunderson, Ronningstam, & Bodkin, 1990), and the borderline personality (Zanarini, Gunderson, Frankenburg, & Chauncey, 1989). Each includes questions geared to traits associated with its respective construct, as manifest in various domains of functioning. The Diagnostic Interview for Narcissism, for example, assesses narcissism in terms of grandiosity, interpersonal relations, reactiveness, affects and mood states, and social and moral adaptation. Because these interviews focus closely on one personality alone, they require only about an hour to administer.

Psychotherapy of the Personality Disorders

The history of psychotherapy is fraught with dogmatism. Popular forms of therapy reflected various popular schools and inherited their disciplinary rivalries. The arguments were fueled by different theoretical assumptions. The behavioral school, for example, denied the existence of mind and asserted that therapy should proceed through classical and operant principles of reinforcement. In contrast, the psychodynamic school held that behavior reflects only the surface expression of deeply repressed or transformed motivations, percolating up from their origin in a deeper, biologically instinctive nature. A psychodynamically trained therapist would administer psychodynamic therapy. A behaviorally trained therapist would administer behavioral therapy. Rather than fit therapy to the patient, clinicians fit the patient to their own preconceived dogma. While such loyalties reigned, psychotherapists were condemned to treat only a part of the whole person.

In the past few decades, however, dissatisfaction with school-oriented therapy, together with a new emphasis on efficacy motivated by managed care, has led to the development of compromise approaches. As in previous decades, the total number of therapies continues to explode. Nevertheless, three trends currently dominate. First, brief therapy claims to achieve as much or greater progress in less time by carefully selecting patients and providing highly structured forms of intervention specific to the presenting problem. Second, the common factors approach seeks to unify much of psychotherapy by identifying factors common to all effective therapies. The argument here

FOCUS ON HISTORY

Albert Ellis and Carl Rogers

Finding Your Own Therapeutic Style

Although Albert Ellis was originally trained as a psychoanalyst, he is an important figure in the history of the cognitive therapy movement. His transformation is striking, as it represents a philosophical shift from that which is deep and mysterious in human nature, namely the unconscious, to that which is more or less obvious, the rational process and errors of reasoning.

The movement Ellis founded is called **rational-emotive therapy.** According to Ellis, logical reasoning is the foundation of mental health. Psychopathology is the product of illogical inferences and other irrational beliefs. From this, it follows that mental unhappiness, ineffectuality, and other disturbances can be eliminated when people learn how to maximize rational thinking. Correct your reasoning, and your emotions will follow. The task of the therapist, then, is to identify errors in the reasoning process, showing patients that their difficulties result largely from distorted perceptions and erroneous beliefs. Not surprisingly, then, rational-emotive therapy tends to be more confrontive than supportive: The patient is doing something wrong, and this must be identified and exterminated. Patients' mistakes are their disease. Like other cognitive theorists, Ellis's thinking does not generate a series of personality constructs, but instead addresses cognitive processes as they cut across most mental disorders.

Carl Rogers, perhaps the single most influential theorist on therapy from the 1960s through the 1970s, is opposite Ellis, both philosophically and in bedside manner. Whereas Ellis is confrontive and highly directive (you must show patients their errors), Rogers impressed patients as a kind grandfather, always listening and reflecting their own emotions as a gentle commentary, intended to make them feel understood rather than thrusting their mistakes into awareness. According to Rogers, each person is innately right; that is, individuals possess their own innate sense of what is required for their own growth as a unique person. Healing emerges from the quality and character of the therapeutic relationship. Rogers' movement, therefore, became known as **client-centered therapy.** Growth could be facilitated through certain therapist attitudes, notably genuineness and authenticity.

Rather than learn complicated techniques founded in some abstract theoretical model, therapists should "be themselves," expressing their thoughts and feelings in a constructive way that honors the person, but without pretension or the cloak of professional authority. For Rogers, "unconditional positive regard" was the key. Clients should be respected as beings of intrinsic worth and dignity, no matter how unappealing and destructive their behaviors might be. However, Rogers also emphasized that clients must assume full responsibility for their own growth. Through accurate empathy and positive regard, the therapist lays the foundation. Only the client can follow through.

is that all therapies are more alike than different, and a better psychotherapy can be created by returning to the core principles and techniques from which particular therapies diversify. Third, therapeutic eclecticism holds that the techniques of various schools should be incorporated into treatment as necessary, without regard for the theoretical model in which the technique was first developed. By divorcing theory from techniques, therapists are free to draw on any technique to optimize the therapy of any particular case.

These movements, however, are only the latest in a long series of adaptations, not the final word. More appropriate to the symptom disorders of Axis I, they represent only an intermediate step toward a psychotherapy logically coordinated to the personality disorders. Personality pathologies are notoriously resistant to treatment. They not only make for fragile gains that are often suddenly and dramatically reversed, but also complicate transference and countertransference reactions with unanticipated issues and just naturally tend to generate Axis I symptoms. The borderline personality, infamous among therapists, provides an outstanding example. Borderlines often improve, only to suddenly become depressed and suicidal again as termination approaches. Moreover, contemporary therapies fail to recognize an intrinsic contradiction between the formal properties of therapy as it is currently practiced and the formal properties of psychotherapy that personality disorders logically require. The premise is simple: Because personality is more than the sum of its parts, therapy must be also (Millon, 1999).

To provide a background against which **synergistic psychotherapy** can be understood, we first provide an overview and critique of the contemporary trends identified previously. Next, synergistic psychotherapy is discussed as a logical outgrowth of the personality construct itself. Finally, barriers to the synergistic psychotherapy are presented, namely, the content shortcomings of the *DSM* and its lack of coordination to personality theory.

CONTEMPORARY TRENDS

Brief therapy, the common factors approach, and therapeutic eclecticism are the dominant reactions to the dogmatic past. Their greatest virtue lies in putting the emphasis on efficacy and the importance of treating the individual case.

Brief Therapy

Modern times have seen the development of an entire species called **brief therapies.** With names such as the Focused Approach (Malan, 1976), the Anxiety-Provoking Approach (Sifneous, 1972), the Confrontational Approach (Davanloo, 1980), Experiential Group Therapy (Budman, 1981; Budman & Gurman, 1988), Planned Single Session Therapy (Bloom, 1992), and the Brief Personality Approach (Horowitz et al., 1984), these therapies seek to accomplish as much or more than the long-term approaches of the past. All share certain common features: They are defined not so much by any therapeutic school as by the time interval in which therapy is practiced. Therapy must be structured so that something gets done. The therapist becomes more directive, and the patient is expected to take an active role in treatment. The themes to be discussed are often agreed on in advance and formalized in a therapeutic contract. If therapy stalls, anxiety-provoking techniques may be engaged to get things going again. Where brief therapy draws on some substantive guiding theory, it mainly seeks to adapt the techniques of a particular perspective to the time frame preferred by contemporary economic constraints.

Common Factors Approach

The **common factors approach** seeks to identify what is common to all therapies and then associate these factors with positive outcomes. Common factors enthusiasts are often fond of noting that most psychotherapies appear to be about equally effective. One of the original common factors proponents, Garfield (1957), for example, notes that treatment begins when an individual experiences a degree of discomfort sufficient to lead to consultation with a therapist as a socially sanctioned healer. Patients are universally afforded the opportunity to express their difficulties, to confide personal matters, and to unburden themselves of confusing or troubling thoughts and feelings. In turn, the therapist exhibits attentive interest and asks questions that elaborate what is presented. Further, every patient develops a relationship with the therapist. Most are good alliances with a reasonable level of mutual respect and trust. The patient gains the opportunity to rethink both self and situation and gains perspective on reality as well as a sense of increased competence and good fortune. Last, most therapists believe in the effectiveness of whatever therapy they practice. By conveying this positive outlook to the patient, they strengthen the conviction that their particular approach will be successful. J. D. Frank (1961) suggested that trustworthiness, competence, and the level of caring of the therapist are fundamental for effective psychotherapy. Also significant are arousing hope, encouraging behavioral change, stimulating emotional arousal and the corrective emotional experience, and developing new ways of understanding yourself. Further, all therapies, according to Frank, must confront demoralization, particularly loss of self-esteem and feelings of incompetence, alienation, and hopelessness. In the contemporary era, the number of common factors has multiplied greatly.

Therapeutic Eclecticism

More and more, clinicians identify themselves as **eclectic,** borrowing tools and techniques from wherever necessary to make treatment most effective. Accordingly, eclecticism is regarded as being open-minded and centered on what actually helps people, humanitarian virtues that are difficult to criticize. In contrast, school-oriented forms of psychotherapy dictate the perspective from which cases are conceptualized and often dictate the specific techniques to be employed in therapy as well. Nevertheless, almost everyone would agree that the therapy should be tailored to the patient, not the patient to the therapy. Eclecticism thus constitutes a giant step forward. Lazarus (1973, 1976, 1981), for example, argues that therapy techniques can be drawn from any number of schools and matched to the presenting problems, without necessarily accepting the theoretical orientation with which these techniques were originally associated. Evaluation, according to Lazarus, should proceed according to the BASIC IB—behavior, affect, sensation, imagery, cognition, interpersonal relationships, and biology—but also be selected on the basis of actual empirical evidence for their effectiveness. Developing their own brand of technical eclecticism, Beutler and Clarkin (1990) stress that outcome depends on numerous factors other than any specific treatment technique, including the outlook of the therapist and patient personality and history, as well as other specific and interactive aspects among treatment methods. In contrast to other eclectics, Beutler (1986) acknowledges that the number and diversity of variables and interactions among patient, therapist, situation, history, and current problems are so potentially vast that theory should be used as a guide to therapeutic selectivity.

APPRAISAL OF CONTEMPORARY TRENDS

Although the preceding contemporary trends represent an innovative improvement over the past, they nevertheless share an important shortcoming: They fail to develop forms of psychotherapy specific to Axis II and, therefore, implicitly treat the personality disorders as if they were identical with the symptom disorders of Axis I.

Brief Therapy

A corollary to Murphy's Law, "Anything that can go wrong, will go wrong," states that "Work expands to fill the time allotted it." With the rise of managed care, however, psychotherapists are now required to accomplish more in less time. The emphasis on efficiency has produced a variety of short-term and brief therapies, listed previously. Unfortunately, such therapies are unified only by their emphasis on the duration of therapy, not its substance. The duration of therapy should be dictated by the nature of the problem, not by economic necessity. Modes of therapy constructed to fit a given time frame naturally home in on the presenting problems. The goal is to resolve immediate difficulties and terminate therapy.

Personality, however, is enduring across time and situation. Moreover, personality disorders create a vulnerability to the development of other psychopathologies that endures across time and situation. Once additional Axis II disorders develop, their course and treatment are further complicated by the presence of personality problems. Clinicians know that a depressed patient with a personality disorder is much more difficult to treat than one without a personality disorder. The tendency of brief therapies to focus exclusively on the most severe immediate problem reflects a bias toward what is overt and easily operationalized. To optimize outcome, therapy should combine multiple interventions in a way that they become more than the sum of their parts, as is personality itself.

Common Factors

Enthusiasts of this approach seek elements common to all successful psychotherapies. In itself, this is a laudable beginning. However, it is doubtful that a single necessary and sufficient set of characteristics will prove uniformly effective for all mental disorders. Instead, these characteristics provide a foundation for effective therapy, against which the efficacy of specific treatments can be evaluated. We should certainly require that cognitive therapy for depression be more effective than simple warmth and empathy from a likable therapist, for example. In the same way, it would be very surprising if all subjects could be treated effectively with cognitive therapy alone, regardless of their personality disorder. The finding that all forms of school-oriented therapy are about equally good shows not that all therapies have common factors, but that no partial view of personality can be expected to succeed more often than any other. Because personality is the patterning of variables across the entire matrix of the person, efforts to treat the total phenomenon through a single perspective are doomed in advance. When applied to the personality disorders, the truth is not that all forms of therapy are about equally good, but that they are all about equally bad.

Technical Eclecticism

There is no doubt that eclecticism is an advance over the school-oriented psychotherapy of the past. Unfortunately, therapists are heard to say, "I consider myself an eclectic," as if eclecticism were like a political party to which you might belong rather than an attitude toward the practice of therapy. Technical eclecticism is a laudable effort to move forward in the face of stubborn difficulties, not the least of which is the contentious climate of hundreds of psychotherapies and perhaps an equal number of theories of psychopathology and personality. By appealing to whatever works, change as the ultimate goal of therapy moves to the forefront. Psychological theories are prevented from laying claim to certain disorders and thereby preempting other forms of treatment.

Eclecticism, however, is only an intermediate stage in the development of psychotherapy. In the absence of a complete theory of human nature, one that encloses each individual nature inside a matrix of psychological laws, we must all remain eclectics. In this case, eclecticism simply co-opts whatever techniques seem to go farthest given the nature of the difficulties to be resolved, essentially functioning as a means of coping with the complexity of persons and their pathologies until some better theory or better means is developed. Eclecticism thus reflects the relative immaturity of the field, not its essential nature.

Even if eclecticism were successful in almost every case, it would not be scientific until research could determine why it was effective. Knowing that it works is not enough. A technique or instrument may work well and even be used to great social benefit, but while its inner mechanisms remain a mystery, it begs for scrutiny. As an applied science, then, psychotherapy cannot advance by simply documenting the effectiveness of a particular technique with a particular disorder. Discovering a highly effective therapy may make you famous and may endear you forever to various managed care concerns, but it does not make you a scientist.

SYNERGISTIC PSYCHOTHERAPY

The process of therapy must be coordinated to the substance of that which is treated. To be both successful and scientific, therapeutic logic and technique should derive from a taxonomy that sorts essential kinds of personality pathology into a coherent framework. From the perspective of the physical sciences, this statement must seem obvious. Physics has the Standard Model, and chemistry has its Periodic Table. The first groups together the various subatomic particles; the second sorts the various elements. A chemical engineer who wants to perfect the chemical process used to make a particular compound, for example, may indeed examine what is common to other approaches, but only in connection with the logic of chemistry itself, to develop a superior solution that makes sense. Features from other approaches cannot be adopted simply according to their frequency. Instead, the laws of chemistry, in conjunction with the characteristics of the particular compound, dictate what will be successful.

Likewise, therapists must understand the characteristics and dynamics of the patients they treat, for these determine the outcome of therapy. Far from showing that psychotherapy has evolved, then, the contemporary approaches described previously reflect a broken and disjoint psychopathology, one in which the pure and applied branches of the science have developed independently. In the final analysis, we can only conclude that it is the formal synthetic properties of personality that dictate new forms of psychotherapy, provide a pathway to the integration of the historical dogmatic schools, and account for the rather startling finding that most psychotherapies are about equally effective.

In retrospect, the revolution against the dogmatism of the historical schools was inevitable. Whether psychoanalytic, cognitive, behavioral, or biological, each constitutes only a partial view of human nature. In the hard sciences, advancement occurs through attempts to falsify established models. The results support one theory while rejecting others. In contrast, the social sciences are intrinsically less bounded; advancement more often occurs when some new content area surges to the center of scientific awareness, creating a new way of looking at the field, a new paradigm. Thus, the psychodynamic school stresses the importance of the unconscious, defense mechanisms, and early object relations; therapy should make the unconscious conscious or unravel the noxious residuals of early caretaker relationships. The interpersonal school stresses the principles of correspondence and complementarity; therapy should not become ensnared in the same old vicious cycles, but instead promote the development of novel modes of conduct through noncomplementary responses. The cognitive school stresses the importance of automatic thoughts and cognitive distortions and beliefs; therapy educates clients to identify such thoughts and replace them with functional alternatives. Each perspective illuminates important domains of personality, but provides no necessary integrating principles. Instead, an intelligent eclecticism, a selectivity based mostly on past experiences with similar clients, is the current norm in psychotherapy.

The definition of personality, however, the patterning of variables across the entire matrix of the person, cannot support this norm. Personality is an inextricably interwoven structure of behaviors, cognitions, and intrapsychic processes. The interpenetration of psychic structures and functions is what distinguishes the disorders of personality from other clinical syndromes. The resulting synergism lends the whole personality an emergent tenacity that makes personality disorders exceedingly difficult to resolve, at least for traditional forms of therapy. Accordingly, a therapy of personality must have much the same formal structure as personality itself. Therapy must be more than the sum of its parts, just as personality is more than the sum of its parts. Therapy should be as integrated and, therefore, as potentially efficacious, as personality is integrated and, therefore, tenacious. In what the senior author of this text has termed **synergistic psychotherapy,** each intervention technique should be selected not only for its efficacy in resolving a singular pathological feature, but also for its contribution to the overall constellation of treatment procedures, of which it is but one. Personality pathologies thus represent that class of disorders for which the logic of the integrative mind-set is explicitly required. Any other choice is suboptimal. Otherwise, the personality disorders are simply misnomered and would be better regarded as the "cognitive disorders," the "interpersonal disorders," or the "psychodynamic disorders" (Millon, 1999).

The idea that personality is a functional-structural system makes certain predictions about personality and its most appropriate modes of therapy. First, it explains why personality disorders seem so clinically difficult. Every system naturally seeks the internal stability of homeostasis. For example, the stresses of everyday life make demands on the disordered personality, just as they do on the normal personality. These range from the mundane, such as getting up in the morning, to the profound, such as the death of a parent or the possibility of failing at a lifelong dream. Subjectively, such stressors make the person feel anxious, which can be dealt with in any number of ways. Rational coping mechanisms can be engaged in pursuit of a realistic solution;

alternatively, defense mechanisms can be used to repress, rechannel, or transform anxiety. Either way, however, the goal is always stability, not change. For personality, each domain uses the others as ballast, reinforcing the entire structure. As enduring and pervasive ways of thinking, feeling, and perceiving, personality disorders have as their goal a homeostasis that is intrinsically at odds with the psychosocial world, leading to vicious circles that perpetuate their same dilemmas repeatedly. By definition, theirs is a stable, pervasive, enduring pathology that has the whole matrix of the person as its ballast. Accordingly, the very nature of personality predicts that strongly school-oriented interventions, those that issue from a single perspective, should be notoriously infectious with the personality disorders. And that is the real-world experience of clinicians everywhere.

To return to the theme presented at the beginning of this section, strictly linear interventions cannot succeed with disorders that are maintained by reciprocal causality. By fighting fire with fire, by applying multiple techniques in coordination with the substantive characteristics of the individual case as identified in the assessment, therapy can be applied so that the equilibrium of the personality is "punctured," setting into motion change processes that build on and reinforce each other, leading to change across the entire system. Synergistic psychotherapy is thus concerned with the application of multiple techniques, potentially drawn from every domain of personality, but selected specifically to exhibit an emergent efficacy beyond what would be expected from the application of any technique alone. In contrast, school-oriented therapy can be regarded only as linear and Newtonian, and the efficacy of therapeutic eclecticism, which lacks any theoretically derived taxonomy and its coordination with the personality domains, through which individuals are understood, can be regarded only as random. Synergistic psychotherapy, school-oriented psychotherapy, and eclectic therapy are contrasted in Figure 4.2.

Potentiated Pairings

Potentiated pairings (Millon, 1990, 1999) draw on two or more techniques applied simultaneously to overcome problematic characteristics that might be refractory were each technique administered separately. Such therapeutic composites pull and push for change on a variety of fronts, leading to a therapy of integrated techniques sufficient to address the tenacity of personality pathology itself.

Catalytic Sequences

Potentiated pairings are designed to be applied simultaneously. In contrast, **catalytic sequences** plan the order of interventions as a means of optimizing their impact. The catalytic sequence is the psychotherapeutic equivalent of the one-two punch in boxing. In effect, it is the opposite of a vicious circle, in that it constitutes a constructive arrangement of techniques designed to produce a spiral back toward psychological health.

Designing Synergistic Arrangements

The ability to borrow and interweave techniques from multiple perspectives gives synergistic psychotherapy tremendous scope: Because personality is cognitive, interpersonal, psychodynamic, and biological, the nature of the personality construct itself dictates that techniques can, should, and must be pulled from any of these perspectives as needed. Eclecticism is simply opportunistic concerning techniques, but the nature of personality

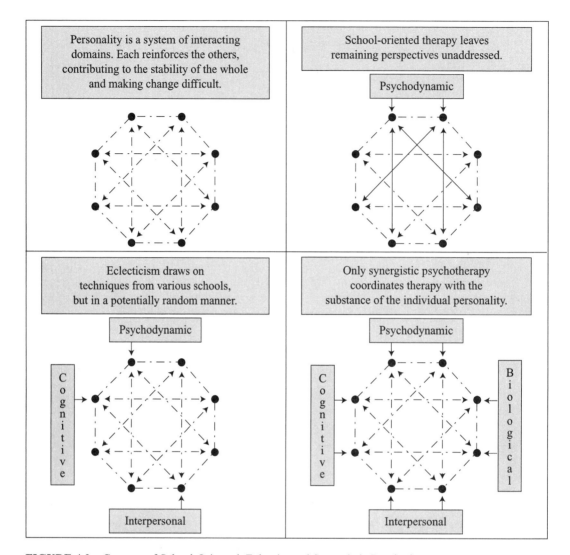

FIGURE 4.2   Contrast of School-Oriented, Eclectic, and Synergistic Psychotherapy.

as a construct specifically predicts the inutility of therapy administered from any single perspective alone. Accordingly, synergistic psychotherapy specifically requires that multiple techniques be pulled from the various perspectives and coordinated to the substance of the pathology. As such, the design of synergistic arrangements assumes extensive knowledge of the individual case. Assessment must be carried beyond the level of simple diagnosis. The important questions are the same for any assessment: What defense mechanisms are typically employed by the person? What are the sensitive issues that evoke these mechanisms? How do they impact relationships with others? How do they exacerbate long-standing problems? What cognitive style and interpersonal conduct descriptors best capture the flavor of the case? How do others react to the individual's interpersonal attitude? How does this attitude prevent or promote the solution of problems

---

FOCUS ON TREATMENT PLAN

Maximizing Supervision

Finding the Most Suitable Therapeutic Approach

Having learned much from her first supervisor, a psychodynamic sage, Jenna was eager to begin studying with her second supervisor, known for his knowledge of cognitive techniques. When her first client, a depressed male graduate student, scored in the narcissistic range on the MCMI-III, her new supervisor recommended that she educate the client in the principles of cognitive therapy, focusing particularly on the discovery of automatic thoughts and their connection with his self-image, which featured quickly vacillating appraisals of his ability, ranging from godlike to pathetically inadequate. After the first two sessions, however, she noticed that the client seemed increasingly condescending, apparently chaffed by her attempts. Realizing that the personality disorder was the most important factor driving his depression, Jenna suggested to her new supervisor that perhaps the automatic thoughts underlying the transference itself could be discussed as a means of synergizing the psychodynamic, interpersonal, and cognitive approaches. By allowing therapy to temporarily refocus on the exploration of the narcissistic self, the client's mood lifted and the discovery of automatic thoughts proceeded more quickly. Thus led to the edge of insight, the client soon discovered that the transference relationship formed an instructive microcosm of his relationships outside the therapy office.

---

in relationships? What cognitive distortions perpetuate maladaptive appraisals of personal and social realities? And so on.

Diagnostic labels assist somewhat in answering these questions, but are rarely definitive. By allowing multiple secondary diagnoses, even the *DSM-IV* recognizes that an antisocial-narcissist overflows what is merely an antisocial or that a dependent-avoidant overflows what is merely a dependent. Most individuals, in fact, combine aspects of two or more personality disorders. Because each personality disorder is strongly associated with certain defense mechanisms, with a particular cognitive style, with certain interpersonal attitudes, and so on, these prototypal features become hypotheses for the individual case that can be checked against the actual assessment data. Narcissists, for example, tend to rationalize; they look at their conduct after the fact and try to imagine how it might be made reasonable. This suggests that your narcissistic patient probably does the same thing, a hypothesis that can be checked against other information or in therapy itself. However, if the subject is diagnosed as a narcissistic-dependent, this suggests that dependent features infiltrate the primary diagnosis. Rather than rationalize, dependents tend to introject, strengthening bonds with caretakers in order to co-opt their instrumentalities in the real world. Most individuals do, in fact, combine aspects of two or more personalities, creating assessment and therapy cases that are naturally complex. Does the narcissistic-dependent lean more toward rationalization or introjection? If both, which is preferred in what kind of situation? Considering such questions takes the assessment far beyond mere diagnostic labels, falsifying the classification system while building idiographic validity. And this is exactly how it should be. Clinicians do not treat prototypes; they treat persons.

Focus on Therapeutic Process

The Sequence of Techniques

From the Immediate Problem to Underlying Issues

A sophomore presented at the university counseling center complaining of stuttering during her speech class. Her next speech, due in three weeks, was to be the longest yet, and she felt terrified. By using guided imagery to recreate the actual event of giving a speech, Jenna was able to explore changes in her anxiety level and automatic thoughts on a moment-to-moment basis, from preparing the speech the night before, to getting up to give the speech, to saying her first words, to starting to stutter, and then to finishing and sitting down again. Most of these cognitions focused on making a fool of herself. To deal with the immediate threat, the upcoming speech, graded exposure through imagery was used to help extinguish her anxiety reaction. Although the speech was not the very best in the class, it was also not the catastrophe she feared. Following this, therapy began to focus more broadly on self-esteem issues that had punished all attempts at self-assertion almost from her earliest memories. By addressing the immediate problem and then shifting the focus to broader personality issues that would otherwise tend to reinstate the original problem, the client was able to take an advanced speaking course, receiving a B+ for her effort.

BARRIERS TO SYNERGISTIC PSYCHOTHERAPY

Although synergistic psychotherapy provides a powerful means of treating personality pathology, several impediments stand in its way.

Confusion of Personality Styles and Personality Traits

The constructs derived from the evolutionary model may be described either as personality styles or personality disorders. Styles and disorders are distinguished in terms of their relative level of pathology: Personality styles shade gently into personality disorders, with styles falling in the normal range and disorders falling in the pathological range. Both are higher order constructs composed of personality traits. More significantly, styles and disorders refer to constructs that integrate the part-functions of personality, whereas traits are simple behavioral consistencies within the various personality domains or perspectives. The distinction between these two levels is essential. When viewing traits as unitary, clinicians have no impetus for assessing the subsidiary domains of personality, such as interpersonal conduct or cognitive style. The assessment process may be prematurely foreclosed by the conclusion that the subject is high on the trait of dependence, for example. In turn, this makes impossible more sophisticated forms of therapy such as potentiated pairings and catalytic sequences. Personality styles and disorders are operationalized in terms of the various perspectives on personality; traits are not.

Current Diagnostic Standards

To be truly useful to therapists, diagnostic criteria should be addressed to everything that personality is; that is, the diagnostic criteria of the *DSM-IV* should be coordinated

FOCUS ON DIAGNOSTIC ACCURACY

Looking beyond the Obvious

Presuming Diagnosis Undermines the Clinical Process

An intelligent-looking undergraduate senior majoring in mathematical physics presented at the university counseling center complaining that his grades were slipping and that he felt "incredibly anxious." During the clinical interview, he announced that he was much more intelligent than the other students and always received the highest grades in his mathematics and physics classes, at least until recently. Further exploration revealed that his father was a mathematical physicist at the same university, but had recently accepted the position of department chair at another institution on the opposite coast. Although intellectual testing in fact showed superior intellectual ability, it was also true that the son identified strongly with his father and greatly enjoyed the time he spent with his father, who tutored him through the most difficult problems. Several weeks into counseling, he was able to admit that he feared that without his father, he would no longer receive such high marks and others would revise their opinion of his intelligence accordingly. He received a presumptive diagnosis of narcissistic-dependent personality disorder, later changed to narcissistic-dependent style. Although his self-image was somewhat inflated, he could not be called grandiose, he did not dominate and exploit others shamelessly, and he was not void of empathy (features typical of a pure narcissistic personality disorder). Cognitive techniques focused on identifying and refuting catastrophic cognitions associated with the possibility of receiving a low grade ("My father won't love me anymore"). Simultaneously, his narcissistic needs, along with his dependency on his father for esteem, were addressed by suggesting that he tutor other students in mathematics or physics, all of whom praised his command of the material.

with the various perspectives on personality. Unfortunately, this is not the case. Often, the diagnostic criteria are redundant, weighting the diagnosis heavily toward one perspective while omitting another perspective completely. Personality criteria should do more than classify persons into categories, a rather minimalistic function. Instead, diagnostic criteria should encourage a substantive and integrative understanding of the patient across all domains in which personality is expressed. Future *DSMs* will probably gravitate toward this position, but the *DSM-IV* just isn't there yet. As a result, a therapist relying exclusively on the *DSM-IV* may remain unaware of important aspects of functioning that work to reinforce and perpetuate a patient's difficulties, thus sabotaging the outcome of therapy. If the constraints on therapeutic change lie elsewhere in the personality, the therapist may be left treating abnormalities peripheral to the real problem.

Lack of Criterion Standards for Outcome Studies

Unfortunately, the *DSM* is viewed as the diagnostic gold standard, and there is no gold standard for the gold standard. The goal of any measurement system is the appraisal of all relevant properties of the objects to be measured. Because the *DSM-IV* weights certain domains on personality and omits others, criterion groups selected for outcome research would be weighted in accidental ways. Moreover, no effort has been made in the

---

FOCUS ON OTHER SUPERVISION

Peer Consultation

Viewing Colleagues as Other Supervisory Resources

During Jenna's second semester at the counseling center, a beginning therapist, Mark, asked her what intervention might be appropriate for a client who scored high on the trait of dependency. By misunderstanding the relationship between personality styles and personality traits, Mark was naturally looking for the single best approach. Once he understood, however, that his new case was better described as a dependent style, he was able to look deeper into the client's personality and tailor a variety of interventions to her interpersonal conduct, use of defense mechanisms, and cognitive distortions.

DSM to equate diagnostic thresholds across disorders with their associated level of severity. Individuals who meet the minimum diagnostic threshold for a personality disorder, Axis II, should be relatively equal in terms of the severity of their pathology, Axis V. No such studies have ever been done. Consequently, research questions that ask whether a particular technique is more effective with dependents than with borderlines are impossible to answer, for the latter are likely to be more pathological from the moment of sample selection. In the future, it is hoped that the understanding of personality pathology as anchored to the entire matrix of the person will lead to more adequately operationalized criteria sets for the Axis II disorders and, in turn, to a synergistic form of therapy as integrative as are the disorders themselves.

Professional Education

Synergistic psychotherapy can initially be demanding of a therapist's education and knowledge base. Many therapists in the United States are acquainted with behavioral and cognitive principles, for example, but fewer receive training in the interpersonal school, and far fewer receive instruction concerning the importance and operation of

---

FOCUS ON CLINICAL JUDGMENT

Beyond the DSM-IV Criteria

Understanding the Client as Multidimensional

While comparing a highly introverted client against the *DSM-IV* criteria for schizoid personality disorder, Jenna noticed that the diagnostic criteria focused mainly on the interpersonal perspective. Cognitive style, defense mechanisms, and object representations were not mentioned at all. Her supervisor explained that because the *DSM* followed the medical model, its diagnostic criteria neglected some personality domains and emphasized others. Together, they decided that a complete understanding of the client would require a broader knowledge base than was represented in the *DSM-IV* criteria.

defense mechanisms. Such therapists engage their clients through the same domains of personality repeatedly, practicing school-oriented psychotherapy because their education permits nothing more. Even worse, such therapists discover pathology only in those perspectives through which they were trained. As a result, they recruit change processes only from these same domains, making an optimized idiographic therapy impossible. No single school-oriented modality gives therapists access to all the change processes that might be called on to maximize therapeutic efficacy. Synergistic comprehensiveness is the wave of the future in the therapies of the twenty-first century.

Summary

The theme of this chapter is that assessment and therapy should be continuous with personality as an integrative construct. Assessment is the basis of therapy. The clinician should gain a complete scientific understanding of the interaction of current symptoms, personality traits, and psychosocial factors. The axes of the multiaxial model should be separately assessed and then integrated into a single composite, the case conceptualization.

In the relationship between pure and applied science, the nomothetic approach seeks to find universal principles applicable to all individuals in a population. The idiographic approach emphasizes the complexity of the individual seeking to understand the totality of a single person. In diagnosing a person, the *DSM* attempts to retain the best of a construct-centered approach, while allowing for a measure of individuality. First, the *DSM* allows multiple personality disorder diagnoses to be assigned. Combinations of two, three, or even four personality disorders are not uncommon. Second, each personality disorder is operationalized as a prototype that consists of many characteristics. There are probably hundreds of ways of satisfying the diagnostic criteria for any two personality disorders. Such vast possibilities are intended to accommodate individuality within the diagnostic system, while the shorthand of diagnostic labels nevertheless recognizes that all subjects who receive the same diagnosis bear a family resemblance. In any categorical classification system, the question is which labels the subject will receive. The idiographic perspective, however, reminds us that taxonomies take us only so far—that diagnostic constructs are only reference points that facilitate understanding, against which the individual should be compared and contrasted. Because the goal is an idiographic understanding of the person, assessment is really an endeavor to show the limitations of the diagnostic system with respect to the person at hand.

In contrast to the physical sciences, measurement instruments in personality and psychopathology are inherently imprecise. Five broad sources of information are available to help describe the clinical problem. Each has its own advantages and limitations. In the first source, the self-report inventory, subjects literally report on themselves by completing a standard list of items. In the second source of information, rating scales and checklists, a person familiar with the subject completes this form in order to provide an alternative perspective. Third, in the clinical interview, the clinician asks the questions and the subject responds verbally, often in a free form style. The clinician is free to following any particular line of questioning desired and usually mixes standard questions with those specific to the current problem. Finally, the fourth source, projective techniques, is an attempt to access unconscious structures and processes that would not ordinarily be available to the subject at the level of verbal report. The use of intimates of the subject who can act as informants, perhaps a spouse, teacher, parent, or good friend, someone who can provide perspective on the problem, might also be considered a source of information. Physiological measurements, neurotransmitter or hormone levels, for example, provide a final source, though these are not available to most therapists.

Measurement in all sciences is limited by biasing and distorting factors. Certain distortions arise because of the personality style of the respondent or interviewer. Different personalities construe the world in different ways. Other limitations on clinical information arise from subjects' motives and their level of personality pathology. In other cases, some personalities consciously distort information to somehow take advantage of the system or avoid some unpleasant consequence of their own behavior. Most self-report instruments have indexes that can detect attempts to fake good or fake bad, though they must be interpreted cautiously in the context of other test information. Whatever the situation, clinicians are always advised to keep the principle of self-interest firmly in mind.

Most patients who require psychological testing present with one or more Axis I disorders. Traits refer to long-standing personality characteristics that endure over time and situations. In contrast, states refer to potentially short-lived conditions, usually emotional in nature. Anxiety, depression, and loss of reality contact can all affect the results of personality testing. Crossover effects from state to trait are an expectable part of assessment and must be considered by whomever interprets the test results.

Psychological tests can be interpreted at different levels: items, scales, and profiles. The item is the standard stimulus in psychological assessment. Since every subject who completes an instrument answers the same items, their responses can be directly compared to those of others. A scale is composed of many items that tap the same psychological construct, so that a scale score reflects a summary of the particular behaviors expressed in those same item responses. A set of scale scores is referred to as a profile or profile configuration. The profile stands in place of the person as a collection of scales, just as a collection of items stands in place of the construct they assess.

A variety of self-report instruments are available to assess the personality disorders. With more than 550 items, the Minnesota Multiphasic Personality Inventory-2 (MMPI) is not so much a standardized test as a standardized item pool that belongs to psychology itself. Literally hundreds of personality scales have been derived from the MMPI throughout its long career. In fact, there are now more auxiliary scales than there are items on the MMPI. The Millon Clinical Multiaxial Inventory (MCMI), now in its third edition, is far the most widely used personality disorder test. A principal goal in constructing the MCMI-III was to keep the total number of items constituting the inventory small enough to encourage use in all types of diagnostic and treatment settings, yet large enough to permit the assessment of a wide range of clinically relevant behaviors. At 175 items, the final form is much shorter than are comparable instruments, with terminology geared to an eighth-grade reading level. As a result, most subjects complete the MCMI-III in 20 to 30 minutes. The inventory is intended for subjects believed to possess a personality disorder and is generally not used with normals. The MCMI is frequently used in research. More than 650 publications to date have included or focused primarily on the MCMI, with approximately 60 to 70 new references currently published annually. Both the MMPI and MCMI have variants designed for use with adolescents.

A number of clinical interviews are available for the personality disorders. The Structured Clinical Interview for *DSM-IV* Axis II Personality Disorders (SCID-II) is a semistructured diagnostic interview assessing the 12 personality disorders included in *DSM-IV.* The Structured Interview for *DSM-IV* Personality (SIDP-IV; Pfohl et al., 1997) is a semistructured clinical interview that assesses all the personality disorders of the *DSM-IV,* plus the self-defeating personality from the revised third edition of the *DSM* (the sadistic personality is not included).

The history of psychotherapy is fraught with dogmatism. In the past few decades, however, dissatisfaction with school-oriented therapy (e.g., behavioral, psychody-namic), together with a new emphasis on efficacy motivated by managed care, has led to the development of compromise approaches. Three trends currently dominate: First, *brief therapy* claims to achieve as much or greater progress in less time by carefully selecting patients and providing highly structured forms of intervention specific to the presenting problem. Second, the *common factors approach* seeks to unify much of psychotherapy by identifying factors common to all effective therapies. The argument here is that all therapies are more alike than different, and a better psychotherapy can be created by returning to the core principles and techniques from which particular therapies diversify. Third, *therapeutic eclecticism* holds that the techniques of various schools should be incorporated into treatment as necessary, without regard for the theoretical model in which the technique was first developed. While these contemporary trends all represent an innovative improvement over the past, they nevertheless share an important shortcoming: They fail to develop forms of psychotherapy specific to Axis II and, therefore, implicitly treat the personality disorders as if they were identical with the symptom disorders of Axis I.

Synergistic psychotherapy, on the other hand, is concerned with the application of multiple techniques, potentially drawn from every domain of personality, but selected specifically to exhibit an emergent efficacy beyond what would be expected from the application of any technique alone. *Potentiated pairings* draw on two or more techniques applied simultaneously to overcome problematic characteristics that might be refractory were each technique administered separately. Potentiated pairings are designed to be applied simultaneously. In contrast, *catalytic sequences* plan the order of interventions as a means of optimizing their impact. The ability to borrow and interweave techniques from multiple perspectives gives synergistic psychotherapy tremendous scope: Since personality is cognitive, interpersonal, psychodynamic, and biological, the nature of the personality construct itself dictates that techniques can, should, and must be pulled from any of these perspectives as needed.

Chapter 5

The Antisocial Personality

Objectives

- What are the *DSM-IV* criteria for the antisocial personality?
- What is *psychopathy* and how does it differ from the *antisocial personality?* What is the difference between *psychopathy* and *sociopathy?*
- The adventurer and dissenting personalities are normal variants of the antisocial. Describe their characteristics and relate them to the more disordered criteria of the *DSM-IV.*
- Do antisocial women show a pattern of behavioral pathology different from the pattern of antisocial men?
- Explain how different personality styles combine to form each of the subtypes of the antisocial personality.
- What is the historical significance of the terms *moral insanity* and *psychopathic inferiority?*
- The behavior of antisocials appears to be highly influenced by biological factors from early on. What is Lykken's position as to the most effective parenting for a child with strong temperamental qualities? What is the meaning of *semantic aphasia?*
- Summarize the biological evidence for the antisocial personality.
- What is meant by the psychoanalytic notion that antisocials lack a mature superego?
- Why is the interpersonal behavior of the antisocial characterized as "pure interpersonal hostility" and "irresponsible"?
- How does the antisocial cognitive style, which appears to be highly vulnerable to the influence of immediate rewards and gratifications, contribute to the overall expression of this personality disorder?
- What are the core beliefs of the antisocial?
- Antisocials share characteristics with other personality disorders. List these other disorders and explain the distinction between each and the antisocial.
- Why is substance abuse so prevalent among antisocials?

- Why are countertransference issues so important in therapy with antisocials?
- List therapeutic goals for the antisocial personality.

In the antisocial personality, badness and madness seem to shade together. Sometimes, antisocials' crimes are so incomprehensible and morally repugnant that the act alone makes us doubt their sanity. For example, the normal person has no way of identifying with Jeffrey Dahmer, who killed, had sex with, and ate the bodies of many of his victims, or with Herman Mudgett (see Stone, 1993), whose evil adventures ended when he was hung just before the end of the nineteenth century. Mudgett, a graduate of the University of Michigan's Medical College and a practicing pharmacist in Chicago, excelled at insurance fraud and the seduction of young women, at least 27 of whom were killed after signing papers that made Mudgett the recipient of their insurance and savings. Drugged with chloroform after a night of prenuptial sex, each would awaken trapped in the elevator shaft of an elaborate three-story office building, specially designed by Mudgett to conceal his nefarious activities. This building, outfitted with trap doors, soundproof rooms, peepholes, enormous furnaces, and vats of acid to dissolve human remains was dubbed his "Castle." Savoring the terror of the trapped girls, he would pump in poison gas and then haul their lifeless bodies onto the dissecting table for the removal of parts that held for him a special fascination.

Fortunately, Dahmer and Mudgett are extreme examples. In fact, not all antisocials are criminals (Alexander, 1930), and not all criminals are antisocials. Serial killers, in particular, are extremely rare (Hare, 1993), despite public fascination with them. In fact, only a minor subset of the antisocial pattern comes into conflict with the law. Cast in scientific clinical terms, the social consequences of the disorder are not necessarily repugnant. In fact, individuals with normal-range antisocial traits are often rewarded by our competitive society, where the ability to act tough and bend the rules is admired as necessary for success and survival in a dog-eat-dog world. Between the extremes of normal adjustment and the most brutal abuse of human life lie many shades of gray. Some antisocials jealously guard their autonomy, striking preemptively at anyone who might restrict or condemn their behavior. In contrast, although normal variants do sometimes impulsively transgress social standards, most find a place for themselves in the rugged side of business, military, or political life.

Consider the case of Toni, a 23-year-old female introduced in Case 5.1. Like most antisocials, Toni has a reputation of being "difficult to get along with." She probably likes it this way, and she probably feels that anything else would be a sign of weakness and others would only take advantage of her. In fact, she works hard at creating a formidable and aggressive image (see criterion 4 in Case 5.1), thus identifying her to the world as someone to be taken seriously—someone you'd better keep your distance from. Her posture, clothes, attitude, and remarks cultivate that image. She wants to impress the listener with her callousness and self-sufficiency. Not surprisingly, Toni has a police record; possession and theft seem to be her favorites, though an arrest for prostitution also appears, probably in connection with a drug habit. The immediate cause of her problems, however, is a peace disturbance for fighting with her neighbor. Ask her why, and she'll tell you, "I don't take anybody's shit," without ever breaking eye contact.

Toni's problems go back a long way. Like many antisocials' families, her history includes a conspicuous absence of prosocial role models. Toni's father died of mysterious

Toni presented for therapy as mandated by court order.[1] She was recently charged with disturbing the peace, after a fight with her neighbor escalated into punching and shouting, and with possession of narcotics with intent to sell. People in her apartment building describe her as "impossible to get along with, with a real chip on her shoulder." She puts forward an image of provocation and challenge that the other residents find intimidating. She dresses the part well, with a black leather jacket, numerous body piercings, and tattoos on every knuckle. Her hostility and penchant for lying about every detail from the important to the insignificant make history-taking difficult. When asked what started the fight that led to her latest arrest, she replies, "Cause I don't take anybody's shit."

Although Toni is only 23 years old, her tough exterior and hard lifestyle make her appear much older. She scoffs when asked about her religious affiliation: "Jesus don't love nobody, or at least he don't love me. The only religion I have is 'do unto others before they do unto you.'" Her police record corroborates this life philosophy. It includes multiple arrests for possession, theft, and prostitution. Toni is known by a variety of different names throughout the city, some based on stolen identities of real people and some purely invented. She has a collection of driver's licenses and social security cards that help her set up lines of credit across town. She proudly boasts that she has perfected the art of obtaining huge lines of credit in electronics stores based on false identities and then selling the goods for quick cash.

Toni is the middle of five children, including two stepchildren, and she does not maintain contact with any of her siblings. Her father died when she was 5 years old under mysterious conditions, possibly drug-related. Her stepfather paid little attention to the children and worked away from home most of the time. Discipline was administered sporadically and violently by her mother, who would often explode in alcohol-induced rages. During these episodes, Toni usually ran away and stayed overnight with friends, until things "cooled down."

The quality of her home life appears to have deteriorated as the years went on. Her school attendance became irregular when her mother took an early morning job at a bakery near their home to pay the bills. With no one at home to monitor her behavior, Toni found it much more interesting to spend the day at the riverfront than at school. Eventually, she began using marijuana and then selling it casually as a means of supporting her own habit. Robbing strangers, usually women, at knifepoint was something she did "a couple of times a month." By the time she was 15, her visits home became infrequent, which Toni attributes to her mother's explosive temper. By the time she was 18, she had been arrested three times, once for possession, once for shoplifting, and once for animal abuse when she lit a stray cat on fire with hairspray and a cigarette lighter. When asked if she feels guilty for any of this, she says, "No way, no one ever felt guilty for what they did to me." She admits to heroin use and occasional needle sharing and says she is not afraid of HIV. "Whatever happens, happens, you know."

When asked about her family of origin, Toni states, "Don't have one, don't need one!" When asked how she supports herself, she says with a smirk, "I get by." In fact, she has never held a job for more than three weeks. "I'm not the kind of person that can get up in the morning and be somewhere on time," she says, "and besides, who could make it on what they want to give you? I am looking for bigger and better things." As the interview moves on, Toni clearly states that she has entered therapy only to avoid prison time for trying to sell cocaine to an undercover cop. She is quick to rationalize and blame others for her current plight: "The apartment was my boyfriend's. I just knew where the stuff was. That cop was a good actor cause I thought he would kill me if I hadn't sold it to him." To hear her tell it, she was an innocent victim, just in the wrong place at the wrong time.

4

B

1

2

C

7

5

6

2

Antisocial Personality Disorder
DSM-IV Criteria

A. There is a pervasive pattern of disregard for and violation of the rights of others occurring since age 15 years, as indicated by three (or more) of the following:

(1) failure to conform to social norms with respect to lawful behaviors as indicated by repeatedly performing acts that are grounds for arrest

(2) deceitfulness, as indicated by repeated lying, use of aliases, or conning others for personal profit or pleasure

(3) impulsivity or failure to plan ahead

(4) irritability and aggressiveness, as indicated by repeated physical fights or assaults

(5) reckless disregard for safety of self or others

(6) consistent irresponsibility, as indicated by repeated failure to sustain consistent work behavior or honor financial obligations

(7) lack of remorse, as indicated by being indifferent to or rationalizing having hurt, mistreated, or stolen from another

B. The individual is at least age 18 years.

C. There is evidence of Conduct Disorder with onset before age 15 years.

D. The occurrence of antisocial behavior is not exclusively during the course of Schizophrenia or a Manic Episode.

[1]Numbers mark aspects of the case most consistent with *DSM* criteria, and do not necessarily indicate that the case "meets" diagnostic criteria in this respect.

causes when she was 5. According to family lore, his death was probably drug-related, a memory that may have somehow encouraged her own drug use. Her stepfather paid little attention to the kids and worked away from home most of the time. Her mother provided only inconsistent discipline and was prone to fly into alcohol-induced rages. For Toni, running away seems to have been a matter of survival, a way of taking time out from a toxic family. Eventually, she found it easier to drop out of school and leave home rather than battle it out. With her mother and father as role models, we can imagine that life must have seemed discouraging, if not futile. Antisocial personality disorder requires evidence of conduct disorder (CD) before the age of 15 (see criterion C in Case 5.1). By this age, we find Toni robbing others at knifepoint and smoking and dealing marijuana on a casual basis to support her own habit. By age 18, her problems have escalated, with arrests for possession, shoplifting, and animal abuse.

Like most antisocials, Toni appears to lack a conscience. Her statement, "No one ever felt guilty for what they did to me," is probably partly true and partly manipulative, intended to evoke pity, give insight into her past, and justify her absence of remorse (see criterion 7) all at the same time. She sneers at religious faith and instead puts forward her own moral principle: "Do unto others before they do unto you." With no obvious prosocial impulses and no internal moral restraints on action, Toni is free to do whatever she wants, whenever she wants. The only barrier to her actions is society itself, and the only constraints she respects are those that society can enforce through its police presence and the threat of punishment or those that others can enforce through their own threats of harm or revenge.

Her lack of conscience creates and amplifies a variety of other antisocial characteristics. Toni is chronically deceitful (see criterion 2). Her use of aliases and stolen identities is a calculated means of pursuing illegal activities while avoiding detection, either by the law or anyone else. There is no way of knowing for what crimes she might actually be responsible. She also has no conscience where her own safety or that of others is involved (see criterion 5), as indicated by her admission of needle sharing, followed by the irresponsible and frankly stupid statement that she is not afraid of HIV. Toni is also unable to maintain steady employment, preferring to obtain money by racking up huge debts in other people's names with no intention of honoring the obligations (see criterion 6). For her, illegal activities provide much more money and immediate reward than legitimate employment. The concept of creating a satisfying life for herself is probably not even within her scope of contemplating at this point.

Although Toni would qualify for a diagnosis of antisocial personality disorder, the terms **psychopath** and **sociopath** also compete for clinical currency in describing individuals who flagrantly and pervasively violate the rights of others. Antisocial personality disorder is currently the official term used in *DSM-IV* (APA, 1994). However, the terms psychopath and sociopath are often bantered about to describe the people who commit heinous crimes. A writer's choice of one term versus the other is often arbitrary or a matter of preference rather than based on concrete scientific differentiations. However, one often used distinction between psychopath and sociopath is the user's belief in the origins of the disorder. Psychopaths are believed to possess some constitutional disposition to the syndrome. In contrast, sociopaths are biologically normal, but develop antisocial characteristics through incompetent or hostile socialization, mainly defective parenting.

The psychopath and sociopath are probably best viewed as existing on a continuum. Development is always an interaction between the individual and social environment.

Thus, some psychopaths receive defective parenting and maltreatment from infancy, like the sociopath, whereas others come from loving homes. Likewise, some sociopaths could possess a biological predisposition to the disorder, perhaps through an irritable temperament, for example, but nevertheless experience incredible levels of neglect and abuse. The pure psychopath and pure sociopath, then, are really just abstractions, not mutually exclusive syndromes. For any given individual, the focus is not, "Which one?" Instead, understanding the particular person requires understanding the interaction of biological and social influences, starting at conception and running across the life span. Nevertheless, these terms are often used loosely, with all three overlapping one another to some extent. This chapter is concerned primarily with the antisocial personality, but often refers to the psychopath where its empirical literature is more highly developed.

The construct of psychopathy was made famous by Hervey Cleckley's *The Mask of Sanity,* first published in 1941. Vivid case examples, compelling writing, and a list of defining characteristics combined to make the work an instant classic. Whereas the noxious behaviors of the antisocial are often obvious, Cleckley held that psychopaths often cloak themselves in the trappings of normality. Unlike the stereotype of the common criminal, psychopaths were believed to come from "good homes" with loving parents, but nevertheless damage or destroy lives without remorse, shame, or conscience. Most are pathological liars adept at sizing up situations and feigning sincerity, thus allowing them to literally flourish undetected behind a "mask of sanity." According to Cleckley, such individuals possess a deep-seated inability to understand the emotional dimension of language, particularly those aspects connected with feelings of attachment and empathy.

Unlike the antisocial personality, the Cleckley psychopath gives us a rich appreciation for the inner detachment with which such individuals destroy life. We diagnose the antisocial, but we "know" the psychopath. By subjecting Cleckley's list of defining characteristics to rigorous methods of scale development, Robert Hare and his associates constructed a clinical rating scale, now revised. Twenty items define the psychopathic prototype (Hare et al., 1990); some focus on long-standing personality traits and others on characteristic behaviors and life events. The total portrait suggests an individual who is not only antisocial, as evidenced by early behavior problems, multiple short marriages, juvenile delinquency, a versatile criminal past, a parasitic lifestyle, and sexual promiscuity, but also narcissistic, as evidenced by traits such as egocentricity, grandiosity, intolerance of boredom, lack of empathy, manipulativeness, and an inability to feel remorse. Stone (1993) suggests the additional item of imperviousness to shame to illustrate the psychopath's complete lack of internal behavioral controls.

Given this portrait of Toni, we are now in a position to approach additional issues, which form the plan of this chapter. First, we explore the continuum from normal antisocial traits to the pathological or "abnormal" antisocial personality disorder; then we move on to variations on the basic antisocial theme. After that, biological, psychodynamic, interpersonal, and cognitive perspectives on the antisocial personality are described. These sections form the core of what is scientific in personality. By seeking to explain what we observe in character sketches like Toni's, we hope to move beyond literary anecdote and enter the domain of theory. We present history and description side by side, noting the contributions of past thinkers, each of whom tends to bring into focus a different aspect of the disorder. Developmental hypotheses are also reviewed but are tentative for all personality disorders. Next, the section " Evolutionary Developmental

Perspective" shows how the existence of the personality disorder follows from the laws of evolution. Also included are a comparison between the antisocial and other theory-derived constructs and a discussion of how antisocial personalities tend to develop Axis I disorders. Finally, we survey how the disorder might be treated through psychotherapy, organizing our material in terms of classical approaches to the field: the biological, psychodynamic, interpersonal, and cognitive perspectives.

From Normality to Abnormality

Many readers will be surprised that some of their best and most admired qualities express characteristics associated with the antisocial personality, though certainly in a muted form. Adaptive traits of the more normal style include a capacity for self-sufficiency, ambition, competitiveness, and a constructive pursuit of individuality and self-determination. Oldham and Morris (1995, p. 217) describe **adventurers,** intrepid individuals who pushed the frontiers by crossing oceans, breaking records, and even walking on the moon. Adventurers live on the edge, these authors state, challenging boundaries and restrictions. Risk and discovery are their rewards. Real-life examples likely include famous explorers such as Christopher Columbus, as well as John Glenn and other test pilots. For such persons, adventure provides a route to freedom that is socially acceptable, even admired as stereotypically masculine. According to Oldham and Morris, they are nonconformers with their own internal value system, they love challenges, they assume people can take care of themselves, and they are interpersonally persuasive and reluctant to settle down. Though mischievous as children and adolescents, they are courageous and tough as adults.

The **dissenting personality** (Millon, Weiss, Millon, & Davis, 1994) represents a somewhat different and slightly more pathological normal-range variant of the antisocial. Dissenting personalities are unconventional; they do things their own way and are willing to take the consequences, regardless of how others might judge them. Inclined at times to finesse the truth, they sometimes flirt with legal boundaries in pursuit of their own goals and desires. Rather than accept customary responsibilities, they see themselves as independent or creatively autonomous. Authority is viewed contemptibly as belonging to Big Brother, that part of society charged with replacing individuality with a socially acceptable identity. Such individuals dislike daily routine and are often criticized by others as being impulsive and irresponsible. In general, they are action-oriented, independent thinking, enterprising, and confrontational. They stretch the limit of established social standards and push forward by means of sheer will, overturning obstacles with clever maneuvers or an aggressive and intimidating posture. Self-motivated and often extremely resourceful, they seize the initiative to make matters work toward their own ends. Many make masterful leaders, ready to take charge with confident, decisive action.

At the very boundary of normality and pathology, we find persons who have never come into conflict with the law, but only because they are very effective in covering their tracks. Although these individuals share with most antisocials a guiltless willingness to deceive and exploit others, they are not overtly physically cruel. Instead, their premeditated restraint often makes them seem more sadistic than antisocial. Stereotypes include industrialists and entrepreneurs who flourish in the gray area of legal technicalities, as well as savvy corporate executives who exploit some market position, monopoly power, or regulatory loophole for huge advantage, even at great costs to others. Individuals who systematically dismember corporations for their own self-gain through hostile takeovers, for example, cannot be regarded as completely normal, much less altruistic.

Similarly, for many politicians, the deception of doublespeak is a talent necessary for survival. Skirting the edge of deceitfulness, they "spin" objective events by minimizing negatives and exaggerating positives. When cornered, they focus attention on mitigating circumstances and lie by omission by failing to report the total circumstances and full motives of their actions. Moreover, they deliberately create public policy so complex that any particular aspect might be singled out to impress the special interest of the moment. All are "premeditating antisocials." In everyday life, they flourish in the form of the smooth-talking businessman and the less-than-forthcoming used-car salesman. Their damage to society is not as vivid as that of the murdering psychopath, but it is more common and just as great and constitutes an important reminder than any scientific theory of the antisocial personality must span both normality and pathology.

Characteristics of an antisocial personality style rather than disorder can also be developed by normalizing the diagnostic criteria of *DSM-IV* (see Sperry, 1995). Whereas the disorder consistently violates social norms through illegal activities (see criterion 1), the style puts its own value system above that of the group and is occasionally caught up in conflict thereby. Whereas the disorder uses various forms of deceit to achieve its own ends (see criterion 2), the style is "slippery," tending to finesse critical points and spin objective events to its advantage without engaging in outright deception. Whereas the disorder is too impulsive to consider the consequences of its actions (see criterion 3), the style is naturally spontaneous and self-indulgent, but knows when failure to delay gratification would violate social norms or lead to substantial harm to self or others. Whereas the disorder is irritable and aggressive to the point of repeated fights or assaults (see criterion 4), the style is assertive in creating a felt physical presence.

For each of these applicable contrasts, in Case 5.1, Toni falls more toward the pathological side. Her arrest record argues that she readily shortcuts accepted social norms for her own ends, whatever they might be. Her conflict with the public interest has nothing to do with an internal value system that might direct behavior through principle in an individualized fashion. Instead, her moral code is summarized succinctly as, "Do unto others before they do unto you," a proactive pursuit of self-gratification at the expense of society. Moreover, Toni's use of deception goes far beyond simply slanting an interpretation of the facts. For example, she has already invented an alibi for her possession charge: Her boyfriend was dealing; she was simply on the scene and feared what would happen if she refused the undercover cop, who she thought was a dangerous drug addict. Outside the context of her own previous arrests and behavior, her rationale has plausibility; inside that context, however, its deceptive purpose is clear. Finally, instead of being simply assertive and physically imposing, Toni uses aggression interpersonally to cow opposition to her will. A charge of peace disturbance is one reason she is being seen in therapy.

The remaining diagnostic criteria of the antisocial personality can also be put on a continuum with normality. Whereas the disorder recklessly disregards the safety and welfare of both self and others (see criterion 5), those with the style simply see themselves as being more resistant to risk than the average person but are not impulsively careless or foolhardy. Whereas the disorder is consistently irresponsible as to work and financial obligations (see criterion 6), the style prefers to remain free of external

FOCUS ON GENDER

Antisocial Women

Rarely Is a Woman Wicked . . .

We have already presented the argument that there are possibly different pathways for the development of antisocial behavior and personality disorder in men and women, but what are some of the other differences that distinguish male and female antisocials? For one, the rate of antisocial personality disorder is usually considered to be higher for men than women. In the community at large, the *DSM-IV* indicates that about 3% of men and 1% of women warrant such a diagnosis with rates of antisocial personality disorder increasing and the rate for women increasing faster than for men. The rates for conduct disorder (CD) in adolescents are considerably higher. One large epidemiologic study of 15-year-olds found that 7.5% to 9.5% of girls and 8.6% to 12.2% of boys met criteria for CD (Fergusson, Horwood, & Lynskey, 1993).

Despite the high prevalence rate of females with CD and antisocial personality disorder, few empirical studies include females in their samples. A few notable exceptions include Mulder, Wells, Joyce, and Bushnell (1994), who compared the characteristics of an equal number of women and men who met criteria for antisocial personality disorder in a community sample. Both groups report parental disharmony during childhood, although this finding was significant only for women. In terms of antisocial symptoms, women most commonly reported relationship problems, job troubles, and violence. In contrast, men reported job troubles, violence, and traffic offenses. Other studies have followed antisocial girls through adulthood and have found that they have higher mortality rates, are at 10- to 40-fold increased risk for criminality, have higher rates of other psychiatric disorders, and are in dysfunctional and often violent interpersonal relationships (Pajer, 1998).

There have also been arguments that males and females express their antisocial behavior in different ways. Historically, women who behaved in antisocial ways were thought to be somehow sicker than their male counterpoints. An old Italian proverb illustrates this nicely: "Rarely is a woman wicked, but when she is she surpasses the man" (Lombroso & Ferrero, 1916, p. 147). Somehow, because it was more rare than male antisocial behavior, it must be more aberrant and severe. Alternately, rather than sicker, female deviance was often viewed as largely sexual misbehavior rather than criminal, and the woman was to be treated and cured rather than punished. Along these lines, it was widely thought that when women committed crimes, it was not out of their own impetus, but rather to aid a male partner, an idea still with us today. More recent models have drawn the distinction that males exhibit more verbal and physical aggression from threatening to hitting while females are more likely to exhibit what has been termed "relational aggression" such as spreading malicious rumors and gossip and rejecting other females from their social groups (Crick, 1995; Crick & Grotpeter, 1995). However, in refute of these supposed differences is the finding that if violent crimes against family members or same-sex peers are analyzed separately, the gap closes considerably (Balthazar & Cook, 1984). Similarly, although girls commit fewer overall antisocial behaviors, the rank ordering of the most common ones are almost identical to those committed by boys (Robins, 1986).

constraints and to spend on the joys of the present rather than save prudently for the future. Finally, whereas the disorder lacks a conscience (see criterion 7) and rationalizes exploitation of others, the style can be aggressively or impulsively self-serving, but within moral, social, and legal boundaries.

Once again, Toni falls more toward the pathological end of the applicable contrasts between style and disorder. Far beyond seeing herself as simply more resistant to risk, Toni admits to abusing heroin and sharing needles and asserts that she is not afraid of HIV. Far beyond wanting to remain free of the constraints that work might put on her time, she has never held a job for more than three weeks, instead preferring to make a lot of money in very little time. If that requires her to do something illegal, that's okay. Finally, far beyond being aggressively self-serving within moral, social, and legal boundaries, Toni shows herself to be devoid of conscience. She not only admits that she does not feel guilty for what she has done, but also rationalizes away her guiltlessness by arguing, "No one ever felt guilty for what they did to me," as if moral principles should be extended and suspended based on the actions of others, rather than held consistently according to one's own internal values.

Variations of the Antisocial Personality

Subclassifying antisocials, psychopaths, and criminals has been a hobby of social scientists for more than a century. Some schemes are based on the types of crimes committed or the severity of the crime, rather than on clusters of trait characteristics. Other schemes are based on methodology-driven approaches, such as cluster analysis. All such schemes fail to recognize the importance of considering other personality characteristics in addition to those of the major pattern. In contrast, the antisocial variants summarized in Figure 5.1 are described as combinations of constructs descended directly from the evolutionary theory (Millon, 1990). Note that other subtypes are possible, and not all antisocials fall neatly into one of the categories.

THE COVETOUS ANTISOCIAL

The **covetous** antisocial is a variant resembling a "pure" prototypal pattern. Here, aggrandizement, the desire to possess and dominate, is seen in a distilled form. These individuals feel that life has not given them "their due"; they have been deprived of their rightful amount of love, support, or material reward; and others have received more than their share. Jealous of those who have received the bounty of a good life, they are driven by an envious desire for retribution to take what destiny has refused them. Whether through deceit or destruction, their goal is compensation for the emptiness of life, rationalized by the assertion that they alone can restore the imbalance fated to them. Seething with anger and resentment, their greatest pleasure lies in taking control of the property and possessions of others. Some are overtly criminal. Many possess an enormous drive for revenge, manipulating others like pawns in a power game.

Regardless of their success, however, covetous antisocials usually remain insecure about their power and status, never feeling that they've been compensated for life's impoverishments. Ever jealous and envious, pushy and greedy, they may make ostentatious

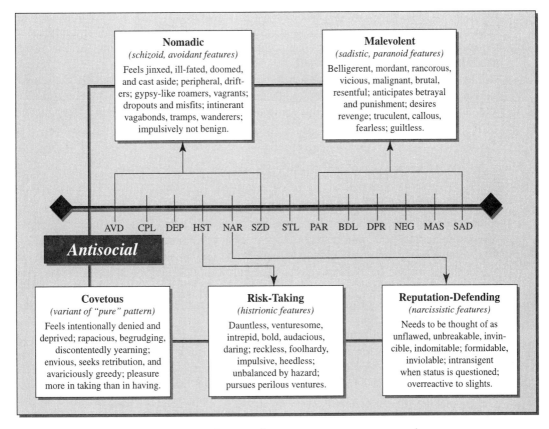

FIGURE 5.1   Variants of the Antisocial Personality.

or wasteful displays of materialism and conspicuous consumption such as buying exotic cars, mansions, and elaborate jewelry as a means of exhibiting their power and achievements to others. Most feel a deep sense of emptiness, juxtaposed with vague images of how different life might have been had opportunity blessed them, as it has so many others. Some are simple thieves, while others become manipulative entrepreneurs who exploit people as objects to satisfy their desires. Although they have little compassion for or guilt about the effects of their behavior, they never feel that they have acquired quite enough, never achieve a sense of contentment, and feel unfulfilled regardless of their successes, remaining forever dissatisfied and insatiable.

THE REPUTATION-DEFENDING ANTISOCIAL

Not all antisocials covet material possessions or power. Those who share traits with the narcissistic personality are motivated by the desire to defend and extend a reputation of bravery and toughness. Antisocial acts are designed to ensure that others notice them and accord them the respect that they deserve. As such, they are perpetually on guard against the possibility of belittlement. Society should know that the **reputation-defending** antisocial is someone significant, not to be easily dismissed, treated with indifference, taken lightly, or pushed around. Whenever their status or ability is slighted, they may erupt with ferocious intensity, posturing, and threatening until their rivals back down. Some reputation-defending antisocials are loners, some are involved in adolescent gang activities, and still others simply seek to impress peers with aggressive acts of leadership or violence that secure their status as the alpha male, the dominant member of the pack. Being tough and assertive is essentially a defensive act intended to prove their strength and guarantee a reputation of indomitable courage.

THE RISK-TAKING ANTISOCIAL

Minor risk taking within a controlled environment provides a normal outlet for excitement and sensation seeking; many people love a roller coaster, for example. However, there are individuals for whom risk taking is intended to impress others with a front of courageous indifference to potentially painful consequences. **Risk-taking** antisocials, who combine antisocial and histrionic traits, wish others to see them as unaffected by what almost anyone else would surely experience as dangerous or frightening. While others shrink in fear, they are unfazed by the possibility of gambling with death or serious injury. Risk is proactively sought as its own reward, a means of feeling stimulated and alive, not a means of material gain. Although their pretense is being dauntless, intrepid, and bold, their hyperactive search for hazardous challenges is seen by normals as foolhardy, if not stupid. In effect, they are thrill seekers infatuated by the opportunity to test their mettle by performing for the attention, applause, and amazement of an audience. Otherwise, they would simply feel trapped by the responsibility and boredom of everyday life. The most important factors making them antisocial is the irresponsibility of their actions and their failure to consider the consequences for their own life, or the lives of others, as they pursue ever more daring challenges.

THE NOMADIC ANTISOCIAL

Although the most widely held impression is that antisocials are incorrigible criminals who undermine the values of the surrounding culture, some seek simply to run away from a society in which they feel unwanted, cast aside, or abandoned. Although most antisocials react antagonistically to social rejection, these individuals drift along at the margins of society, scavenging whatever slim resources they come across. The **nomadic** variant combines antisocial with schizoid and/or avoidant characteristics. Most see themselves as jinxed or doomed and desire only to exist at the edge of a world that would almost certainly reject them. Mired in self-pity, they drop out of society to become gypsy-like roamers, vagabonds, or wanderers. With little regard for their personal safety or comfort, they may drift from one setting to another as homeless persons involved in prostitution and substance abuse.

Adopted children who feel uneasy about their place in the world sometimes follow the path of the nomadic antisocial, wandering from place to place in an apparently symbolic search for their true home or natural parents. Their sense of "being no place" signifies alienation from self and others. For this reason, nomadics often appear vaguely disconnected from reality and lack any clear sense of self-identity. Compared to other variants, nomadic antisocials often seem relatively harmless because of their attitude of indifference and disengagement. Some are indeed vacant and fearful, but others are deeply angry and resentful. As a consequence of alcohol or substance abuse, they may act out impulsively, discharging their frustrations in brutal assaults or sexual attacks on those weaker than themselves.

THE MALEVOLENT ANTISOCIAL

As a blend of the antisocial and paranoid or sadistic personalities, **malevolent** antisocials are often seen as the least attractive antisocials. Belligerent, rancorous, vicious, malignant, brutal, callous, vengeful, and vindictive, they perform actions charged with a hateful and destructive defiance of conventional social life. Like the paranoid, they anticipate betrayal and punishment. Rather than merely issue verbal threats, however, they seek to secure their boundaries with a cold-blooded ruthlessness that avenges every mistreatment they believe others have inflicted on them in the past. For them, tender emotions are a sign of weakness. They interpret the goodwill and kindness of others as hiding a deceptive ploy for which they must always be on their guard. Where sadistic traits are prominent, they may display a chip-on-the-shoulder attitude and a willingness to confirm their strong self-image by victimizing those too weak to retaliate or those whose terror might prove particularly entertaining. When confronted with displays of strength, malevolents are experts at the art of posturing and enjoy pressuring their opponents until they cower and withdraw. Most make few concessions and instead escalate confrontations as far as necessary, backing down only when clearly outgunned.

Early Historical Forerunners

The antisocial personality has been known since at least the ancient Greeks. In the 1800s, the origins of antisocial behavior were associated with the philosophical debate between free will and determinism. Given such a context, the physicians of the 1800s naturally wondered whether antisocial persons could understand the consequences of their own actions. Philippe Pinel (1801, 1806) referred to a form of madness known as **la folie raisonnante,** a tendency toward impulsive and self-damaging acts in the presence of unimpaired intelligence and full awareness of actions. Pinel's observation was intended to be descriptive, not value-laden. The idea that psychopathology could occur in the absence of mental confusion then spread throughout Europe but was still hotly debated.

Other physicians regarded antisocial individuals as being defective in character and, therefore, worthy of moral condemnation. The term **moral insanity,** first used by Prichard (1835), crystallized this notion. Prichard held that despite understanding the choices before them, their conduct was swayed by overwhelming compulsions. He also broadened the syndrome to include diverse emotional and mental conditions, all of which shared a common inability to guide themselves according to an inner sense of rightness, goodness, and responsibility. Though unscientific, the idea of moral insanity still has a certain appeal, if only because the normal person often has no way of identifying with the more pathological actions of antisocials and psychopaths. Dahmer and Mudgett, discussed briefly at the beginning of this chapter, provide two examples. Toni is certainly less extreme, though we still wonder why she cannot understand the consequences her actions will have on her life.

Subsequent writers suggested parallels between anatomical defects and defects of character, though in a way that would be considered amusing today. For example, some believed that a specific cerebral center controlled morality (Maudsley, 1874). Just as some individuals are colorblind, some were regarded as morally blind. Other writers held that antisocials were born delinquents possessing common physical features, such as a large, projecting lower jaw, outstretched ears, sloping forehead, left-handedness, robust physique, precocious sexual development, insensitivity to pain, and muscular agility (Lombroso, 1887). Stone (1993) suggests that society needs the comfort of believing that criminals somehow look different to reassure ourselves that we are protected from true psychopaths, who cloak themselves with the trite and ordinary.

Toward the end of the nineteenth century, psychiatry began to turn away from moral classification and toward observational research. Koch (1891) proposed that the term moral insanity be replaced by **psychopathic inferiority,** explicitly casting the syndrome as an "inferiority of brain constitution" (p. 54). Though his intentions were the same as those of Pinel—to classify scientifically rather than morally—the choice of words was poor. "Inferiority" was eventually dropped in later usage, after the term traveled to the United States. The term **psychopathic,** literally meaning "psychological pathology," endured for the first three decades of the twentieth century, referring to a broad range of conditions far beyond our contemporary antisocial personality. Cleckley's 1941 work crystallized the construct of psychopathy in its modern form, thus launching a research tradition that has flourished ever since.

The Biological Perspective

Biological factors may be divided into two kinds: those known to directly affect the development of the organism and those that often accompany the appearance of a syndrome but with an uncertain developmental role. The former include temperament and some genetic conditions; the latter include congenital factors, physical constitution, hormonal patterns, brain structure, and neurotransmitter patterns. The most definitive and interesting line of research that links biology with the violation of shared standards of social living is associated with the construct of psychopathy. The following findings might, or might not, generalize across psychopathic, antisocial, and sociopathic individuals.

Casual observers have often remarked that antisocials and psychopaths appear to have inborn temperaments that make them seem tough, aggressive, fearless, impulsive, hotheaded, and sensation seeking. Naturally, such traits tend to send the individual down certain life trajectories rather than others, namely, toward the development of delinquent and antisocial behaviors and away from the development of prosocial or altruistic attitudes. In an interesting chapter, one of the leaders of the field, David Lykken (1995) discusses his pet bull terrier, a breed that crosses the strength and temperament of a bulldog with the agility of a terrier, thus providing, according to Lykken, something of an "animal model" of psychopathy. Pups easily and playfully destroy household items with their powerful jaws, he states, and are almost indifferent to punishment. Consequently, raising a bull terrier requires patience and fortitude. Drawing on four parenting styles described by Baumrind (1971, 1980), Lykken suggests that the authoritarian style produces an adult who is obedient when faced with strength, but surly and dangerous to the weak. Permissive parents fail to set limits, thus producing an animal that is ultimately uncontrollable. Neglectful or rejecting parenting produces a "bully outlaw." Only a firm but loving authoritative style, Lykken argues, yields an animal that is ultimately sociable, loyal, and controllable, despite its aggressive genetic heritage.

Presumably, the same holds true for the socialization of antisocials and psychopaths. Parents often report that children who chronically act out were just born that way, unimpressed by punishment, rigidly resistant to control, and almost unmanageable from birth. Such children explore the environment more assertively, frequently intrude on others, and just naturally get into trouble more often. Without firm limit setting and competent parenting, their destiny is that of the unsocialized bull terrier pup, who pursues its own will without deterrence. The hope is that patience, consistent discipline, and prosocial role models will produce internalized value systems sufficiently strong to contain a biologically fueled aggression or at least channel it in socially acceptable ways—what the psychodynamic perspective calls sublimation.

Nevertheless, even among human beings, it appears that there are children who even the best parents could not socialize—children born to normal, traditional, loving, nuclear families, who go on to gross violations of social norms. Cleckley (1988) provides such examples, including many who have murdered, conned, and swindled. Cleckley (1950) argued that these individuals, then termed primary psychopaths, suffer what he called a "semantic aphasia." Semantic refers to meaning, and aphasia is broadly considered a class of disorders related to the understanding or production of language. What Cleckley believed, however, is that psychopaths suffer an inborn inability to understand and express the meaning of emotional experience, even though their understanding of language is normal.

Unable to understand the suffering their behavior creates, they do not develop a conscience and thus are left without empathy or remorse. Many are shrewd and calculating and struggle to learn the emotional mechanics of interpersonal communication, thus masking their disorder. Nevertheless, the significance of embarrassment, shame, or fearfulness, for example, is just lost on them. For psychopaths, statements such as, "I apologize," or "You have made me so happy!" are meaningless social conventions. Some psychopaths have even been known to purchase psychology books explicitly to develop an understanding of human emotional reactions, of "what makes people tick," a "necessary evil" in adapting to an alien world of the empathic and socialized.

In the past several decades, Cleckley's conjecture has been pursued experimentally, with a number of interesting findings. For example, most people process linguistic data faster when they are received through the right ear than through the left ear. Because the auditory nerve from each ear connects directly to the opposite brain hemisphere, the pathway connecting the right ear to the language centers of the left hemisphere is simply shorter. In contrast, information from the left ear must first travel to the right hemisphere and then on to the language centers of the left, a longer pathway. Studies have shown, however, that psychopaths possess a smaller speed advantage for the right ear than do normals (Hare & McPherson, 1984). Presumably, then, their language skills are not as strongly lateralized to the left hemisphere.

Many studies have found other strange discrepancies in the language of psychopaths. Normal subjects react strongly to the emotional dimension of statements or pictures, but psychopaths do not (Williamson, Harpur, & Hare, 1991), nor do they emphasize distinctions between neutral and emotional words as much as do normals in ordinary speech (Louth, Williamson, Alpert, Pouget, & Hare, 1998). Cerebral blood flow studies, which tap patterns of information processing in the cortex, have found that the processing of emotional words differs between psychopaths and nonpsychopaths (Intrator, Hare,

Stritzke, & Brichtswein, 1997). Gillstrom and Hare (1988) argue that the language of psychopaths is broken into smaller conceptual units. Collectively, these and many other studies converge in supporting Cleckley's original hypothesis.

Other researchers have examined brain functioning, broadly conceived. Because the frontal lobe is implicated in executive functions such as long-term planning, coordination of goals and subgoals, judgment, and attention, its study is naturally relevant to the study of psychopaths. Brain wave recordings show that the EEG patterns of adult psychopaths resemble those of young children, suggesting a developmental delay in the physical maturity of the brain, though these findings are controversial (Hare, 1993). Some (Elliott & Gillett, 1992) even argue that deficits in frontal lobe activity help explain the psychopath's inattention to morality. Deckel, Hesselbrock, and Bauer (1996) have shown that increased activity in the left frontal lobe is associated with a lower likelihood of antisocial personality disorder. Compared to Alzheimer's subjects, individuals with dementia of the frontal and temporal lobes exhibit more antisocial behavior (Miller, Darby, Benson, & Cummings, 1997), including assault, indecent exposure, and shoplifting. Furthermore, acting-out behavior is a well-known effect of traumatic injury to the frontal lobes. Siever, Klar, and Coccaro (1985) suggest that antisocial personalities are less cortically aroused but more motorically disinhibited and, therefore, tend to act before they can take time to reflect.

Another research tradition (Eysenck, 1964; Lykken, 1957; Quay, 1965) suggests that psychopaths are difficult to arouse physiologically. Physiological reactions are closely linked to the experience of many emotions, especially fear. Unable to become aroused, such individuals seem fearless under conditions of objective threat and are unable to profit from experience. Numerous studies have shown that whereas the heart rate of normal subjects increases in anticipation of some aversive stimulus, such as a loud noise or electric shock, the heart rate of psychopaths tends to remain the same or increases only at the last moment (Hare, 1978). Unable to appraise a potentially dangerous situation by gauging their own fear, they plow ahead violently, regardless of risk—a deficiency that eventually develops into a lifestyle. A lower autonomic baseline did, in fact, predict the development of delinquency a decade later in Danish adolescents (Loeb & Mednick, 1977). Other writers have suggested that such individuals experience life as chronically boring and might, therefore, require voracious amounts of sensation and excitement simply as a means of feeling alive. The penchant of many antisocials and psychopaths to "stir up some excitement" is well known.

Many other biological bases for psychopathy or antisocial personality have been proposed. Cloninger (1987b) regards the primary psychopath as being high in novelty seeking, low in the desire to avoid harm, and low in dependence on external rewards, the three main dimensions of his neurobiologic model of personality. Such individuals, according to Cloninger, are aggressive, oppositional, and opportunistic, essentially resembling the Cleckley psychopath. Gray (1987) suggests that three brain systems control emotional behavior. Individual differences in one of these, the behavioral inhibition system, leads some persons to react strongly to experiences associated with past aversive events, while others react very little. If this system is weak, the person tends to condition poorly to fear and exhibits an absence of anxiety.

A variety of other neurochemical findings have been reported. Low serotonin levels are associated with displays of aggression, violence, and impulsivity in the personality disorders generally (Siever & Trestman, 1993). They are also associated with antisocial personality disorder and comorbid substance abuse (Moss, Yao, & Panzak, 1990). Similarly, decreased levels of the hormone cortisol have been found in violent adult male

FOCUS ON RESEARCH

Understanding Alcoholism Through Personality

Different Types of Drinkers

One of the reasons alcoholism resists treatment is that every alcoholic is different. Recognizing that people drink for different reasons, researchers have turned to personality to better understand the variety of forces that drive the disease. Cloninger (1987a) proposed two types of alcoholism based on his model of neurobiological personality dimensions. His Type 1 alcoholic is high in harm avoidance and reward dependence and low in novelty seeking, a combination of traits similar to the dependent and avoidant personalities. His Type 2 alcoholic is high in novelty seeking but low in harm avoidance and reward dependence, a combination of traits similar to the antisocial personality. Cloninger's speculations are interesting, if only because two personality types identified as being at risk fall at opposite corners in the space defined by his conceptual model (see Figure 1.5 in Chapter 1). The avoidant-dependent type appears to drink as a retreat from the stresses of life, and the antisocial type appears to drink more for the pure reinforcement of intoxication.

Because theory can only suggest possibilities, it must always be followed up by empirical research. Studies have shown that the antisocial is indeed the most common personality disorder among alcoholics (Hesselbrock, Meyer, & Keener, 1985). Other personality disorders, however, have also been observed. In addition to the antisocial, Morgenstern, Langenbucher, Labouvie, and Miller (1997) found high numbers of borderline and paranoid personalities. Although these disorders have no exact parallel in Cloninger's model, their vulnerability to alcoholism can nevertheless be understood in terms of their characteristic traits. As noted in *DSM-IV,* borderlines are disposed to indulge themselves impulsively in self-damaging ways, including excessive spending, reckless driving, binge eating, and substance abuse. Excessive alcohol consumption serves the same end. Moreover, as the borderline personality has frequently been associated with mood swings and chronic depression, it is likely that alcohol consumption represents a means of self-medicating; that is, it is an attempt to "even out" the highs and lows of their chaotic life. A similar story holds for the paranoid personality. Because paranoids are, by definition, saturated with intense social avoidance, it is likely that they find alcohol reinforcing because it calms otherwise ever-present fears. In contrast, further research has found that alcoholism occurs only rarely in the dependent personality. Although Cloninger's original theory of alcoholism and personality disorders now appears somewhat imperfect, the larger proposition—that alcoholism must be understood in the context of the total personality—is nevertheless an enduring finding.

offenders (Virkkunen, 1985), in conduct-disordered boys (McBurnett, Lahey, Rathouz, & Loeber, 2000), and in adolescent girls with conduct disorder (Pajer, Gardner, Rubin, Perel, & Neal, 2001). High levels of the male hormone testosterone have been associated with antisocial behavior in male veterans (Dabbs & Morris, 1990), though not in college students (Dabbs, Hopper, & Jurkovic, 1990). Evidence linking antisocial or criminal behavior to heredity can be found in numerous studies (e.g., Cloninger, Reich, & Guze, 1978; Grove, Eckert, & Heston, 1990), thus indicating some genetic basis for these syndromes.

The Psychodynamic Perspective

Classical psychoanalysis holds that the individual is forever gripped by inexorable conflicts between the instincts of the id and the forces of socialization. Freud imagined three structures in the mind: id, ego, and superego. The id, the most primitive part of the personality and the only part present at birth, works on the pleasure principle. Sexual and aggressive urges are to be gratified immediately and directly: If someone angers you, you kill them; if someone excites you, you mate with them.

This strategy certainly has its appeal, but real life requires that such impulses be rechanneled or postponed. Within the psychodynamic perspective, normal development works toward the delay of self-centered, immediate gratification. First, reality itself imposes certain constraints on free action that make delay necessary. Sometimes, reward can be obtained only following a particular sequence of behaviors; for example, a new car requires enough money, which requires a decent job, which usually requires some kind of training. The job of relating the needs of the organism to the practical constraints and opportunities of the real world belongs to the ego, which works on the reality principle.

Second, constraints on immediate gratification are imposed by the superego. Socialization is a long and complex process that begins with early attachment experiences and continues until early adulthood. Through firm but loving role models, normal children learn that others are separate beings who have their own lives, feelings, and potentials that are different from, but just as valuable as, their own. In normal persons, a mature superego develops as parental values and prohibitions are internalized as the conscience and ego ideal. The conscience consists of restrictions and prohibitions—what you should not do—and the ego ideal consists of values that direct self-actualization—what you should do to obtain self-esteem and fulfill your unique potential as a human being. The process by which the superego forms is called **introjection,** which literally means "a putting inside." Because the superego operates according to what Freud called the moral principle, breaking moral codes results in feelings of guilt, and satisfying the ego ideal results in feelings of pride and self-respect.

The antisocial personality is easily understood from within this classic psychoanalytic framework. The ego develops, but the superego does not. Instead, the total personality remains dominated by the infantile id and its pleasure principle (Friedlander, 1945). Because intellectual functions and reality testing remain intact, such individuals appear, in the words of Prichard, "morally insane." Just as classical psychoanalytic theory holds that the id is completely centered on its own immediate needs, antisocials impulsively and egocentrically violate shared standards of social living. Just as the id is dominated by sex and aggression, so is the behavior of most antisocials. Just as the id demands immediate gratification, antisocials focus on the short term, failing to think ahead or anticipate the consequences of their actions. Just as the id is seen as closed off from the outside world, antisocials are egocentric and unable to appreciate the entityship of fellow human beings. Just as the id knows only its own urges, antisocials know mainly the selfish pursuit of their own satisfaction, acting without reflection, remorse, or regard for others. Just as the moral principle is irrelevant to the id, social conventions and ideals have no intrinsic value to the antisocial personality. Just as the id has no tolerance for frustration, neither do antisocials, who seem incapable of delaying action in the face of reward, unless deterred by the threat of concrete punishments.

In fact, lack of conscience is perhaps the most stunning characteristic of the antisocial personality, if only because the inhibitory controls that the superego normally provides appear necessary to its development. Though Freud was not much concerned with such individuals, he did recognize (1916/1925, p. 333) that among criminals are those who "commit crimes without any sense of guilt, who have either developed no moral inhibitions or who, in their conflict with society, consider themselves justified in their actions." Antisocials have little in the way of an inner voice or internal censor to moderate their actions. Compared to the immediacy of their own impulses, urges, and desires, societal constraints seem abstract, nebulous, distant, and irrelevant, hardly salient enough to interrupt and inhibit impulsive, destructive, and reckless behaviors. Without a conscience, other persons become the raw material for gratification. Convicted for rape, one antisocial stated, "She had a nice ass, so I helped myself" (quoted in Hare, 1993). In fact, the social and legal consequence of massive violations of fundamental human rights and dignities may never enter conscious awareness. When social rules do interrupt behavior, they exist mainly as nagging nuisances to be circumvented in whatever way might prove successful.

Although a deficient conscience would seem to be common to all antisocials and psychopaths, there are individual differences in the degree to which the reality principle is developed that strongly affect their presentation. Some are highly intelligent in circumventing social constraints to exploit others and satisfy their own needs. Just as remorseless and egocentric as more impulsive antisocials, these individuals are more subtle and planful and, therefore, more deceptive and more dangerous. As Hervey Cleckley (1988) would say, they wear the "mask of sanity." Without a conscience to restrain it, the ego is free to pursue any avenue to gratification that the intellect might imagine. Other human beings are part of the furniture of existence, to be manipulated, used selfishly, and then discarded. Honoring social rules is a practical necessity connected to the avoidance of punishment, not a moral consideration.

Although most antisocials and psychopaths find the tender emotions incomprehensible, these individuals learn to adapt to a world in which emotional expression is the very currency of communication, developing a sensitive intellectual awareness of social conventions and an ability to size up interpersonal situations. Their knowledge of human relations allows them to feign empathy when necessary, to deceive and manipulate (Bursten, 1972) their victims with chameleonlike charm, even to make their way in the most respected professions of society (Cleckley, 1988). Cold and calculating, their existence shows us what happens when the id is mated with intellectual cunning. Moreover, it also shows us that the capacity to reason cannot alone define what it means to be human.

In terms of defense mechanisms, antisocials are especially sparse. Because their personality works mainly on the reality principle, they have little to defend against. Most persons experience anxiety and guilt in connection with the expectations of others. We fear letting someone down, people will be disappointed in us, they will believe we have not done a good job, and so on. These are our parental introjects, the socializing internalized voice of mother and father and other role models. When feelings of hostile aggression exist in normals, they are repressed, displaced, transformed, or converted into overconformity, as with the compulsive personality. Anxiety thus requires a capacity for empathy, an ability to take the perspective of others and evaluate how the self might be perceived. Many antisocials are impervious to shame or embarrassment (Stone, 1993), affects that assume a capacity to understand how others might view some unattractive aspect of the self in comparison to his or her own ego ideal.

Many brag about their violent crimes to impress their listeners but do not disclose more petty offenses. Such antisocials enjoy "getting one over on someone" as a means of indulging a sense of narcissistic grandiosity (Bursten, 1973). As an innocent man convicted of murder noted on his release: "At least it was murder, 'because then you get some respect' " (quoted in Lykken, 1995).

With no life goals and no capacity to appreciate the opinion of others, antisocials seek a life of untroubled indulgence. Neurotic worry is not part of their existence. When they do experience anxiety, it relates mainly to fears of getting caught and being punished: the realistic anxiety of the ego, not the moral anxiety of the superego. When caught in a lie, for example, antisocials learn how to lie better, if they learn anything at all. Normal persons rationalize their behavior to themselves; antisocials, however, rationalize to develop accounts of their behavior that are plausible to others. When held accountable for their actions, they regularly minimize major violations of socials norms (McWilliams, 1994). Thus, a case of domestic violence becomes a "difference of opinion" and theft becomes a case of "poor judgment." When frustrated, antisocials do not contain themselves; they act out, transforming conflict into action. Projection may accompany acting out as a means of justifying preemptive aggression. Thus, antisocials read malevolence into the motives of others and then "defend" themselves by counterattacking. The need for restitution warrants actions by the antisocial, who now sees himself or herself as the persecuted victim.

The Interpersonal Perspective

Whereas the psychodynamic perspective was classically concerned with internal conflict, the interpersonal tradition focuses on relationships between persons and the impact of their communications, both developmentally and in the here and now.

Within the interpersonal tradition, behaviors are often organized in terms of the interpersonal circle. According to Kiesler (1996), the antisocial personality represents almost pure interpersonal hostility. Offering descriptions at two levels of severity, he summarizes the actions of the moderately pathological form of antisocials as oppositional, irritable, and rude (p. 14). In addition, they are quick to argue, ignore the feelings of others, resist cooperation, and readily provoke disputes. Their extreme form Kiesler regards as rebellious, vicious, and vulgar (p. 15). Moreover, they exhibit blatant defiance and ruthlessly attack, torment, and abuse others who thwart their intentions.

Using her SASB model, Benjamin (1996) paints a similar picture. Unlike Kiesler, however, her model suggests that antisocials also seek to control others, while vigorously resisting any and all attempts by others to control them. They may refuse to make child support payments, for example, mainly because they have been exacted by external authority. According to Benjamin, this provides an important distinction between antisocial behaviors and those that are merely criminal. Criminal behaviors are antisocial only when they contain the additional interpersonal element of establishing or perpetuating some form of control over others, without regard to the impact of their actions. Accordingly, criminal actions geared exclusively toward personal gain, for example, do not qualify as evidence of an antisocial personality.

Antisocials not only seek control, according to Benjamin, but also do so pridefully. The exploitation of others, whether by conning or coercion, for example, makes them proud, regardless of how the lives of others are affected. Thus, they may guiltlessly abuse others physically, even critically injuring them, to secure control over a relationship or express their own autonomy. For example, a spouse who confronts her antisocial husband too forcefully about his infidelity potentially faces an ambulance ride to the emergency room. Antisocials' willingness to assault others violently, even jeopardizing life itself, serves an important instrumental purpose: causing others to think twice about taking any control for themselves or even about asking that their rights or welfare be respected. Instead, the antisocial believes that others should automatically assume a posture of submission.

Consider the case of Oscar, introduced in Case 5.2. Oscar's aggressive urges are hardly sublimated by his supervisory role. Whereas constructive intervention requires knowing the strengths and limitations of those supervised, Oscar would rather intimidate and coerce. He argues even with his own supervisor, which is the immediate reason for his referral. He refers to his wife as "the bitch" and demeans everything she does. Prideful aggression features strongly in his history. Moreover, he is rarely at work on time, is absent without explanation, collects overtime pay that is apparently undeserved, and lets substance use interfere with his job. When he presents for therapy, he attempts to excuse his actions through a fabrication that would make him out to be the sympathetic party. He is not interested in the consequences of his actions; instead, his strategy is to be so threatening that no one dares get in his way. He even views therapy as a punishment and vows revenge, saying that those who have wronged him have "brought it on themselves."

Like Oscar, many antisocials see the world as suspended in what Thomas Hobbes referred to as a "state of nature": Competition is the rule, survival is the goal, and no one can be trusted. To the extent that antisocials reflect on the content of human nature, people are seen as inherently selfish creatures whose motives are power and control. Toni (from Case 5.1) comments on this worldview when she sneers at religious feeling, asserting, "Jesus don't love nobody, or at least he don't love me," and again when she declares, "No one ever felt guilty for what they did to me." Likewise, instead of working out his problems, Oscar is interested in avenging himself. Such attitudes are characteristic of antisocials, for whom morality is an illusion, goodness is weakness, and trust is naïve.

Given such a world, the behaviors of the antisocial, particularly lack of remorse, can be seen as a functional adaptation. Because others are only too willing to exploit and hurt, it is a well-developed conscience that is pathological. Giving in to guilt would only mean leaving yourself open to domination and exploitation at some future date. Success in taking advantage of someone yields a sense of triumph in a game where everyone has exploitation as his or her hidden agenda.

How does the antisocial personality develop from the interpersonal perspective? Children exposed to neglect, indifference, hostility, and physical abuse are likely to learn that the world is a cold, unforgiving place. Such infants lack normal models of empathic tenderness. Rather than learn how to be sensitive to the emotional states of others, they instead develop enduring resentments and an unwillingness to reflect on the consequences of their own actions. Without adequate parental controls, future antisocials never learn to control aggression adequately. In fact, they usually learn that physical intimidation and violence can be used instrumentally with peers and siblings to coerce their behavior. Further, a violent parent provides a violent role model. Children who watch one parent verbally threaten or beat the other into submission eventually imitate this pattern in their later relationships.

CASE 5.2

Employed as a maintenance supervisor, Oscar was referred to the university's employee assistance program (EAP) because of a harsh, dictatorial interpersonal style. He missed two previous appointments and was 20 minutes late today. His history is marked by a long series of arguments with coworkers, which appear to be increasing in frequency.[1] Although he is rarely at work on time, he has somehow managed to collect overtime pay from the university for the past three pay periods, and his time sheets are being examined for evidence of fraud. He is belligerent with both his supervisor and the crew he manages. On several occasions, staff has complained that they smelled alcohol on his breath.

(margin markers: 6, 1, 4, B)

Oscar is 33 years of age, about 6 feet tall, with an average build and dark good looks. Edgy and irritable, he remains seated only with difficulty. He simmers as he discusses the details that have brought him here. He immediately takes the position of one who has been wronged and launches into a heart-wrenching story of how life has mistreated him cruelly. He regales an elaborate tale of how his mother is sick in the hospital, and there is no one but him, the dutiful son, to take care of her. He has been late or absent from work to take care of her, and he needed the extra money to pay her medical bills and her rent as well as take care of his alcoholic brother and his eight shoeless children. These are interesting claims in light of the fact that his mother died six years ago and he hasn't seen his bachelor brother in more than two years.

(margin marker: 2)

Eventually, pieces of Oscar's history unravel. He came to the United States illegally at age 4. The family subsisted as seasonal pickers on farms throughout the Southwest. He speaks condescendingly about his parents, noting that they pretended to be what they were not, never had a home, had too many kids, were usually without running water, and were never home. Verbally, they insisted he keep clean, show respect, and study the books they carried from farm to farm. Nevertheless, any chance for learning was apparently undermined by Oscar's aversion to authority. Occasionally, his parents would rise up to assert their authority, but these episodes were short-lived. During his teenage years, he was in and out of juvenile detention centers mostly for truancy and assault.

(margin marker: C)

Trust is the theme of this first meeting. Married at 18, Oscar refers to his wife simply as "the bitch." Apparently, her cooking is inadequate, she puts the kids and her job before him, and worse, she gets angry if he does not come home after work. Furthermore, he draws an angry comparison between "the bitch" and his coworkers, both supervisors and subordinates alike. Like her, they fail to appreciate him and would "fall flat on their faces" if he suddenly disappeared. "They have it easy," he says with obvious resentment. "I carry all the responsibility." Oscar is angry, viewing therapy as a disciplinary action and punishment. He makes it clear that the actions of his supervisors and subordinates will not soon be forgotten.

(margin marker: 7)

Oscar speaks with a cool calculation. Not ruled by anger, his actions are instead planful, but punctuated by an underlying rage. He believes the world to be a hostile place requiring deliberate defensive and offensive actions. When asked about his plans of revenge, he replies with cold and unblinking eyes, "They brought it on themselves."

---

[1]Numbers mark aspects of the case most consistent with *DSM* criteria, and do not necessarily indicate that the case "meets" diagnostic criteria in this respect.

Antisocial Personality Disorder
DSM-IV Criteria

A. There is a pervasive pattern of disregard for and violation of the rights of others occurring since age 15 years, as indicated by three (or more) of the following:

(1) failure to conform to social norms with respect to lawful behaviors as indicated by repeatedly performing acts that are grounds for arrest

(2) deceitfulness, as indicated by repeated lying, use of aliases, or conning others for personal profit or pleasure

(3) impulsivity or failure to plan ahead

(4) irritability and aggressiveness, as indicated by repeated physical fights or assaults

(5) reckless disregard for safety of self or others

(6) consistent irresponsibility, as indicated by repeated failure to sustain consistent work behavior or honor financial obligations

(7) lack of remorse, as indicated by being indifferent to or rationalizing having hurt, mistreated, or stolen from another

B. The individual is at least age 18 years.

C. There is evidence of Conduct Disorder with onset before age 15 years.

D. The occurrence of antisocial behavior is not exclusively during the course of Schizophrenia or a Manic Episode.

Benjamin (1996) makes a crucial distinction: Early abuse explains antisocial aggression, but not a need for autonomy and a resistance to and resentment of control. Neglect and abuse are rather nonspecific factors, implicated in the early childhood of many personality disorders, perhaps especially borderlines, as well as a host of Axis I disorders. What shifts the child down a specifically antisocial pathway? For Benjamin, the answer lies within the context of parenting. Although usually neglectful, the parents of future antisocials, she states, sporadically become stern disciplinarians. A cocaine-abusing mother or an alcoholic father, for example, might suddenly decide to "put the house in

---

FOCUS ON CURRENT ISSUES

Domestic Violence

Who Commits Domestic Violence?

A 26-year-old male was arrested following the multiple stabbing death of his wife. Intoxicated during the incident, he positioned the corpse so that he could perform vaginal intercourse while he watched pornographic films on television. Psychological testing performed after his arrest revealed diagnoses of antisocial personality disorder and major depression (Meloy, 1996).

Although this case is obviously an extreme example, psychologists are often called on to make judgments about what is called "dangerousness." It is difficult to distinguish between those who are likely to become violent and those who are not, but Hare's (1991) revised Psychopathy Checklist is often helpful. Psychopathy consists of two underlying dimensions. The first reflects interpersonal and emotional aspects of the disorder and includes traits such as callousness, selfishness, exploitative use of others, and lack of remorse. The second more closely parallels the DSM's antisocial definition, which refers to a socially deviant lifestyle. Violent offenders generally score higher on the instrument (Cornell, Warren, Hawk, & Stafford, 1996). Moreover, research has shown that on release, psychopaths are four times more likely to commit a violent offense than are nonpsychopathic inmates (Harris, Rice, & Cormier, 1991).

Other investigators have attributed the psychopath's propensity for violence to a malfunction of a "violence-inhibition mechanism" (Blair, 1995; Blair, Jones, Clark, & Smith, 1995). Most animals have mechanisms that regulate aggression, causing them to terminate attacks when submission cues are displayed. For example, a dog will stop fighting when its opponent bares its throat. Blair, Jones, Clark, and Smith (1997) suggest that in psychopaths, such mechanisms are either inoperative or underresponsive. Their research shows that psychopaths underrespond to cues of distress, for example, a close-up of the face of a crying child.

The psychopath's apparent inability to inhibit aggression has implications for the area of domestic violence. Exactly who will become abusive is difficult to determine. Although domestic violence occurs at all levels of society, sociodemographic variables indicate that younger, lower income, less educated men with a history of parental violence and current diagnoses of antisocial personality disorder, depression, and alcohol or drug abuse are more likely to be perpetrators (L. E. Keller, 1996). In this text, psychopaths are more clearly depicted as the malevolent antisocial subtype.

order." As unenlightened despots, they overcompensate for their earlier neglect by becoming superauthoritarians who control, degrade, and blame rather than persuade with love or protect with firmness. Harsh discipline builds resentment, and its inconsistent application makes it seem arbitrary and exerted from a position of domination. As a result, Benjamin states, antisocials develop a seething resentment of any and all intrusions, while strongly valuing independence. When parents do try to show concern, it usually shows little awareness for the real welfare of the subject. Her example comes from the mother of a 14-year-old prostitute, who asserts that her daughter's occupation is probably just a stage.

As young antisocials move into adolescence and toward delinquency, they survive by further developing their self-image of independence and strength. Expressed against the backdrop of the larger society, they may revel in unconventional behaviors that not only assert their individuality, but simultaneously disdain social customs, flout conventional rules, and undermine what is socially admired, while idealizing disrespect, deviancy, and self-sufficiency. Their fundamental desire is to be free of all constraints, including personal attachments, responsibilities, and routines. What others would call irresponsible, they call freedom and autonomy. For them, manipulation, dishonesty, and deceit are the rule rather than the exception.

The Cognitive Perspective

Although the cognitive perspective and the interpersonal perspective inform each other through their emphasis on the internal models of self and others, the cognitive perspective is also concerned with beliefs, expectations, attributions, appraisals, and the unique and highly subjective ways in which individuals construe their worlds.

Like all personalities, antisocials run the entire range of intellectual ability. Some, like Gary Gilmore, have near-genius IQs; others suffer mental retardation (Hurley & Sovner, 1995). Many antisocials and psychopaths are capable of both clarity and logic, an observation made in Pinel's (1801, 1806) earliest writings. Nevertheless, their failure to plan ahead, to anticipate the consequences of their actions, often shows much less foresight than would usually be expected on the basis of their intellectual ability alone. For them, right and wrong are irrelevant abstractions. Morality is a ponderous and boring issue that complicates and constrains free action. Shapiro (1965) provides an interesting discussion of impulsiveness considered as a cognitive style, with specific attention given to psychopathic insincerity and lying. The following discussion draws on his work, but also profits from more recent developments in the cognitive tradition and from advances in research on psychopathy.

The cognitive style of the antisocial is best described as deviant, egocentric, and impulsive, characteristics that derive from the mental architecture of the breed. For contrast, consider the stream of consciousness as it exists in the normal person. Over the course of everyday life, the events of the day naturally populate the stream with any number of chance associations and images, all which appeal to the person and suggest some immediate course of action. For example, a pizza delivery ad is intended both to crystallize desire and to suggest the object of its satisfaction. If the ad works, the ongoing flow of activity is interrupted with a spike of hunger, causing a commandment to be issued from the frontal lobes: "Go to the phone, order it, and they will come." Not all such impulses are as dramatic. Some live out a moment of fleeting awareness and then evaporate forever. Others are considered to some depth but found to be incongruent with overarching long-term life goals or moral ideals and are rejected. Still others are superseded by competitors that promise to be even more rewarding.

In normals, life events often suggest possibilities that require extended deliberation. When dropping or adding a class, for example, students must examine how future job opportunities and the timetable for graduation will be affected, as well as whether the class will prove interesting or boring and how much work it might require. Because the short term feeds into the long term, such possibilities must be assessed in the context of an entire system of higher level, more intangible self-actualization goals, such as "feel financially secure and start a family," even though their fulfillment lies at some indeterminate point in the future.

Higher order goals thus serve an important function: They guide short-term action and help the organism manage what would otherwise be an indefinite number of competing lower level possibilities. When conscious reflection is engaged, attention moves back and forth between higher level considerations and the practical considerations of the immediate context, selecting, ordering, and fine-tuning subgoals and possible actions to optimize some overall set of purposes. Instead of adding that interesting class now, you might wait until next semester, when your overall load will be easier to manage and the professor teaching it is one who doesn't give pop quizzes and cumulative final exams, for example. Considering everything, immediate gratification should be deferred. In the work world, for example, sending out a business letter to valuable contacts helps secure profitable orders for the company, which helps in getting promoted, which leads to a larger salary, which increases the money available to the family, which makes the birth of another child reasonable.

For the antisocial, however, such overarching layers of higher order goals and moral constraints, the contents of what would be called the ego ideal and conscience from the psychodynamic perspective, are only vaguely developed, if not absent. After all, both depend on the internalization of values derived from parental models. As such, it is the egocentric significance of the moment that grips the antisocial mind. Largely devoid of self-actualization goals and moral values, their stream of consciousness is populated mainly by associations and imagery related to possibilities of immediate gratification and potential frustrations to immediate gratifications. Both Toni and Oscar exemplify this point. Any action that seems satisfying is free to be pursued in any way permitted by the laws of physics. For normal individuals, the presence of higher order goals gives substance and continuity to life. For the antisocial, however, the stream of consciousness consists of a discontinuous series of fixations and frustrations (Shapiro, 1965) that have for their horizon mostly the considerations of the moment, hence, their lack of insight, poor behavioral controls, and self-indulgent, predatory actions.

Even where their actions are not always flagrant or extreme, antisocials often suffer frequent setbacks. Life gains may evaporate quickly as superordinate goals succumb to the gratification of some comparatively concrete, lower level pleasure so salient that its stimulus pull fills the mind and eclipses everything else. Despite a poor work history, for example, an antisocial might charm his way into a desirable job, only to be dismissed for thieving some trivial item temporarily left unattended. Asked to explain, he might reply, "I just wanted it, so I took it." This is apparently what is happening to Oscar. Despite somehow making it into a supervisory position, he is consumed by the idea of avenging himself on his supervisor and coworkers. Whether he might have real problems has not yet crossed his mind.

Such incidents strongly suggest that antisocials are either deficient in creating mental models that relate actions and consequences or such models are highly vulnerable to the influence of immediate rewards and gratifications. They cannot detach from their own egocentric desires long enough to process potential consequences. They cannot be planful or considerate, and, more important, they cannot accumulate wisdom, which assumes a capacity to profit from experience. Instead, they are at the mercy of the moment. Asked to appraise his actions in retrospect, for example, Gary Gilmore replied, "Until I got caught or shot by police or something like that . . . I wasn't thinking, I wasn't planning, I was just doin' " (quoted in Hare, 1993).

Two other cardinal traits of the antisocial, intolerance of boredom and a need for excitement, can also be understood through this framework. For normal persons, much of life consists of activities that ultimately serve higher order goals, yet antisocials know only their immediate circumstances and their immediate desires. When the moment is empty, life is empty. For normal persons, boredom sets in after the parameters of a given situation have been explored, be it a career, a relationship, or a new video game. For antisocials, boredom refers to any time period lacking short-term stimulus opportunity. This may explain why substance use is so attractive to the antisocial mind. A "good buzz" is relatively instantaneous and provides internally generated sources of stimulation that either distract from the emptiness of the present or fill the present through artificially generated perceptions.

Not surprisingly, then, many antisocials find that the best way to relieve boredom is to stir up some excitement themselves. Callous and predatory acts, flagrant violations of social norms, and outrageous deceits are all diversions that help them create a sense of excitement that saturates the moment with sensation. Others read such actions as irresponsible and morally reprehensible, but to antisocials, this is the only thing that makes life meaningful or at least as meaningful as it can be to them. Otherwise, the moment would be empty, and life nihilistic.

Although the cognitive style tradition examines the interplay between cognitive architecture and thinking style, the cognitive therapy tradition holds that thought mediates behavior. To explain behavior, you must look at the actual beliefs that a person holds. Beck et al. (1990) distinguish three types of beliefs: core, conditional, and instrumental. **Core beliefs** usually function below the level of conscious awareness with an absolute, enduring validity that mediates views of self, world, and future. Core beliefs are a powerful influence in organizing other beliefs, especially in predicting the consequences of various courses of action, called **conditional beliefs.** Such if-then statements relate behavior to probable outcomes. **Instrumental beliefs,** in turn, refer to action that should be taken on the basis of core and conditional beliefs (Beck et al., 1990). Instrumental beliefs are beliefs about what the person should do.

Congruent with the interpersonal perspective outlined previously, Beck et al. (1990) hold that the core beliefs of antisocials are organized around a need to see themselves as strong and independent. Because the world is seen as an intrinsically hostile place, survival demands survival-oriented core beliefs, such as, "I must look out for myself," and "If I am not the aggressor, then I will be the victim" (Beck et al., 1990, p. 55). To justify their actions, antisocials appeal to a stunted sense of morality, an eye for an eye, a tooth for a tooth. If someone harms you, you harm him or her back; if someone infringes on your turf, you have a turf war. Retaliation becomes a moral imperative. Ordinary persons may be viewed by antisocials as weaklings just begging for exploitation. Core beliefs here include, "It's okay to take advantage of someone who allows it."

The Evolutionary-Neurodevelopmental Perspective

Although perspectives are necessary to knowledge, no single perspective ever tells the whole story. Both antisocials and narcissists may be thought of as independent types who turn only to themselves to derive rewards from life (Millon, 1969). Although the *DSM-IV* presents the personality disorders as separate syndromes, in the evolutionary theory (Millon, 1990), antisocial and narcissistic personalities can be viewed as existing on a continuum. In the normal range, both are oriented to the satisfaction of their own needs and desires. In the pathological range, they not only put themselves first, but also satisfy their own needs and desires to the exclusion, expense, or injury of others.

Despite their similarities, the two personalities also have differences. Narcissists turn passively to themselves for gratification, exhibiting a sublime self-confidence deeply rooted in a belief that they are superior human beings. They expect others to defer to them automatically, contributing to their notorious sense of entitlement. In contrast, antisocials are actively oriented to satisfying themselves by intruding on and manipulating the social environment, often through aggression, threat, or intimidation. Their independence stems not so much from a belief in self-worth as from a mistrust of others to protect their own autonomy or control others preemptively. Finally, narcissists often have a childhood history of parental indulgence, in contrast to many antisocials' history of neglect or abuse. Antisocials usually have a history of conduct disorder before the age of 15 (see criterion C in Case 5.2 box); narcissists typically do not.

Any individual who is primarily self-oriented risks running afoul of social standards. In the disordered range, enlightened self-interest easily slips into total self-interest. When self-concern takes criminal expression, either narcissistic or antisocial features may dominate. Some individuals will be more narcissistic than antisocial, and some will be more antisocial than narcissistic. Viewed as opposite ends of a continuum, every individual may be located between these two extremes, so that combinations of traits become the rule rather than the exception. In contrast, the *DSM-IV* depicts these two personalities as separate syndromes. These two variants of antisocial behavior were referred to by Millon (1969) as representing the narcissistic and antisocial psychopaths, the former being essentially the primary psychopath described in the tradition of Cleckley and Hare.

Similarly, the distinction between psychopathy and sociopathy, inner constitutional versus external socializing causes of antisocial behavior, need not be mutually exclusive. The evolutionary model maintains that personality is the patterning of variables across the entire matrix of the person. For some antisocial individuals, biological determinants dominate. A deficit in the ability to process the meaning of emotional experiences, for example, may lead to psychopathy even when the individual comes from a "good home" (Cleckley, 1950). For other antisocials, socializing influences dominate. An otherwise physically normal child, for example, may experience intense, hostile abuse and neglect; develop a baseline of hostility and resentment as a result; receive rejection from other children in school; fall in with a deviant peer group; and eventually develop a delinquent pattern. For most antisocials, however, environment and biology interact in almost inextricable ways. Some, for example, may be born with a choleric temperament that puts them at the upper end of a normal distribution for anger and irritability (Lykken, 1995), leading to abuse and neglect by already stressed caretakers. Figure 5.2 puts the antisocial and narcissistic personalities at opposite ends of a continuum, illustrating their relationship with psychopathy and

FOCUS ON RESEARCH

Differences in Developmental Pathways

Once a Criminal, Always a Criminal?

There has been tremendous interest in developing models to explain the different pathways for developing antisocial behaviors and personality that clinicians have observed. Predicting which kids who commit crimes as juveniles will continue to commit crimes as adults has long frustrated psychologists, school officials, the justice department, and the community at large. Just as not all antisocials are criminals and not all criminals are antisocial, by no means do all kids who commit juvenile offenses grow up into offending adults. However, most offending adults also committed crimes as juveniles. In recent years (see Silverthorn & Frick, 1999, for an excellent review), several theorists have offered up compelling models to explain two distinct trajectories for the development of antisocial behavior in boys. In one trajectory, the onset of severe antisocial behavior begins in childhood; in the other, the onset is not until adolescence (Hinshaw, Lahey, & Hart, 1993; Moffitt, 1993).

Even the *DSM-IV* has incorporated this conception of two distinct and meaningful pathways by distinguishing **Childhood-Onset Type** versus **Adolescent Onset Type** as subtypes of conduct disorder. One reason for the success of these models is that they provide good predictive validity. It has been found repeatedly that children who develop severe conduct problems prior to adolescence are the most likely ones to continue showing these symptoms into adulthood (Frick & Loney, 1999; Loeber, 1991). Juveniles with childhood-onset typically demonstrate more aggression; possess what seems more analogous to adult conceptualizations of antisocial personality disorder with a cold, callous, and suspicious interpersonal style; and come from families with higher rates of pathology, conflict, and dysfunctional parenting practices.

However, these models were developed solely on the male pattern of antisocial behavior. Do these same trajectories apply to females as well? Silverthorn and Frick (1999) think that at least in part they do, but require some serious modifications to be a useful model for conceptualizing antisocial girls. After reviewing the limited research that has been published on antisocial girls, they hypothesize a third developmental pathway for girls they label "delayed-onset." They found that while many of the mechanisms that are thought to contribute to the development of antisocial behavior (i.e., cognitive and neuropsychological deficits, conflict-ridden family environment, parental pathology, and a cold and callous interpersonal style) are operating throughout childhood, in girls, antisocial behaviors are not expressed until adolescence for a variety of speculated social and biological reasons. They predict that this delayed-onset pathway in girls in analogous to childhood-onset in boys in terms of predicting future course and outcome and that there is no comparable pathway in girls to the adolescent-onset in boys.

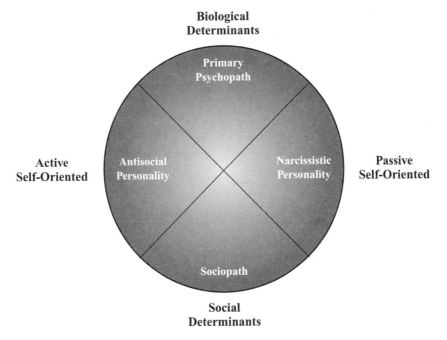

FIGURE 5.2   Psychopathy, Sociopathy, and the Antisocial and Narcissistic Personalities.

sociopathy. Table 5.1 summarizes the antisocial personality in terms of eight clinical domains.

CONTRAST WITH OTHER PERSONALITIES

Most personalities share certain essential traits. Some psychologists have complained that this overlap makes the personality disorders difficult to understand and contributes to situations in which three, or even more, personality disorders are diagnosed in the same subject. Understanding the diverse roles that the same or similar traits may play in different personalities, however, is an important part of any clinical education. Where two or more personalities have several traits in common, the key lies in understanding the function of each trait in the context of the total personality. Two different personalities may possess the same trait for different reasons, just as two individuals sometimes behave in exactly the same way, but with different goals in mind.

The antisocial and the paranoid share numerous characteristics. Both tend to be hypersensitive and may interpret innocent or benign comments as thinly veiled insults. Likewise, both are readily angered, are often overly concerned with protecting their own self-determination, and sometimes run into problems with the law or with other social norms of behavior. Moreover, both read malevolent motives into the actions of others, thus justifying preemptive aggression. Antisocials, however, often find themselves in trouble for any number of impulsive actions, ranging from minor thefts to gratuitous violence. Their enemies are created through their own malevolent behaviors. In Oscar's case, his coworkers and family have all been targets of his aggressive behavior and unempathetic outlook. Further, antisocials often put up a façade of apathy

TABLE 5.1   The Antisocial Personality: Functional and Structural Domains

Functional Domains		Structural Domains	
	Impulsive	**Self-Image**	**Autonomous**
Expressive Behavior	Is impetuous and irrepressible, acting hastily and spontaneously in a restless, spur-of-the-moment manner; is short-sighted, incautious, and imprudent, failing to plan ahead or consider alternatives, much less heed consequences.		Sees self as unfettered by the restrictions of social customs and the constraints of personal loy0alties; values the image and enjoys the sense of being free, unencumbered, and unconfined by persons, places, obligations, or routines.
	Irresponsible	**Object-Representations**	**Debased**
Interpersonal Conduct	Is untrustworthy and unreliable, failing to meet or intentionally negating personal obligations of a marital, parental, employment, or financial nature; actively intrudes on and violates the rights of others, as well as transgresses established social codes through deceitful or illegal behaviors.		Internalized representations comprise degraded and corrupt relationships that spur vengeful attitudes and restive impulses that are driven to subvert established cultural ideals and mores, as well as to devalue personal sentiments and to sully, but intensely covet, the material attainments of society denied them.
	Deviant	**Morphologic Organization**	**Unruly**
Cognitive Style	Construes events and relationships in accord with socially unorthodox beliefs and morals; is disdainful of traditional ideals, fails to conform to social norms and is contemptuous of conventional values.		Inner morphologic structures to contain drive and impulse are noted by their paucity, as are efforts to curb refractory energies and attitudes, leading to easily transgressed controls, low thresholds for hostile or erotic discharge, few subliminatory channels, unfettered self-expression, and a marked intolerance of delay or frustration.
	Acting-Out	**Mood/ Temperament**	**Callous**
Regulatory Mechanism	Inner tensions that might accrue by postponing the expression of offensive thoughts and malevolent actions are rarely constrained; socially repugnant impulses are not refashioned in sublimated forms, but are discharged directly in precipitous ways, usually without guilt or remorse.		Is insensitive, irritable, and aggressive, as expressed in a wide-ranging deficit in social charitableness, human compassion, or persona remorse; exhibits a coarse incivility as well as an offensive, if not reckless, disregard for the safety of self or others.

Note: Shaded domains are the most salient for this personality prototype.

about the possibility of arrest or punishment, that is, real action against them by the agents of society.

In contrast, paranoid personalities are intrinsically suspicious and hypervigilant. They have great difficulty relaxing, as they are always guarding themselves against the deceitful machinations of imagined enemies. This tense or edgy quality is unusual in most antisocials and even more unusual in the glib and charming psychopath. Moreover, the desire of the paranoid to uncover hidden motives imparts an intermediate step between impulse and action that many antisocials do not possess. Whereas the paranoid acts rationally given his or her assumptions about the world, the impulsive antisocial is better characterized as arational. Although it is commonly said that "paranoids have enemies, too," their problems tend to arise from the interpersonal aversiveness that others experience from being cast in the role of plotter or persecutor. Unlike antisocials, most paranoids are too fearful and guarded to give others a legitimate basis for taking action against them.

Antisocials, histrionics, and borderlines are often manipulative and impulsive, and all three tend to act out dramatically at times. However, they do so for different reasons. In antisocials and psychopaths, manipulation reflects a need to dominate, seize power, gain material reward, or satisfy some concrete need. In borderlines, manipulation usually reflects some desperate attempt to evoke support and nurture from others. In histrionics, manipulation usually reflects some attempt to occupy and hold the center of attention or a means of getting others to provide them with some resource or reward. The histrionic pulls, and the antisocial pushes. As such, histrionics do not characteristically exhibit the overt hostility and socially repugnant behaviors of the antisocial.

All three personalities also exhibit impulsivity. In the antisocial, however, impulsivity reflects a shortsighted fixation on immediate gratification. Borderlines sometimes fixate on short-term gratification, but become impulsive in reaction to anxious feelings of emptiness or depersonalization. In the histrionic, impulsivity is part and parcel of a scattered cognitive style. Attention moves from one thing to the next, each of which receives its own emotional dramatization. Although all three personalities act out dramatically at times, the antisocial and borderline are characteristically more intense. In the antisocial, acting-out takes the form of intense verbal threat or violence, but in the borderline acting-out often takes the form of suicidal gestures. Finally, borderlines often engage in self-mutilation, damaging themselves; antisocials and psychopaths are more likely to damage others.

Although the sadistic personality was dropped from *DSM-IV,* comparison with the antisocial is still informative. Both break social norms, damaging the lives of others. Sadistic personalities, however, are more violent and explosive, primarily oriented to the destruction and derogation of others. In contrast, antisocials are not necessarily sadistic, just focused exclusively on their own gratification. When their actions damage or hurt, it reflects their willingness to use others as a means to an end in fulfilling their own desires. Others are regarded more as furniture than as real persons. In contrast, most sadists appreciate the genuine personhood of others, without which their suffering would not be nearly as powerful or satisfying. Moreover, antisocials and psychopaths are more likely to manipulate or deceive others cleverly for personal gain. Sadists manipulate others to effect and then observe their personal grief.

PATHWAYS TO SYMPTOM EXPRESSION

Although antisocials are usually seen as being emotionally insensitive, they are nevertheless vulnerable to a variety of symptom conditions. As always, it is important to remember that there is a logic that connects the personality pattern with its associated Axis I syndromes. As you read the following paragraphs, try to identify the connection between personality and symptom.

Anxiety Disorders

For some personality patterns, such as the avoidant and the dependent, anxiety tends to build and build without limit. In contrast, antisocials are not disposed to ruminate or reflect on their feelings, much less express feelings verbally. Instead, they find anxiety to be an intolerable poison that must be acted out, usually in some impulsive and thoughtless way. In fact, the aggressive drive that often seems to define antisocial behavior can be seen as anxious energy redirected toward the manipulation, confrontation, or domination of others. Feelings of helplessness are thus discharged by making others feel helpless before the wrath of the antisocial. As such, chronic feelings of anxiety are rare. When they do occur, it is usually because the antisocial finds that some insuperable barrier cannot be knocked down, making discharge impossible. Antisocials may experience intense dread at the possibility of being controlled by others or by circumstances, dread retaliation by those they have damaged, or dread an inevitable prison sentence, for example. Increases in sustained acting-out behavior, therefore, are likely to signal some enduring life circumstance or external constraint not easily overcome through impulsive physical action.

Substance Abuse

Antisocial traits and substance abuse go hand-in-hand. Alcoholics with antisocial personality disorder, for example, usually experience their first intoxication at an earlier age, and their disease has a more severe and chronic course than for alcoholics without antisocial personality disorder (Holdcraft, Iacono, & McGue, 1998).

Many pathways of reinforcement lead antisocials toward drug use. First, antisocials have no moral qualms that might moderate substance use and usually have little regard for any constructive direction in life that might be damaged as a result. Instead, the immediate gratification offered by most substances resonates well with the tendency of antisocials to seek sensation in its raw, uncut form. Second, a variety of substances are usually readily available, providing both a sense of defiance of the ruling culture and a sense of brotherhood in the subculture of a deviant peer group, the only positive feeling that may exist in the lives of some antisocials. Third, substance use diminishes or distracts from residual negative affects, such as anxiety, depression, and guilt. These may be replaced with feelings of confidence and power, thus playing to a strong self-image while allowing fearless displays of aggression. Other antisocials may be attracted to the money, power, and sexual opportunities that dealing in substances provides. Alcohol, marijuana, heroin, cocaine, and other stimulants form a pantheon of substances that might be abused singly or in almost any combination. Finally, substance use may also represent a form of self-medication when the individual has some additional symptom disorder, not only an anxiety or mood disorder but also schizophrenic or dissociative symptoms.

Consider the case of Jim, the drunken father (see Case 5.3). Jim has a long history of substance abuse that stretches back to his teen years, when he was wondering across Kansas, staying with one relative after another. When he joined the Navy, he lied about these activities and apparently entered a relatively abuse-free period. At 30, however, he married a girl 10 years younger, who apparently had her own problems, namely, prostitution to support her heroin habit. Jim couldn't take the nausea of a heroin high, so he started using cocaine and soon began dealing himself, drifting from city to city. Arrested in a sting operation, he turned state's evidence and received a reduced sentence.

If Jim were just an addict, he would not be diagnosed as an antisocial personality. However, his substance use is part of a more general pattern of violation of social norms and illegal activities, including robbery, dealing, domestic violence, lying his way into the Navy, and dishonorable discharge. Thereafter, he seems to have tried to go straight

A 20-year-old female business major sought counseling because her father, Jim, age 50, was arrested by local police outside a bar (B) about 70 miles from his home in western Kansas.[1] According to the police report, he was drunk, attempted to provoke a fight with several bar patrons, made lewd and lascivious remarks to two women inside, and seemed confused about his whereabouts and purpose. (1) At the jail, he seemed stuporous, apathetic, and barely capable of communicating. After repeatedly refusing to answer the officers' questions, he was transferred to the state hospital for observation.

Gradually, the sad story of Jim's childhood unfolded in therapy. He had been the third of seven children. His mother was hardworking but died when Jim was 11; his father was a drifter and periodic drunkard who died when Jim was 10. The younger siblings became wards of the state and were eventually placed in foster care. Jim, however, ran away when he was 14, wandering from town to town (C) across Kansas, occasionally staying with relatives until he became so disruptive he was thrown out. In the meantime, he sampled any illicit drug he could lay his hands on.

At 18, Jim enlisted in the Navy, lying about his history of substance (2) abuse. He found the structure stifling and greatly resented taking orders, getting up early day after day, and being forced to be respectful to those in authority. Within 18 months, he was court-martialed for assaulting an officer and being intoxicated while on duty. After a brief stint in the brig, he was handed a dishonorable discharge. Upon release, he took up residence in a rundown part of (6) Kansas City, working irregularly as a dishwasher and cook. Between jobs, he admitted that he sometimes mugged vulnerable elderly women "for fun" and as a means of securing rent money. (1)

At age 30, he met and married an apparently histrionic female barely 20 years old, who occasionally worked as a prostitute to support her own pattern of heroin addiction. Jim tried heroin but found it nauseating and decided to stick with rock cocaine. (5) Together they lived miserably for three years. Their only child was born six months into the marriage. After a particularly brutal marital fight that left the wife with a broken arm and fractured skull and Jim with a month's sentence in jail, Jim's wife left him for a new boyfriend, though they were never legally divorced.

Over the next few years, Jim became more heavily involved in drug-related crime. Drifting from Kansas City to St. Louis to Memphis and (1) finally to New Orleans, he began dealing drugs in earnest. Eventually arrested in a sting operation, he agreed to turn state's evidence in exchange for a reduced sentence of five years.

His relationship with his daughter has been one of broken promises (2) and disappointments. On the rare occasions he would breeze into town, he would make grand promises to her that he had transformed his life and was going to try to win custody of her. He would then describe all of the gifts he was going to buy her and the blissful life they would lead together. He would then disappear just as quickly as he had entered, once stealing her new bike and another time persuading her to steal a ring from her mother's bureau drawer. No matter how desperately she wanted him to love her, he seemed incapable of showing her any affection or feeling.

Currently, Jim has been paroled for four years and again lives on the outskirts of a small Kansas town. He prefers not to bother people and likes to be left alone. About once a year, however, he goes on a binge, spending most of his money, brawling, and landing in jail. He (4) is known by the judge and the local police, who now consider him more as an annoying nuisance than a major threat to society. He is usually confined in the county jail for about a month, after which he is released to alleviate overcrowding. Between these sprees, he is typically sober.

Antisocial Personality Disorder *DSM-IV* Criteria

A. There is a pervasive pattern of disregard for and violation of the rights of others occurring since age 15 years, as indicated by three (or more) of the following:

(1) failure to conform to social norms with respect to lawful behaviors as indicated by repeatedly performing acts that are grounds for arrest

(2) deceitfulness, as indicated by repeated lying, use of aliases, or conning others for personal profit or pleasure

(3) impulsivity or failure to plan ahead

(4) irritability and aggressiveness, as indicated by repeated physical fights or assaults

(5) reckless disregard for safety of self or others

(6) consistent irresponsibility, as indicated by repeated failure to sustain consistent work behavior or honor financial obligations

(7) lack of remorse, as indicated by being indifferent to or rationalizing having hurt, mistreated, or stolen from another

B. The individual is at least age 18 years.

C. There is evidence of Conduct Disorder with onset before age 15 years.

D. The occurrence of antisocial behavior is not exclusively during the course of Schizophrenia or a Manic Episode.

[1]Numbers mark aspects of the case most consistent with *DSM* criteria, and do not necessarily indicate that the case "meets" diagnostic criteria in this respect.

but was derailed when he met his wife. After a lifetime centered on substance use, Jim now lives in a small Kansas town. Like most antisocials, his pathology has burned out as he has aged. Apparently to minimize problems, Jim lives at the outskirts of town, where no one can bother him. Nevertheless, he still gets drunk from time to time, becomes belligerent, and wants to fight, but only ends up in jail.

Mood Disorders

Some antisocials exhibit a long history of depression. Vague feelings of helplessness and futility make such individuals even less likely to reflect on the consequences of their actions. Constructive courses of actions are irrelevant, because life cannot be changed, has already been wasted, or presents too many barriers to be overcome in the face of too few resources. Rejection by significant others or residual remorse for past actions may feed into an already irritable mood, exacerbating relationship conflicts and further lowering the threshold for hostile or aggressive action. The net effect is a link between depressive feelings and an increase in the acting-out behaviors that typify the antisocial pattern.

Therapy

Treatment is usually forced on antisocials by some form of threat, perhaps expulsion from school, termination of employment, impending divorce, or possible imprisonment. Many subjects have abused repeated opportunities to reform, even after many proclamations that they have finally "learned their lesson." Because antisocials are possessed of an absent or defective conscience, restraints must usually be provided by external forces. The consequences of their behavior do not concern them, nor do its effects on others. Antisocials display lack of empathy, lack of insight, and a deficient conscience. Ordinary forms of therapy, particularly individual therapy, are likely to be highly ineffective. Most interventions, in fact, are implicitly focused on containment, with only modest goals for change. This makes practical sense. Because antisocials are lacking in conscience, society must either function as the conscience they lack or suffer the consequences.

Nevertheless, some clinicians believe that the chances for real gains increase with advancing age of the clients. As the disorder begins to burn out from physical decline, perhaps accelerated by years of substance abuse and fast living, some antisocials eventually tire of aversive encounters with the forces of society.

THERAPEUTIC TRAPS

For antisocials, therapy is just another game, another annoying encounter with the constraining forces of society. From their perspective, the goal is simply to make them into something other than what they are. Because antisocials are basically interested in shrugging off external constraints, the antisocial in therapy must seem to develop a sense of conscience, must seem to express guilt and contrition, and must express a sincere desire to reform and make amends. Antisocials know that apparent change must be paced, for quick reform naturally undermines any aura of sincerity. Instead, they should change slowly and mostly in response to the searching and confrontive questions of the therapist.

The antisocial, then, seems to have returned to the flock, with the therapist as his or her proud shepherd. Any therapist who consistently works with antisocial subjects will probably be duped many times over by seemingly sincere expressions of regret, ranging from guilt about the destruction of life and property, to an almost existential despair about the wasting of the potential of their own life. Beginning therapists may be especially naïve to the antisocial's wiles, as are those who "need" to cure their subjects and those who might compete against fellow therapists by displaying their pet psychopath, the one who grew a conscience.

Therapists often exhibit a variety of intense countertransference reactions to antisocial subjects. Some become so suspicious, angry, and resentful that they may miss opportunities to catalyze real change in the few subjects where a genuine therapeutic alliance can be created. Most antisocials have been rejected by others all their lives, and a cynical therapist simply becomes another in a long line. Another problem is that antisocials frequently feel threatened by their therapists, and therapists frequently feel threatened by antisocial subjects. Particularly when both are male, they may challenge each other for domination. Many subjects may even take a sadistic delight in sabotaging their own progress, and some therapists may even take a sadistic delight in allowing it, because any victory is ultimately a loss. Frances (1985) suggests that the therapist openly acknowledge the vulnerability of the therapy setting to the possibility of manipulation, as many subjects appreciate such frank disclosure.

Therapists with compulsive traits may be at risk for presenting themselves as dogmatic symbols of deference to the establishment. Compulsives rigidly adhere to social norms, and antisocials carelessly violate them; the two are likely to despise each other. As the antisocial acts out to test a compulsive therapist, the therapist may become implicitly condemning, thus sabotaging therapy. Such countertransference reactions indicate therapist issues and should be evaluated as objectively as possible. Beck et al. (1990) suggest that self-assurance, a reliable but not infallible objectivity, a relaxed and nondefensive interpersonal style, a clear sense of personal limits, and a strong sense of humor are particularly valuable when working with antisocial clients.

STRATEGIES AND TECHNIQUES

The ultimate goal of therapy with antisocial persons lies in their developing a sense of nurturing attachment (Benjamin, 1996). The object of attachment is technically unimportant. The first object of therapy, however, is to find some way of bonding with the antisocial person, to develop a therapeutic alliance that transcends a desire to con the counselor. Coerced into therapy, many antisocials feel a deep underlying sense of hostility that must be addressed before a sense of trust can develop. Likewise, if the therapist is perceived as an agent of Big Brother, nothing authentic will occur. Accordingly, the therapist may wish to suggest that because external forces have mandated a course of therapy, the time might as well be used constructively, even though the therapist has no personal investment in the outcome. Another difficulty that arises in developing this bond is the challenge to the therapist in regards to his or her reaction to the antisocial person. Antisocials, by virtue of their willingness to destroy others' lives, are capable of eliciting feelings of moral disgust in the counselor, and they are often aware that this has the capacity to derail intervention attempts. Psychodynamic treatments are not discussed because antisocials are not typically capable of change through insight.

Interpersonally, Benjamin (1996) suggests that antisocial subjects lack constructive socializing experiences administered through dominance or warmth. Antisocials learn early that they do best by anticipating and reacting to an indifferent and unreliable environment with defensive autonomy, if not suspicion and hostility. Extrapolating from Benjamin, treatment from a position of benevolent power, the basic assumption of effective parenting, would likely involve a highly structured environment in which both rewards and punishments are known well in advance of common misbehaviors.

When transgressions occur, punishment can be administered reluctantly, but consistently. Reluctance models continuing care and attachment to the welfare of the subject and consistency shows that the system cannot be exploited in the service of shameless antisocial motives and will not tolerate antisocial acting-out. Benjamin further notes a number of strategies that can be used to help antisocials internalize values. One method particularly effective with children and adolescents uses sports figures to model warm and benevolent attitudes. Another strategy puts the antisocial in a potentially nurturing position; the antisocial may be given a pet or allowed to instruct children in some supervised context, such as a skill or a sport. The hope, according to Benjamin, is that such dependency can draw nurturance from the antisocial.

Writing in Beck et al. (1990), D. Davis describes the use of cognitive therapy with the antisocial personality. Rather than attempt to induce shame and anxiety, these authors advocate a strategy that helps move the subject from a primitive to a more abstract level of moral reasoning. Most antisocials function at the lowest level, constructing the world in terms of their own immediate self-interest. The goal of therapy is the next level, which features a longer term, more enlightened self-interest that includes limited recognition of the effects of the individual's own actions on others. Specific problem areas can be identified through a thorough review of the subject's life. Following this, the use of cognitive distortions relevant to each problem is identified. Antisocials may believe that just wanting something justifies any subsequent behavior, thoughts and feelings are always accurate, their actions are right because they feel right about what they are about to do, and the views of others are irrelevant. If antisocials can recognize that their actions affect others and have reciprocal consequences for themselves, they can at least move to a position of enlightened self-interest.

Further, these authors realistically suggest that antisocial behavior be described as a disorder with long-term negative consequences, such as incarceration, possible physical harm from others, and broken contact with family and friends. This minimizes the possibility that subjects will feel accused and thereby increases their chances of continuing therapy. Throughout therapy, therapist and subject draw clear priorities, evaluating a full range of possibilities and discussing advantages and disadvantages before making important decisions. This models delay of gratification and teaches skills necessary to make enlightened self-interest a reality.

Summary

Not all antisocials are criminals, and not all criminals are antisocial. Quite the contrary, there are many normal-range antisocial traits that are admired and encouraged in our competitive society. In fact, most antisocials find comfortable places in society, often becoming business tycoons, politicians, and military professionals. Oldham and Morris's adventurer and Millon's dissenting personalities are examples of these normal variants, who are often the heroes and conquerors described in our history books.

Several subtypes of the antisocial personality have been identified using Millon's evolutionary theory: covetous antisocials, who feel that life has not given them their due; reputation-defending antisocials, who share traits with the narcissistic personality; risk-taking antisocials, who share qualities with the histrionic personality and seem unfazed by brushes with death; nomadic antisocials, who share characteristics with the schizoid or avoidant personality; and malevolent antisocials, who, in their belligerent and vicious manners, share qualities with the paranoid and sadistic personalities.

The concept of an antisocial personality has been around for a long time. In the early 1800s, Philippe Pinel introduced the notion that the antisocial personality was a unique form of madness where the person was impulsive and destructive yet maintained all intellectual faculties, la folie raisonnante. Although Pinel's term was intended to be a value-free label, other physicians of the time began to argue that the antisocial possessed a character deficiency, and in 1835, Prichard coined the term moral insanity to describe these kinds of patients.

Of all of the personality disorders, the antisocial has the most extensive and persuasive biological evidence supporting it. It appears that there are some children who from birth are likely to explore the environment more assertively, resist control, and be undeterred by punishment or parental efforts at curbing acting-out behavior. Cleckley proposes what he calls semantic aphasia, or an inability for antisocials to understand and process emotional experiences, hence leading to their failure to develop a conscience and ability to empathize. Other researchers have found evidence that antisocials have additional specific language-processing deficiencies that all support Cleckley's original concept. Other biological research has found frontal lobe abnormalities in antisocials and lower levels of physiological arousal that may account for the antisocial's constant search for dangerous and novel experiences as well as a host of neurochemical differences that may contribute to the disorder.

Psychodynamics provides an easily understood model for comprehending the antisocial personality: a strong ego development with a failure to develop a superego. Instead, the id and the pleasure principle dominate the entire personality. With the id in control, the antisocial has no tolerance for frustration and seems able to delay action toward a reward only in the face of concrete punishment. Some antisocials have more developed reality principles that enable them to wear a "mask of sanity" that allows them to move in normal social circles. Although they are just as remorseless as other antisocials, they have relatively more control over their impulses and are better at manipulating others.

Interpersonally, antisocials can be characterized as hostile. Using SASB, Benjamin describes antisocials as also seeking to control others while vehemently trying to prevent others from controlling them. Developmentally, interpersonal theorists propose that antisocials are not exposed to models of empathic tenderness and never learn to control their aggression. Parental models that are also violent tend to produce violent children as well. Although neglect and abuse are rather nonspecific factors for many types of psychopathology, Benjamin predicts that a specific pattern of general parental neglect punctuated by sporadic outbursts of authoritarian rule and harsh discipline is what creates the anger and resentment seen in the antisocial.

Cognitively, antisocials are notorious for poor planning abilities and inability to foresee consequences to their actions. Their cognitive style is deviant, impulsive, and egocentric. One hypothesis that explains why they are such poor planners is that they are unable to generate mental models of consequences of actions or are too susceptible to their desire for instant rewards to process consequences. Beck et al. add that antisocials have a need to see themselves as strong and independent and often have core beliefs such as, "If I am not the aggressor, then I will be the victim."

From an evolutionary perspective, antisocials are actively oriented to satisfying themselves by manipulating the environment. Their behavior is driven by their basic mistrust of other people and often ends up violating even the most basic standards of social living.

Antisocials share many qualities with other personalities, namely paranoids, histrionics, borderlines, and sadists. They are not particularly vulnerable to anxiety disorders, although they often suffer from substance abuse disorders and occasionally from symptoms of depression.

Antisocials are a frustrating group to treat. They are often in therapy against their will and as a punishment for transgressions against society. Advancing age seems to increase the chances for progress in therapy, but in general, antisocials see therapy as a game where the goal is to con and to best the therapist by pretending to be contrite and redeemed but ultimately returning to their previous behaviors. For this reason, developing a therapeutic alliance has the best chance of enacting real change. Because antisocials are most likely incapable of achieving change through insight, other strategies might include cognitive-behavioral techniques, becoming a parent to the patient using more effective parenting techniques from the position of a benevolent power, or placing the antisocial in a position requiring nurturing.

Chapter 6

The Avoidant Personality

Objectives

- What are the *DSM-IV* criteria for the avoidant personality?
- The sensitive, vigilant, and hesitating personalities are normal variants of the avoidant. Describe their characteristics and relate them to the more disordered criteria of the *DSM-IV.*
- How does the avoidant personality manifest itself in a collectivist society?
- Explain how different personality styles combine to form each of the subtypes of the avoidant personality.
- List the contributions of the psychodynamic perspective to the conceptual development of the avoidant personality.
- What is *phobic character?*
- Explain how the content and structure of cognition interact in the avoidant to perpetuate this disorder.
- What is *cognitive interference?*
- What are the core beliefs of the avoidant?
- Because of their fears and anxieties, avoidants withdraw from interpersonal contacts. What are some of the consequences of their interpersonal reticence?
- How does anxiety inhibition contribute to the development of the avoidant personality?
- Avoidants share characteristics with other personality disorders. List these other disorders and explain the distinction between each and the avoidant.
- Avoidants are particularly prone to anxiety disorders. Are social phobia and avoidant personality distinct disorders?
- List therapeutic goals for the avoidant personality.

You may have seen individuals in your classes who seem to earnestly desire participation in discussions, but they say little to nothing and seem awkwardly self-conscious on those very rare occasions when they speak a few words. Perhaps you have noticed someone at a party who shows up early and stays late but spends most of the time anchored to a corner of the room, hoping someone else will approach him or her to make conversation. If you are that person who approaches, you will likely notice the person's immediate discomfort upon your initiating even the most pleasant, innocuous, non-threatening conversation. You might wonder what keeps people this socially "wrapped up" and defended and how such individuals perceive themselves and the world they share with you. You might correctly perceive that they are filled with chasms of self-doubt, they intensely fear any sort of humiliation, and they would not dare knowingly (or even unwittingly) expose themselves to other people or a competitive and cut-throat world for which they feel they are no match.

These individuals demonstrate the **avoidant personality** pattern. They may have just one or two trusted friends, perhaps a spouse or partner, or even a sole family member. Few others, if any, would be able to pass their strict tests of uncritical support and acceptance to gain access to their more private circle of existence. Does this mean that such a person is content with this very secretive, isolated way of life? Quite the contrary. Their pain wrought from loneliness and seclusion hurts them to the core of their existence, but rather than allow themselves to be vulnerable to the "inevitable" social humiliation that would follow from their perceived incompetence and awkwardness being put on naked display, they take their silent, lonely pain and make themselves nearly invisible—out of the trajectory of others' "harsh but deserved" criticisms. Because of their way of exaggerating potential for embarrassment, they do more to themselves than forego social enhancement. They resist any life change that may bring them more openly into the public eye, including occupational promotions and other life rewards. While they may deeply wish for love, genuine intimacy, and greater life enjoyment or satisfaction, their souls are seen as so disgraced that they must withdraw into a private world of shame, where they can at least be alone with their inadequacies.

Consider the case of Allison (see Case 6.1), who seems to meet diagnostic *DSM-IV* criteria for avoidant personality disorder in a rather straightforward manner. This pattern exhibits social inhibition caused by deep feelings of inadequacy and fears of ridicule and rejection. As it is virtually impossible to predict what others may think of them and nearly as difficult to know how they themselves should "ideally" behave, avoidants are in a constant state of threat and alarm when they must interact with others. They are hypersensitive to negative evaluation, doubt that they have anything to offer others, and thus find it terrifying to interact with anyone they do not already know. This may be an apt description of Allison's internal, subjective existence. Hypersensitive to a marked degree, she panics on having to interact, as she quickly feels that the critical eyes of everyone are on her. Her self-consciousness convinces her that others are taking great pains to notice her; this possibility is recycled unremittingly in her mind, her anxiety snowballs, and she feels forced to flee. Although this is typical of avoidant patterns, it is not exclusive to them. What is unique, however, is how this is experienced. Whereas some personalities, such as the narcissist or histrionic, may find the spotlight irresistible, avoidants dread it and must take flight for the relative safety of obscurity. Life is left with very little joy, but at least it holds no pain.

Similar themes permeate many, if not all, aspects of the avoidant person's life. Fears of evaluation will likely cause avoidants to restrict their occupational activities

CASE 6.1

Allison is a 22-year-old undergraduate at a local community college. She is clearly shy and uncomfortable in the clinical interview, but nevertheless complains of panic attacks so immobilizing that her contact with the outside world is limited to a bare minimum. With a new semester starting, she does not know if she will be able to attend classes.[1] The pattern is always the same. Suddenly she notices her heart quicken, then she begins to sweat as the fear of an attack grows, then her heart begins to race faster and faster and she is overtaken by panic. ← (1)

There is little joy in Allison's life. She tries to work each day, takes care of necessary errands, and shops for food every few weeks. Generally, she lets things accumulate and then tries to do them all at once, to get it over with. In the past, she occasionally enjoyed volunteer work at a botanical garden, but has never held a real job. ← (1) When asked about her social life, she has difficulty naming friends. "My fear," she states, "is that others won't like me if they really find out about the real me!" Although her words are deeply felt, she never makes eye contact with the interviewer. She concedes that although others may be capable of succeeding in the world, she desperately wants to be left alone. Even when she is just sitting in class, she has difficulty believing that others who are laughing are not making fun of her. ← (2) ← (4)

Allison's history goes far toward making sense of her symptoms. She has been reminded many times that her birth was an accident, something unpleasant that her mother and father "had to go through." She cannot recall a time when she felt loved by her parents. "Not that they were neglectful," she quickly points out, "but I always felt like a burden to them." Life at home was without warmth or joy, with much time spent fantasizing alone in her room, something she still does today. Worse, her parents, themselves highly successful, had high expectations for her but were often excessively critical, even of the smallest mistakes. Because of her shyness, she had to endure hours of merciless teasing from the other children, ← (6) apparently the origin of a crippling self-consciousness that has followed her ever since. Unable to defend herself, she withdrew socially, as if to become smaller and less noticeable to others.

When asked about relationships, Allison refers to her only boyfriend, when she was a high school senior. "Even then," she reflects, "I was ← (3) afraid to be myself or voice any kind of opinion of my own. I was afraid he would dump me." When asked about marriage, Allison admits she has dreams of being accepted unconditionally, but doubts ← (2) that it will ever happen. Instead, she prefers to be alone, "where it's safe, where no one can see your faults, much less judge you or criticize you for them." "If you keep with what you know," she says, ← (7) "you at least don't have to worry about embarrassing yourself."

[1] Numbers mark aspects of the case most consistent with *DSM* criteria, and do not necessarily indicate that the case "meets" diagnostic criteria in this respect.

(see criterion 1). Their job suffers under imagined nightmares that their performance will somehow be defective or inadequate. Depending on the severity, they may simply quit or may remain stuck in positions with no challenge, where adequacy is easy. As we saw, Allison formerly volunteered at the botanical gardens. She probably enjoyed its beauty and tranquility and was not expected to perform to any particularly difficult measure, as would an employee. Thus, Allison created her own means of escape. If her fears became too great, she could simply say that school or something else in her life was more important, and everyone would understand. It seems, however, that her fears have intensified to the point that she can no longer tolerate the demands of school. More than likely, Allison has never spoken to any of her professors, who are required to grade her and note areas in which she may improve. Allison has become far too sensitive for this process, and we may speculate that she is unable to profit from feedback of almost any kind, whether good or bad. Therefore, Allison plays everything safe.

There is only one way that she may ever involve herself with others: She must be absolutely certain that she will be liked (see criterion 2). This is, however, extremely difficult to accomplish. She has an abiding faith in her own defectiveness, in her ability to bring shame on herself simply by existing. Whereas most of us are insecure about something, Allison's insecurities constitute her perceived reality. Accordingly, the notion that someone might like her and might accept her for who and what she is, is virtually unthinkable. To develop a friendship, Allison needs repeated overtures of nurturance and assurance. Moreover, she needs consistency. Let some small criticism slip just once, and like a frightened turtle, she recoils in terror, withdrawing to the sanctity of her shell, shutting out the world. Because the shell is so thick, few people ever gain the trust of an avoidant person.

Even when Allison does overcome her hypersensitivity long enough to let someone in, her belief in her own imagined inadequacies has another unfortunate consequence: Allison is afraid to be herself. To grow, relationships must balance between self-conscious commitment and spontaneity. But Allison can't afford to be herself because she is hyper-aware of the faults and imperfections all humans carry (which she feels are hers and hers alone), and the price of authenticity is too high (see criterion 3). Were she in a relationship, Allison would find it extremely difficult to reveal her true self, to share a secret, or even to tell her partner about her real likes and dislikes. Any of these could poison the thin illusion of genuine companionship that her insecurities afford and leave her with nothing. So Allison sacrifices the potential of a romance for a steady trickle of togetherness, which is at least more certain. There are no flings of infatuation, weekends away, or sweep-you-off-your-feet dreams-come-true for Allison. No one would ever like her that much, or so she believes; if someone did like her, it would only be because she had the wisdom never to show her true self. She sees herself just as her parents likely saw her—as a burden that no one would want.

These descriptions constitute Allison's work, school, and relational perceptions; these are but a subset of her experience. Avoidant personalities feel this way in nearly all social situations (see criterion 4). Wherever they go, they feel people always have expectations of them. They fear criticism and rejection, as the *DSM* notes, but they also live in fear of simply disappointing others. That is, rejection doesn't need to be actually voiced to summon up the fears of people like Allison. Just the idea that someone might privately judge them as having failed or fallen short is enough to make avoidants want to disengage. Worse is the possibility that someone might take a stern attitude toward them, presuming to judge them from a position of authority, where the verdicts are more powerful and absolute in their condemnation.

It is of little wonder, then, that avoidants are inhibited in interpersonal situations (see criterion 5). Feelings of inadequacy make them shrink back, as Allison did, "to become smaller and less noticeable to others." We often think about pathology in connection with shutting others out, but avoidants take the additional measure of shutting themselves in. For them, the key is to limit exposure. By revealing very little of themselves, avoidants leave little that can be attacked. The philosopher Hegel said, "To be is to be perceived." For Allison and others like her, however, the existential truth is just the reverse. The only way to be is not to be perceived, at least if you want to be safe and salvage a marginal quality of life. Accordingly, whereas some personalities, such as the narcissist and histrionic, surge forward in social situations, seizing the limelight and demanding admiration, avoidants inhibit themselves and withdraw to a niche where they can at least be alone and, therefore, feel some comfortable. Avoidants should always be aware of others, but others should never be aware of the avoidant.

As with many personality disorders, positive change and improvement of life circumstances is very difficult for the avoidant person. Personal growth requires a measure of risk. Because Allison sees herself as inept and unappealing (see criterion 6), it is doubtful that she will ever, as humanistic psychologists would say, actualize her potential in life. To expand our horizons, we must push the boundaries. Or, as the old adage goes, experience is the best teacher. Avoidant personalities, however, refuse to take risks that might leave them open to public view (see criterion 7). They can be highly creative in the privacy of their apartment or become superheroes in their own fantasy life, but in the real world, it's best not to attempt anything that might bring attention to themselves. When you're inadequate and you know it, attention becomes the enemy.

As in the previous chapter, we now move from this introductory case example of an avoidant personality to examine conceptual, theoretical, and historical issues. First, we compare normality and abnormality; then we move on to the various incarnations and admixtures of avoidant patterns. Psychodynamic, cognitive, interpersonal, and biological perspectives, the core of the science of personality, are then described. By seeking to explain what we observe in character sketches such as Allison's, we move beyond literary anecdote and enter the domain of theory. As always, we present history and description side by side, noting the contributions of past thinkers, each of whom tends to bring into focus a different aspect of the disorder. Developmental hypotheses are also reviewed but are tentative for all personality disorders. Next, the section "Evolutionary Neurodevelopmental Perspective" shows how the existence of the personality disorder follows from the laws of evolution. Also included are a comparison between the avoidant and other theory-derived constructs and a discussion of how avoidant personalities tend to develop Axis I disorders. Finally, we survey how the disorder might be treated through psychotherapy, again organizing our material in terms of classical approaches to the field: the cognitive, interpersonal, and psychodynamic perspectives.

From Normality to Abnormality

You may be noticing a tinge of "medical student syndrome"; that is, in reading this and the previous chapter, you may identify aspects of your own personality that coincide with the personality patterns already described. Take heart: This is not unusual! A healthy personality maintains shades of many of the personalities described in this book, albeit in a greater state of balance and flexibility. You must also recognize that there is no sharp boundary between normality and pathology. Instead, personality styles (which we all have) are on a continuum with personality disorders. As the level of pathology and number of rigid traits increase, however, so does the likelihood that difficulties will be created in multiple venues of human life, including job, family, school, and recreation. At the border between normality and pathology, these difficulties can often be attributed to a few maladaptive traits, and these characteristics can be treated in relative isolation. At more pathological levels, however, there are fewer personality strengths and many more extreme traits. These interweave so completely that the total person becomes the driving force behind most of his or her problems.

Several normal-range variants of the avoidant personality (i.e., people exhibiting a slightly higher balance and preference for avoidant styles) have been proposed in the literature. Of the better-known variants are Oldham and Morris's (1990, 1995) **sensitive** and **vigilant** personality styles. Sensitive persons generally are comfortable in familiar surroundings and thrive within the context of a small group of trusted intimates. They are deeply concerned about the feelings and opinions of others and need their approval to flourish. Interpersonally, they are courteous and restrained. They avoid ambiguity, instead preferring situations where the expectations of others are well known and easily confirmed. Sensitive persons do not readily reveal themselves to others; they share their thoughts and dreams only after some time and only when they feel safe. Because they are very private persons, they may self-disclose too infrequently to deepen their relationships, frustrating others to the point that a real sense of intimacy is lost. Many are lovers of art and literature, and some express their vivid imaginations by becoming absorbed in acts of artistic creation. Combining the sensitive with the following characteristics of the vigilant style results in a more complete representation of the normal-range avoidant. Vigilants are hyperalert to criticism and prefer to deal with others cautiously. They are highly aware of goings-on in their surroundings and are ever on the outlook for potential threats to their safety or esteem.

Millon et al. (1994) describe a **hesitating** pattern that combines slightly more pathological aspects of the sensitive and vigilant styles. Such persons are sensitive to social indifference and rejection, feel unsure of themselves, and are unusually wary in new social or interpersonal situations, especially with strangers. Ill at ease and self-conscious, they anticipate difficulties in relationships and fear embarrassment. Most prefer to work alone or in small groups where they know that people have accepted them. Once established in a social milieu, they are likely to open up, be friendly and cooperative, and participate with others productively.

Allison exhibits many of these more normal characteristics, but in an exaggerated and uncompromising form, so she falls into the range of pathology. Sensitive persons, as described by Oldham and Morris (1995), are comfortable within a small group of trusted intimates; Allison's social circle, however, has shrunk to almost nothing. If she could be sure of approval, she might indeed open up to someone. As it is, however, she has difficulty naming friends, so she is unlikely to have the chance. That keeps her safe, but it also keeps her isolated, part of the vicious circle that sustains her pathology. Whereas sensitives self-disclose too little to grow in intimacy in their relationships, they at least have some relationships. Allison can remember only one real boyfriend, to whom she was too afraid to reveal anything about herself for fear of being dumped. Like the vigilant style, she is highly aware of her social surroundings. However, she is so highly aware of her own presence in her social surroundings that feelings of self-consciousness have escalated into panic attacks.

Characteristics of an avoidant personality style can also be developed by creating a less intense or extreme version of existing *DSM-IV* criteria, an approach pursued by Sperry (1995). Thus, those at the disordered end of the spectrum exaggerate the difficulties and dangers involved in deviating from conventional routine, while those in the normal range simply prefer the familiarity of habit and are more comfortable with the known than the unknown but do not resist novelty when clear benefits are shown. Similarly, the disordered has no close friends or confidantes and avoids interpersonal interactions. In contrast, the normal simply feels a close allegiance with family and friends and tends to be a homebody but can venture forth as necessary and deal effectively with the world at large. The disordered is hypersensitive to criticism and refuses to become involved with others unless certain of being liked; the normal is simply cautious and deliberate.

Allison falls on the pathological side of each of these contrasts. She could not, for example, venture out at will to engage the world on her own terms, even for substantial benefit. Instead, she minimizes her expeditions into the social world, leaving her house perhaps only for absolutely necessary errands and the regularly scheduled grocery store trip. She makes no effort to make small talk with anyone she may come in contact with on such occasions because she prefers to stay under the radar of any watchful, potentially critical eyes, rather than develop a familiar relationship with any store or business owner. Far beyond being interpersonally cautious and deliberate, her hypersensitivity to disapproval does not even allow her to make eye contact with the interviewer, whose role is by definition to be constructive and empathic.

Other diagnostic criteria can also be put on a continuum. The disordered individual fails to share himself or herself socially and may present a false face; the normal is simply shy and reserved but also truthful. The disordered is most often an underachiever whose social anxiety makes consistent job performance difficult; the normal is more likely to maintain consistent employment but work behind the scenes. Again, Allison falls consistently more toward the pathological end of these contrasts. She is far beyond shy and reserved, as was evidenced by her false face she presented to her former boyfriend and by her ongoing attempts at anticipating and conforming to all expectations of others when she is forced into social situations. As a volunteer at the botanical gardens, she is also an underachiever. Far beyond a simple anxiety that might make consistent job performance difficult, Allison has never held a real job.

Variations of the Avoidant Personality

Allison represents a reasonably "pure" or "prototypical" representation of an avoidant personality. However, as with most personality patterns, whether problematic or not, not all avoidant patterns closely resemble our panicky undergraduate. While Allison's style doesn't really combine characteristics of other disorders with her basic avoidant pattern, most avoidants exhibit features of other personality disorders, such as the schizoid, dependent, depressive, negativistic, schizotypal, and paranoid patterns. The resulting moods and actions that these individuals manifest give different colorations to the basic avoidant pattern that makes them unique from pure cases like Allison's. Such subtypes of the avoidant personality are reviewed in Figure 6.1. Actual cases may or may not fall into one of these combinations.

THE CONFLICTED AVOIDANT

A defining feature of avoidant personality disorder is the conflict of longing for intimacy versus the fear of vulnerability that naturally ensues in a close relationship with another. In a similar manner, those with a negativistic personality (formerly referred to as

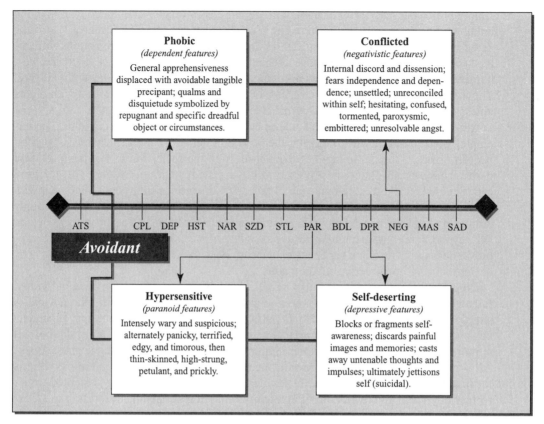

FIGURE 6.1   Variants of the Avoidant Personality.

"passive-aggressive") are basically ambivalent about themselves and others. They ideal-ize their close friends and companions, but should their sense of autonomy be threat-ened, they seek to undermine or humiliate them. What we are terming the **conflicted** avoidant is an avoidant pattern that combines features of the negativistic personality. Here, we may expect to see basic withdrawal tendencies of the avoidant pattern but ex-pressed in a manner akin to the negativist's penchant for "interpersonal guerilla warfare."

If not withdrawn into isolation, conflicted avoidants may be experienced as petulant and sulking. They may attack others for failing to recognize their needs for affection, but accuse those who offer nurturance of seeking to compromise their independence. Disposed to anticipate disappointments and fearful of facing others openly, they may strike out indirectly by obstructing their actions and misrepresenting their wishes. They often report feeling misunderstood, unappreciated, and demeaned, and their mood is generally much more erratic than in the basic avoidant pattern. During periods when stresses are minimal, they may deny past resentments and portray an image of general contentment. Under slight pressures, however, their pacific surface quickly gives way to impulsive hostility. Unable to orient emotions and thoughts logically, they may at times become lost in personal irrelevancies and autistic asides, further alienating them from others. Relating to such individuals, undoubtedly, is an arduous process, requiring far more patience than most people are likely to offer. This interpersonal strategy, as you

FOCUS ON CULTURE

Taijin Kyoufu and Avoidant Personality Disorder

Taijin kyoufu, literally "interpersonal fear," is a syndrome characterized by interpersonal sensitivity and fear and avoidance of interpersonal situations (Ono et al., 1996, p. 172). Presumably, its origins lie in the belief that blushing, eye contact, ugliness, and body odor are noticeable and troubling to others. Apparently common in Japan, the disorder is recognized as a culture-bound syndrome in the *DSM-IV* (APA, 1994) that resembles social phobia.

Ono and his associates (1996), however, argue that taijin kyoufu is really more closely related to the avoidant personality. In collectivist societies, such as Japan, the self is defined externally through its relationships with others. The self is, therefore, subordinated to the concerns of the group. In individualistic societies, such as the United States, the self is more an internal construct regarded as the individual's exclusive identity.

Because Japanese and American concepts of the self are so radically different, it is logical that the same disorder should be manifested in different ways in each culture. In individualistic societies, the avoidant personality fears criticism from others, negative evaluation, and rejection. This is followed by what Okonogi (1996) calls a Western-style type of shame: "One is concerned that one is not behaving as expected according to one's own ego ideal" (p. 175); that is, "I have failed to live up to my own standards." In a collectivist society, however, the avoidant personality is more likely to be manifest as a fear of offending others with one's behavior, with the discomfort that one's own characteristics may be causing to others. Logically then, taijin kyoufu subjects tend to be more concerned with their appearance and the impact that it may have on others.

Such cultural distinctions make another prediction as well. You would expect that social phobia, being more concerned with embarrassment to self, would be more prevalent in individualistic societies such as the United States and that avoidant personality disorder, taijin kyoufu, would have a higher prevalence rate in collectivist societies such as Japan. Although there are no studies of differential prevalence rates between these two countries, Ono and his colleagues (1996) offer data showing that the avoidant personality was the most frequently diagnosed personality in their study. More research is required on prevalence rates of personality disorders in different cultures.

can see, fulfills the avoidant's circular struggle; it vilifies others and discourages their closeness (keeping them safe from harm), yet ensures the avoidant's unwanted isolation.

Let's revisit our pure avoidant, Allison. It would seem far-fetched to imagine her seething with thoughts of revenge at those who fail to recognize her need for affection. Whereas the conflicted avoidant feels misunderstood, Allison believes that others see her for the inadequate person she sees in herself. She is far too fearful of negative evaluation to intentionally obstruct anyone.

THE HYPERSENSITIVE AVOIDANT

In contrast with the conflicted pattern, the **hypersensitive** avoidant incorporates features of the paranoid personality, but exhibits greater reality contact. Whereas persons with paranoid personality disorder are generally autonomous to a fault and cannot acknowledge any personal vulnerabilities, even to themselves, hypersensitive avoidants are well aware of their own shortcomings but will attribute them as much to the maneuverings of others as to themselves. Both are high-strung and prickly, vigilant to signs of rejection and abuse, and excessively wary of the motives of others. Moreover, their pervasive apprehensiveness is often accompanied by intense and labile moods that feature prolonged periods of edginess and self-deprecation. Hypersensitive avoidants strongly expect that others will be rejecting and disparaging but alternate between the profound gloom that often accompanies the basic avoidant pattern and the irrational projection of the paranoid. Either way, their usual strategy is a protective withdrawal that maintains a safe distance from all emotional involvement. Retreating defensively, some become more and more remote from others and from needed sources of support. Those who are more avoidant may express guilt and contrition, while feeling misunderstood, unappreciated, and demeaned by others. Those with a greater abundance of paranoid traits, however, find it difficult to contain their anger toward anyone who has been unsupportive, critical, or disapproving.

As the self-esteem of the hypersensitive avoidant approaches collapse, many take on more severe paranoid features and come to believe that their "pathetic self" is the product of covert actions by others to undermine them or make them inhibit themselves. Those with preexisting paranoid traits may find it easier to believe that others are the cause of their inadequacy, an external attribution, than to believe that they are naturally inadequate, an internal attribution. The former shifts the blame and perhaps allows a remedy; the latter leads only to resignation. Avoidants who have paranoid traits, therefore, may find that these traits intensify as conditions become more stressful.

Allison exhibits some paranoid traits, but there are important differences; therefore, some very fine distinction must be made to correctly identify these distinctive patterns. Here, we must look to the origin of presenting features. For example, it is nearly impossible for Allison to sit in a class without believing that people who are laughing are laughing at her. This resembles an idea of reference, a classic paranoid characteristic where the perceiver gets the notion that people or things happening in the environment are somehow referring to her via a conspiracy of these people or things. Allison's, however, are produced by her intense self-consciousness because she sees the laughing as the natural product of what she is, evoked because she is laughable.

THE PHOBIC AVOIDANT

Like the avoidant, dependent personalities desire close personal relationships; unlike the avoidant's basic sense of mistrust, however, dependents invest their trust (and much of their sense of self) in a significant other and relentlessly dread the potential loss of that relationship. **Phobic** avoidants combine features of these two personalities. Trapped between desire and the possibility of abandonment, phobic avoidants find a symbolic substitute onto which to project or displace their fear and anger. A free-floating and barely tolerable sense of anxiety or dread is thus concretized and shifted away from its true object: It's not the boyfriend or girlfriend, but the dog next door that is to be feared. By fleeing the phobic object or situation, such individuals seek to free themselves by symbolically leaving fear behind. Such phobias express the avoidant's fear of personal rejection, humiliation, and shame. For many phobic avoidants, the expression of fear in the presence of the phobic object also represents a cry for compassion, a desire to make instrumental use of fear as a means of disarming rejection and abandonment threats by eliciting support from otherwise unsupportive persons. Thus, phobic avoidants may successfully distance themselves from anxiety-producing situations, while also soliciting a degree of tolerance from others: You can't really hate her for not wanting to take the job at the dam; she has a fear of drowning. Unfortunately, such attempts often backfire, for the phobia itself may elicit mockery.

Our case study, Allison, does not seem to fit this pattern, either. Note that while she does experience similar acute symptomology, hers are clearly panic attacks that relate directly to her interpersonal world, rather than displaced phobic reactions to inanimate "replacement" objects. She is not attempting to make her worries tangible and concrete as a phobic avoidant may do in projecting fears onto a dreaded stimuli. She is also not attempting to elicit support by her panic attacks; quite the contrary, these are an instrumental method of escape.

Note, too, that many personalities experience phobic syndromes. Some exhibit dramatic displays; others, being more constrained, show a motor restlessness and worry about being exposed as weak and inadequate. Irritable personalities seem always on edge, even when the phobic object is not present; avoidants hide their fears under a quiet public reserve.

THE SELF-DESERTING AVOIDANT

A clear example of the influence of different personality domains is found in this last subtype of avoidant patterns. **Self-deserting** avoidants combine the social (interpersonal) retreating of the avoidant with the ruminative (cognitive) self-devaluation of the depressive personality. These individuals immerse themselves in a surrogate fantasy existence to avoid the discomfort of having to relate to others. They are not, however, unaware of their use of these tactics (unless, for example, they are concurrently experiencing a major depressive episode with psychosis), and this makes them painfully aware of their perceived inadequacies. Fantasy gradually becomes less effective, and their thoughts center more and more on the misery of their lives and the anguish of past experiences. Waking dreams are displaced by painful ruminations.

Thus totally interiorized, the feelings that motivated their initial withdrawal reverberate unremittingly. More and more, they cannot tolerate being themselves and seek to completely withdraw from their own conscious awareness, an existential abnegation of selfhood. Some become increasingly neglectful psychologically and physically, even to the point of neglecting basic hygiene. Some plunge into despair and are driven toward suicide, abandoning life as a means of ridding themselves of inner anguish and horror of their own identities. Others regress into a state of emotional numbness in which they are completely disconnected from themselves. In particularly severe cases, the structure of consciousness itself may split or fragment, leaving a regressive disorganization reminiscent of the schizotypal personality. As this process proceeds, self-deserting avoidants become outside spectators, observing from without the drama of their frightening transformation.

Allison's considerable alone time, which encourages her negative self-focus typical of this subtype, may suggest that she bears some resemblance to this pattern. However, the use of fantasy, as well as the nagging cognitions, is notably absent in her presentation.

While there are no absolute pure textbook avoidants, Allison's presentation, aside from a few notable traits that resemble those typically found in the preceding variants, seems to be most in line with the theoretically derived prototype.

Early Historical Forerunners

The avoidant personality has been described in several sources as far back as the early 1900s, although the personality style was not so named for some time. In 1911, Bleuler (1950) studied schizophrenia and its various developmental pathways. Some of his patients were noted to "shun contact with reality because their affects are so powerful they must avoid everything which might arouse their emotions. The apathy toward the outer world is then a secondary one springing from a hypertrophied sensitivity" (p. 65). Other theorists described traits essential to the avoidant, without hitting on this key contrast. Schneider (1923/1950), for example, described the "insecure self-distrusting psychopath," individuals who are chronically dissatisfied with themselves and always blame themselves when things go wrong but keep such feelings deeply hidden. Avoidant and schizoid patterns were frequently either confused or referred to synonymously, until Kretschmer (1921), in providing the first relatively complete description, developed a distinction. He divided active and passive forms of withdrawal into a continuum between two extremes: anaesthetic and hyperasesthetic. Anaesthetics, the obvious forerunners of the contemporary schizoids, were said to be affectively insensitive, dull, and lacking in spontaneity. In contrast, hyperasesthetics, although also withdrawn, were described as excitable and anxious, but also tender, shy, sulking, and distrustful of others. In particular, they seek "as far as possible to avoid and deaden all stimulation from the outside" (p. 161), which is a classic avoidant trait.

In the following four sections, we offer a detailed portrayal of the avoidant personality as expressed through the biological, psychodynamic, interpersonal, and cognitive perspectives. Each of these domains interacts to form the whole person. We have chosen to present history and description side by side. Avoid the temptation to see this material simply as a historical progression of "who did what when" because you will miss out on the descriptive bounty that each theoretical background brings to the construct. By the time you finish these sections, you should have a good grasp of the avoidant prototype. Developmental pathways are also described, though these pathways are currently speculative and indistinct. Read not only for history but also for the characteristics that each author unearthed and their significance to the total personality. References to the cases are included.

The Biological Perspective

The emotional vista of the avoidant personality is one of constant and confusing undercurrents of anxiety, sadness, and anger. Anguished by most all actions and events, they vacillate between unrequited desires for affection and pervasive fears of rebuff and embarrassment. The confusion and emotional irresolution they experience frequently lead to a general state of numbness. As noted, avoidant personalities have a deep mistrust of others and a marked deflated image of their own self-worth. They have learned to believe, through painful experiences, that the world is unfriendly, cold, and humiliating, and that they possess few of the social skills and personal attributes by which they can hope to experience the pleasures and comforts of life. They anticipate being slighted or demeaned wherever they turn. They have learned to be watchful and on guard against the ridicule and contempt they expect from others.

Portraits similar to the avoidant personality have been put forward by psychobiological researchers. In 1970, before the avoidant appeared in the *DSM-III,* Klein distinguished two schizoid subtypes. The first was noted by an asocial disposition, which he believed was accurately labeled in the *DSM.* A second type was described as a "shy, socially backward, inept, obedient person who is fearful and therefore isolated but appreciates sociability and would like to be part of the crowd" (p. 189). These characteristics, Klein noted, occurred in conjunction with anticipatory anxiety and low esteem. Other researchers (Siever & Davis, 1991, p. 1655) regard anxiety inhibition as providing one of the core psychobiological dispositions in the development of personality. Exploring beyond the safety of a nearby caretaker is an important development task for all children; those with a low threshold for anxiety would be seen as shy, inhibited, and fearful. They would not form new relationships easily, would avoid new situations, and would be particularly alert to the possible negative consequences of their actions. In turn, inhibition would interfere with learning new assertive behaviors and prevent such children from competing effectively with peers.

The biological development of most personality disorders is still speculative, but much exploration in this realm is underway. Still, a biological disposition alone is likely insufficient to result in the adult expression of the disorder; we are not exclusively biological beings. We may say with some certainty, however, that the deep inadequacy of some avoidant personalities may have a basis in physical maturation. Slow or uneven physical development can elicit teasing from peers that compounds a deep sense of awkwardness or inferiority; children who are already somewhat self-conscious for other reasons might then become even more so, eventuating in an avoidant pattern. The likelihood is probably increased when parents respond to atypical development with embarrassment or disappointment. Those who expect their children to progress rapidly through the usual stages of physical and psychological development may experience considerable anxiety and dismay over even small deviations and shortcomings.

As the child matures, feelings of shame expressed by parents in response to lack of achievement are likely to instill a sense of defectiveness or incompetence, even when the child performs above the norm. An athletic father who becomes frustrated and disappointed with his lanky and uncoordinated son, for example, implicitly communicates the idea that love and acceptance are contingent on superior performance. Similarly, an intellectually normal child whose mother is a highly intelligent college professor and has the same ambitions for her daughter may internalize her mother's disappointment and damn herself for not being smart enough. In both cases, the covert message is, "You are not good enough to be my child. You have not become what I expected or wanted. It is a chore to love you." Such examples are not exclusively biological, but instead highlight the interaction of the biological and social in producing characteristics observed in the total organism. The case of Sean (Case 6.2) illustrates this dynamic. When children are somehow never good enough, they internalize as their own self-image the shame their parents apparently felt just by having them.

There is evidence that the avoidant personality has a basis in temperament. Although shyness is not specific to the avoidant personality, its presence does suggest a sense of inner shame or self-doubt characteristic of the avoidant. Kagan, Reznick, and Snidman

CASE 6.2

A first-year college student, Sean hardly associated with anyone. In the clinical interview, he seemed to want to make contact, but he frequently stuttered, causing him to retreat in embarrassment. Otherwise, he expressed almost no emotion.

His second computer programming course was the immediate problem.[1] Though he was fluent in several computer languages, his professor wanted the students to work in groups, to collaborate in building chunks of a single large project. Sean was scared. "I try to work on it, but I can't concentrate." His voiced shrank to a whisper. "They're g . . g . . going to think I'm an idiot." His solution was to drop the class, though he had an A average going into this, the last assignment of the semester. In fact, his grades were exceptional overall. Nevertheless, Sean could report no friends, and confessed, "I'm lousy at meeting people. I guess I think they won't like me or something. I'm awkward. I'm a clutz. I just don't have many qualities others are interested in, I guess. But I'm great with computers."

In the first several sessions of therapy, he seemed to be holding back, as if he were looking for what a therapy client should do, in order not to disappointment expectations for progress. These transference issues were difficult to discuss at first, though eventually they led to a breakthrough, whereby Sean was able to see the link between present and past, and began to express his emotions more freely.

Sean's problems had their origin with his father, an aggressive and financially successful physician, noted for authoring a breakthrough surgical procedure. His mother was a shy woman who had worked as a high school teacher before they were married. From birth, he was an unusual baby. He cried incessantly and failed to develop a coherent schedule of feeding and sleeping. Worse, he was easily upset, and cried at the sight of anyone other than his mother.

From the start, Sean's father had little tolerance for his son. When he found out that Sean, now age 7, was afraid of the dark, he locked his son in the pitch black basement for hours, until the crying stopped. As Sean grew up, he failed to meet developmental milestones as fast as his older brother, thus disappointing his father again and again. Even his younger brother outgrew him. In physical education class, he was always picked last for teams. He dreaded coming up to bat, and he dreaded that the ball might somehow find its way to him. The other kids called him simply "The runt."

Sean's performance in school, though below that of his older brother, was nevertheless well above average. Even so, his father joked that the other boys would go on to good medical schools and Sean would go to nursing school. As Sean himself was acutely aware, his anxiety about measuring up to the other boys in his programming group had its origin in the many unfavorable comparisons he suffered at home.

---

[1] Numbers mark aspects of the case most consistent with *DSM* criteria, and do not necessarily indicate that the case "meets" diagnostic criteria in this respect.

(1988) studied 2-year-old children who exhibited either extreme behavioral restraint or extreme spontaneity in an unfamiliar context. At 7 years of age, the children were examined again. The majority of the restrained group remained quiet and socially avoidant, whereas those who were spontaneous became talkative and social. Although at 2 years, individuals have already passed through the phase at which early attachments are formed, it is possible that avoidants possess a constitutionally based fearful or anxious temperament, that is, a hypersensitivity to potential threat that accounts for such surprising continuity between age ranges.

The Psychodynamic Perspective

As mentioned previously, there has historically been a tendency to lump together schizoid and avoidant patterns, based on the tendency of both to withdraw. This may be traced to the historic psychodynamic tradition, where anyone whose personality was best described as withdrawn was classified simply as schizoid. Avoidants and schizoids were thus grouped together, as if their development and functioning were essentially the same. Even today, many analysts regard the avoidant simply as a nonpsychotic portion of the "schizoid spectrum," defined by withdrawal into imagination as the characteristic defense, something that Allison has been engaged in since childhood.

Psychodynamicists, however, did separate the constructs for study on several occasions and described character types akin to what we would now term the avoidant personality. Menninger (1930) described "isolated" individuals who demonstrated the capacity for normal emotional expression but who had "been artificially withheld from human contacts to the point of developing curious deficiencies, mannerisms, attitudes, odd behaviors, which serve to preclude their absorption or amalgamation into the group" and who "suffer constantly and sometimes acutely with feelings of inadequacy, diffidence, self-dissatisfaction and a pervading discouragement because of such feelings" (pp. 64, 71). Fenichel (1945), in line with the psychoanalytic school's long-term interests with inhibition, fear, and avoidance of our most basic drives, formulated a conception reflecting a phobic character but did not emphasize its social dimension. Other classical analytic investigators have also focused on phobia as a characterologic feature, as is seen in Rado's "phobic avoidance mechanism" (1969, p. 182), which he describes as a progressive reinforcer of more and more psychic safeguards in patients with "overreactive disorders," and in the "phobic character traits" described by MacKinnon and Michels (1971), which imply a generalized disposition to phobia where avoidance becomes the key feature.

Ego analysts, another faction of analytic thought, moved away from personality conceived through the conflict between basic drives and social forces and began to emphasize the interpersonal and reality-oriented nature of the ego, which was not driven by the battle between internal and external forces but instead operated synthetically to bind together and assimilate them (Greenberg & Mitchell, 1983), thus becoming capable of adding its own unique stamp to human behavior. Anticipating modern formulations, Horney (1937, p. 99) developed the concept of the detached type, individuals who believe, "If I withdraw, nothing can hurt me." Far from making themselves invulnerable, however, Horney believed that such individuals develop a sense of self-hatred and self-contempt and in turn are led to the conclusion that others regard them exactly as they regard themselves. As a result, they feel strained when relating to others, distance themselves from social encounters, and seek to never become attached to anyone. These theorists submit that a central goal of the avoidant personality is to deny anxiety and discomfort by denying all emotional feeling, actively derailing their painful preoccupations and tensions by introducing irrelevant thoughts or distorting the meaning of their thoughts, and effectively escaping the pain and anguish of simply being themselves by blunting and diffusing their internal perceptions and emotions.

Additionally, ego analysts describe avoidants as markedly indulgent in fantasy and imagination, both as a means of replacing anxiety-arousing cognitions of inadequacy and low self-worth and as a means of gratifying needs that cannot be met due to social withdrawal but may be explored in an isolated fashion. Because feelings of being unwanted are always close to the surface, they may imagine that they are deeply loved and involved in a whirlwind, fairytale romance. Allison, as you may recall, does not say what she fantasizes about, but the odds are strong, especially with her admission that she "has dreams" of unconditional acceptance, that the fantasy world version of herself is not just adequate but immensely talented and highly admired, complete with a "romantic someone" who fervently seeks to know everything about her. This is just the reverse of what she believes in real life—that others are not only disinterested in her but regard her as defective and shameful. Other avoidants, especially those who have comorbid paranoid or negativistic traits, may see themselves dispatching their enemies with a swift, confident fury.

Inevitably, however, such fantasies serve only to highlight just how impoverished their lives tend to be. Rather than employing a flexible and well-rounded array of defense mechanisms as would a healthy personality, the avoidant personality relies virtually exclusively on escape and fantasy. If these defenses are not possible or are highly impractical, they may quickly be overwhelmed or simply repress emotions of every kind, leaving only a flat, bland, unemotional exterior that belies a painful inner turmoil. This is one of the principal reasons avoidant personalities are often mistaken for schizoids, even by therapists. You can easily imagine Allison, if forced into a social encounter, choosing not to share anything of herself at all. In that case, she would appear to be completely without emotion or motivation, cardinal characteristics of the schizoid personality.

The experience of anxiety in the avoidant personality is complicated and fueled by several defining conflicts. First is the struggle of affection versus mistrust or, as Allison might say, having a boyfriend or getting dumped. As noted, avoidants wish for intimacy with others but cannot shake the belief that these desires inevitably end in pain and disillusionment. This characteristic provides one of the key distinctions between the avoidant and the dependent, who trusts readily and easily approaches others in time of emotional need. Second, avoidants deeply want to actualize their potentials but have strong doubts about their own competence and abilities. In particular, the idea of venturing into society and competing against others who are much more self-confident is especially frightening to them. You can imagine how Allison might feel knowing that professors are fond of students who raise their hands in class and contribute to the discussion. You can probably imagine a professor's puzzlement with such a bright girl who sits in the corner, out of sight, saying nothing.

For avoidants, then, virtually all roads to happiness seem blocked: Not only are they unable to act effectively on their own behalf, but their pervasive sense of inadequacy and mistrust prevents them from relying on others. Both roads lead to pain and discomfort. Avoidants are trapped in the worst of both worlds, seeking to avoid both the distress of moving forward socially and the emptiness within them that accrues from neglecting their own self-actualization. For some, like Allison, the conflict eventually becomes so acute that they present for therapy and begin working to resolve the dilemma.

Finally, though a later section covers broad, contextual developmental aspects of the avoidant personality, it is important to understand this pattern's early experience through the lens of object relations. This imperative branch of psychoanalytic thought is concerned with the influence of early memories and images of caretakers formed during infant development, no longer accessible to consciousness, which exert an ongoing influence on adult behavior. One of the basic tenets of psychoanalytic theory holds that children internalize the standards of important others, such as parents, teachers, and other role models, in the superego, which has two parts. First, the ideal self, or ego ideal, consists of wished-for characteristics, standards of behavior, accomplishments, and other things the individual would like to become. Because a highly developed ego ideal leads to effort to realize that ideal, this part of the superego can be connected to individual differences in levels of aspiration and self-actualization, the desire to fulfill your own unique potentialities as a living being. The conscience is the second part of the superego, containing all manner of prohibitions, rules, and commandments that detail behaviors that are off limits. Manifestations of the mature superego are felt in adult life through pangs of guilt or the voice of conscience.

The avoidant personality typically has a highly developed ego ideal complete with high aspirations and desires for self-actualization, but it is paired with an intensely condemning superego that constantly faults and disapproves of every behavior. In effect, they have internalized parental standards of high achievement and social success, combined with blame and shunning for the smallest mistakes. Allison states that during her childhood, her parents were very successful and had equally high expectations for her. Unfortunately, they also criticized her excessively for every small mistake. Allison carries both internalized voices, one demanding achievement and the other so critical that she is convinced of her inadequacies as a social leper. In effect, the distance between her ego ideal and her perceived actual self, who she believes herself to be, is so great that she is humiliated before her own judgment and panics when she thinks others might regard her in the same way.

The strong emphasis on standards of behavior sometimes leads to the development of traits that are characteristic of the compulsive personality, as well. In particular, the desire to avoid the small faults that elicited surges of parental dismay may frequently lead to the preoccupation with detail characteristic of the compulsive. Whereas the compulsive seeks to perform flawlessly, however, the avoidant usually refuses to perform at all; the risk is too great.

The Interpersonal Perspective

We have previously described much of the interpersonal spectrum of the avoidant personality because a pervasive sense of interpersonal unease may be the most noticeable domain of this personality pattern. Occasionally, you are likely to feel somewhat uncomfortable when confronted with a big crowd; by contrast, avoidants feel uncomfortable when confronted with even a single strange individual. Just one new person can activate all their fears of inadequacy and rejection. At best, they hesitate in expressing their own thoughts or opinions; at worst, they misread innocent comments and facial expressions as indicating an attitude of critical judgment or rejection.

As the tension mounts, their speech may become slow and constrained, with noticeable fragments of confused or irrelevant digressions. They may stutter through their lack of confidence, as with the case of Sean (Case 6.2). Because avoidants often feel that others are watching for their gaffes, their body posture may seem stiff and highly controlled, though with periodic bursts of fidgety movements. Overt expressions of emotion are kept in check for fear that others might detect their anxiety, much to their own shame. Inevitably, the feeling of being awkward contributes to their awkwardness. This is especially true of avoidants, for whom every miskeyed movement is scrutinized and judged, or so they believe.

Anxiety often precludes the avoidant's ability to speak fluidly and coherently, causing some avoidants to conclude that it would be best to not speak at all and attempt to melt into the woodwork. Such physical manifestations of interpersonal anxiety are likely to be especially acute in forced social situations, for example, when a school demands that all students attend a graduation ceremony, and many people are milling around and talking while waiting for things to start. Formal occasions are likely to be especially dreaded because they come with amplified codes of dress and behavior. Everyone knows what to expect and everyone is trying to conform, so discrepancies become magnified and errors stick out like a sore thumb. Allison would likely wait in the restroom and pray for the event to be over.

Avoidants do not confront this interpersonal anxiety. Instead, they escape social encounters whenever possible as a means of saving themselves from "inevitable" negative judgments. Any event that requires communication with others constitutes a potential threat to their fragile security. They may even deny themselves simple possessions to protect against the pain of loss or disappointment. Most find that efforts to comply with others' wishes, much less to assert themselves, prove fruitless and painful. They may feel that repeated appeasements have cost them their personal integrity, leading only to greater feelings of self-contempt. The only course they know to reduce shame and humiliation is to back away, withdraw within themselves, and keep a watchful eye on any incursion into their solitude. Distance guarantees safety, but trust invites pain.

To encourage even a modicum of social and functional efficacy, those who interact with avoidants, and especially those who have a stake in the avoidant's interpersonal interactions, must tread with extreme caution. For example, in a work situation, the avoidant's supervisor would need to approximate a good boxing manager. You don't start the avoidant out on something critical to an important project. You can imagine Allison's reaction if her boss were to say, "Okay, I know this is your first day, but there are a lot of people depending on you, and if this isn't done right, well, there'll be hell to pay." She would most likely go home for an early lunch and never return. Instead, avoidants need to be started out slowly, preferably on tasks for which they already feel some sense of competence—not so easy to cause them to think, "Gee, I guess he really sees through me and doesn't want to risk giving me any responsibility at all," but something manageable nonetheless.

Further, avoidants need to have a crystal-clear picture of others' expectations, with clear communications, well-defined interpersonal situations, and sequences of operations fully explained for them. Definition makes anxiety more manageable and keeps the avoidant from making mountains out of molehills. Consequences for mistakes should also be clearly defined and, if possible, minimized. A boss who is comfortable enough to self-disclose some of his or her own gaffes is also helpful. The risk is always that once their anxiety gets out of control, avoidants will leave with a courteous smile, as if nothing were the matter, and never come back. Because avoidants fear the expectations and judgment of others, cultivating a sense of trust with an avoidant worker is always a plus. Avoidants will not be the first to speak up when problems arise, especially if the problem mainly inconveniences them.

We previously mentioned the interpersonal relationships of avoidant personalities, especially through Allison and her high school boyfriend. Avoidant personalities frequently develop a façade that seems more adequate to them for dealing with the outside world. This façade is then used as a means of securing relationships against their perceived inadequacies that seem to them so egregious as to invariably sabotage the relationship, if ever discovered. Oftentimes, spouses begin to collaborate with their avoidant partners to some degree, doing things for them that permit them to stay at home, thus insulating them from the expectations or judgments of strangers. As the years wear on and the avoidant remains an underachiever, such collaborations may eventually wear thin. In effect, the more able spouse functions as an enabler of personality pathology. Some spouses, to their great disappointment, even sense that the avoidant affects a certain degree of pretense in the marital relationship as well. Some end the relationship, feeling that the intimacy they thought was there never really was and that they never knew the avoidant person at all.

In general, avoidants' protective shell of isolation serves only to perpetuate their problems. First, by narrowing their range of interpersonal experiences, they preclude the possibility of learning new ways of behaving that might bring them greater self-confidence or a sense of personal worth. In the most severe cases, they are left completely alone with their own turmoil and conflict. Though they have succeeded in minimizing external dangers, many find themselves trapped in their own skin, alone with their own self-contempt. These avoidants continue to recycle past humiliations, often losing touch with reality by becoming more and more caught up in the past and more and more estranged from the everyday current world. Second, like dependent personalities, their apparent weakness and self-doubt does occasionally attract those who enjoy shaming and ridiculing people who cannot defend themselves. The additional humiliation they experience thereby works to confirm their mistrust of others and causes them to place faith in a very few.

The interpersonal development of the avoidant personality has been described succinctly by Benjamin (1996) through her SASB model. Much like dependent and negativistic personalities, avoidants begin life with normal, healthy attachments, thus accounting for their wish to enjoy interpersonal relationships of genuine intimacy. As they mature, however, caretakers begin to exert intense control directed toward creating an impressive and admirable social image, casting mistakes and imperfections as extremely embarrassing to the family. You can see this in both Allison's and Sean's histories. Flaws are degraded and mocked, thus creating an extreme sensitivity to the possibility of humiliation. From Sean's history, we can see that his father was invested in making offensive comparisons between Sean and his two brothers. In the last paragraph of the case, his father even indicates that he doesn't respect him as a male.

What might the future avoidant do to safeguard against these invectives? First and foremost, they begin to conceal anything that might be seen as an imperfection or that might be fuel for further negative commentary. In fact, they become hypersensitive to the possibility of mistakes, which contributes to the development of a generalized fear of the negative evaluations of others. This also, not surprisingly, chips away at an already un-dermined self-image. Benjamin (1996) also notes that avoidants are usually shunned by the rest of the family as evidence of the family's shame and harsh judgment. Rather than be welcomed as part of the group, avoidants are forced to "go it alone," because the group won't have them. From the perspective of future avoidants, there is apparently a consensus about their defectiveness. Sean saw this both in his own family and at school, where he was picked last for teams and referred to as "the runt." Allison's mother and fa-ther even supplied supporting evidence, telling her that her birth was an accident and treating her as a burden.

To survive, future avoidants develop a sense of autonomy that is intrinsically linked to punishment (Benjamin, 1996). For example, avoidants are more likely to be "over-looked" for an invitation to a family reunion, or, as a child, the birthdays of their friends or even siblings are celebrated, but not theirs. In avoidance of the shame of such segre-gation, such shunned individuals withdraw in advance. Though they regret their defec-tiveness, they continuously strive to win over caregivers, who in turn often infuse the message that the family is the only genuine source of love and support, and loyalty is valued above all else. The implicit message is, "Although we tolerate your flaws, no one else ever will. Stay in the place where you at least *have a chance* to feel safe."

Whereas most avoidant personalities develop as the result of repeated exposure to developmental experiences that instill a sense of shame and low self-esteem, clinical experience indicates that certain traumatic childhood experiences, such as physical brutalization, incest, or molestation, may also be sufficient to produce a lifelong pat-tern of social avoidance and interpersonal fearfulness that resembles the avoidant pat-tern (Stone, 1993). Sexually abused children, for example, are often made to feel that they have something to be ashamed of, either by the perpetrator or by their own family. They may feel or be made to feel, "If I weren't defective in some way, this wouldn't have happened in the first place."

The Cognitive Perspective

The information-processing perspective, which you may have encountered in cognitive and experimental courses in psychology, is particularly relevant to the avoidant person-ality. In general, there are several information-processing models that attempt to explain cognitive process in humans. Some of these models are focused on neural networks (e.g., a particular cue, such as the word *flower,* primes linguistic systems for words such as *pretty, rose, red,* and each of these, in turn, primes other associations), while others are rule-based production systems (e.g., a sound leaves a sensory imprint, which is then translated into the multilevel memory system, prompting a comparative match from previous experience already stored in memory, all of which is necessary for the ensuing response). All of these cognitive process models have a common thread: The system is limited. There is but a finite capacity for attention and processing in humans. When at-tention becomes divided or fragmented, essential features of the stimulus world are ne-glected, all inputs are processed to a more shallow depth, and the overall quality of processing degrades substantially.

Generally, when cognitive theorists discuss personality, they focus on the contents of cognition—on how core and conditional beliefs influence and sustain a vicious circle of pathological interpersonal behavior, for example (Beck et al., 1990). In the avoidant personality, however, the contents of cognition establish a pathological reciprocity with the *structure* (i.e., the information-processing apparatus) of cognition, which in turn helps perpetuate the entire disorder. Here, hypervigilance is central. Avoidants constantly scan their environment for signs of danger. Sensitive to the most subtle feelings and intentions of others, they are acutely perceptive observers who appraise every movement and expression of those with whom they come into contact. Their incredibly sensitive instruments pick up and magnify incidental actions and reinterpret them as indications of derision and rejection.

What results from this flooding is an information-processing system overwhelmed with excessive stimuli that prevents attending to many of the ordinary, yet also relevant, features of the environment. In effect, the baseline expectancy of danger is so high that even innocuous events cross the avoidant's threshold at a point where they are appraised as harmful. Bombarded with a superabundance of potential threats, no single piece of information is processed at depth. The hypothesis that every source of stimulation is harmful is sustained because the consequences of uncertainty, of letting even one threat go unnoticed, are simply too great. As a result, anxiety increases, sensitivity to cues of threat increase, and depth of processing suffers further. Eventually, the entire cognitive processing system becomes so overburdened that everything is threatening, and the avoidant must withdraw to a safe haven, where the sources of stimulation (e.g., a few trusted others) are known to be safe. If unable to withdraw, they are left with a mind full of free-floating associations and a vague but powerful sense of danger. Figure 6.2 diagrams this vicious circle.

Your intuition may have already informed you that hypervigilance is likely a key contributor to Allison's panic attacks. As she moves from the safety of her home and into the surrounding world, Allison becomes increasingly attuned to the facial expressions and mannerisms of everyone around her. She notes where people are looking and at what. If she thinks they are looking at her (a not-too-uncommon finding for her), her self-consciousness escalates, since she will typically think that they are always looking just a little too long. She checks her dress and makeup for some social gaffe. She finds nothing, but her vigilance increases. Maybe she just can't see what they can. With her

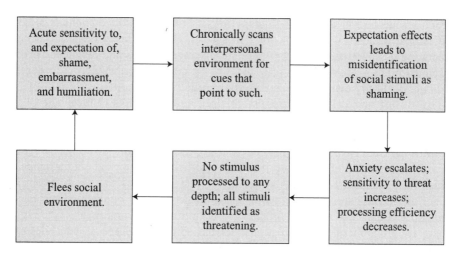

FIGURE 6.2   The Vicious Circle of the Avoidant's Information Processing.

attention heightened, she notes even more looks. At this point, time slows down for her, and she begins to feel "found out." With her defects public, she begins to feel shamed, and her anxiety level shoots off the scale, a full-fledged panic attack.

Many avoidant persons engage a form of cognitive defense designed to short-circuit this self-perpetuating vicious circle. To regain a measure of tranquility, they engage a series of reinterpretations and digressions, actively blocking, destroying, and fragmenting their own thoughts, seeking to disconnect relationships among what they see, what meanings they attribute to their perceptions, and what feelings they experience in response. Defensively, they intentionally destroy the clarity of their thoughts by intruding irrelevant distractions, tangential ideas, and discordant emotions. Rather than let the associations to threat further overwhelm them, they consciously introduce irrelevant thoughts and emotions into the cognitive stream to displace anxiety-ridden content with more neutral associations. In effect, they have learned to disrupt the automatic processing of stimulation with a form of self-consciously practiced cognitive interference. For some, this strategy assumes an automaticity of its own, giving it the characteristics of a personality trait. At least superficially, such individuals may resemble the schizotypal personality.

Much like an intoxicating drug, this strategy of cognitive interference may win anxiety reduction, but at the expense of cognitive clarity. By habitually interfering with the natural flow of cognitive processes, avoidants further diminish their ability to deal with events efficiently and rationally. No longer can they attend to the most salient features of their environment, nor can they focus their thoughts or respond rationally to events. Moreover, their thinking becomes too scattered and cluttered to learn new ways of coping. Social communications may also become tangential and irrelevant, further distorting others' responses to the avoidant. In their attempt to diminish intrusively disturbing thoughts, they fall prey to a coping mechanism that further aggravates their original difficulties and ultimately intensifies their alienation from both themselves and others. Allison does not appear to be this severe; although she is certainly overwhelmed cognitively, she does not seek (actively or automatically) to disrupt the coherence of her own self-awareness as a means of protecting herself against pain, as does the young man in our second case example (see Case 6.2).

In addition to information processing, the cognitive perspective also informs us that beliefs about the world, self, and others (i.e., the aforementioned *contents of* cognition) are critical in determining behavior (Beck et al., 1990). The influence of schemata in mediating behavior can be shown by reinterpreting the traits and diagnostic criteria of a given disorder, as we do in the following paragraphs. Cognitivists refer to **core beliefs,** as beliefs held to be absolutely and eternally true; factors in the world may change, but the validity of such beliefs endures essentially forever, usually at a level below conscious awareness. Core beliefs are a powerful and pervasive influence in organizing other beliefs, especially in predicting the consequences of various courses of action, expressed as **conditional beliefs,** if-then statements that are contingent on the subject's behavior. In turn, conditional beliefs feed into **instrumental beliefs,** notions about the mode through which the individual can affect the world.

The *DSM-IV* criteria for the avoidant personality can be conceptualized in terms of two core beliefs, two conditional beliefs, and three instrumental beliefs (see Figure 6.3). There are probably other formulations, depending on the degree of detail desired at the level of core beliefs. For example, is the first box in Figure 6.3 a single core belief, as shown here, or is it really four beliefs—one core belief for each piece of the self-image?

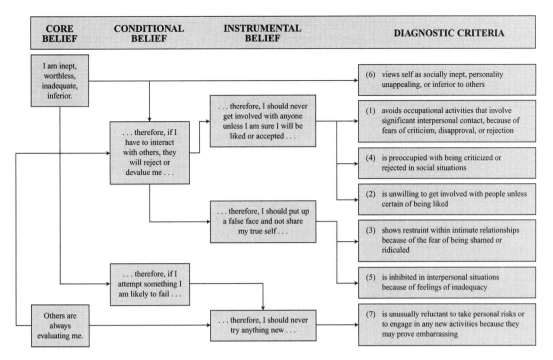

CORE BELIEF	CONDITIONAL BELIEF	INSTRUMENTAL BELIEF	DIAGNOSTIC CRITERIA

FIGURE 6.3   Belief and the Avoidant Personality (some beliefs from Beck & Freeman, 1990).

Because there are only fine distinctions among such descriptors, we have chosen to group them together. Core beliefs should be global and generalized, for they influence all other beliefs below them in the schematic hierarchy. Accordingly, Figure 6.3 maps the first *DSM-IV* diagnostic criterion directly to a single core belief. Such direct translations are rare and occur mainly in the self-image realm. Thus, the first criterion, "Views self as socially inept, personally unappealing, or inferior to others" (p. 665), is directly translated into the belief, "I am inept, unappealing, and inferior."

Moreover, Figure 6.3 shows that some diagnostic criteria reflect the same instrumental belief, only expressed in different situations. For example, the first and fourth criteria are almost the same, except that the first refers to vocational concerns and the fourth to social concerns. The second criterion essentially repeats the same theme. Such redundancy suggests that some taxonomy of situations should be developed so that the same belief does not become needlessly multiplied, weighting the disorder too much in a particular direction. For example, each instrumental belief might be expressed through a single criterion in the vocational, educational, recreational, and interpersonal domains. This criticism applies to nearly every personality disorder, not just the avoidant.

As mentioned before, the avoidant's instrumental beliefs of ineptitude and unworthiness, which create a perpetual downward spiral of depleting self-esteem, also tend to manifest significant underachievement. Given that many of these people are talented and intelligent, this is a very unfortunate hindrance. Because they internalize their parents' high expectations, many avoidants acquire considerable skills but never judge themselves "good enough" to apply what they have learned in front of others. Alternatively, other avoidants try to develop an interest in something, only to quit prematurely because they judge their own performance as inadequate, just as mother and father did.

Although the case discussion does not say so, this may contribute to why Allison feels she may not be able to attend classes. She may not be motivated to, because she may believe that no matter how expert her teachers, she would just screw things up anyway. Why learn to be anything when you'll never do anything with it anyway? Better to save yourself the agony of trying, especially with panic attacks in your way.

You can easily see the relevance of the cognitive perspective on beliefs to the personality disorders in Allison. Her core belief in her own inadequacy has been amplified, with cascading influences down the hierarchy to the level of conditional and instrumental beliefs. Allison is no longer certain that she will be able to attend classes, a variation of, "If I try something, I am likely to fail." She consolidates her shopping trips to avoid others, an expression of the underlying belief, "If I have to interact with others, I will be rejected." She notes the context in which her inadequacy beliefs were formed, under high parental expectations and equally strong parental criticism. She was afraid to be herself with her former boyfriend, a behavioral manifestation of the instrumental belief that she must put up a "false face" or be rejected. Other examples could be noted. Consult Beck et al. (1990) for a discussion of these and other avoidant beliefs.

The Evolutionary-Neurodevelopmental Perspective

Perspectives such as biological, cognitive, interpersonal, and psychodynamic are useful for illuminating a given personality from a particular angle but do not permit holistic conceptions. Whereas most other personality disorders have ample historical precedent, the avoidant personality was originally formulated from Millon's biopsychosocial theory of personality in 1969 as the actively detached pattern, as distinctive from the passively detached schizoid personality. This conception shares many features with its modern evolutionary counterpart (Millon, 1990; Millon & Davis, 1996) that describes the avoidant as *active* and *pain* oriented in its evolutionary structure, while the schizoid is markedly *passive,* largely insensitive to either *pleasure* or *pain,* and only very moderately attuned to *self* over *others* in orientation. For schizoids, interpersonal detachment is ego-syntonic: Social isolation is simply solitude and does not trouble the individual. In contrast, the avoidant is actively detached. This sets up a conflict in which such individuals strongly desire involvement, love, and intimacy but fear exposing themselves to shame in seeking it. For them, social isolation is loneliness. Allison and Sean share this crucial characteristic though, in Sean, it is moderated through his intense interest in computers. Although he has not yet progressed to a point that he may recognize it, we could speculate that for Sean, computers are a substitute for real relationships. Therefore, he expresses his interpersonal needs far less than does Allison.

Before the crucial distinction between active and passive detachment, the central features characterizing the avoidant personality were scattered across the clinical literature. Although they have now been collected into a single syndrome, there is no strong parallel between past and contemporary conceptions, as there are for most other personality disorders. Because both avoidants and schizoids avoid interpersonal contact, they share the superficial feature of social detachment. Early object relations thinkers found this phenomenon to be particularly interesting (Fairbairn, 1940) but, paradoxically, emphasized withdrawal from the social world rather than the underlying reason for withdrawal, thereby mixing avoidant and schizoid features together. The error is understandable, as both personalities conceal their innermost thoughts and motives and both resist scrutiny and evaluation. The schizoid lacks the rich inner life of the avoidant, but neither offers the aspiring taxonomist much information. Accordingly, history classifies the two together. Some of this can be seen in Sean, who presents in a state of emotional numbness caused by intense fear. Table 6.1 summarizes the total avoidant personality in terms of its clinical domains.

The evolutionary model suggests several hypotheses in terms of the neurodevelopment of avoidant behavior. There are many structural elements and physiological processes that comprise the biophysical undergirding for the complex psychological functions of this pattern, such as affective disharmony, interpersonal aversiveness, and so on. Studies demonstrate that a higher than chance correspondence within family

TABLE 6.1   The Avoidant Personality: Functional and Structural Domains

Functional Domains		*Structural Domains*	
	Fretful		*Alienated*
Expressive Behavior	Conveys personal unease and disquiet, a constant timorous, hesitant, and restive state; overreacts to innocuous events and anxiously judges them to signify ridicule, criticism, and disapproval.	**Self-Image**	Sees self as socially inept, inadequate, and inferior, justifying thereby isolation and rejection by others; feels personally unappealing, devalues self-achievements, and reports persistent sense of aloneness and emptiness.
	Aversive		*Vexatious*
Interpersonal Conduct	Distances from activities that involve intimate personal relationships and reports extensive history of social anxiety and distrust; seeks acceptance, but is unwilling to get involved unless certain to be liked, maintaining distance and privacy to avoid being shamed and humiliated.	**Object-Representations**	Internalized representations are composed of readily reactivated, intense, and conflict-ridden memories of problematic early relations; limited avenues for experiencing or recalling gratification, and few mechanisms to channel needs, bind impulses, resolve conflicts, or deflect external stressors.
	Distracted		*Fragile*
Cognitive Style	Warily scans environment for potential threats and is preoccupied by intrusive and disruptive random thoughts and observations; an upwelling from within of irrelevant ideation upsets thought continuity and interferes with social communications and accurate appraisals.	**Morphologic Organization**	A precarious complex of tortuous emotions depends almost exclusively on a single modality for its resolution and discharge, that of avoidance, escape, and fantasy; hence, when faced with personal risks, new opportunities, or unanticipated stress, few morphologic structures are available to deploy and few backup positions can be reverted to, short of regressive decompensation.
	Fantasy		*Anguished*
Regulatory Mechanism	Depends excessively on imagination to achieve need gratification, confidence building, and conflict resolution; withdraws into reveries as a means of safely discharging frustrated affectionate as well as angry impulses.	**Mood/Temperament**	Describes constant and confusing undercurrent of tension, sadness, and anger; vacillates among desire for affection, fear of rebuff, embarrassment, and numbness of feeling.

Note: Shaded domains are the most salient for this personality prototype.

groups in social apprehensiveness and withdrawal behavior can be attributed in large measure to learning, but there is reason to believe, at least in some cases, that this correspondence may partially be assigned to a common pool of genotypic dispositions within families.

Some infants display hyperirritability, crankiness, tension, and withdrawal behaviors from the first days of postnatal life. The apparent "avoidant" constitutional disposition of these babies may then prompt rejecting and hostile attitudes from the caregivers. But it is neither necessary, nor sufficient, to be possessed of such a disposition. Normal, attractive, and healthy infants may also encounter parental devaluation, hypercriticism, and rejection. Reared in a family setting in which they are belittled, abandoned, and censured, these youngsters will have their natural robustness and optimism crushed and acquire in its stead attitudes of self-deprecation and feelings of social alienation. These harsh, self-critical attitudes may then have far-reaching and devastating consequences. The child who belittles his or her own worth will not be possessed of a self capable of healing psychological wounds or gaining rewards unobtainable from others. They are caught in a web of social *and* self-reproach, and they, themselves, become the agent of negative reinforcement.

Signs of avoidant behavior are usually, but not always, evident well before the child begins to participate in the give-and-take of peer relationships, school and athletic competitions, dating with its attendant anxieties, and so on. These early signs may reflect the operation of constitutional dispositions or attitudes and habits conditioned by the circumstances of family life. Whatever its origins, many school-age children already possess the social hesitations and aversive tendencies that will come to characterize them more clearly in later life. But for many other youngsters, the rudiments of social withdrawal and self-alienation have only developed minimally when they first encounter the challenges of peer-group activities. For them, the chances of enhancing their competencies and for developing the requisite skills for effective social adaptation remain good, unless they experience rejection, isolation, or the devastating ridicule that often can be meted out by their age-mates.

CONTRAST WITH RELATED PERSONALITIES

Avoidants share traits with several other personalities. Both avoidants and schizoids withdraw from the world of interpersonal relationships, though for different reasons. True schizoids are socially indifferent, or passively detached. They lack strong drives and emotions and appreciate few of the subtle nuances of human communication. In contrast, avoidants overflow with anxiety and are hypersensitive to even minor criticisms. Schizoids do not find interpersonal relationships reinforcing; avoidants find them punishing. Whereas the mental landscape of the schizoid is largely a vast, empty, unbroken plain, avoidants often develop a rich fantasy life as a means of compensating for their social inadequacies. Their need for affect and closeness may pour forth in poetry, be sublimated in intellectual pursuits, or be expressed in sensitively detailed artistic activities. In effect, they invent an imaginary world to substitute for the real world they avoid. Sean, for example, is deeply interested in programming languages. Because the computer always does exactly what he asks without judging him, it has become his playground.

Finally, the thought processes of both avoidants and schizoids sometimes seem disrupted or tangential. Given their scant drives, schizoids find neither life, thought, nor fantasy reinforcing. They have no interest in exploring the implications of a particular concept or developing a line of argument. For this reason, their thought processes are inherently diffuse. Seldom do they focus on any one idea for long. In contrast, avoidants are easily overloaded by external stimulation and may actively interfere with their own cognitive processes as a means of distracting themselves from overwhelming levels of anxiety or fear. Sean's stuttering, even in the safety of the therapy office, is a prime example, as is his inability to concentrate on his programming task knowing its social dimension.

The cognitive interference, pervasive social anxiety, and preoccupation with an internal fantasy world of some avoidants can also resemble the eccentricities, social detachment, and low self-esteem of the schizotypal personality. The cognitive intrusions of avoidants, however, rise and fall with their level of anxiety. When alone or with a few trusted intimates, the avoidant is often capable of sustained, goal-oriented cognition. In contrast, the schizotypal is characterized by a baseline of eccentricity, though this can sometimes be treated with the appropriate medications. Schizotypals are more dramatically bizarre and more prone to periods of psychotic decompensation. They may believe, for example, that they can read the thoughts of others, see through walls, or hear sounds emanating from far distant locations. Such ideas are highly unusual in an avoidant.

Both paranoids and avoidants are chronically tense and mistrustful, and both fear that they will suffer humiliation or embarrassment at the hands of others. Avoidants, however, believe their own inadequacies are the cause of social derogation, whereas paranoids believe that others are actively attempting to undo them. Both avoidants and paranoids are reluctant to confide in others. Avoidants, however, mainly fear embarrassment; paranoids feel that they will be betrayed and that the information conveyed will someday be used against them. Both personalities tend to be desperately lonely, a fact of which avoidants are often acutely aware. In contrast, paranoids see themselves as an island fortress under perpetual external assault and thereby disavow loneliness as an annoying vulnerability. Moreover, paranoids tend to be aloof, humorless, and aesthetically blunt, whereas avoidants show sensitivity, a good sense of humor, and often, a well-developed artistic capacity.

Finally, avoidants, dependents, compulsives, and negativists are all part of the so-called anxious cluster, personalities for whom anxiety is a prominent life concern. Avoidants and dependents are alike in sharing deep feelings of personal inadequacy but differ in their response to perceived inadequacy. When threatened with feelings of helplessness, dependents seek to bind others even closer to them by increasing their submissiveness and attempting to please others all the more. In contrast, the avoidant is often very effective in nonsocial situations; the dependent is not. Avoidants run away at the first sign of negative evaluation; dependents stay and try to please. Both avoidants and compulsives share performance anxiety and a fear of evaluation, which they modulate with extraordinary self-control. Compulsives, however, are usually able to sublimate their anxiety into a preoccupation with rules, details, lists, and such; avoidants are more likely to simply withdraw from social venues.

PATHWAYS TO SYMPTOM EXPRESSION

Avoidants are often thought of as the "anxious personality"; it is not surprising that they are highly vulnerable to the development of any number of clinical syndromes, more so than just about any other personality pattern. Accordingly, this section is somewhat longer than its counterparts in other chapters. As always, remember that there is a logic that connects the personality pattern with its associated Axis I syndromes. Avoidants who develop panic attacks, for example, like Allison, do so for reasons different from dependents. As you read the following paragraphs, try to identify the connection between personality and symptom.

Anxiety Disorders

Because their interpersonal skills are often sorely lacking due to chronic rejection, sharply critical caregivers, hereditary disposition, or the like, avoidant persons are highly inadequate in managing everyday social strains and challenges. Many of these individuals attempt to adjust by minimizing their social world as much as possible. However, this becomes a vicious, self-perpetuating circle, as the more insulated the person becomes, the more social phobia he or she manifests. Others who fail to adjust develop an anxiety disorder. Generalized anxiety and social phobia are probably the most frequent of the anxiety-spectrum disorders, though obsessive-compulsive disorder is also commonly found (Rodrigues & Del Porto, 1995). Panic attacks are also possible; just ask Allison.

Subjects with generalized anxiety disorder seem perpetually on edge and unable to relax, easily startled, tense, worried, preoccupied with possible calamities, and prone to nightmares. When asked what it is they fear, they report only a vague and diffuse awareness that something dreadful is imminent, though they are not sure what it is they dread or from where it will strike. Hypervigilance, an attention that is chronically active in searching for threat, even when the individual is alone, is probably the source of continuity between the avoidant personality and the clinical syndrome. In essence, the individual continues to scan the environment for sources of threat, even when other persons are not physically present. Without some concrete focus, it is possible that these individuals turn their ruminations inward, scanning their memories and recent interpersonal interactions for something that has been overlooked, for example.

The fear of social situations characteristic of generalized social phobia is so much a part of the avoidant that it is difficult to determine where the personality disorder ends and the clinical syndrome begins. The association is so close, in fact, that many researchers have questioned whether the two are separate syndromes (e.g., Fahlen, 1997) or whether they may represent points on the same continuum, both manifesting personality dimensions and clinical syndromes such as shyness, depressive symptoms, neuroticism, introversion, social phobic avoidance, and social or occupational impairment (e.g., Rettew, 2000; van Velzen, Emmelkamp, & Scholing, 2000). Some (e.g., J. Reich, 2000) find extensive diagnostic criteria and treatment approach overlap and advocate reconceptualization of the Axis I and II constructs according to "empirical findings." Still others argue that their overlap is an artifact of the committee process through which the *DSM* is revised. The *DSM-IV* specifically asks clinicians to consider the additional diagnosis of avoidant personality where social phobia is generalized to most social situations.

Although both may be simultaneously diagnosed, several important distinctions should be remembered. First, the personality disorder includes a variety of traits that need not be associated with generalized social phobia. Avoidants, for example, typically attempt to maintain a social façade of poise and self-control that conceals an inner anger, inherited from a developmental history that includes mockery for faults and foibles. In contrast, social phobias need not possess the full developmental picture expressed by the avoidant. Likewise, avoidants deeply wish for love and acceptance but doubt that such luxuries are possible, at least for them. Social phobics are not required to be distressed in this way.

Tentative therapy-outcome research suggests that the Axis I and II disorders frequently overlap, and those with a diagnosis of both avoidant personality disorder and social phobia are more impaired at the beginning of therapy, have more comorbid diagnoses, and remain more impaired after therapy and three months thereafter (Feske, Perry, Chambless, Renneberg, & Goldstein, 1996). This seems to suggest that avoidant personality includes additional enduring trait characteristics that social phobia does not, yet others have argued that the avoidant is only a more severe form of social phobia (Dahl, 1996; M. R. Johnson & Lydiard, 1995). The controversy is not yet settled and remains an important frontier in research on the personality disorders.

Obsessive-compulsive disorder is frequently found among avoidant personalities (Rodrigues & Del Porto, 1995). Obsessions are intrusive thoughts, impulses, or images that the individual experiences as stressful or anxiety provoking. The *DSM-IV* maintains that obsessions are usually unrelated to real-life problems and are experienced as unwanted, outside the person's control, and occurring unexpectedly. Fear of germ contamination is an example. In contrast, compulsions are unwanted behaviors, such as checking or washing rituals, which the person feels compelled to perform. If the compulsion is resisted, an inner sense of anxiety develops and increases. By giving these symptoms a functional interpretation, continuity can be established with the personality disorder. First, obsessions and compulsions serve to distract avoidants from constantly dwelling on their perceived inadequacies. Likewise, obsessive or compulsive preoccupations may counteract feelings of estrangement or depersonalization by providing especially withdrawn avoidants with thoughts and behaviors that assure them that there is some tangible reality to life. Disordered attention undoubtedly plays a role, though explaining why an obsession or compulsion takes on a particular theme seems to step outside the bounds of the cognitive perspective.

Physical Symptoms

Many personality disorders exhibit physical symptoms, referred to in the *DSM-IV* as somatoform disorders. In each case, the common thread is the presence of physical symptoms that cannot be explained by a medical condition or actual illness. Numerous factors make physical symptoms an ideal candidate for some hidden psychological purpose: All medical tests have some degree of error, physical perceptions are largely subjective, and medicine is an inexact science. Moreover, almost everyone has heard horror stories about incompetent physicians who overlook real problems, forcing their patients to complain even more loudly just to receive adequate care.

Physical symptoms can be used by avoidants to solve a number of coping problems. First, somatic concerns can be used to counter impending feelings of depersonalization or dissociation by assuring subjects of their own physical reality. In severe cases, social isolation may cause these bodily preoccupations to be elaborated into bizarre delusions. Second, somatic symptoms can be used as a distraction from an internal world of shame. If everyone is focused on the problem, they're at least not focused on the person. Third, unexplained feelings of fatigue or disabling pain may be used to justify social withdrawal, particularly in cases where significant others are at their limits and demand that the avoidant seek employment or otherwise engage the world on its own terms. Here, the physical problem functions as a distractor for all parties.

Although speculative, it appears that one physical symptom disorder, body dysmorphic disorder, might frequently present in the context of an avoidant pattern. Individuals with this condition are preoccupied with an imagined or very minor defect in their physical appearance, perhaps the shape of their nose, the size of their jaw, or a thinning hairline. So intense is their concern that they report feeling tormented and shamed. Some isolate themselves from society completely or travel only at night, when the darkness conceals their "ugliness." Some may spend hours examining their defect in a mirror. Obviously, the extreme avoidance of social engagement due to intense shame suggests characteristics of the avoidant personality. Stone (1993) presents such a case. Similarly, avoidants would not want to have some physical defect that might call attention to their other defects.

Dissociative Disorders

Avoidants, borderlines, and self-defeating (masochistic) personalities sometimes experience dissociative states (Ellason, Ross, & Fuchs, 1995, 1996). For the avoidant, feelings of self-estrangement may arise as a protective maneuver to diminish the impact of excessive stimulation, the pain of social humiliation, or a devalued sense of self. Without an integrated inner core to which experience can be anchored, events may seem disconnected, ephemeral, and unreal. Dissociative states can also be traced to the intentional use of cognitive interference, through which avoidants disconnect themselves from their own thoughts and feelings. Experiences of amnesia may sometimes occur as an expression of the rejection of self, a protective disowning of an individual's own identity.

Depressive Disorders

Avoidants are highly vulnerable to feelings of depression. Although Allison was diagnosed as experiencing panic attacks, her situation is objectively depressing. Though avoidants seek to insulate themselves from the fears and pains of interpersonal encounters, most are only partially successful. Moreover, isolation is bittersweet and conflict arousing, as avoidants continue to desire a successful and confident existence, intimate companionship, and freedom from self-contempt. The ideal self continues to seek expression, and critical internal voices continue to carp. Accordingly, most avoidants continue to feel unloved, alone, and ineffective. These feelings may be displayed either through full-blown depressive episodes or quietly endured periods of despondency and futility.

Schizophrenic Disorders

Historically, schizophrenia and the psychotic disorders have always represented a loosely bound collection of clinical symptoms. Despite considerable clinical observation and empirical research, it is not clear whether schizophrenia is one disorder or several, how restrictive the definition of the disorder should be, or how it might break down into subtypes. Some theorists believe that a genetic predisposition is a necessary factor (Meehl, 1962, 1990a, 1990b), whereas others hold that the disorder can occur through disordered family communication patterns alone. Despite problems in defining the disorder, most clinicians recognize the importance of distinguishing between positive and negative symptoms. Positive symptoms represent pathological exaggerations or distortions of normal cognitive functioning and include hallucinations, delusions, and disorganized speech and movement. Such persons often seem overaroused or hypersensitive. Negative symptoms represent deficits relative to normal behavior. Such persons are notable not so much for what they do, but for the lack of richness in their experience and existence. Their emotions seem flat, perhaps barely experienced. They have no purpose, goals, motives, interests, pursuits, hobbies, or passions, and they are not bothered by the absence of these things.

The distinction between positive and negative symptoms is similar to the distinction between the passively detached schizoid personality and actively detached avoidant personality (Millon, 1969) drawn earlier in this chapter. This suggests that schizoids are more likely to develop the negative symptoms of schizophrenia, and avoidants are more likely to develop the positive symptoms. Schizoid schizophrenics would thus display a chronic hyporeactivity and an absence of emotional depth. Cognitively, their lack of interest and motivation would cause them to drift aimlessly from one sparse and tangential thought to another. They would be completely apathetic about their lack of interpersonal involvement. In contrast, avoidant schizophrenics would display hyper-alertness and emotional turmoil. Cognitively, their tendency to distract themselves from pain and shame by interfering with their cognitive clarity would cause them to appear disorganized, fragmented, or incoherent. Interpersonally, they would tend to develop paranoid delusions as a defense against critical parental voices internalized during childhood. In effect, their fear of criticism develops into delusions of persecution, the idea that others are actively hunting for their faults, scheming to expose their inadequacies, or secretly planning a humiliating attack.

Therapy

Although the avoidant is one of the most common personality disorders encountered in clinical practice, many factors combine to make its prognosis unusually poor. The most basic characteristics of the avoidant run counter to the basic requirements of psychotherapy. Simply put, avoidants avoid. So intense is their desire to flee shame and humiliation that many employ defensive strategies designed to block such feelings from their own self-awareness. In contrast, effective therapy requires that thoughts and emotions be discussed openly, at least at some point, which in turn requires a focus on the self and its perceived deficiencies. Just considering the very first question of therapy—"What is it about me that I would like to change?"—may prove to be extremely terrifying for more severe cases, many of whom never present for therapy or drop out after just a few sessions. As we saw with Sean, perceived defects can be difficult to discuss, even with someone whose role it is to help.

THERAPEUTIC TRAPS

Avoidants require tremendous patience and care. Because almost everyone in avoidants' lives is perceived as a painful fountain of negative evaluation, avoidants are extremely reluctant to share themselves openly. Accordingly, they need to know that the therapist is different and that the therapeutic relationship will be different. Reassurance, pacing, and acceptance are essential. When avoidants sense impatience, they feel judged, criticized, and attacked, and their immediate impulse is to withdraw. Conversely, avoidants are often so afraid of disappointing others that they may fake real progress or report what they believe the therapist wants to hear, effectively setting themselves up to simply drop out when further expectations cannot be met. This often leaves the therapist in a state of confusion and astonishment.

Avoidants need to know that they can say, "You're pushing me too hard right now" without destroying the relationship or incurring the wrath of those they respect. Every other relationship in their lives operates on the assumption that disclosure will be punished. The therapeutic relationship should be perceived as safe enough and authentic enough that avoidants can assert themselves without fear of being condemned, as Sean eventually did. This is an index of progress, but it is also true that such levels of trust constitute a breakthrough for many patients, one that grows out of the total process of therapy. Many avoidants find any discussion of transference and countertransference too threatening, at least at first.

Because trust is such an important issue, avoidants have ways of testing those they encounter to determine who can be trusted and who cannot. Minor frustrations may be imposed on others as a means of gauging their reaction. They may find an excuse to cancel appointments, reschedule at an inconvenient time, or just not show up. Here, the questions behind these behaviors are: How easily or willingly will this individual become an extension of my own punitive superego? Will he or she seek to punish me like everyone else? Or can he or she be trusted as safe? Becoming critical, hostile, impatient, or indifferent fails the test.

THERAPEUTIC STRATEGIES AND TECHNIQUES

Trust will likely remain an issue throughout therapy, but the therapist will have more freedom to focus on difficult problems once a basic sense of safety becomes established. The inept self-image of avoidants, their interpersonal fears of exposure and rejection, and their defensive use of distraction to diffuse the pain of mere self-conscious awareness, of just being themselves, are all deeply connected.

Working from a cognitive perspective, Beck et al. (1990) suggest that once this modicum of safety is established, feelings of low self-worth can be addressed by actively disputing automatic thoughts, such as, "I am no good, inadequate. I am defective. Others will mock me." This helps patients discover errors in thought that they commit in the course of everyday living that contribute to their own painful feelings and problems. In addition, most avoidants possess a variety of admirable traits that get lost in their relentless focus on their own faults. Global feelings of worthlessness can be moderated and counterbalanced by integrating these positive characteristics into a fuller and more balanced sense of self. An objective assessment of Sean, for example, would emphasize his excellent grades and his ample computer talents, things of which he can be proud. If these can be integrated into his self-schema, his esteem should rise and, with it, his willingness to experiment socially.

Other techniques mix cognitive and behavioral elements. Tolerance to interpersonal situations can be increased by imagining social situations that evoke negative emotions and exploring them together with the therapist in the privacy of the therapy room. Automatic thoughts (Beck et al., 1990) can be elicited and tested along the way. This technique combines cognitive and interpersonal elements and can be used to try out new behaviors that prediffuse feelings of anxiety before the behaviors are implemented in the outside world. After the avoidant begins to feel more comfortable with these experimental rehearsals, an entire hierarchy of anxiety-provoking topics can be constructed and the subject can be asked to predict exactly what will happen in each situation.

Ideally, each of these predictions is eventually reality-tested by the patient, with the results discussed in session. The avoidant moves forward as comfort with each succeeding step grows. If subjects are reluctant to test their predictions, they can be asked to role-play, with the therapist assuming the part of the other person. To aid in preventing relapse, avoidants can be taught to use anxiety as a signal that automatic thoughts are active, to keep logs of avoidant thinking, to actively discredit their own irrational beliefs, and to plan realistic coping strategies in advance of difficult situations. This approach would probably be particularly effective with Allison because anxiety is so much a part of her life.

Finally, because cognitive techniques implicitly involve disagreeing, interrupting, or redirecting the subject, transference feelings created as a result of these activities should probably be explored at the very beginning. Otherwise, the avoidant may paint the therapist as critical or rejecting and conclude, "I'm so defective that I can't even do therapy right." Beck et al. (1990) suggest that patients rate feedback from their therapist on a trust scale ranging from 0 to 100%, thus providing very specific information that allows progress in this area to be charted concretely. All such activities work to increase social competence while falsifying the automatic thoughts that any amount of embarrassment at all will be too painful to bear.

The social detachment that avoidants employ to defend against criticism works to confirm their pessimistic expectations. From an interpersonal perspective, Benjamin (1996) stresses the internal experience of avoidants, its basis in their developmental history, and its effect on the therapeutic process. She again emphasizes that the poor self-concept of avoidants makes them vulnerable and easily hurt by the therapist. For example, Sean or Allison would probably be more comfortable with Carl Rogers than with Albert Ellis.

Unlike other formulations, however, Benjamin also suggests that beneath a surface of reluctance and unease lies a deep reservoir of anger. Because of their hypersensitivity, even minor suggestions may be viewed as put-downs. Afraid to share these hurts, avoidants hold them inside until the day they simply boil over. According to Benjamin, the antidote to this pattern is accurate empathy and uncritical support. Because the covert interpersonal message to the avoidant during childhood was, "Do not trust others. You are so defective only your family could love you," these subjects may experience feelings of disloyalty when sharing details of their family history. Presenting therapy as a warm sanctuary helps avoidants express these feelings safely.

Family, couples, and group therapy can be beneficial in breaking patterns that perpetuate avoidant behavior. Frequently, one spouse functions as an enabler who interacts with the world at large, allowing the avoidant the freedom to restrict social contacts to a bare minimum with no adverse consequences. Enablers must understand their role in reinforcing avoidance behavior. After years of encouraging avoidant spouses who suddenly quit jobs for no reason or burst into anger without first sharing feelings of resentment, many partners are themselves under considerable stress. Avoidants are hypersensitive to rejection even from their most intimate partners and readily become involved in triangulated relationships, including extramarital affairs (Benjamin, 1996). These relationships are considered *safe* in that they provide the intimacy of sexual relationship but also a degree a distance. As Benjamin notes, couples therapy cannot be conducted while such secret relationships are active. The secret lover who provides comfort and protection when the spouse is angry or withdrawn must be given up to improve the marital relationship.

Because avoidants are especially fearful of social situations, group therapy conducted in a context of acceptance and support can be invaluable if the group is sensitive to the individual's fears and can respond empathically. Warm acceptance from a variety of people in a group provides a strong counterpoint to early rejection from the family. Moreover, groups can often be effective in identifying positive characteristics in avoidants that they cannot see in themselves or simply devalue. Avoidants should not be forced into interacting but rather should be allowed to observe from the sidelines until they feel ready to risk exposure. Such groups allow the person the unique opportunity to acquire and practice behavioral and social skills in a microcosm of the social world. Given the subject's needs, groups with members who are critical for no reason are probably to be avoided (Millon, 1999).

Psychodynamic theories see avoidant behavior as being driven by the shame of not measuring up to the ego ideal. By this formulation, avoidants fear the opinions of others because they fall short of their own internalized standards and see themselves as weak, defective, or even disgusting, sometimes even to the point of dissociation as an escape from the pain of basic self-conscious existence. Treatment emphasizes a strongly empathic understanding of the experience of humiliation and embarrassment and insight into the role of early experiences in creating present emotions. Childhood memories are analyzed to clarify the roots of the disorder. Because avoidants use fantasy as a major coping mechanism, they often bring rich interpretive material to the therapeutic process. Fantasies of success, acceptance, and self-actualization can be contrasted with their present life and related to early childhood recollections. Feelings of embarrassment may be seen as deriving from a comparison of the self against the standards of a harsh, punitive superego. Accordingly, particular attention must be given to the role of parental figures in creating patterns of self-condemnation. Avoidants need to separate from such vicious introjects. Allison and Sean may have problems, but their families provided the toxic environment in which these problems could take root and grow.

Summary

Avoidants are painfully sensitive to humiliation and social disapproval, and they actively seek protection from the perceived inevitable threats of others in the environment. The *DSM-IV* describes avoidants as exhibiting a pattern of inadequacy and a fear that their shortcomings will expose them to judgment and ridicule. Several normal variants have been proposed, including Oldham and Morris's sensitive and vigilant styles and the hesitating pattern by Millon, Weiss, Millon, and Davis.

The basic avoidant pattern is often mixed with other personality traits that are evidenced in several subtypes. The conflicted avoidant includes features of the negativistic personality where the basic withdrawal of the avoidant pattern is combined with the negativist's tendency toward interpersonal guerrilla warfare. The hypersensitive avoidant includes features of the paranoid personality but exhibits greater reality contact. Phobic avoidants combine features of the dependent and avoidant personalities, being especially prone to experiencing social phobias. The self-deserting avoidant combines social avoidance with the ruminative self-devaluation of the depressive personality.

Most psychodynamic thinkers still consider the avoidant as part of the schizoid personality. However, three major psychodynamic theorists described personality patterns that are distinctly like the avoidant. Menninger (1930) described the isolated personality,

Fenichel (1945) formulated the notion of a phobic character, and Horney (1937) developed the concept of the detached type, individuals who believe, "If I withdraw, nothing can hurt me." As a defense, avoidants actively interfere with their painful preoccupations and tensions by intruding irrelevant thoughts or distorting their substantive meaning. In addition, avoidants indulge themselves excessively in fantasy and imagination, both as a means of replacing anxiety-arousing cognitions of inadequacy and low self-worth and as a means of gratifying needs that cannot be met due to social withdrawal. Avoidants may be seen as having a highly developed ego ideal, including a high level of aspiration and desires for self-actualization, paired with an intensely condemning superego that constantly finds fault with and disapproves of their every behavior. In effect, they have internalized parental standards of high achievement and social success, combined with blame and shunning for the smallest mistakes.

From a cognitive perspective, an information-processing model seems particularly useful in understanding the avoidant personality. The very contents of the cognitions seem to establish a pathological reciprocity with the structure of cognition, perpetuating the disorder. As avoidants consistently scan their environment for signs of danger, their information-processing system becomes flooded with excessive stimuli that prevent them from attending to other features. The cognitive perspective also holds that beliefs about the world, self, and others are critical in determining behavior (Beck et al., 1990). Avoidants' core beliefs, which are usually below the level of conscious awareness, are held to be unconditionally and eternally true. They influence how other beliefs are organized, especially when predicting the consequences of various courses of action, expressed as conditional if-then beliefs.

From an interpersonal perspective, the avoidant has a perpetual sense of social unease. This is not limited to a crowd of people; a single person can activate these feelings. Instead of confronting their anxiety, they escape social encounters whenever possible, only serving to perpetuate their problems. By narrowing their range of interpersonal experiences, they fail to learn new ways of behaving that might bring them greater self-confidence or a sense of personal worth. Their personality also seems to attract those who enjoy shaming and ridiculing them. Benjamin's SASB model captures the interpersonal development of the avoidant personality: Beginning life with normal attachment, caretakers' criticisms of flaws eventually result not only in avoidants' developing a poor self-image but also in helping them develop strong self-control and restraint that causes their hypersensitivity to error. Certain traumatic childhood experiences such as physical abuse, incest, or molestation may be sufficient to produce a lifelong pattern of social avoidance and interpersonal fearfulness that resembles the avoidant pattern (Stone, 1993).

Although in most cases a biological disposition is insufficient to result in an avoidant personality, there is evidence of some biological influence; however, specifics remain highly speculative. Some researchers (Siever & Davis, 1991) regard anxiety inhibition as providing one of the core psychobiological dispositions in the development of the avoidant personality. Some of the feelings of inadequacy in avoidants may have a basis in slow or uneven maturation, as this can elicit teasing from peers. The avoidant personality may also have a basis in biological temperament; although shyness is not specific to the avoidant personality, its presence does suggest a sense of inner shame or self-doubt characteristic of the avoidant.

The avoidant personality was originally conceived in 1969 as the actively detached pattern from Millon's biopsychosocial theory of personality. This means that there is a conflict between the person's desire for social contact and fear of exposure to shame for seeking it. Millon's more contemporary evolutionary theory (1990; Millon & Davis, 1996) maintains the active-detachment hypothesis but more clearly posits the motivating aim of protection against pain, to the extent of a virtual denial of life-enhancing possibilities. Whether by hereditary predisposition, a caustic and critical upbringing, or some blend of these two influences, the avoidant continually learns that psychic safety is a first priority worthy of taking all actions to ensure. As he or she gets more isolated by virtue of this approach, interpersonal skills among peers fail to develop, and those abilities that have developed dissipate.

Avoidants share characteristics with other personalities including schizoids, schizotypals, and paranoids. They are also part of the anxiety spectrum. Historically, the central features characterizing the avoidant personality have been scattered throughout clinical literature. The avoidant was often confused with other personalities, such as the schizoid, and even confused as a pathway to developing schizophrenia. Avoidants are especially vulnerable to developing other clinical syndromes. Anxiety disorders, particularly generalized anxiety, social anxiety, and obsessive-compulsive disorder, are common in avoidants. They are also vulnerable to developing somatoform disorders, particularly body dysmorphic disorder, dissociative disorders, depressive disorders, and schizophrenic disorders.

The therapeutic prognosis for the avoidant personality is remarkably poor. The most basic characteristics of the avoidant run counter to the basic requirements of psychotherapy. Because of their intense sensitivity to negative evaluation, the therapeutic relationship is critical. Patience seems to be a key quality for the therapist to build a trusting relationship with the avoidant. Cognitive and cognitive-behavioral techniques seem to have some benefits, all designed to help avoidants overcome their social fears and gain a better sense of self-worth. Working from an interpersonal perspective, Benjamin (1996) suggests that avoidants possess a deep reservoir of anger and that the antidote to this pattern is accurate empathy and uncritical support. Family, couples, and group therapy can be beneficial in breaking patterns that perpetuate avoidant behavior. Psychodynamic treatment emphasizes a strongly empathic understanding of the experience of humiliation and embarrassment and insight into the role of early experiences in creating present emotions.

Chapter 7

The Obsessive-Compulsive Personality

Objectives

- What are the *DSM-IV* criteria for the compulsive personality?
- The conscientious and conforming personalities are normal variants of the compulsive. Describe their characteristics and relate them to the more disordered criteria of *DSM-IV.*
- Explain how different personality styles combine to form each of the subtypes of the compulsive personality.
- Explain the meaning of the terms *anal-retentive* and *anal-expulsive* as used in early psychoanalytic tradition.
- How do the defense mechanisms of reaction formation, sublimation, undoing, and isolation of affect work in the compulsive personality?
- Explain the significance of guilt and shame in modern object-relations theories of the compulsive personality.
- Why is the interpersonal behavior of the compulsive described as hypernormal, contrived, and deliberate?
- Explain how parental overcontrol and an emphasis on perfection lead to the development of the compulsive personality.
- How can the compulsive cognitive style best be characterized?
- What is the fundamental core belief of the compulsive?
- Compulsives share characteristics with other personality disorders. List these other disorders and explain the distinction between each and the compulsive.
- What is the relationship between obsessive-compulsive disorder and the compulsive personality?
- Why are compulsives prone to body dysmorphic disorder?
- Why are compulsives difficult psychotherapy patients?
- List therapeutic goals for the compulsive personality.

Are there people in your life who seem just a little too efficient, well-ordered, and organized? You may have noticed these virtuous workers dutifully putting in long hours, attempting to ensure that their performance measures up to their self-imposed standard of flawlessness. They try to do everything they do perfectly to avoid the slightest mistake or flaw that would induce mountains of guilt and cause them to regard their performance as marred, if not ruined. Rigidly devoted to productivity, they rarely take time out for themselves or their families. Instead, they are known for arriving early and staying late and persevering until the job is not only done, but done to perfection. They set high, often unrealistic standards for themselves and expect the same from others, especially those who work under them. Anyone who takes too much free time is branded a "slacker" and gets no respect. In contrast, they are routinely appeasing to those in authority, seeking opportunities to prove themselves as selflessly committed to the "greater cause." In their private lives, they are often rigidly dogmatic in matters of morality, ethics, and values. Everything is by the book; nothing is on the sly. What they believe they hold as absolute truth, so much so that others see them as exceptionally stubborn.

Such individuals exemplify the obsessive-compulsive personality pattern; for convenience, they are referred to simply as **compulsives** in this chapter. As Donald (see Case 7.1) demonstrates, they seek to assuage their anxiety about any number of factors by plunging themselves ever deeper into detail (see criterion 1). "Success by micromanagement" might be their motto: If you can just gather enough information and organize that information in the right fashion, things will work out okay and you will be protected from harm or at least from disapproval. We might speculate, for example, that Donald probably has his socks and pants color-coded and systematized, which can be sorted in advance so that everything matches, thus saving time in the morning.

The opening paragraph of Donald's case is particularly striking. Donald can detail everything to which his stomach is sensitive. When he goes in for a checkup, the doctor need not be concerned that the patient will omit some small piece of crucial information. He may, however, run into the opposite problem, which may be the greater of two evils. Donald's responses are comprehensive to a fault. If allowed, he will undoubtedly indulge in a lengthy treatise about his dietary habits, outlining specific foods and quantities, and sharing any relevant research he has already done on the subject, leaving the doctor in the awkward position of having to either agree or risk losing any rapport with his patient. Donald thrives in the details, but he tends to overwhelm others with it because he expects them to value it just as much as he does. In fact, he becomes condescending when they don't. Others are subject to fault, but not Donald. To him, any doctor who doesn't hear him out is simply not being professional.

In his work life, Donald's devotion to detail supports his perfectionism (see criterion 2). He prides himself on his ability to get work done (see criterion 3) and get it done perfectly. We can imagine that his desk is cleaned off at the end of each day, with every pencil sharpened so that tomorrow starts smoothly. Indeed, Donald is probably proud that he has parlayed this character trait into occupational success. In his view, the rapid promotion to a middle-management position validates the superiority of his approach to life and justifies his contempt for the "average worker," whom he no doubt considers "sloppy" or "neglectful." Donald will always be tapped whenever there's paperwork to do and details to control, but he isn't likely to be the person that the board of directors looks to develop some imaginative new product or to construct broad corporate strategy.

Donald sought assistance because of unexplained stomach pains and nightmares. "My stomach has always been queasy," he noted. "I'm very sensitive to dietary factors." These he enumerated in burdensome detail, ranging from exotic brands of spices, to cabbage, certain brands of soda pop, and on to smog and stuffy interiors.[1] Recently, though, the discomfort has begun to interfere with his sleep. The nightmares, in which he loses complete control, he finds frightening and intolerable.

At the same time, he was quick to note that he could usually bear the discomfort in silence and go about his day normally. Without fail, he arrives at work early so he can "smooth things out" before the day officially starts. Donald also stays after the others have left to anticipate "kinks" they might otherwise confront in the morning. "Even though my wife complains I don't spend enough time with her, and even when the discomfort is intense," he states, "I can maintain an efficient operation in the workplace." Privately, his wife notes that Donald is someone who "tends to make up his mind about things, and keep it made up."

By his own admission, he is a perfectionist, a characteristic that has allowed him to advance quickly to a middle management position. He scrupulously supervises the work of his subordinates and is quick to discipline them for their mistakes. "People don't understand that work is a virtue, " he states with a certain indignation. For this reason, he is often reluctant to trust a job to others, "cause I know they'll screw it up." When forced to deviate from this rigid style, he begins to experience physical discomfort, including stomach pains and nightmares.

Donald seems invested in being a "good patient." He prides himself on being able to answer the intake questions with precision, even though his responses are often time-consuming and unnecessarily qualified. He flounders, however, without the aid of a formal structure. His comfort returns when it is suggested that he speak about his "average day." In the lengthy description that follows, Donald relishes detail, accuracy, predictability, and efficiency. He believes dogmatically in the virtues of a healthy lifestyle, exercising daily, eating balanced meals, sleeping eight hours a night, and attending church regularly. He is offended by implications of the slightest impropriety. He has never drunk or smoked, has always been a good saver, and has never taken a vacation from work.

Donald's history explains much of his current situation. As a child, he secured approval by doing as he was told and showing interest in primarily solitary activities such as reading and coloring. He remembers trying to color between the lines, and feeling that the picture was ruined if there was one errant mark, a metaphor for his entire life. He remembers his parents as distant and stern. Any horseplay met with swift discipline. Outside school, Donald rarely played with other children, because his parents disapproved of their poor manners. His parents affectionately called him "our little man." Two years ago, Donald married Rachel, who is eight years older. When asked about the age gap, he explains that he was attracted to her mature attitude and serious approach to life. They have a stable, if somewhat unromantic, relationship. Rachel and Donald have lunch with his parents on Sunday after church, and Donald visits them alone every other Wednesday after work.

[1] Numbers mark aspects of the case most consistent with *DSM* criteria, and do not necessarily indicate that the case "meets" diagnostic criteria in this respect.

Compulsive Personality Disorder
DSM-IV Criteria

A pervasive pattern of preoccupation with orderliness, perfectionism, and mental and interpersonal control, at the expense of flexibility, openness, and efficiency, beginning by early adulthood and present in a variety of contexts, as indicated by four (or more) of the following:

(1) is preoccupied with details, rules, lists, order, organization, or schedules to the extent that the major point of the activity is lost

(2) shows perfectionism that interferes with task completion (e.g., is unable to complete a project because his or her own overly strict standards are not met)

(3) is excessively devoted to work and productivity to the exclusion of leisure activities and friendships (not accounted for by obvious economic necessity)

(4) is overconscientious, scrupulous, and inflexible about matters of morality, ethics, or values (not accounted for by cultural or religious identification)

(5) is unable to discard worn-out or worthless objects even when they have no sentimental value

(6) is reluctant to delegate tasks or to work with others unless they submit to exactly his or her way of doing things

(7) adopts a miserly spending style toward both self and others; money is viewed as something to be hoarded for future catastrophes

(8) shows rigidity and stubbornness

Donald constantly appears to be restrained and defended, as if he were anticipating some impending catastrophe. For example, he fears that he will make a mistake and that his superiors will secretly take note of it, recording it somewhere in the dreaded database created specifically for Donald's failings. He can already imagine them saying in a stern voice, "Donald, that's your second mistake this year. We're watching you." He carries this condemning voice around inside him, and it ensures that he labors perpetually under the same kind of threat that he inflicts on those under him. That's why he doesn't trust his subordinates to do their own jobs competently (see criterion 6). Donald would tell you, "You can't take your eyes off them." They can't be trusted to perform up to his standards, and without constant supervision, it is likely that even the best of them would soon regress into what, for him, would be regarded as "irremediable slackership." Worse, if they screw up, Donald has his own voice to atone to. So, he anticipates problems, stays late, and puts in the hours necessary to make sure everything runs shipshape.

If you lived down the block from Donald and his family, you would probably know him as a morally sound, upstanding citizen of your community. As you got to know him better, however, you would begin to see more and more of his rigidity in matters of values, ethics, and morality (see criterion 4). He and the family always make it to church and always make it there in a timely manner, with the kids neatly dressed. For Donald, God is just the top-level manager in the hierarchy, the ultimate superior whom he must please, but he does not feel this at a conscious level. Donald does have rebellious tendencies, but he cannot afford to be aware of them. Instead, he buries them so deep that not even he can see them; then he does just the opposite so that he can be absolutely comfortable with himself. Donald is dogmatic in his beliefs, a quality he and others sometimes mistake for passion. He overconforms to armor himself against impropriety. His religion and morality are entirely by the book, but he is not known to be a forgiving person despite his religion's teachings to the contrary. Instead, he tends to be self-righteous, and he is not above using the rules to bring a little sorrow to someone who doesn't know how to follow orders or doesn't have the kind of serious attitude that he respects; this includes the people who work for him.

Donald's dogmatism, in fact, extends beyond matters of morality and religion to just about everything in his life, and this is expressed in his considerable stubbornness (see criterion 8). In fact, Donald can't afford to change his mind about anything because that would imply that he was wrong, and he must be on his guard against mistakes. To him, people who change their minds are wishy-washy. They lack the courage of their convictions. So, Donald stands pat and argues his points, stringently committed to his point of view, regardless of genuine convictions.

Given the portrait of Donald, we are now in a position to examine additional issues, which form the plan of this chapter. First, we compare normality and abnormality; then we move on to variations on the basic compulsive theme. After that, psychodynamic, interpersonal, and cognitive perspectives on the compulsive personality are described. These sections form the core of what is scientific in personality. By seeking to explain what we observe in character sketches like Donald's, the goal is to move beyond literary anecdote and enter the domain of theory. As always, we present history and description side by side, noting the contributions of past thinkers, each of whom tends to bring into focus a different aspect of the disorder. Developmental hypotheses are also reviewed but are tentative for all personality disorders. Next, the section

"Evolutionary Neurodevelopmental Perspective" shows how the existence of the personality disorder follows from the laws of evolution. Also included are a comparison between the compulsive and other theory-derived constructs and a discussion of how compulsive personalities tend to develop Axis I disorders. Finally, we survey how the disorder might be treated through psychotherapy, again organizing our material in terms of classical approaches to the field: the interpersonal, cognitive, and psychodynamic perspectives.

From Normality to Abnormality

Don't be surprised if you recognize aspects of yourself in these descriptions of the compulsive personality. This pattern, in particular, is prevalent in developed societies, where traits such as efficiency, punctuality, a willingness to work hard, and orientation to detail are valued as necessary prerequisites to social and financial well-being. Self-discipline and organization are personality features encouraged by many modern societies. It is almost a prerequisite, for example, to possess at least a few compulsive traits when seeking an advanced graduate degree. How else could you be diligent and motivated enough to do all the reading and write all the papers necessary to get through school? Many professors have strong compulsive traits, as well. Running subjects, managing effective research, and writing papers for peer review all require precision and a detailed knowledge of the field. Compulsive traits are often a key to excelling in such endeavors.

Several normal-range variants of the compulsive personality have been proposed. Each emphasizes a slightly different constellation of traits. The **conscientious** style (Oldham & Morris, 1995) is characterized by a dedication to hard work, deeply held convictions of conscience and moral principle, a need to do things perfectly and in a socially approved manner, perseverance in pursuits, preference for orderliness and detail, cautious consideration of alternatives before acting, and the need to save or collect things. Conscientious individuals tend to emphasize work more than any other aspect of their lives. For example, they may spend long hours at the office to bring a project to completion or strive hard to eliminate some minor imperfection that most people would simply gloss over. They enjoy detail, thrive on accomplishment, set high standards, and just seem to keep on going long after others have called it a day. With such self-discipline, it is not surprising that many become top managers. Emotionally, they tend to be somewhat reserved, distant, and rather unromantic.

In contrast, the **conforming** style (Millon et al., 1994) is constructed around conventionality, a preference for following established rules and standards. Conforming individuals are proper, conventional, orderly, and perfectionistic. They respect tradition and authority, uphold established rules and standards, and follow regulations closely. They seldom exhibit spontaneity and can be rather rigid and inflexible in their relationships. Moreover, they are intolerant of deviance and tend to be judgmental of those who are not as earnest. Ever diligent in their responsibilities, they dislike having work pile up and worry about finishing projects. Because of these characteristics, others perceive them as highly dependable and industrious. Though they always attempt to think things through before acting, they are sometimes given to dogmatic thinking, perceiving the world around them and controversial issues in terms of black-and-white, right-or-wrong extremes.

Donald has most of the preceding characteristics, though in a much more exaggerated form. In fact, most of his life is about being in control, the real source of his somatic concerns. Work is the core of his life, and his need for control is most clearly expressed there. In somewhat prideful and stilted language, he "maintains an efficient operation in the workplace." He requires the approval of his superiors, to whom he presents an image of industriousness and diligence. Like the conforming style, he has a respect for tradition and values, though he is more dogmatic and rigid. He favors intellectualism over emotionality and reservedness over spontaneity. It would be difficult to imagine Donald ever stopping by the florist on his way home from work on a whim and bringing a bouquet of roses home to his wife. If he would, that otherwise charming act would likely be done so rigidly as to neatly remove any hint of spontaneity from the gift. This rigidity follows Donald throughout his romantic life, including making love. He is likely to have that act divided into stages, so as to keep control and reduce discomfort arising from any unexpected deviations in the routine.

As with other personality patterns, normal and pathological variants of the compulsive personality may be seen as existing on a continuum; more normal variants will typically display lesser frequency and intensity of the disordered traits described in the *DSM-IV,* and some of those more balanced traits may serve the individual well (see Sperry, 1995). Whereas the disordered individual becomes so preoccupied with rules and lists that the big picture is lost (see criterion 1), the more balanced individual with this style takes pride in the finer points of an accomplished work, without overwhelming the self and without letting some detail dominate the overall plan or final production. Although the compulsive personality disorder is characterized by a constant emphasis on perfectionism in every single task (see criterion 2), individuals with a compulsive style know where to draw the line. They simply do the best possible job they can within the constraints of time, resources, and, more important, their own desires. Whereas the disordered person is so rigidly devoted to work that fun, friends, and family fall by the wayside (see criterion 3), a person possessed of the style is able to work hard and consistently but recognizes the importance of intimacy in relationships.

For each of the preceding contrasts, Donald falls more toward the pathological side. He is happy to tell you that he takes pride in his work, but he probably doesn't really understand what that means. People like Donald tend to bombard themselves with information before beginning a job. They try to work everything out in advance, and they hate to make accommodations along the way. Accommodations mean that they've failed to anticipate something, which is an uncomfortable state for people who must work with the known rather than the unknown. In fact, they detail themselves endlessly so that they can diminish the influence of uncertainty to the very margins of what rationality allows. What Donald feels when he completes something that has challenged him is not so much a sense of pride and fulfillment as it is a sense of relief. He got through it without incurring the wrath of someone he's accountable to, perhaps a boss or just his own severe superego.

It is these qualities that drive Donald's perfectionism, as well as the side effect of his inability to make time for his wife or family. They don't stand over him, and they're not really part of his conscience. Donald acquired the dictum, somewhere in his development, that a good husband should spend time with the family. But even then, it's not quality time generated from a sense of genuine love and desire for connection. Rather, it's an obligation, a duty to the family to be performed like any other duty. Odds are his family knows this at some level. He can cover it up in a variety of ways, perhaps by making a virtue of being a "good provider" or insisting that times are tough and he has to work hard to get ahead, but it's a loss for everyone, including Donald.

The remaining diagnostic criteria of the compulsive personality can also be put on a continuum with normality (Sperry, 1995). Dogmatic attitudes rigidly devoted to moral, ethical, and religious principles (see criterion 4) lie on the disordered end of the spectrum; a personal sense of integrity and recognition of life's complexity are examples of more balanced personality features. Individuals who are more in line with the style recognize that individual values and situations must sometimes trump the blanket application of rigid moral absolutes. Whereas the disordered individual is unable to discard what is worn out or worthless (see criterion 5), most people with conscientious or conforming styles recognize that these things might come in handy someday, but draw the line when saving them becomes too inconvenient. Another feature of the disordered personality is the inability to delegate tasks to others (see criterion 6) or rigidity in insisting that things be done a certain way. Those with the more normal style recognize that others may have valuable contributions and are then flexible enough to shift their mindset to make room for new ideas. The disordered side of the spectrum often features stinginess (see criterion 7), whereas the more flexible personality style is savings-conscious, but not at the cost of relationships or occasional episodes of spontaneity. Finally, disordered persons are stubborn and rigid (see criterion 8), while normals are capable of weighing the facts dispassionately and having a change of mind.

Again, when we compare Donald to the preceding contrasts, he usually falls more toward the pathological side of the continuum. From the information contained in the case, Donald does seem dogmatic with respect to morality (see criterion 4), ethics, and values. First, he is offended by examples of moral impropriety, and he pursues important lifestyle choices with radical religious zeal. His emphasis on health, for example, is not only a reaction to his somatic concerns, but also an example of how he makes lifestyle choices into absolutes. As noted, Donald finds it nearly impossible to delegate tasks to other workers (see criterion 6). When he does, he finds that his own anxiety level begins to increase. He starts thinking about all the ways things might go wrong, and he wonders whether his coworkers will anticipate this or safeguard against that. He has to be absolutely sure they follow his flowchart because he needs a sense of control to protect himself against the uncertainty of what he fears might happen. As for miserliness, the case notes that Donald has "always been a good saver," a characteristic of the compulsive style, but not extreme enough for the disorder. Finally, as Donald's wife says, "Once his mind is made up, it stays made up," an example of black-and-white thinking typical of compulsive patterns. He can't change his mind because he hates the thought that he might have been wrong, and he can't give ground because he rarely, if ever, sees shades of gray.

Variations of the Compulsive Personality

Having described the pure compulsive in some detail, we now move on to variations of the basic pattern. The compulsive combines with several other personality disorders, giving a different coloration to the resulting pattern. A brief guide to the subtypes of the compulsive personality is given in Figure 7.1. Actual cases may or may not fall into one of these combinations.

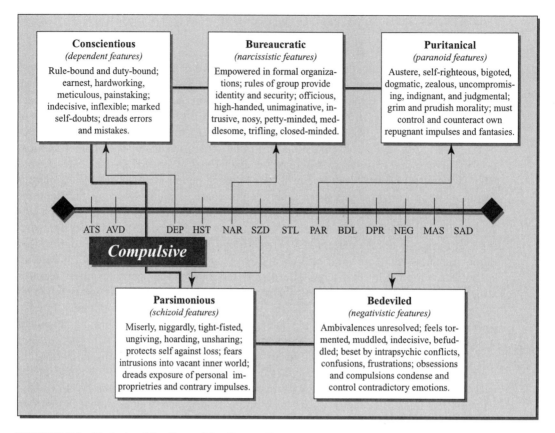

FIGURE 7.1   Variants of the Compulsive Personality.

THE CONSCIENTIOUS COMPULSIVE

More than any other variant, the **conscientious** compulsive exhibits a conforming dependency, compliance to rules and authority, and a willing submission to the wishes, values, expectations, and demands of others. Conscientious compulsives see themselves as considerate, thoughtful, and cooperative. They often voice a strong sense of duty, which masks underlying feelings of personal inadequacy. As such, they tend to minimize their accomplishments, underplay their abilities, and grade their success in terms of how well the expectations of others are fulfilled. Though they are usually described as earnest, hardworking, and thorough, these characteristics compensate for deep feelings of self-doubt and hesitation and serve to keep them in the good graces of those they rely on for esteem.

You may note from the preceding description that conscientious compulsives exhibit insecurity in a manner similar to the dependent, although they still compensate for feelings of inadequacy much like the typical compulsive. They hold fast to the belief that they will be cared for, valued, and loved in direct proportion to their hard work and monumental accomplishments. This belief structure comes with a significant liability: They fear that failure to perform perfectly will provoke both abandonment and condemnation, which creates considerable inner sensations of tension and guilt. So dreadful is the thought of making mistakes or taking even the smallest risk that they perpetually rework their efforts, never attaining a true sense of satisfaction for a job well done, all the while feeling perennially anxious over their perceived inadequacy to handle any unanticipated hitch. This blend of dependent and compulsive features gives rise to a distinct submissive interpersonal manner with superiors and an air of propriety and restraint with all others. This is in direct conflict with intense contrary feelings that frequently lurk beneath this veneer, and on occasion, these more primitive qualities sneak through their tightly controlled coping skills. Their occasional experience with such security breaches teaches them to hold even tighter to self-control, thereby creating an existence that is overorganized, devoid of spontaneity, and dramatically upset by any deviation in routine. Understand, however, that this is primarily a private battle and is usually masked by a front of equanimity and social agreeableness.

Like the other variants, conscientious compulsives do sometimes attach themselves to institutions or religious organizations, both for interpersonal support and as a means of participating vicariously in a social aura of respect or holiness. In general, however, the conscientious variant is the most sublimated of the compulsive subtypes, jettisoning some of the more self-righteous and forceful qualities that produce interpersonal discomfort. This subtype tends to shade much more readily into normality than the other variants described next.

THE PURITANICAL COMPULSIVE

As originally emphasized by analytic authors (e.g., Rado, 1959) and later expanded by object-relations and interpersonal theorists, all compulsives experience a deep ambivalence between obedience and defiance, which they resolve through sublimation, reaction formation, and displacement. Those who sublimate this conflict seem more normal, those who displace their aggression seem more forceful, and those who react strongly against their internal anger become self-righteous. W. Reich (1933) wrote that over the course of development, each person's defensive operations settle into a defensive style that armors him or her against the world. Using Reich's metaphor, we might say that the drives and impulses lurking within **puritanical** compulsives are so strong, yet so strongly reacted against, that these individuals seek the armor of God's righteousness to purify, transform, and contain them. Most feel the persistent press of irrational and repugnant aggressive and sexual drives and adopt an ascetic and austere lifestyle to prohibit their dark impulses and fantasies.

All variants of the compulsive pattern experience a conflict between obedience and defiance on some level, but the puritanical variant experiences this much more intensely than any other. Though sharing aspects of zealous defensiveness and guardedness with the paranoid, the puritanical subtype presents as an exaggeration of the basic compulsive pattern. Their hostility, then, is also greater and more likely to be vented through vicious displacements, which usually identify a common enemy or seek to scapegoat the weak. Dichotomous thinking reinforces these urges: In their mind, the world is composed of the all good and the all bad, us versus them, the justified and the unjust, the saved and the sinners, along with the saints (i.e., the compulsives themselves).

Naturally reviled by perceived moral laxity, puritanicals use their wrath as a "vengeful sword" of righteousness bestowed with a sacred mandate to dispel sin and iniquity. Most are pleased to be this instrument through which justice is administered. In fact, puritanicals naturally gravitate toward radical fundamentalism, as the literalism inherent in such beliefs creates a clear picture, not only of who deserves punishment, but who deserves absolute punishment. Thus, injustice is made just and they are free of any residual guilt. Many of these puritanical compulsives secretly enjoy punishing others, as they are strengthened by this judgment of their superego.

People respond in very diverse ways to such a personality. A large part of our society admires the seeming combination of strength and purity that such individuals project. Moreover, puritanical compulsives are not limited to religious dogma. Over the course of history, and even in current politics, they have been an influential force in stirring na-tionalistic fervor. On a smaller scale, they can be found in virtually any institution, large or small, assuming the mantle of righteousness, preaching the transgressions of their as-sociates, and demanding purges. In fact, excessive interpersonal control may be geared toward eliciting behaviors of defiance from others, so that the enemy can be uncloaked. Some succeed in their pursuit, but eventually, most come to view them as harsh, de-manding, abrasive, irritating, and prudish. Some are simply exceptionally straitlaced. Here, the function of the straight and narrow path is transparent, intended to contain and civilize drives that would otherwise be almost uncontrollably intense.

Although this description does not neatly match Donald, he does have a streak of this variation in him. His high contempt for "lazy" subordinates gives a glimpse of this ten-dency. His indignant tone when he says, "People don't understand that work is a virtue" also has an element of this. Indignation and allegiance to absolute principles are closely connected.

THE BUREAUCRATIC COMPULSIVE

Bureaucratic compulsives ally themselves with traditional values, established authori-ties, and formal organizations. Most other compulsive subtypes feel conflicted, angered, and even oppressed by these influences, although their overt awareness of this conflict is suppressed. Bureaucratic compulsives are somewhat more aware of this conflict than their counterparts, and instead of allowing their feelings to cause even the slightest dif-ficulty, they wholeheartedly embrace the order and structure inherent in recognized in-stitutions, authorities, and social mores. They flourish in organizational settings, feeling comforted, strengthened, and empowered by clearly defined superior and subordinate relationships, definite roles, and known expectations and responsibilities. Once estab-lished, they function loyally and dependably. In effect, these individuals use highly de-veloped and formalized external structures to compensate for the internal sense of ambivalence and indecisiveness that plagues the average compulsive pattern. Many fuse their identity with the system as a means of achieving place, purpose, and protection, and this frees them from any anxiety related to making independent decisions. Their su-periors know them as trustworthy, diligent, and faithfully committed to the goals and values of the institution, which fortifies their self-esteem and gives them a direction. Be it church, police, union, university, or business, without the organization most would feel lost or aimless in life. Punctual and meticulous, they adhere to the work ethic like worker ants in a colony, appraising their own and others' tasks with black-and-white ef-ficiency, as done or not done.

The status gained by their alliance with their "greater cause" offers these generally rigid and constrained individuals better than a modicum of pride and self-importance. Deeply committed to all of the trifling and inconsequential directives of their beloved in-stitutions, bureaucratic subtypes gain a sense of status by fusing their identity with a much larger force and becoming an indispensable part of this important structure. As such, they often share hallmarks with the narcissistic personality, although these more inflated qualities are but skin-deep. Like the conscientious compulsive, the bureaucratic compulsive often shades gently into normality, but individual differences run the spectrum from nearly normal to wholly forceful. At a moderately disordered level, their rigid adherence to policies and rules makes them seem officious, high-handed, close-minded, and petty. At a severely disordered level, they may use their knowledge of the rules, effectiveness with red tape, and ingratiating attitude with superiors to terrorize subordinates or anyone else who crosses their path without paying them the proper dues and respect. Donald has some traits of the bureaucratic compulsive in that he is obviously a company man, but he doesn't derive pleasure from control. As a middle-level manager, he could potentially exert a great amount of control over his underlings, but he does not take advantage of this opportunity. Holden, in Case 7.2, is a better example. Notice his relationships with his superiors and with his students.

THE PARSIMONIOUS COMPULSIVE

The **parsimonious** compulsive resembles Fromm's hoarding orientation (1947). For these individuals, miserliness takes on an almost symbolic significance. Ever wary of the possibility of loss, they are selfish and niggardly and keep a tight, self-protective grip on everything they possess, lest it somehow be wrested from them. Here, the concern shifts from identification with authority or organizational codes to the security value of material goods. Having been deprived of so many wishes and desires in childhood, they nurture and protect what little they have, ever suspicious that others might scavenge their few prized possessions. They draw sharp boundaries and behave with an unnecessary stinginess. In effect, their behavior says, "What is mine is mine, and what is yours is yours."

Fromm's (1947) conceptualization suggests that as children, such individuals were often deprived of wishes and desires. Their basic needs were not necessarily neglected by their parents, but perhaps few if any of their wants were fulfilled in a manner that seemed reasonable to them. Perhaps under the best of intentions, the caregivers attempted to instill a deep sense of duty and self-responsibility by radically avoiding any measure that could potentially spoil the child. Undoubtedly, it is far healthier to allow children to experience a modicum of unfulfilled wishes than it is to indulge them with everything they could ever imagine. However, when this otherwise healthy approach to child rearing is taken to an illogical extreme, an orientation evolves wherein individuals seem to have an almost one-dimensional focus on nurturing and protecting anything earned or achieved. They become self-sufficient to a fault, disallowing anyone who may potentially deprive them of their resources and acting as if any loss in their nest egg could not be replenished. This miserliness also masks a deeper need. By effectively shutting out anyone else from permeating their world of possessions, they are, in effect, guarding against any discovery of the barrenness of their attainments and competencies. Even more important, this is a safeguard shared with other variants of the compulsive personality, in that keeping an air of propriety and privacy staves off any possible unearthing of their dreaded rebellious urges or irrational anger. This cool distancing from others and this protection of monetary and material possessions from external intrusions are qualities shared with the schizoid personality.

Holden reported self-doubt, guilt, and prolonged periods of diffuse anxiety. Though not overwhelming, these feelings had become more difficult to control. He now had trouble sleeping at night and experienced growing indecisiveness at work.

The immediate problem was a coming change of academic position. A new administration asked that he resign his deanship and return to teaching history. In the initial sessions, he focused on the details of the transition.[1] He was particularly concerned about facing students in the classroom again, worried about organizing his materials, and doubted his ability to interest and discipline students. Though he had been a competent teacher before, he kept reviewing old lecture notes again and again, but with little comfort.

No mention was made about any anger regarding his demotion, or the fact that Holden had poured his life into the position, working long hours and coordinating personally with the various department heads on matters that other deans would have assigned to their secretaries. Instead, he voiced his "complete confidence in the rationality of the process" that had led to the choice of another dean. Nevertheless, he stuttered and trembled whenever he engaged members of the administration.

The second of two sons, Holden was younger than his older brother by three years. Both parents held high-level positions, and both were regarded as efficient, strict, and orderly. Life at home was always "well-planned," with charts and schedules posted in common rooms detailing cleaning responsibilities, appointments, and even yearly physicals. Nothing was left to chance. Holden and his brother knew what they could count on in life and what was expected in return. If they failed to meet expectations, it would be treated almost as misbehavior: punishment would be swift and severe. Neither parent would tolerate expressions of anger in the family. Holden felt his brother "got away with" everything, but could only vent his feelings by tattling, which he derived great pleasure from. Not until after many sessions did Holden recognize that this was not a matter of "sticking to the rules," but a means of dealing with his jealously of his older brother.

At 27, Holden completed his Ph.D., married a "stable girl from a good home," and began teaching at a small college. His "fine work" in advising freshmen led to his becoming dean of freshmen, and eventually dean of students. Although he conscientiously "kept the rules," he was accused of being a stuffed shirt lacking real human compassion. Moreover, the department heads were often angered by his refusal to bend the rules. Anyone without an earnest attitude could become an object of his wrath, to be reined in with burdensome forms and guidelines. Because of his lack of warmth and occasional harsh decisions with students, he was asked to step down.

---

[1] Numbers mark aspects of the case most consistent with *DSM* criteria, and do not necessarily indicate that the case "meets" diagnostic criteria in this respect.

Compulsive Personality Disorder
DSM-IV Criteria

A pervasive pattern of preoccupation with orderliness, perfectionism, and mental and interpersonal control, at the expense of flexibility, openness, and efficiency, beginning by early adulthood and present in a variety of contexts, as indicated by four (or more) of the following:

(1) is preoccupied with details, rules, lists, order, organization, or schedules to the extent that the major point of the activity is lost

(2) shows perfectionism that interferes with task completion (e.g., is unable to complete a project because his or her own overly strict standards are not met)

(3) is excessively devoted to work and productivity to the exclusion of leisure activities and friendships (not accounted for by obvious economic necessity)

(4) is overconscientious, scrupulous, and inflexible about matters of morality, ethics, or values (not accounted for by cultural or religious identification)

(5) is unable to discard worn-out or worthless objects even when they have no sentimental value

(6) is reluctant to delegate tasks or to work with others unless they submit to exactly his or her way of doing things

(7) adopts a miserly spending style toward both self and others; money is viewed as something to be hoarded for future catastrophes

(8) shows rigidity and stubbornness

THE BEDEVILED COMPULSIVE

The **bedeviled** compulsive is blended with the negativistic personality. For average compulsives, the strategy of self-denial works reasonably well, allowing them to submerge their oppositional desires and put forth a proper and correct front. The bedeviled variety, however, appears on the surface to be maintaining a controlled and austere front but struggles incessantly with a desire to conform to the wishes or agendas of others one minute and the desire to subvert others and assert their own interests the next. When expected to act decisively, they vacillate and procrastinate, feel tormented and confused, become cautious and timid, and use complex rationales to delay making decisions as long as possible. Unable to crystallize their own identity and feeling wave upon wave of ambivalence, they may express their dissatisfaction by becoming exhausted, grumpy, and discontent. Many feel caught between heart and head, between what one part of them sees as reasonable and another part as emotionally satisfying.

Perpetually overwhelmed by the conflict between the will and better decisions, the bedeviled variant's existential experience is that of being caught between a rock and hard place. Painfully aware of their inner impulses, many engage in a form of self-torture, an act of punitive resolution that symbolically undoes that which bedevils them. In this context, the obsessions and compulsions that emerge signify a futile attempt to control that which is illogical, irrational, or even abstract about themselves and their desires. Unfortunately, this is not all that such attempts signify. Generally, the more extreme the obsessions and compulsions, the more the individual's routine coping skills are failing. Their inner ambivalence is the inability to confront what is upsetting to them, and outward behaviors such as compulsions are an outlet for their contradictory feelings. As individuals become more severely disordered, they may see themselves as driven by ego-alien forces, perhaps demons. Helpless, in their perspective, to escape the clutches of corruption, the more decompensated individuals may come to feel as though they are on the edge of psychic dissolution.

Early Historical Forerunners

Not surprisingly, the history of the obsessive-compulsive personality is intertwined with the history of obsessive and compulsive symptoms. Richard von Krafft-Ebing introduced the German equivalent to compulsion, Zwang, in 1867 but employed it only in reference to the constricted thinking of depressives. A paper by Griesinger (1868) used the same term in a more modern sense, referring to compulsive questioning, compulsive curiosity, and compulsive doubting, somewhat similar to what we have seen in the case of Holden, who seems to keep questioning himself about what to do and how to proceed. Toward the end of the nineteenth century, a debate arose concerning whether hidden emotions might underlie compulsive behavior. By this time, however, differences in its translation led the term Zwang to acquire different meanings on either side of the Atlantic. In London, it referred to obsessions; in New York, it referred to compulsions.

Both Schneider (1923/1950) and Kretschmer (1918) wrote important treatises on the personality disorders in the first third of the twentieth century. Discussing anakasts, Schneider noted their inner uncertainty and tendency toward overcompensation, stating that "outer correctness covers an imprisoning inner insecurity" (p. 87) and describing them as "carefully dressed people, pedantic, correct, scrupulous and yet with it all somehow exceedingly insecure" (p. 92). We see this in both our cases, with both Donald and Holden being outwardly correct and scrupulous and incredibly insecure. Of the two, however, Holden is definitely the more uncertain because Donald conceals his self-doubts with the armor of dogmatism. Under the label, "sensitive" types, Kretschmer described persons burdened by intrapsychic complexes they are unable to externalize or discharge. Unable to take decisive action, they likewise become uncertain over both large and small matters. To compensate, they hold fast to standards set with conviction by others, often becoming "men of conscience." There is somewhat of a developmental pathway that runs from Holden to Donald. Despite the influence of these theorists, however, the most important role would be played by Freud and his disciples.

In the following sections, we offer a detailed portrayal of the compulsive personality as expressed through the psychodynamic, interpersonal, and cognitive perspectives. Each of these domains interacts to form the whole person. We have chosen to present history and description side by side. Do not be tempted to see the material simply as a historical progression of who did what when, because you will miss out on the descriptive bounty that each author brings to the construct. By the time you finish these sections, you should have a good grasp of the compulsive prototype. Developmental pathways are also described, though these are now speculative and indistinct. Read not only for history but also for the characteristics that each author unearthed and their significance to the total personality. References to the cases are included.

The Psychodynamic Perspective

According to Freud, human development proceeds through various psychosexual stages. In each, a particular area of the body becomes an erogenous zone, the focus of libidinal energy during that particular period. Sexuality was conceived as an instinctual force that naturally seeks discharge. For most people, progress through the psychosexual stages is largely unremarkable. Some individuals, however, experience either excessive frustration or excessive indulgence, resulting in the fixation of sexual energy on the concerns of a particular stage, thus coloring the total personality. During the oral stage, for example, sexual energy is focused on the mouth. Excessive gratification of oral needs was believed to lead to the development of an oral character, the psychodynamic equivalent of the contemporary dependent personality.

As children begin to move into toddlerhood, they leave the oral stage and enter a period of toilet training, the anal stage, beginning at about 18 months. As Freud (1908) noted, whereas the oral stage requires only suckling at the breast, an inborn reflex that comes naturally to all infants, the anal stage begins a period of anal eroticism that instead requires an inhibition of what is natural. In particular, the anal stage requires self-control, a delay of instinctual gratification that accompanies an immediate expulsion of feces. The pleasurable drive of the id thus runs directly into the desire of parents, so the anal stage plays an important role in the formation of the superego and the control of aggressive impulses.

The exact influence of the anal stage on personality development was believed to depend on the attitude taken by parents toward toilet training. A rigid, impatient, or demanding attitude could result in the formation of anal-retentive traits, the characterological counterpart of the compulsive personality. Essentially, the child reacts against the parents by holding back and refusing to perform, leading to adult traits such as stubbornness, stinginess, and hidden anger. Anal-retentive types were also believed to be punctual, orderly, conscientious, and preoccupied with cleanliness, the very traits that led their parents to demand that they perform on schedule, with everything in its place and with no mess. Alternatively, children might react to overcontrol by becoming an anal-expulsive type. Here, the child goes on the offensive; feces become a weapon. Whereas the anal-retentive strategy is simple refusal, now the strategy shifts to the active destruction of parental wishes, a desire to make others regret they had ever exerted any control at all. Naturally, adult traits are the opposite of the anal-retentive type and include destructiveness, disorderliness, and sadistic cruelty.

If we look at what the case studies say about Donald's and Holden's early childhood, we do find elements of parental overcontrol. Donald, in fact, struggled to do what he was told, remembering his mother and father as stern and intolerant of the horseplay that is part of the early life of most boys. Holden had a similar experience, being required to meet his parents' expectations and follow their rules, with "severe consequences" for misbehavior. Parental overcontrol is different from fixations of libidinal energy, but as these examples show, there is indeed some wisdom encapsulated in these old analytic conceptions.

As psychoanalysis began to develop into ego psychology and object relations, conceptions of the anal character broadened as well. W. Reich (1933) depicted the compulsive as preoccupied with a "pedantic sense of order," as living life according to preset patterns but also tending to worry and ruminate, characteristics seen especially in Holden. Perhaps more important, W. Reich (1949) regarded the compulsive as exceptionally reserved emotionally, not given to displays of love and affection, a characteristic he referred to as "affect-block." As we have seen, neither Donald nor Holden seems to have much room for fun in his life. We can't imagine either of them telling jokes "with the boys" or reacting to a serious situation with too much levity. Neither are they romantic.

A variety of theorists have made important contributions. Combining influences from economics, culture, and existentialism, Fromm (1947) described the hoarding orientation. Such persons build a protective wall around themselves to prevent anything new from entering. As if always expecting a famine or disaster, they hoard, save, and fortify themselves for lean times and, like the anal-retentive described previously, only rarely share anything with others. For them, orderliness signifies an existential victory over the ungovernable complexities of life, giving them a feeling of mastery and control over the world (see "Focus on History" box for more information on Fromm's scheme of character orientations). Like other theorists before and since, Rado (1959) described the compulsive as overly concerned with minutiae, details, and petty formalities. He also noted continuities between normality and pathology. Thus, the scrupulously honest person may give way to the hypocrite, and sensitivity to hurt may give way to destructiveness, criticism, and vindictiveness. For Salzman (1985), the compulsive's unrelenting need to control internal and external forces provides an illusion of certainty and security in a threatening and uncertain world. To minimize the possibility of unanticipated misadventure, compulsives become cautious and meticulous, even phobic. There are other interpretations, but Donald's stomach pains could be seen as reaction to the feeling that too much about his life remains beyond his control, a feeling too threatening to be allowed into conscious awareness and thus channeled into his body.

We have seen that compulsives, more than any other personality, intrinsically require order, detail, and perfectionism as a means of coping with what is unpredictable or unsure in the world around them. But that is not the limit of these requirements; compulsives demand the same sense of order and security from their internal world, as well. At any moment, a little self-examination shows that most of us are seething with conflicting feelings that pull us one way or another and prevent black-and-white assessments, even of simple situations. You take a class, for example, and although the instructor is superb, the workload gets in the way of other classes and causes you anger and regret. You take a class, and although the workload is easy, you definitely could be getting more substance for your tuition dollars. You love your mother, but she smothers you; then again, when she doesn't meddle at least a little, you wonder if she still loves you. The issues may be different, but everyone is caught in such conundrums. Most of us just acknowledge both sides of the coin and tolerate the complexity of life. Nothing is all good or all bad.

For compulsives, however, such contrary feelings and dispositions create intense feelings of anger, uncertainty, and insecurity that must be kept under tight rein. To do so, they make use of a whole host of defensive strategies, more than any other personality pattern. Research argues that the first, and perhaps most distinctive, is reaction formation (Berman & McCann, 1995). Here, compulsives reverse forbidden impulses of hostility and rebellion to conform to a highly rigid ego ideal. For example, when faced with circumstances that would cause dismay or irritability in most persons, compulsives pride themselves in displaying maturity and reasonableness, just as Donald does, when noting that even when his wife is griping and his pain is intense, he manages to keep things under control. In effect, compulsives symbolically purge themselves of unclean and shameful feelings by embracing what is diametrically opposite.

Second, compulsives often displace anger and insecurity by seeking out some position of power that allows them to become a socially sanctioned superego for others. Here, compulsives enact their anger by making others conform to precise standards that are unworkably detailed or strict. Holden is almost the incarnation of this pattern. Those who fall short either pay their dues by acknowledging the compulsive's superior authority and knowledge or fall victim to a swift judgment that conceals a sadistic and self-righteous joy behind a mask of maturity. Punishment becomes a duty; humanitarianism, a failing. Fiercely moralistic fathers and overcontrolling mothers provide examples of camouflaged hostility. Despite their efforts at control, research shows that compulsive traits are strongly related to impulsive aggression (Stein, Trestman, Mitropoulou, & Coccaro, 1996).

Although usually capable of exquisite self-control, compulsives sometimes transgress their own standards or incur the disapproval or disappointment of authority figures. When their ego defenses fail, they may become filled with feelings of guilt. Whereas hostility can be transformed or vented, guilt must be expiated or exorcised, a defense referred to as undoing. Compulsives go to great lengths to atone for their perceived sins. Such compensation seeks not only to repair the damage but also to put things back the way they were before and return them to a position of good standing in their own eyes and those of others. At the moment, for example, Holden is working so hard to organize and rememorize his old lecture notes that he's overloading himself and experiencing nightmares. We might expect, however, that when Holden returns to his teaching position in the history department, he may work harder than he ever has before to make up, at least in his own mind, for his previous rigid strictness. Paradoxically, he might even work hard at being merciful with the students in his new class.

Another defense mechanism used by compulsives, isolation of affect, connects the psychodynamic and cognitive domains, at least for these personalities. The same demand for order and perfection that compulsives demand of their environment, they demand of their own mental landscape. To keep oppositional feelings and impulses from affecting one another and to hold ambivalent images and contradictory attitudes from spilling over into conscious awareness, they organize their inner world into tight, rigid compartments. In effect, compulsives seek to suffocate instinct, passion, and emotion by deconstructing experiences into little bits that are easily classified and talked about rather than felt. For normal persons, memory is not just a mechanism of recall, but also is a means of rewinding and replaying episodes from our lives to recapture the fullness of the original experience, with all the emotions and sensations that accompany it. Although some are frightening and some are cherished, all of us have such memories that we return to many times.

Compulsives, however, are different. Their mental contents resemble highly regimented repositories of shriveled or dehydrated facts, each of which is carefully indexed but kept separate from the others. In effect, their goal is the opposite of poetry. Whereas poetry embellishes experience by providing symbolic and metaphorical links to related experiences, compulsives seek to contain each aspect of experience in its own little compartment. They database their memories and make only intellectual associations among them. By preventing their interaction, compulsives ensure that no single facet of experience is able to catalyze any other to produce an unanticipated emotion or drive of significant depth. Consequently, most compulsives view self-exploration as a waste of time. Psychotherapy may be seen as too much of a soft science to warrant their time or attention. For the compulsive, isolation of affect and mental structure protectively reinforce each other. We don't see Donald or Holden breaking forth in laughter or tears because some aspect of their immediate environment took them back to an old memory.

Modern conceptions of the compulsive personality are put forward from an object-relations framework. As noted previously, the psychodynamic development of the compulsive personality is linked closely to the anal stage. Freud emphasized frustration and the resulting fixation of psychosexual energy. Later psychodynamic thinkers reinterpreted the psychosexual stages in object-relations terms, making central the role of caretakers, not the fixation of psychic energy. The essential conflict is between the parent's desire to interfere and control and the child's growing sense of autonomy. Toilet training is then only a small part of the total interaction between parent and child, and it is out of this total interaction that personality grows. We don't need to know how Donald or Holden were toilet-trained to see the continuity between their parents' treatment of them and their adult characteristics.

In addition to overcontrol, contemporary psychodynamic accounts also emphasize expectations of perfection by caretakers. As noted in Gabbard (1994), compulsives internalize a harsh superego and search for flawlessness as a means of regaining lost parental approval (for further discussion of childhood expression of these symptoms, see "Focus on Childhood" box). From the beginning, they are taught to feel a deep sense of responsibility and a deep guilt whenever their responsibilities are not met. Frequently, they are moralized to by others to inhibit any impulse toward frivolous play and are instilled with a sense of shame whenever their sense of responsibility sags. When Donald's parents refused to let him play with other children because they disapproved, at first he probably conformed simply to do as they said. Eventually, however, Donald incorporated their moral sense of superiority into himself. Now, he disapproves of others for any number of reasons, seemingly as part of the substance of what he is.

By the time they reach adolescence, future compulsives have fully incorporated the strictures and regulations of their elders. By now, they are equipped with an inner gauge that ruthlessly evaluates and controls them, relentlessly intruding to make them doubt and hesitate before acting. External sources of restraint have been supplanted with the inescapable controls of internal self-reproach. Compulsives are now their own persecutor and judge, ready to condemn themselves not only for overt acts but for thoughts of transgression as well. By promoting a sense of guilt, the child acquires a self-critical inner voice ready with rebuke even when caretakers are physically absent or even dead. Religious elements often play an important role. Some are told the terrifying consequences of mischief and sin; others are told how troubled or embarrassed their parents will be if they deviate from the "righteous path." Sometimes, they turn their sense of morality into a sense of moral superiority and use this to fuel an indignation that excuses the expression of anger and focuses it toward a suitable target, as Holden often did by using bureaucracy as a weapon.

The Interpersonal Perspective

As we learned in previous chapters, the interpersonal perspective is concerned with patterns of communication between individuals and whether these communications are congruent or incongruent with the definition of the self on both sides. Timothy Leary (1957) referred to the compulsive as the "hypernormal" personality. Such persons make normality a goal and want others to perceive them as reasonable, successful, and mature. Perceptions of weakness or childishness are the antithesis of how compulsives wish to be seen by others. In Leary's formulation, the capacity for playfulness, childlike indulgence, and the capacity to show deep feelings would all be regarded as an unconscious or suppressed portion of their personality. Kiesler (1996, p. 161) regards the compulsive pattern as a form of hostile submission, describing them as emotionally nonexpressive, hyperrational, perfectionistic, indecisive, and uncertain. Also included were tendencies that blend the interpersonal and cognitive, such as "censoring and premonitoring."

We can conclude that compulsives are highly deliberate in their interpersonal interactions. Whereas normal persons have the capacity for spontaneity, compulsives actively monitor their own actions and messages. Their communications may seem to be preceded by a flowchart rigidity, perhaps looking a little like this: First, formulate an interpersonal plan. Second, check the plan scrupulously for deficiencies in precision and maturity, adopting a low threshold at which to delete behavioral possibilities to eliminate any possibility of embarrassment or incompetency. Third, formulate new behaviors if necessary, and check as before. Fourth, enact selected behaviors, gauge the reactions of others, and return to step one. Rigidity increases when the other participants in the transaction have some rank or status that exceeds that of the compulsive so that the importance of censoring mistakes increases.

The interpersonal process of compulsives requires that they invest much time and energy in it. For this reason, compulsives are often seen by others as reserved, cheerless, or even grim. Although they are invariably polite, this flows from their desire to adhere to social convention, not from an intrinsic warmth. Their posture and movement may seem tight and controlled. Their words are carefully chosen to be accurate and objective. Whatever the topic of conversation, compulsives prefer to remain distant and impersonal, disdaining subjective assessments or opinion in favor of intellectualized or abstract formulations that reveal nothing of themselves. They may speak in a stilted and impersonal manner that universalizes their commentary, raising it to the level of a rule. For example, a compulsive might say, "One often finds in life that experience is one's best teacher," rather than, "You make mistakes, learn what you can, and go on." For this reason, their interpersonal impression is one of propriety, formality, and restraint. Holden would almost certainly strike others this way. A hint of his need for restraint is seen in the absence of anger he feels toward the new administration that asked him to step down.

The inner dynamics of the compulsive personality are made especially clear when contrasting their interpersonal conduct with superiors and subordinates. Given their conscientiousness and preoccupation with detail, efficiency, and perfection, compulsives make good "organization men or women," adopting the needs and goals of the business as their own, almost as part of their own superego. Most relate to others in terms of rank or status. They are deferential, even obsequious, to their superiors, but authoritarian or dictatorial with subordinates. By allying themselves with powerful others, compulsives enjoy a measure of protection and indirectly assume a mantle of strength and respect. At the same time, they use their position of power to induce fear into their subordinates, the same fear they themselves experience when "called on the carpet" before more powerful others. To vent their repressed hostilities, compulsives may antagonize their workers with rules, regulations, codes of conduct, and conformity to a job description. All three of the cases depicted in this chapter exhibit this characteristic: Holden with his students, Donald with his workers, and Elsa, discussed in Case 7.3.

How does the compulsive personality develop from an interpersonal perspective? Two features are prominent. The first is parental overcontrol. Overcontrol is similar to overprotection, important in the development of the dependent personality. Both betray an intrusiveness that affects the growing child's sense of autonomy, though in different

Elsa is a graduate teaching assistant who presented at the university counseling center at the suggestion of her supervising professor. She is to teach two classes, Introduction to Sociology and Research Methodology, and was given free rein to choose the textbooks, develop the lecture content, and create homework assignments and exam materials. When asked why she was given such latitude, her professor remarked, "I've worked with her, I know she likes things her own way."[1] According to Elsa, she knows the material in great detail, having studied the entire summer rather than allow herself time off to spend with friends. Yet, there has been a swell of protest from students in both classes.

Elsa became a fixture at the bookstore for several weeks before the beginning of the semester. She was obsessed with choosing just the right text, but paralyzed by the many alternatives. Although the students feel that her lectures are well-organized and informative, they also feel that she imposes her own academic values onto them, and expects too much work, including weekly reports, a comprehensive final, and a term paper, and expects everything to be proofread and flawless. Worse, they note that she is extremely critical of everything they turn in, and seems so focused on sentence structure and writing style that she overlooks content and meaning. Due to her meticulous analysis, papers are often not returned for many weeks.

Elsa presents as a mature young lady. With her conservative hairstyle, gray suit, and serious manner, she seems much older than she really is. For her, therapy is just another responsibility, to be carried out earnestly. She admits wanting to please her supervising professor, but in the same breath reproaches her students, who "want a college degree without doing college work." As a teaching assistant, she has made it her duty to weed out those who see school as a four-year vacation from responsibility. She does not address, or emotionally acknowledge, the rather awkward reasons that brought her to the counseling center.

Elsa is the first person in her family to attend college. She describes her father as a proud but angry man, ruling the house by fear. Her mother insisted she do well in school and rise above their "immigrant heritage." Elsa attended church regularly, kept house for the family, and did well enough to win a college scholarship, which paid most of her tuition. She is ashamed of her sister, who left home at 15 and contacts the family only in dire circumstances. Elsa still lives at home, which "allows me to save rent money." She has no social life beyond church, but states that she neither needs nor has the time for one. Her days are well organized, with intense devotion to her work. She becomes angry thinking about others who fail to use their time wisely, namely, the students in her two classes.

Circled markers in margin: 6, 3, 1, 4, 2, 1, 3

[1] Numbers mark aspects of the case most consistent with *DSM* criteria, and do not necessarily indicate that the case "meets" diagnostic criteria in this respect.

Compulsive Personality Disorder
DSM-IV Criteria

A pervasive pattern of preoccupation with orderliness, perfectionism, and mental and interpersonal control, at the expense of flexibility, openness, and efficiency, beginning by early adulthood and present in a variety of contexts, as indicated by four (or more) of the following:

(1) is preoccupied with details, rules, lists, order, organization, or schedules to the extent that the major point of the activity is lost

(2) shows perfectionism that interferes with task completion (e.g., is unable to complete a project because his or her own overly strict standards are not met)

(3) is excessively devoted to work and productivity to the exclusion of leisure activities and friendships (not accounted for by obvious economic necessity)

(4) is overconscientious, scrupulous, and inflexible about matters of morality, ethics, or values (not accounted for by cultural or religious identification)

(5) is unable to discard worn-out or worthless objects even when they have no sentimental value

(6) is reluctant to delegate tasks or to work with others unless they submit to exactly his or her way of doing things

(7) adopts a miserly spending style toward both self and others; money is viewed as something to be hoarded for future catastrophes

(8) shows rigidity and stubbornness

ways. Overprotection usually reflects loving parental concern, the implicit message being, "We love you, let us do for you, because you are incapable on your own." In contrast, overcontrol is based on the appraisal that children can never be trusted with any amount of autonomy. Overcontrolling parents thus keep a close watch on their children and quickly punish even minor transgressions, even when the child does not yet have the cognitive capacity to fully understand what went wrong and why.

Overcontrol is thus similar to hostility, an important developmental factor for the antisocial and sadistic personalities. Hostile parents, however, punish regardless of actual behavior, whereas overcontrolling parents punish only when they believe the child has misbehaved. Nevertheless, the parents of the future compulsive set the threshold for misbehavior very low. As noted in the case of Holden, he and his brother "knew what they could count on in life. . . . If they failed to meet expectations . . . punishment would be swift and severe." The interpersonal message to the future antisocial is, "You are bad"; the interpersonal message to the future compulsive is, "You'd better be careful, because you are mighty close to being bad." As a result, future compulsives grow up living in fear of making a mistake, without knowing when the next thrashing or tirade will come or what its justification will be. Naturally, they are plagued by indecision and self-doubt and stick closely and rigidly to the rules, which represent, as much as possible, a position of relative safety. Thus we have Elsa, who describes her father as a "proud but angry man."

Second, the parents of future compulsives almost never reward the child's legitimate achievements. Instead, they expect order and perfection and condemn anything that falls

FOCUS ON HISTORY

Erich Fromm

Early Explorations of the Social Development of Personality

Erich Fromm (1947) was one of the early theorists to reinterpret Freud along social lines. Although constructing his model in accordance with the same themes, Fromm questioned the relevance of biological forces as the prime element in character development. Instead, he emphasized the interpersonal transactions between parent and child. For example, the compulsive pattern was seen to result not from frustrations experienced at the anal stage, but from the behavioral models exhibited by a rigid and meticulous parent.

According to Fromm, four problematic character orientations develop from early interpersonal learning experiences. The first, the receptive character, is characterized by a deep need for external support from parents, friends, and authorities. All things that are good or necessary are found outside the self. The second, the exploitative character, extracts what it wants from others, either by force or cunning. Pessimistic, suspicious, and angry, these characters feel incapable of producing on their own. The third, the hoarding character, achieves a sense of security by saving and keeping. Rigid and orderly, they are miserly about their possessions and thoughts, sharing almost nothing. Finally, the marketing orientation is ever ready to adapt itself to what others expect or require. As such, they have little that is stable and genuine in their own makeup because they are always "selling" themselves to others.

short of this. Real achievements are taken for granted and rarely acknowledged. Given these parents' low threshold for criticism and condemnation, for projecting an all-bad image into the child without rewarding the positive, future compulsives grow up living in fear of some inadvertent transgression, ever circumspect of the possibility of making a mistake, while feeling guilty that not enough has been done to secure parental approval. Donald's parents, for example, were so "stern" that "He remembers trying to color between the lines and feeling that the picture was ruined if there was one errant mark."

Working from her SASB model, Benjamin (1996) sketches a similar picture. The parents of future compulsives emphasize perfection and orderliness, while offering the child little warmth and no respect of his or her developmental level. In other words, the parents of compulsives-in-training often behave with a stern, cold formality, Benjamin states, and demand that the child not only perform tasks of which he or she is developmentally incapable, but also perform these tasks with perfection. Failure is met with blame. Displays of affection in the household are not tolerated, and the child is expected to behave like a highly rational miniature adult; Donald's parents, for example, took pride in calling him "our little man." Because children learn to regard themselves as others regard them, these standards and expectations are then put into the superego, with the result that the child comes to demand perfection not only of the self but also of others. Finally, as Benjamin further emphasizes, parents who are angry and moralizing in addition to being cold and controlling produce children with a self-righteous streak loaded on top of other compulsive characteristics. Perhaps this is the case with Elsa, who has made it her mission to weed out the slackers among her students.

The Cognitive Perspective

The strong cognitive traits of the compulsive personality were recognized and written about by analytic theorists long before the cognitive perspective was ever popular. Whereas contemporary information-processing accounts are concerned with flow-charting the architecture and processes of cognition, analytic accounts were more concerned with cognitive style and the close connection between character and cognition. W. Reich (1933, p. 211) regarded compulsives as indecisive and doubting, and "just as ill disposed toward affects as [they are] acutely inaccessible to them."

Other psychoanalytic theorists noted compulsives' intolerance of ambiguity. Compulsives treat their mental contents as they treat their work: They like to have things specified concretely; everything should fit neatly into some system of classification; anything not easily organized becomes either a source of anxiety or an object of contempt. Devoted to the classical concept of the anal character, Rado (1959, p. 326) described these persons as concrete, factually oriented, and contemptuous of fancy and imagination. Such cognitive traits can perhaps be traced back to the family environment: When your parents are harsh, punitive, and righteous, you naturally prefer the concrete because it's easier to judge and it keeps you out of trouble, especially if you're a child and, therefore, without a mature cognitive apparatus.

Realizing that attention is an essential aspect of information processing, Shapiro (1965) emphasized that whereas most people have the capacity to move their attention about freely, the attention of compulsives is sharp yet acutely restricted, principled, and always concentrated. Shapiro was thus able to link level of attention to the intrusiveness of irrelevancies that plague compulsives' mental life. Their focus on detail never flags, so it must seize on something; rather than relax when nothing of urgency exists to occupy it, it moves from some small detail of their work to a piece of dirt on the floor or to a minor personal foible. As we saw with the indecisive dean, in anxious situations a preference for a high level of detail becomes maladaptive; he keeps reviewing old lecture notes but never feels ready.

Anything at the farthest edges of the compulsive personality's attention has the potential to be transported directly to the center of awareness and put under the person's exquisite magnifying glass. These individuals are not only typically incapable of grasping the "big picture" but also generally unable to sense the overall emotional tone of interpersonal situations, contributing to the interpersonal impression that they are reserved or cold. Because compulsives focus on detail in communications and fail to adequately judge the interpersonal atmosphere, they cannot relax or be spontaneous or empathic. Shapiro also connected compulsives' level of attention to their lack of intuition, noting that they rarely get hunches. Finally, for this same reason, compulsives are largely hardened against aesthetic appreciation of art or literature. The level of attention works in conjunction with the defense of emotional isolation, for example, to make them insensitive to tragedy or any other human drama. If Elsa could just gauge the atmosphere of her classroom, she would have responded to student feedback and wouldn't be sitting in the counseling center.

In fact, unaware of their insensitivity to emotional nuance, it is likely that compulsives fail to realize that the emotional lives of others are far richer than their own. Whereas most people would pity the compulsive's immersion in detail as being foreign to the immediacy and vividness of feeling truly alive, most compulsives have no insight into the impoverishment of their lives. Instead, they sterilize and dehumanize their existence by organizing their thinking rigidly in terms of conventional rules and regulations, formal schedules, and social hierarchies. Some do so with condescension and contempt, regarding others as disorganized, ineffective, and primitive. Such types flourish in bureaucratic settings, where their desire for specificity and detail can be used as a weapon against anyone who crosses them, pays them inadequate respect, or just seems a little too carefree, as with the indecisive dean. By complicating the lives of others, compulsives vent their inner anger while justifying their behavior as required by organizational codes.

Moreover, because compulsives analyze the emotion out of experience, the sadistic quality of their actions is usually not accessible for conscious reflection. Those who shred the lives of others on some technicality may rationalize their actions by asserting that life requires someone to filter out those who are unworthy, to eliminate those unable to make the grade, as with Elsa. Here, the cognitive, interpersonal, and psychodynamic domains shade more closely together than for most personalities. Such compulsives are bent on following the rules, but deeply resent being bound by them and resent even more the idea that someone might "get away" with something. The idea of others laughing about getting away with something fills them with rage. Some actively seek omissions or foibles on the part of others, whom they victimize with regulations, red tape, endless forms and applications, the "fine print," and intolerance for the slightest error or transgression, however human. They have no pity for those they injure. By doing so, they seek revenge against the strictures of their own condemning superego by displacing their hostility onto others, frustrating others' wishes, and sabotaging others' attempts at self-actualization. There are no shortcuts. Here, Holden provides the best example.

Other compulsives, however, seem to cling to order and detail almost as a cognitive defense against uncertainty and ambiguity. Unlike the preceding sadistic variety, they are more submissive and fearful of condemnation, possessing an intense need to be sure. Such compulsives deeply dread making mistakes, restricting themselves to situations that are familiar and approved. They avoid the dangerous unknown by maintaining a tight and well-organized approach to life. The same dull routines allow them to play it safe but prevent them from developing new perceptions or approaches to problem solving.

Such individuals are naturally indecisive, endlessly seeking out every source of information, advice, and authoritative opinion before making even minor decisions. Often, their quest leaves their judgment overwhelmed by hundreds of details they feel helpless to integrate conclusively. Thus stuck and forever fearful of error, they may become mired in a paralysis of analysis that prevents them from making any decision at all. In effect, they are caught in an information-processing vicious circle: The more detail they gather, the more the facts fail to converge on a single course of action or conclusion, and the more their anxiety increases. The solution is to redouble their efforts and gather even more detail (see Figure 7.2).

Beck et al. (1990) have written extensively about the cognitive perspective on personality and its disorders. These theorists hold that beliefs about the world, self, and others are critical in determining behavior. Although traits may indeed refer to consistencies in behavior, cognitive theorists would argue that behind every behavioral consistency lies a cognitive consistency. Characteristic ways of construing the world are, therefore, even more fundamental than traits themselves, which give only a surface view. Core beliefs, which may be either conscious or unconscious, are held to be true regardless of time, place, or circumstance. Conditional beliefs express the interactive role between person and situation: If such-and-such occurs, then such-and-such will result. In turn, conditional beliefs feed into instrumental beliefs, which concern what persons can or can't do to affect the world around them.

Given their developmental history and superego formation, the most fundamental core belief of the compulsive personality is, "I should" (Beck et al., 1990). Schemata

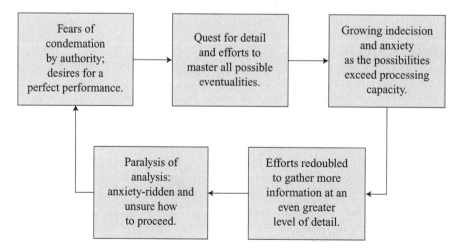

FIGURE 7.2   The Vicious Circle of the Compulsive's Information Processing.

for control, responsibility, and systematization, these authors state, become overdeveloped, and those related to spontaneity and playfulness are neglected and, therefore, weak. If a "should" cannot be identified, compulsives begin to feel uncomfortable, as if drowning in ambiguity. Whereas many would occasionally reflect deeply before making a decision, compulsives are always focused on justifying their actions and how candidate actions might be criticized or evaluated by an observer, especially an authority figure. As such, their minds are forever entangled in a web of, "I should . . ." and "I fear . . . ." Cognitively, then, they need the structure of scripted situations, because known scripts tell you what to do, as well as how and when to do it. Donald, for example, fell apart in the clinical interview but rebounded nicely when told to describe his average day. For most compulsives, structure is their total reality. Most know nothing else, which often leads them into paradox. When compulsives go to a party, for example, they work at enjoying themselves, for that is the purpose of a party. The absurdity never dawns on them.

In turn, the moral imperatives that rule their existence are reinforced and perpetuated by several key cognitive errors (Beck et al., 1990). Perhaps most notably, compulsives view the world in black-and-white terms. Their "should" statements constitute absolutes unqualified in terms of situation, personal ability, or the availability of resources. Instead, compulsives are governed by commandments dispensed from an almighty Superego: "Thou shalt not fail. Thou shalt be always in control. Thou shalt not be caught in a mistake, however small," and so on. Given their dichotomous, moralistic view of the world, it is not surprising that the consequences of violating even one of these commandments are grim, even catastrophic. Compulsives cannot do what they desire; they must do what they should, in every case. As a result, life has but little potential for small joys and a large potential for anxiety. We see some of this in the case of Donald, who is overflowing with anxiety but who can neither afford to consciously acknowledge it nor surrender any measure of control. Much of compulsives' lives are spent in the past or future, lost in rumination about what they should do about a certain person or situation or how what they have already done might fall short. Sometimes their intense deliberation can make them seem distracted. Only rarely are they centered in the present moment, home to most of the joys and intimacies of life.

The Evolutionary-Neurodevelopmental Perspective

Because personality refers to the matrix of the total person, each of the preceding perspectives offers limited insight into the compulsive personality as a total phenomenon. Each of these theories explores important facets of a given personality within a particular domain (e.g., cognitive, intrapsychic), but none sufficiently embrace the totality of the person.

The compulsive personality, according to the evolutionary theory of personality (Millon, 1990; Millon & Davis, 1996), is one of two interpersonally conflicted styles, the other being the negativistic personality (or the passive-aggressive personality disorder, as it is referred to in *DSM-III-R*). Although the dependent, histrionic, narcissistic, and antisocial personalities are all interpersonally imbalanced, they still relate to others in a consistent fashion. Because their needs and agendas are definite, life can be experienced as satisfying, fulfilling, or complete. Dependents, for example, seek support and assistance from others; as long as these resources are forthcoming, their lives are happy. Compulsives and negativists, however, are beset by a severe internal schism; they are deeply ambivalent about their relationships and attachments. Sometimes, they feel they must put their own needs and priorities first; sometimes, they feel they should defer to what others desire. Their fundamental struggle is between obedience and defiance (Rado, 1959).

What separates these two patterns is how this conflict is displayed. Passively conflicted compulsives pursue a strategy of containment. Given their early interpersonal development with demanding, overcontrolling, and perfectionistic parents, they develop introjects that demand self-control and self-containment. Inside, they struggle with issues of conformity and rebellion but transform anger into obedience through the mechanism of reaction formation. In contrast, actively conflicted negativists act out their ambivalence by alternating between actions that are impressively loyal and obedient and actions that are impressively frustrating. Compulsives overconform to rules and strictures; negativists become overly resentful of such impositions. The two personalities appear very different, but they are fundamentally connected by theory. The negativistic personality is discussed in more depth in Chapter 15.

In early development, children begin the struggle to acquire autonomous skills and to achieve a sense of self-competence. During this period, most children become assertive and resistant to parental direction and admonition. Overcontrolling parents respond to these efforts with firm and harsh discipline; they physically curtail the child, berate the child, withdraw love, and so on; in short, they are relentless in their desire to squelch troublesome transgressions. Children who are unable to find solace from this parental assault submit entirely, withdraw into a shell, or become adamant and rebel. However, if children uncover a sphere of operation that leaves them free of parental condemnation, they are likely to reach a compromise; they will restrict their activities just to those areas that meet parental approval. This, then, becomes the action available to the compulsive child; the youngster sticks within circumscribed boundaries and does not venture beyond them.

However, several consequences frequently result from taking this course. Autonomy has been sharply curtailed; these children will not develop adequate self-competence that other, less restricted children acquire. As a result, they have marked doubts about their adequacy beyond the confines to which they have been bound, they fear deviating from the "straight and narrow path," they hesitate and withdraw from new situations, and they are limited in spontaneity, curiosity, and adventurousness. Thus, having little self-confidence and fearing parental wrath for the most trivial of misdeeds, these children submerge impulses toward autonomy and avoid exploring unknowns lest they transgress the approved boundaries.

Overcontrolling parents are generally caring but display their concern within the context of "keeping the child in line," that is, of preventing trouble not only for the child's sake, but for theirs, as well. Thus, overcontrolling parents frequently are punitive in response to transgressions, whereas overprotective parents restrain the child more gently, with love rather than with anger or threats. Overcontrol, then, is similar in certain respects to the techniques of parental hostility, a training process more typical of the antisocial and sadistic developmental patterns. But there is an important distinction here, as well. The hostile parent is punitive *regardless of* the child's behavior, whereas the overcontrolling parent is punitive *only if* the child misbehaves. Thus, the parents of compulsives expect their children to live up to parental expectations and condemn them only if they fail to achieve the standards they impose. We may speak of overcontrol as a method of contingent punishment; that is, punishment is selective, occurring only under clearly defined conditions.

Another feature found commonly in the developmental history of the compulsive personality is exposure to conditions that instill a deep sense of responsibility to others and a feeling of guilt when these responsibilities have not been met. These youngsters often are "moralized" to inhibit their natural inclinations toward frivolous play and impulse gratification. They are impressed by the shameful and irresponsible nature of such activities and are warned against the "terrifying" consequences of mischief and sin. This learned sense of guilt diverts the child's anger away from its original object and turns it inward toward the self, where it can be used in the service of further curtailing rebellious feelings. The child is made both fearful of the consequences of aggressive impulses, as well as guilt-ridden for possessing such "ugly" and "sinful" attributes. Any deviant behavior is most assuredly curtailed by this attitude.

Largely because of these early experiences, the clinical profile of the adult compulsive personality emerges as one that not only defers to authority, but often worships it, internalizing all aspects of conformity and responsibility in an effort to eschew any shadings of oppositional character or action in self. This mandate of compliance and responsibility permeates all aspects of compulsives' existence, especially work. From the perspective of superiors, compulsives seem like the model of conscientiousness. To their subordinates, however, they are often sadistic taskmasters, demanding of their workers exactly what their parents demanded of them, while offering only slim mercy to those who shirk their duties. At a surface level, compulsives resemble the dependent personality, but underneath, they possess characteristics of the antisocial. To bind their oppositional urges and reinforce their controls, compulsives become overly conforming and overly submissive. They not only follow rules and customs but also vigorously defend them, overcompensating so much that they become caricatures of order and propriety. Resisting their impulses and repressing their antagonisms, they proceed systematically, meticulously, and rigidly through their daily routine, fearing that any deviation from their regimen could lead to angry outbursts or a loss of self-control. The compulsive personality is described through the clinical domains in Table 7.1. In the following section, it is contrasted with other constructs also derived from the evolutionary theory.

CONTRAST WITH RELATED PERSONALITIES

Perhaps more than any other personality, the traits that make up the compulsive pattern are tightly interwoven. As a result, the disorder is only rarely confused with other personality patterns. However, there are theoretical relationships and similarities to other personality patterns. Both compulsives and dependents, for example, conform to the expectations of others and often fail to make progress in their goals, but for different reasons. The dependent conforms out of deep feelings of inadequacy and fears losing supportive partners. In effect, dependents borrow the maturity and efficacy of their significant others as a means of insulating them from the demands of adult responsibility. Failure to conform puts the relationship at risk, leading to fantasies of abandonment and helplessness and on to episodes of anxiety, worry, and even panic. Wishes are the opposite of fears, and the dependent wishes to remain childlike—to be forever cared for in a world of love and happiness where infant and caretaker are magically fused as a single being.

TABLE 7.1   The Compulsive Personality: Functional and Structural Domains

Functional Domains		Structural Domains	
	Disciplined	**Self-Image**	**Conscientious**
Expressive Behavior	Maintains a regulated, highly structured and strictly organized life; perfectionism interferes with decision making and task completion.		Sees self as devoted to work, industrious, reliable, meticulous, and efficient, largely to the exclusion of leisure activities; fearful of error or misjudgment, hence overvalues aspects of self that exhibit discipline, perfection, prudence, and loyalty.
	Respectful	**Object-Representations**	**Concealed**
Interpersonal Conduct	Exhibits unusual adherence to social conventions and proprieties, as well as being scrupulous and overconscientious about matters of morality and ethics; prefers polite, formal, and correct personal relationships, usually insisting that subordinates adhere to personally established rules and methods.		Only those internalized representations with their associated inner affects and attitudes that can be socially approved are allowed conscious awareness or behavioral expression; as a result, actions and memories are highly regulated, forbidden impulses sequestered and tightly bound, personal and social conflicts defensively denied, kept from awareness, maintained under stringent control.
	Constricted	**Morphologic Organization**	**Compartmentalized**
Cognitive Style	Constructs world in terms of rules, regulations, schedules, and hierarchies; is rigid, stubborn, and indecisive and notably upset by unfamiliar or novel ideas and customs.		Morphologic structures are rigidly organized in a tightly consolidated system that is clearly partitioned into numerous distinct and segregated constellations of drive, memory, and cognition, with few open channels to permit interplay among these components.
	Reaction Formation	**Mood/Temperament**	**Solemn**
Regulatory Mechanism	Repeatedly presents positive thoughts and socially commendable behaviors that are diametrically opposite deeper contrary and forbidden feelings; displays reasonableness and maturity when faced with circumstances that evoke anger or dismay in others.		Is unrelaxed, tense, joyless, and grim; restrains warm feelings and keeps most emotions under tight control.

Note: Shaded domains are the most salient for this personality prototype.

In contrast, adult self-control and maturity are core values of the compulsive's self-image. Whereas dependents flee demands of work, maturity, and achievement, compulsives view such things as fundamental to their very identity. Although some compulsives are indecisive and easily overwhelmed cognitively by their inability to select a single option from a large number of possibilities, it is not the lack of fundamental competencies that prevents them from moving forward as it is for the dependent. Elsa is a fine picture of self-control and maturity. However, she is unable to complete the task of choosing a text and exhibits other patterns of compulsive behavior, including overconscientiousness about grading papers and correcting sentence structure.

Similarities are also seen between compulsive and schizoid personalities. Compulsives' devotion to institutional rules and social conventions colors their interpersonal behavior with a passivity that superficially resembles the schizoid. You can imagine that Holden, regarded as being a "stuffed shirt lacking real human compassion," might approach this on his more formal and less emotional days. Moreover, both compulsives and schizoids lack richness in their emotional life. For the schizoid, however, the absence of emotion reflects a basic incapacity for affective experience beginning in infancy, with a basic lack of attachment to caretakers, and continuing into adulthood. In contrast, the impoverished emotional life of the compulsive is connected to a self-image of earnestness and interpersonal reserve and the effort to block, stifle, or transform affect, wherever it is found. Accordingly, compulsives are best described as emotionally constricted, whereas schizoids are best seen as emotionally vacant.

Both compulsives and paranoids often possess deeply hidden feelings of hostility. The compulsive's anger, however, is more readily concealed behind a smiling façade of conformity, whereas the paranoid's anger is much closer to the surface and is even occasionally acted on. Moreover, paranoids readily show their irritability, whereas compulsives are more likely to transform hostility into overconformity through reaction formation or shift the expression of their anger from authority figures toward subordinates through the mechanism of displacement. In reaction formation, for example, an individual with both strong aggressive urges and strong strictures against their expression may overconform to superego demands in an attempt to compensate for guilty feelings. In displacement, aggressive feelings are redirected away from figures who might retaliate in kind and toward objects or persons who are incapable of any real threat. Thus, rather than scream at their supervisors, angry compulsives may use their position of power and knowledge of institutional rules to sabotage those who they feel have not accorded them sufficient respect or whom they simply view as not having paid their dues in life. In contrast, paranoids transform aggression by projecting feelings of hostility; in effect, they avoid responsibility for such emotions by attributing them to others and thus become the object of attack and persecution themselves.

The indirect expression of hostility and the presence of interpersonal conflict between their own desires, urges, and agendas and those of others also tie together the compulsive and negativistic personalities. However, as seen previously, the compulsive has a variety of means available to transform aggression, including its total sublimation. Frequently, this creates the façade of normality seen in certain traits, such as calm, reserve, and organization. In contrast, the actively conflicted negativist vacillates between passive-aggressive behavior that, like the compulsive's, conforms to expectations of others but only at a superficial level. Both are responses to overcontrolling authority, but whereas the compulsive follows the rules to please those in positions of power, the negativist uses the rules as a means of undermining those in power. Donald probably wouldn't have such intense somatic concerns if he could only, like a good negativist, allow himself to "throw a wrench into the works" once in a while and enjoy the resulting chaos.

PATHWAYS TO SYMPTOM EXPRESSION

Like most people with personality disorders, compulsives are naturally prone to express certain symptoms when faced with periods of prolonged or intense stress. As always, it is important to remember that many Axis I syndromes derive logically from deeply engrained personality patterns and the same Axis I syndrome has different significance to different underlying dynamics. Compulsives who develop somatic concerns, for example, like Donald, will do so for reasons different from avoidants. As you read the following paragraphs, try to identify the connection between personality and symptom disorder.

Obsessive-Compulsive Disorder

On initially examining the *DSM-IV,* you may naturally conclude that obsessive-compulsive disorder (OCD), which refers to unwanted and intrusive thoughts and actions, is obviously related to the obsessive-compulsive personality. After all, the two are identically named, as if some theoretical or empirical basis linking them were already established. However, although the relationship between these two disorders has been the subject of a great deal of speculation and empirical research, their relationship remains highly controversial. A review of the literature concluded that only a small minority of subjects diagnosed with obsessive-compulsive disorder are also diagnosed as compulsive personalities (Black & Noyes, 1997). Many are instead diagnosed as avoidants (Skodol, Oldham, Hyler, & Stein, 1995) or even as dependent, histrionic, or paranoid (Rodrigues & Del Porto, 1995). Moreover, tentative outcome studies suggest that where both disorders do exist in the same person, obsessive-compulsive disorder may be successfully treated while leaving the compulsive personality unaffected (McKay, Neziroglu, Todaro, & Yaryura-Tobias, 1996).

These findings, however, show only that obsessions and compulsions are not specific to the compulsive personality but instead occur in a variety of other patterns, which we would expect. Psychodynamic theorists, for example, have also linked obsessions to the narcissistic personality (see McWilliams, 1994). Whereas compulsives need perfection to avoid superego condemnation, the intrusive thoughts of narcissists are related to perceived flaws or limitations within themselves. Compulsives must satisfy the demands of a carping internalized parent, but narcissists need to believe in their own intrinsic superiority.

Both may, therefore, develop obsessive-compulsive disorder, but the content and meaning of such symptoms are likely to be different. The compulsive personality is, therefore, linked to obsessive-compulsive disorder, but through logic that relates the nature of the personality to the nature of the disorder. Obsessive checking, for example, appears to be more strongly associated with the compulsive pattern than is compulsive washing (Gibbs & Oltmanns, 1995; Rosen & Tallis, 1995) and with the trait of perfectionism in particular (Ferrari, 1995). The association of checking with compulsive personalities can be regarded as an attentional pathology that might be related to their characteristic level of attention (Shapiro, 1965) in conjunction with fears of error. Thus, the checker seems to be asking, "Did I really turn off the stove?" perhaps in response to a chronically activated internalized parental voice that keeps asking repeatedly, "Are you sure you've done everything right?" To keep this voice quiet, sooner or later you'll check the stove again, just to get a little peace.

Other Anxiety Disorders

Compulsives are frequently among candidates for the development of other anxiety disorders as well, including social phobia (Turner, Beidel, Borden, & Stanley, 1991) and generalized anxiety disorders (Nestadt, Romanoski, Samuels, Folstein, & McHugh, 1992). Many compulsives, especially those who have endured prolonged periods of stress (perhaps brought on by their own indecisiveness), develop the fear that their social façade will disintegrate, either because they are found to be inadequate and, therefore, become shamed beyond measure or because they themselves might snap under pressure and vent their aggressive feelings directly. Because most compulsives seem driven internally to accomplish their goals, the constant presence of tension often becomes part and parcel of their being. As a result, it can be difficult to distinguish the personality pattern from the clinical syndrome. On the positive side, however, many compulsives use the energy derived from anxiety to fuel their characteristic diligence and conscientiousness. Anxious energy is redirected into containment.

Somatoform Disorders

The somatoform disorders include conversion disorder, pain disorder, hypochondriasis, and body dysmorphic disorder. Although Case 7.1 features a compulsive personality and intensified somatic concerns, little research is available that relates these syndromes to the compulsive personality. Rost, Akins, Brown, and Smith (1992), however, found that although other personality patterns are more common, notably avoidant, paranoid, and self-defeating, somatization disorder is often diagnosed with compulsive personality disorder as well. Symptoms include pain, gastrointestinal illness, sexual dysfunction, and pseudoneurologic symptoms, none of which can be explained by a legitimate medical condition.

For compulsives, bodily ailments may be used as a means of rationalizing failures and inadequacies or a means of "saving face" by ascribing shortcomings to causes obviously beyond their control. Compulsives who succeed in spite of their illnesses reap a secondary gain: Those in charge reward them for their noble suffering or for persevering in the face of adversity, thus turning illness into an opportunity for praise and respect. Moreover, sickness allows them to escape the condemnation of a sadistic superego that is always ready with blame. The manifestation of physical symptoms can also be seen as an expression of accumulated tension and anxiety turned inward toward the body. For some, there is nowhere else anxiety can be expressed, for its presence destroys their façade of competency. Sometimes, the accumulation of tension and secondary gain work hand-in-hand, as with our queasy compulsive Donald, who must be under incredible pressure yet can maintain an "efficient operation" at work even when the discomfort is intense. Undoubtedly, he thinks his managers respect him for keeping at it rather than giving in to some nagging physical ailment.

Although the idea of being ill probably runs counter to their logical, rational, intellectual, sober, and controlled self-image, compulsives do exhibit a drive toward perfection that can cause them to become obsessed with minor imperfections that cannot be eliminated or overcome. Perhaps for this reason, compulsive personalities sometimes develop body dysmorphic disorder (Neziroglu, McKay, Todaro, & Yaryura-Tobias, 1996), a preoccupation that some part of the anatomy or appearance is defective. Once identified, the supposedly deformed part becomes the focus of constant and intense scrutiny. Such persons might examine their "wrinkled lips" or "crooked nose" in the mirror repeatedly many times a day, for example, or even make repeated suicide attempts (Veale, Boocock, Gournay, & Dryden, 1996).

Once established, body dysmorphic disorder is probably driven by a combination of compulsives' distorted level of attention (Shapiro, 1965), described previously, and their tendency toward black-and-white thinking. By allocating their total attention to the perceived defect, it becomes magnified completely out of proportion, consuming their entire awareness. At the same time, their dichotomous thinking makes a realistic assessment impossible. Rather than falling somewhere in the middle of the aesthetic range, they judge their nose or lips to be all bad, thus creating a vicious circle from which there is no release. Other personalities may be diagnosed with body dysmorphic disorder as well but probably for somewhat different reasons. Avoidants, for example, feel shamed by their defect and fear that it will bring them into public scrutiny; narcissists feel deflated; and histrionics, whose cognitions are remarkably imprecise, just feel globally ugly. Compulsives, however, probably feel that their defect causes others to take them less seriously or otherwise distracts others from properly focusing on their public image or position of power.

Dissociative Disorders

Avoidant, borderline, and compulsive personalities are common in subjects diagnosed with dissociative experiences (Simeon, Gross, Guralnik, & Stein, 1997), defined as "a disruption in the usually integrated functions of consciousness, memory, identity, or perception of the environment" (*DSM-IV,* 1994, p. 477). Many kinds of dissociation are possible. In dissociative amnesia, the individual is left with gaps in memory, usually due to some traumatic or highly stressful experience that cannot be recalled. Dissociative fugue is similar to dissociative amnesia, but features sudden flight away from home. In effect, the person wishes to not only forget but also get away. In dissociative identity disorder, formerly called multiple personality disorder, seemingly separate selves coexist within the same person.

Compulsives would seem naturally vulnerable to experiences of depersonalization, particularly a sense of detachment or estrangement from self and the idea that the surrounding world has somehow become unreal or dreamlike. The link between the disorder and the larger personality pattern derives from the compulsive's characteristic overcontrol of feeling, excessive intellectualization, and distorted attentional processes. Because emotions are so threatening to them, compulsives stultify and dichotomize their world as a means of making it more controllable. Taken to the extreme, however, perceptions of self, others, and environment can become completely purged of life. At this point, the compulsive becomes a machine functioning in a mechanical world governed by deterministic rules. Obviously, the line between depersonalization and delusion can become rather thin. W. Reich (1933), in fact, spoke of these persons as "living machines."

Depression and Other Mood Disorders

Compulsive personalities are naturally inclined toward depressive feelings. By overcontrolling and denying emotions and wishes and focusing themselves on detail work, they exist at a greater level of safety, but without much joy. In effect, their daily lives are deprived of the positive emotions that most of us take for granted, as all three of the cases presented illustrate. Whereas most people have their good days and bad days, compulsives just keep grinding forward with an emotional state best described as grim, reserved, or barren. As such, they experience few reinforcements in their interpersonal relationships. Others simply find them either boring or controlling and seek simply to minimize their interactions, leaving the compulsive feeling puzzled or rejected. Unfortunately, their tendency to sublimate conflict and quash any expression of affect leaves most compulsives so estranged from their own emotions, yet so dedicated to hard work and performance, that many just plod onward, unaware of how depressed they appear. Elsa, for example, could not emotionally acknowledge the reasons that brought her to the counseling center; we don't know if she is angry with her class or depressed because at some level she recognizes her shortcomings and the disappointment of others.

Compulsives whose defensive controls remain intact exist perpetually in a dysthymic twilight, but those in the grips of major depression are more likely to have suffered some kind of defensive breach related to their own intrinsic ambivalences. Psychodynamic theorists, for example, have long regarded depression as anger turned inward, directed against the self. Unable to resolve the conflict between obedience and defiance, compulsives may belittle their own competencies and become mired in feelings of guilt, condemnation, and shame. Some may come to resent or even hate themselves for displaying weakness and indecision and use depressive feelings as a means of self-punishment, believing that they deserve to suffer. Alternatively, compulsives with more insight may come to hate themselves for the happiness they have given up in conforming to external pressures or criticize themselves for imagined failures or for letting others take advantage of their drudgery.

Therapy

Compulsives make frustrating clients. Ironically, although they tend to work in earnest in therapy, many eventually fold under the collective weight of their own traits. For one thing, a corrective emotional experience is often part of successful therapy, but compulsives often find it difficult to connect emotionally with anything. Emotions are equated with being out of control, and that scares them. Some eventually complain that their time, money, and, ironically, their hard work have all been wasted.

THERAPEUTIC TRAPS

At the beginning of therapy, most clients naturally defer to the therapist as an authority or expert. The therapist, after all, holds an advanced degree, has thousands of hours of clinical experience, and so on. As therapy proceeds, however, these expectations loosen somewhat as client and therapist develop a sense of mutual trust and get to know each other as genuine human beings. Clients may initially believe that therapists have all the answers, but they eventually learn that every person is different and, consequently, that psychotherapy is based on a body of principles that rest on probabilities, and there is no "direct line" to normal functioning. They also learn the importance of sharing and reflecting on their innermost feelings and experiences and of using these to help identify dysfunctional patterns in their relationships.

Compulsive personalities, however, possess several characteristics that undermine this natural progression. First, most compulsives are cooperative, friendly, and conscientious as a result of their developmental history and the dynamics of the therapeutic situation. Thus, Donald seems invested in being the perfect patient and provides exhaustive answers to the intake questions. Motivating this façade, however, are punitive introjects. Donald would not dare give an incomplete answer; the therapist, representing authority, may be seen as an extension of Donald's own harsh superego. Consequently, there is the risk that any therapeutic interpretation could be transformed into something judgmental and condemning.

Therapists who are naturally more directive or confrontational, then, may inadvertently recapture compulsives' early developmental experiences, thus reinforcing their tendency toward self-criticism, suppressed defiance, and unvoiced irritation. In the worst-case scenario, a vicious dynamic develops: The therapist feels mystified and frustrated with the compulsive, who repeatedly intellectualizes and rigidly refuses to open up; in turn, the compulsive feels rebuked and shamed, withdraws even further, and fights the therapist behind a barricade of logic and rationality.

Second, even when the therapist is consistently warm and accepting, the desire to pull emotion from compulsives must be controlled and their exposure to affect paced. Unstructured therapies can evoke anxiety in the compulsive, who feels most comfortable only when conforming with some known structure. Therapists who like to move things along, especially with insight-oriented approaches, may find themselves frustrated by the compulsive's need to consider things factually, to deliberate over the possibilities, and to squelch emotional conflict to the point that insight becomes impossible. Constancy is a form of defensive armor, purposely constructed to resist emotional experience, even the corrective emotional experience of therapy. Change means vulnerability, and affect means vulnerability, instability, and insecurity. Compulsives typically not only minimize emotions but also do not know what emotions to feel. Therapy thus becomes an ambiguous situation in which they feel paralyzed by indecision and terrified by novelty.

THERAPEUTIC TECHNIQUES AND STRATEGIES

Working from an interpersonal perspective, Benjamin (1996) emphasizes that therapy with the compulsive personality may degenerate into a struggle for power. Sometimes, compulsives want control; sometimes, they want others to take control. However, compulsives can be engaged through their rationality. Benjamin advocates her SASB model, but compulsives should be interested in any therapeutic plan explained to them in a point-by-point, logical manner. Compulsives are also likely to agree that exploration of early developmental influences is necessary to the understanding of current problems. The notion that each person is the product of experience connects the past and present in a way that should appeal to them. By casting therapy as a process not unlike scientific research, their rational mode can be engaged, while the therapist helps them gain perspective on and establish empathy for that young, malleable child who was subjected to such cold and demanding parental control. Such compassion frees them from a constant, overbearing need to secure approval from internalized, condemning parental images and opens the way to warmth in current relationships. Identification with critical parents and the internalization of their relentless faultfinding can then be seen as an adaptation to a pathological family situation that is now no longer necessary and is maladaptive in the present. Excessive self-criticism, for example, is a major pathway to subtle feelings of depression.

Broader interpersonal interventions may also be helpful. As Benjamin (1996) also notes, couples therapy may be especially helpful because compulsives tend to marry other personality patterns whose dependency complements the compulsive's need to control, such as dependents and histrionics. Sexual problems are frequent and often crystallize larger pathologies in the relationship. For example, compulsive females may feel such a strong need for constant self-control that orgasm becomes impossible. When their mate does not want to have sex, male compulsives may feel that sexual withholding is really a play for control. Finally, compulsives can be enlisted to help establish rules for negotiating trouble spots in the relationship, be it money, leisure time, or sex. Because compulsives understand rules, this technique serves as a paradoxical means of coercing them into relinquishing control while establishing precedents of egalitarianism with their spouse. Other interventions include having the compulsive parent begin to spend time playing with the children, who naturally pull for joy, affection, and spontaneity. Otherwise, compulsives may remain so engrossed and engulfed by work that they continue to neglect their families.

Techniques drawn from other domains of personality can be useful in amplifying the effectiveness of interpersonal interventions. Because compulsives are vulnerable to chronic tension and anxiety, behavioral techniques such as relaxation training may be used to help them cope in anxiety-provoking situations and can be effective in loosening them up at the beginning of a session, prior to other interventions. Cognitive interventions should follow the general plan of cognitive therapy using techniques aimed at modifying the compulsive's maladaptive beliefs as well as emotions. Listing goals and assigning value and ranking to these objectives will likely appeal to the compulsive's sense of structure. Easy goals can be solved first to give a sense of accomplishment, providing support for the idea that change is possible and motivating patients with experiences of success. Once rapport has been established, beliefs can be tested with an attitude of scientific discovery rather than confrontation, which only recaptures the developmental past. Thought stopping can be used between sessions to decrease the amount of time spent in ruminative worry.

Psychodynamic approaches can be used to interpret displaced and repressed elements that have manifested as overt symptoms. Object-relations approaches are particularly relevant. Although discussion of the transference relationship provides a starting point, many patients are so affect-denying that other techniques must be called into play. Dream interpretation and free association can be helpful in getting past intellectual guardedness and uncovering deep-seated fears, such as making a mistake or incurring the disapproval of authority figures. Subjects may be surprised at the blatant and emotionally revealing content of their dreams. Uncovered fears can then be discussed in the context of the therapeutic relationship and linked to compulsives' rigidity and their insistence on discipline, perfection, prudence, loyalty, and, especially, reaction formation. Unfortunately, many compulsives defend against such psychodynamic techniques, viewing them as an unscientific waste of time.

Summary

The obsessive-compulsive personality struggles to contain conflict between obedience and defiance by overconforming to rules and strictures, becoming almost a caricature of order and propriety. Western society seems to encourage these traits by valuing hard work, efficiency, and attention to detail, but at the disorder level, order turns into perfectionism and discipline into rigidity. Compulsives become preoccupied with rules and lists, force others to conform to their rules, and become so overwhelmed by details of life that decisions become impossible.

Within a normal range, Oldham and Morris (1995) describe the conscientious style, who is particularly hard working and devoted to moral principles and order, while Millon's (Millon et al., 1994) conforming style is more concerned with following rules and conventions, tending to exhibit black-and-white thinking, and shunning emotionality. The compulsive personality is rarely confused with other personality patterns, although it is theoretically related to the dependent personality, the schizoid personality, and the paranoid personality.

A variety of adult subtypes of the compulsive personality exist. Conscientious compulsives exhibit a strong conforming dependency, puritanical compulsives are particularly troubled by ambivalence and prone to displacing their aggression in sadistic ways, bureaucratic compulsives use external structures to compensate for their internal ambivalence and may become sadistic, parsimonious compulsives are preoccupied with hoarding, and bedeviled compulsives are blended with the negativistic personality.

Freud explains the compulsive personality as a fixation at the anal stage of psychosexual development. Anal-retentive types are believed to be caused by a rigid, impatient, or demanding attitude taken by parents toward toilet training and children subsequently internalizing a harsh superego, ready to condemn themselves for thoughts and actions. Alternatively, children may react by becoming anal-expulsive types, a strategy of resisting parental controls. Later, ego psychologists and object relationists shifted the focus to the compulsive personality's intolerance of ambiguities, with the use of a host of defense mechanisms such as reaction formation, displacement, undoing, and isolating affect to overcome feelings of anger and insecurity aroused by the conflicts.

From an interpersonal perspective, we can see that compulsives are extremely deliberate in their social interactions. They seem incapable of spontaneity, instead following almost a flowchart for personal interactions. Their interpersonally distant and calculating qualities can be seen clearly in the work setting by their interactions with superiors and subordinates. As in the psychodynamic perspective, parental overcontrol is one factor contributing to the development of the compulsive personality. Interpersonal psychologists believe that parental failure to reward real achievements is also a contributing element.

Cognitions seem to play a large part in the functioning of the compulsive personality. Abhorring ambiguity, compulsives need to categorize their thoughts into discrete compartments and cling to order and rules as a defense against the dangerous unknown. Having an unflagging focus on minute detail, compulsives often miss the big picture and usually fail to recognize the emotional nuances of a situation. So fearful of making an error, many compulsives become mired in a paralysis of analysis. Compulsives have overdeveloped schemas for control, responsibility, and systematization and are trapped by black-and-white thinking, "should" statements, and ruminating about the past and future, causing them to miss out on most of the joys of life.

The compulsive personality is prone to displaying other symptoms when experiencing stress; obsessive-compulsive disorder (OCD), other anxiety disorders, somatoform disorders, dissociative disorders, and depression are the most common.

In therapy, compulsive personalities are likely to intellectualize their experiences and refuse to open up emotionally, but this does not mean that therapy cannot be successful. Couples therapy, psychodynamic therapy with dream analysis and free association, and framing therapy as scientific research are all useful techniques in treating the compulsive personality. Issues of control and power are likely to take center stage in therapy.

Chapter 8

The Dependent Personality

Objectives

- What are the *DSM-IV* criteria for the dependent personality?
- The devoted and agreeing personalities are normal variants of the dependent. Describe their characteristics and relate them to the more disordered criteria of the *DSM-IV*.
- Explain how different personality styles combine to form each of the subtypes of the dependent personality.
- How do men and women differ in their willingness to admit dependency?
- How does oral fixation lead to the development of the dependent personality in the psychoanalytic tradition?
- How do the defense mechanisms of introjection, idealization, and denial work in the dependent personality?
- Explain the role of parental overprotection in the development of the dependent personality.
- What are the core beliefs of the dependent?
- How does the inability to make good judgments contribute to the development of the dependent personality?
- Dependents share characteristics with other personality disorders. List these other disorders and explain the distinction between each and the dependent.
- Explain why dependents are prone to depression.
- Is there a relationship between separation anxiety disorder and the dependent personality?
- Why are issues of transference and countertransference important in psychotherapy with dependents?
- List therapeutic goals for the dependent personality.

Dependent personalities, referred to here simply as **dependents** for the sake of linguistic convenience, are caring to a fault, allowing others' well-being to come first no matter what the cost may be to themselves or their identity Ever helping and giving, they are committed to their personal relationships, especially to their spouses and the institution of marriage. Essentially, they live their lives through others and for others, to whom they offer warmth, tenderness, and consideration. When people they care for are happy, they are happy. Not surprisingly, they tend to assume the more passive role in their relationships, deferring to the opinions and desires of those they love, whose pleasure and fulfillment they then enjoy vicariously. They prefer harmony in their relationships and tend to be apologetic even when others should take the greater part of responsibility for a disagreement.

Many characteristics associated with the dependent personality are prized and admired in our culture. These include the quality of being happy when loved ones are happy and making personal sacrifices for the good of others, including volunteering to perform many selfless acts. On the surface, they are warm and affectionate, but underneath, they see themselves as helpless and fear doing anything on their own. They need to be taken care of and seek competent instrumental surrogates who reward submission by facing down the problems of the world in their place. Many are incapable of making even routine decisions without first seeking advice. By putting their lives in the control of others, they suffocate their partners with their clinginess and in turn leave themselves vulnerable to abandonment. To protect against this possibility, dependents quickly submit to their partners' wishes or become so pleasing no one would possibly want to leave them. Often, they arrange their lives so that they can avoid acquiring competencies that might allow them to stand on their own. When a relationship does finally dissolve, their self-esteem is devastated. Deprived of support or attachment, they withdraw into themselves and become increasingly tense and despondent.

As the case of Sharon demonstrates (see Case 8.1), dependents find it almost impossible to take the initiative on their own behalf or to provide direction to their lives or careers. Instead, they bond themselves to those they perceive as confident or in control and constantly solicit advice and reassurance before committing to almost anything (see criterion 1). In effect, they piggyback themselves on the talents, abilities, and fortitude of others, often even in trivial matters, such as what to have for lunch or what clothes to buy. Even after working as a teacher's aide for nine years, for example, Sharon still relies on the teachers to tell her what to do. After such a long time in a nondemanding position, Sharon should already know the possibilities and be able to judge for herself what is best given the lessons of the day.

Sharon was lucky enough to have been born into a traditional family and have a big sister to look out for her. She has always been taken care of by others, so much so, in fact, that she never developed a sense of self-identity and never learned to take control of her own life. She needs people to assume control and responsibility in almost everything (see criterion 2). Just look at her childhood: If something went wrong in school, Sharon ran to Brandy, who protected her and made things right again. The whole family participated in infantilizing her; Sharon was their precious little "porcelain doll," put on a shelf and rewarded just for being sweet and cute. You can almost imagine little Sharon with a pink bow in her hair running up to Mommy and Daddy with a big bright smile and receiving a pat on the head and a big hug in return. At every stage of life, her needs were always met; she never learned to drive, for example, because Brandy took her wherever she wanted to go. For Sharon, her early treatment became an interpersonal

Sharon, a 32-year-old teacher's aide, first sought therapy at the suggestion of the school principal, someone she is particularly close to. The principal had "taken her under her wing."[1] Although Sharon has worked as an aide at the same school for nine years, she still requires the advice and encouragement of other teachers before starting any new project for the students, sometimes needing reassurance multiple times in the same day.

Sharon is the younger of two sisters. She describes her childhood as "traditional" and "perfect," with her father being the strong figure on whom the rest of the family relied. Her mom was old-fashioned and took good care of everyone. From almost the day Sharon was born, everyone treated her like a "precious porcelain doll." All of her needs were met before she even knew there was a void. In school, her sister Brandy became her guardian. If anything went wrong, Sharon ran to Brandy to make it right, whether it was to protect her from bullies or help her in her classes. Sometimes, Brandy even did Sharon's homework herself. Although Sharon was only an average student, the teachers liked her because she was "sweet and well-behaved." As a teenager, Sharon never learned to drive. Instead, Brandy always took her wherever she wanted to go.

The Saturday after graduating from high school, Sharon married Tom, an appliance mechanic who reminded her of her father. And like her father, Tom loved the idea of having a wife at home who didn't work and didn't mind catering to him, having his meals ready when he got home. He even thought it was "cute" that she was so helpless at many daily tasks. For the most part, Sharon adored Tom and loved playing the role of the traditional wife although she occasionally found it difficult to assert herself in the relationship, fearing that Tim might become angry with her.

Soon, however, Tom began to see Sharon as needy and suffocating. Without her own circle of friends, she insisted they spend every free moment together. Tom eventually convinced Sharon to take a job as a teacher's aide when they were experiencing some financial difficulties, and he encouraged her to keep it once the problems were settled. However, because Tom drops her off at work every morning and picks her up again in the evening, he can never hang out with guys after work or even stay late to earn extra money. Responding to her neediness, Tom eventually decided that Sharon should have more of an identity of her own and insisted that she enroll in junior college. She asked Tom to pick out her classes and warned him that he would likely have to tutor her in the evenings as well as drive her to and from classes. Sharon has reluctantly agreed to go but doubts that she has the confidence or ability to follow through.

Six months into couples therapy, Sharon had begun to take driving lessons. About this same time, however, Brandy was killed in a car accident. The effect on Sharon was devastating. With Brandy gone, Sharon began to slip into depression and began to cling to Tom even more tightly. She dropped all of her classes and stopped going to work. In response, Tom now seems to be in a process of extended emotional withdrawal and is threatening divorce. Sharon feels destroyed, as though, "I have lost a part of myself I can never get back," and cannot imagine how she will possibly make it alone. Though Tom insists that there is still a chance for reconciliation and though Sharon realizes that there were problems all along that she didn't want to face, she nevertheless "knows" he will divorce her.

Dependent Personality Disorder
DSM-IV Criteria

A pervasive and excessive need to be taken care of that leads to submissive and clinging behavior and fears of separation, beginning by early adulthood and present in a variety of contexts, as indicated by five (or more) of the following:

(1) has difficulty making everyday decisions without an excessive amount of advice and reassurance from others.

(2) needs others to assume responsibility for most major areas of his or her life.

(3) has difficulty expressing disagreement with others because of fear of loss of support or approval. **Note:** Do not include realistic fears of retribution.

(4) has difficulty initiating projects or doing things on his or her own (because of a lack of self-confidence in judgment or abilities rather than a lack of motivation or energy).

(5) goes to excessive lengths to obtain nurturance and support from others, to the point of volunteering to do things that are unpleasant.

(6) feels uncomfortable or helpless when alone because of exaggerated fears of being unable to care for himself or herself.

(7) urgently seeks another relationship as a source of care and support when a close relationship ends.

(8) is unrealistically preoccupied with fears of being left to take care of himself or herself.

[1]Numbers mark aspects of the case most consistent with *DSM* criteria, and do not necessarily indicate that the case "meets" diagnostic criteria in this respect.

dictum: "Please others, and you will be special and they will love you and care for you forever." Sharon's life has always taken whatever direction others might give it, so it is their creation, not her own.

Although Sharon is all grown up, psychologically, she remains a child in many ways. In her private moments, her immaturity scares her, but it is an interpersonal strategy she will continue to pursue, if only because she has failed to develop any other mature strategies of her own. Independence is anathema to her. Instead, Sharon will forever present herself as precious and adorable. In her mind, she must always be pleasing and never disagree with those on whom she depends (see criterion 3). Conflict is not only inconsistent with her self-image but also risks her continued protection, either explicitly by evoking others' anger or implicitly by establishing a separate identity to be respected, a dangerous precedent for any dependent. It seems a better strategy for the dependent to play it safe and submit to the opinions and desires of others. As she herself says, she finds it difficult to assert herself in the marriage because "Tom might become angry with me." Now that Brandy is gone, much of Sharon's insurance against standing on her own has evaporated.

Having others take responsibility for everything in her life has affected Sharon in a variety of ways. She has difficulty starting projects and doing things on her own (see criterion 4). Because others have always been there to take control, her expectation is that all she needs to do is to be sweet and pleasing and everything will be taken care of by others. To the casual observer, her lack of initiative might make her seem depressed. However, Sharon has plenty of energy; she simply lacks direction. She cannot commit to a decision without first knowing that others approve of it. She lacks confidence to set her life on a course of her own making and then follow through. On the surface, she might agree to learn how to drive or to attend college, but she becomes suspicious when other people push such an agenda too hard. If she were to be successful, others might demand that she do even more. They may even demand that she assume a measure of control over her own life, a trend that frightens her. Even the request that she do something on her own might be perceived as rejection. "What happens after I learn to drive?" she wonders. "What else will they expect? Why does Tom really want me to attend college? Is he setting me up to leave me?" Sharon believes that the less she initiates on her own, the better chance she has of holding on to people.

In fact, Sharon's goal is to maintain things as they have always been, a kind of timeless childhood in which she is passive and pleasant and is ensured protection and a comfortable attachment to others. We cannot say exactly what the future holds for her. The case does not state whether Sharon and Tom were able to work out their problems. We do know, however, that Tom feels suffocated, and we can infer that he has begun to see their relationship as something Sharon needs more than she wants. Tom thinks that Sharon should have more of an identity of her own. He may even doubt that she honestly loves him or is mature enough to know what love means. Now that Tom has begun to withdraw, Sharon is feeling the distance, and her desperation and panic are increasing. She will probably react by doing even more for Tom, even volunteering for tasks that are unpleasant (see criterion 5) to secure the relationship. Especially with Brandy gone and her marriage in jeopardy, Sharon is terrified of being left alone (see criterion 6). Worse, there is no one else to whom she can appeal for nurturance and support (see criterion 7), something that is undoubtedly always on her mind (see criterion 8).

With Sharon, we have seen a portrait of the more pathological side of the dependent personality. However, we have also touched on how some of these qualities manifest themselves in healthy and normal personalities. The following section explores this continuum more fully.

From Normality to Abnormality

Several normal variants of the dependent personality have been proposed, and these include characteristics that many readers will undoubtedly find in themselves. The **devoted style** (Oldham & Morris, 1995) is caring and solicitous, generally putting the welfare of others first. Similar to the devoted style is the **agreeing style** (Millon et al., 1994), built around the traits of cooperativeness, consideration, and amiability. Rather than risk upsetting others, they adapt their preferences to be compatible with those around them. Trusting others to be kind and thoughtful, they readily reconcile differences and make concessions to achieve peaceable solutions to conflict.

Healthy variants of the dependent are capable of genuine empathy for others, possessing a tremendous capacity for sustained unconditional love. Moreover, they are among the most trusting people, with a modest, uncritical, gentle demeanor that communicates almost unquestioned acceptance. Easy to please and demanding little, they never set unattainable standards for approval and are almost always encouraging of their mates and loved ones. Most have deep reservoirs of goodwill and are genuinely pleased by the good fortunes of others. Often, they are gracious even to those whom they may dislike. Despite the high esteem in which they are held, the more people value them, the more humble they become. Some are close to what we would consider saints but are simply pleased at being well thought of and embarrassed if regarded as special. Charitable in giving of themselves, they put a positive light on all life events and stress the virtues and good they find in others.

Unfortunately, the healthy and adaptive traits described previously are easily turned toward pathology. Dependents tend to fuse their own identity with that of others, a strategy that certainly carries its own risks, even for those in the normal range. At their very core, dependents hate to be alone. Because their identity is inextricably enmeshed with those they love, the idea of separation causes them intense anxiety, as we saw with Sharon. Whereas most normal persons acknowledge that separation is sometimes necessary for self-actualization, this thought is anathema to the dependent. When relationships end, dependents often feel dominated, used, depleted, and desperate. Having constantly blurred the boundaries between themselves and others, the loss of a relationship is effectively a loss of self. Considerateness turns to suffocation, and the ever-present voice of encouragement shades into a desperate subservience. To protect their investments in other people, they may infantilize themselves and refuse to learn adult skills of independent living as a means of holding onto their significant other. Sharon is reluctant to attend college or even learn how to drive. Some dependents may become so devoid of life skills that it is almost impossible for them to survive on their own.

Another way of contrasting the normal style with the disorder is by constructing more normal versions of the *DSM-IV* diagnostic criteria (see Sperry, 1995), paraphrased here. Whereas decisions, even everyday decisions, provoke excessive advice-seeking from the disordered individuals (see criterion 1), the style seeks out the opinion of others, weighs the advantages and disadvantages, but makes the decision based on their own analysis. Whereas the disordered require that others take responsibility for the largest part of their life (see criterion 2), the style is comforted by the support of others and enjoys their company but can perform adequately without it. Whereas the disordered often subordinate their own feelings and agree with others out of fear of separation (see criterion 3), the style prefers interpersonal harmony but is able to speak up when necessary and hold their ground. Whereas the disordered lack the confidence to start new projects or carry out their own responsibilities (see criterion 4), the style is capable of functioning autonomously but prefers to work in close proximity to others.

For each of these contrasts, Sharon falls more toward the pathological end of the continuum. She does not seek out advice to add to a database of information that she will ultimately process on her own; she is incapable of weighing the advantages and disadvantages. Better to trust such an important task to someone else. Instead, Sharon seeks advice before making everyday decisions because she would rather be advised by those she wants to please than risk offending them. Similarly, Sharon requires support from others to the extent that she must forfeit responsibility for major areas of her life. In school, she needed Brandy to "make it right," protect her from bullies, and sometimes do her homework. She is not merely comforted by support, then; she is lost without it. In her relationship with Tom, Sharon does not remain silent simply because she values interpersonal harmony; instead, she is afraid of the consequences of disagreeing. Finally, her attachment concerns are so intense that she lacks the confidence to follow through on new projects, such as going to college.

The remainder of the diagnostic criteria can also be put on a continuum. Whereas the disordered personality desires nurturance and support to the point of volunteering to perform unpleasant jobs (see criterion 5), the style is considerate and occasionally self-sacrificing, keeping the best interest of others foremost in mind. Whereas the disordered greatly fears being unable to cope when left alone see (see criterion 6), the style prefers the company of others but can enjoy occasional solitude. Whereas the end of a relationship results in a desperate search for a new partner in the disordered (see criterion 7), the style is nostalgic about lost intimacy but does not immediately seek to merge with another. Whereas the disordered are afraid of being left to fend on their own (see criterion 8), the style enjoys the affection of others as expressed through thoughtfulness but is not terrified of abandonment.

Again, for each of the preceding contrasts, Sharon falls more toward the pathological extreme. Whether the fifth diagnostic criterion applies to Sharon is debatable, because her domestic activities, such as having Tom's meals ready on time, are consistent with the stereotypical housewife role she enjoys. Nevertheless, we can imagine her struggling to keep the house especially clean or making Tom especially delicious meals when the relationship becomes strained, whatever the cost of time and labor to herself. Likewise, Sharon's need for others is exaggerated beyond what is normal. She seems to fear taking care of herself and prefers instead to have someone she trusts nearby at all times. She seeks therapy at the suggestion of the school principal. Tom even has to drop her off at work in the morning and pick her up again in the evening. Time alone is not experienced as solitude, but instead as the uncomfortable shadow of what she would very much like to avoid. Sharon cannot imagine not having a major attachment figure physically present in her life at all times. Although she does not seem to be seeking another relationship now that Brandy is gone, the spirit of the seventh criterion can be seen in the desperation with which she clings to Tom. Finally, Sharon is terrified that Tom will leave her and cannot imagine how she will make it on her own. In fact, it appears that she cannot remember Brandy without thinking about the significance of Brandy's loss to herself.

Variations of the Dependent Personality

In addition to the more prototypal cases described in this chapter, there are several variations of the dependent that express its combination with other personalities. Figure 8.1 provides a summary of these subtypes. Actual cases may or may not fall into one of these combinations.

THE DISQUIETED DEPENDENT

A mixture of both the dependent and avoidant patterns, the **disquieted** dependent is often found in an extreme form in institutional settings that minister to chronic ambulatory patients. Most live a parasitic existence sustained by institutional rewards and requirements. Whereas all dependents are submissive and self-effacing, relying on others for guidance and security, disquieted dependents possess an underlying apprehensiveness that overlies a lack of initiative and an anxious avoidance of autonomy. They seem easily disconcerted and experience a general sense of dread and foreboding. They are particularly vulnerable to separation anxiety and greatly fear loss of support and nurturance. Unlike most dependents, disquieted dependents sometimes express these fears

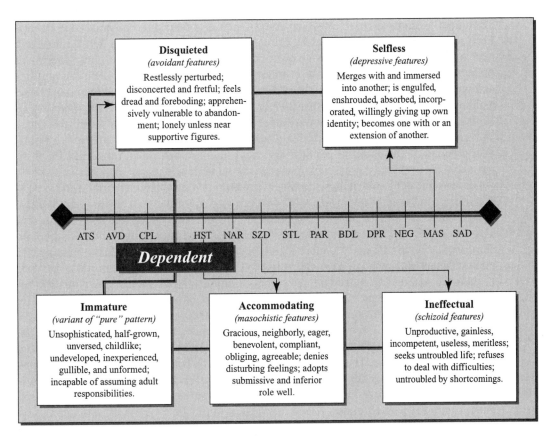

FIGURE 8.1   Variants of the Dependent Personality.

through outbursts of anger directed at those who fail to appreciate their needs for security and safety.

Because the disquieted dependent is usually sustained by some institutional or environmental structure, they have acquired a pattern of withdrawing from social encounters. Loneliness and isolation are commonly experienced. Although such individuals attempt to be pleasant and agreeable like other dependents, they experience underlying tension, sadness, and guilt. On the surface, they appear quiet and affable in the face of difficulties, but underneath they may be overwhelmed by fears of abandonment and isolation. Complaints of weakness and tiredness may reflect an underlying depression. Having experienced continuing rebuff from others, these dependents readily succumb to physical exhaustion and illness. Under these circumstances, simple responsibilities demand more energy than can be mustered. Life is seen as empty but heavy.

THE ACCOMMODATING DEPENDENT

Accommodating dependents are more submissive, agreeable, and hungry for affection, nurturance, and security than other subtypes. Fears of abandonment lead them to be overly compliant and obliging. Some become socially gregarious and charming and seek to become the center of attention through self-dramatizing behaviors. As such, they are similar to the appeasing histrionic, described in the next chapter. Both are gracious, neighborly, benevolent, and compliant in their relationships with others, preferring to avoid conflict and seek harmony even at the expense of their internal values and beliefs. Further, both are preoccupied with external approval, so both may be left without any real inner identity, valuing themselves not for their intrinsic traits but only in terms of their relationships with others. By submerging or allying themselves with the abilities and virtues of others, they bolster themselves through an illusion of shared competence and are comforted by the belief that the bond achieved thereby is firm and unbreakable. Both evidence a naïve attitude toward life's problems. Maintaining an air of pleasantry and good spirits, they deny disturbing emotions and cover inner conflicts with self-distraction. Critical thinking is not their strong point. Having had others do for them most of their lives, most areas of knowledge are underdeveloped or immature.

Unlike appeasing histrionics, however, accommodating dependents tend to be self-sacrificing and readily adopt the role of inferior or subordinate. They are sympathetic toward the needs of their partners, who almost always feel stronger and more competent as a result. They avoid self-assertion and leave responsibilities in the hands of others. In contrast, the histrionic takes a more active posture, maneuvering and manipulating life circumstances rather than passively sitting by. The self-sacrificing and inferior posture of the accommodating dependent somewhat resembles the masochistic personality, described briefly in Chapter 15. All that matters is that others like them, are pleased by them, and are willing to accept their smiles and goodwill as sufficient.

Unfortunately, most accommodating dependents are accommodating for a reason: Agreeableness is designed to encourage others to take control, thereby compensating for their incompetence. They always have a smile and a friendly word, but rarely follow through on adult responsibilities. In fact, they usually feel helpless whenever autonomy or initiative is required. The loss of a significant source of support or identification may prompt severe depression. Open displays of guilt, illness, anxiety, and depression are common but serve the purpose of deflecting criticism and transforming threats of disapproval or abandonment into support and sympathy. Sharon has several features of the accommodating dependent.

THE IMMATURE DEPENDENT

Different individuals mature at different rates. Moreover, even within a single person, mathematical or musical abilities may mature relatively early and language abilities later or vice versa. Some individuals, however, never achieve even a modest level of accomplishment at any point in life. Instead, they remain childlike throughout their existence, prefer childhood activities, find satisfaction relating mainly to children, and thoroughly dislike all adult activity and responsibility. Such persons are not only dependent through their childlike outlook and level of achievement but also seem satisfied in being so.

Going beyond the simple naïveté of the average dependent, the **immature** variant is underdeveloped, inexperienced, and unsophisticated. Some simply lack ambition and energy, which makes the expectancies of adulthood overwhelming and frightening. Others are overly passive and easygoing and simply never developed competencies or confidence in their own abilities. Many appear to lack a strong gender identity and to find the assumption of adult roles to be somewhat distasteful or frightening. For the most part, these individuals are pleasant and sociable as long as they are permitted to remain pre-adult in their preferences and activities. They become difficult, however, when others begin to expect more or demand that they mature and get down to the business of life. To their troubled parents or spouses, they often seem irresponsible and neglectful. Eventually, their failure to develop the abilities necessary to survive on their own leaves them completely incapable of ever maturing to an adult level. Sharon has some characteristics of this subtype as well. Her position as a teacher's aide is nondemanding and allows her to relate to children all day long, perhaps a throwback to her own childhood, when she was the precious porcelain doll. She cannot drive or perform many other tasks that are age appropriate.

THE INEFFECTUAL DEPENDENT

The **ineffectual** dependent represents a combination of the dependent and schizoid patterns. Both exhibit a general lack of vitality, low energy level, fatigability, and weakness in expressiveness and spontaneity. Schizoids usually possess an anhedonic temperament, meaning that they are unable to experience pleasurable emotions in great depth. Moreover, they shun social relationships, including being part of a family, and almost always choose solitary activities. The ineffectual dependent, however, is more able to empathize and understand the basic emotions of others. Additionally, the thought processes of schizoids often seem unfocused, tangential, or even absent, especially concerning human relationships. While interpersonal subtleties escape the understanding of most schizoids, they are understood by most ineffectual dependents, who do not shun close personal relationships. Like the immature dependent, the ineffectual variety seeks an untroubled life completely free of responsibility, though mainly because of a lack of drive rather than a childish nature. Through their schizoid characteristics, they often simply tune out life's demands. Not wanting to deal with reality, they often appear to sleepwalk through life, half disengaged and half dependent. They typically do not want to engage in anything or think too deeply, so they often exhibit a certain fatalism that allows them to ignore difficulties. They have a belief that nothing ever changes on the basis of human efforts, and they have neither the drive nor the desire to act on their own behalf. Sharon does not fall into this subtype.

THE SELFLESS DEPENDENT

For the **selfless** dependent, idealization and total identification are the major themes. Like all dependents, they subordinate themselves to others but in a much more extreme fashion. Attachment concerns take on a new meaning for these individuals, who totally merge themselves with others, forfeiting their own identity in the process. Their own unique personal potentials are denied and left to atrophy as the residuals of an unwanted independence. Through fusion, they secure a sense of significance, emotional stability, and purpose in life. Eventually, everything they do is performed in the service of extending the status and significance of another, be it a person or an institutional entity. In extreme cases, they are completely defined through their relationships, existing as an extension of their significant other, with no sense of themselves as independent beings at all. Because of this fusion, they may adopt values and attitudes that are different from their ordinary preferences. Sometimes, they seem confident and self-assured but only by assuming for themselves the qualities of the persons or institutions with whom they have identified.

Despite the loss of their own identity, many selfless dependents do seem fulfilled by their self-sacrificing lifestyle. Whereas all dependents are submissive, adopting the values and beliefs of more powerful others to whom they attach themselves, the very essence of the selfless dependent rests on those to whom they sacrifice themselves. The more they fuse with their idealized others, the more they become emotionally attached and the more they feel themselves to have significance in the world. Stereotyped examples include the overbearing stage mother who lives through her successful child and the wife who submerges herself totally in the life and career of her husband.

Although most selfless dependents feel vitalized and valuable through their relationships, some eventually wonder whether they have lost too much of themselves. By deriving their identity through external sources, they make themselves extremely vulnerable to loss. When relationships run into difficulties, selfless dependents, more than other people, experience episodes of anxiety and depression, which fluctuate in intensity depending on the quality of the attachment. All dependents are devastated when relationships end, but selfless dependents are almost completely destroyed, having essentially been voided of themselves. Sometimes, the anticipation of loss is sufficient to leave them with a chronic hopelessness, a characteristic of the depressive personality.

Early Historical Forerunners

Despite repeated attempts to develop the concept of an antisocial personality free from the implications of "moral insanity" (Prichard, 1835), it continued to influence subsequent conceptions, including early conceptions of the dependent, which were contaminated by the idea that such persons simply reflect a seldom-seen variant of moral degeneration.

Both Kraepelin (1913) and Schneider (1923/1950), for example, made little reference to the dependent's need for external support, stressing instead their malleability of will and the ease with which they could be influenced by others. Schneider noted that "as far as their pliable natures will allow they are responsive to good influences, show regret for their lapses and display good intentions" (p. 133). Kraepelin considered these types to be a product of delayed maturation, a remarkably contemporary view. Nevertheless, to these early theorists, the "shiftless and weak-willed types" were easy prey to social misdeeds such as addiction and thievery. Unless motivated by powerful external forces, such outcomes are not typically characteristic of the dependent personality.

In the following three sections, we offer a detailed portrayal of the dependent personality as expressed through the psychodynamic, interpersonal, and cognitive perspectives.

FOCUS ON GENDER

Measurement Issues

Gender Differences in Dependency

Do men and women differ in their willingness to admit dependent feelings, attitudes, and behaviors? Studies using self-report measures have found significantly higher levels of dependency in women than in men. Similar results have been obtained using school-age children rather than adults and using subjects from other cultures.

Because self-reports measure what is accessible to conscious awareness, Bornstein (1993) asked whether the difference between males and females would be found when using projective tests intended to tap motives outside conscious awareness, in the realm of the unconscious, not available for self-report.

Similar levels of dependency were found for men and women. Bornstein concluded: "Women report higher levels of dependency than do men on self-report measures, but men and women obtain comparable dependency scores on projective measure" (1993, p. 47). Women are thus more willing to admit dependency; men are just as dependent but unwilling to admit it. In fact, there is a consistent relationship between the face validity of the measure used and the extent to which gender differences are found when assessing dependency. As face validity increases, so does the magnitude of the gender differences found when using that measure (Bornstein, Rossner, Hill, & Stepanian, 1994).

Because face validity is largely a function of how easy it is to figure out what a test assesses (the item, "I feel helpless without someone to protect me," is face valid for dependency), such differences between men and women can only be a function of self-presentation and social desirability. As it becomes easier to figure out that a test measures dependency, men refuse to admit their dependency needs. Traditionally, men have been socialized to express dependency indirectly, whereas women express dependency in a more direct and overt manner (Maccoby & Jacklin, 1974; Mischel, 1970).

Future studies of the dependent personality must take into account the potential masking effects of self-presentation and social desirability. Valid assessment of a personality trait so closely linked to sex-role orientation argues for an unobtrusive approach to assessment, at least where males are concerned.

Each of these domains interacts to form the whole person. We have chosen to present history and description side by side. If you see the material simply as a historical progression of "who did what when," you will miss out on the descriptive bounty that each author brings to the construct. By the time you finish these sections, you should have a good grasp of the dependent prototype. Developmental pathways are also described, though these are currently speculative and indistinct. Read not only for history but also for the characteristics that each author unearthed and their significance to the total personality.

The Psychodynamic Perspective

According to classical psychoanalytic theory, the dependent personality is characterized by fixation during the oral stage, the first stage of psychosexual development. Because character types were named after their respective stage of psychosexual fixation, the dependent personality is usually called the **oral character** in classic psychoanalytic theory (Abraham, 1927c). Whereas the relationship between psychosexual fixation and subsequent personality traits seems rather obscure for some character types, for the oral character it was believed to be relatively straightforward. Because the role of the mouth in adult life has always been approved and accepted, oral characteristics could be more easily expressed without first requiring great transformations to mask them and make them acceptable. Thus, it is relatively self-evident that oral characters should enjoy eating, talking, and other forms of oral stimulation.

As with all psychosexual character formation, fixation occurs either through indulgence, leading to oral-receptive traits, or frustration, leading to oral-sadistic qualities. If the mother was always available to nurse her infant, the resulting intense gratification was assumed to lead to an optimistic spirit not easily shaken. However, it could also produce passiveness and inactivity, reflected in the implicit belief that some mother figure would always be available to meet the individual's needs. In effect, such children grow into adults who have never been weaned. Symbolically, they expect their mother's breast to just keep on giving, and they feel completely helpless, even astonished, when it stops. Although her relationship with Tom is now in jeopardy, Sharon would seem to be very much an oral character. She has been optimistic for most of her life that others will always offer themselves to meet her needs and she need never be weaned into adult independence.

In contrast, frustration during the oral stage was believed to result in an enduring ambivalence between hunger and hostility. Such children are unsure whether to nurse or bite. As adults, they seem to always require something more but remain hostile even when their needs are met. The psychoanalytic idea of oral fixation thus leads to a connection between the dependent and negativistic (passive-aggressive) personalities. Later psychoanalytic thinkers generalized Abraham's basic thesis beyond the nipple. Fenichel (1945), for example, argued that fixation in the oral stage led to identification with the caretaker, resulting in an inability to care for oneself, but also a desire to become a mother figure to others.

Dependent personalities tend to emphasize two defense mechanisms. As a result of their desire to remain childlike, they fail to develop the more mature defenses of normal adults. The first defense mechanism is called **introjection,** which literally means "to put inside," hence their need for fusion with more powerful and instrumentally

---

FOCUS ON HISTORY

Karen Horney

Three Modes of Interrelationships

Karen Horney's descriptive eloquence is perhaps without peer, but it is difficult to sum up concisely what she regarded as the major solutions to life's basic conflicts. Although her primary publications were written over a short period, she sometimes used different terms to represent similar conceptions.

Considering the insecurities and inevitable frustrations of life, Horney identified three broad modes of relating: moving toward others, moving against others, and moving away from others. Those who move against others are aggressive types with expansive solutions; they glorify themselves and rigidly deny weakness and inadequacy. Those who move away from others have become alienated from life; they achieve peace, not by investing themselves in any aspiration, but by curtailing needs and wishes. By employing neurotic resignation, they go through each day as detached onlookers.

Those who move toward others, the parallel to the dependent personality in Horney's schema, are compliant and self-effacing. They have a marked need for affection and approval, along with a willingness to forgo self-assertion. Because their self-esteem is determined by the opinions of others, they subordinate their own desires, sometimes to the point of self-accusation, helplessness, passivity, and self-belittlement. For them, love solves all problems.

---

competent others. When dependents look inside themselves, they see inadequacy and incompetence, reflecting their basic lack of skills and knowledge. Such insights in turn provoke feelings of worthlessness and, moreover, an existential terror at the possibility of being left alone to care for themselves; this is what Sharon feels now.

To escape this terror, dependents seek to incorporate the presence, strengths, and competencies of a stronger figure. The bond achieved is much more than the average relationship. First, dependents seek to put the other person's identity inside themselves to create an amalgamation of weaker and stronger, of incompetence and skill, of worthlessness and confidence. In the economics of the relationship, the dependent borrows strength, ability, and self-esteem in exchange for a willingness to serve the goals of another. Thus, dependents tend to become like their partners, whose identity and needs become their own.

Second, dependents tend to idealize their partners. No longer are their partners human beings with their own strengths, foibles, and frailties; instead, they may become superhuman protectors with near omnipotent power to provide a safe haven that keeps the dependent from harm. As young children, we all pass through a period during which we believe our parents are omnipotent and omniscient. Parents have the power to make it snow, the wisdom to make it stop, and the money to buy us whatever we want for our birthdays. And because they are all-knowing and all-loving, we can always trust that their actions will work toward our good, at least in the end. As our first case notes, Sharon describes her childhood as traditional and perfect, with her father being the strong figure on whom the family relied. As a little girl looking up to her daddy, he must have seemed the very incarnation of strength and ability.

The idealization of attachment figures is a normal part of growing up. Though we inevitably discover that our parents are not the infallible beings we thought they were, idealization lives on as romantic love. Surely no one is as perfect as your romantic partner. When Sharon met Tom, for example, he reminded her of her father, her previous prototype of strength. Eventually, most people work through their fantasies of idealization and see their girlfriend or boyfriend, spouse, or lover in the light of realism. At that point, it is time to work on the relationship, as Tom and Sharon have discovered. Dependents, however, outgrow their early idealization only with difficulty. They continue to inflate their partners much in the same way and for much the same purpose that the narcissistic personality inflates the self. In part, their awe of their protectors can be seen simply as a by-product of an artificially delayed development. However, it also transmits worth to the dependent, for if this quasi-deity, someone important and valuable, loves the dependent, then he or she must also be valuable. For Tom and Sharon's relationship, this means that Sharon has worth because Tom, being the amazing person that he is, loves her. Someone of his importance and brilliance would never squander his love on an undeserving person. In addition, the illusion further strengthens dependents' belief that their protector has the power to keep them safe from harm.

This is a principal reason that dependents are often so completely devastated when relationships end. In effect, abandonment becomes the final verdict of someone whose opinion they have previously accepted as unquestioned truth. Should the marriage fail, Sharon may experience the divorce as not only a break from Tom but also an abandonment by everything Tom symbolizes, including her father. In effect, she is being abandoned by an introjected ideal that forms an important cornerstone of her identity. If she cannot succeed in therapy in drawing a distinction between Tom and this internalized image, the future may prove particularly crushing.

Another way of coping with a problematic, hostile world is simply to deny that it is hostile at all. Although introjection creates soothing feelings of being allied or fused with a powerful other, it cannot eliminate all sources of anxiety. Accordingly, dependents make extensive use of denial to damp down whatever feelings of doom or apprehension introjection does not eliminate. All normal persons use denial, but dependents do so to wall themselves off from objective difficulties, to maintain the illusion of an internal utopia untroubled by external demands and harsh realities. Flight from a hostile world is easily seen in Sharon, who realizes some six months into couples therapy that her idealization hid many problems that were lurking behind the scenes all along. By creating a universe devoid of objective struggles, dependents make it easier to remain naïve, childlike, and syrupy sweet.

The second function of denial is to protect dependents from acknowledging their own hostile impulses. For dependents, anger is extremely threatening. First, it undermines their view that the larger adult world is really an extension of the playground. Second, if the sweet dependent is allowed to acknowledge anger, the next logical questions are: "Of what are others capable?" and "How do they really feel?" Such thoughts cannot be allowed to enter conscious awareness, for they effectively destroy the dependent's illusion of security and protection. This is not directly seen with Sharon, though by inhibiting feelings she was afraid to express toward Tom, she has probably built up a reservoir of anger, now closer to the surface given her fears of abandonment. Part of her may even be feeling a mixture of astonishment and anger, as if to exclaim, "How can you leave someone as sweet as me? Damn you for accepting all my goodwill!"

The Interpersonal Perspective

Harry Stack Sullivan (1947) described the inadequate personality—individuals who learn helplessness from parental models and require a stronger person to make decisions. Timothy Leary (1957) systematized many aspects of Sullivan's thinking. Together with his associates, Leary developed the Interpersonal Circle, which describes interpersonal conduct across a continuum from normal to abnormal. Leary's docile-dependent was characterized by a trustful conformity at more adaptive levels of functioning and by helpless dependency at more pathological levels.

Friends usually see the dependent personality as generous and thoughtful, overly apologetic, or even obsequious. Neighbors may be impressed by their humility, cordiality, and graciousness. By denying points of difference and avoiding expressions of power, dependents forfeit control over their own lives, believing that only others possess the talents or experience necessary to navigate the intricacies of a complex world. By acting weak, expressing self-doubt, and displaying attitudes of compliance and submission, dependents seek the complementary interpersonal response from others—namely, nurturance, protection, and displays of strength and confidence.

Beneath their warmth and friendliness, however, lies a desperate search for acceptance and approval, needs that are especially apparent under stressful conditions, as Sharon shows. At these times, dependents seek to narrow the interpersonal responses of others by becoming even more helpless and clinging. Only by being impressively submissive and loyal can they be assured of evoking consistent care and affection. When relationships are genuinely jeopardized, a depressive tone colors their moods, and they may become excessively self-sacrificing, adopting the role of inferior to provide their partner with the feeling of being strong, competent, and superior, precisely the qualities that dependents seek in their mates. In psychodynamic terms, these qualities are projected onto their significant others. Their posture, voice, and mannerisms convey an increased lack of self-confidence. They may speak so softly that they are barely heard. Their facial expressions convey meekness and vulnerability, and they seem to be pleading for help. They may become even more childlike to attract others to their purity and innocence.

Interpersonal formulations of the development of the dependent personality emphasize parental overprotection, overconcern, overnurturance, and active discouragement of autonomy as the major developmental pathways. Newborns are helpless and entirely dependent on their caretakers for protection and nurturance. During the first few months of life, children become attached to persons who provide them with nourishment and remove noxious sources of stimulation, such as a soiled diaper. Adequately nurtured, most children develop a sound attachment to their caretakers, including a basic capacity to trust (Erikson, 1959) and the feeling that the world is a place of security that will provide for their fundamental biological and emotional needs. Eventually, as toddlers, they begin to develop their own independent agency, including a burning curiosity about the surrounding world. As they learn to crawl, they make brief excursions to explore their environments, using their caretakers as a secure base to which they can return for protection and reassurance. As the naturally reinforcing power of curiosity takes hold, children become driven to develop their own exciting potentials. Eventually, children challenge the authority of their parents and learn one of the worst words that a parent can hear: "No!"

Some parents, however, never allow their children to develop independently. Rather than allow curiosity and agency to unfold naturally, they cater to the habits and needs of their children, memorize the idiosyncrasies of their biological rhythms and temperament, and constantly fret over their comfort. In effect, they remove any need to explore the world by bringing the world to the child. Such children are often so pampered that there is simply no reason for them to develop competencies that might generalize beyond the microcosm created by their caretakers. In effect, the increasing sophistication that accompanies psychological maturity fails to occur as normal developmental stages become drawn out over time. Even talking may be delayed. Constant attention to every need and nuance of their emotional state leaves children with little motivation to develop symbolic and linguistic capacities to name the objects they want or want removed. Fortunately, some children eventually come to resent the implicit intrusiveness of protection and successfully develop their own identity through some form of separation or rebellion.

Other children, however, never outgrow early overprotection and remain dependent on the care and nurturance of more powerful figures. Such parents often pathologically discourage independence for fear of "losing their baby." They seldom let the child out of their sight and express anxiety that normal maturational challenges will inevitably be harmful, as if learning to ride a bike or playing on the monkey bars would hurt or strain the child. Rather than let experience be the best teacher, they carry the child well beyond the walking stage, continue to spoon-feed, and discourage any motion that promises greater independence. Many children enjoy the intensified attachment and attention. Sharon, for example, remembers her own childhood as "perfect."

Chance factors may also play an important developmental role. Unusual illnesses or prolonged health issues may prompt normal parents to become overconcerned and tend to their child well beyond what is medically necessary. Conversely, an excessively worrisome and anxious parent may be hyperalert to the real needs of a normal child, resulting in undue attention and cuddling in infancy, followed by efforts to restrict natural curiosity and exploration later. Occasionally, special circumstances may throw parent and child together into an emotional symbiosis, as when one parent goes off to war or suffers some extreme accident or dies.

Parents play the dominant role in creating dependent pathology, but other family members and peer group experiences are often contributing factors. If one child is much more dominant or aggressive, the other may be forced to adopt a submissive posture and run to parents for protection. Alternatively, a hostile or difficult child may inspire another sibling to become the "little angel" who always seeks Mommy's advice and always does what she says, rewarding her attention and praise with warmth and affection. Feelings of dependency may be amplified when children with dependent traits begin school and must separate for the first time from parents who have thus far been their lifelong protectors. Feelings of unattractiveness and competitive inadequacy, especially during adolescence, may result in social humiliation and self-doubt, causing children to return to previous attachments in compensation.

Extending the ideas of Leary and his associates some years earlier, Benjamin (1996) emphasized that the dependent begins life with warmth, care, and attention and forms a normal attachment. Thereafter, however, caretakers refuse to let the child develop autonomy, either because they enjoy the intimacy that a dependent child affords or because they fear that frustration of any kind might result in later problems. At first, the protection and nurturance of caretakers inspires normal trust. Unfortunately, as the child grows older, the level of nurturance and protection remains constant, eventually being transformed into control, what Benjamin calls "relentless nurturance" (p. 227). In turn, control pulls for submission, and at the same time, all efforts to regain autonomy are greeted with blame. The result is a submissive child for whom being controlled is normal and for whom independence violates the standards of previous relationships, thus creating intense feelings of guilt. The child then internalizes the belief that although others are instrumentally adequate, he or she is not and never should be.

The Cognitive Perspective

The interpersonal strategy of dependents, designed to secure care and protection, has important negative consequences for their self-image and cognitive development. The helpless façade that dependents project eventually works its way into their self-concept. You cannot act helpless without believing it to some extent yourself. Dependents usually describe themselves as weak, fragile, inadequate, inept, or incompetent. When their incapacities become too clearly focused, anxiety and panic may result. To keep their vulnerability controlled, many dependents prefer not to look too deeply into themselves, preferring instead to limit their awareness to the pleasantries of life, seeing only the good and never the bad. When difficulties are acknowledged, it is often with a saving silver lining that effectively undoes the problem by assuming that things will work out in the end. Denial, discussed in the psychodynamic perspective, thus gradually develops into a broader cognitive style.

The self-schema of dependents includes both positive and negative qualities. On the positive side, dependents see themselves as considerate, thoughtful, and cooperative. By disavowing legitimate achievements, they seem humble and self-effacing. Secretly, they may hope for praise and commendation, but not too much, as expectations of independence and self-sufficiency would surely follow. The good qualities that dependents attribute to themselves, however, are also balanced by a number of pathological core, conditional, and instrumental beliefs (Beck et al., 1990, p. 45). At the core level, dependents believe, "I am completely helpless," and "I am all alone." To cope with these core beliefs, they form conditional beliefs, including, "I can function only if I have access to somebody competent," and "If I am abandoned, I will die." A variety of instrumental imperatives follow, including, "Don't offend the caretaker," and "Cultivate as intimate a relationship as possible." We have seen all of these before in other contexts.

Many dependents are not terribly sophisticated cognitively. To others, they seem naïve, childlike, and innocent—an image they often reinforce by minimizing their own achievements and abilities and magnifying their instrumental incompetencies. Fewer demands are made of inadequate persons. Because others always come to their aid, dependents may develop few coping strategies that go beyond basic life skills. Sometimes, even these are impaired. Some cannot balance a checkbook or require so much instruction and advice that even holding down a basic job becomes impossible. Other dependents closer to the normal range may be competent within restricted domains, though these instrumentalities are usually formed in the service of protecting a nurturing relationship. Here, the notion, "I must learn how to do such-and-such well if I am to enjoy the safety and protection of this relationship," functions as an additional, and highly adaptive, conditional belief. Such persons perform for the approval of others and may become skilled within an encouraging framework, as with the dependent wife who puts in long hours to further the career goals of her husband.

Writing in Beck et al. (1990), Fleming notes a number of cognitive distortions that sustain the disorder. Two seem crucial: First, dependents see themselves as "inherently inadequate and helpless"; second, their self-perceived shortcomings lead them to conclude that they must seek out someone who can handle the troubles of life in a dangerous world. This much is really just a repetition of what they have already learned. However, between premise and conclusion lie several logical errors that distort reality (Fleming, 1990) and thus invalidate the whole argument. Foremost among these is dichotomous thinking, a style that forms the world into polar opposites, with no shades of gray in between. If dependents are not cared for, they see themselves as being totally and utterly alone in the world. Similarly, if they are not absolutely sure how to do something, surely the problem must be insurmountable, at least for them.

Dichotomous thinking inevitably leads to a third cognitive distortion: Dependents tend to catastrophize, especially about relationships. Breakups are painful for everyone, but for the dependent, they are shattering. A healthy interpretation might reframe a breakup as an opportunity to discover your own role in why the relationship failed. A tragedy is thus transformed into a growth experience. To dependents, such an argument is unthinkable. Instead, every fluctuation in the quality of their attachments is catastrophic, a total abandonment, a verdict that they are worthless and unlovable. In fact, because core beliefs are so central to self-identity, it is unlikely that such adaptive lines of thought ever reach consciousness. More often, they simply do not exist, and someone else, perhaps a therapist, is required to calm the catastrophe, creating shades of gray that the subject never perceives. If Sharon, for example, could just calm down long enough to establish some perspective on her relationship and see that Tom really wants to work things out, she might stop suffocating him long enough to lay the foundations for her own identity.

How might dependents develop and maintain their dichotomizing and catastrophizing ways? The answer might be found in the core beliefs of their caretakers, who often model appraisal processes that present the life of the future dependent as one narrowly averted crisis after the next. There are some parents who believe their children are always in extreme danger; even when the children are sleeping peacefully in bed, they are convinced the risk of death or injury is always lurking around the corner. As the children begin to develop normal autonomy, these parents imagine outrageous scenarios of doom, each of which points to a single absolute result, "Freedom is the enemy of safety." Other auxiliary beliefs include, "Under no circumstances can children be trusted not to hurt themselves," and "The consequence of trusting my child is his or her death." Complex, balanced appraisals of maturation as the process of picking themselves up and learning from experience are resisted as being too risky. Future dependents thus internalize the extreme fear projected by parents, learning appraisal processes that always conclude, "To trust in myself is disaster," and "Others must save me from myself." Such an explanation shows the interplay of the interpersonal and cognitive perspectives.

A second aspect of the cognition of dependents is their cognitive style, which features thought patterns especially likely to remain global and diffuse. Introspective individuals constantly search within themselves and create definite ideas about who they are, what they want to become, and what they want from life. Because dependents seldom look inward, they necessarily develop only vague ideas about their self-identity and direction. When asked about her life plan, for example, Sharon might think to herself: "Continue on with Tom and enjoy life together." Because the strategy of the dependent is essentially to rely totally on an all-powerful, all-protecting other, further probing would be unlikely to reveal anything of greater depth.

A full understanding of the cognitive characteristics of dependents requires some knowledge of the normal pattern of cognitive development. According to Piaget (1954), the last stage of cognitive development is the development of formal operations, when children acquire the capacity to represent the world abstractly. More recent thinkers, however, have argued that beyond formal operations lies another stage of thought, which is concerned with the development of judgment. Having applied our abstract abilities to construct the world in many different ways, we inevitably discover that no one way or philosophy of life captures everything that life is. Instead, the world is naturally complex, so complex, in fact, that it cannot be put completely into any single philosophical system. All philosophies and perspectives are necessarily simplifications of the world, and as simplifications, certain things are necessarily omitted. No matter how good any perspective sounds in the abstract, it eventually fails in the concrete. In this case, knowing what to do and why becomes a matter of judgment and rests on a knowledge of the alternative possibilities, how likely each is to succeed or fail and why, and the costs and benefits to all parties involved. Most important, however, good judgment requires the self-confidence necessary to construct a reasoned plan laid open and exposed to the scrutiny of those it affects, all of whom have definite public and private expectations about the outcome.

Most dependents, with their lives micromanaged by competent authority figures since infancy, never develop the potential for making such qualitatively sophisticated judgments. Others either assume dependents are incapable or naturally take control themselves and decide, for every life question, what the best outcome would be and how to get there. Either way, dependents repeatedly find themselves encapsulated in a world that actively discourages the development of cognitive sophistication. Necessity may be the mother of invention, but it is also the mother of a variety of cognitive talents, especially the ability to form plans, to hold a variety of alternatives in mind, to determine the criteria for a good outcome for self and others, and to assess the probabilities that a given course of action will be successful. And paradoxically, it is precisely through persistent mothering that these sophisticated cognitive skills never develop fully in dependents, for whom all needs are already someone else's responsibility.

However, this does not mean that dependent personalities are necessarily ignorant or uneducated. For example, in a school environment, where the concrete expectations of good grades wins approval, praise, and affection from parents and teachers, many normal-range dependents readily conform and produce better-than-average report cards. Some even become the teacher's pet. But placed in a context where future evaluations are inevitable and the course of action is ambiguous, even more normal-range dependents are likely to feel anxious or depressed. Those with a diagnosable disorder are likely to simply flee or break down in tears. Their overall lack of cognitive sophistication preempts the possibility of weighing all alternatives and calculating benefit-loss ratios from the perspectives of every individual affected. Moreover, their fear of disappointing others prevents them from even attempting it. Instead, the key to dependent cognition lies in constructing a simplistic but much more manageable world, albeit one lacking in complex appraisals. Cognitively, the dependent needs simplicity, just as the compulsive needs an internal world of control and order.

The Evolutionary-Neurodevelopmental Perspective

There are many perspectives on personality; the view of personality as holistic must integrate diverse concepts into a single composite. Along with the histrionic, narcissistic, and antisocial, the dependent is one of four interpersonally imbalanced personality styles. In the evolutionary theory (Millon, 1990; Millon & Davis, 1996), the dependent personality is formulated as the passive-dependent pattern. Recall from Chapter 2 that passivity in an evolutionary context refers to a tendency to accommodate to your surrounds, that is, to make the most of whatever the environment offers. Whereas the narcissist and antisocial seek the fulfillment of their own selfish concerns and wishes, dependent personalities rely on others to make life meaningful, deliberately undermining their own self-sufficiency to avoid independence from those on whom they rely. They arrange their lives to ensure a constant supply of nurturance and guidance from their environment, searching for an all-powerful magic hero—someone who will take care of them, save them from the competitive struggles of life, and protect them from any possibility of harm in a hostile world. This strategy is opposite that of the active personalities, particularly antisocials, who seek to alter the environment to suit their own needs, albeit in an impulsive and destructive form.

The characteristics of the dependent personality reviewed in each of the preceding perspectives support its passive nature. Such individuals avoid instrumental competencies that might allow them to adapt their surroundings to their own needs in any significant way. Seeing themselves as inept, they seek instrumental surrogates—stronger, more experienced figures to go forth into an unfriendly world. To bond their caretakers close to them, they maintain a disposition of sweetness and naïveté. Their world is kept simple and unsophisticated, their growth suspended at the edge of childhood. The dependent personality is summarized in terms of the eight domains of personality in Table 8.1. We consider its contrast with other theory-derived constructs in the next section.

Despite the paucity of concrete data and the unquestioned influence of learning, common sense tells us that an individual's inherited biological machinery may incline him or her to perceive and react to experiences in ways that result in his or her learning a passive and dependent style of behavior. Dependency per se is never inherited, but certain types of genetic endowments have high probabilities of evolving, under "normal" life experiences, into dependent personality patterns.

All infants are helpless and entirely dependent on their caretakers for protection and nurturance. During the first few months of life, children acquire a vague notion of which objects surrounding them are associated with increments in comfort and gratification; they become "attached" to these objects because they provide positive reinforcements. All of this is natural. Difficulties arise, however, if the attachments they learn are too narrowly restricted or so deeply rooted as to deter the growth of competencies by which they can obtain reinforcements on their own.

It seems plausible that infants who receive an adequate amount of reinforcing stimulation but obtain that stimulation almost exclusively from one source, usually the mother, will be disposed to develop dependent traits. They experience neither stimulus

TABLE 8.1   The Dependent Personality: Functional and Structural Domains

	Functional Domains		*Structural Domains*	
	Incompetent	**Self-Image**	*Inept*	
Expressive Behavior	Withdraws from adult responsibilities by acting helpless and seeking nurturance from others. Is docile and passive, lacks functional competencies, and avoids self-assertion.		Views self as weak, fragile, and inadequate. Exhibits lack of self-confidence by belittling own attitudes and competencies; hence, feels incapable of doing things independently.	
	Submissive	**Object-Representations**	*Immature*	
Interpersonal Conduct	Needs excessive advice and reassurance, as well as subordinated self to stronger, nurturing figure without whom may feel anxiously alone and helpless.		Internalized representations are composed of infantile impressions of others, unsophisticated ideas, incomplete recollections, rudimentary drives, and childlike impulses, as well as minimal competencies to manage and resolve stressors.	
	Naïve	**Morphologic Organization**	*Inchoate*	
Cognitive Style	Rarely disagrees with others and is easily persuaded. Unsuspicious and gullible. Reveals a Pollyanna attitude toward interpersonal difficulties, watering down objective problems and smoothing over troubling events.		Entrusting others with the responsibility to fulfill needs and cope with adult tasks, there is both a deficient morphologic structure and a lack of diversity in internal regulatory controls, leaving multiple undeveloped and undifferentiated adaptive abilities, as well as an elementary system for functioning independently.	
	Introjection	**Mood/ Temperament**	*Pacific*	
Regulatory Mechanism	Is firmly devoted to another to strengthen the belief that an inseparable bond exists between them; jettisons independent views in favor of those of others to preclude conflicts and threats to relationships.		Is characteristically warm, tender, and noncompetitive. Works diligently to avoid social tensions and interpersonal conflicts.	

Note: Shaded domains are the most salient for this personality prototype.

impoverishment nor enrichment but are provided with stimuli from an unusually narrow sphere of objects. Because of this lack of variety, the infant forms a singular attachment, a fixation, on one object source to the exclusion of others.

Any number of factors may give rise to this exclusive attachment. Unusual illnesses or prolonged physical complications in the child's health may prompt a normal mother to tend to her infant more frequently than is common at this age. On the other hand, an excessively worrisome and anxious mother may be overalert to real and fantasied needs she sees in her normal child, resulting in undue attention, cuddling, and so on. Occasionally, special circumstances surrounding family life may throw the infant and mother together into a symbiotic dependency.

Many youngsters who were not especially attached to their mothers in the earliest stages of life also develop the dependent pattern; experiences conducive to the acquisition of dependency behaviors can arise independently of an initial phase of exclusive maternal attachment.

Not uncommon are children's own deficit talents and temperamental disposition, such as their physical inadequacies, fearfulness of new challenges, anguish when left to themselves, and so on. Some children, by virtue of constitutional temperament or earlier learning, elicit protective behaviors from others; their parents may have unwillingly acceded to overprotective habits because the child "forced" them to do so. Similarly, children who have suffered prolonged periods of illness may be prevented from exercising their maturing capacities either because of realistic physical limitations or the actions of justifiably concerned parents.

Barring the operation of constitutional dispositions and physical deficits, the average youngster in this stage asserts his or her growing capacities and strives to do more and more things for himself or herself. This normal progression toward self-competence and environmental mastery may be interfered with by excessive parental anxieties or other harmful behaviors; for example, some parents may discourage their children's independence for fear of losing "their baby"; they place innumerable barriers and diverting attractions to keep their children from gaining greater autonomy. These parents limit their children's ventures outside the home, express anxiety lest they strain or hurt themselves, make no demands for self-responsibility, and provide them with every comfort and reward so long as they listen to mother. Rather than let them stumble and fumble with their new skills, the parents do things for them, make things easier, carry them well beyond the walking stage, spoon-feed them until they are 3, tie their shoelaces until they are 10, and so on. Time and time again, they are discouraged from their impulse to "go it alone."

Ultimately, because of the ease with which children can obtain gratifications simply by leaning on their parents, they forego their feeble efforts at independence, they never learn the wherewithal to act on their own to secure the rewards of life, and they need not acquire any self-activated instrumental behaviors to obtain reinforcements; all they need do is sit back passively and "leave it to mother."

Similar difficulties conducive to dependency may be generated in experiences with an individual's peer group. Feelings of unattractiveness and competitive inadequacy, especially during adolescence, may result in social humiliation and self-doubt. These youngsters, however, are more fortunate than the avoidant adolescent because they usually can retreat to their home where they will find both love and acceptance; in contrast, avoidant youngsters receive little solace or support from their families. Although the immediate rewards of affection and refuge at home are not to be demeaned, they may, in the long run, prove a disservice to these children because ultimately they must learn to stand on their own. It is implicit in parental overprotection that children cannot take care of themselves. Pampered children are apt to view themselves as their parents do—as people who need special care and supervision because they are incompetent, prone to illness, oversensitive, and so on. Their self-image mirrors this parental image of weakness and inferiority.

When they are forced to venture into the outside world, they find that their sense of inferiority is confirmed and they objectively are less competent and mature than others of their age. Unsure of their identity and viewing themselves to be weak and inadequate, they have little recourse but to perpetuate their early pattern by turning to others again to arrange their life and provide for them.

CONTRAST WITH RELATED PERSONALITIES

The dependent shares a variety of traits with other personality disorders, most notably the histrionic, avoidant, masochistic, and borderline personalities.

Histrionic and dependent personalities are usually easy to distinguish, but they do share certain characteristics. Both dependents and histrionics possess an intense need for social approval and affection. Both seek to please those to whom they are attached, and their search for love leads both to deny their own thoughts and feelings, especially when these might displeasure their partner. Both avoid putting forward an identity of their own, which might give others something concrete to find objectionable. Finally, both are often exceedingly sensitive to disapproval and are likely to experience any form of disinterest or criticism as devastating.

The crucial difference between the dependent and histrionic personalities lies in their interpersonal strategy for making others the center of their lives. Dependents passively lean on others for protection, nurturance, safety, and guidance. By their attitude of helplessness, they encourage others to be active to intercede for them to arrange and manage their life. In contrast, histrionics are active. Rather than sit on the sidelines, they take the initiative to modify their life circumstances to ensure, first and foremost, that the attention and approval they need from others is forthcoming. They do not sit passively, waiting for the competencies and skills of others to give shape to their lives. Moreover, they do not cling or seek nurturance, as does the dependent personality. Instead, histrionics reassure themselves that their relationships are solid by doing things that make attention pour in. As long as others do not become bored or disinterested, histrionics know their attachments are solid. The dependent evokes attention, but the histrionic provokes it. Thus, dependents are submissive, self-effacing, and docile, whereas the histrionic is gregarious, charming, and seductive. If attention is not forthcoming, the histrionic may sulk and become angry, whereas the dependent is afraid to express anger at caretakers.

The distinction between the avoidant and the dependent is often more difficult to make, at least on the basis of surface behavior. Both dependents and avoidants may seem shy, lacking in confidence, and fearful of criticism, and both have strong needs for protection and nurturance. Dependents, however, often play the shy, innocent role to encourage others to encroach upon them and take control. Their submission automatically pulls for dominance from others. Dependents could not adopt such a tactic without believing that others are fundamentally trustworthy. They withdraw so that others will seek, with the goal of finding an enlightened despot who will shepherd them through life while rewarding their loyalty with protection and kindness. The dependent, therefore, is fundamentally receptive to interpersonal overtures. In contrast, avoidants actively shrink from others because they fear rejection and humiliation. Instead of trusting others, they trust that others will put them under a microscope and scrutinize their every shortcoming for public review. Moreover, dependents are largely incapable of taking the initiative on their own behalf, whereas avoidants desperately wish to develop their potentials and can act autonomously when social judgment is not a possibility.

Likewise, both the dependent and the masochist are often self-effacing and submissive but for different reasons. Dependents seek to form good alliances that insulate them from the trials of life and ensure their continued protection. Their helplessness may appear as if it undoes their possibilities for success, but it serves the larger purpose of getting others to assume the instrumental role. In contrast, masochists readily work for their own benefit but then feel guilty or fearful of success and undermine their opportunities. Whereas dependents fail out of passivity, masochists actively work for it.

Finally, dependents and borderlines share certain traits, particularly a fear of abandonment. Borderlines also tend to blur the boundary between self and others and very often idealize their partners at the beginning of a relationship. Borderlines, however, readily express anger and rapidly shifting emotions and often intimidate others with their intensity, whereas dependents are rarely forceful. Likewise, borderlines may attempt to control their partners to avoid abandonment, but dependents wait passively to see what happens and trust that the outcome will be good. Moreover, dependents function well as long as their caretakers provide them with love and guidance. In contrast, the rapidly shifting emotions of the borderline reflect a greater degree of psychological decompensation. In periods of intense stress, borderlines may experience temporary loss of contact with reality, whereas dependents are more likely to develop panic attacks or other anxiety disorders.

PATHWAYS TO SYMPTOM EXPRESSION

Dependents are naturally predisposed to develop a variety of clinical syndromes. Although different individuals vary in terms of their specific characteristics and thus develop different disorders, in each case, the logic that connects the personality disorder and the ensuing syndrome is easily seen. As you read the following paragraphs, try to identify the connection between personality and symptom. Because more is known about the connection between dependent traits and the development of other psychopathologies, this topic is discussed in more detail here than in other chapters.

Anxiety

Dependents are extremely vulnerable to develop anxiety disorders, especially panic disorder and agoraphobia (Marshall, 1996; J. Reich, 1987; Starcevic, 1992). Those who develop generalized anxiety disorder are beset by persistent background worries. Most of their concerns are related to the possibility of being abandoned or being unable to cope or even to survive. Alternatively, their meager competencies may lead to intrusive worries about task performance, especially if they are under pressure to undertake more adult responsibilities. Such persons are likely to feel restless or tense, fatigue easily, and experience sleep difficulties. For example, they may lie awake for hours going over conversations with their significant other to ensure that nothing offensive has been said to jeopardize their relationship. A vicious circle may develop where anxiety feeds back and interferes with what problem-solving skills the dependent does possess (Turkat & Carlson, 1984). Where threats to their security are restricted in scope, dependents may develop specific phobias. These not only anchor anxieties to concrete threats but also inform others in a very objective way about the kind of stimuli the dependent wishes to avoid.

For many dependents, the anticipation of abandonment or helplessness may become so real that they suddenly find themselves overwhelmed by catastrophic thoughts, resulting in a full-scale panic attack. Some may use these attacks for manipulative purposes, first, as concrete proof that a disabling condition prevents them from undertaking any further responsibility and, second, as a means of evoking nurturance, sympathy, and support from others. For the dependent, then, the net effect of secondary gain, what the individual gets out of the disorder, is doubled. Not surprisingly, panic attacks in dependents are frequently accompanied by agoraphobia, a fear of being left alone or of being left without help in situations from which escape is nearly impossible. The higher the number of dependent traits, the more difficult recovery becomes (Hoffart & Hedley, 1997). In situations such as traveling away from home, waiting in line or in a crowd, or riding with strangers on a bus or train, the fear usually becomes tolerable when the dependent is accompanied by the reassuring presence of a companion. From a psychoanalytic perspective, the companion functions as a protecting mother figure who comforts the phobic anxiety aroused by infantile dependence (Kleiner & Marshall, 1985).

Depression

The link between depression and dependency is well researched. In fact, the two are often so frequently associated that some researchers have sought to determine whether they can be measured separately at all (Overholser, 1991). Cognitive theorists frequently emphasize feelings of hopelessness and helplessness as two key components in depression. The connection is obvious: Subjectively at least, hopeless persons have nothing to look forward to, and helpless persons have no means of putting their life on a better course. Both characteristics are closely related to the dependent personality. Because dependents have few competencies of their own, they may have only a few strained relationships and a sense of utter helplessness. Likewise, with no possibility of ever learning how to master the complexities of life on their own, they easily become mired in hopelessness. Real abandonment may prompt the dependent to plead for reassurance and support. Excessive guilt and self-condemnation are also common as means of evoking sympathy while preempting further expressions of criticism from former protectors.

Once an individual is depressed, dependency complicates the road to recovery. Bad things happen to everyone in the normal course of life, but adverse events are particularly devastating to depressed persons, whose coping resources and motivation are already compromised. Dealing with normal adversity is often a major issue in psychotherapy, for subjects who experience adverse life events are more prone to relapse. Moreover, if these events affect aspects of life that are highly valued, relapse becomes even more likely: Removing one of the few things a recovering depressive feels is most reinforcing or pleasurable in an already sad existence lays the foundation for disaster. However, by considering each individual's level of dependency, predictions of who will relapse and the number of weeks to relapse can be improved (Lam, Green, Power, & Checkley, 1996). Highly dependent recovering depressives relapse more quickly than those with lower levels of dependency, even if the level of adversity is the same for both. The association between dependency and relapse in major depression has even been found in subjects assessed six years after first being studied (Alneas & Torgersen, 1997).

Eating Disorders

There is also evidence that dependents suffer from higher than expected rates of eating disorders (Tisdale, Pendeliton, & Marler, 1990; Wonderlich, Swift, Slotnick, & Goodman, 1990). Bornstein (2001), in a meta-analysis of the relationship between interpersonal dependency and eating disorder symptoms, found that there is a positive association between the two in both anorexia and bulimia. However, there are symptoms of other personality disorders as well as dependency that are also implicated in eating disorders. Additionally, when eating disorder symptoms remit, dependency levels decrease as well. So, while there is a significant relationship, it is relatively modest and nonspecific.

Physical Symptoms

Because dependents cannot cope instrumentally by taking control of their lives and changing their circumstances directly, they must cope indirectly. Theoretically, they should develop syndromes that function both to relieve them of responsibility and to bond their protectors to them even more closely, thus doubling their secondary gains. Phobic disorders provide one route; physical disorders provide another. Functionally, they are probably almost equivalent, with one important exception: An anxiety disorder leaves the dependent open to blame and derision, either for being weak or for refusing to adjust to a level of adult maturity.

The connection between dependency and a physical disorder, however, is more obscure, more easily denied, and more readily elicits sympathy and allegiance from others, who may even complain that it's a cruel world in which someone as sweet and innocent as the dependent must be so afflicted. Such illnesses divert attention from the true source of dismay, the feeling that others might be losing interest and that the bonds of relationships are somehow strained or failing. Alternatively, for some dependents, feigned physical disorders may represent an attack on themselves for being so objectively helpless and incompetent, disguised in the form of bodily ailments and physical exhaustion. Most of the time, the relationship between dependency and physical disorder operates on an unconscious basis. However, it is possible that particularly severe cases may consciously fabricate physical symptoms in order to assume the sick role and thereby manipulate their physical status directly to ensure that appropriate levels of attention and solicitation are forthcoming.

Consider the case of Jack, who is now unemployed and, like Sharon, on the edge of divorce (see Case 8.2). Jack is obviously a dependent personality. He has never held down a real job, working instead in his father's bookkeeping business and even then only bringing coffee, cigarettes, and other items to the staff. With a naïve and childlike demeanor, he finds it difficult to disagree with anyone. When asked about his chronic back pain, Jack consistently looks to his wife, Joan, to decide what to say. Indeed, she has always taken charge of the house and finances. Whereas another husband might be troubled by his inability to provide for the family, Jack is not troubled by his lack of achievement, but instead has enjoyed having others take care of him all his life. Joan is simply the latest in a long chain. Like many somaticizing subjects, Jack's problems seem a little too convenient. He is not nearly as troubled as you might expect for someone on the edge of being declared physically disabled. The fact that his pain developed suddenly on the day the divorce papers were to be served argues that his symptoms are more functional than real.

Therapy

Psychotherapy with the dependent personality generally has a good prognosis, although with their social support systems intact, most dependents do not seek therapy; their needs for protection, nurturance, and instruction are already met by others. When they do seek therapy, it is usually because some aspect of their social world has been disrupted, as with Sharon and Jack. Whereas self-oriented personalities, such as the antisocial and narcissist, often terminate prematurely, most dependents are highly motivated to continue. The therapeutic relationship itself naturally supplies them with the very resources they feel are deficient in their everyday lives. In effect, the therapist

Jack, a 54-year-old unemployed male, was referred for therapy by his family physician. His wife, Joan, accompanies Jack to all of his appointments. He had just been laid off from his job of 22 years.[1] Joan was adamant that Jack suffered from fatigue and crippling back pain, although Jack himself seemed oblivious to why he should be seen and constantly looked to his wife to take the lead in responding to questions. He was seriously physically disabled, she maintained, and should be collecting disability insurance. When no physical cause could be found for his pain, he was referred for a psychological assessment. ← (1)

Jack is the youngest child and only son in a family with six children. His mother kept careful watch over him, limited his responsibilities, and restricted most of his outdoor activities, fearing that he would be hurt. Throughout childhood and adolescence, Jack's sisters and parents protected him so much that he either learned many important skills late or not at all. Because he seemed naturally unassertive, Jack accepted this comfortable role. Jack recalls that he never went through that "teenage rebellion thing."

In high school, Jack's mother and sisters arranged his social life, even finding him a date for his senior prom. They chose his electives and after-school activities. At the age of 20, Jack's mother fixed him up with Joan, the daughter of a family friend. Joan was five years older than Jack and very eager to take care of him. They were married six months later. Joan efficiently ran the home, assuming all responsibilities for bill paying and household management. ← (2)

Jack worked for many years as a general assistant in his father's bookkeeping business. Instead of assuming some managerial responsibilities of the company, as his father hoped, Jack failed to learn even the most basic computer or administrative skills. As a consequence, he became the office gopher, fetching coffee for others and delivering the office mail. He was known as a good-natured fellow afraid to disagree with anyone, but he was also the butt of much joking behind closed doors. His daily responsibilities grew to include getting sandwiches, coffee, and cigarettes for the office staff. Joan often ridiculed Jack's lack of ambition and his lack of competence. ← (3) ← (5)

Throughout the years, Jack has been content to have others take care of him. He is aware that he has not attained the goals that others have set out for him, but he is not troubled by it. Indeed, he seems ambitionless by almost every standard, desiring simply to "fit in," never to lead. He never followed through on a single company project assigned to him. There is a naïveté and childlike quality to him. His expression conveys the question, "What is everyone making such a big fuss over?" ← (2) ← (4)

With money already tight, tensions between Joan and Jack escalated. On multiple occasions, she has threatened to leave him. Each time, Jack would make some half-hearted attempt to work, but he would eventually slide back into his old form and beg her to stay, arguing that he'll be helpless without her. On the day the divorce papers were to be served, Jack developed debilitating back pain that forced him to remain in bed with Joan as his constant attendant. She has agreed to remain in the marriage until he recovers. ← (6)

[1]Numbers mark aspects of the case most consistent with *DSM* criteria, and do not necessarily indicate that the case "meets" diagnostic criteria in this respect..

Dependent Personality Disorder
DSM-IV Criteria

A pervasive and excessive need to be taken care of that leads to submissive and clinging behavior and fears of separation, beginning by early adulthood and present in a variety of contexts, as indicated by five (or more) of the following:

(1) has difficulty making everyday decisions without an excessive amount of advice and reassurance from others.

(2) needs others to assume responsibility for most major areas of his or her life.

(3) has difficulty expressing disagreement with others because of fear of loss of support or approval. **Note:** Do not include realistic fears of retribution.

(4) has difficulty initiating projects or doing things on his or her own (because of a lack of self-confidence in judgment or abilities rather than a lack of motivation or energy).

(5) goes to excessive lengths to obtain nurturance and support from others, to the point of volunteering to do things that are unpleasant.

(6) feels uncomfortable or helpless when alone because of exaggerated fears of being unable to care for himself or herself.

(7) urgently seeks another relationship as a source of care and support when a close relationship ends.

(8) is unrealistically preoccupied with fears of being left to take care of himself or herself.

becomes a kind of surrogate caretaker who listens attentively, offering acceptance, security, and empathy as a counterbalance to the criticism, blame, and guilt that dependents naturally heap on themselves. The strength and authority of the therapist is comforting and reassuring and provides the idealized omnipotent figure that dependents seek to rescue them in time of need. Moreover, dependents are usually ready to trust and to talk, and the therapist is ready to listen. Therapy almost inevitably gets off to an auspicious beginning, creating the impression that progress will be rapid and sure.

THERAPEUTIC TRAPS

The readiness of the dependent to please the therapist and the promise of quick improvement are the principal barriers to effective psychotherapy. The dependent talks when talking is required. The dependent listens when listening is desired. The dependent follows all instructions and basks in every word of praise and sign of approval.

Not surprisingly, many beginning therapists, faced with intractable borderlines or insufferable narcissists, at first feel they have found the dream client in the dependent. Even experienced therapists with strong narcissistic and maternal needs are vulnerable. More narcissistic therapists are tempted to take up the reins and become more directive, responding to the dependent's underlying message, "Help me, and I will do exactly what you say. I will please you, and I will admire, even worship, your intelligence, strength, and courage." Such covert communications make the therapist feel powerful. The dependent gives up responsibility for the outcome and bonds closer and closer, and the therapist takes up the responsibility, subscribes to the delusion that he or she is actively curing the dependent, and glows godlike in projections of omnipotence and omniscience.

Such therapeutic relationships are pathological, only recapture the client's larger pattern of interpersonal dependency in the microcosm of the therapy office, and inevitably succumb to the same vicious circles that have defined the client's life and provided the very reason for coming to therapy from the beginning. Similar outcomes are likely for therapists with strong maternal needs, for whom the interpersonal pull is to become even more supportive than usual. Here, the dependent effectively seeks to make the transition from lonely orphan to adopted child.

THERAPEUTIC STRATEGIES AND TECHNIQUES

The strategic goals in working with dependents are the same as for any other personality. Clients can only become a more functional variant of themselves; they cannot be transformed into something completely different. The sweet, innocent, needy dependent will not become a ruthless corporate executive or an intrepid explorer of new frontiers, and it would be pathological to hold him or her to such expectations. Instead, all personalities must learn to play their strengths and minimize their weaknesses. Doing so assumes both a knowledge of these weaknesses and a willingness to step in and interrupt old patterns of relating and perceiving that lead to vicious circles. None of this changes the basic personality pattern, but it does bring them within the normal range of functioning, from which more adaptive possibilities can emerge, both during and after therapy. As is always the case with personality disorders, the key lies in addressing the personality pathology at multiple levels simultaneously, though the exact combinations and order in which these techniques are applied depend on the individual subject.

FOCUS ON RESEARCH

Childhood Syndromes

Separation Anxiety and Dependent Personality

A number of personality disorders have parallel diagnoses in children. Separation anxiety disorder, first introduced in *DSM-III* (1980) and elaborated in *DSM-IV* (1994), provides a diagnostic label for children who experience intense anxiety upon separation from home or from important attachment figures. When separated from caretakers, many children become frightened, requiring frequent reassurance that they will eventually be reunited. Separation may lead to fearful fantasies that the caretaker or the child will suffer a horrible accident or illness and never return. Younger children may fear becoming lost, after which they never find their way home or see their parents again. In more extreme cases, they have nightmares, rarely leave their parents' side, and may not be able to be left alone in a room without one parent present. Many of these children cannot stay overnight with a friend; they resist going to school or even being left with relatives.

Although separation anxiety reflects a pathology of attachment, theorists nevertheless distinguish between attachment and dependence (Ainsworth, 1969, 1972; Bowlby, 1973; Sears, 1972). **Attachment** is generally regarded positively and refers to an exclusive relationship in which the individual seeks proximity to another individual who is usually stronger or wiser. This proximity increases feelings of security in the individual. **Dependency,** on the other hand, refers to generalized behaviors that are not directed at any specific individual but designed to elicit assistance, guidance, or approval (Hirschfeld et al., 1977).

Current conceptualizations of dependent personality disorder appear to include components of both attachment and dependency. The sixth diagnostic criterion states, "feels uncomfortable or helpless when alone"; the seventh, "urgently seeks another relationship . . . when a close relationship ends"; the eighth, "is unrealistically preoccupied with fears of being alone to take care of self." Livesley, Schroeder, and Jackson (1990) obtained two factors when studying the dependent personality criterion of the *DSM-III-R*. One had as its central feature lack of confidence or assurance about themselves and their abilities. People who scored high on this factor were probably "impressionable, dependent on advice and guidance from others, and prone to establish submissive relationships" (p. 138). The second factor was descriptive of insecure attachment and related to persons who are "unable to function independently, and that require the presence of attachment figures to feel secure" (p. 138).

Accordingly, persons could presumably be diagnosed as dependent personalities in two different ways, either suffering the effects of insecure attachment or lacking confidence and assurance in themselves. This duality may help explain the results of some research that shows that many adult patients who can be diagnosed as suffering from separation anxiety disorder do not suffer from dependent personality disorder (Manicavasagar, Silove, & Curtis, 1997). For example, some might have a secure attachment but no self-confidence. Others may have developed a level of self-confidence but nevertheless experience an insecure attachment. These are the individuals who are likely to have had separation anxiety concerns as children.

Interpersonally, dependents must learn to interact with others in a way that encourages individuation rather than submission. The key to a successful outcome lies in making use of dependency without indulging it. Although the therapist can be used as a secure base to which the dependent can return, both parties should understand from the beginning that dependency is precisely the problem and that the purpose of therapy is to outgrow the therapeutic relationship. The therapist is obligated to make the a social response (Kiesler, 1996), that is, to be sensitive to the emotional nuances of the therapeutic relationship—what psychotherapists call **transference** and **countertransference**—and relate to the dependent in a way that pulls for autonomy. An anxiety hierarchy of instrumental and assertive behaviors can be set up and implemented gradually. Role playing and modeling allow the dependent to rehearse independent living skills and new ways of relating in the safety of the therapy office. Assertiveness training can be used to target submissive behaviors as they occur in session. Group therapy may be particularly useful. Most groups are naturally accepting, and veteran group members are often adept in identifying maladaptive patterns of relating. Abandonment issues may

---

FOCUS ON LIFESPAN

Dependent Personality and Partner Illness

Separation Anxiety and Dependent Personality

The connection among aging, depression, and dependency is a burgeoning frontier of research. The quality of life for many aging dependent personalities is complicated by the health status of the partner they have always relied on, in many cases for most of their life. Dependents seek out those who are willing to face a cruel and uncertain world and make major life decisions for them. Their chosen protector, usually a spouse but sometimes a mother or father, provides structure and resources intended to shelter dependents from responsibility. Dependents are just along for the ride, so to speak. And that's exactly how they prefer it.

What's a dependent to do, however, when the all-powerful protector begins to succumb to the effects of aging? Because age and stability usually go together, it is not uncommon for the protector to already be many years older. Eventually, the protector may require steady in-home care or even begin to develop a dementing illness, such as Alzheimer's, eliminating his or her role as chief decision maker. Because many families cannot afford round-the-clock nursing care, the burden often shifts to the dependent personality. A role-reversal may occur in which dependents are required to assume control of the family and take charge of financial and legal responsibilities. They may also be required to administer medications on a schedule, watch over the activities of the ailing partner, coordinate their partner's day, or perform a series of medical chores in a routine program. As the illness worsens, dependents must take control of two lives, whereas previously, they sought to forfeit control of their own. In a study examining the relationship between personality and caregiving, Alzheimer's caregivers who were distressed were found to be six times more likely to possess dependent traits (J. T. Olin, Schneider, & Kaser-Boyd, 1996). As the population of the United States continues to age, individuals with dependent traits can be expected to complicate an already troublesome crisis in health care.

be less intense in group therapy, as the dependent has more than just the therapist on whom to rely.

The effectiveness of interpersonal techniques can be combined with cognitive techniques, which help confront the black-and-white thinking of the dependent. In fact, cognitive techniques may be most useful at the very beginning of therapy, for their black-and-white world causes most dependents to see therapeutic change as sink-or-swim and not a gradual deepening of adaptive competencies. Clients can be asked to record their perceptions and feelings in a thought diary throughout the week, and the contents can be processed in session as a means of illuminating automatic thoughts that put them in the submissive mode. Interactions with significant others are particularly important. Whatever cognitive technique is employed, the goal is to actively engage dependents in a more active style of problem solving that disconfirms life as an existence of total helplessness and total isolation and moves them toward a more competent self-image. Moreover, dependents can use the therapist as a sounding board during a session to perform a reality check for their automatic thoughts.

Interpersonal and cognitive techniques are primarily useful in helping the individual understand pathological patterns in current functioning, but they do not explain the developmental basis from which these patterns arose. Psychodynamic exploration may be effective in helping dependents understand the source of such problems, though insight alone is unlikely to be sufficient in producing personality change. If dependents can be led to an understanding of the role of caretakers in their early lives, they will also understand that without their own conscious intervention, their future will be determined by their past. Understanding the role of introjection and idealization in the present is important in interrupting the reemergence of pathological patterns of relating once some level of progress has been achieved. Achieving less idealized images of others inevitably may involve confronting intense feelings of guilt related to more realistic images of parents and spouse as less than perfect, but the role of guilt in perpetuating submission and low self-esteem should be understood; otherwise, its background presence continually erodes any achievements of autonomy.

Although dependents often make rapid progress, for every individual and every therapy, the solidity of gains is checked at termination. For the dependent, the end of therapy means a loss of attachment with the therapist and a possible return to feelings of aloneness and helplessness: The crutch is gone. When the therapist begins to talk about the future, phobic symptoms and depressive feelings may suddenly escalate. If therapist and subject are somehow covertly aligned in maintaining the dependent pattern, they may spend many, many sessions trying to understand the meaning of these events, only to endure through yet another relapse as termination again approaches. Many therapists remain caught in this cycle, and eventually, most find it absolutely exasperating. The majority of cases, however, are likely to have a happier outcome.

Summary

Dependents arrange their lives to ensure a constant supply of nurturance and guidance from their environment. They can be described as self-effacing, obsequious, docile, and ingratiating. Many search for an all-powerful magic hero, someone who will take care of them, save them from the competitive struggles of life, and protect them from any possibility of harm. Given a nurturing and understanding partner, dependents often function with ease, being sociable, warm, affectionate, and generous. One normal variant of the dependent is Oldham and Morris's (1995) devoted style, who is caring and puts the needs of others first. Another is Millon's (Millon et al., 1994) agreeing style, who is cooperative and amiable. A healthy dependent is capable of genuine empathy for others and has the capacity to give unconditional love. The more pathological variants fuse their identity with that of others and become inextricably enmeshed with others.

There exist several adult subtypes of the dependent personality. The adult subtypes include the disquieted dependent, who displays a mixture of avoidant and dependent personalities; the accommodating dependent, who has an insatiable need for affection and nurturance and often shares traits with the histrionic; the immature dependent, who never develops competencies and remains childlike; the ineffectual dependent, who reflects a combination of schizoid and dependent features; and the selfless dependent, who is known for idealization and total identification.

Psychodynamically, the dependent can be thought of as fixated at the oral stage of development. For the dependent, this fixation is thought to have occurred through indulgence at the oral stage rather than through frustration. They tend to rely on introjection and idealization, generally of partners, as defense mechanisms. They may also use denial to avoid feelings of anxiety that introjection does not abolish.

Interpersonally, dependents are often seen as generous and thoughtful, overly apologetic, or even obsequious. Beneath their warmth and friendliness, however, lies a solemn search for assurances of acceptance and approval. To achieve their interpersonal goals, dependent personalities attach themselves to others, submerge their own individuality, deny points of difference, and avoid expressions of power. Interpersonal formulations of the development of the dependent personality emphasize parental overprotection, overconcern, overnurturance, and active discouragement of autonomy as the major developmental pathways. Some parents never allow their children to develop independently. In effect, they remove any need to explore the world by bringing the world to the child. Other family members and peer group experiences can also contribute to the development of a dependent personality.

The cognitive perspective asserts that the helpless façade that dependents project eventually works its way into their self-concept. Accordingly, the self-schema of dependents includes both positive and negative qualities. On the positive side, dependents see themselves as considerate, thoughtful, and cooperative; on the negative side, they often tell themselves that they are helpless and completely alone in the world. To remedy these deficits, dependents often form conditional beliefs; for example, they can survive only if someone protects them, or if they are alone, they will die. Dependents are cognitively immature. They seldom look inward and possess only vague ideas about their self-identity and direction.

The evolutionary developmental perspective conceptualizes dependents as arranging their lives to ensure a constant supply of nurturance from the environment, but doing so in a passive way. They avoid developing competencies that would allow them to actively adapt to their surroundings.

The dependent personality disorder is related to several other personality disorders including the histrionic, avoidant, and masochistic. Dependents are extremely vulnerable to developing anxiety disorders such as generalized anxiety disorder, phobias, agoraphobia, and panic attacks. Additionally, dependents often develop depression, dissociative reactions, and display physical symptoms such as assuming the "sick role."

Psychotherapy can be effective in treating the dependent personality. Most dependents are highly motivated to remain in therapy, as the therapeutic relationship itself naturally supplies them with the very resources they feel are deficient in their everyday lives. The strength and authority of the therapist is comforting and reassuring and provides the idealized omnipotent figure that dependents seek to rescue them in time of need. Moreover, dependents are usually ready to trust and to talk with a therapist. Cognitive techniques can be used to challenge dependents' propensity toward black-and-white thinking with the goal of engaging dependents in a more active style of problem solving that disconfirms life as an existence of total helplessness and moves them toward a more competent self-image. Psychodynamic exploration may also be effective in helping dependents understand the developmental basis from which maladaptive patterns arose, though insight alone is unlikely to be sufficient in producing personality change.

Chapter 9

The Histrionic Personality

Objectives

- What are the *DSM-IV* criteria for the histrionic personality?
- The dramatic and outgoing personalities are normal variants of the avoidant. Describe their characteristics and relate them to the more disordered criteria of the *DSM-IV*.
- Explain how different personality styles combine to form each of the subtypes of the histrionic personality.
- What is the historical significance of hysteria and its contribution to the development of the histrionic personality?
- Modern psychodynamic theorists distinguish between the hysterical and the histrionic personalities. Explain that distinction.
- How do the defense mechanisms of repression, sexualization, dissociation, and projection work in the histrionic personality?
- Are histrionics likely to be good sexual partners?
- Explain what is meant by the statement: "Histrionics have an impressionistic cognitive style."
- Explain how early family dynamics led to the development of the histrionic personality.
- Do histrionic and antisocial personality disorders have common etiology?
- Histrionics share characteristics with other personality disorders. List these other disorders and explain the distinction between each and the histrionic.
- List therapeutic goals for the histrionic personality.

At some point in your academic career, you may have encountered a classmate or two who invariably claimed the center of attention. Typically dramatic and often seductive, these individuals made every attempt to impress the teacher and classmates with witty remarks and suggestive behaviors. Perchance you may have noticed that their interaction with other classmates involved a frequent interrupting or reframing of discussions to sustain themselves as the focus. Anything falling short of others' admiration or reverence toward themselves would inevitably invoke feelings of resentment and depression. Yet, these negative moods would have been fleeting as their relentless striving for approval prompted a more suitable affect. In addition, you would have noted to yourself how easily influenced they were, especially as you witnessed their opinions and behaviors conform on a whim to suit whomever they sought to interact with. Once in conversation, they communicated with flamboyant headlines at the expense of substantive details. This bold pattern of expression was usually perpetuated by their physical appearance, whether it was their hairstyle, make-up, clothing, or a memorable combination of the sort. In the end, you would have felt these people were the "life of the party."

The pattern displayed by these individuals is that of the **histrionic personality.** Yvonne (see Case 9.1) clearly illustrates such a pattern. To her, attention bestows its narcotizing effects as it is something she "can't do without" (see criterion 1). Bolstering her sense of worth, Yvonne can readily interact with others whose attention she's captured. Without it, she feels subpar and scrambles to redirect all interests back to her. Over the years, she has developed ingenious ways of doing so with a sensitivity to the qualities and behaviors that others might find interesting and attractive. Indeed, most of Yvonne's strategies are seductive or sexually provocative (see criterion 2); her repertoire of behaviors contributes to her success as an exotic dancer. Such behaviors are conducive to her profession and are not considered pathological when in that environment. However, her chronically seductive maneuvering outside of work is inappropriate and ill-suited. For example, she throws out double entendres in the clinical interview but then retreats to the safer interpretation if pursued. Her purpose in the interview should be to report her own experience, not charm or attract the interviewer. Nonetheless, Yvonne is just being herself.

As males are the stereotypical antisocial personality, females are that of the histrionic personality. In many ways, Yvonne seems to epitomize this female stereotype. Her tendency to hyperemotionalize overshadows her rationale as she exhibits an ever-changing stream of consciousness and its respective, uncensored emotional expressions (see criterion 3). Her emotional life has the trappings of depth and seems vividly alive but, on deeper inspection, lacks authenticity. Always a little exaggerated and theatrical (see criterion 6), her emotional shifts are sometimes so rapid and overplayed that the observer may wonder whether Yvonne's feelings are genuine or else wonder about the underlying conflicts and insecurities her never-ending kaleidoscope of affect conceals. On reflection, Yvonne seems too concerned with her own universe. She talks freely but, for the most part, she tends to avoid serious matters, causing her words to lack detail and substance (see criterion 5).

Like most histrionics, Yvonne uses her physical appearance to direct attention toward herself (see criterion 4). Although the case talks more about her gesture and speech than her dress, her job as an exotic dancer can be seen as an exaggeration of this characteristic. On any day ripe with social opportunity, Yvonne probably tries to look flashier, sexier, and more colorful than everyone else, for these are the qualities that she believes will win friends and influence people. Though Yvonne is right some of the time, her interpersonal postulate comes at a substantial cost. She tends to confuse attraction and intimacy (see criterion 8), apparently because she has as little insight into others as she has into herself. She openly states, "Most guys just want me for my body," for example, yet she also says, "I think I find it easy to get to know others, and that's why I get so

CASE 9.1

Yvonne is a 23-year-old, single female referred for psychological as- ④
sessment by her gynecologist. She is outgoing and effusive,
"dressed to kill," and yet coquettishly reluctant to disclose the nature of her difficulties.[1] When directly asked, she avoids open dis- ③
cussion and seems to free associate to any number of topics, some
happy, some sad, but all tangential to the clinical interview. She
talks a lot, but doesn't really say much. She states, for example,
that she is on a first-name with her physician, that she has been a ⑤
dancer since she was a little girl, and that she is "blessed" with
countless good friends.

After a period of direct questioning, Yvonne reveals that she has
been experiencing debilitating pain continually for over half a year.
"I just lay in bed and feel like I will absolutely expire!" she ex- ⑥
claims, closing her eyes and dropping her head forward to feign
death. Extensive medical testing reveals no sufficient basis for her
complaint.

During the clinical interview, Yvonne's nonverbal affectations are numerous. Her head is cocked slightly down, eyes wide with invitation.
Her facial expressions, intended to underscore the meaning of her
words, are exaggerated far beyond those of normal persons. She skips ⑥
quickly from one topic to another. Apparently theatrical by nature,
she measures the reaction of her audience and adjusts her performance accordingly. She periodically throws out double entendres, but ②
retreats to the safer, more demure meaning if others begin to act on
her suggestions. At times, she seems to parade through a succession
of persons to find the one that best fits the role of therapy client.

Despite Yvonne's interpersonal intensity, her history seems mostly
unremarkable. She describes a happy and well-adjusted family,
though she admits some conflict with her mother. Her two brothers,
much older than she, still treat her like a baby. She remains very
close to her parents, especially her father, and calls home on a
daily basis. At present, she is not involved in a serious relationship,
but notes with a giggle that "most boys find me very attractive."
Nevertheless, she feels that she has been unlucky in love, and
openly admits that most guys "just want me for my body." "I think ⑧
I find it easy to get to know others," she says, "and that's why I get
so bored with people so fast." Instead, she prefers the excitement
of new experiences, including occasional episodes of intoxication
and substance abuse.

Currently, Yvonne works as a dancer at an adult club, but asserts ④
forcefully that she is different from the other girls, an artist plying
her trade. When asked what drew her to this mode of expression, she
says she likes the attention and the money, "two things I can't do ①
without." She expresses disgust with both the after-hours practices
of the other dancers and with the clientele. Her family believes that
she is teaching ballet. The source of her pain remains uncertain.

[1] Numbers mark aspects of the case most consistent with *DSM* criteria, and
do not necessarily indicate that the case "meets" diagnostic criteria in this
respect.

Histrionic Personality Disorder
DSM-IV Criteria

A pervasive pattern of excessive
emotionality and attention seeking, beginning by early adulthood
and present in a variety of contexts, as indicated by five (or
more) of the following:

(1) is uncomfortable in situations in which he or she is not the
center of attention

(2) interaction with others is
often characterized by inappropriate sexually seductive or
provocative behavior

(3) displays rapidly shifting and
shallow expression of emotions

(4) consistently uses physical appearance to draw attention to self

(5) has a style of speech that is
excessively impressionistic and
lacking in detail

(6) shows self-dramatization,
theatricality, and exaggerated expression of emotion

(7) is suggestible, i.e., easily
influenced by others or
circumstances

(8) considers relationships to be
more intimate than they actually
are

bored with people so fast." This boredom results from her innate disinterest in detail and
preference for headlines. As in life, headlines are fleeting and so, too, is the shelf life of
her interpersonal relationships. In fact, she becomes bored because she has little substance of her own through which to connect with others. Yvonne knows many people,
but she doesn't know anyone deeply, and that likely includes not knowing herself. In

this sense, her cascade of exaggerated emotions serves as a distraction from the emptiness of her experience.

With this portrait of Yvonne, we are now in a position to examine additional issues that form the plan of this chapter. First, we compare normality and abnormality and then move on to variations of the basic histrionic theme. After that, biological, psychodynamic, interpersonal, and cognitive perspectives on the histrionic personality are described. These sections form the core of what is scientific in personality. By seeking to explain what we observe in character sketches like Yvonne's, the goal is to move beyond literary anecdote and enter the domain of theory. As always, we present history and description side by side, noting the contributions of past thinkers, each of whom tends to bring into focus a different aspect of the disorder. Developmental hypotheses are also reviewed but are tentative for all personality disorders. Next, the section "Evolutionary Neurodevelopmental Perspectives" shows how the existence of the personality disorder follows from the laws of evolution. Also included are comparisons between the histrionic and other theory-derived constructs, as well as a discussion of how histrionic personalities tend to develop Axis I disorders. Finally, we survey how the disorder might be treated through psychotherapy, again organizing our material in terms of classical approaches to the field: the interpersonal, cognitive, and psychodynamic perspectives.

From Normality to Abnormality

Many readers will find aspects of the histrionic in their own personality. American standards, in particular, reward those who are friendly, expressive, and sociable. Several normal-range variants of the histrionic personality have been proposed, each capitalizing on a slightly different constellation of characteristics. The **dramatic** style (Oldham & Morris, 1990) emphasizes feeling, color, and attention. Such persons process their world effectively, value the impact of emotion, and display their emotions easily and openly. They experience life through sensation and romance, deliberately make themselves physically attractive, consciously dress with the opposite sex in mind, and become engaging, charming, or even seductive when "on stage." Many are highly intuitive and quickly sense what to talk about and how others wish to be regarded. Most trust others easily and readily involve themselves in relationships.

The **outgoing** style (Millon et al., 1994) focuses more on sociability than on theatrics. Possessing great confidence in their influence and charm, such persons go out of their way to be popular and just naturally know how to make others like them. Usually, they are described as warm, lively, dramatic, energizing, or provocative. Most see themselves as cheerful and optimistic. Their joy in life is infectious, stimulating others to equal exuberance. Many act and think like young adolescents, even into their middle and older years. Most are open to new possibilities and find tremendous joy in new experiences.

By working backwards from the disordered traits that underlie the criteria of the *DSM-IV*, a sketch of the normal-range histrionic can be developed (see Sperry, 1995). Histrionic personality-disordered individuals usually become angry, depressed, or envious when not the center of attention, whereas those with a more outgoing style enjoy compliments and praise without depending on them. Moreover, the outgoing, too, enjoy entertaining others, yet can relinquish the floor and become part of the audience.

Interpersonally, histrionics rely on a blanket sexual allure. This contrasts with the outgoing, who are more fittingly charming, engaging, and subtle. Emotionally, histrionics are fickle with their rapidly shifting moods. The outgoing, on the other hand, have a more appropriate control of their emotions. Also, physical attraction by way of style, fashion, and designer apparel is of utmost importance to histrionics. The outgoing, too, possess such interests though they fall short of a disordered obsession.

For each of the preceding contrasts, Yvonne seems to fall more toward the pathological end. Compliments and praise are not enough; she must be the center of attention at all times, as she herself admits. Moreover, Yvonne is more sexually provocative than subtle, as seen by her use of posture and double entendre. As she speaks with the interviewer, her emotions change quickly, often in response to her own free associations. Finally, she is inappropriately dressed for the clinical interview. Looking more as if she were destined for a nightclub than a psychological assessment, she is obviously invested in creating an attractive physical presence.

The remainder of the diagnostic criteria can also be put on a continuum with normality (see Sperry, 1995). The disordered are cognitively global, diffuse, and impressionistic, whereas the styled are more constructive in qualifying and detailing appraisals, given their authenticity of emotion (Kernberg, 1992). As opposed to the disordered, who are constantly engaged in dramatic and theatrical expression, the styled are less amplified without the interest of taking center stage. While the disordered are easily swayed by the influences of others, the styled are capable of making their own decisions, even at the expense of attention and approval. Finally, the disordered consider relationships to be more friendly or intimate than they really are, whereas the styled are anchored to a more solid sense of self, allowing for a greater sense of continuity over time and more insight into the nature of personal relationships.

Yvonne falls more toward pathology than normality. At the beginning of the interview, she seems unable to hold a point and explore it in depth, but instead digresses from one superficiality to the next, perhaps somewhat deliberately as a means of avoiding conflict or unpleasant emotions; for example, she is on a first-name basis with her physician, she has been a dancer since she was little, and so on. She overdramatizes her physical pain with theatrics obviously intended to impress the listener and uses facial expressions to exaggerate and underscore her emotions far beyond what ordinary communication would require. Finally, far from being able to appreciate others on their own terms, Yvonne instead remarks on how easily she gets to know others and how quickly she becomes bored with them.

Before moving on, you should be aware that this chapter makes an important simplifying assumption. Like all such assumptions, it makes the material easier to understand but distorts reality somewhat in the process. Just as the antisocial chapter implicitly assumes the vast majority of antisocials are men, this chapter assumes that the vast majority of histrionics are female (see "Focus on Feminist Psychology" box). According to the *DSM-IV-TR* (2000), females more than males have been clinically diagnosed as histrionic personality, yet this difference is consistent within gender ratios of each clinical setting. Many males have manifested histrionic traits, such as a chronic need to call attention and approval to themselves through exaggerated sex role stereotypic behaviors. Kernberg (1992) describes two kinds of male histrionics: the first, a caricature of the masculine stereotype; the second, more infantile and subtly effeminate. As society condones the braggadocios male for his athletic prowess or corporate proficiency, it is conceivable that such histrionic traits go unnoticed. Rather, it is typically considered of poor taste when a woman boasts her splendor and irresistible charm. Because of this societal masking of male histrionic characteristics, it has been difficult to ascertain the true cognitive, interpersonal, and psychodynamic similarities between males and females. Although both are constant attention-seekers, the developmental pathways, associated symptoms, and preferred treatment modalities could well be different. Accordingly, this chapter focuses on the histrionic personality as it occurs in women.

Variations of the Histrionic Personality

The norm is to receive more than one personality disorder diagnosis. Combinations with secondary patterns lead to colorations of the primary pattern, though occasionally subtypes appear merely as a combination of the major traits. Frequently seen subtypes of the histrionic personality are described in the following sections and summarized in Figure 9.1. Actual cases may or may not fall into one of these combinations.

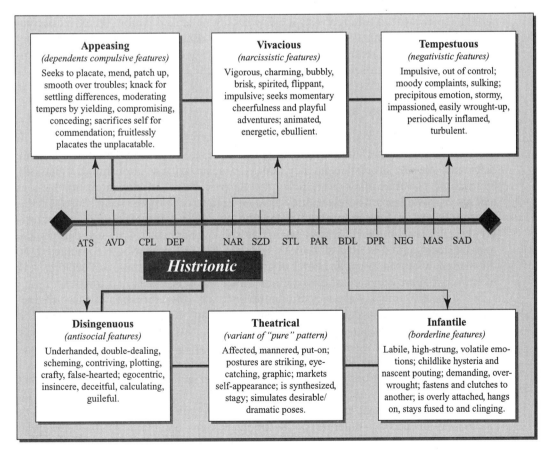

FIGURE 9.1 Variants of the Histrionic Personality.

THE THEATRICAL HISTRIONIC

Especially dramatic, romantic, and attention seeking, the **theatrical** histrionic is the epitome of the basic histrionic pattern. Described by Fromm's "marketing orientation," such individuals essentially live as commodities, marketing themselves as chameleons on social demand, and changing the characteristics they display depending on audience and circumstance. For them, nothing is intrinsic. Instead, the self is subordinated to the requirements of the social economy—transformed, synthesized, fabricated, and packaged to optimize their appeal to the given market niche. Style is not only valued over substance but also valued to the exclusion of substance. As a result, the theatrical histrionic exists largely without depth, as having inner identity limits potential maneuvering. Rather, reading the motives of others and reflecting back to them what is attractive, pleasing, and seductive is their prominent endeavor.

Within the theatrical subtype lie several subvarieties. Among women, such histrionics personify the female gender by adorning themselves with bright, sexy clothes and jewelry. Some create a good composition and resemble fashion plates; others, however, look gaudy, accessorizing beyond all sensibility, as if level of attractiveness were directly proportional to the number of earrings and bracelets. Among men, theatrical histrionics include some bodybuilders and many "pretty boys," who embody the male sex role by creating a look that suggests superpotency. Somewhat less obvious, but still within the theatrical subtype, are those who dramatically exhibit their intellectual achievements or financial success, perhaps through ostentatious displays of consumer goods. Whether male or female, theatrical histrionics are always mating, at least symbolically. Yvonne is probably not exaggerated enough to qualify for this subtype.

THE INFANTILE HISTRIONIC

The **infantile** histrionic, similar to Kernberg's (1967) infantile personality, represents a blend of the histrionic and borderline personalities. As indicated previously, many histrionics possess strong dependency issues. By sexualizing relationships prematurely and pulling powerful others into their orbit, histrionics experience more indulgences and fewer frustrations. Therefore, they have no need to develop the solid sense of identity that begins its formation with what analysts call the reality principle, the realization that life is so intrinsically frustrating that some generalized psychic apparatus, the ego, will be required to deal with it. As such, the life of the histrionic continues to be dominated by a need to be the center of attention, by persistent sensation seeking, and by primitive regressions into fantasy, all of which serve the pleasure principle.

In the more primitively organized infantile histrionic, the expression of these characteristics is even more severe. Given their lack of identity formation, their attachment to significant others is highly dependent and demanding. Most constantly seek reassurance to maintain their stability and vacillate between overcompliance and profound depression when approval is not forthcoming. With no sense of self to buffer or modulate their basic drives, their emotions change quickly, easily, and unpredictably, running the gamut from intense love to intense rage to intense guilt, all of which may be expressed simultaneously. In more pleasant moments, they may behave with a childlike agreeableness or fascination but become sullen or pouty the next. Many complain that they are either unloved or treated unfairly, attitudes that quickly escalate into tantrums when anyone disagrees.

THE VIVACIOUS HISTRIONIC

The **vivacious** histrionic synthesizes the seductiveness of the histrionic with the energy level typical of hypomania. The result radiates attractiveness, charm, playfulness, verve, and intensity. More than just bubbly or perky, vivacious histrionics are interpersonally cheerful, optimistic, spontaneous, and impulsively expressionistic, often without regard to future consequences. Driven by a need for excitement and stimulation, many are easily infatuated, attaching themselves to one person after another in quick succession. Behaviorally, their movements are quick and animated. They both enter and leave with a flourish. Even though they are only superficial thinkers, their ideas often flow so quickly and easily that others become infected by their excitement. Those who are more normal race around, get things done, start projects, and persuade others to join them with an energy and friendliness that make for a natural salesperson. Others, however, pursue momentary whims without completing much of anything—leaving broken promises, empty wallets, and distraught associates. Not surprisingly, many vivacious histrionics also possess narcissistic traits.

THE APPEASING HISTRIONIC

The **appeasing** subtype combines histrionic, dependent, and compulsive features. Approval is their one mission in life: You must like them; you must become their friend. To achieve this goal, they continually compliment, praise, flatter, commend, and make you feel that they would do anything for you: "You are so ingenious! You have done a perfect job! You look so beautiful! How can I help you?" Whenever they sense indifference, they immediately step up their activities, positioning their appraisal back toward the positive. In effect, they present the image of absolute goodwill, someone for whom appreciation becomes a moral imperative. When disagreements do occur, they immediately begin smoothing things over, even when they must sacrifice ground, compromise their own desires, or concede important points. Rather than retaliate against those who cannot be placated, they choose simply to suffer injuries, painting themselves as innocent victims caught in a cruel world, martyrs who suffer the slings and arrows of outrageous fortune, ever deserving of sympathy and pity.

The implication of such a conciliatory lifestyle is the compensation for a substantial void. Beneath their friendly smiles lie the emptiness of the histrionic, the guilt of the compulsive, and the inferiority and helplessness of the dependent. Most feel that they are problem persons who are unloved and inadequate. As such, they become superpleasers, ever alert to any subtle means whereby appreciation and approval might be secured. More developmentally advanced than the basic histrionic, these individuals have internalized condemning parental voices that rain down from on high with criticism and admonishment. Whereas compulsives hyperconform, these individuals appease their tormentors, conscientiously anticipate their needs, and offer only goodwill and kind gestures in return for anger and hostility. Essentially, they become so nice and good and sweet they could make even a sadistic superego feel guilty.

THE TEMPESTUOUS HISTRIONIC

The **tempestuous** variant combines features of the histrionic and negativistic personality. Such individuals are best described as intensely moody and emotionally variable.

During better periods, they enact mainly histrionic features, presenting an attractive front, being superficially friendly and sociable, engaging others in conversation, and adding their own free emotional expression in return. Like the theatrical histrionic, they are easily bored, overly dramatic, hyperreactive to external stimulation, and impulsively sensation-seeking. When combined with borderline features, the result is emotional overdrive. Like the borderline, tempestuous histrionics are hypersensitive to criticism, intolerant of frustration, and socially immature—characteristics that almost ensure that the good times won't last. Most alternate between periods of extreme emotional excitement and impulsive acting-out, followed by fits of anger that transition to depressive-like symptoms of fatigue and sleep and eating pattern changes.

Whereas normal persons develop a strong sense of self-identity that wraps and conceals basic drives and moderates emotions, tempestuous histrionics are not only more thinly veneered than the basic histrionic pattern but also somewhat fragmented like the borderline. Consequently, they are much more vulnerable to unmoderated displays of raw and rapidly changing emotions. When tweaked, they lose control, reacting with storm and turbulence to even minor provocations. Deprived of attention, they may search frantically for approval, becoming contentious, dejected, or hopeless when it is not readily forthcoming. Over time, these individuals may become less and less histrionic and more and more disgruntled and critical of others, begrudging others' good fortune. They may also develop preoccupations with body functioning and health, and dramatically exhibit their illnesses or complain endlessly about ailments to recapture lost attention and support.

THE DISINGENUOUS HISTRIONIC

The **disingenuous** subtype synthesizes histrionic and antisocial features. A somewhat different picture is created, depending on the relative influence of histrionic and antisocial traits. In the beginning, they make a good first impression and seem sociable and sincere, exhibiting such spontaneity and charm that others quickly lower their defenses. The combination of histrionic and antisocial features, however, makes the disingenuous subtype more manipulative than the basic histrionic pattern and for ends other than simple attention and approval. For some, their histrionic traits serve simply as a convenient method of making contacts and opening doors but overlay and temporarily conceal characteristics fundamental to the antisocial, including a willingness to violate social conventions, break promises and shatter loyalties, behave irresponsibly, and sometimes erupt with anger and physical confrontation. For some, the antisocial influence stops here with traits attributable to simple delinquency.

Others, however, combine histrionic and more psychopathic characteristics. These individuals synergize the histrionic's more adaptive social skills, charm, and ability to read the motives and desires of others with a rather calculated malevolence. Obviously, this variant is more egocentric, more willingly insincere, and probably more conscious of their manipulations than is the basic histrionic pattern. They often seem to enjoy conflict, gaining a degree of gratification or amusement from the excitement and tension thereby produced. Because antisocials usually interpret kindness as weakness, their friendly histrionic traits sometimes make them afraid that others will come to view them in exactly that same way. If they sense this is true, they may avenge this wrong impression by becoming particularly predatory.

Early Historical Forerunners

The histrionic personality was first officially recognized in *DSM-III,* published in 1980, replacing the psychoanalytic school's older, gender-biased **hysterical personality.** No longer an officially recognized term, hysteria nevertheless remains in widespread currency. Its several meanings refer to a state of intense emotional overexcitement, the neurosis that presumably eventuates in such states, and the conversion of emotional conflicts into physical symptoms (also known simply as conversion hysteria). In psychodynamic thought, these ideas are intimately connected. Historically, the relief of hysterical conversion symptoms through hypnosis by Charcot eventually led Freud to the discovery of the unconscious. Ironically, the evolution of early ideas on hysteria holds some similarity to the evolution of psychoanalysis itself. In the beginning, both the psychosexual stages of early analysis and the hysteria of the Greeks were directly connected to the functioning of sexual organs. Eventually, however, both were interpreted more broadly. Hysteria detached itself from the uterus and grew into a collection of traits and symptoms. Classical psychoanalysis detached itself from psychosexual stages and the determinism of the libido, growing into ego psychology and object relations.

Hippocrates, the famous Greek physician, believed hysteria was caused by a wandering uterus that traveled the body and took up residence in the brain, exciting its neural tissues during menstruation. More sophisticated views did not become established until nearly the second half of the nineteenth century. Gradually, the interpretation of the syndrome shifted away from female anatomy and toward a collection of co-occurring symptoms. Ernst von Feuchtersleben (1847) depicted women disposed to hysterical symptoms as being sexually heightened, selfish, and "overprivileged with satiety and boredom." Attributing such traits to the nature of female education, he argued that the disorder "combines everything that can heighten sensibility, weaken spontaneity, give a preponderance to the sexual sphere, and sanction the feelings and impulse that relate to it." Griesinger (1845/1867) described hysterics as notable for their volatile humor, senseless caprices, and inclination to deception, prevarication, jealousy, and malice. Briquet (1859) wrote that any number of painful emotions might produce the disorder, including sadness, jealously, fear, and even boredom or disappointment (Stone, 1993). By 1875, Charcot had established that hypnosis was effective in relieving hysterical physical problems.

The famous descriptive psychiatrists of the early 1900s also recorded the existence of hysterical syndromes. Kraepelin (1904, p. 253), for example, noted that such an individual delights in novelty, enthusiasm, vivid imagination, great excitability, mood lability, romantic preoccupation, capriciousness, and impulsiveness and tries "ruthlessly to extort the most careful attention of those around her." Presaging the shift from hysterical to histrionic, Schneider (1923/1950) chose the label attention-seeking for such individuals, claiming that the hysterical was too broad and vague and implied a moral judgment. Schneider's account highlighted histrionics' proclivity to exaggeration and pathological lying employed to make themselves seem more interesting and attractive to others. Finally, Kretschmer (1926, p. 26) strongly echoed contemporary positions, viewing these persons as having a preference for the theatrical and preferring the "loud and lively," but also as disposed to threaten suicide as a means of manipulating others. All three psychiatrists were contemporaries of a still young but emerging psychoanalytic movement.

FOCUS ON FEMINIST PSYCHOLOGY

Why No Wandering Penis?

Effects of a One-Gender Dominated Field of Psychology

The origins of hysteria reach deeply into both history and human nature. As all women and most men know, men do not understand women. Worse, men cannot understand why they cannot understand women. Rather than keep trying, men have instead created diagnostic syndromes to contain aspects of female behavior they find particularly perplexing. Because the history of humankind has thus far been dominated by males, perhaps it is not surprising that hysteria was one of the first mental disorders to be discussed. For the ancient Greeks, hysteria was caused by a wandering uterus that could become detached, tour the body, and settle in the brain, thus producing the behavioral excesses that most men naturally fear, such as wild emotion and female lust. Hysteria thus embodies the male belief that all women are crazy or at least constitute subthreshold cases easily exacerbated into a frenzy by some stray comment or unintended oversight. The "bad hair day" crystallizes this notion.

Eventually, the glory of ancient Greece and Rome disappeared. In the Middle Ages, the world was viewed through a religious paradigm. Faith in God offset hard times for humanity, including mass starvation, disease, pestilence, and war. By some estimates, a third of the population of Europe was killed by the Black Death alone. Humans naturally sought explanations to such paradoxical calamities. How could such horrors occur if God were just and loving? Again, women were to blame. Those who ran afoul of social standards became natural scapegoats, being "diagnosed" according to the standard of the times as witches, in league with Satan. Through their sorcery, these evil beings could summon famine, plague, bad luck, and worst of all, impotence. Eventually, the widespread dread of witches found religious sanction in the *Malleus Maleficarum,* or *Witches' Hammer,* written by two German monks in 1496, a kind of Stephen King version of our modern *DSM,* complete with its own form of therapy: burning at the stake.

Though the witch hunts would eventually subside, it seems that every era unveils some new syndrome for which only women are at risk. The contemporary premenstrual dysphoric disorder may be seen as a modern parallel, the idea that women's natural cycles naturally cause them psychological problems. Although many would admit to emotional and behavioral changes related to their period, women might also argue that these changes occupy only a few days a month, whereas a penis distorts behavior most of the time. Strangely, history holds no such wandering member that might become detached, take up residence in the brain, and distort perception in order to explain antisocial behavior among males.

The Biological Perspective

The biological perspective recognizes that purely physical factors are often strongly associated with various personality traits. The value of biology in unraveling the origins of personality, however, is complicated by the nature of the personality disorders themselves, which exist as constellations of co-occurring traits, not single dimensions.

Moreover, many aspects of biology may be studied, including genetics and heredity, temperament, neurotransmitter profiles, brain morphology and irregularities, evoked potentials, constitution, and birth complications. How these various proximal, or biologically near, influences might interact and combine to influence personality development is largely unknown. Most factors are studied in isolation, if at all.

Some research has been directed toward the role of genetics, a distal influence on immediate behavior that comes down to us across millions of years of evolutionary time. The heritability of certain personality disorders is clearer, though the exact pathways remain speculative. Pedigree studies have shown that antisocial and criminal behavior is much more frequent in the fathers of antisocial children, even when the child is adopted away at birth so that the psychological influence of coping with an antisocial parent is eliminated (Cadoret, Troughton, Bagford, & Woodworth, 1990). Antisocial behavior in a fraternal or identical twin also raises the possibility that the other twin will also be antisocial, whether raised together or separately. If histrionic personality disorder is considered a dramatic caricature of what is female, just as the antisocial personality may be considered a dramatic caricature of what is male, we might expect that both disorders represent the same underlying genetic construct.

Cloninger and Guze (1975) argued essentially this thesis, showing that hysteria is common in families where the father is sociopathic. Cloninger (1978, p. 199) concluded that "hysteria is a more prevalent and less deviant manifestation of the same process which causes sociopathy." However, their definition of hysteria included a substantial illness-related component, today classified as part of the somatization disorders. The notion that antisocial and histrionic personalities might represent different expressions of the same underlying genetic pattern has been reexamined by Hamburger et al. (1996), who assessed major antisocial, psychopathic, and histrionic personality traits in conjunction with traditional masculine and feminine gender roles. The relationship between psychopathy and antisocial and histrionic personality traits was moderated by biological sex, not by gender role, thus arguing that antisocial and histrionic personality disorders may be considered a single entity whose expression depends on gender.

Recently, Cale and Lilienfeld (2002) based their research on the aforementioned Hamburger et al. (1996) study as they sought to demonstrate that the gender-differentiating behaviors between the histrionic and antisocial personality disorders are merely gender variants of psychopathology. Specifically, females would demonstrate the psychopathic features associated with histrionic personality disorder, whereas males would demonstrate that of the antisocial personality disorder. Their findings, however, were both "weak" and "inconsistent" in supporting this hypothesis. Though there was evidence that psychopathic females exhibited histrionic features while their male counterparts demonstrated antisocial features, the results were not statistically consistent enough to substantiate their hypothesis. With the limitations of the study considered, conclusions drawn from it do support sex-based differences between the two personality disorders in addition to confirming the common trait, impulsivity, shared between the two personalities. Clearly on the right track, this trend for determining biological bases for personality disorders is warranted. Meanwhile, further explanations for similarities between histrionic and antisocial personalities are considered.

The association between antisocial and histrionic personality disorders may also be understood as an example of assortative mating. Across many species, traits attractive to the opposite sex tend to become amplified over many generations; individuals possessing a superabundance of attractive traits simply have more mating opportunities.

Some individuals, however, accumulate so many of these characteristics that they are biologically disposed from birth to caricature their sex. From this perspective, the histrionic and antisocial personalities become evolutionary inevitables. The histrionic is attracted to the hypermasculine antisocial, whose apparent strength, self-confidence, and risk-taking provide masculine displays she naturally finds attractive. In turn, the antisocial is naturally attracted to the childlike hypersexuality and impulsive sensation seeking of the histrionic.

The Psychodynamic Perspective

Although the preceding contributions anticipate the modern view, arguably the most important historical development came in 1895 with the publication by Breuer and Freud on unconscious mechanisms in hysteria, stimulated by the famous case of Anna O. Both were fans of hypnosis, used to gain insight into Anna's unconscious conflicts, including her dislike for her father and her love for Breuer, who then left the case to Freud. Eventually, the two formed the theory that hysterical symptoms resulted from early sexual molestation, leaving memories so distressing that they were intentionally forgotten and could only be fully remembered under hypnosis. Once such symptoms were recalled fully to consciousness, Freud found that they vanished, never to return. These findings became the basis for a momentous development, the first theory of neuroses, which holds that behind every neurotic conflict lays a forgotten childhood trauma. Such experiences are said to be repressed. Making the unconscious conscious is still one of the primary goals of psychotherapy. The idea that the mind can somehow forget things that it really knows has provided both enlightenment and perplexity to psychologists ever since.

Eventually, Freud made yet another discovery, even more important. He discovered that, far from being completely trustworthy, the hypnotic recollections of his hysterics instead reflected the presence of unconscious wishes, fantasies superimposed on memory. Hysterical symptoms could now be seen, not as resulting from childhood trauma, but rather as reflecting unconscious instincts threatening to break into consciousness awareness. The effect on psychoanalytic theory was broad and transforming. With hysterical wishes obviously formed during early development while relating to the opposite-sex parent, the discovery of childhood sexuality and the consequent development of psychosexual stages and their associated character types were now on the horizon. In fact, without this insight, there might be no field of personality disorders, as there would be no characterology from which the study of personality disorders could emerge. Eventually, the importance of wishes led Freud to dreams as the "royal road to the unconscious" and to the use of free association as the technique that defined psychoanalysis as an applied science. Even into the 1950s, analytic theorists would continue to regard conversion hysteria as the cornerstone on which the whole of classical psychoanalysis was constructed (Fenichel, 1945).

Modern psychodynamic theorists have sought to distinguish between the hysterical character and the histrionic personality as presented in various editions of the *DSM*. Most analysts see the two as existing on a spectrum of severity. Kernberg (1992), for example, places the hysterical personality at a higher level of functioning and the histrionic personality at a lower, infantile level of functioning. The higher level hysteric, Kernberg states, is more socially adaptive, with more genuine, authentic, and predictable emotions. Affective control, he elaborates, is lost only in connection to others with whom there exist intense sexual or competitive conflicts. Gabbard (1994, pp. 559–560) paints a similar picture: Histrionics are more florid, more labile, more impulsive, and more sexualized and seductive; hysterical personalities, in contrast, are more subtle in their exhibitionism and express sexuality in a more coy or engaging manner. Whereas hysterical personalities can be successful, even ambitious, at work, Gabbard states, histrionics fail due to aimlessness, helplessness, and dependence. Finally, hysterical personalities tolerate separation from love objects, but histrionic patients are overcome with separation anxiety. We have contrasted Yvonne across the normal and pathological ends of this continuum. Again, she falls more toward the pathological side.

Although the analytic account of these personalities continues to evolve, adult traits nevertheless are recognized in a variety of historical works. Freud (1931/1950) developed a conception of the erotic character, for whom the desire for love and the possible loss of love are key themes. W. Reich (1933, pp. 204–205) provided a more detailed description, including "coquetry in gait, look or speech" in women and "softness and excessive politeness" and femininity in men. Reich also noted fickleness, suggestibility, a tendency to change emotions quickly and unexpectedly, being excited one moment but quickly disappointed the next, and a tendency to confuse fantasy with reality. In terms of defenses, he regarded histrionics as only thinly armored, with few of the sublimations and reaction formations common in the compulsive, in many ways the histrionic's theoretical opposite. Fenichel (1945, p. 528) amplified Reich's conceptions, noting that hysterical characters sexualize all their relationships and act as if entertaining an audience in an attempt to "induce others to participate in [their] daydreaming."

The psychoanalytic school of thought has historically based the framework of a histrionic personality around female stereotypes, hence, the abundance of female-typed descriptors evidenced here and in forthcoming paragraphs. However, modern-day schools of thought, including that of the psychoanalytic, recognize the prevalence of histrionic personality patterns among both males and females. Arriving at this equitable plateau has, nonetheless, become a welcomed reality as the science of psychology continues to build on the works of its forerunners.

The defensive style of the histrionic personality has been an especially fertile area of psychodynamic investigation. Across the decades, psychodynamic theorists have been repeatedly astonished by their use of massive repression, which Freud called a splitting of consciousness. Histrionics specialize in actively excluding most of what is factual, detailed, and precise from conscious awareness (see Shapiro, 1965). Instead, they possess a need to keep it simple; for them, the devil is in the details, literally. In contrast to compulsives, who isolate similarities and differences, ponder small points, and agonize over the possibilities to the point of indecision, histrionics are sensitive only to the overall emotional tone; they pick up vibrations and give off vibrations, but everything else is excluded from awareness as being too dangerous for consideration. We've noted this already in Yvonne at the beginning of the interview, where she seems to have a problem focusing on reporting her actual problems.

Given this need to repress, histrionics do not routinely startle you with their abstract power or their ability to see compelling connections among ostensibly diverse phenomena. Instead, they create a barrier between themselves and the world, filtering what is logical and reasonable and letting in only what is affectively charged, a style most of us would consider grossly superficial. By refusing to reflect on their own goals, attitudes, and identity, histrionics free themselves from worry and are thereby excused from the existential albatross the rest of us bear. Histrionics repress the emptiness of the marketed self, the conflicts their sexualized relationships create in others, and even their own unfulfilled desires. In essence, they lack the fervor for intense personal growth.

In addition to repression, hysterical personalities make use of sexualization, dissociation (considered in a subsequent section), and projection. Sexualization, in particular, serves complex adaptive and defensive purposes. W. Reich (1933), in fact, regarded hypersexuality as the defining characteristic of these personalities, suggesting that seduction is used as a defense against the fear or threat of masculine aggression. In other words, frightened by the possibility of violence, the histrionic summons another drive in the aggressor, replacing hostility with attraction. In part, this explains a curious paradox in their behavior: Histrionics exude sexual potential but are simultaneously intensely frightened and repelled by actual sexual activity (Easser & Lesser, 1965).

In fact, histrionic personalities are often shocked when asked to confront their provocative sexual messages. Apparently, conscious awareness of the instrumental use of the physical body is completely incompatible with a self-image of sweet innocence, an example of massive repression in action. Histrionics are more likely to turn the tables, projecting hypersexual interest onto their accuser and deflecting attention from themselves. With righteous indignation, they may maintain that they cannot express how hurt they are by such a suggestion, thereby leaving their prospective suitors feeling angry, confused, or even amazed. For Yvonne, this tendency is perhaps seen with her insistence that she is "not like the other girls," as she insists forcefully that she is an artist, dancing presumably for the aesthetic value. Histrionics may also use sexualization to distract themselves from feelings of anxiety or emptiness or to compensate for their perception that women lack power in a male-dominated world. By evoking sexual desire in others, by creating demand but rarely satisfying it, histrionics level the interpersonal playing field. Whatever the reason, their pervasive use of sexuality has caused many analytic writers to remark that these personalities display a false maturity, effectively, a false presentation of self. Rather than join the mature world, histrionics remain childlike with superficial efforts to disguise their seductive wiles.

Within psychodynamic circles, the development of the hysterical character remains controversial. Freud suggested fixations revolving around the opposite-sex parent, a doctrine reinforced by Fenichel (1945) but questioned by later writers (Marmor, 1953; Sperling, 1973). Ironically, it would seem that psychodynamic thinkers are still debating the very issue on which psychoanalysis itself was founded. Current thinking is that low-functioning hysterics display predominantly oral concerns, and high-functioning hysterics display issues related to the oedipal stage of development, during which a growing sense of sexuality creates an unconscious desire for the opposite-sex parent. Accordingly, the more primitive *DSM-IV* histrionic personality should be plagued by oral dependency, together with more profound disturbances in object relationships and interpersonal conduct. In contrast, hysterical personalities should be relatively more intact and experience greater overall success in most areas of functioning (Blacker & Tubin, 1991). The difference is one of degree: Analysts speak of a spectrum running from the relatively more oedipally fixated "good hysteric" to the more primitive and orally fixated "bad hysteric" (Zetzel, 1968).

In contrasting the oral and oedipal hysteric (Blacker & Tubin, 1991; Easser & Lesser, 1965; McWilliams, 1994), the most important tasks are to account for the presence of excessive dependency together with massive repression. Whereas the message from caretakers to the future dependent personality is, "We will do for you, because you cannot do for yourself," the analytic perspective sees the mothering of future histrionics as often inadequate, cold, and insensitive. Feeling afraid, isolated, unsafe, or unappreciated, the little girl must seek some source of nurturance beyond the primary caretaker. Eventually, she turns strongly to her father while devaluing her mother, thereby refusing a normal female identification. Males are strong and exciting, and females, including herself, come to be seen as weak and wanting. The part of her personality that might have developed a genuinely full and female selfhood given an adequate female role model is thus left to atrophy (McWilliams, 1994). Without any realistic anchor, it becomes caricatured into a loose set of behaviors that conform to social stereotypes about what elicits male desire (Blacker & Tubin, 1991). The conflict with her mother that Yvonne acknowledges, together with her closeness to her father and brothers, might fit this pattern, though more exploration would be needed.

At the same time that the little girl is turning to her father, she finds attention-getting efforts to win his approval are made more effective by nuances of seduction. Subtle sexual overtones thus begin to catalyze relationships. Awareness of this attraction is mutually threatening to both father and daughter and must be forcefully repressed, though comments may be made on the little girl's beauty, cuteness, sweetness, or innocence (McWilliams, 1994). As a result, a pattern of repressed sexual desire and sexual manipulation takes form and continues throughout life. Naturally, this also leads to conflicts between mother and daughter, whereby the mother is devalued. In effect, the future histrionic or hysteric, now "Daddy's cute little girl," learns to throw herself at male figures with the false maturity of hypersexualization, but at the same time develops a shallow or superficial sense of self that betrays her lack of an adequate female role model. We can easily imagine, for example, that at the beginning of therapy, Yvonne might state simply, "My mother and I have never been close," which might evolve into, "My mother was a cold person who was frightened by my relationship with my father."

The consequences of such a dynamic are easily seen by returning to the fundamental principles of psychoanalysis. Recall that in normal development, mental life is at first dominated by the id, which operates on the pleasure principle: I want what I want, and I want it now. Because the demands of the id almost always run into frustration, the ego emerges to coordinate its demands with the constraints of the external environment. Based on the reality principle, the ego operates as the executive branch of the personality. At first, the ego is free to consider any available route to satisfaction. Eventually, however, parental figures and other role models forbid some actions and idealize others. Thus, the superego develops, consisting of the conscience and the ego ideal, that is, what one should and should not do and become. Frozen in developmental

FOCUS ON SEXUALITY

Histrionic Personality and Sex

Personality and Sexual Well-Being

Histrionic personalities demonstrate, usually in a mildly caricatured form, what our society fosters and admires in its members: to be popular, extroverted, attractive, and sociable. Interpersonally, they use seductive maneuvers to attract the attention they crave.

But do they follow through and sustain that initial impression? Are they good lovers? Apparently, the answer is no. Apt and Hurlbert (1994) studied a sample of women who had been diagnosed as histrionic using the MCMI-II and compared them to a matched sample of other nonhistrionic women in a series of measures of sexual behaviors and attitudes. Histrionic women were found to have significantly lower sexual assertiveness, greater erotophobic attitudes toward sex, lower self-esteem, and greater marital dissatisfaction; they were found to be more preoccupied with sexual thoughts; and they reported having lower sexual desire and more sexual boredom. They also reported a greater incidence of orgasmic dysfunction and indicated a greater likelihood of entering into an extramarital affair. Despite such negative findings, histrionics reported greater sexual self-esteem.

Although the results of this particular study referred to histrionic women, there is no reason to believe that histrionic men are any more sexually competent. In fact, a similar pattern of high sexual self-esteem and difficulties has been identified for males and labeled sexual narcissism by the same authors (Hurlbert & Apt, 1991).

time, histrionics do not develop a strong superego because they have few qualms about transgressing commitments or manipulating those around them.

Consider Monique (Case 9.2), who has a lot going for her, but she cannot seem to remain monogamous. Like Yvonne, she seems to have a need for stimulation. New relationships excite her, though she quickly becomes bored, to the point that she feels the need to "return to partying and drinking." Now that her writer husband has settled down, she feels the urge to return to the same pattern that produced her two previous divorces, the desire to begin a secret and exciting affair. When she presents for therapy, she exhibits many of the classical symptoms. Her emotions run the gamut from laughter to sadness. She sexualizes her interaction with the interviewer by deliberately creating sexual imagery. Her need for attention is consistent with her social butterfly, cheerleading history, becoming pathological in her depressive reaction when her girlfriend was voted homecoming queen and again in her interest in extramarital relationships. The impressionistic cognitive style of the histrionic is evident in her description of her high school years, and a theatrical, exaggerated emotionality can be seen in the dramatic flourish that accompanies it. Finally, there is evidence that she considers relationships to be more intimate than they really are. She married her first husband after having known him only three weeks, though, "It felt like we'd known each other all our lives." She probably feels the same way about her lovers, something that justifies each affair and contributes to its beginning.

If Monique's superego development were more robust, such desires would either be inhibited or never reach consciousness. Moreover, if her ego identity were more solidly anchored, she would long ago have developed goals that would further define her place in the world and give meaning to her existence, and she probably would not have a history of nontraditional life choices or alcohol abuse. Like other histrionics, Monique has short-circuited her natural developmental process. By sexualizing relationships prematurely, histrionics lure powerful others toward them so they may ease their way, reward their desires, and reduce their frustrations. Like other histrionics, Monique has no desire to develop a deep, abiding, solid sense of identity. Thus, histrionics remain, as W. Reich (1933) noted, "thinly armored," with only a veneer of selfhood to cover the drives and dependencies of an infantile id. As such, they continue to be dominated by the pleasure principle, as expressed through their need to be the center of attention; persistent stimulus-bound and sensation-seeking behavior; dramatic, theatrical displays; and even primitive regressions into fantasy, called primary process thinking. When anxiety threatens, their thin self tends to fragment or dissociate under the strain, regresses into primitive fantasy, or redirects stress somatically into the body, where it reappears as symptoms not easily accounted for by a legitimate medical condition, possibly Yvonne's situation.

The development of the higher functioning hysterical personality is similar to that of the histrionic, in that both have oral-dependency concerns. However, the hysteric runs into difficulties mainly during the oedipal phase, that is, at the point in development when budding sexuality creates an unconscious desire for the opposite-sex parent. At this stage, children naturally begin to compete with the same-sex parent, who becomes a rival. Some unusual circumstance, however, is required to intensify the dynamic and produce lasting personality traits. Zetzel (1968), for example, found that many of her hysteric patients had experienced real separation or loss of the opposite-sex parent during this period, presumably intensifying their unconscious wish to possess their parent-lover, thereby making resolution of the conflict more problematic. This provides a second pathway leading to the development of the hysterical personality.

CASE 9.2

Monique, an attractive and vivacious woman, sought therapy hoping to prevent the disintegration of her third marriage.[1] As she describes her problem, her emotions run the gamut from laughter to sadness. Whenever in a relationship, she would eventually become "bored," (laughter) start showing interest in "more exciting males," and eventually return to partying and drinking. "Can you imagine me in a s-e-x-u-a-l affair?" she asks the interviewer playfully with a feigned innocence. As a recovering alcoholic, Monique thought she might be "on the brink," but wanted to take a good look at herself before ruining her marriage to the loving husband who had bonded so well with Jacqueline, her daughter from her first marriage.

Monique's history foreshadows her current situation. She is four years older than her sister, her only sibling. Her father, a wealthy businessman and gifted salesman, regarded the girls as "display pieces," trotting them out at social gatherings so that others could admire the successful family man. Her mother was an emotional but charming woman who took great pains that the children grew up "beautiful and talented." Both entered childhood pageants and talent shows. Monique's most precious memory is running into her father's arms after winning one such contest at age 8.

During the teen years, Monique was very popular, a social butterfly who dated often and never wanted for attention from the opposite sex. She busied herself with a variety of extracurricular activities, including the high school choir and artwork for the school paper. In her junior and senior years, she made the varsity cheerleading team. She describes these years with a flourish as "just the most wonderful and exciting and stimulating time that a person could ever, ever have." She does, however, recount becoming depressed and lying in bed for days when her best girlfriend was voted homecoming queen. "She wasn't nearly as cute as me," Monique states solidly.

After high school, Monique decided on art school instead of a traditional college. As a freshman, she married a fellow student, a handsome boy three years older with good grades but a reputation for causing trouble. Though they had known each other for only three weeks, "It was like we'd known each other all our lives . . . I could tell we were meant!" she states. She recounts the course of subsequent events as if building up the plot of a soap opera, introducing dramatic pauses at just the right points. Both craved excitement and eventually decided on an open marriage. She is still not certain her first husband is Jacqueline's real father. Seven months later, they were divorced. Three years later, she married an older man in his forties who gave both mother and daughter a "comfortable home and lots of love and attention." Again, however, she eventually became bored and started several affairs, but broke off each one for fear her husband would find out. Eventually he did, and they were divorced. For the next four years, she was on her own, partying, using drugs, and drinking heavily. Her mother and sister took care of Jacqueline.

Her wild days came to an end, however, when she met her present husband, a talented writer. But now that she has settled down, Monique again feels herself at the threshold of destroying the relationship, either by her own potential infidelity or by the distraction of alcohol abuse.

[1] Numbers mark aspects of the case most consistent with *DSM* criteria, and do not necessarily indicate that the case "meets" diagnostic criteria in this respect.

Histrionic Personality Disorder
DSM-IV Criteria

A pervasive pattern of excessive emotionality and attention seeking, beginning by early adulthood and present in a variety of contexts, as indicated by five (or more) of the following:

(1) is uncomfortable in situations in which he or she is not the center of attention

(2) interaction with others is often characterized by inappropriate sexually seductive or provocative behavior

(3) displays rapidly shifting and shallow expression of emotions

(4) consistently uses physical appearance to draw attention to self

(5) has a style of speech that is excessively impressionistic and lacking in detail

(6) shows self-dramatization, theatricality, and exaggerated expression of emotion

(7) is suggestible, i.e., easily influenced by others or circumstances

(8) considers relationships to be more intimate than they actually are

Reproduced with permission from the *Diagnostic and Statistical Manual of Mental Disorders, Fourth Edition.* Copyright 1994 American Psychiatric Association.

For subjects who received adequate mothering, oral issues are absent and object relations are relatively intact. In other words, adequate mothering leads to trust and relatively solid ego development. Such hysterics have a solid female role model, do not devalue the mother or turn strongly to the father for nurturance prior to the development of their adolescent sexuality, and, therefore, do not sexualize their adult relationships as overtly. Instead, they are more subtle, the expression of their sexuality is more constructive, and they exhibit fewer psychological symptoms under conditions of stress. Subjects following the first pathway fall victim to a developmental double whammy: With the father already idealized and no good female role model with which to identify and sublimate their blooming sexuality, the desire to possess the father is more easily magnified. Communications that before were sexualized mainly through reinforcement and shaping are now fueled unconsciously by real sexual force.

The Interpersonal Perspective

Although Sullivan is usually regarded as the father of the interpersonal perspective, later interpersonal thinkers have been much more systematic. Leary (1957), for example, was the first to actualize the potential of the interpersonal circle. His cooperative-overconventional personality comes closest to the contemporary histrionic. Such individuals are characterized by extroverted friendliness and sociability and a striving to be liked and accepted. On the positive side, Leary noted that they are ever optimistic, if somewhat bland, and "continually strive to please, to be accepted, to establish positive relations with others" (p. 304). On the negative side, however, he also noted that they are intolerant of criticism, seek to void themselves of all guilt, and refuse to see their own behavior as hostile or power mongering.

Researchers following Leary have further refined the geometry of the original interpersonal circle through more sophisticated statistical methods. In a particularly fine-grained analysis, Kiesler (1983, 1996) divides the circle into 16 segments described at two levels of functioning, normal and pathological. Although many personality disorders possess characteristics that do not map neatly onto the interpersonal model, the histrionic can be described succinctly in terms of two main segments. In the normal range, Kiesler (1996, pp. 14–15) uses the descriptors *uninhibited, dramatic, perky, neighborly, approachable,* and *interested.* At the pathological extreme, these become *unbridled, melodramatic, flamboyant, always available,* and *intrusive.*

Histrionics have many distinctive interpersonal qualities, most notably their self-image and the immediate impression they make on others. At least at a conscious level, they usually see themselves as attractive, friendly, and fun to be around. In the beginning, they can seem most charming. The ease with which they open up and relate their feelings seems to establish a quick intimacy that is both alive and refreshing, qualities that alone are often very attractive. More severe histrionics, however, inevitably become volatile, provocative, theatrical, and capacious. Their one-on-one charm becomes a talent for grabbing the headlines, marketed to entire social groups. If not the life of the party, the histrionic at least has a retinue of smiling followers eager for eye contact. To make themselves more appealing, they may alternate playing the naïve, innocent waif and the worldly sophisticate, tailoring their display as the audience desires. Attentiveness to such signals allows them to quickly maneuver their interpersonal impression to minimize any possibility of rejection or indifference, while maximizing ongoing attention and attracting numerous potential suitors, their resources, and their helpfulness. Dramatic gestures, attractive coiffures, frivolous comments, and shocking clothes—all are designed to stimulate interest and draw attention, as Case 9.3 demonstrates.

Although histrionics are often experienced as being attractive at first, their intimate relationships usually have a superficial quality. Because most require constant attention and stimulation, their partners may eventually feel enslaved by their neediness, tire of the burden, and simply withdraw emotionally, leaving the histrionic terminally bored and actively looking for alternatives. More pathological individuals may move quickly through friendships and companions, who become burned out by their intensity and mood swings. By contrast, the less pathological individuals maintain relationships by using their good looks and charm, for example, the illustrious trophy wives, whose mission is to look good and ornament their husbands' achievements. Not surprisingly, many histrionics find the self-confidence of the narcissistic style to be very attractive. One is as empty as the other is full. Although hardly satisfying, such relationships may endure as long as each member keeps up his or her end of the bargain. The male must continue his ascent up the ladder of social status; the female must appear as attractive as possible and combat the process of aging with grace. The unfortunate reality for these women relying on their appearance to gauge success is the Darwinian effect of survival of the fittest or, in this case, prettiest. Inevitably, younger and prettier competition surfaces and creates insurmountable stress for the aged vixen.

An example of superficial interpersonal relationships is the case of Sheila. When she presents for evaluation and therapy, she exhibits many of the classic features of the histrionic personality, with characteristics of the infantile subtype. In the message left at the counseling center, Sheila threatens suicide but apparently feels that she will not be taken seriously. She seeks to guarantee a response by following up her threat with, "I'm not kidding." In the interview, she readily admits using such suicidal gestures manipulatively, noting that it gets attention and "always works on the parents." Although she is probably being truthful, it is also possible that Sheila fears that she has underestimated the impact of her message and wants to head off interventions she most definitely would not enjoy, perhaps hospitalization, by suggesting that she was being deliberately manipulative. Moreover, her behavior with the male interviewer is suggestive and inappropriate, and there is a curious discrepancy between the depression she acknowledges and her animated style. Her responses to questions seem overemotionalized and poorly detailed, often with no real segue between succeeding emotional states.

Although probably exaggerated, the impression we get from Sheila's message is that she sometimes feels alienated from almost everyone. She has been arguing with her roommates since the beginning of the semester because she borrows their things without permission, parties too late, and brings intoxicated visitors back to the apartment she shares. Her boyfriend is "extremely and unreasonably jealous," probably in part because she denies the role of her seductive style in actively soliciting male attention. "I can't help it if they find me attractive," we can imagine her saying. Despite their problems, her boyfriend is nevertheless described as "the closest person in the world to me," an exaggeration consistent with the tendency of histrionic individuals to assume that their relationships are more intimate than they are. The fact that he has "turned on" her only makes matters worse, and that is what prompted her call to the counseling center. Almost every relationship has problems, but we can imagine that Sheila's are probably more chronic than most, with themes of crisis and betrayal that are repeated again and again. Indeed, this is one of the defining characteristics of personality disorder.

CASE 9.3

Sheila called the university counseling center just after midnight. She spoke softly into the answering machine and seemed to be fighting back tears. "Uh, I feel really shitty and I'm mad at everyone I know and I need to talk with someone who cares or I'm going to kill myself right now and I'm not kidding either!"[1] Although she left her phone number at her dorm room, attempts to reach her by the on-call therapist were unsuccessful. According to her roommate, Sheila was out "making the rounds." After a second call the next morning, she agreed to come in for evaluation. ◄ (6)

Sheila arrived 30 minutes late, chewing bubble gum and dressed scantily in a shocking black outfit. When her male interviewer paused immediately upon seeing her, she stated simply, "It symbolizes the way I'm feeling right now. Do you like it?" A turban covered her hair, and dark stones adorned her fingers, ears, and neck. The whole getup seemed chosen for its obvious shock value. An assessment of suicidal potential was the first objective, but Sheila denied that she was really serious. "If I was serious," she quipped dramatically, "I wouldn't be here, now would I?" "It's a good way of getting attention . . . I don't like to be ignored . . . always works on the parents. You'd be surprised what you can get if you try hard enough." At that moment, she blew a big bubble, and then suddenly sucked the air out of it, all without losing eye contact with the interviewer. ◄ (4) ◄ (6) ◄ (1) ◄ (2)

Sheila reports problems in many areas of life. First, she is doing poorly in school and fears she may be thrown out if her grades do not improve. She is already on academic probation. When asked about her attendance, she admits that she rarely makes it to classes, because most of them are in the morning, and her social activities get started after midnight. However, "a lot of the guys in class have volunteered to take notes for me." Second, Sheila and her roommates have had problems getting along since the beginning of the semester. They object to her "borrowing" their things, her late nights, and her frequent male visitors, who often stay overnight in various states of intoxication. Finally, her boyfriend, whom she regards as extremely and unreasonably jealous, wants to break up, objecting to her flirtatious behavior, even though she swears she has been completely faithful to him over the month they have been together. Sheila states that she is overwhelmed that "the closest person in the world to me would turn on me all of a sudden like that." And that, she notes, is what prompted her call to the counseling center. ◄ (8)

Although Sheila speaks of her great distress and depression, her demeanor belies her words. She is animated and demonstrative, perhaps even slightly manic. She flits from topic to topic and from emotion to emotion with only minimal insight and no real transition in between. No follow-up appointment could be made, because Sheila is "too busy." She denies continued feelings of suicidality. When asked if she wants to continue next week, she remarks teasingly "I'll get back to you," blowing another bubble and then pressing the gum under her seat on the way out. ◄ (6) ◄ (5) ◄ (3)

[1] Numbers mark aspects of the case most consistent with *DSM* criteria, and do not necessarily indicate that the case "meets" diagnostic criteria in this respect.

Histrionic Personality Disorder *DSM-IV* Criteria

A pervasive pattern of excessive emotionality and attention seeking, beginning by early adulthood and present in a variety of contexts, as indicated by five (or more) of the following:

(1) is uncomfortable in situations in which he or she is not the center of attention

(2) interaction with others is often characterized by inappropriate sexually seductive or provocative behavior

(3) displays rapidly shifting and shallow expression of emotions

(4) consistently uses physical appearance to draw attention to self

(5) has a style of speech that is excessively impressionistic and lacking in detail

(6) shows self-dramatization, theatricality, and exaggerated expression of emotion

(7) is suggestible, i.e., easily influenced by others or circumstances

(8) considers relationships to be more intimate than they actually are

The development of the histrionic's interpersonal style can be understood from a social learning perspective (Millon, 1969, 1981), without invoking the somewhat obscure jargon of psychoanalysis and its associated psychosexual assumptions. Here, the parents of future histrionics rarely criticize or punish but instead reinforce only behaviors that are parentally approved, but on a variable schedule. Sometimes a behavior is rewarded, and sometimes it is not. Because nothing they do works consistently, such children experience frustration in getting their parents' attention and exaggerate behaviors basic to their gender stereotype to secure compliments and affection. Otherwise, they are ignored. For example, dressing up to look cute and pretty might produce a positive comment one day but not another. Eventually, only caricatured behaviors cross the threshold beyond which parents notice them and comment approvingly. Competent behaviors or achievement strivings inconsistent with the gender stereotype go unnoticed.

When parents fail to identify this dynamic, they instead set into motion a vicious circle in which more and more desperate and exaggerated efforts are required to sustain the same level of nurturance. Such children enter adolescence with a nearly insatiable thirst for attention and love. Naturally, they find that by exploiting their own growing sexuality, they quickly become a magnet for sustained sexual interest, whereas before, they could sustain nothing. While being Daddy's cute little girl worked some of the time, this strategy works all of the time, and it works well. When preadolescent tactics designed to get the opposite-sex parent's attention combine with the biologically motivated attraction of a developing libido, deprived histrionics are catapulted from the agony of being perpetually ignored to the ecstasy of social center stage, a role they will not soon relinquish. This developmental one-two punch is not unlike the emphasis on oral and oedipal concerns voiced by the psychodynamic perspective, though the language is different.

Such early interpersonal dynamics have further psychological consequences. First, they shuttle the histrionic down the pathway toward poor identity development. Social interactionists anticipated later developments in the interpersonal school, asserting that the self develops through the appraisals of others, a position not too different from that of contemporary object relations. Essentially, we learn who we are, consciously and unconsciously, from the reflections of others. As these reflections are internalized, they give the self content. Because histrionics are often ignored by parental figures, they simply have fewer reflections to internalize, and those they do have are centered on the exaggeration of stereotypic gender roles. Monique's case provides a prime example. Her father was interested in advertising himself as the successful family man with two beautiful daughters, and her mother took great pains to ensure that the girls grew up to be talented pageant winners. Neither parent seems to have been interested in nurturing Monique's unique potential as a person.

Given such a history, histrionics develop only a thin margin of self to cover basic emotions and contain or transform their drives, a fact that makes them vulnerable to dissociation and fragmentation of the self under conditions of intense anxiety or stress, Sheila being the example here. Histrionics don't just sometimes feel empty; they are empty, at least relative to the average person. The interpersonal message that histrionics internalize results in a crushingly low self-esteem. Essentially, their developmental mantra is, "You are ignored because you deserve to be ignored, because you do not merit more, and to merit more, you will have to try very, very hard." Because the very actions that produce validation on one occasion do not on the next, histrionics never feel that their self-worth is secure. In this sense, their sexualization represents a compensation that functions to control those on whom they depend, making nurturant resources more dependable and less variable. All the cases in this chapter seem to have followed this pathway.

Working from her SASB model, Benjamin (1996) paints a similar picture. Like most accounts, Benjamin emphasizes the classic father-daughter dynamic, noting that value within the family system depends on "good looks and entertainment value" (p. 168). The mother is symbolically dismissed from the marital relationship as the little girl becomes Daddy's new sweetheart. Although the father dotes on her, meeting all her needs, it is a pseudonurturance that rewards appearance and cuteness, not behaviors appropriate to the full female role. In turn, she learns that looking good and being charming and entertaining provide the keys to the castle, as Benjamin notes, and can be used coercively for control. The future histrionic is thus led into an active dependency on others (Millon, 1969), for knowing how to care for herself is not required. Surface behaviors map into what the SASB would call "friendly trust," but underneath, the agenda is to use sex-role exaggeration to milk others for attention, nurturance, and love.

In addition, Benjamin draws out other distinctive nuances of family dynamics. Echoing W. Reich (1933), she notes that the seductive charm of the future histrionic often provides power over a violent, and perhaps alcoholic, father who threatens the mother or other siblings. Here, the agenda is to protect the family and defuse a precarious situation by offering innocent dependency and other tender emotions directly in the face of potential violence. Such dynamics tend to be self-perpetuating, with both positive and negative effects. The safety of the family depends on her success, although there is no knowing whether the explosive caregiver can be successfully calmed. As a result, cues that signal impending violent episodes, Benjamin states, become associated with anxiety and panic. Gradually, they may become generalized to any flaw in future caregivers, so that anxiety and panic ensue whenever attention and approval fall below some almost unsustainable level. Finally, Benjamin notes the existence of a sickly, coquettish subtype of the histrionic personality, who coerces attention and exploits dependency through apparent disability.

The Cognitive Perspective

In the histrionic personality, cognition and defense merge to support a single protective purpose (see Shapiro, 1965). As opposed to compulsives, whose memory and description of the surrounding world is precise, highly detailed, technical, or even encyclopedic, the cognition of histrionics is notoriously vague, diffuse, global, impressionistic, scattered, and flighty. Rather than compare and contrast perspectives to illuminate all sides of an issue, histrionics seek to minimize cognitive complexity whenever possible. In fact, histrionics cannot really be said to appraise anything, because appraisal naturally requires conscious awareness of the various dimensions on which the evaluation occurs. Their cognitive-defensive filter actively protects them from anything too precise, factual, concrete, abstract, reasoned, logical, systematic, philosophical, or existential. The factual or concrete is too boring. The abstract or reasoned is too tedious. The philosophical is too long and tiresome. The existential is too deep and too threatening.

Instead, histrionics perceive the world through the single channel of their own colorful and dramatic, but imprecise, hyperemotional impressions. When asked for a description, for example, they may respond in overdramatized emotion words: "I just love it!"; "Isn't she cute!"; "I can't stand her!"; "I felt like I would die!" (Shapiro, 1965).

Their attention flits about here and there, pulled by sensory stimulation and fleeting internal associations. Anything that occupies the focus leaves only a temporary imprint and few memory traces. Rarely does anything get processed to any significant depth. As such, well-developed schemata for classifying and ordering the world or for comparing future possibilities to past experiences are limited. Yvonne's description of the pain she feels fits this classic histrionic pattern. She states that she lies in bed all day and yet apparently finds time to dance. She says she feels "like I will absolutely die!" but somehow lives to party on.

Histrionics, in fact, do not ponder, concentrate, contemplate, reflect, conduct controlled experiments, or give sage advice. In fact, they often seem to lack a basic curiosity about the world around them. Instead, they prefer to ignore fine discriminations and parse the world in terms of cognitive categories that are broad, overgeneralized, and loosely boundaried. In part, their capriciousness reflects an avoidance of potentially disruptive unconscious images and urges, especially those that might bring to awareness their deeply hidden dependency needs and sexual manipulations. By ignoring the details of their world and relationships, they reinforce the mechanism of repression. By allowing their cognitive structures to remain loose and poorly formed, they not only allow themselves a measure of distractibility when life becomes too upsetting but also support a tendency to dissociate defensively under more intense stress.

The cognitive characteristics of histrionics are easily observed in everyday life, and they sometimes appear on conventional tests of intelligence. Most of us, when faced with a difficult problem, formulate several strategies and learn something from each failure until the problem is solved. If the answer is already known, we may even reconstruct the solution by working backwards. Big problems can be dissolved into smaller parts, each of which is tackled individually. More difficult problems may require pencil and paper, consultation with others, or even library research. Whatever the exact route, typically a person tries various approaches and gradually uncovers the root of the problem.

In contrast, histrionics often simply give up and report, "This is too hard." Faced with an entire series of puzzles, they may become irritated or express fatigue. Concentration may seem tedious, boring, or incongruent with their self-image. Historically, the need to solve problems has proven unnecessary for histrionics; their modus operandi is to relieve themselves of such burdens by eliciting the aid of others. They may also give up due to insufficient background knowledge. Given their impressionistic style, histrionics frequently fail to accumulate a reservoir of facts about the world around them. Their "crystallized intelligence" (Cattell, 1971) should grow more slowly than for others simply because they fail to process the world to any depth, failing to connect facts and storing little about the world that is definite (Shapiro, 1965). Consequently, situations necessitating substantial acquired knowledge are avoided, thereby limiting their exposure to any significant intellectual challenges.

The final consequence of an impressionistic cognitive style is lack of knowledge about their own identity. Most persons see the self as a substance. The belief that each person has a soul echoes this view, for presumably, the soul contains the timeless essence of a human being. Social psychologists, however, hold that our beliefs about ourselves are formed in much the same way as those about the external world. Like scientists, we form theories, make connections among ideas, and draw conclusions. Some such beliefs are consensually shared; others are purely personal constructs (Kelly, 1955). Someone who repeatedly experiences feelings of attraction to members of the same sex, for example, may eventually conclude that he or she is homosexual. Thus, the self is a construct, much like any other scientific construct, and the process of self-development is as much a process of discovery as of choice. Like any other construct, the connections between the theory of self and adjacent ideas and experiences that inform and define it can be either more dense or more sparse. Some people, for example, know themselves absolutely, whereas others have only feeble notions.

Because the impressionistic, unfocused, global style of histrionics makes for a very poor scientist, they seldom develop a well-formed, qualified, principled sense of identity, complete with long-term goals and a detailed life plan. Instead, their impressions of self resemble their impressions of the surrounding world, being global, vacuous, and superficial. We would expect neither Yvonne nor Monique to spontaneously launch into a thorough and precise description of herself, how she is similar to yet different from her mother and father, how they have influenced her life choices and the goals she has set for herself, and what she sees as the primary challenges to her personal growth and identity in the next five years.

Contemporary cognitive therapy focuses as much on the contents of cognition, mainly the central beliefs of each personality disorder, as on cognitive style. Writing in Beck et al., Fleming (1990, p. 215) emphasizes that, like dependent and depressive personalities, histrionics believe, "I am inadequate and unable to handle life on my own." However, unlike depressives, who dwell on their own personal inefficacy, or dependents, who seek an instrumental surrogate, histrionics actively seek out ways that others can be persuaded to care for them. Like dependents, histrionics see others as holding the keys to the quality of life. However, whereas the helpless dependent is at the mercy of external forces, histrionics take the initiative in soliciting attention and praise to draw potential caretakers more closely to themselves. Rather than take control of their lives directly, they seek to control those who control their destiny. As Fleming further argues, this strategy has its own implications. Histrionics go out of their way to make themselves desirable, and they feel devastated when not desired or simply ignored. After all, working hard without success says much more than failing without putting in much effort.

Writing in the same volume, Beck et al. (1990) paint a similar picture. Histrionics see themselves, according to Beck, as glamorous and impressive. As such, they feel justified in being the center of attention and form strong bonds with others who indulge them and play the part of the admiring audience. Whereas the same is true of narcissists, histrionics do not remain aloof and superior to others, but instead engage them directly in ways that solicit a continuous flow of praise and appreciation. Like most personality disorders, the core beliefs of histrionics are intensely negative. In fact, those schemas lead to compensatory beliefs, which literally insulate individuals from what they believe to be the dismal truth. Histrionic core beliefs are variants of, "I am basically unattractive," and "I need others to admire me in order to be happy"; compensatory beliefs include, "I am very lovable, entertaining, and interesting," and "People are there to admire me and do my bidding" (p. 50). Conditional beliefs flow from core beliefs and include notions such as, "Unless I captivate people, I am nothing," "If I can't captivate people, they will abandon me," and "If I can't captivate people, I am helpless" (p. 50). Beck et al. also emphasize an important instrumental belief that connects the cognitive contents of histrionics to their effusive emotional displays: "I can go by my feelings" (p. 51). Rather than delay expression, then, histrionics act on their emotions, even when reflection would serve them better, crying when they feel sad or throwing a tantrum when angry.

The Evolutionary-Neurodevelopmental Perspective

Although the preceding perspectives are valuable, they are only part of the whole story. In the evolutionary theory, the histrionic personality is referred to as the active and other-oriented, whereas the dependent personality is referred to as the passive and other-oriented. Both feel helpless and make others the center of their lives. Dependents seek an instrumental surrogate, someone to compensate for feelings of helplessness and inadequacy. To bind others to them, dependents create a sweet, innocent, passive, and childlike façade. By perfecting this image, they dare others to confront the guilt of abandoning them.

In contrast, the histrionic actively seeks to create an image so compelling it consumes the consciousness of others with one single-minded desire: Get closer to me! If the ideal relationship is symbiotic, the dependent is comparable to the functions of a parasite and the histrionic to that of a black widow spider. Whereas the dependent mates for life, the histrionic mates covertly and symbolically across every medium the senses offer, attracting as many potential suitors as possible. Whereas the dependent invests in a single relationship, the histrionic hedges bets by cultivating backup alternatives. Whereas the dependent fuses exclusively with a single all-powerful other, the histrionic projects the secret wish of an omnipotent lover so powerfully that others easily become caught up in the web of fantasy themselves. Table 9.1 summarizes the histrionic personality in eight clinical domains, abstracted in part from the preceding discussion of perspectives.

The overarching question is: How does such a personality, like that of the histrionic, evolve? In keeping with the evolutionary perspective, for a personality to ultimately become what it is, it must survive, adapt, and replicate. As scientists delved into the origins of man to discover the process of evolution, so, too, do we examine the origins of the histrionic personality.

In searching for the biological origins of the histrionic pattern, the role of neurodevelopment is our first source of explanation. The neural and chemical substrate for tendencies such as sensory alertness and autonomic or emotional reactivity may logically be traced to genetic influences. Evidence demonstrating a high degree of family correspondence in these traits is suggestive of physiological commonalities but can be explained also as a function of experience and learning. The need for research is obvious, not only in establishing factually the presence of family correspondence but also in tracing the manner in which such alleged genetic factors unfold and take shape as psychological traits.

However, equally important to genetic influences are the environmental experiences, which inevitably contribute to and mold a newly born personality. The constitutionally alert and responsive infant experiences greater and more diverse stimulation in the first months of life than the less aware or receptive infant. As a consequence of these early stimulus gratifications, the tendency to look outward to the external world for rewards is reinforced rather than looking inward. In a similar manner, normally alert infants may develop this exteroceptive attitude if their caretakers, by virtue of sensory indulgence and playfulness, expose them to excessive stimulation during early life stages.

Histrionics appear to have been exposed to a number of different sources that provided brief, highly charged, and irregular stimulus reinforcements. For example, the histrionic may have had many different caretakers in infancy (parents, siblings, grandparents, and

TABLE 9.1   The Histrionic Personality: Functional and Structural Domains

Functional Domains		*Structural Domains*	
	Dramatic	**Self-Image**	*Gregarious*
Expressive Behavior	Is overreactive, volatile, provocative, and engaging, as well as intolerant of inactivity, resulting in impulsive, highly emotional, and theatrical responsiveness; describes penchant for momentary excitements, fleeting adventures, and shortsighted hedonism.		Views self as sociable, stimulating, and charming; enjoys the image of attracting acquaintances by physical appearance and by pursuing a busy and pleasure-oriented life.
	Attention Seeking	**Object-Representa-tions**	*Shallow*
Interpersonal Conduct	Actively solicits praise and manipulates others to gain needed reassurance, attention, and approval; is demanding, flirtatious, vain, and seductively exhibitionistic, especially when wishing to be the center of attention.		Internalized representations are composed largely of superficial memories of past relations, random collections of transient and segregated affects and conflicts, as well as insubstantial drives and mechanisms.
	Flighty	**Morphologic Organization**	*Disjointed*
Cognitive Style	Avoids introspective thought, is overly suggestible, attentive to fleeting external events, and speaks in impressionistic generalities; integrates experiences poorly, resulting in scattered learning and thoughtless judgments.		There exists a loosely knit and carelessly united morphologic structure in which processes of internal regulation and control are scattered and unintegrated, with ad hoc methods for restraining impulses, coordinating defenses, and resolving conflicts, leading to mechanisms that must, of necessity, be broad and sweeping to maintain psychic cohesion and stability, and, when successful, only further isolate and disconnect thoughts, feelings, and actions.
	Dissociation	**Mood/ Temperament**	*Fickle*
Regulatory Mechanism	Regularly alters and recomposes self-presentations to create a succession of socially attractive but changing facades; engages in self-distracting activities to avoid reflecting on and integrating unpleasant thoughts and emotions. Sexualization is used to influence relationships, projection to deny this influence. Both are examples of massive repression.		Displays rapidly shifting and shallow emotions; is vivacious, animated, impetuous, and exhibits tendencies to be easily enthused and as easily angered or bored.

Note: Shaded domains are the most salient for this personality prototype.

foster parents), who supplied intense, short-lived stimulus gratifications that came at irregular or haphazard intervals. Such experiences may have not only built a high-level sensory capacity, which requires constant "feeding" to be sustained, but also conditioned the infant to expect stimulus reinforcements in short concentrated spurts from a mélange of different sources. (Irregular schedules of reinforcement establish deeply ingrained habits that are highly resistant to extinction.) Thus, the persistent yet erratic dependency behaviors of the histrionic personality may reflect a pathological form of intense stimulus seeking traceable to highly charged, varied, and irregular stimulus reinforcements associated with early attachment learning. As such, the shifting from one source of gratification to another, the search for new stimulus adventures, the penchant for creating excitement, and the inability to tolerate boredom and routine all may represent the repercussions of these unusual early experiences.

In other words, the parents of the future histrionic rarely punish their children and distribute rewards only for what they approve and admire, yet often fail to bestow these rewards even when the child behaves acceptably. Such behaviors have personality consequences: strategies designed to evoke rewards, a feeling of competence and acceptance only when others acknowledge their performances, and a habit of seeking approval for its own sake. All three of these traits are characteristic of the histrionic personality. We next detail their development.

Children who receive few punishments and many rewards develop a strong and inambivalent inclination to relate to others. If they learn that the achievement of rewards is dependent on fulfilling the expectations and desires of others, they will develop a set of instrumental behaviors designed to please others and thereby elicit these rewards. However, if these strategies succeed sometimes but not always—that is, if they are sporadically reinforced—these children will persist in using them or variations of them, well beyond all reason, until they do succeed, which eventually they will. As do most anything intermittently reinforced, these instrumental behaviors will not easily be extinguished, even if they fail much of the time.

As a consequence of this pattern of experiences, children become actively rather than passively oriented toward others. Furthermore, they learn to look to others rather than to themselves for rewards since their behavior is only preliminary and not a sufficient condition for achieving reinforcements; the same behavior on their part elicits a reward one time but fails on another. Despite the fact that they continuously aim to please and perform for others, it is always others who determine whether and when they will be rewarded. They await others' judgment as to whether their efforts will bring recognition and approval; as a consequence, it is others who define the adequacy of their behavior; that is, their competence is judged by the reaction of others, not by their own efforts or behaviors.

There is little question that children learn, unconsciously, to mimic that which they are exposed to. The prevailing attitudes and feelings and the incidental daily behaviors displayed by family members serve as models, which growing children imitate and take as their own long before they are able to recognize what they are doing or why. This process of vicarious learning is made especially easy if parental behaviors and feelings are unusually pronounced or dramatic. Under these circumstances, when parents call attention to themselves and elicit emotional reactions in their children, the children cannot help but learn clearly how people behave and feel. Thus, many female histrionics report that they are "just like" their mother, emotionally labile women "bored to tears with the routines of home life," flirtatious with men, and "clever and facile in their dealings with people." The presence of a histrionic parent, who exhibits feelings and attitudes rather dramatically, provides a sharply defined model for vicarious and imitative learning.

Children who struggled long and hard to capture the attention and affection of their parents under conditions of sibling rivalry often continue to use the devices that led to their periodic successes long after the rivalry ceased to continue. Not only are these behaviors reactivated when they seek attention in the future, but they often misperceive innocuous situations (perceptive distortion) and recreate competitive situations (repetition compulsion) in such ways as to bring forth the strategies they learned in the past. If the child learned to employ cuteness, attractiveness, and seduction as a strategy to secure parental attention, these interpersonal behaviors may persist and take the form of a life-long histrionic pattern.

Aesthetically appealing girls and likable or athletic boys need expend little effort to draw attention and approval to themselves; their mere being is sufficient to attract others. As rewarding as these experiences may be in building up a high sense of self-esteem, they do have their negative consequences. These persons become excessively dependent on others because they are accustomed to approval and have learned to expect attention at all times. They experience considerable discomfort, then, when attention fails to materialize. To ensure the continuation of these rewards and thereby avoid discomfort, they learn to play up their attractiveness. For example, the formerly pretty young girl, to elicit the attention and approval that came so readily in youth, goes to great pains as she matures to remain a pretty woman; similarly, the formerly successful young athlete struggles to keep his muscular and trim figure as he progresses into middle life. Both of these attractive individuals may have failed to acquire more substantial talents in their youth because they needed none to elicit social rewards. What we observe in their later life, then, is a childish exhibitionism and an adolescent, flirtatious, and seductive style of relating, all of which characterize the histrionic personality.

CONTRAST WITH RELATED PERSONALITIES

Given their drama and theatrics, the histrionic is one of the most reliably identifiable personality disorders. In addition to similarities with the dependent, the histrionic shares important traits with several other disorders as well. In general, personalities that are self-oriented, such as the narcissist and antisocial, tend to develop paranoid traits under conditions of intense or prolonged stress, whereas personalities that are other-oriented, such as the dependent and histrionic, develop traits that are more borderline. Accordingly, both dependent and histrionic personalities, for whom fantasies of fusion with caretakers are an important feature, tend to develop symptoms related to identity diffusion or dissociation, though borderlines are usually more severe. Likewise, both borderlines and histrionics exhibit rapidly shifting emotions, and both experience feelings of profound emptiness. Both may attempt to manipulate others with suicidal gestures. However, actual self-destructive behaviors, such as cutting, are more frequently seen in borderlines. Despite their contrasts, the two disorders do shade into each, as histrionics may develop borderline traits. Developmentally, histrionics enjoy a special relationship with their opposite-sex parent that stops short of actual incest and develop repression as a means of keeping such forbidden desires out of consciousness. In contrast, for borderlines, incest or other sexual abuse is often a reality.

Both histrionics and narcissists are exhibitionists, sharing a desire to be the absolute center of attention, though for different reasons. As noted, histrionics exhibit their wares and read the desires of others to create intense interest and attraction. Narcissists are aloof from such concerns and feel that they should be desired just as they are; tailoring their image betrays too much vulnerability. Histrionics believe the world is dominated by the sexual instinct and specialize in creating such wishes in others, though not necessarily in fulfilling them. Narcissists, in contrast, believe the world is dominated by their own self. They seek the realization of grandiose wishes for infinite power, success, and superiority. Histrionics exhibit themselves to others to create desire. In contrast, narcissists exhibit themselves to elicit admiration; they enjoy the worship they give themselves as much as the attention they receive from others. Histrionics follow popular fads and conventions and feign fragility and neediness as necessary to pull others back to them. Narcissists, in contrast, disdain dependency, viewing themselves as being above activities that subordinate their personal charisma to mundane group norms. For this reason, the narcissist remains above it all, calm and insouciant, whereas the histrionic is given to emotional displays that seem shallow, labile, and often desperate.

Finally, we revisit the antisocial and histrionic personalities. They both are impulsive, manipulative, stimulus-bound, and unable to anticipate the consequences of their behavior. Histrionics, however, often seem impulsive because of their dramatic, hyperemotional behavior, which is used to secure attention and nurturance. Alternatively, they may seem impulsive because of their cognitive style. Because histrionics are both hyperemotional and easily distracted, their attention may seem to move impulsively from one stimulus to the next, each receiving its own affective exclamations. Consequently, histrionics are less often engaged in blatant criminal behavior, with the exception of drug abuse. In contrast, antisocial impulsivity stems from an inability to delay gratification, especially where the release of aggressive impulses is concerned. Antisocials are bound by their drives; they fail to think ahead because their consciousness is absorbed by the possibility of immediate reward. In contrast, histrionics fail to think ahead because they want to minimize cognitive effort; awareness of the future invites the responsibility of choice, and histrionics repress that burden. Their distractible and impressionistic style is constructed to prevent deliberate consideration and cautious evaluation of a variety of alternatives.

PATHWAYS TO SYMPTOM EXPRESSION

Each personality style finds a path to dysfunction in its own particular way. In each case, a logic can be constructed that links expressed symptoms directly to the personality, development, and circumstances of the individual concerned. In general, the degree of symptom expression is associated both with the severity of the disorder and with the intensity of current life stressors. Thus, an individual who might be diagnosed as disordered, whose life is currently without stressful concerns, might easily be symptom-free, whereas a normally high-functioning individual encountering severe stress might develop an Axis I disorder. As you read the following paragraphs, try to identify the connection between personality and symptom.

Somatoform Disorders

Historically, the psychodynamic perspective has always considered illness-related symptoms, especially conversion symptoms, to be part of the hysterical personality. Today, such symptoms have been separated from their associated personality traits and classified as part of the Axis I disorders, irrespective of their association to the hysterical personality. Therefore, we see many other personalities exhibit somatic symptoms, notably, the dependent personality. Hueston, Mainous, and Schilling (1996) found that medical care use was highest for subjects at risk for histrionic and dependent personality disorders as opposed to all other personality disorders, a finding in keeping with our dancer, Yvonne, who suffered from pain for months with no apparent cause.

For histrionics, hypochondriacal concerns—the fear that you have some serious disease—and somatization disorder—physical complaints lacking a substantial basis—are used instrumentally to draw attention, comfort, and nurturance from others. Whenever the histrionic feels empty, isolated, or bored, the secondary gains become more tempting, so the disorder seems to be exacerbated. Finally, as noted by Benjamin (1996), frequent complaints of illness have often been associated with the female gender role, as it was with the patients Freud studied in his seminal investigations. For Benjamin, these somatic aspects are considered so important that they form a distinct subtype of the histrionic personality.

Dissociative Disorders

As with somatic symptoms, dissociation also has a historical association with the hysterical personality as viewed through the psychodynamic perspective. The hysterical phenomenon of forgetting what you know to be true, a motivated amnesia, was the original conundrum that led Freud to the discovery of the unconscious. Breuer and Freud, for example, noted two distinct states of consciousness in their famous patient, Anna O. For the histrionic, dissociation is simultaneously both a defense and a symptom. Because histrionics make extensive use of repression, they fail to integrate their various experiences into a single integrated conception of the self. As such, their mental architecture creates an enduring vulnerability to identity diffusion and other forms of dissociation during stressful periods.

However, dissociation also serves a protective purpose. By disconnecting their true selves from the theatrical poise they present to the world, histrionics prevent painful experiences from being processed to any depth. In effect, the existence of an integrated self is temporarily suspended until the storm blows over, preventing anguish, despair, or anxiety from surging into full conscious awareness. Note that because dissociative symptoms are so frequently associated with a history of childhood abuse, their presence should motivate clinicians to inquire about such a possibility.

Anxiety Disorders

Both dependents and histrionics are vulnerable to separation anxieties, though for different reasons. Histrionics increase their potential for anxiety through their tendency to seek diverse sources of support and stimulation. Because they quickly get bored with old attachments and excitements, their relationships are never truly solidified. Consequently, they often set themselves up to feel isolated and alone. Like borderline subjects, they may find themselves frantically searching for attention and approval until some new romance or excitement captures their interest. Subjectively, their discomforts are real but again tend to be overdramatized as a means of soliciting attention and support. Agoraphobia is probably more rare among histrionics than dependents, for histrionics naturally love to take center stage and become the center of attention in a social gathering. Likewise, phobias are probably rare, except where they constitute an image the histrionic wants to present.

Mood Disorders

In the histrionic personality, major depression usually stems from feelings of emptiness, boredom, or loss of dependent security, probably related to relationship problems; recall the case of Sheila, the semisuicidal sophomore. Given histrionics' characteristic tendency toward sensationalism, agitated symptoms are most common, accompanied by dramatic verbalizations of abandonment and helplessness. Their agitation, however, does not reflect the internal struggle that can occur with the negativist and obsessive-compulsive, but instead represents the direct expression of their feelings, though probably in an exaggerated form. Because histrionics think globally, they may simply report that they feel "incredibly awful" or "bad," emphasizing the intensity of their feelings without much further qualification. Consistent with their socially exuberant style, histrionics may also be susceptible to the development of manic or hypomanic disorders. Confronted with severe separation anxieties or anticipating loss of social approval, some histrionics intensify their habitual behaviors, becoming frantically congenial and hyperactive. Sheila may fall into this category.

Substance Abuse

Histrionics sometimes become involved in substance abuse. Alcohol, for example, liberates their already dramatic tendencies, while further deadening the self-insight that histrionics characteristically repress. The function of the abuse varies among these individuals. For Yvonne, substance abuse is consistent with a partying lifestyle, where it enhances stimulation and excitement. For Monique, substance abuse may have started the same way; after her second divorce, however, alcohol seemed to become important in distracting her from larger life problems. Stimulants may also be used to escape feelings of emptiness, helping the subject feel alive and energetic while supporting a natural tendency toward sensation seeking. Because histrionics are usually concerned about physical appearance, stimulants also provide a faster means of becoming slim and attractive. Those with an abundance of neurotic anxiety may use heroin or methadone as a means of self-medication. Given their lack of solid internal controls, the prognosis for histrionic substance abusers is probably poor.

Therapy

Histrionics rarely seek therapy for a variety of reasons. First, because our society confuses appearance and essence, high-functioning hysterical personalities readily find reward for good looks and charm. Implicitly or explicitly, they always have a source of rewards. Moreover, because their emotions are more authentic, hysterics are more likely to experience the subtle but nagging feeling that something is missing from life rather than full-blown depressive episodes. If their primary relationships remain solid, they may convince themselves that nothing is really wrong. After all, how could things go awry if all the technical indicators of house, car, and kids all look so good? Second, the more severe somaticizing variants have appropriate sources of attention: the care of their immediate family and the medical community. Because somatization is an unconscious mechanism, this subtype will not seek therapy directly, though they may be unsuccessfully referred. After a breakup, these individuals are usually found in the emergency room with mysterious symptoms or pain. When the couple reunites, the symptoms disappear. Third, histrionics who seek therapy do so mainly in hopes of finding immediate relief for anxiety or depression. Therapy requires introspection and objectivity, both of which are threatening or boring to histrionics; accordingly, when symptoms seem to remit somewhat, they move on. Finally, the demographic trends operating in psychotherapy run counter to what histrionics naturally prefer as their source of attention and support. As more and more women become psychologists, more and more female histrionics are deterred from therapy because they view women not only as contemptible but also as competitors with motives similar to their own. Rather than seek counsel with the enemy, female histrionics naturally seek male therapists.

THERAPEUTIC TRAPS

Therapy always involves potential unseen problems. For the histrionic, two complicating factors are particularly important to recognize. First, histrionics secure attention and approval by being charming and entertaining. Although they may seem emotionally forthcoming at first, their pseudo-intimate maneuvers betray a secret wish to simply find someone who will take care of them. The same pattern is likely to manifest in therapy. Because histrionics project omnipotence onto prospective mates, unaware therapists are particularly vulnerable. Supportive work comes naturally to many therapists and provides a good starting point for most cases once the patient's histrionic personality has been recognized.

For the patient, however, support can easily indulge pathological neediness. Here, the therapist may lose sight of the client's questions while reflexively dispensing emotional resources and falling prey to the wiles of the histrionic. Eventually the therapist feels drained of attention, support, and nurturance, as is expected, because that is how most individuals eventually experience the histrionic. Not surprisingly, this is the very pattern that therapy must divert; otherwise, when issues of termination arise, histrionics may shift from a demanding to a desperate dependence, featuring flairs of illness and manipulative suicidal gestures. As the client becomes more infantile, the therapist becomes more and more of a magical savior.

Whereas the first complicating factor is primarily interpersonal, the second contains two related themes that originate with the histrionic's feelings of incompetency. Over the course of normal development, most individuals acquire skills that enable them to survive as adults. In contrast, histrionics were reinforced for being attractive, not for developing valuable instrumentalities. As such, histrionic women frequently have a distorted impression of the female role in that their greatest fear is to be less feminine and unattractive—an inevitability for women who engender qualities beyond their appearance. Therefore, independent capacity equals differentiation between self and caretakers, which equals separation. In therapy, the implication is that getting better somehow entails hostile termination. The belief is that if they improve, the therapist may become angry and abandon them. Only slightly different from this is the requirement that therapy focus on the histrionic. Most therapists try to set goals with their patients; however, because histrionics want to be perceived as attractive, they may suggest goals that they feel will be alluring to the therapist (Fleming, 1990). Fortunately, these goals are often easily recognized, being vague and stereotypic of how therapy is portrayed in the media.

STRATEGIES AND TECHNIQUES

The need for attention and approval with the inappropriate sexualization of interpersonal relationships potentially manifests in therapy. Somehow, therapy must help histrionics give up the manipulative, demanding, and desperate dependence that causes them to orchestrate every social interaction. If subjects could simply be taught adult competencies outright or if their self-esteem could be magically raised, the problem would be eminently treatable. As with all personality disorders, however, the therapeutic mission is complicated by the tightly knit nature of different aspects of the personality, which serve the same functional purpose. In the histrionic, for example, a diffuse, impressionistic, distractible cognitive style merges with the need to keep the self protected from any reflection on its grave vulnerabilities. What is superficial is also protective. If this passive form of nonperception fails, repression is always at the ready.

Accordingly, the usual goals of therapy, which include making the unconscious conscious and producing a deep corrective emotional experience, run up against the needs of the histrionic style.

Writing from a cognitive perspective, Fleming (1990) suggests that histrionics must first learn to focus their attention. Given their flighty thought patterns, a detailed agenda can be invaluable, not only in terms of structuring long-terms goals but also in bringing order to a single session. Otherwise, patient and therapist may become distracted by tangential themes without problem solving anything in depth—talking about everything but doing nothing. Such is their style. Many are content to talk away the hour by reviewing every emotional nuance of their intersession activities. Fleming suggests that a brief period of time be set aside for this, if necessary.

Moreover, he suggests that it is important that goals be desirable to the patient, who may otherwise become threatened or bored and quit, but also reasonable for the pursuit of therapy. Goals that promise more immediate gratification can help keep subjects in therapy while helping them focus on one thing at a time. As noted previously, histrionics want to please their therapists, so it is important that their goals be their own. Globalized items can be further broken down into subgoals by asking patients how their purpose might be achieved. Introspection can be linked to reward by asking them how they would change were their goal achieved and why they chose a particular goal rather than something else. The act of thinking about and setting goals is conducive to identity development. Focusing also helps histrionics learn to identify automatic thoughts and confront impulsive tendencies, though unlike patients who naturally tend to ruminate, histrionics are not likely to record thoughts in a diary without repeated prompting and examples. Because this can be unstimulating, histrionics can be encouraged to write vividly and to challenge dysfunctional thoughts with dramatic defiance.

Interpersonally, histrionics often define themselves in terms of the individuals to whom they are attached. As noted in Benjamin (1996), the development of a personal identity that transcends relationships is a major objective. Assertiveness training can be used to help patients constructively put forward their own thoughts and agendas, rather than seduce others into solving their problems for them. Instruction in active listening skills, paraphrasing, and reflection can be instrumental in helping the client learn to pay more attention to the feelings of others (Turkat, 1990). Focusing on such previously unexamined matters, including major identity choices in adolescence (Benjamin, 1996), often helps integrate past experiences and sets the foundation for recognizing repeating patterns and their futile consequences. For example, many histrionics flit from relationship to relationship, without ever establishing a sense of security that they so much desire. Insight into relationship patterns should lead to less childish coping behaviors as well as greater levels of personal independence.

In addition, patients should understand that their theatrics and sexualization, particularly manifested in group social situations, signal an intense underlying desperation (Benjamin, 1996). If the subject makes this connection, dramatizing behaviors should become ego-dystonic, increasing motivation to change and, therefore, the likelihood that histrionics will remain in therapy long enough for change to occur. Many histrionics experience anxiety when they are no longer controlling the action as the center of attention. Mixing the interpersonal and behavioral, graded exposure may be used to delay enacting impulses to seize social center stage and to tolerate increasingly long periods during which attention is directed at others. Whether these goals are reasonable and whether they are successful depend on subjects' level of insight, which in turn depends on their level of object-relations pathology. More infantile subjects are more impulsive, more egocentric, less able to see themselves in context and, therefore, less able to understand how they perpetuate their own problems. In such cases, it is almost impossible for therapist and client to develop an alliance against the patient's maladaptive behavior patterns. Benjamin, for example, suggests that therapy begin with warmth and support but not indulge a position of neediness. What the therapist supports is change, seeking an alliance with the patient against patterns that perpetuate old problems.

Finally, the psychodynamic perspective assumes that problems have an origin in early family dynamics. Again, excessive dependency is seen as the unresolved unconscious. Fortunately, unconscious patterns of relating are repeated in the transference relationship, where they can be brought to the attention of the subject and related back to childhood dynamics. If the therapeutic relationship is sexually charged, a connection can be drawn between seductive in-session maneuvers and the subject's relationship with potential partners in general. If the therapeutic relationship is one of sexual competition, a relationship can be drawn between contempt for the therapist and the contempt that histrionics feel toward similar others, generally. Any such attempts to induce insight must wait until the therapist-client relationship is solid. Even so, many therapists find themselves frustrated by histrionic pseudo-insights or dramatized episodes during which the subject claims to suddenly understand or put the whole picture together, which are somehow forgotten by the next session. A brief period of review at the beginning of each session helps establish continuity across time and defeat tendencies toward distractibility, diffusion, and, especially, repression of previous gains. Histrionics need high praise for self-reliant and nonsexual behaviors, the reverse of their psychodynamic childhood pattern.

Summary

Histrionics can be described as seductive, indecisive, overemotional, demonstrative, and attention seeking, yet at the root of their character lies a basic feeling of helplessness and a need to make others the center of their lives. Histrionics put much of their energy into cultivating many superficial relationships and lack fidelity and loyalty not only to sexual partners but across all interpersonal relationships. Histrionic characteristics are a valued part of our culture. Friendly, expressive, and sociable people are often the life of the party (recall the classmate scenario at the beginning of the chapter). Oldham and Morris (1995) describe the dramatic style as those living their lives through sensation and romance in almost a theatrical way. The outgoing style (as described by Millon) is charming, with a zest for life that is contagious. The disorder, however, has a deficient sense of self-esteem, is cognitively global and diffuse, and uses sexual provocativeness inappropriately.

Several variants of the histrionic personality exist. Theatrical histrionics are chameleons, transforming themselves to fit each new situation. The infantile histrionic is a blend with the borderline personality, with rapidly changing emotions. The vivacious histrionic is a blend of extremely high levels of energy with many narcissistic traits. The appeasing histrionic is a combination of dependent and compulsive features, becoming syrupy sweet and good. The tempestuous histrionic personifies many borderline personality features, being intensely moody and having the least developed self-identity of the histrionics. The disingenuous histrionic is a blend with antisocial features, being manipulative and revengeful.

The modern-day histrionic personality grew out of a long history of the hysterical personality that can be traced back to ancient Greece but was really the cornerstone of the psychoanalytic movement. In the 1890s, Breuer and Freud hypothesized about the unconscious mechanisms that were at work in their famous hysterical patient, Anna O. Eventually, Freud discovered the defense mechanism of repression and, even more important, he proposed that hysterical symptoms were the result of unconscious instincts threatening to seep into consciousness. This discovery of secret wishes and unconscious desires has led to most of the major developments in psychoanalysis. A host of analysts who have written about various histrionic character types, including Kernberg, Reich, and Fromm, included the defense mechanisms—repression, sexualization, and dissociation—as integral personality components maintaining the histrionic type. The development of the hysterical character is still feverishly debated. Freud believed oedipal fixations were key, but modern analytic thinkers believe low-functioning hysterics have oral concerns and higher functioning hysterics, as Freud suggested, have issues related to the oedipal stage of development.

Cognitions and defense mechanisms are closely intertwined for histrionics. Their cognitions are scattered, diffuse, global, and overly simplistic. They possess a filter to keep out any ideas that are too detailed, philosophical, or concrete. Instead, they view the world through their own imprecise and overemotional lens. Their attention is extremely limited; thus they possess few schemas for making sense of our complex world and tend to make broad overgeneralizations. The histrionic also fails to develop a well-formed sense of identity, never identifying goals and putting together a life plan. Many believe that histrionics fundamentally feel inadequate and are unable to handle life; hence, they actively seek help from others by making themselves attractive and desirable. At the core, however, remain intensely negative beliefs despite the admiration and adoration of others.

Although at first histrionics seem attractive and charming interpersonally, eventually most people tire of their neediness and shallowness. Hence, histrionics cycle through friendships and sexual relationships quickly. From a social learning perspective, it is fairly easy to make sense of the development of a histrionic. Parents who reinforce desirable behaviors on a variable schedule force children to become more and more extreme and exaggerated in their behaviors to secure needed attention and nurturance. These behaviors cross over into other social interactions when they enter adolescence and learn to exploit their developing sexuality to capture others' attention.

There is some evidence of the role of biology in the development of the histrionic personality. Most of the evidence comes from research in sociopathy and the theoretical assumption that histrionic personality is the female expression of the antisocial personality. Assortative mating theory proposes that traits attractive to the opposite sex tend to become amplified over many generations and that histrionics have amassed a superabundance of these traits.

From an evolutionary neurodevelopmental perspective, the histrionic is referred to as the active and other-oriented personality. Histrionics actively work to bind others to them but only with the goal of collecting back-up alternatives to ensure a steady supply of affection.

While histrionics are easy to identify because of their drama and theatrics, they do share characteristics with the dependent and borderline personalities as well as the narcissistic and antisocial personalities. Histrionics are prone to developing certain Axis I disorders such as somatoform disorders, dissociative disorders, anxiety disorders, mood disorders, and drug and alcohol abuse.

Histrionics rarely seek therapy. However, several techniques may be of use in treating histrionics. The therapist must be alert to the histrionic's attempts to manipulate the therapist into indulging the client's need for endless nurturance. In addition, the client may have difficulty setting goals as self-improvement may run counter to the purposes of therapy. Cognitively, histrionics must learn to focus their attention and set goals for therapy. Interpersonally, they need to work on developing their own identity. What may prove useful in therapy is assertiveness training and active listening skills geared toward changing their old patterns of interaction.

Chapter 10

The Narcissistic Personality

Objectives

- What are the *DSM-IV* criteria for the narcissistic personality?
- How is narcissism expressed in a collectivist culture?
- The self-confident and asserting personalities are normal variants of the narcissistic. Describe their characteristics and relate them to the more disordered criteria of the *DSM-IV.*
- Explain how different personality styles combine to form each of the subtypes of the narcissistic personality.
- What are the distinctions between phallic and compensatory narcissists?
- How do narcissists use grandiosity, rationalization, and fantasy as defense mechanisms?
- How does the narcissistic personality disorder develop in the psychodynamic perspective?
- How do narcissists manifest their sense of entitlement interpersonally?
- Are the origins of narcissism a defense against early deprivations or the product of overvaluation?
- Explain the role of fantasy in an expansive cognitive style.
- What are the core beliefs of the narcissist?
- Narcissists share characteristics with other personality disorders. List these other disorders and explain the distinction between each and the narcissist.
- Are narcissists more likely to have extramarital affairs?
- Explain how narcissists can be vulnerable to Post Traumatic Stress Disorder (PTSD) and major depression.
- How is narcissism related to substance abuse?
- List therapeutic goals for the narcissistic personality.

We have all met people who constantly present themselves as superior, often with an inviolable arrogance. They seem to reflect on themselves in an exaggerated manner, getting lost in their self-generated fantasies of godlike power, infinite riches, master-mind intelligence, or unparalleled celebrity. They not only perceive themselves as better than others but also hold others in contempt for being inferior, if not just for being average. They are self-proclaimed shining stars, and we are expected to watch and admire. For them, the rest of us are simply worker bees, worthy only of taking and carrying out their every direction but not worthy of ever having an original thought, much less a life independent of their plans and desires. To balance out our indebtedness to them for the honor of their association, we must anticipate their every need and excuse them from any mundane duty, while working tirelessly toward the realization of their glory. Other people in their lives frequently come to feel as though they are possessions of such individuals, existing to be used and exploited without shame. Their egocentricity makes them indifferent to the rights and welfare of others and, sometimes, indifferent to the laws of society as well. To justify their actions, they rationalize ad nauseam, presenting convenient reasons that excuse their inconsiderateness and superior attitude, thus placing themselves in the best possible light. When pressed or confronted, they are likely to become even more haughty, dismissive, and, in some instances, enraged.

Such individuals demonstrate the *DSM-IV* **narcissistic personality** pattern. For the people who must interact with them, they are among the most difficult of the personality disorders. Consider the case of our self-proclaimed genius, Gerald (see Case 10.1), who obviously exhibits a grandiose sense of self-importance (see criterion 1). He identifies himself with Einstein and Salk, individuals who "had suffered nobly for being ahead of their time, just like me." Undoubtedly, Gerald's grandiosity is what fuels many of his behaviors. His arrogance leads him to assert that his problems lie in the company, not him, ignoring the fact that his relationships with both his supervisors and his subordinates are already strained to the breaking point. Others in this position would likely take time to reflect on their behavior when faced with a united front, rather than plow ahead foolishly in the face of negative feedback from both above and below in the organizational hierarchy.

Gerald, however, shows such self-importance as to persevere in spite of what he sees as others' ignorance. His grandiosity feeds a fantasy life where unbridled brilliance and success are realized (see criterion 2). He mentions, for example, that he sees himself as president of a new company that will put his ideas into action and he can only imagine that success is just a matter of time. More than likely, Gerald needs these fantasies, which support and protect a superior image of the self against intrusions from an above-average but much less stellar reality. Undoubtedly, his need for superiority has evolved in connection with the worship he receives from his mother, who insists that he will do something important, implying that he will become famous by somehow contributing to human history.

Though Gerald is obviously intelligent, as evidenced by a career that otherwise would likely have ended long ago, his perception is still distorted to magnify his aptitude. His estimation of his own abilities and his expectations that others should bow to his every whim speak to a considerable discrepancy between reality and his own aggrandized self-image. He believes that he is special, and he is pleased that he is being treated by a psychiatrist, for only someone with a medical degree would have a chance of understanding his situation (see criterion 3). Moreover, he feels so special that he is entitled to invent new ways of doing things that disrupt organizational patterns, without worrying about their effects on the lives of others (see criterion 7). Instead of offering sympathy, Gerald expects that his subordinates should simply recognize and automatically effect the wisdom of his intellectual mandate (see criterion 5). If there

CASE 10.1

Gerald stormed out of his supervisor's office, furious that he was on the edge of being terminated. He stubbornly resisted the demand that he seek counseling, asserting that the problem was the company, not him.

The immediate issue was his strained relationship with his supervisor and the subordinates in his office. Although his credentials were excellent, Gerald had ways of inventing new procedures that impacted standard routines without much sympathy for those affected.[1] Everyone was automatically expected to follow his whim. Sometimes his novel notions worked out, and sometimes they didn't. Regardless, the staff resented each such imposition on their time and their job descriptions. When things did work out for the better, Gerald gave only lip service to the role of his coworkers. — (7) (5) (6)

Worse, Gerald never gave up any of his ideas. He was sure they were superior to the "old ways" and would work if the staff could just "get their head out their ass long enough to see the big picture and just adjust for the better." "I do not know why the magnitude of my innovations isn't obvious to everyone," he has been heard to state. When asked how he sees himself in five years, Gerald remarks, "I'm a firm believer in the power of positive thinking. For the most part, it's old ways that hold us down. Wherever I've gone I've found new ways, new efficiencies, some of them startling. I can only imagine that in time I will be fantastically successful. It is my destiny." — (9) (2)

In fact, Gerald has been pushed out at other companies for making life difficult, just as he is creating problems now. Others, he asserts loudly, "either do not recognize my ability, or else are envious when they do." The problems with the office staff he attributed to jealousy. "They want to get me fired so I don't make them all look bad. In fact, I think some of them might be deliberately sabotaging me." The same was supposedly true of his supervisor. — (8)

Gerald also spoke about the "cretins" he was forced to work with, and how their incompetence constantly delayed him from finishing his own projects and implementing his latest ideas. Having been forced to associate with inferiors all his life, he was glad that a psychiatrist was treating him, because a medical doctor would have a better chance of understanding him and sympathizing with his plight. Asked to name people with whom he felt a bond, he mentioned Einstein and Salk, individuals who "had suffered nobly for being ahead of their time, just like me." — (9) (3) (1)

Gerald is the only child of a widowed mother, her "pride and joy." She has told him all his life that he would do something important. Ever thinking of others, he maintains an apartment next door so that she won't feel "so alone." The arrangement is ideal: he pays no rent, she does his laundry and makes his meals, and he has all the privacy he needs, as he always has. Indeed, he has come to expect such treatment from everyone. — (6)

[1] Numbers mark aspects of the case most consistent with *DSM* criteria, and do not necessarily indicate that the case "meets" diagnostic criteria in this respect.

Narcissistic Personality Disorder *DSM-IV* Criteria

A pervasive pattern of grandiosity (in fantasy or behavior), need for admiration, and lack of empathy, beginning by early adulthood and present in a variety of contexts, as indicated by five (or more) of the following:

(1) has a grandiose sense of self-importance (exaggerates achievements and talents, expects to be recognized as superior without commensurate achievements)

(2) is preoccupied with fantasies of unlimited success, power, brilliance, beauty, or ideal love

(3) believes that he or she is "special" and unique and can only be understood by, or should associate with, other special or high-status people (or institutions)

(4) requires excessive admiration

(5) has a sense of entitlement, i.e., unreasonable expectations of especially favorable treatment or automatic compliance with his or her expectations

(6) is interpersonally exploitative, i.e., takes advantage of others to achieve his or her own ends

(7) lacks empathy: is unwilling to recognize or identify with the feelings and needs of others

(8) is often envious of others or believes that others are envious of him or her

(9) shows arrogant, haughty behaviors or attitudes

are costs of extra time and effort to their own lives, these are inconsequential and not worth worrying about, at least from Gerald's perspective. Given such a sense of entitlement, Gerald can only exploit those around him (see criterion 6) and shamelessly does so repeatedly (see criterion 7).

Gerald has also created the perfect way of dealing with the displeasure of those he makes miserable: He sees them simply as jealous. Again, it is not Gerald who has the problem. As he sees it, everyone recognizes his outstanding abilities and realizes that he is on his predetermined road to success and riches. Therefore, they inevitably recognize their own unworthiness and, out of spite, put obstacles in his way (see criterion 8). Compared to him, they are just aspirants who can only want for something better but never achieve what they desire, as Gerald is destined to do.

In this chapter, we first compare normality and abnormality; then we move on to variations on the basic narcissistic theme. After that, biological, psychodynamic, interpersonal, and cognitive perspectives on the narcissistic personality are described. These sections form the core of what is scientific in personality. By seeking to explain what we observe in character sketches like Gerald's, the goal is to move beyond literary anecdote and enter the domain of theory. As always, we present history and description side by side, noting the contributions of past thinkers, each of whom tends to bring into focus a different aspect of the disorder. Developmental hypotheses are also reviewed but are tentative for all personality disorders. Next, the section titled "Evolutionary Neurodevelopmental Perspective" shows how the etiology and existence of the personality disorder follow from the laws of evolution. Also included are a comparison between the narcissist and other theory-derived constructs and a discussion of how narcissistic personalities tend to develop Axis I disorders. Finally, we survey how the disorder might be treated through psychotherapy, again organizing our material in terms of the classical approaches to the field described in the earlier parts of this chapter.

From Normality to Abnormality

Although it has appeared across the globe and throughout history among the royal and the wealthy, the narcissistic personality seems to have gained prominence only in the late twentieth century. Narcissism may manifest differently in other cultures (Warren & Capponi, 1995); our experience derives mainly from the more advantaged American middle and upper classes. The *International Classification of Diseases,* the international equivalent of our *DSM-IV,* does not include this personality disorder, indicating that its more American expression does not occur with frequency in other nations.

Instead, narcissism may be associated with higher levels of Abraham Maslow's (1968) hierarchy of needs. Individuals in disadvantaged nations must navigate the slings and arrows of disease and famine; they are too preoccupied with basic safety and survival needs and cannot afford the luxury of a passive existence where the riches of the world are, in their eyes, owed to them. However, as basic survival needs become satisfied, the quest for self-actualization moves into the foreground, at times along with pathologies related to more extreme forms of that quest, including the narcissistic personality disorder. Indeed, the risk is likely to be much lower in a collectivist society. Many Western societies, such as the United States, stress individualism and self-gratification at the expense of community. Moreover, the disorder seems more prevalent in professions that are unusually respected, including law, medicine,

FOCUS ON CULTURE

Culture and Narcissism

How Does Narcissism Differ in Collectivist Cultures?

Because individualistic cultures value self-identity over group identity, pathological narcissism fits well in that cultural climate. But how might it arise and be expressed in a collectivist society? In an individualistic culture, the narcissist is "God's gift to the world." In a collectivist society, however, the narcissist is "God's gift to the collective." Because of this special status, the collectivist narcissist is granted privileges within the group not generally available to others. For example, in fifteenth-century Spain, a collectivist culture, first-born males were regarded as *hidalgos* (literally, sons of something) and stood to inherit the family's wealth. Sons born subsequently were known as *segundones* (literally, second ones) and, because of their lower status in the family, had to make their own fortune. Not surprisingly, many Spanish conquistadors who came to the New World in search of their fortune were segundones.

Because the self develops in accordance with cultural patterns, you would expect different forms of the self to develop in different societies. Roland (1992) discusses the familial or we-self, more characteristic of collectivist cultures, and the individualized or I-self, more characteristic of individualistic cultures. In the United States, an individualistic society, the inner representation of the self emphasizes individuality and a self with outer boundaries that are rather impermeable. Accordingly, "individualistic narcissistic structures of self-regard . . . are relatively self-contained and independent" (Warren & Capponi, 1995, p. 79). In collectivist cultures, such as Japan, the development of the inner self "involves intensely emotional intimacy relationships" (p. 80), symbiotic reciprocity, and ego boundaries that are permeable and accessible to those in the collective. Accordingly, "narcissistic configurations of the we-self . . . denote self-esteem derived from strong identification with the reputation and honor of the family, groups, and others in hierarchical relationships" (p. 80).

and science, or those that boast celebrity status, such as entertainment, sports, and politics. For most of us, our immediate impression is that narcissists are more likely to be male than female (Rienzi et al., 1995), perhaps because males are widely considered more exploiting and entitled (Tschanz, Morf, & Turner, 1998).

This personality style is unusual, as the relationship between disordered narcissism and adaptiveness is less clear and direct than with other personality disorders. As with most personality styles, only a fine line separates normality from pathology—in this case, normal self-confidence and an artificially inflated sense of self-worth. On the other hand, because narcissism is intimately connected with self-regard, too little can be just as pathological as too much. Deficient self-regard typically implies feelings of incompetence, ineffectiveness, unworthiness, and inferiority, whereas excessive self-regard implies feelings of superiority, arrogance, grandiosity, and lack of empathy for others. Low self-regard can be paralyzing, if only because the individual hesitates to risk what little self-regard remains. The smallest possibility of failure is interpreted as another chance to lose. In contrast, individuals with an inflated self-regard may falsely believe that they can accomplish anything or that their accomplishments or contributions far exceed their true worth. Overconfidence causes them to dismiss realistic risks as somehow inapplicable to them.

The relationship between self-regard and pathology thus resembles the letter *U*. Being somewhat self-confident helps make you seem sociable and confident, but being too self-confident makes you seem arrogant and exploiting. Those in the middle—the so-called "healthy narcissists"—should demonstrate social concern and interpersonal empathy, a genuine interest in the ideas and feelings of others, and a willingness to acknowledge their personal role when problems occur (see Figure 10.1).

Several normal-range variants of the narcissistic style have been proposed, each built around some slightly different aspect of the total pattern. Because our society often values narcissistic traits (Lasch, 1978), you are likely to even find aspects of yourself in these brief portraits. Individuals with a **self-confident** style (Oldham & Morris, 1995) have a strong faith in themselves, believing they are special, exceptional, or even destined to do great things. Many have a powerful vision of themselves as hero, conqueror, or expert. Most often, they are frank about their ambition to realize their goals. Often, their enthusiasm and natural leadership create an aura that makes it easy to recruit others to their purpose. Most aim high and enjoy the battle to succeed. They enjoy the vision of being on top of their game, at the top of their field or profession, though they are not above envying others who may be more accomplished. Ever aware of their strengths, their equanimity is untouched by self-doubt. They expect others to acknowledge their specialness and treat them with respect, if not admiration. Sometimes, they may show their temper when crossed or slighted.

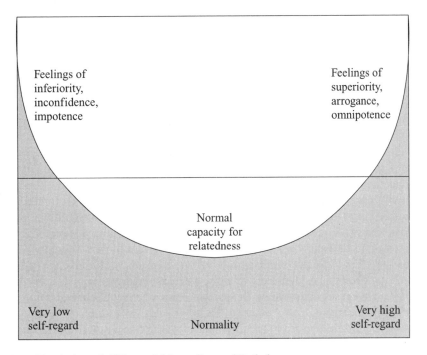

FIGURE 10.1 Narcissism, Self-Regard, Normality, and Pathology.

Millon et al. (1994) describe a similar, **asserting** pattern, though this style is more strongly competitive and self-assured. Such individuals exhibit a sense of boldness that stems from an unwavering belief in their own talent or intelligence. Ever ambitious, they naturally assume the role of leader, act decisively, and expect others to recognize and defer to their superior abilities. Beyond mere self-confidence, they are audacious, clever, and persuasive, charming others to their cause. At times, however, their self-regard may create a sense of entitlement—the feeling that they are special and, therefore, entitled to special treatment beyond what is merited by their role or by the conventional social courtesies.

The normal-range narcissistic style can also be portrayed by examining normal variants of the pathological traits found in the *DSM-IV* (see Sperry, 1995). The narcissistic personality exhibits a grandiose sense of self-regard, expecting their superior talent, ability, and intelligence to be recognized even in the absence of commensurate performance (see criterion 1). In contrast, the narcissistic style has a healthy sense of self-esteem based on genuine achievements but one that may overestimate inherent talents and endowments. Whereas the disordered individual is preoccupied with fantasies of almost infinite success, power, brilliance, beauty, or accomplishment (see criterion 2), those with the style project confidence rather than omnipotence and have more well-formed plans concerning how their goals can be achieved. Whereas the disordered feels a sense of specialness and affiliates only with others who are likewise special (see criterion 3), the style simply prefers the company of talented others, without feeling a strong contempt for individuals not similarly gifted. Whereas the disordered actively requires admiration and seeks to evoke displays of admiration from others (see criterion 4), the style gracefully accepts compliments and praise without excessive ego inflation.

For each of the preceding contrasts, Gerald falls more toward the pathological end of the continuum. Rather than value his ability at the extreme upper end of what realism might afford, Gerald compares himself with Einstein and Salk. In fact, his history argues that he has few actual accomplishments, as he has repeatedly been fired from one company after another. Instead of projecting confidence, Gerald needs to be fantastically successful. In fact, he sees this as his destiny. Far from enjoying the company of talented others, Gerald requires that those he associate with be "at the same level" as he. Anyone who runs afoul of his sense of greatness is automatically demeaned as an inferior, someone who lacks in the necessary ability to appraise Gerald appropriately.

Other diagnostic criteria can also be put on a continuum with normality. Whereas the disordered feels entitled to special treatment (see criterion 5), those with the style feel a sense of self-confidence and poise that often enables, rather than eliminates, humility. Whereas the disordered exploit others as a means to their own goals (see criterion 6), those with the style play the strengths of those around them, without making excessive demands of time or effort. Whereas the disordered is unable to empathize with the feelings of others (see criterion 7), those with the style can take distance from their own preoccupations and show sensitivity for others. Whereas the disordered is often envious of those who are more accomplished or successful (see criterion 8), the style is capable of admiring others as role models. Finally, whereas the disordered acts in an arrogant or haughty manner (see criterion 9), the style is simply self-confident and not incapable of generosity or altruism.

Again, Gerald falls more toward the pathological side. In putting his new ideas into play, Gerald automatically expects that others will see their merit and give him special treatment by making the necessary accommodations. Whereas the narcissistic style might draw the workers together, confidently present new ideas, and then actively solicit advice, thus helping others feel like part of a larger mission, Gerald exploits his subordinates' time and effort, while giving only lip service to their role in contributing to ideas that actually succeed. Rather than put himself in the shoes of those he affects, Gerald shamelessly shoves his new practices down their throats. Rather than take credit for both success and failure, Gerald attributes success to himself and failure to the envy of others working to undermine him behind the scenes. Finally, whereas the narcissistic style finds companionship or friendship in others regardless of their social or intellectual status, Gerald insists on associating only with those he perceives to be as gifted or credentialed as he.

Variations of the Narcissistic Personality

Few individuals in real life exist as the incarnation of an abstract psychological ideal. Instead, most persons combine aspects of two or more personality styles, though some combinations are more common than others. Whereas the previous section sharpened the contrast between various prototypes for explanatory purposes, in this section we portray narcissistic variants that are found as the disorder begins to shade toward other personalities (see Figure 10.2 for a summary). Actual cases may or may not fall into one of these combinations.

THE UNPRINCIPLED NARCISSIST

Unprincipled narcissists combine the self-confidence of the narcissist with the recurrent aberrant behavior of antisocial personality patterns. Many of these individuals achieve success in society by exploiting legal boundaries to the verge of unlawfulness. Others may inhabit drug rehabilitation programs, centers for youth offenders, and jails and prisons. Still others are opportunists and con men, who take advantage of others for personal gain. Most people who demonstrate a pattern combining these styles are vindictive and contemptuous of their victims. Whereas many narcissists have normal superego development, unprincipled narcissists are skilled in the ways of social influence but have few internalized moral prohibitions. They are experienced by others as unscrupulous, amoral, and deceptive. More than merely disloyal and exploitive, these narcissists show a flagrant indifference to the welfare of others, a willingness to risk harm, and fearlessness in the face of threats and punitive action. Vengeful gratification is often obtained by humiliating and dominating others. Joy is obtained by gaining the trust of others and then outwitting or swindling them. Their attitude is that those who can be taken advantage of deserve it.

Because they are focused on their own self-interest, unprincipled narcissists are indifferent to the truth. If confronted, they are likely to display an attitude of justified innocence, denying their behavior through a veneer of politeness and civility. If obviously guilty, they are likely to display an attitude of nonchalance or cool strength, as if the victim were to blame for not having caught on sooner. To them, achievement deficits and social irresponsibility are justified by expansive fantasies and frank lies. Those who display more antisocial traits may put up a tough, arrogant, and fearless front, acting out their malicious tendencies and producing frequent family difficulties and occasional legal entanglements. Relationships survive only as long as the narcissist has something

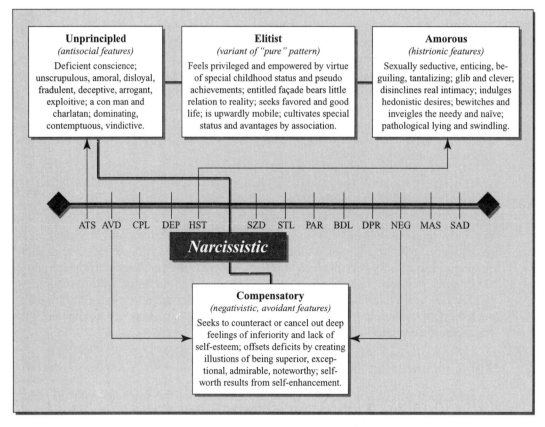

FIGURE 10.2   Variants of the Narcissistic Personality.

to gain. So strong is their basic self-centeredness and desire to exploit others that people may be dropped from their lives with complete indifference to the anguish they might experience or how their lives will be affected. In many ways, the unprincipled narcissist is similar to the disingenuous histrionic (a combination of histrionic and antisocial patterns; see Chapter 9). The unprincipled narcissist preys on the weak and vulnerable, enjoying their dismay and anger. In contrast, the disingenuous histrionic seeks to hold the respect and affection of those they dismiss in their pursuit of love and admiration.

THE COMPENSATORY NARCISSIST

The **compensatory** variant essentially captures the psychoanalytic understanding of the narcissistic personality (discussed in a later section of this chapter). The early experiences of compensating narcissists are not too dissimilar to those of the *avoidant* and *negativistic* personalities. All have suffered "wounds" early in life. Rather than collapse under the weight of inferiority and retreat from public view, like the avoidant, or vacillate between loyalty and anger, like the negativist, however, the compensating narcissist develops an illusion of superiority. Life thus becomes a search to fulfill aspirations of status, recognition, and prestige. Every small certificate and plaque the individual has ever received may be displayed on the office wall, for example. At other times, they may bore others while they present a complete biography of their most minuscule successes and achievements.

Like avoidant personalities, compensating narcissists are exceedingly sensitive to the reactions of others, noting every critical judgment and feeling slighted by every sign of disapproval. Unlike avoidants, however, they seek to conceal their deep sense of deficiency from others and from themselves by creating a façade of superiority. Though they often have a degree of insight into their functioning, they nevertheless indulge themselves in grandiose fantasies of personal glory and achievement. Some procrastinate in doing anything effective in the real world for fear of evaluation. Instead of living their own lives, they often pursue the leading role in a false and imaginary theater unrelated to the real world. When threatened with reality, they may defend themselves by becoming more and more arrogant and dismissive until the offending stimulus withdraws. If reality overturns their illusion completely, compensating narcissists may retreat more and more into an imaginary world of others who recognize their supposed accomplishments.

THE AMOROUS NARCISSIST

Amorous narcissists, who represent a blend of the core narcissistic temperament with traits of the histrionic, are often defined by the game of erotic seduction they play with objects of their affection. Their skill lies in enticing and tempting the emotionally needy and naïve, while fulfilling their own hedonistic desires and sexual appetites as they deem necessary. Although their game plan usually implies the possibility of an exclusive relationship, they are not inclined toward genuine intimacy, instead choosing to romance a number of potential conquests simultaneously. Some are sexual athletes whose designs call simply for sexual exploitation. They may seem to desire the warm affection of a genuine relationship, but when they find it, they usually feel restless and unsatisfied. Repeated demonstrations of sexual prowess often become an obsession, with "victory" only reinforcing their sense of narcissistic power. Having won others over, they quickly devalue their lovers and feel the need to continue their game elsewhere.

For the most part, their partners simply provide a warm body that they can temporarily exploit before boredom overtakes them. As such, amorous narcissists leave behind them a trail of sexual excesses and intricate lies as they maneuver their way from one pathological relationship to another. Confrontation, criticism, and punishment are unlikely to make them change their ways. Narcissists quickly dismiss such carping as the product of jealous inferiors. More than most, the amorous variety is likely to exhibit substantial *body narcissism,* attending scrupulously to physical appearance, clothes, and other external attributes.

THE ELITIST NARCISSIST

The **elitist** narcissist is somewhat reminiscent of Wilhelm Reich's (1933) "phallic-narcissist character." Such individuals are self-assured, arrogant, energetic, "impressive in . . . bearing" and "ill-suited to subordinate positions among the rank and file" (W. Reich, 1949, pp. 217–218). Like the compensating variant, these individuals construct a false façade, but one that amplifies an already superior self-image, not one that compensates for deep feelings of inferiority. Theirs is a fear, not of being inadequate, but of being ordinary.

Reich's phallic-narcissists, he asserted, were to be found among military men, pilots, and athletes. Real-world historical figures Napoleon and Mussolini serve as examples of the classic character. In today's Western society, we might add to this list many modern-day lawyers, surgeons, entrepreneurs, and other professions that naturally resonate with a swollen, aggressive courage Reich regarded as the cardinal trait of the phallic-narcissist. When carried to the logical extreme, such individuals fancy themselves as demigods who stand as a race apart from ordinary human beings, competing against one another for victory on the world stage with only a handful of worthy competitors. Many hold the common person in such contempt that they may be said to possess traits of the sadistic personality as well. However, the concept of the elitist narcissist is somewhat broader than Reich's phallic-narcissist. Whereas elitist narcissists revel in displays of power, the exhibitionism of raw self-assertion may also be focused on intellectual ability or the privilege of accumulated wealth; there are many ways to be swollen with aggressive confidence. Such individuals attend the most prestigious schools and academies, join exclusive fraternities, and associate only with members of their own social class.

Moreover, elitists are known to flaunt symbols of their status and achievement. Most idolize recognition and engage heavily in self-promotion. In whatever domain of activity interests them, they advertise themselves, brag about their achievements (whether substantive or fraudulent), and make everything they have done appear wonderful and impressive. Unrivaled in the pursuit of becoming "Number 1," many elitists actively create comparisons between themselves and others, turning personal relationships into public competitions and contests. By making excessive claims about themselves, elitist narcissists expose a great divide between their actual selves and their self-presentation. Many other narcissistic personalities recognize such disparities in themselves, but elitists are absolute in their belief of their grandeur. Rather than backing off, withdrawing, or feeling shamed when responded to with indifference, elitists accelerate their efforts all the more, acting increasingly and somewhat erratically to exhibit deeds and awards worthy of high esteem. They may present grandiose illusions about their powers and future status, amplify their limited accomplishments, and compete foolishly against others who have already eclipsed them in reality. Through such self-protective behaviors, elitists frequently alienate those around them, depriving themselves of the admiration and recognition they so desperately require, thus contributing further to their own troubles.

An example of two of the variations is the case of Leonardo (see Case 10.2), who might best be described as a mixture of the elitist and amorous subtypes. Leonardo describes himself as narcissistic, but asserts that he falls within the normal range. Moreover, he alleges that his self-confidence must be considered an example of the narcissistic style because someone disordered would not possess such considerable insight. Unfortunately, Leonardo is more correct than incorrect. Paradoxically, by preempting the therapist to create a rationale that seeks to discredit the possibility that the extremes in his personality style are problematic for him, Leonardo only exposes a need to protect an inflated and empty self-esteem. His lack of insight is expected given the defensive purpose of his assertion and only supports the diagnosis.

Other aspects of Leonardo's presentation are strongly consistent with the narcissistic personality disorder, particularly the elitist and amorous variations. Although it is conceivable that his family is indeed "one of the richest in Spain" and that his father has "greatly influenced the history of that nation," odds are that he is greatly exaggerating,

CASE 10.2

Leonardo is a second-year resident in the Department of Psychiatry. He is handsome, fair-skinned, with piercing blue eyes and blonde hair. His family owns several banks scattered throughout Spain. Both parents are noted for their service on the boards of charitable organizations. "My family is one of the richest in Spain," he says. "My father greatly influenced the history of that nation, as will I, and my sons after me."[1]   **(1)**

Leonardo has been asked to speak with a therapist because he believes psychotherapy training to be ridiculous. Apparently as a defensive maneuver, he attempts to head off a possible diagnosis by stating frankly, "I am, without doubt, a narcissistic personality. Everyone has a personality, and the narcissistic is the most adaptive. Were I in the disordered range, I would not be capable of such insight." When asked how he had arrived at this conclusion, Leonardo explains, "I am unique in many ways. I am well aware of my good looks. I've been successful with every woman I ever really wanted." Adjusting his tie, he immediately assumes the posture of a superior individual, with the therapist as his captive audience. "Medical school was easy," he continues. "I believe in destiny, and I believe that I am destined to be successful in everything I do. Furthermore, I have a very high IQ, and I doubt that there is anything of which I am not capable."   **(2) (2) (1)**

Apparently because the therapist was male, Leonardo began to use the session to discuss something of which he was truly proud, his many "conquests." Glowing with pride, he bragged about the women he had "bedded," offering details of their performance, giving each one a rating from 1 to 10 based on their looks and performance. He remarks that after sex, he makes them sleep on the couch, asserting, "I require the whole bed, or almost certainly will not awaken feeling refreshed."   **(4) (6) (7)**

Over the course of many sessions of therapy, Leonardo showed virtually no understanding of how his "narcissistic style" might lead to interpersonal problems, instead maintaining that "reality contact requires that I acknowledge my superiority. Anything else would be delusional." Moreover, he shows no insight into the pain those he had seduced and exploited might feel, even though he made them undying promises of love. When the point is pressed, he becomes angry, apparently believing that his looks and charm entitle him to such liaisons. "You wish only that you were like Leonardo," he charges, leaving the session in a huff.   **(7) (5)**

[1] Numbers mark aspects of the case most consistent with *DSM* criteria, and do not necessarily indicate that the case "meets" diagnostic criteria in this respect.

Narcissistic Personality Disorder *DSM-IV* Criteria

A pervasive pattern of grandiosity (in fantasy or behavior), need for admiration, and lack of empathy, beginning by early adulthood and present in a variety of contexts, as indicated by five (or more) of the following:

(1) has a grandiose sense of self-importance (exaggerates achievements and talents, expects to be recognized as superior without commensurate achievements)

(2) is preoccupied with fantasies of unlimited success, power, brilliance, beauty, or ideal love

(3) believes that he or she is "special" and unique and can only be understood by, or should associate with, other special or high-status people (or institutions)

(4) requires excessive admiration

(5) has a sense of entitlement, i.e., unreasonable expectations of especially favorable treatment or automatic compliance with his or her expectations

(6) is interpersonally exploitative, i.e., takes advantage of others to achieve his or her own ends

(7) lacks empathy: is unwilling to recognize or identify with the feelings and needs of others

(8) is often envious of others or believes that others are envious of him or her

(9) shows arrogant, haughty behaviors or attitudes

thus creating the aura of an impressive background that might somehow justify his arrogance and sense of entitlement. Although he does not have the swollen aggressive courage typical of the phallic-narcissist, an interpersonal quality, he is nevertheless interpersonally overbearing through his insistence on his own superiority, particularly his good looks and self-proclaimed high IQ, and his belief that he is destined for success in everything he does. Like other elitist narcissists, his beliefs are absolute.

Leonardo also has qualities of the amorous subtype. Evidently, his success at seduction forms the foundation of a hypersexualized masculine self-image. He creates the illusion of genuine affection, though it is obvious that his goal is really sex. Typically, he quickly loses interest in his current conquest, becomes restless, and seeks out a new female body to entertain him. His bragging to the therapist and his rating of the women are further evidence of a lack of empathy and a willingness to exploit those around him. In all likelihood, Leonardo believes that his impressive heritage and superior abilities entitle him to casual sexual access to most women and that his likely exaggerated autobiography of sexual triumphs only provides further evidence of his superiority.

Early Historical Forerunners

In spite of an apparent dearth of reported clinical cases of narcissistic personality disorder across the globe, this potential for excessive self-regard leading to involuntary self-destructiveness is apparently well recognized across culture and time. Ancient Greek mythology teaches us the perils of excessive *hubris* (roughly translated as "lack of humility") in the myth of Narcissus, a beautiful young man who, though loved by everyone, will not love anyone in return. His refusal eventually catches the ire of the goddess Aphrodite, who curses him. Ironically, he gazes into a pool and falls desperately in love with his own reflection. Each day is spent alone with his reflection, pining after what he cannot possess. Not knowing that it is his own image that he loves, he proceeds to seek "oneness" with his self-glorified image, and he promptly drowns himself in the pool. The myth thus seems to say that narcissists are unaware both of the intensity of their own self-love and how it affects the lives of others and that the act of unknowingly taking yourself as a lover ultimately leads to desperation and loneliness. If Leonardo were to be dismissed from his residency, a rough equivalent of drowning in an insufferable self-inflation, he could probably be regarded as a contemporary incarnation of this myth.

A variation on the same theme associates narcissism with a need for power (Joubert, 1998). In Christian history, for example, a pathological level of pride is painted as the original source of all evil. Sin enters the world because Satan is caught up in his own fantasies of omnipotence and brilliance, while refusing to humble himself before God. In a slightly different twist, some Eastern religions regard attachment to the self as part of the normal psychopathology of everyday life that must be dispelled before the person can achieve enlightenment. Though the exact nature of their beliefs is different, these traditions seem to agree that a preoccupation with the self is a formidable barrier to growth. Again, there are parallels in our cases. You can imagine, for example, Leonardo arguing with the chief of psychiatry about a diagnosis and refusing to back down. The same can be said for Gerald, our long-suffering Einstein, who has already run afoul of superiors and subordinates alike. The self is their entire life, and giving up a devotion to the self would be tantamount to death.

The following three sections offer a detailed portrayal of the narcissistic personality as expressed in its psychodynamic functioning, interpersonal behavior, and cognitive style and contents. As with the other clinical chapters of this text, history and description are presented side by side. As you read these sections, you will gain a broad-based perspective of the narcissistic prototype. Read not only for history but also for the characteristics that each thinker unearthed and their significance within the total personality pattern.

The Biological Perspective

The role of biological influences in the narcissistic personality seems especially unclear. Although evidence adduced in support of biogenic determinants for most of the other personality patterns was largely of a speculative nature, there was some, albeit tenuous, logic for these speculations. In the case of the narcissistic pattern, however, where the existence of distinctive biophysical precursors seems lacking, conjectures would have unusually weak grounding; thus, none are proposed. However, some observations about mood and temperament, presumably of a biophysical nature, are noted here.

Narcissists are often seen as being possessed of a buoyant mood and an optimistic outlook under usual circumstances, provided they have managed to settle into an environment that does not meaningfully threaten their sense of superiority. Cheerful and carefree in affect, this personality pattern enjoys an unusually relaxed demeanor, likely because of established self-glorifying cognitions that may routinely and immediately pacify any temperamental tendencies toward reaction to everyday annoyance. However, should this shield be penetrated, a rapid turn may take place. This change may take the form of either an edgy and irritable mood marked by interpersonal friction, or it may be manifest in repetitive bouts of dejection characterized by feelings of emptiness, worthlessness, or humiliation.

Since little evidence for the development of the narcissistic personality can be provided from biological sources, we must trace the roots of this pattern among psychogenic influences.

The Psychodynamic Perspective

After the ancient historical incarnations of this personality pattern, many centuries passed before narcissism was given an explicit psychological definition. In 1898, Havelock Ellis, an English psychologist, used the term *narcissus-like* (A. P. Morrison, 1986) in reference to excessive masturbation, whereby the individual becomes his or her own sexual object. Rank (1911) published the first psychoanalytic paper specifically concerned with narcissism, linking it to vanity and self-admiration (cited in Pulver, 1970). Amazingly, Freud published only a single paper devoted exclusively to narcissism in 1914, discussing it as a libidinal investment in the self that, in healthy and reasonable quantities, would ultimately give way to mature object-relationships. The central question to Freud was how the infant, living in a universe composed only of the self, which he called *primary narcissism,* developed an appreciation for the existence and identity of others.

Today, the psychoanalytic literature about narcissism is so voluminous that it resists summary. The term continues to have multiple meanings that are not easily distilled into single formulation. As noted by Pulver in 1970, narcissism has become somewhat of a paradox, being one of the most important, yet most confusing, contributions of psychoanalysis. Stone (1993) regards the problem of its definition as being rivaled only by the term borderline. Currently, psychoanalysis remains divided between rival formulations of narcissism, namely the self psychology of Kohut (1971, 1977) and the object-relational theory of Kernberg (1975, 1984, 1989b, 1989c), which provide two alternative and competing accounts of narcissism.

The route from Freud's 1914 paper to contemporary conceptions is long and twisted, and space does not permit its review here. Whatever the underlying dynamics proposed, however, adult traits reminiscent of the personality disorder saturate historical portrayals, allowing continuity with contemporary conceptions. W. Reich (1933, pp. 217–218), for example, described the phallic-narcissistic character as "self-assured, sometimes arrogant, elastic, energetic, often impressive in his bearing," exhibiting a "flagrant display of superiority and dignity." Significant reactions to psychoanalytic theory began in the mid-1930s, including the emergence of the neo-Freudian schools of ego psychology, object relations, and social theory. These theorists stressed the primacy of relatedness rather than of self and, therefore, began to develop a deficit model of narcissism as stemming from problems in early relationships with caretakers (McWilliams, 1994). In contrast, because Freud's instinct model was purely intrapsychic, he could speak of narcissism only as an exaggerated self-cathexis, that is, a libidinal investment of self, as if the self were taken as a lover. If relatedness is primary, however, it follows that narcissism can only derive from a pathology of early relatedness, that is, a pathology of object relations.

These developments did not take place all at once but instead accrued slowly over time. Karen Horney (1939, pp. 89–90) regarded narcissism as essentially representing self-inflation, which, "like economic inflation, means presenting greater values than really exist," loving and admiring the self without adequate foundation, and expecting the same from others. Fenichel (1945) regarded narcissists as racing from one achievement to another but with no real satisfaction, only later realizing that the purpose of their pursuit lay in concealing a deeper emptiness. A. Reich (1960, p. 58) developed the compensatory theme that many analysts believe underlies narcissism, noting that the "exhibitionistic drive contains contempt for those whose admiration is needed." Rosenfeld (1964) noted narcissists' idealized self-image and their tendency to pervasively deny any and all deviation from perfection. Can you identify such personality facets in Leonardo and Gerald?

Although narcissists use a variety of defense mechanisms, contemporary psychoanalytic accounts stress grandiosity, rationalization, and fantasy. Narcissistic patients are often talented, with some sustained period of success or creativity (Ronningstam, Gunderson, & Lyons, 1995), yet they possess a highly unrealistic self-image. In classical analytic terms, narcissists convince themselves that they have become the ego ideal incarnate (Freud, 1914/1925), living a perfect and superior existence that they believe everyone should admire. Their grandiosity may become so extreme that they see themselves as omnipotent and invulnerable. They are capable of anything and resistant to everything. Similarly, they may assert that they do not need others because needing someone would imply some boundary to their power or imply that they are incomplete.

Narcissists have a tough job because perfection is viewed as either all or nothing: If you are not perfect, you are imperfect, and if you are imperfect, you are nothing. This ego ideal must then be projected as a public persona whom others must appease with sacrifices of admiration and submission. Anything short of this ideal tarnishes the self, squashing perfection outright and leading to chronic feelings of emptiness or shame. Gerald is very resistant to making any accommodations to his workplace because this would imply that he was wrong or had failed to consider something important. Similarly, even after many sessions of therapy, Leonardo shows no insight into how his actions might hurt the women he's exploited. Narcissists cannot tolerate any flaw, however small, in the perfection of the self.

Because of this intolerance, narcissists must find ways of dealing with information that is foreign to their perceptions—data that tell them that they exploit others, they make mistakes, it is they who are envious, and so on. Much of this information is simply denied or repressed, but more elaborate defenses are also frequently employed. Narcissists often use rationalization to construct alternative realities that draw on the actual substance of events but change their significance to excuse blunders and exploitations. Once a scenario is found that saves face and puts the narcissist in the best possible light, it replaces the previous version of events and becomes the working model of reality on which the narcissist proceeds. This may lead to some strange role reversals: The narcissist does not exploit others; others should be flattered that the narcissist consorts with them. The narcissist doesn't make mistakes; the narcissist is a visionary who pursues dreams others cannot possibly understand. The narcissist is not a dictator, but an enlightened autocrat. Many more variations routinely take place in the experience of these individuals. Almost undoubtedly, Leonardo believes that his conquests should be thankful they were judged worthy to be conquered by him, just as Gerald probably believes that his subordinates are privileged to work in his presence.

Such extensive use of rationalization gives us insight into the architecture of the narcissistic mind. On first impression, the internal world of the narcissist seems intelligent, solid, and substantial. Few ideas are so cherished, however, that they cannot be tailored for the admiration of an audience. When incriminating evidence surfaces, narcissists put a subtle spin on events, convincing both themselves and others that they were right all along, everything was worked out in advance, and it was all part of their grand plan. Far from being ideologically grounded, the internal world of the narcissist is wrought with flimsy constructions put together for temporary, convenient, or defensive purposes. Current rationales need not be defended as absolute, for they can always be reconfigured for new purposes as they arise. A convenient, rather than principled, interpretation of the world and a willingness to shift interpretations as necessary to support their own egocentric goals speak to a laissez-faire superego that afflicts many narcissists. Morality and values are simply a constraint on the subject's unbounded desire for omnipotence.

One of the foremost contemporary descriptions of these personalities is expressed in the Diagnostic Interview for Narcissism. As previously mentioned in Chapter 4, one of the best ways to study a construct is by examining the content of established instruments. By surveying the content on which the instrument is focused, clinicians quickly gain an appreciation for how traits of the larger personality pattern combine. In a series of studies, Gunderson and Ronningstam constructed the Diagnostic Interview for Narcissism, now in its second edition (Gunderson & Ronningstam, 1990). They began by reviewing three prominent diagnostic systems: the *DSM-III* (APA, 1980), Akhtar and Thomson (1982), and Kernberg (1983, 1985b). Augmented with comparisons with their own clinical experience, they created a tentative item list describing pathological narcissism as it might be expressed in the clinical interview. After evaluating the ability of each statement to discriminate narcissistic patients from other patients with a mixed group of personality disorders, the first edition of the interview was formed. In its second edition, 101 questions are grouped into 33 descriptive statements, which in turn are grouped into five topic areas. Listed in Table 10.1, these statements provide a quick and empirically supportable summary of pathological narcissism.

How does the narcissistic personality disorder develop from the psychodynamic perspective? Freud (1914, p. 48) was aware that pathological narcissism could develop because of parental overvaluation, stating that parents "are impelled to ascribe to the child

TABLE 10.1   Summary Statements from the Diagnostic Interview for Narcissism

Grandiosity (The person . . .)
   . . . Exaggerates talents, capacity, and achievements in an unrealistic way.
   . . . Believes in his invulnerability, or does not recognize his limitations.
   . . . Has grandiose fantasies.
   . . . Believes that he or she does not need other people.
   . . . Regards self as unique or special compared to other people.
   . . . Regards self as generally superior to other people.
   . . . Behaves self-centeredly and/or self-referentially.
   . . . Appears or behaves in a boastful or pretentious way.

Interpersonal Relations (The person . . .)
   . . . Has a strong need for admiring attention.
   . . . Unrealistically idealizes other people.
   . . . Devalues other people, including feelings of contempt.
   . . . Has recurrent and/or deep feelings of envy toward other people.
   . . . Reports being or behaves entitled, i.e., has unreasonable expectations of favors or other special treatment.
   . . . Appears or behaves in an arrogant, haughty, or condescending way.
   . . . Is exploitive, i.e., takes advantage or uses other people.
   . . . Lacks empathy (is unable to both understand and feel for other people's experiences).
   . . . Has been unable to make close, lasting emotional commitments to others.

Reactiveness (The person . . .)
   . . . Is hypersensitive.
   . . . Has had unusually intense feelings in response to criticism or defeat.
   . . . Has behaved or felt suicidal or self-destructive in response to criticism or defeat.
   . . . Has reacted with inappropriate anger in response to criticism or defeat.
   . . . Has had hostile, suspicious reactions in response to the perception of others' envy.

Affects and Mood States (The person . . .)
   . . . Has sustained feelings of boredom.
   . . . Has sustained feelings of meaninglessness.
   . . . Has sustained feelings of futility.
   . . . Has sustained feelings of hollowness.
   . . . Often feels emotionally impoverished: Yearns for deeper emotional experiences.

Social and Moral Adaptation (The person . . .)
   . . . Has superficial and changing values and interests.
   . . . Shows disregard for unusual/conventional values or rules of society.
   . . . Has corruptible moral and ethical standards.
   . . . Has broken laws one or a few times under circumstances of being enraged or as a means of avoiding defeat.
   . . . Has recurrent antisocial behavior (scored negatively in this section, does not indicate narcissism).
   . . . Exhibits sexual behavior that includes perversion, promiscuity, and/or lack of inhibitions.

Adapted from Gunderson and Ronningstam, from "The Diagnostic Interview for Narcisstic Patients" in *Archives of General Psychiatry,* copyright © 1990.

all manner of perfections which sober observation would not confirm, to gloss over and forget all his shortcomings" and even "the laws of nature, like those of society, are to be abrogated in his favour." Only and oldest male children were especially vulnerable. Horney (1939, p. 91) remarked, "Parents who transfer their own ambitions to the child and regard the boy as an embryonic genius or the girl as a princess, thereby develop in the child the feeling that he is loved for imaginary qualities rather than for his true self." The case of Gerald, for example, mentions that he is the only child of a widowed mother, her "pride and joy," and his mother has told him all his life that he would do something important.

More recent psychoanalytic opinion has often been divided between the object-relations theory of Otto Kernberg (1975, 1984) and the self-psychology of Heinz Kohut (1968, 1971, 1977). Both theorists are summarized in Summers (1994), to which the following is indebted. For Kernberg (1975, 1984), the narcissistic personality is essentially a defensive organization. Narcissists fail to develop integrated conceptions of self and other object-images. In other words, their object-representations are split into all-good and all-bad components, much like other personalities functioning at the borderline level (see Chapter 14 on the borderline personality for a more extensive discussion of this concept). Narcissists, however, develop an intrapsychic organization that compensates somewhat for identity diffusion and rapidly changing emotions. To achieve a more cohesive self, narcissists fuse the ideal self, ideal object, and self-image, an explanation reminiscent of Freud. Although such a fusion distorts reality, it nevertheless permits greater continuity of experience and a measure of social adaptation.

In Kernberg's formulation, then, the narcissistic personality is a compensation, a defense against early developmental arrest. Fusion of self-image and ideal self leads to conceptions of grandiosity and omnipotence, as exemplified in notions that one is brilliant, ahead of the times, deserves to be famous, and so on. It is clear from this perspective, then, how any minor faults in this unyielding personality landscape would tear at the soil composing the person's psychic defenses, opening pathways to acute psychological symptoms. Gerald, for example, probably fears that his abilities do not measure up to his ambitions, yet if his insecurities and true beliefs about the self were available for conscious inspection, he would probably be overcome with depression and would accomplish nothing. His self-deception is both created and supported by his mother, who long before set his standard for "what is worthy and unworthy," as for his conviction that his destiny is incontrovertibly to "do something important." This is also why Gerald is so angry with his coworkers. By resisting his changes and insisting on realism, they fall far short of the admiring ideal other who automatically complies with the narcissist's desires.

While this fusion of ideal self and self-image explains the grandiosity of narcissists, the fusion of the ideal other and self-image explains their need for admiration and sense of entitlement. The ideal other is admiring to the point of being reverential and fully devoted to sustaining the illusion of the narcissist's central and unrivaled importance. Moreover, because the ideal other is merged with the ideal self, those who associate with the narcissist should be perfect as well. Imperfections in others are incongruent with the self-image and often lead to expressions of ridicule and contempt. This is one reason Gerald expresses such disdain for his coworkers; rather than automatically dispense admiration and automatic compliance with his notions, they understandably resist his entitlement and press for realism, an enemy of grandiosity. As Kernberg (1967, p. 655) notes, narcissists "present an unusual degree of self-reference in their interactions with other people, a great need to be loved and admired by others, and a curious apparent contradiction between a very inflated concept of themselves and an inordinate need for tribute from others."

Kernberg's theory stresses that the family environment is fundamental in instigating the development of grandiose fantasies. On the one hand, caretakers are likely to be cold and indifferent, perhaps even sending messages that are implicitly spiteful and aggressive. Obviously, this damages the self-concept and sets the stage for the development of some pathological means of self-esteem regulation. Given an inferior or inadequate self-concept, the child is ready to embrace some saving defensive mechanism. The family supplies this by finding in the child some exceptional talent, perhaps the role of family genius, which becomes a refuge from the inferior or inadequate self, thus offsetting parental neglect and rejection. If circumstances rule out an integrated, normal self-identity, a grandiose self becomes attractive, if only because this is the only self the caretakers are willing to accept. Although pathological, such love requires adoption of the compensatory genius or special role, a means of up-regulating self-esteem in the face of a family environment devoid of authentic warmth and love.

Most of the time, according to Kernberg (1975, 1984), the grandiose self holds control. Remember, though, that the grandiose self is an adaptation that conceals not only an inadequate, defective self, but also oral rage—an intense, hidden aggression originally intended for caretakers unwilling to offer unconditional love. This rage is always lurking in the unconscious, ready to be vented against anyone who withholds a steady supply of compliments or, worse, anyone who is critical. Lovers or spouses who were the subject of idealization may suddenly find themselves completely devalued as the all-good image is replaced by an all-bad, persecutory image. Because the grandiose self is a compensation, narcissists are highly sensitive to comments that seem to disparage the qualities of their sacred self-image. The more fragile the grandiose self, the more sensitive narcissists are and the more easily oral rage is brought to the surface.

The writings of another analytic theorist, Heinz Kohut, focused largely on narcissistic personality development. The movement spawned by his writings, which were considered esoteric even for psychoanalytic literature, is now influential well beyond psychoanalytic circles. This movement has become known as **self-psychology,** named for Kohut's integral addition of the self to the classical analysts' pillars of human nature: the instinctual sexual and aggressive drives of the id and the moderating psychic structures of ego and superego. In the classical model, the self is considered a function or subset of the ego. In contrast, Kohut makes the self the central focus of development, the essence of what it means to be human. Kohut regards the self as complementary, as finishing the natural evolution of psychoanalysis that began with the drive model, not as its replacement. Again, this summary is indebted to Summers (1994).

As with Freud, Kohut holds that development begins in a state of unawareness called **primary narcissism,** in which no self yet exists. Fortunately, the child begins life with a mother who responds to his or her needs, nursing and nurturing empathically. Soon, the infant realizes that rewards come not from inside the self, but from the external world, and develops what are called **self-objects.** These are not just basic images of others, but perceptual interpretations of others as they are important to the self. In the beginning, the infant expects absolutely perfect nurturing—to be changed or fed immediately as needed. However, because no mother is capable of perfect nurturance, the child soon begins to feel uncertain about whether needs will continue to be met. With this uncertainty comes an overwhelming sense of vulnerability. To compensate, the child seeks to return to the bliss of primary narcissism by idealizing the parent, once again perfectly nurturant, and by developing a grandiose self, which provides a sense of omnipotence. Kohut thus paints the grandiose self not as a pathological intrapsychic structure, but instead as a normal developmental phenomenon. As normal empathy subsequently develops, the grandiose self will eventually be given up and incessant, infantile demands will gradually be transformed into realistic ambitions. Developmental arrest occurs, however, when maternal empathy at this stage is grossly defective; then, the grandiose self continues as a defense against the vulnerabilities of an unkind world. See Summers (1994) and Greenberg and Mitchell (1983) for more comprehensive discussions of self-psychology.

The Interpersonal Perspective

As stated in previous chapters, the interpersonal perspective focuses on transactions between sender and receiver in interpersonal communication. Each participant negotiates the content of the exchange so that, ideally, both parties receive messages congruent with their self-image and feel validated. Communications that are not validating support some alternative conception of self and are experienced as anxiety provoking.

Leary (1957) developed the interpersonal circle in an effort to refine and systematize the insights of Sullivan and the socioanalytic perspective of Horney, both of whom reacted to Freud's instinct model by developing psychoanalysis in an interpersonal direction. For Leary, narcissists demonstrated a competitive self-confidence founded on "adjustment through competition." Such individuals, he states, seek superiority and are terrified by dependence. Subsequent interpersonal circles have refined Leary's original contribution using more contemporary methods. Kiesler (1996, p. 21) regards narcissists as acting "presumptuously forward," "incapable of self-criticism," and "impossible to embarrass." He uses descriptors such as brazen, cocky, boastful, pushy, egotistical, self-enthralled, and "unable to ask for help with anything." Leonardo certainly demonstrates these qualities, and we can see that neither he nor Gerald acknowledge needing anyone else for anything.

Although the descriptors offered by Leary (1957) and Kiesler (1996) provide a concise summary of the interpersonal conduct of the narcissistic personality, other classic characteristics might be mentioned as well. Entitlement, as described frequently in previous sections of this chapter, is a central, defining feature of this personality pattern. Narcissists consistently expect special treatment, often as if they should hold diplomatic immunity to rules and conventions. Whereas ordinary persons should be required to abide by behavioral codes, many narcissists, especially those with a poorly developed superego, believe they should be exempted from shared standards of social living; conformity simply does not apply to their circumstances. Rules, laws, and oaths are instruments designed to keep the masses in line. Accordingly, rules should be evaluated on a case-by-case basis and dismissed where the end justifies the means or where abiding by the rule introduces too much red tape or otherwise constitutes an unreasonable restriction on free action. Making such an evaluation would be a sticky affair for any normal superego, but narcissists somehow always find themselves qualified.

Moreover, many narcissists break accepted interpersonal and social standards in a concerted effort to establish themselves as exceptional, to reinforce their own self-image of being special and unique, or to avoid defeat (Gunderson & Ronningstam, 1990). After all, only someone special can go unpunished. Some even flaunt their transgressions to competitors, and fellow narcissists may even compete to determine who can successfully take the most shortcuts; the most flagrant rule-breaker wins. Such individuals hug the boundaries between the narcissistic and antisocial personalities. In extreme cases, their self-centered exploitiveness may take on an almost diabolical quality. M. Scot Peck's (1983) portrayals of evil have been seen by some as mixing narcissism and moral corruption (Klose, 1995). Not all narcissists are like this. There are certainly those with good superego development; this alternate variant of the personality pattern often incorporates moral values into an exaggerated sense of superiority. Here, moral laxity is seen as evidence of inferiority, and it is those who are unable to remain morally pure who are looked on with contempt.

The sense of entitlement characteristic of narcissistic personalities also extends to the person, identity, and time of other human beings, where it merges with another cardinal trait: lack of empathy. Sometimes, it extends to the physical bodies of others, as with sexual harassment or domestic violence (Rothschild, Dimson, Storaasli, & Clapp, 1997). Narcissists are entitled to expect special favors, without offering anything in return. To simply do unto others as you would have them do unto you is insufficient, perhaps even mocking. Because others must know that the narcissist is an exceptional person, normal courtesies are often viewed as insulting.

Nowhere else are the interpersonal difficulties of narcissistic personalities so evident than at home, where the family is mandated not only to willingly defer to their desires but to anticipate their needs, excuse them from the pedestrian chores of everyday life, and remove obstacles from their way. It is not uncommon for narcissists to experience several divorces over the course of their lives (Beck et al., 1990), largely because of their sense of entitlement and tendency to berate others for the slightest imperfection, while putting their own actions in an unrealistically positive light (Gosling, John, Craik, & Robins, 1998). Not surprisingly, their mates often possess masochistic traits or at least a near-pathological measure of self-doubt. The masochist is attracted to the self-confidence of the narcissist, who accepts the deference of the masochist and his or her willingness to sacrifice the self to the entitlement of the narcissist. Unfortunately, the masochist always falls short of the idealized other, earning the masochist unending contempt. Worse, narcissists often fear that intimacy may be used to control them (Nelsen, 1995) and, therefore, may act out angrily against others when, in fact, they are reacting against feelings of vulnerability common to all relationships.

It may be obvious by now that the families of narcissists customarily must play second fiddle in terms of personal priorities. Anyone without direct relevance to the pursuit of personal glory is left at the periphery of the family system. Family members are not perceived as real persons with their own hopes, dreams, and aspirations, who need shared time with a caring mother or father, but as part of the furniture of existence. The family is valued only in terms of what its members might mean to the narcissist, rather than in terms of what they might mean to themselves. Children may be exhibited as baubles for their smarts or beauty, but the love they receive is contingent on their remaining so. This egocentric worldview makes it almost impossible for narcissists to grasp their abuses of others, either explicitly, through a sense of entitlement, or implicitly, by failures of authenticity in relationships. This, according to McWilliams (1994, p. 175), is the most "grievous cost" of narcissism, a "stunted capacity to love."

As with all of the personality patterns, not all narcissists exhibit flagrant, obvious hallmarks of the disorder. At this point in your study of personality patterns, you are likely realizing that there is not a singular pattern for each disorder, but many admixtures; likewise, the intensity of a disordered pattern ranges from muted to highly brazen. Our next case (see Case 10.3) concerns familial imbalance. Chase clearly demonstrates many aspects of narcissistic personality disorder and could be diagnosable as such, but he also is much less grandiose than Gerald or Leonardo. Chase and his wife are in family therapy because everything in their lives revolves around him. His wife admits that he is talented and imaginative, characteristics to which she was probably attracted from the very beginning. Now, however, she has realized that despite his good qualities, Chase is simply not emotionally available to her and takes her for granted in the relationship. This problem extends to the entire family; Chase's wife notes that he tends to "objectify" their two children. In addition, rather than spending time with the family, Chase is spending all of his free time on his novel, an achievement he feels will bring him national fame and tremendous wealth, which would alleviate any monetary concerns he or the family could possibly face. In the interim, however, he earns only a small check for his ghostwriting, and the financial difficulty this presents only exacerbates the couple's presenting problem. Probably because he fears criticism, he lets no one read his masterpiece, although he hints that the therapist might be allowed, as he may just "make the cut" of who is qualified and capable of appreciating his work.

The grandiose self usually makes a good first impression, appearing calm and carefree. These are qualities frequently mistaken for evidence of genuine strength, and only later do they become painfully transparent as arrogance or snobbishness. Many narcissists see themselves as too superior to be bothered by everyday hassles and instead prefer that others see them as unruffled by the strains of ordinary existence. To stress over meeting a deadline, for example, is simply beneath them, for it would indicate that they are just like everyone else. Instead, many present the image of just floating along through life, effortlessly enjoying their gifts of intelligence and success. Reversing Edison's dictum, they would have us believe that their life is 99% inspiration and just 1% perspiration. The good that happens they attribute to their own control (Ladd, Welsh, Vitulli, & Labbe, 1997), for their superior abilities ensure that the normal prerequisites to achievement, hard work and struggle, are suspended.

Other narcissists do not wish to be perceived as carefree but rather as confident and in control. They are the movers and shakers, manifesting power over their dominion by calling the shots and making the deals. Such individuals invest a great deal in their public image, frequently holding positions such as corporate executives, lawyers, and stockbrokers. For these individuals, impressive displays of material wealth and power—the prominently displayed sports car or elegant mansion—are all calculated to induce awe and admiration in the observer. Their conspicuous consumption and intense hypercompetitiveness in interpersonal relationships go far beyond what normal and adaptive levels of self-esteem require (P. Watson, Morris, & Miller, 1998) and speak clearly to underlying feelings of inadequacy.

Also noteworthy in the interpersonal domain is the extraordinary sensitivity to perceived slights. Many narcissists combine a conscious image of specialness with deep, unconscious feelings of inferiority, and this conflict renders them particularly disposed to perceive injury or insult. Therapists, for example, may run afoul of narcissistic vulnerability simply by making supportive comments. Attempting to induce hope

CASE 10.3

Chase entered marital counseling at the demand of his wife, who insisted that he was "selfish and totally preoccupied with work." "Our world," she states, "revolves completely around Chase. His desires. His moods. His comfort. Everything is catered to him."[1] She admits that "he's a good guy, basically, with talent and imagination," but that was no longer enough. She wanted an equal partner, someone to spend time with, someone to feel intimate with, someone who would appreciate her, whereas he wanted, she stated, "a mother, a maid, and an occasional sex slave."

In therapy, Chase seemed friendly but self-satisfied and faintly disdainful. He talked at length about his writing, a novel that he hoped would bring him national fame and tremendous wealth. All his time was spent working on it, making chapters and creating dialogue. His only source of income was his ghostwriting, from which he earned a small paycheck. "Expressing creativity," he explained, "is my way of fulfilling myself." Nevertheless, he would let no one read his masterpiece. He hinted, however, that he might show it to the therapist, because "both of us have a deep concern for character and its development. I think a psychologist might be able to appreciate it."

In the third session of couples therapy, Chase revealed that alcoholism was an important factor that created problems in the marriage. During occasional bouts of drinking, he became self-condemning and irritable. Sometimes, his anger was displaced toward his wife, whom he accused of being the cause of his failures, having seduced him into marriage, putting obstacles in his way, and failing to appreciate the work he showed her. "She doesn't like anything I write!" he blurted out. "That's not true," she replied in disbelief. "I like most everything you write, and when you ask for feedback, I give it. I don't need to lie to you, do I?"

Chase recalls an isolated childhood during which he was expected to perform above and beyond the other children. Usually, he was successful, but occasionally suffered tirades from his own alcoholic father, for whom "nothing was ever good enough." Nevertheless, for the most part, his parents regarded him as "the boy wonder, the little genius of the family." Peer relationships were pleasant, but never close. Others thought of him as snobbish, an impression he admits he still encourages, because it signified that he was "more intelligent than the rest of the kids."

---

[1] Numbers mark aspects of the case most consistent with *DSM* criteria, and do not necessarily indicate that the case "meets" diagnostic criteria in this respect.

Narcissistic Personality Disorder
DSM-IV Criteria

A pervasive pattern of grandiosity (in fantasy or behavior), need for admiration, and lack of empathy, beginning by early adulthood and present in a variety of contexts, as indicated by five (or more) of the following:

(1) has a grandiose sense of self-importance (exaggerates achievements and talents, expects to be recognized as superior without commensurate achievements)

(2) is preoccupied with fantasies of unlimited success, power, brilliance, beauty, or ideal love

(3) believes that he or she is "special" and unique and can only be understood by, or should associate with, other special or high-status people (or institutions)

(4) requires excessive admiration

(5) has a sense of entitlement, i.e., unreasonable expectations of especially favorable treatment or automatic compliance with his or her expectations

(6) is interpersonally exploitative, i.e., takes advantage of others to achieve his or her own ends

(7) lacks empathy: is unwilling to recognize or identify with the feelings and needs of others

(8) is often envious of others or believes that others are envious of him or her

(9) shows arrogant, haughty behaviors or attitudes

in a depressed client, a therapist might comment, "Many others just like you have traveled the same road and yet gone on to recovery." Sensing that similar problems mean similar outcomes, most people would feel reassured. Narcissists, however, are likely to feel insulted, as if thinking, "What do you mean others just like me? There is no one else like me, and if you have the ability to understand me, you would already know that!" Some narcissists realize that anger would only disclose their vulnerability, so they hide their sensitivities. Others perceive themselves as belonging to some exceptional class of human beings and may not react at all, even to overt insults, especially if received from someone of obviously inferior status. Those who hurl insults are beneath contempt. By remaining unruffled, narcissists conceal the vulnerability of the self and prove that others are unworthy of upsetting them.

Not surprisingly, most narcissists eventually make boring conversationalists. At first, their sense of self-confidence and talk of their grand schemes are interesting and entertaining. Narcissists usually respond enthusiastically, because every willing listener is an opportunity for them to hear themselves talk and soak up yet more admiration and attention. Yet, when listeners share an event from their own life, they are likely to be interrupted as the narcissist either reasserts control over the conversation or resumes self-referential oration. Again, egocentricity prevents them from taking any interest in the inner world of others, who are not permitted to talk about themselves for long. The only thing of importance is the narcissist and what affects the narcissist. The achievements and agendas of others are irrelevant, except where they might provide a stepping stone for the narcissist's own ambitions. Eventually, most persons tire of such friendships, realizing that their destiny is to remain self-objects (Kohut, 1971), never to be known for who and what they are. For this reason, many narcissists excel at making acquaintances but fail at making friends. When asked who their friends are and what they enjoy most about them, narcissists often talk around the question.

Lacking genuine friendships and believing in the superiority of the self, many narcissists replace intimate friendships with a circle of loyal admirers. Because they see their ideas as revolutionary, they often invoke religious metaphors to describe their quest. Rather than mere associates, their loyal followers are regarded as disciples or aspirants, members of the inner circle, much as Freud's followers were in the early period of psychoanalysis. Such individuals walk a fine line. They must be special enough to rise above the ignoble horde of humanity. However, they must also be flawed in some way that prevents them from rivaling the narcissist. As extensions of the ego, they glow only by virtue of the master's own reflected light. Fortunately, if they are completely loyal and admiring, their leader's projections of grandiosity will transform them into idealized, perfect beings, whose brilliance is ensured through their participation in the glory of the great guru. Moreover, they must not have their own independent ideas, but only ideas that reinforce those of the leader, without adding anything substantial. Originality is not met with enthusiasm, but with disdain, as it implies that the prophesy of the master is as yet somehow incomplete—something must be integrated that the prophet could not supply. Freud's feuds with his disciples are notable illustrations of this point; certainly Gerald would be much happier if his coworkers would just conform to his self-image and begin admiring him.

Many narcissists have a degree of insight into their situation. Given their inability to connect with others and develop a shared history of love or work, narcissists often report feeling a sense of boredom or meaninglessness. Needing to be above everyone, narcissists salvage their own esteem and create an aura of specialness but doom themselves to a pretty lonely life. After all, emotional intimacy requires that two people strip away the illusion of power and status differences between them, creating a vulnerability intolerable to the narcissist. Realizing this, some narcissists long for more authentic and deeper emotional experiences to offset the empty worship they give themselves and receive from others.

The interpersonal development of the narcissistic personality has been sketched in detail by Benjamin (1996). Her account differs from the contemporary psychoanalytic accounts of Kernberg and Kohut, both of whom portray the disorder as a compensation or defense against early deprivations. Although narcissists seek to perfect the self, Benjamin holds that the force behind their development is actually parental overvaluation or at least a need for the child to be perfect. Following Freud (1914), Benjamin refers to the narcissist aptly as "His Majesty, the Baby." As she sees it, the early history of the narcissist personality is full of intense warmth and love, an adoration tantamount to worship. So exclusively focused are the parents on making the child feel special that they fail to disclose their own feelings and needs. As a result, the child fails to learn that others are separate beings with their own legitimate identity who might be fulfilled in ways other than basking in his or her presence.

Toddlerhood, the period of time characterized by the psychoanalytic schools as the "anal stage," is perhaps the most critical period in the development of pathological narcissism, according to the interpersonal perspective. It is here that the infant's budding sense of omnipotence runs headlong into the frustrations of reality. Whereas in early infancy, caretakers necessarily respond quickly and automatically to every demand, toddlerhood features the development of autonomy, important for the definition of the self. According to Benjamin (1996), the discipline that normal parents administer during this period teaches children that their actions affect others and that others are real persons, too. The parents of future narcissists, however, continue to indulge their children, remove all barriers to their progress, and fail to indicate how the children affect them. Without such messages, children can develop only an inconsiderate and insensitive egocentricity, a total lack of empathy. When no one is there to anticipate their needs, Benjamin states, such children are astonished. Naturally, as adults, they expect favors and indulgences and become rageful when these things are not immediately forthcoming, requiring instead "great dedication, overwork, and heroic performance from the people associated with him or her—without giving any thought to the impact of this pattern on their lives" (p. 150). Gerald again fulfills this pattern. His mother makes his meals and does his laundry, as she always has. This is exactly the unquestioning conformity that Gerald expects from everyone.

The final factor that Benjamin suggests is a subtle but "ever-present threat of a fall from grace" (1996, p. 146), an element that perhaps accounts for the emphasis on perfection of the self. The caretakers admire the child excessively but do not permit mistakes. The child is to be glorious and perfect, and the parents refuse to tolerate any hint of error, for then the child would be glorious and perfect no more. The covert message might be phrased, "You are glorious and perfect, and we love you for it. But don't screw it up, because if you do, it's over." All of us have both good and bad things about ourselves, but for the narcissist, the result is failure to tolerate any hint of imperfection, which immediately leads to feelings of emptiness and severe self-criticism. We see this in the case of Chase, who was expected to perform above and beyond the other children. For the most part, he succeeded, becoming the "little genius" of the family. Nevertheless, Chase has a vicious introjection: the condemning voice of his alcoholic father.

When Chase drinks, this voice surfaces, and he becomes irritable and self-condemning, finally blaming his wife for his own shortcomings.

The Cognitive Perspective

As with many other personality disorders, the cognitive style and defensive needs of narcissists merge almost seamlessly, always operating to support their sense of grandiosity. Narcissists play fast and loose with reality, altering and recomposing facts extemporaneously to reinforce their pet notions, a style Millon (1990) termed *expansive*. Some leaders of third-world governments or extremist political movements, for example, may mix dreams of omnipotence with paranoid trends (Miliora, 1995). Likewise, on a smaller scale, the association between narcissism and abuse of power by grandiose charismatic types within organizations is well known (Sankowsky, 1995); reality is refashioned as needed to retain followers and preserve a special status.

Whereas normal persons have realistic goals that balance their own needs with those of others, narcissists project themselves into an idealized future featuring unbounded fantasies of success and admiration. Their imagination is often so vivid that the future may seem to lack any dimension of contingency. Instead, fantasy is experienced with a compelling intensity that rivals reality itself, as with Leonardo, who "knows" his destiny holds immeasurable success. The power, ability, and glory of the self become a spectacle to be played and replayed repeatedly in the imagination. And because the narcissist provides both actor and applause, the applause is always a standing ovation, and the plot never becomes worn or tiresome, however often it is repeated. Those who admire the narcissist often make their own contribution, as did Gerald's mother, who has always told him he will do "something important," and Chase's parents, who insisted he become the "boy wonder." Interestingly, but not terribly unusual for intelligent, creative narcissists, we find with Chase that fantasy has actually been harnessed for an adaptive purpose—his writing.

By substituting fantasy for reality, narcissists reinforce their sense of omnipotence and justify their arrogance in the real world. Commoners become kings, and kings become gods. For the compensating narcissist, imagination provides a means of both protecting the underlying vulnerable self and warding off shame. In effect, were it not for the presence of a grandiose self, these individuals would resemble the avoidant personality, who feels shamed because of the pathetic and defective person they believe themselves to be. In contrast, with Millon's earlier biopsychosocial (1969, 1981) and contemporary evolutionary (Millon, 1990; Millon & Davis, 1996) conceptions of the narcissistic pattern, fantasy serves to exhibit the self for its own pleasure. Compensation is not required, and fantasy functions more to extend the indulgence of early caretakers than to defeat some obnoxious inadequacy lurking at the edge of conscious awareness.

The use of fantasy is not limited to the future but also extends into the past. We have noted the continuity between cognition and defense and have already remarked in our discussion of the psychodynamic perspective that narcissists rationalize and reconstruct. As cognitive theorists emphasize, there is no objective reality that the mind records and remembers. Instead, overlying sensation and perception is a layer of interpretation consisting of individualized constructs (Kelly, 1955), that is, personal concepts about ourselves, others, and the surrounding world. Although the significance of objective events is open to discussion, most of the time we share a consensual reality with those close to us, and we can at least agree on the events the past contains. In contrast, narcissists write personal fables. They revise their personal history to amplify objective successes and excuse, minimize, or transform failures in an effort to protect their own vulnerable self-esteem or reinforce their current positions. They remember the past as they would have wanted it to occur, not as it actually happened. Such reconstructions might not be called lies, because they often shift the emphasis of events or aspects of the situation. The future provides the narcissist an opportunity for glory, and the reconstruction of the past provides the continuity through which fantasies of brilliance or success can be given a substantial basis.

Many narcissists make the past and present much more hostile to their ambitions than it really was or is. In so doing, the individual feeling and experiencing personal failures has a means of deflecting personal responsibility. They may contemptuously assert, for example, that years of their life have been lost to the ignorance of others, who failed to recognize the true merits of their ideas or achievements or inadvertently stood in their way out of narrow-minded conventionalism or lack of courage to change. On the other hand, those experiencing personal triumph may then magnify their success still further by creating scenarios in which only omniscience or omnipotence could possibly overcome the trials and tribulations set forth before the conquering hero. Either way this is directed, it is an example of the narcissistic pattern's expansive cognitive style serving to execute a reversal of depressive realism, operating in the service of self-inflation rather than self-criticism. Gerald certainly comes to mind here. According to his assertions, he has been forced to work with "cretins" all his life, and their incompetence constantly delays the implementation of his brilliant ideas. If he does succeed, he will not only feel justified and vindicated but also want to advertise the ignorance of others to the world, making himself that much more impressive because of his victory.

Excessive use of fantasy also contributes to lack of empathy for others. While immersed in their reveries, narcissists focus their mind on a vague time in the future, at a point where their aspirations have already been realized. Achievement here is not a process or a personal growth experience. Questions about how their fantasies are to be logically and tangibly realized get in the way of feeling the glory. Worse, such detail work is incongruent with their self-image as synthesizers of information, visionaries, or strategists attuned to the big picture. Again, Gerald is a good example. He doesn't stop to think how his changes might affect others. He has no appreciation of how the particular cogs of the business come together from the ground up, instead seeing only the big picture painted in his own mind.

After the big decisions are made, the rest is merely grunt work, to be delegated to some toiling troglodyte whose job is not to question why, but only to effect the narcissistic will. As mere mortals, rather than original thinkers, such individuals work behind the scenes and inevitably receive little or no credit for the final production. Nevertheless, they are held responsible when things go wrong. Because narcissists refuse to involve themselves in the actual work of pulling off their objectives, they typically fail to realize the magnitude of what is required of their subordinates. When their workers fail to do the impossible, it is not that narcissists have overreached what is realistic but that the talent of their underlings is lacking. By confusing wish and reality and refusing to break goals into subgoals, narcissists act as if their will alone were sufficient to alter reality and bring their goals into being. For narcissists, what has been delegated has already been accomplished, an attitude that both controls and pressures those who work with them. Ultimately, this is why Gerald's coworkers resent him.

In many ways, the cognitive style of the narcissist is opposite that of the compulsive. Whereas the narcissist can't see the trees for the forest, the compulsive can't see the forest for the trees. Narcissists fail to fill in the details and instead paint the future with broad, confident, impressionistic strokes. In contrast, compulsives are plagued by detail; they meticulously hunt down every piece of missing information and eventually get lost in the indecision that results from trying to predict all possible outcomes for every possible action. The narcissist plunges ahead as if there were no barriers to what might be achieved but somehow forgets the logistics and mechanics of the actual work involved. In contrast, the compulsive frets endlessly about every small item, to the point that the overall purpose of the work is lost. The fantasies of the narcissist are wishes that focus on bringing about a future in which the self succeeds and is thus glorious and admired. In contrast, the fantasies of the compulsive are fears that focus on preventing a future in which the self errs and is thus contemptible and condemned. Both seek perfection but embrace only half of the equation. The narcissist is too proactive and ambitious; the compulsive, too preventative and cautious. Contrast the case of the indecisive dean or the hypercritical graduate assistant (Cases 7.2 and 7.3) with the long-suffering Einstein or the Romeo resident (Cases 10.1 and 10.2).

Writing in Beck et al. (1990), Denise Davis notes that the desire of narcissists to be unique encourages a number of cognitive distortions. First, narcissists are prone to dichotomous appraisals of themselves and others. Particularly during periods of stress, narcissists vacillate between an all-good and an all-bad image of the self. Sometimes, they see themselves as worthy and omnipotent; at other times, however, reality breaks through and they see themselves as worthless and powerless. Their opinion of others may also vacillate, depending on their perceived level of gratitude or loyalty. Narcissists with paranoid trends, for example, usually believe that others have become envious of their position or ability. Such individuals may see their friends, family, and coworkers as completely loyal and trustworthy on one occasion but as possibly having secretly conspired with the enemy on the next. This is especially likely where the narcissist has constructed a house of cards on the edge of collapse, perhaps some entrepreneurial or quasi-legal misadventure.

Second, Davis notes that narcissists often take notice of small differences between themselves and others. Again, their purpose is the justification of self-esteem. Because narcissists naturally eclipse all others, they cannot afford to be too similar to those around them, as this jeopardizes their special status. To support a sense of superiority they secretly doubt, narcissists search for differences and then build on these differences as a means of preserving their unique status. Whatever it is that stands out about the narcissist is amplified and reconstructed as objective evidence of his or her exceptional stature. The cognitive view is thus not too different from the psychodynamic perspective, which holds that narcissists idealize others but are ready to find fault with them.

The cognitive contents, the fundamental beliefs of the narcissistic personality, are easily inferred on the basis of their behaviors and traits. Core beliefs are those held by the individual as timeless truths. For example, because narcissists act arrogant and dismissive, we can safely assume they possess a strong belief in their own superiority. Beck et al. (1990, pp. 50–51) list their core beliefs as including, "Since I am special, I deserve special dispensations, privileges, and prerogatives," "I'm superior to others and they should acknowledge this," and "I'm above the rules."

Whereas core beliefs are universal and eternal, conditional beliefs express possibilities contingent on certain assumptions. For the narcissist, Beck et al. (1990, pp. 50–51) list examples such as, "If others don't recognize my special status, they should be punished," and "If I am to maintain my superior status, I should expect others' subservience." In addition, Beck lists, "Strive at all times to insist upon or demonstrate your superiority." Such statements crystallize the assumptions through which the narcissist approaches and interacts with the surrounding interpersonal world. Many others could be added to capture additional dimensions of the narcissistic personality not mentioned by Beck. Thus, "If I am not perfect, I am nothing," might be listed as a conditional belief for the compensating narcissist, as might, "If I get involved in working out my plans at too great a level of detail, I will fail."

The Evolutionary-Neurodevelopmental Perspective

By definition, perspectives offer only limited insight into any given phenomenon. Because personality refers to the matrix of the total person, a theory adequate to embrace personality must exist at a level of analysis equal to personality itself. Perspectives are only parts, not wholes, and cannot accomplish this goal.

According to the biopsychosocial-evolutionary theory (Millon, 1990; Millon & Davis, 1996), the narcissistic personality is passively self-oriented. Such individuals turn primarily to themselves for gratification and do not perceive a need to engage in the requisite give and take necessary to live in a community. The developmental pathway to this strategy is often relatively straightforward, as portrayed in the interpersonal tradition. Here, caretakers overvalue the self-worth of the future narcissist by providing noncontingent praise, attention, and tribute. Narcissists fail to develop the motivation and skills ordinarily necessary to elicit these rewards. Merely being who they are is sufficient; thus, narcissists come to value themselves regardless of their real attainments. Nothing should be required to elicit admiration or performance from others. Instead, narcissists feel nothing more is needed than to just be themselves.

Indeed, parental overvaluation through the stages of neuropsychological development may be seen as a core factor in the development of narcissistic patterns. Feelings of omnipotence begin shortly after birth but do not take hold in a meaningful fashion until the sensorimotor-autonomy stage. Every minor achievement of future narcissists is responded to with such favor as to give them a deluded sense of their own extraordinary self-worth. Extreme confidence in your child need not be a disservice if it is well earned. In the case of the future narcissist, however, a marked disparity exists between the child's actual competence and the impression he or she has of it.

Failures in parental guidance and control play an important role during the intracortical-initiative stage. The child is encouraged to imagine, explore, and act without discipline and regulation. Unrestrained by the imposition of parental limits, the child's thoughts and behaviors may stray far beyond accepted boundaries of social reality. Untutored by parental discipline as to the constraints of fear, guilt, and shame, the child may fail to develop those internal regulating mechanisms that result in self-control and social responsibility.

At other times, the developmental route to narcissism is circuitous. Both Kohut and Kernberg, for example, see the inflation of the self as a compensation for early deprivations. Contemporary psychoanalytic theorists recognize both possibilities. Stone (1993), for example, states:

Narcissistic traits can develop, curiously, when there are deviations from ideal rearing on either side: pampering or neglecting; expecting too much or too little. Excessive praise of a child . . . can give rise to . . . feelings of superiority, of being destined for greatness. . . . But compensatory feelings of a similar kind can arise where there has been parental indifference and neglect. (p. 260)

Ramsey, Watson, Biderman, and Reeves (1996) have given some research support to the idea that dual developmental pathways underlie pathological adult narcissism, noting that narcissistic subjects often report either highly permissive or highly authoritarian parents.

Table 10.2 presents a full cross-domain synopsis of the narcissistic personality.

CONTRAST WITH OTHER PERSONALITIES

As with the personalities you have encountered in earlier chapters, the narcissist shares many traits with other personality patterns. As before, examining the evolutionary model for the functional significance of these shared traits within the total personality highlights important distinctions.

Both narcissists and histrionics can be charming, and both enjoy being the center of attention. The histrionic actively and constantly seeks the attention of others, often to repress a subtle but uncomfortable sense that the self is void or empty. Psychodynamic thinkers contend that the narcissist shares this self-impression, using a grandiose self to cover up a deep sense of inferiority. However, histrionics view themselves as attractive and sociable, whereas narcissists view themselves as talented and exceptional. They feel so exceptional, in fact, that they expect others to recognize and admire them without any effort. When this does not occur, they socialize with the singular goal of redirecting others back to where the attention must be focused; after this point, they may then return to being a passive receptacle of worship. Too much interpersonal involvement would convey dependence, and dependence is a weakness. Narcissists thus prefer to remain above the need for relationships. In contrast, histrionics may desperately desire relatedness and work to create a "fund of attachments" that can be exploited. Moreover, in the normal range, histrionics can be warmly expressive and involved in the conventions and fashions of life. Narcissists, however, are above convention: It is only others who must live by rules and subordinate themselves meekly to standards. The rules narcissists live by are those they incidentally accept or those they create for themselves.

Disdain for shared standards of social living often leads to confusion between the narcissistic and antisocial personalities. Both exploit others to their own advantage. Narcissists, however, are passive in so doing and largely unaware of the relevance of manipulating others. Theirs is not the scheming, promise-breaking exploits of the antisocial. Instead, their self-centered convictions of entitlement lead them to believe that others simply owe them, whereas the antisocial is deliberately deceptive and ruthless. Moreover, the two disorders differ markedly in their daily worldview. The narcissist manifests an attitude of insouciant calm, being above the stresses of everyday life. In contrast, the antisocial sees the world as an intrinsically hostile place where everyone is a potential aggressor and impulsive anger serves a functional purpose: The best

TABLE 10.2   The Narcissistic Personality: Functional and Structural Domains

Functional Domains		Structural Domains	
	Haughty	**Self-Image**	**Admirable**
Expressive Behavior	Acts in an arrogant, supercilious, pompous, and disdainful manner, flouting conventional rules of shared social living, viewing them as naïve or inapplicable to self; reveals a careless disregard for personal integrity and a self-important indifference to the rights of others.		Believes self to be meritorious, special, if not unique, deserving of great admiration, and acting in a grandiose or self-assured manner, often without commensurate achievements; has a sense of high self-worth, despite being seen by others as egotistic, inconsiderate, and arrogant.
	Exploitive	**Object-Representations**	**Contrived**
Interpersonal Conduct	Feels entitled, is unempathic, and expects special favors without assuming reciprocal responsibilities; shamelessly takes others for granted and uses them to enhance self and indulge desires.		Internalized representations are composed far more than usual of illusory and changing memories of past relationships; unacceptable drives and conflicts are readily refashioned as the need arises, as are others often simulated pretentious.
	Expansive	**Morphologic Organization**	**Spurious**
Cognitive Style	Has an undisciplined imagination and exhibits a preoccupation with immature and self-glorifying fantasies of success, beauty, or love; is minimally constrained by objective reality, takes liberties with facts, and often lies to redeem self-illusions.		Morphologic structures underlying coping and defensive strategies tend to be flimsy and transparent, appear more substantial and dynamically orchestrated than they are in fact, regulating impulses only marginally, channeling needs with minimal restraint, and creating an inner world in which conflicts are dismissed, failures are quickly redeemed, and self-pride is effortlessly reasserted.
	Rationalization	**Mood/ Temperament**	**Insouciant**
Regulatory Mechanism	Is self-deceptive and facile in devising plausible reasons to justify self-centered and socially inconsiderate behaviors; offers alibis to place self in the best possible light, despite evident shortcomings or failures.		Manifests a general air of nonchalance, imperturbability, and feigned tranquility, appears coolly unimpressionable or buoyantly optimistic, except when narcissistic confidence is shaken, at which time either rage, shame, or emptiness is briefly displayed.

Note: Shaded domains are the most salient for this personality prototype.

defense is a good offense. Thus, narcissists call others to worship and seek respect through the fact of their superior existence; the antisocial often draws territorial boundaries and obtains respect through fear.

Despite their differences, the two disorders can occur together (see sections titled "The Unprincipled Narcissist" earlier in this chapter and "The Covetous Antisocial" in Chapter 5 for two characterizations of these variants). The result catalyzes the worst qualities of both, with particularly vicious consequences for society. When the egocentricity, lack of empathy, and sense of superiority of the narcissist cross-fertilize with the impulsivity, deceitfulness, and criminal tendencies of the antisocial, the result is a psychopath, an individual who seeks the gratification of selfish impulses through any

FOCUS ON SEXUALITY

Who Will Cheat?

What Personality Traits May Influence Fidelity?

Does personality influence who is likely to be unfaithful and who is not? Apparently so. D. M. Buss and Shackelford (1997) studied the relationship between a variety of personality traits and infidelity in recently married couples. After completing self-report personality inventories at home, subjects were asked to come into the lab and rate the probability that both they and their partners would engage in each of six levels of extramarital interest: flirting, passionate kissing, a romantic date, a one-night stand, a brief affair, or a serious affair. As part of the assessment, they also reported on their own narcissism, as well as that of their mates.

Not surprisingly, a strong correlation was found between conscientiousness and extramarital interest. This finding is perhaps expectable, as conscientiousness can be considered a tendency to do the right thing, to inhibit impulses, and to have social standards foremost in mind. Subjects low in conscientiousness rated themselves as more likely to engage in extramarital behaviors. Moreover, the partners of those low in conscientiousness also rated them as being more likely to engage in extramarital behaviors.

Also associated with extramarital interest was narcissism for both men and women. Because narcissism can be viewed as a focus on the interests of self, this result was not unexpected. The surprising finding, however, was that narcissism in women was more strongly correlated to extramarital interest than was narcissism in men across all of the six levels of behavior, with an emphasis on flirting, dating, and a brief affair. Perhaps even more interesting, husbands' ratings of their wives confirm their wives' opinion. Husbands were able to predict, to some extent, that their wives might cheat based on the wife's personality.

For anyone seeking to sort out the cheaters from the noncheaters in advance on the basis of personality characteristics, a combination of low conscientiousness and high narcissism is especially predictive of extramarital interest. Such individuals are more likely to focus on their own desires to the exclusion of social standards and then to act on their impulses.

means, without empathy or remorse. When the superiority of the narcissist is also especially prominent, such persons validate their feelings of omnipotence by exploiting the average person, who is contemptible simply by virtue of being ordinary.

Narcissists also share numerous traits with the paranoid personality. Whereas narcissists pull others toward them, paranoids separate from others to defend their autonomy. Whereas narcissists are preoccupied with unlimited success or brilliance, paranoids are preoccupied with maintaining their own firm boundaries, often in an effort to remain compensated, to resist further psychotic deterioration. Whereas narcissists evoke loyalty and admiration, paranoids are mistrustful and inspire mistrust in return. Finally, whereas narcissists are typically calm and aloof, paranoids are often irascible and confrontational, drawing all data into support of their persecutory ideas.

The last personality with which the narcissist shares some resemblance is the sadistic. The passive exploitation of the narcissist is often mistaken for the active exploitation of the sadist. In the narcissist, however, exploitation is incidental to egocentricity. In contrast, the sadist dominates others self-consciously and deliberately constructs scenarios that demean others to force their inferior status to consciousness. The narcissist wants your worship; the sadist wants to inflict impotence on others. Further, whereas the sadistic personality is characteristically destructive and cruel and enjoys watching others suffer, narcissists become rageful only when their sense of specialness is compromised. Otherwise, narcissists are content to go forth with benign insouciance, surveying their dominion and soaking up tributes and comforts "owed" to them by lesser others. If Leonardo returns to Spain, he will do so with just this mentality.

PATHWAYS TO SYMPTOM EXPRESSION

In a review of more than 100 studies on the comorbidity of narcissism and narcissistic personality disorder with major mental illness, Ronningstam (1996) found that narcissism is not linked systematically to any specific Axis I disorder. Instead, it would appear that a narcissistic personality only colors the expression of any Axis I disorder that develops. Although the energy, dominant control, and love of hearing themselves talk suggest some fundamentally biological relationship between the narcissistic personality and bipolar disorder, Stormberg, Ronningstam, Gunderson, and Tohen (1998) found that bipolar patients exhibit most of the criteria of pathological narcissism only while in the manic phase. When not manic, their levels of pathological narcissism are no higher than other general psychiatric patients. Some reports suggest that narcissistic personality disorder may exacerbate the severity of posttraumatic stress disorder (B. Johnson, 1995), perhaps because the omnipotent narcissist is confronted repeatedly with evidence of mortality (see box titled "Focus on Pathology: Narcissism and Posttraumatic Stress"). As you read the following paragraphs, try to identify the connection between personality and symptom.

Anxiety Disorders

Given narcissists' image of strength, ability, and self-confidence, the reported rate of anxiety disorders among narcissists is probably lower than that of other personalities. Nevertheless, narcissists do experience anxiety disorders related to underlying feelings of inferiority or shame, but they are unlikely to seek help in resolving these symptoms. As with the compulsive personality, a major pathway to an obsessive-compulsive disorder is exaggerated concerns with perfection. However, narcissists become obsessed out of fear that the perfection of the self has been tainted. The obsessions of compulsives, in contrast, are often related to fear of condemnation or a fear that they may transgress self-imposed restrictions, whereas narcissists are not inclined to restrict themselves at all. Obsessions may also reflect a need to be all-knowing and all-controlling (Glickhauf-Hughes & Wells, 1995). Social phobia may result from experiences of shame, in which the impotence or shortcomings of the narcissist somehow become available for public consumption.

Mood Disorders

Overall, the defensive self-inflation of the narcissistic personality pattern offers surprising resilience against depressive disorders. After all, narcissists excel at minimizing

FOCUS ON PATHOLOGY

Narcissism and Posttraumatic Stress

Feelings of Superiority and Vulnerability

Imagine that you and your family lived in a small village downriver from a large dam. Now imagine that the dam broke; half the village survived and the others drowned or were crushed by the debris of collapsing structures. Imagine that you watched your mother swept away by the current.

If you survived, you would have experienced a traumatic event far outside the range of normal human experience. Memories of lost loved ones would intrude into your daily thoughts, turn your dreams into nightmares, and set your heart racing. You would reexperience the event again and again and be helpless to stop it. Veterans of war, victims of rape, and even individuals who observe someone else suffer serious threat of physical harm are often diagnosed with posttraumatic stress disorder (PTSD). Nevertheless, of those who experience the same traumatic event, only some develop PTSD. Whatever the event, clinicians now know that its effects must be interpreted within the context of the total personality.

Among the characteristics that increase vulnerability to PTSD is a narcissistic style (B. Johnson, 1995). But why would narcissists be vulnerable? Recall that narcissists use grandiosity and omnipotence as a defense against a fragile self-concept, an empty sense of self-worth. Moreover, their superiority makes them believe that they could not possibly suffer the bad luck of others or be caught up with inferiors in some swirl of uncontrollable events.

Traumatic events shatter these assumptions. Among outpatient veterans who develop PTSD, for example, narcissistic traits are some of the most common (Crosby & Hall, 1992). Far from being invulnerable and immortal, the individual is instead just like everybody else, a speck in a vast cosmos, with random potential for disaster and death. No one is excepted, solid proof that narcissists are not the special persons they believed themselves to be. Among military veterans, Karen (1994) suggests that those with PTSD have fallen far short of the warrior ideal they sought to become. Because narcissists are notorious for idealizing themselves as unusually bright, successful, and admired, we might suppose that traumatic events generally puncture the bubble of these narcissistic fantasies. The individual is brought down to earth in a way that is particularly crushing given the needs of this personality. The persistent question many victims ask, "Why me?" can precipitate feelings of anger and rage in those with a narcissistic style, who feel entitled to better treatment from the universe.

shortcomings and exaggerating real achievements. Given their skill at manipulating those who cater to their needs, narcissists must have multiple layers of defenses broken down before feeling helpless or hopeless. It may not be surprising that low-grade depressive symptoms are probably more common than major depressive episodes.

Compensating narcissists may have a modicum of hidden knowledge of the protective role their grandiosity plays, but other narcissists are likely to meet with recurrent disappointments, all the while failing to grasp this insight. Although many narcissists do possess real talents and intelligence, some never achieve a measure of success but instead limp forward with an air of specialness and entitlement. Afraid to test their own adequacy, they present only the illusion of competence and slip increasingly behind others in actual achievements. As the discrepancy between presentation and reality becomes more pronounced over time, their shortcomings become ever more obvious, making their superiority, the bedrock of their identity, ever more questionable. Eventually, the strain of maintaining the false self converts a pretense of ability or brilliance into deep feelings of fraudulence and emptiness. Even more entitled narcissists, who expect the world on a platter, may eventually realize that others are moving ahead through hard work and thus become unable to suppress their envy and anger. Eventually, the illusion wears thin, confidence gives way to uncertainty, and superiority to nagging feelings of self-deception. Gerald could easily follow this path. He has already moved from company to company, and he is experiencing problems yet again. At some point, the balloon will pop.

Depressive feelings may be expressed dramatically, associated with irritability, or used instrumentally as an excuse to justify current shortcomings. Because narcissists control others and expect to be babied by them, they may complain that their caretakers are insufficiently supportive or should have rescued them from their own deficiencies. Witnesses to their shame and humiliation may be scorned simply for observing their helplessness and inefficacy. If their losses are enduring, they may eventually devalue areas in which their abilities were previously expressed. Kernberg (1975) described one such example in a major political figure, who:

. . . became depressed and developed deep feelings of defeat and humiliation accompanied by fantasies in which his political opponents were gloating with satisfaction over his defeat . . . He went into retirement, but gradually devalued the areas of political science in which he had been an expert . . . a narcissistic depreciation of that in which he was no longer triumphant, which brought about a general loss of interest in professional, cultural and intellectual matters. (p. 311)

Major depression may occur after such public and irreparable blows to self-esteem.

For narcissists, then, grandiosity and depression are two sides of the same coin. If they can convince themselves that perfection and omnipotence can be realized, their grandiose defenses hold firm. If not, they begin to feel "intrinsically flawed rather than forgivably human" (McWilliams, 1994, p. 174). Threats to esteem are perhaps more threatening in the second half of life, with the disappearance of youth, beauty, and energy associated with advancing age. Facing Erikson's (1959) stage of integrity versus despair, some conclude that their entire life has been an inauthentic sham, lived out through the falsity of a self-generated illusion. Many feel overcome by shame and experience thoughts of suicide. Some of these people make impulsive attempts, and a number of them succeed.

Delusional Disorder

When narcissists are faced with recurrent failures or adversities too severe to deny, they naturally attribute such events to the operation of forces external to the self, which is the foundation of paranoid and delusional disorder. Already prone to grandiose fantasies and unwilling to accept the verdict of reality, narcissists sometimes isolate themselves from the corrective effects of shared thinking. Running scared through their private, fictional world, they may lose touch with reality and begin thinking along peculiar and deviant lines. Because narcissists see themselves as both brilliant and superior, obviously their success could be blocked only by some entity equally gifted but malevolent. They may find hidden and hostile meanings in the incidental behavior of others and become convinced that innocent behaviors hide malicious motives and intricate schemes. Such persecutory delusions represent the last-ditch effort to protect the grandiose self from total collapse and establish continuity between pathological narcissism and paranoid and delusional disorders.

Indeed, in some cases, the paranoid presents as a narcissist whose inflated sense of self-esteem has been repeatedly or profoundly flattened, perhaps through ordinary encounters with reality or perhaps by colleagues who have secretly decided among themselves to undo an insufferable supervisor or coworker. Here, paranoid symptoms represent a defensive adaptation to a hostile environment that threatens the narcissist at a fundamental level. The paranoid quality may be expressed through a belief that others are conspiring to deprive these individuals of their sense of specialness or somehow cheat them out of a momentous accomplishment, a testament to their brilliance. For example, the individual may assert that coworkers have stolen the seeds of an invention that would provide the world with a clean source of unlimited energy. The difference between believing that others are envious of you and believing that others are actively trying to undo you sometimes becomes rather thin as stressors mount. We can imagine this happening to Gerald, who already believes that the staff is jealous of him and wants to get him fired.

Substance Abuse

Narcissistic traits are frequently associated with abuse of alcohol, opiates (Calsyn, Fleming, Wells, & Saxon, 1996), cocaine and stimulants (Marlowe, Husband, Lamb, & Kirby, 1995; McMahon & Richards, 1996), and other substances. Although the motives underlying substance abuse are often complex, two possibilities seem likely. First, abuse of alcohol and other substances often provides relief from painful feelings. By numbing their awareness, narcissists whose self-regard is under siege can temporarily put aside painful feelings of inferiority and self-doubt. In fact, by turning reality aside, some may actually reinstate their cherished illusions of superiority and competence for a time. Numbing negatives and reinstating positives thus make substance abuse doubly reinforcing. However, the substance abuse is likely to depend on availability, peer group influences, and personality factors. The sense of power and self-confidence associated with cocaine or its derivatives are notorious, but alcohol is legal, less expensive, and more readily acquired. Even where narcissistic traits occur secondary to an antisocial personality disorder, research suggests that substance abuse may be made more severe (McMahon, Malow, & Penedo, 1998).

With Chase, we see an example of narcissistic personality disorder where substance abuse figures prominently. Like other narcissists, Chase is grandiose and entitled. The way he sees it, his novel will be an unmitigated, overwhelming success. Consequently, he feels justified spending all his time working on it and no time with his wife. Regardless, she is expected to cater to his every need, to the point of being his "sex slave." If Chase seems less pathological than Leonardo or Gerald, it is because his insecurities are closer to conscious awareness, tempering his grandiosity. Moreover, Gerald's mother simply set a high standard, and Gerald is struggling to justify her faith in him. Chase's parents, at least his father, apparently were both exalting and condemning at the same time. As a result, Chase's personality has a dual aspect. A superficial grandiosity keeps him floating along, but underneath, he can't make up his mind whether he's the boy wonder or the boy blunder. The internalized voice of his condemning, alcoholic father keeps intruding and deflating him. Chase drinks excessively because a part of him believes his father. He desperately wants to escape the version of reality his father's voice keeps thrusting on him—a reality in which Chase is inferior, inadequate, and probably a failure, despite his "usually" superior performance. As a result, his drinking often has the paradoxical effect of liberating his own self-condemnation, which he then displaces onto his wife, subjecting her to tirades similar to those he must have endured as a child.

Therapy

If given even a normal measure of reinforcement, most narcissists find an adequate foundation for their exaggerated self-image, allowing them to function somewhat successfully in society. Most are convinced they can get along well on their own, and their pride causes them to reject the defective role of patient. Chase is an exceptional circumstance, then, because narcissists rarely present voluntarily for therapy. Those who do search only for the "best doctor," someone of special status who might understand them. Anyone else is devalued. Either way, narcissists who seek therapy do so with the purpose of finding some relief from nagging feelings of emptiness and inefficacy, to be buoyed back to their former grandiose state, that is, to perfect the self, not to understand it (McWilliams, 1994).

The therapist has different goals. As this becomes apparent, narcissists may resist diagnostic testing or perhaps attempt to debunk the therapist's credentials. They may assume from the beginning that the therapist, whom they personally chose, will simply agree that all their problems are caused by the limitations of others. As the real purpose of therapy sinks in, they are likely to maintain a well-measured distance from the therapist, resist invitations of personal exploration, and become indignant over any comment that implies deficiency. As a result, some struggle for dominance and seek to triumph over their therapist in a war of interpretation: Who can see more deeply into whom? Others just quit outright and do not return. A history of narcissistic rage probably portends a poor outcome; evidence of some genuine concern for others is probably a good sign.

THERAPEUTIC TRAPS

The nature of most therapeutic relationships, paradoxically, is the most significant difficulty in treating a narcissistic personality. Most therapists are accustomed to providing their patients with warm support and encouragement. The more narcissistic the subject, the more likely he or she is to respond to this staple of treatment. Admiration from a supportive therapist provides a warm womb in which the narcissist can successfully stretch his or her wings. And therein lies the problem. If the therapist is too supportive, narcissists may emerge suddenly from their cocoon of self-doubt and abruptly quit therapy. Perhaps other people can't handle their problems, but the narcissist can. Alternatively, they may continue indefinitely, glowing in the reinforcement the therapist supplies, thus perpetuating the very essence of the disorder. Worse, if the therapist is also somewhat narcissistic, the two may form a covert mutual admiration society, commenting on each other's enlightened intelligence and wit, while bemoaning the plight of other poor souls who form the remaining mass of humanity. When this occurs, change becomes impossible.

Interpretation, much less confrontation of their behaviors, often proves just as problematic. First, any interpretation implies that the therapist believes that an interpretation should be made, which implies that the narcissist has overlooked something important or needs to be educated in reality. Second, by attempting to make any interpretation at all, the therapist presumes to understand the narcissist, whose problems are unique and who is too sophisticated for ordinary mortals anyway. Thus, some narcissists quit therapy because they are hypersensitive, secretly fearful that their vulnerabilities will be laid open with each session; others quit because their superior attitude has been insulted.

Alternatively, they may continue but question and devalue the expertise of the therapist, who has now joined the ranks of the commoners (i.e., their critics). Such arrogance is both self-protective and interpersonally aggressive, either silencing the therapist through intimidation or shaping the behavior of the therapist to conform to the narcissist's version of therapy: "I talk, you listen and bask in my glow, admire me, and provide compliments. Anything less is not only aversive, but unrealistic." Or, because they assume others should anticipate their needs, an attempt at interpretation may itself be interpreted as a competitive struggle for control, whatever its content. In response, narcissists may become disapproving, angry, or even rageful. Given their obvious resistances, therapists must be very careful to consider their own countertransference reactions: How do I genuinely feel about this client?

STRATEGIES AND TECHNIQUES

For the same reason that therapy is almost a contradiction, it also walks a fine line. The initial phase of therapy must build a strong working alliance. Confronting maladaptive patterns prematurely will likely lead to termination. On the one hand, enough empathy and attention must be provided to motivate subjects to continue long enough for genuine change to occur. Moderate relief from depressive symptoms can be obtained by reviewing past achievements and allowing narcissists to focus on themselves. On the other hand, if the therapist reinforces subjects too much, they may abruptly reinflate to the point that real motivation to change no longer exists. The narcissist believes that he or she is cured when, in fact, only symptom relief has been obtained; what remains is the underlying personality pathology that drives symptom production in the first place.

From an interpersonal perspective, narcissists must decrease entitlement, envy, and arrogant grandiosity. Benjamin (1996) holds that such persons require gentle, consistent, accurate empathy that reflects their own unpleasant inner experience, while guiding their awareness toward the underlying cause of that experience. Narcissists may consider change if they believe it will produce more favorable responses from others. Determining what elements should be emphasized and validated, however, is crucial. For example, identifying with feelings of arrogance directed at rivals ignores the presence of unconscious envy, thereby enabling the narcissistic pattern.

Instead, Benjamin (1996) suggests the therapist identify individuals in the subject's upbringing who were emotionally centered on the narcissist, connecting their regard to the current situation. If the mother was completely devoted to the client, the therapist might ask, "What would your mother say if she knew your competitor had just been featured in the newspaper?" The idea here is that the subject has failed the mother by failing to become what she treated him or her as: the center of the universe. By increasing awareness of this connection, envy should decrease, if only because the narcissist will not wish to give anyone that much control over his or her own internal world. Benjamin presents another example of a narcissist who becomes enraged at his wife one evening for not greeting him at the door when he arrives from work. If the husband can understand that dinner was burning, he may be able to overcome the vulnerability of requiring her constant attention and admiration.

Many of Benjamin's (1996) suggestions are rooted in the paradoxical approach to therapy, dividing the pathology against itself. By painting grandiosity as a need, it becomes incongruent with a self-image of strength and self-determination. The tendency of the narcissistic personality to externalize blame, according to Benjamin, can be countered by the therapist's taking responsibility for small errors. The narcissist thus sees a status person who is comfortable with his or her own human imperfections, with no need to project blame onto others. The therapist's model allows narcissists an avenue for escape from their early learning history, in which most were unconditionally praised for "perfection" and feel like utter failures if seen as lacking perfection. Other interpersonal strategies may also be effective. Couple and family therapy provide an opportunity for guided negotiation with significant others to help break patterns that support narcissistic behavior, leading to new and more genuinely gratifying interactions.

Interpersonal techniques should be combined with cognitive strategies applied simultaneously toward similar goals. D. Davis (in Beck et al., 1990) suggests that the automatic thoughts of narcissists with depressive symptoms revolve around unfulfilled dreams and expectations, the shortcomings of others, and the uniqueness of their despair, as if the narcissist were the first human being to ever become depressed. She suggests that though long-term treatment goals vary with each subject, they are likely to include "adjustment of the patient's grandiose view of self, limiting cognitive focus on evaluation by others, better management of affective reactions to evaluation, enhancing awareness about the feelings of others, activating more empathic affect, and eliminating exploitive behavior" (p. 248). Grandiosity and fluctuations from all-good to all-bad conceptions of self represent cognitive distortions that should be corrected, creating a more realistic, solid, and integrated self-image.

Likewise, Davis maintains that unrealistic fantasies should be replaced by thoughts about the rewards inherent in more readily obtained accomplishments. Rather than become a rock star, for example, the individual might play in a local band. Such fantasies become realistic rehearsals that desensitize the subject to the possibility of failure while raising self-esteem. Alternative beliefs may be incorporated as functional replacements to maladaptive ones. For example, "One can be human, like everyone else, and still be unique" (quoted in Beck et al., 1990, p. 249). Davis further suggests that rather than elevate themselves above others, narcissists should search for personal similarities. Finding common ground creates the necessary foundation for empathy with others. To further develop empathy, role playing can be used to help narcissists accurately identify the emotions of others and develop beliefs about their significance. Moreover, alternative ways of relating effectively can be suggested, perhaps beginning with something as simple as giving someone a compliment.

Psychodynamic therapy of the narcissistic personality is generally based on the formulation of either Kernberg or Kohut. Kernberg (1984) describes an expressive psychotherapy that tends to be more confrontational, with the goal of helping subjects understand the origin of their conscious and unconscious anger, examining negative transference toward the therapist, and addressing the use of defenses such as splitting, projection, and projective identification. This approach follows the essence of Kernberg's theory, whereby the grandiose self serves as a defense against the incohesiveness of a borderline level of personality functioning but conceals oral rage directed at early attachment figures. Accordingly, therapy focuses on how the consequences of these early relationships are recaptured in the relationship with the therapist. Presumably, once individuals understand the connection, the way is open for insight into the pathologies of their other relationships as well. In contrast, Kohut's model predicts that grandiose narcissism is a developmental arrest caused by inadequate or defective empathy during infancy. As such, the therapy seeks to recreate early frustrations, with the therapist providing constant empathy and appropriate mirroring, thus helping the subject move beyond the need for the grandiose self.

Summary

The narcissistic personality disorder is frequently experienced by others as obnoxious, grandiose, and unempathic. Narcissists' immense arrogance, their belief that they possess unsurpassed intelligence and celebrity, and their degradation of the mere mortals who inhabit the planet make them insufferable as family members, partners, and coworkers. Several normal-range variants of the narcissist exist, such as Oldham and Morris's (1995) self-confident style and Millon's (Millon et al., 1994) asserting pattern; these possess traits that are actually assets when trying to get ahead in a capitalist society. At the disordered level, however, self-confidence and healthy assertiveness turn into grandiose self-regard; complete disregard for other people's strengths, talents, and feelings; and extreme haughtiness.

Several subtypes also exist that combine aspects of these personalities with the narcissistic. The unprincipled narcissist combines elements of a sadistic personality with the narcissist's skills of social influencing but few internalized moral prohibitions. Amorous narcissists are focused on erotic seduction with multiple partners. Compensating narcissists have some elements of the avoidant and negativistic personality. The elitist narcissist is full of aggressive confidence.

Narcissistic characteristics can be traced throughout historical literature, from Greek mythology to the Bible, but it wasn't until almost the twentieth century when it was given explicit psychological meaning by Haveloch Ellis, an English psychologist. The psychodynamic history of the narcissistic personality disorder is extensive and convoluted, but over time it has changed from Freud's purely intrapsychic model of narcissism as self-cathexis to the idea that narcissism is a pathology of early relatedness. Horney, Reich, and Kernberg all contributed to this change. Grandiosity, rationalization, and fantasy are the most common defense mechanisms used by narcissists; in classical analytic terms, they are the ego ideal incarnate. Developmentally, psychoanalysis proposes that the narcissists' parents loved them for imaginary qualities instead of for their true selves. Further, Kernberg proposed that narcissists fail to develop integrated conceptions of self and other object images.

Interpersonally, narcissists are noted for their sense of entitlement and subsequent lack of empathy toward others. This makes intimate relationships nearly impossible, as others are seen only as appendages of the narcissist's ego, not as a partner. Narcissists often make a good first impression, but soon others regard them as arrogant and snobbish because of their seeming calm and confident nature. They are also extremely sensitive to perceived slights and often seek a close circle of admirers who will worship them. Benjamin suggests that developmentally, narcissists' parents failed to disclose their own needs, instead worshipping the infant. As a result, the child failed to learn that others are separate beings with their own desires.

Cognitively, narcissists substitute imagination and daydreams for reality. Their past, present, and future are colored by these imaginings, all adding to their glory. Other cognitive processes protect narcissists' vulnerabilities, such as their refusal to test hypotheses, because their ideas must be innately correct. They are also prone to black-and-white thinking and focus on small differences between themselves and others.

Biophysical hypotheses concerning narcissistic patterns are still unclear, although some observations may be noted in terms of mood and temperament. Under most circumstances, narcissists are possessed of a carefree mood and a positive outlook, enjoying an unusually relaxed demeanor. However, changes taking the form of edginess and irritability or dejection characterized by feelings of emptiness, worthlessness, or humiliation may quickly become their baseline if their sense of superiority is penetrated.

From an evolutionary perspective, the narcissist is passively self-oriented. Narcissists believe they are worthy of unconditional praise and tribute for just being themselves, with no actions or responsibilities required to earn rewards. Oddly, there seem to be two developmental pathways to narcissistic personality disorder: One is overly indulgent parents; the other is neglectful or authoritarian parents.

Narcissists share surface similarities with histrionic, antisocial, paranoid, and sadistic personalities. Although not linked systematically to any Axis I disorders, narcissism certainly colors any that do occur. Narcissists experience fewer anxiety disorders than many other personalities but still may develop social phobias and obsessions. They are also resilient against many depressive disorders but may experience low-grade depressive symptoms. Substance abuse is frequently a problem; for narcissists, it is a way to numb their awareness of events that intrude on their sense of self-worth.

Most narcissists strongly resist psychotherapy. For those who choose to remain in therapy, there are several pitfalls that are difficult to avoid, including the therapist's being too reinforcing of the narcissist and, subsequently, the narcissist's never wanting to leave therapy. Interpretation and even general assessment are often difficult to accomplish. For successful treatment, there must be a strong working alliance established, and confronting the narcissist's behaviors and patterns must be timed properly. A combination of interpersonal and cognitive strategies may prove the most effective treatment to decrease sense of entitlement and increase awareness of others' feelings.

Chapter 11

The Schizoid Personality

Objectives

- What are the *DSM-IV* criteria for the schizoid personality?
- The solitary and retiring personalities are normal variants of the schizoid. Describe some of their characteristics and relate them to the more disordered criteria of the *DSM-IV*.
- List the several subtypes of the schizoid personality and indicate how each relates to other personality types.
- Summarize the genetic, neuroanatomical, and neurophysiological approaches to the schizoid personality.
- Could schizoidal tendencies in personality be due to prenatal insult to the fetus?
- Explain why the psychoanalytic tradition does not make a distinction between schizoid and avoidant personalities.
- Describe the varied attempts of the psychoanalytic tradition to explain the schizoid personality.
- What insights does the interpersonal perspective offer to the understanding of schizoid functioning?
- A sense of identity develops from interactions with others. How does social isolation of schizoids affect the content of their cognition?
- Schizoids share characteristics with other personality disorders. List these other disorders and explain the distinction between each and the schizoid.
- Schizoids generally do not experience anxiety. Explain why social overstimulation or understimulation may trigger an anxiety reaction in them.
- List therapeutic goals for the schizoid personality.

Imagine, as you are walking to class, you spot an individual sitting on the campus lawn, back against a tree, textbook opened and inverted on his lap, gazing distantly to the sky.

You instantly recognize him from your classes, where rambunctious classmates often harangue and berate him, yet to no avail, as though he was emotionally detached and indifferent, appearing almost numb. He is also the one who seems so apathetic when the professor praises him for his academic performances. Nearing him, you glance his way with a nod and smile, acknowledging his presence and inviting a response. He reciprocates the nod and resumes his reading. As a friendly gesture, you invite him to join you at lunch. He declines, which is reminiscent of the many other offers he has rejected, saying, "I much prefer being by myself." Though in keeping with his past behavior, it puzzles you as to whether he is merely fearful of rejection or truly enjoys a life of solitude. Pondering this query, you realize you have never seen him with nor has he sought out friends. Could it be that he truly enjoys a life of solitude and lacks the need for interpersonal relationships? The answer is yes. As we see in this chapter, you have just encountered a **schizoid personality.**

Typically distant and viewed as introverted, these individuals keep to themselves. With the exception of minimal familial relations, schizoid personalities, or schizoids, feel no need for relationships, whether platonic or sexual. This is notably unlike the painfully shy avoidant, who desperately desires intimacy and acceptance but fears shame, humiliation, and embarrassment. Because schizoids choose to be by themselves, they go through life with markedly reduced interpersonal stress, as they are immune to the demands that others might put on them. Neither responding to praise nor criticism, the social dynamics typically held to most of us as important are merely incidental to schizoids. They almost seem incapable of experiencing emotional extremes of pleasure—as they rarely become excited about anything—and anger—as they hardly ever become heated or irate. Their emotional experience and expression may be so flattened that they seem detached from the world and even themselves. Perpetually untroubled and indifferent, they work silently and unobtrusively at their jobs and rarely get noticed by anyone, even by those with whom they have some routine contact. Left to their own doing, they would probably blend into the background indefinitely.

Our first case study, Leonard (see Case 11.1), provides a global illustration of a schizoid personality. Leonard's asocial disposition and the book checkout position proved incongruent. Leonard found it difficult to be friendly to others, to smile, to make small talk, or to follow the niceties of casual social encounters. In fact, the need for closeness is a notion confusing to him; the concept is simply beyond anything his life experience might incur. Rather than having a gregarious lifestyle, Leonard prefers to spend time alone watching television or working on his model airplanes (see criterion 2). It is not that he is hostile, but simply that he is indifferent. When others smile at him or try to develop a conversation, he probably senses that they want a response of some kind, but he either does not know what to say in return or just does not feel like saying much of anything. For this reason, people automatically conclude that Leonard is unlike most and view him as deliberately aloof and condescending, perhaps even too arrogant to speak. In reality, he is merely detached and without proclivity to engage others.

Detachment from human relationships is a central theme of all schizoid personalities. For Leonard, it extends even to his association with his family (see criterion 5). When he changes his residence, for example, Leonard has been known to delay notifying his family for months. Once he does, however, they continue to stay in touch with him, despite his lack of reciprocity. He just doesn't find such relationships rewarding, and he may even find them aversive, overstimulating, and confusing. For that

CASE 11.1

Leonard is a tall, slender man referred to the Employee Assistance Program at the university by his supervisor. When asked why he was being seen, Leonard replied, "Maybe he thought I'd do better by now." He offers no other explanation, cannot explain why his supervisor might be dissatisfied, and does not seem especially concerned.[1] He has worked at the library for not quite a year. At first, he was assigned to book checkout, but was unable to engage the patrons interpersonally and was eventually reassigned to work alone in the stacks, a position he prefers. — ⑥ ②

The most notable aspect of his presentation is an absence of emotion. There is no restrained anger, nor even any sign of fear or annoyance. Nor is there any anxiety or curiosity about what he might experience. In fact, Leonard seems quite detached from the surrounding world, responding slowly but automatically, as if he were just going through the motions. Eye contact is minimal. — ⑦

Gathering information from Leonard takes time. Sometimes, he seems to misunderstand the questions. Sentences loaded with emotional nuance take a long time for him to process. Even when he does understand, his responses are brief and nearly devoid of emotional content. The few facial expressions he uses seem inappropriate to the content of his words.

And yet, Leonard is not malicious. Rather, he is simply not connected to the interviewer, nor to the world. No mention is made of friends, coworkers, or any significant relationships, either past or present. Instead, he prefers to spend his free time alone, watching television or working on model airplanes, which are "all I need." Nevertheless, he cannot name a show or series he likes. He does not understand the idea of a "favorite." When asked if he is close to anyone in his family, he is confused by the idea of "closeness," but does mention that his older sister had suggested that work at the university would give him health insurance coverage. Further inquiry reveals that although his family lives in the area, it is they who stay in touch with him, while Leonard has been known to move without notifying anyone for months. — ⑤ ② ④ ①

Leonard's conduct cannot be seen as insubordinate, because he has no understanding of what "insubordinate" might mean. When it is explained to him that if job improvements were not seen, termination might result, he seems to understand but is not perturbed by the possibility. — ⑦

[1] Numbers mark aspects of the case most consistent with *DSM* criteria, and do not necessarily indicate that the case "meets" diagnostic criteria in this respect.

Schizoid Personality Disorder *DSM-IV* Criteria

A. A pervasive pattern of detachment from social relationships and a restricted range of expression of emotions in interpersonal settings, beginning by early adulthood and present in a variety of contexts, as indicated by four (or more) of the following:

(1) neither desires nor enjoys close relationships, including being part of a family

(2) almost always chooses solitary activities

(3) has little, if any, interest in having sexual experiences with another person

(4) takes pleasure in few, if any, activities

(5) lacks close friends or confidants other than first-degree relatives

(6) appears indifferent to the praise or criticism of others

(7) shows emotional coldness, detachment, or flattened affectivity

B. Does not occur exclusively during the course of Schizophrenia, a Mood Disorder with Psychotic Features, or another Psychotic Disorder, and is not due to the direct physiological effects of a general medical condition.

Note: If criteria are met prior to the onset of Schizophrenia, add "Premorbid," e.g. "Paranoid Personality Disorder (Premorbid)."

same reason, he avoids making friends. Leonard finds that he neither wants nor needs social affiliation. Friends contribute seemingly nothing to his quality of life. When others try to strike up a conversation with him in the library, he may reply only briefly, perhaps bordering rudeness, thus bringing the interaction to a conclusion or otherwise exposing his indifference. In fact, he appears to be much more comfortable in the world of inanimate objects, which is probably why he prefers working in the stacks to working at the checkout. To Leonard, model airplanes are all he needs.

Although Leonard has now found a more comfortable place for himself, it is likely that his detachment from the world of human affairs will continue to create problems for him vocationally. Such difficulties are not limited to simply engaging others but also concern his ability to profit from feedback from coworkers and supervisors. In addition, because he receives so little reinforcement from the social world, he has little incentive to change his behavior in any way. Accordingly, he does not truly grasp why his job performance is perceived as unusual and why others are dissatisfied with it, and he finds no reason to change based on the assessment of his supervisor. He is indifferent to both praise and criticism (see criterion 6). If terminated, he is not likely to feel angry or disturbed. Instead, he will simply go through the motions of getting another job that supports his existence in a basic way.

Why is Leonard so detached? To those unfamiliar with the schizoid personality, he might be characterized as an extreme introvert. To the trained professional, however, Leonard's clinical interview revealed distinct signs of the personality disorder. The similarity between introverts and schizoids extends only to their asocial nature, as introverts are able to experience and express emotion. On the other hand, schizoids are most recognized for flattened affectivity (see criterion 7), and Leonard shows this limited capacity for expression of emotion. In fact, he has a restricted ability to experience pleasure of any kind. Additionally, he has no fear, annoyance, anxiety, or curiosity—just an unwavering absence of feeling (see criterion 4). This was observed by his inability to comprehend the concept of "favorite," his paucity of interests and hobbies, and his monotone speech with unvarying facial expression. Like other schizoids, Leonard's life typically lacks fascination, immersion, intimacy, and perhaps even joy. It is also without transcendental or peak experiences because they require the ability to fuse with something more ultimate than self. To most, humans are commonly regarded as innately expressive, emotional, and social creatures. As such, persons like Leonard, who lack these typically human characteristics, may be perceived as robotic and somewhat mechanical. It is this anomaly that leads us to pursue a greater understanding of this personality disorder.

With the illustration of Leonard, we are now in a position to consider other issues, some of which are preliminary to any further discussion. Although the term schizoid has been in constant use for over half a century, its meaning has never really stabilized. As the case of Leonard shows, the *DSM* diagnostic criteria focus almost exclusively on what is absent from the schizoid personality that might be present in normals. Rather than give the construct its own intrinsic traits, the *DSM* tells us what it lacks, namely, any capacity for emotional experience, motivation, sexuality, or interpersonal sensitivity and relatedness. Defining a personality disorder through what it lacks is highly questionable. Take everything away, and nothing substantive remains. The *DSM* schizoid is somewhat of a contradiction: the ineffective exercise of describing what exists when all qualities have been removed. Who can offer a rich description of a vacuum? For this reason, the various perspectives on the construct do not synthesize as harmoniously as for other personality disorders. Likewise, many experienced clinicians claim never to have seen a true schizoid personality (e.g., Benjamin, 1996).

To clarify the disorder, certain accommodations must be made. First, because the nature of the construct is uncertain, we do not focus on issues of development. The developmental pathways sketched in the biological perspective are too uncertain, and those of the psychodynamic perspective are too tangled by obscure metapsychological formulations. Only the interpersonal perspective offers a straightforward, easily understood account, which is briefly reviewed. Second, the chapter draws certain important theoretical contrasts, giving the disorder a measure of content by putting it on a continuum with constructs that are both more common and more familiar. In the evolutionary theory, the schizoid and avoidant are viewed as interpersonally detached patterns existing at opposite ends of a continuum. The schizoid is passively detached; the avoidant is actively detached. In its prototypal form, the schizoid appears behaviorally inert, interpersonally unengaged, remote, and indifferent; cognitively impoverished or even vacant; and temperamentally unexcitable. In contrast, the avoidant appears behaviorally fretful and hesitant, interpersonally fearful, cognitively distracted, and temperamentally anguished and tense.

Both personalities can be put on a continuum with normal introversion. The distinction between them disappears as they merge near the threshold of normality, where we find individuals with both schizoid and avoidant traits but also a capacity for near-normal adjustment. Thus, although the total schizoid typically lacks the avoidant's fear of social humiliation, many nevertheless possess a degree of emotional capacity and enjoy a well-developed fantasy life, while still preferring a solitary lifestyle. Moving toward higher overall levels of pathology, the continuum between the schizoid and avoidant personalities gradually becomes defined into their *DSM* expressions. Finally, both may be seen as merging into the more unusual and eccentric schizotypal personality, and beyond this, with the more deteriorated schizophrenic syndromes (Millon, 1981). The relationship of the schizoid and avoidant personalities to the schizotypal personality and schizophrenia is considered in depth in the next chapter. Consult Figure 12.2 in the schizotypal chapter to clarify the preceding theoretical contrasts.

With the preceding qualifications, the plan of this chapter is the same as that for the other personality disorders. First, we compare normality and abnormality; then we move on to variations of the basic schizoid theme. After that, biological, psychodynamic, interpersonal, and cognitive perspectives on the schizoid personality are described. These sections form the core of what is scientific in personality. By seeking to explain what we observe in character sketches like Leonard's, the goal is to move beyond literary anecdote and enter the domain of theory. As always, we present history and description side by side, noting the contributions of past thinkers, each of whom tends to bring into focus a different aspect of the disorder. Developmental hypotheses are also reviewed but are tentative for all personality disorders. Next, the section "Evolutionary Neurodevelopmental Perspective" shows how the existence of the personality disorder follows from the laws of evolution. Also included are a comparison between the schizoid and other theory-derived constructs and a discussion of how schizoid personalities tend to develop Axis I disorders. Finally, we survey how the disorder might be treated through psychotherapy, again organizing our material in terms of classical approaches to the field: the interpersonal, cognitive, and psychodynamic perspectives.

From Normality to Abnormality

Although the schizoid construct is somewhat nebulous, many readers may nevertheless recognize some aspect of themselves in the schizoid pattern. Everyone knows someone who is an extreme introvert, for example. We all want to be left alone from time to time, if only to quiet our own thoughts or think things through, to unwind from a long day of boring business meetings, or simply let down that façade of friendliness that is required by burdensome visits from friends and relatives. We love them, but sooner or later, enough is enough. In contrast, individuals with schizoid traits feel this way about their social interactions most of the time. What is interpersonal is intrinsically unrewarding to them; thus, they often turn toward objects and abstractions or toward isolative hobbies such as stamp or rock collecting, mechanical gadgetry, or even mathematics or computer science. More normal schizoids and those with avoidant characteristics, who have some intact capacity for emotional experience, may even develop intricate fantasy worlds in which to stage their dreams and ambitions.

Several normal-range variants of the schizoid personality have been proposed. Each capitalizes on some characteristic feature of the total construct. An example of a normal-ranged schizoid variant is Oldham and Morris's (1995) **solitary style.** These individuals have only a limited need for companionship and social support. They feel most comfortable, most free, and most themselves when alone. For this reason, they prefer to live and work in the relative calm and reassurance of social isolation without concern of boredom or loneliness. Self-contained and self-sufficient, their self is their inner sanctum, where they are independent of the emotional and social worlds. As dispassionate observers of life, these solitary individuals rarely get excited about anything. Their even-tempered calm frees them from noisy social attachments but also makes them intellectually aware of details others would easily miss. In relationships, they need their alone time and seldom become as intimately involved as their partners would prefer. In work, they function efficiently but not as team players.

Similarly, the **retiring style** of Millon et al. (1994) has only a minimal need to give and receive affection or to become involved with others emotionally. For this reason, they have few relationships and do not develop strong ties to others. Instead, they are seen as calm, placid, untroubled, and easygoing but also as possibly being socially awkward or indifferent to the feelings of others. They are private people who enjoy being alone, only rarely expressing their inner thoughts and feelings. Ever unobtrusive, they work quietly and methodically behind the scenes, content to remain in the background. Some are introverts caught up in the joy of mentation. Others often see them as lacking in spontaneity and vitality.

A normal variant or style of the schizoid personality can be uncovered by deductively reviewing diagnostic criteria of *DSM-IV* (see Sperry, 1995). Those who are disordered neither desire nor enjoy any close relationships, including that of family. This can be contrasted with individuals manifesting a schizoid style; though they are comforted by the quiet and solitude of an asocial lifestyle, they possess the capability to relate to others when necessary. A schizoid personality usually selects solitary activities resulting in social isolation. Similar to an extent, a schizoid style prefers minimal to no contact when engaged in an activity, yet, unlike the disordered, is willing and able to productively interact when necessary to accomplish a goal. Sexuality is an undesirable and unexplored realm for a schizoid personality. The schizoid style is also not very sexual, though to a lesser extent; they do occasionally experience sexual feelings.

For each of the preceding contrasts, an underlying theme differential emerges; the feature distinguishing the schizoid style from the schizoid personality is capability. Both the schizoid style and personality prefer to be asocial, isolated, and asexual, yet only the schizoid style is capable of executing the alternative when necessary. Leonard falls more toward the pathological extreme. For example, he lacks the motivation to stay in touch with his family. Despite the convenience and simplicity of living in the same area, he does not seek them out. Leonard's indifference toward family forces them to be the ones to sustain relations. In fact, his level of pathology is so extreme that he probably fails to understand the concept of family itself—its meaning and all its connotations. Whereas the schizoid style is capable of understanding warmth, closeness, and the notion of a shared history with others, to Leonard such concepts seem confusing or foreign. The schizoid style can relate to others when necessary; Leonard cannot. He is unable to understand the nuances of interpersonal situations and is unable to respond appropriately, hence, his fitting reassignment to the stacks.

The remaining diagnostic criteria of the schizoid personality disorder can also be normalized to reveal further attributes of the schizoid style. The disordered find little pleasure in most activities, whereas the style can become engaged in certain hobbies or interests. In addition, the disordered have no close friends or confidants other than those in the immediate family. The styled, on the other hand, have more acquaintances and can sometimes find enjoyment from being part of a small social group. Much of this is attributed to the fact that those with the disorder are so uninterested in the reactions of others that they remain indifferent to criticism or praise. Conversely, the styled are capable of productively receiving feedback and changing their behavior accordingly if needed. Emotionally, the disordered may seem cold and detached, with only feeble emotional experiences. This is contrasted with the styled, who are even-tempered with some range of emotion and are capable of experiencing a degree of pleasure and sadness.

Again, when compared to the preceding contrasts, Leonard falls more toward the pathological extreme. Watching television is pretty generic, but he does seem somewhat invested in his model airplane hobby, possibly a good prognostic sign. Whereas the styled are sometimes able to become involved in small groups, including those you might find while working in a library, Leonard reports having no friends at all. The reinforcement value of social contact seems alien to him. Whereas someone with a schizoid style would realize the need to be more engaging and lively when working at the checkout, Leonard does not. Even criticism from his supervisor was not enough to motivate him. For Leonard, anhedonic life drones on, irrespective of whether he has a job.

Variations of the Schizoid Personality

Although contrasts among personality prototypes sharpen their distinctions, most individuals combine aspects of several personalities. In the real world, there are very few pure schizoid personalities, as is the same with the other patterns. Instead, each personality includes several variations, reflecting its combination with other, secondary constructs that give the major type additional coloration. Subtypes of the schizoid personality are discussed in the following section and summarized in Figure 11.1. Actual cases may or may not fall into one of these combinations.

THE LANGUID SCHIZOID

A combination of the schizoid and depressive personalities, the **languid** schizoid is marked by a slow personal tempo, low activation level, and the absence of vigorous and energetic action. Easily fatigued, with only weak motoric expressiveness, languids seem either too comfortable or too lazy; they are unable to rouse themselves to meet their responsibilities, pursue the simplest pleasures, or behave with spontaneity. Interpersonally, they have a quiet, colorless, and vaguely dependent way of relating, hybridizing the introversion of the schizoid with the lethargy characteristic of the depressive personality. As such, they rarely take the initiative, seem broadly anhedonic and cognitively detached, or vaguely ruminative. Such individuals have few interests, preferring a simple, repetitive, and dependent lifestyle. Unlike the affectless schizoid, described later, languids are not necessarily emotionally void. They do suffer the same type of profound angst often seen in depressives, yet their lack of vitality ensures that their sentiments are rarely expressed strongly.

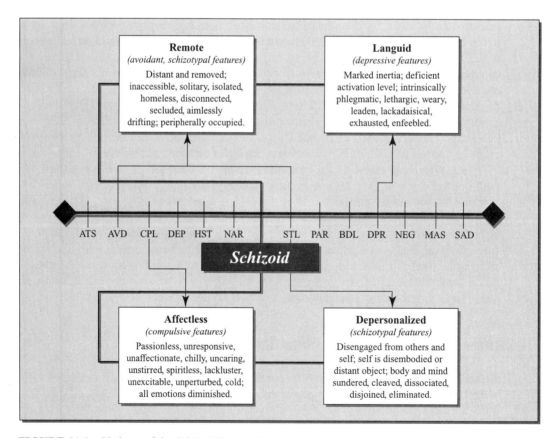

FIGURE 11.1   Variants of the Schizoid Personality.

THE REMOTE SCHIZOID

Although more characteristic of the avoidant personality development, children subjected to intense hostility and rejection very early in life may protectively withdraw so completely that their native capacity for feeling and relating to others becomes permanently reduced. Here, youngsters otherwise capable of normal interpersonal adjustment learn that such desires and emotions yield only anguish and disillusionment. Unlike the basic schizoid, some capacity for feeling and relating remains with the **remote** schizoid, but the wish for affective bonding has been so completely repressed that it no longer enters conscious awareness. Remote schizoids who are more severely impaired may also possess features of the schizotypal personality.

Such individuals are often seen among the homeless, the chronically institutionalized, and the residents of halfway houses. Whereas the basic schizoid is aloof and insensitive to emotional experience, remote schizoids may express a measure of social anxiety as well as frequent behavioral eccentricities, autistic thinking, and depersonalization. At best, their low self-esteem and deficits in social competence allow them only a peripheral, but dependent, role in interpersonal and familial relationships. Most seek solitude and go through life as detached observers closed off from sources of growth and gratification. Some earn a marginal livelihood in low-status jobs, but most follow a meaningless, ineffectual, and idle pattern, drifting aimlessly on the periphery of social life. Many are totally dependent on public support.

THE DEPERSONALIZED SCHIZOID

Often observed simply staring off into space, **depersonalized** schizoids seem dreamy and distant, as if they were contemplating some peaceful vision that draws them more and more away from the everyday existence of the mundane world. Like all schizoids, they are extremely inattentive and disengaged from the affairs of life. More than most, however, depersonalized schizoids have deteriorated into obliviousness. Although they appear preoccupied internally with something substantive, they are in fact preoccupied with nothing at all. Rather, their detachment takes a peculiar, schizotypal-like form: These schizoids feel like disembodied observers viewing themselves from the outside, detached not only from the real world but also from their own thoughts and feelings, from their imagination and fantasies, and from their own corporeal bodies, as well. Focused neither internally nor externally, they possess an ethereal attitude and only a residual physical presence. Whereas the basic schizoid pattern is best described as cognitively vacant, depersonalized schizoids seem cognitively absent.

THE AFFECTLESS SCHIZOID

The isolated, emotionally detached, and solemn characteristics of the **affectless** schizoid suggest constitutional factors, perhaps some abnormality of the neurological systems that support empathy, warmth, and sensitivity in human relationships. Although this might seem to suggest schizotypal features, the schizotypal exhibits a defect in the ability to understand the meaning of human communication. In contrast, the affectless variant combines the apathy of the schizoid with the emotional constriction and formality of the compulsive, effectively eliminating all emotional expression. Like compulsives, they find structured settings comfortable and are more likely to be effective in adult roles than the basic schizoid pattern. But like schizoids, they express the basic conflict of the compulsive, autonomy versus obedience, only weakly if at all.

The Biological Perspective

The history of the schizoid personality begins in early descriptive psychiatry and continues through later temperament and constitutional theorists. Early writers emphasized different characteristics of the modern prototype. For example, Ribot (1890) invented the term anhedonia to describe the diminished ability to experience pleasure, characteristic of the schizoid pattern. Similarly, A. Hoch (1910) described what he called the shut-in personality, using adjectives such as *reticent, seclusive, stubborn,* and *shy.* Likewise, Kraepelin (1919, p. 213) spoke of an autistic personality existing in a healed and stable prepsychotic state, individuals who "narrow or reduce their external interests and contacts and [are notable for] their preoccupation with inward ruminations."

The term schizoid itself, however, can be traced to Bleuler (1922, 1929), who also gave schizophrenia its label in 1911. Schizoidness was seen by Bleuler as expressed to different degrees in everyone, achieving morbid intensity only in schizophrenia. More moderate schizoids were described as "shut in, suspicious, incapable of discussion, people who are comfortably dull" (1924, p. 441). According to Bleuler (1950, p. 40), "even in the less severe forms of the illness, indifference seems to be the external sign . . . an indifference to everything—to friends and relations, to vocation or enjoyment, to duties or rights, to good fortune or to bad." The association between indifference and apathy and the schizoid personality has endured to the present. Leonard reflects both through his indifference to the criticism of his boss and lack of interest in social relationships or the surrounding world.

The essential distinction between the contemporary schizoid and avoidant personalities, outlined previously and recaptured theoretically by Millon (1969), was first put forward by Kretschmer (1925) under the labels anesthetic and hyperaesthetic. The hyperaesthetic, or avoidant, was described using adjectives such as *timid, shy, sensitive, nervous,* and *excitable.* For Kretschmer, "their autism is a painful cramping of the self into itself. They seek as far as possible to avoid and deaden all stimulation from the outside" (p. 161). In contrast, the anesthetic, or schizoid, was described as flavorless and boring. Beneath their nondescript surface lay only "a nothing, a dark, hollow-eyed nothing . . . which twitches uncertainly with every expiring whim—nothing but broken pieces, black rubbish heaps, yawning emotional emptiness, or the cold breath of an arctic soullessness" (p. 150).

According to Kretschmer (1925), indifference was a cardinal trait engendered by lack of affective response: "He draws himself back into himself because he has no reason to do anything else, because all that is about him can offer him nothing" (p. 162). Such individuals were described as being without warmth and humor, but more important, they were regarded as being "affectively lame," that is, temperamentally and constitutionally disposed to lack an "adequate reaction to what we are doing and saying to him . . . he can stand there with a puzzled face and hanging arms . . . in a situation that would electrify [anyone else]" (p. 170). For Kretschmer, then, schizoid characteristics could be traced to inborn biological deficiencies.

Although current theories are speculative, the role that biological factors play in the schizoid personality probably becomes stronger as the disorder becomes more extreme.

FOCUS ON PHYSICAL CORRELATES

Body Weight and Personality

Is Body Type Related to Personality?

A long tradition of clinical speculation compares body characteristics with psychopathology. Kretschmer (1925), for example, categorized individuals according to body build. The asthenic, one of four body types he proposed, was characterized by fragility, poor muscularity, and a frail bone structure. The greater an individual's resemblance to the asthenic prototype, according to Kretschmer, the greater the chance of developing schizophrenia.

Because body types are rather global variables, contemporary researchers have begun to focus on more specific measures. Low birthweight, for example, has been associated with the development of mental disorders later in life (Kopp & Kaler, 1989). Following up on this theme, Hebebrand et al. (1997) examined the relationship between the body mass index (an empirically derived statistic that correlates highly with body weight) and the schizoid personality and Asperger's disorder, a syndrome similar to autism, in a sample of male adolescents diagnosed with one of the two disorders. The body mass index of all patients was significantly below normal.

What mediates the relationship between body weight and the schizoid personality is unclear. Clinical records indicate abnormal eating behavior by some patients, including fussiness about food, preference for unusual foods, habits of eating alone or only when at home, and hypochondriacal fears related to food. One patient commented that he had always been a "poor eater" (Hebebrand et al., 1997). Many schizoids seem to withdraw not only from the social world but also from themselves; they may be relatively insensitive to feelings of hunger. However, schizoids also derive little pleasure from anything. Accordingly, they may simply be anhedonic for eating; they don't enjoy it, so they don't eat much.

Another area of research in psychopathology links exposure to traumatic environmental events to the development of later characteristics. Hoek et al. (1996) studied the relationship between schizoid personality and prenatal exposure to famine, created by the Nazi blockade of western Holland during the winter of 1944 to 1945. Their findings show that the children of pregnant women affected during the first trimester of gestation were at significantly greater risk of developing a schizoid personality. These results were similar to those obtained in a previous study (Susser et al., 1996) that looked at the relationship between prenatal exposure to famine and schizophrenia. Perhaps both disorders, then, can be seen as existing on a continuum of prenatal damage, though this is only speculation.

Because the capacity for a rich emotional life seems so fundamental to human nature, the notion that schizoids suffer some constitutional deficit of emotional capacity provides a simple and compelling explanation for other characteristics of the disorder. Although many introverts are relatively asocial, they nevertheless have numerous interests and a rich inner life. In contrast, extreme schizoids seem impervious to all emotion—even anger, depression, and anxiety—not just to joy and pleasure. Lacking a capacity to experience pleasure and pain, schizoids feel little reinforcement or punishment from the normal activities of human life. They fail to attach to caretakers, find later interpersonal relationships unrewarding, and develop few interests or hobbies, just like Leonard, the librarian. In fact, schizoids have no motivation to think about anything at all. Because emotion and motivation are usually seen as possessing a physical component, they seem chronically underreactive or underaroused, completely lacking energy and initiative. The biological perspective naturally goes far toward explaining the central characteristics of schizoids, at least in the *DSM-IV* version, which exists largely as a disorder built on the absence of normal capacities.

Nevertheless, the specifics of a biological explanation of the schizoid personality are lacking. Individuals closer to the threshold between normal introversion and the schizoid personality disorder, for example, may simply exist at the lower end of a genetically based distribution of emotional capacity, interpersonal sensitivity, physiological arousal, and perhaps even native curiosity. Tentative twin, adoption, and family pedigree studies suggest that schizoid personality disorder belongs with schizotypal personality disorder as part of a schizophrenic spectrum (Siever, 1992), though conclusive data are not yet available (Nigg & Goldsmith, 1994). In the most straightforward polygenetic model, schizophrenia would be expressed through the action of numerous genes. Schizotypal personalities would, therefore, receive either a smaller number of such genes or only some subset of defective genes. Schizoids would receive the fewest schizophrenic genes or some still more restricted subset. Perhaps normal introverts would receive one or two such genes. Alternatively, the expression of more insidious genes might be suppressed by the presence of other genes that compensate in some way. Any number of more complex possibilities might be imagined. Unfortunately, although twin, adoption, and family pedigree studies can establish a role for heredity, identifying the exact genes involved in carrying the expression of a disorder and their interaction is more difficult. Meehl (1962) developed a single dominant gene model, which connects the schizoid and schizotypal personalities with schizophrenia.

Although some genetic basis seems inevitable, other individuals with schizoid traits might suffer focal brain abnormalities, perhaps in the limbic system, which plays an important role in emotional reactions. Alternatively, some deficiency might exist in the reticular activating system, which provides constant excitement to cortical cells in the normal brain during wakefulness and REM sleep, thus accounting for the lack of alertness seen in many schizoids. Perhaps limbic or reticular cells are only thinly branched or defective in some other way. Alternatively, other mechanisms may be at work, with different abnormalities producing different variations within the basic schizoid pattern. Genetic explanations and research on brain structures are not necessarily mutually exclusive; perhaps the density of neural branching in the limbic area is itself under genetic control, for example.

Finally, a neurobiological scheme embracing many of the personality disorders has been put forward by Cloninger (1987b). Here, the adult expression of personality is seen as being strongly constrained by three broad biological temperaments, each of which is associated with a particular neurotransmitter. Schizoids are seen as being low in reward dependence, reflecting their social detachment or lack of interest in obtaining rewards from others; low in harm avoidance, reflecting their self-confidence; and low in novelty seeking, reflecting their behavioral rigidity. Contemporary accounts of the schizoid personality do not typically emphasize self-confidence, which is associated with the narcissistic personality. Instead, their aloof manner is not meant to imply arrogance, but instead refers only to their interpersonal distance. Because Cloninger's schizoid differs from the *DSM* conception, he suggests the term **imperturbable schizoid** be used to convey the more restricted neurobiological definition. We do not, for example, see a kind of encapsulated arrogance in the case of Leonard, the librarian.

The Psychodynamic Perspective

The psychosexual model of character development, seen strongly in formulations of the dependent and compulsive personalities, historically has not been emphasized in the development of the schizoid character. Not surprisingly, the schizoid came to be understood only through the development of the object-relations school and its emphasis on the quality of early interpersonal attachments. Lacking almost completely in these attachments, the schizoid was easily formulated in terms of withdrawal from the object world.

The apparent absence of emotion in schizoid persons has always been of interest to psychoanalysts. Because the unconscious is the center of mental life, the meaning of surface behavior is almost never apparently on the surface; some deeper explanation is always lurking underneath, waiting to be uncovered. Behavior is the product of unseen forces, and what you see is almost never what you get. Thus, psychoanalysts have historically put the avoidant and schizoid together as simply schizoid. Arieti (1955), for example, proposed that the insensitivity of the schizoid actually defends against profound fears of rejection to the point that no social longing remains, a statement definitely more characteristic of the contemporary avoidant. We do not find hidden social longing in Leonard, but instead a comfortable interpersonal detachment.

The essential distinction between the passive detachment of the schizoid and the active detachment of the avoidant was not formally made until 1969 by Millon. As noted previously, schizoids were described as being basically incapable of deep emotional experience, and avoidants were described as exceedingly sensitive, vulnerable, and emotionally needy. Schizoids do not desire interpersonal contact, but avoidants long for the acceptance of intimate relationships. Old habits die hard, however, and even today the psychodynamic perspective still regards the avoidant as basically a less withdrawn and more emotionally intact variant of the schizoid. Accordingly, although the following review uses historical accounts to highlight characteristics of the adult schizoid as distinguished from the avoidant, thus clarifying the disorder, it nevertheless distorts the contemporary psychodynamic position somewhat by doing so.

Even before the development of object relations as a formal school, individuals with a contemporary schizoid flavor were well known to psychoanalytic theorists by the 1930s and 1940s. Because psychoanalysis always seeks to go beyond surface behavior, theorists could only distinguish between a false exterior and a more genuine inner core. Some saw deep conflictual drives; others, such as Kretschmer (1925), discussed previously in the biological perspective, saw a frightening soulless void. Menninger (1930, p. 79), for example, states that schizoids present one front for the world, while retreating into an "inner unseen life" that allows no enduring emotional contact. Some are "seclusive, quiet, reserved, serious-minded, unsociable, eccentric," and others are "dull . . . indifferent, often quite pliable, but more often very stubborn." Likewise, Wilhelm Reich (1933) saw schizoids as being isolated, estranged, and apathetic, with a core of "inner deadness."

Perhaps no other psychoanalytic thinker has been as deeply involved with the working of the schizoid mind as Fairbairn (1940), who regarded what he called the schizoid position as the fundamental situation of life: The infant nurses at the breast, but the breast is not a constant presence; it appears and disappears. Formulated symbolically, such universal early experiences suggest that every human being must come to terms with the possibility that our deepest need may inadvertently destroy the very thing we love the most. According to Fairbairn, the infant concludes that love, the presence of the breast, implies death, the absence that follows, causing the schizoid to withdraw to protect the loved object. Fairbairn further stressed depersonalization, derealization, and a disturbance in the sense of reality. His subjects sensed themselves as "artificial," with a "plate-glass" between themselves and others, exhibiting "an attitude of isolation and detachment, and a preoccupation with inner reality" (p. 15). For Fairbairn, schizoids were regarded as incapable of giving or receiving love—a characteristic traced to the role of caretakers, particularly the mother, who "fails to convince her child by spontaneous and genuine expressions of affection that she herself loves him as a person" (p. 13).

We do see a potential for depersonalization and derealization in Leonard, who takes a long time to answer questions, especially those loaded with emotional nuance. Even then, his answers are brief and his facial expressions inappropriate to his words. Nevertheless, it is not clear whether these characteristics have some deep psychodynamic explanation or are the simple product of social detachment. Because the self is the product of interpersonal transactions, we would expect an impoverished sense of self and consequent inability to make emotional contact with others based on simple detachment alone. Certainly, we do not see in Leonard a "preoccupation with inner reality." Instead, we see a deficiency in the capacity to experience pleasure of all sorts, leading to a deficiency of interest in all things internal and external.

The false self is a related idea first crystallized by Deutsch (1942), with her famous as-if personality. Intellectually, these individuals learn the mechanics of relating, while being unable to experience emotions themselves. Others are aware of their lack of normal emotional response, but the as-if personality is not. Deutsch traced this outcome to the impersonal and formal quality of children's early relationships. As a result, their expressions of emotion have a formal, learned, mechanical quality that may seem technically correct within an interpersonal context but betray the ingrained emptiness of their own internal experience. Whereas others eventually notice that something is amiss, schizoids experience others as being like themselves, fellow robots in a robot world. Based on this description, it is possible that there is substantial overlap between the as-if personality and the affectless schizoid, described previously.

Along the same lines, Winnicott (1956, 1945/1958) described the false-self personality. The function of the false self is to protect the true self and react to its failures and experiences, but the false self cannot feel real or genuine. As elaborated by Guntrip (1952, p. 86), such patients are but "neutral observers," watching from a distance, who report feeling "shutoff, out of touch . . . being out of focus or unreal, of not feeling one with people." Following a more severe thread, Laing (1960, p. 87) regarded their experience with others as always being once removed and lacking in immediacy; instead, "everything is dead, including the self."

McWilliams (1994) offers a description of the psychodynamic schizoid personality at less severe levels of functioning. According to McWilliams, schizoid refers to a type of defensive form of withdrawal, not necessarily to primitive level of functioning. In hospitalized catatonic schizophrenics, for example, the defense operates at a psychotic

CASE 11.2

Hillary, a 22-year-old junior in college, sought counseling at the urging of her dormitory roommate, who felt she might have latent homosexual tendencies. Although this concern proved unjustified, other pathological characteristics were clearly evident.

When asked about her dating experiences, Hillary replied that she never enjoyed herself on dates.[1] Not that she found herself disgusted or repelled by the inevitable sexual overtones of dating, but that "those kinds of things simply aren't fun for me." Relationships with same-sex peers were almost nonexistent. When asked if she would miss her roommate after the semester was over, Hillary seemed confused, as if she could not understand what it would be like to miss someone. She avoids invitations to parties, preferring to stay in her room reading or working at her studies. She is an excellent student, majoring in geology. On several occasions, she had been chosen to assist her professors in fieldwork, but could appreciate only the intellectual aspects of the work, not the joy of a mentoring relationship. ◄①◄③◄⑤◄②

Classmates viewed Hillary as distant and aloof. She turned down an opportunity to join a sorority and could name no close friends, with the exception of one cousin back home. Though she was asked out frequently, she had never had more than two dates with a single boy, with one exception. "I think they find me confusing," she said. "They seem interested in me, but I don't understand why, and I'm not really interested in them." In the dormitory, the other girls sometimes referred to her as "Strange Brain," but Hillary did not seem to care. "At least with that reputation they don't try to involve me in things," she said. ◄⑤◄①◄⑥

Her one significant relationship, with a quiet young man who shared her interest in rocks, lasted only a couple of months. Together, they took nature hikes and commented on the "childish" behavior of their classmates. After a while, however, she found they had nothing to say to each other. Hillary "believes" she would have liked to continue this friendship, but she experienced no dismay over its termination. Indeed, Hillary seems content to sit on the sidelines, while others become perturbed, ecstatic, or hostile about "silly little things." In describing her few relationships, past and present, she seems to be vague, superficial, and naïve, and unable to organize her thoughts. Sometimes, she wanders into irrelevancies, such as what shoes certain people preferred, or the physical characteristics of their parents. ◄⑦

[1] Numbers mark aspects of the case most consistent with *DSM* criteria, and do not necessarily indicate that the case "meets" diagnostic criteria in this respect.

Schizoid Personality Disorder
DSM-IV Criteria

A. A pervasive pattern of detachment from social relationships and a restricted range of expression of emotions in interpersonal settings, beginning by early adulthood and present in a variety of contexts, as indicated by four (or more) of the following:

(1) neither desires nor enjoys close relationships, including being part of a family

(2) almost always chooses solitary activities

(3) has little, if any, interest in having sexual experiences with another person

(4) takes pleasure in few, if any, activities

(5) lacks close friends or confidants other than first-degree relatives

(6) appears indifferent to the praise or criticism of others

(7) shows emotional coldness, detachment, or flattened affectivity

B. Does not occur exclusively during the course of Schizophrenia, a Mood Disorder with Psychotic Features, or another Psychotic Disorder, and is not due to the direct physiological effects of a general medical condition.

Note: If criteria are met prior to the onset of Schizophrenia, add "Premorbid," e.g. "Paranoid Personality Disorder (Premorbid)."

level, as seen in their rigid and oppositional effort to minimize stimulation and shut out the world. In the creative genius, she states, the defense constitutes a constructive autistic withdrawal that distances the individual from humanity at large, allowing a new perspective on conventional practices that permits radical reconceptualizations and innovations. The fundamental strategy of schizoids is simply to stand apart, solidifying boundaries and squelching emotions. Their withdrawal from life and experience causes them to appear emotionally blunted. Intellectualization thus serves as a primary defense mechanism.

Like Cloninger, McWilliams (1994, p. 195) writes that the psychodynamic tradition has often noted a "faintly contemptuous" attitude, an "isolated superiority" of many schizoid individuals, perhaps developed as a reaction against the intrusiveness and over-control of others who would socialize them through forced participation. The deepest fear of schizoid persons is engulfment, the notion that others will enmesh them in relationships, thereby obliterating their individuality and identity. Autism thus becomes a form of opposition or defiance against a "devouring external world" (p. 199) that would digest and assimilate them.

When viewed in this way, the schizoid described by McWilliams (1994) may be seen as opposite to the dependent and histrionic personalities. Whereas the dependent seeks fusion with competent others, the schizoid is frightened, repelled, and perhaps even disgusted. Likewise, the schizoid would see the histrionic as being without boundaries, as encouraging encroachment whenever possible, and worse, as manipulating others through subtle seduction. As the reverse of the dependent and histrionic, the schizoid tolerates abandonment and fears engulfment, seeking strength and identity in isolation. Although Leonard is not contemptuous, he is nevertheless relieved at being removed from book checkout and reassigned to the stacks, where he can work alone.

Consider the case of Hillary (see Case 11.2 on page 385), who demonstrates a pattern of behaviors that point to schizoid personality. Across a variety of social arenas, she remains uninvolved and removed from close relationships. Whether dating, mixing with classmates in the dormitory, or interacting with family, Hillary acts more as an observer than a participant. A main concern for her is that she not be involved with others in her world. She avoids parties, not out of fear, like the avoidant, but rather out of a preference for being alone. She promotes her image of being a "strange brain," thus keeping fellow students at bay while remaining completely unconcerned with peer criticism. Moreover, she appears to have little need for interpersonal stimulation and instead enjoys studying and reading. Rarely angry or excited, she prefers to remain on the sidelines, allowing those around her to interact without her. Unlike most college students, dating is not on her list of enjoyable activities. Her one long-term relationship, lasting only two months, ended because she and her boyfriend had "nothing to say" to each other. Hillary finds social involvement and potential sexual experiences neither painful nor rewarding, further underscoring the impression that schizoids are "lacking" personality. But Hillary does have an aloof and "faintly contemptuous" quality, regarding the behavior of other, more social and involved classmates as "childish."

The Interpersonal Perspective

Although schizoids are detached from social life, they nevertheless exist in a social world and impress others with their behavior. Schizoid traits can be mapped to particular segments (Kiesler, 1996) of the interpersonal circle, some of which also map to the avoidant and schizotypal. Focusing on major traits, Kiesler refers to the interpersonal behavior of the schizoid as escapistic-unresponsive. His description for male subjects states that such a person is likely to:

> . . . *ignore others' presence and refuse to speak or respond. He remains totally unresponsive, is constantly lost in his own thoughts, and appears compulsively uncommunicative. He doggedly ignores all social overtures, and resists intrusions into his privacy. Whenever possible, he avoids others and becomes totally reclusive. When around others, he is totally disinterested and relentlessly stays in his own private world. He strikes others as being disengaged, hermetic, and mute.* (p. 20)

Leonard and Hillary are practically incarnations of this description.

As the preceding paragraph illustrates, schizoids are impressive not for what they do, but for what they fail to do. Again, the schizoid is probably best described as the reverse of the histrionic. Whereas histrionics are turned radically outward toward the social world, schizoids are radically detached. Whereas histrionics are hyperemotional, schizoids lack the capacity for deep emotional experience. Whereas histrionics are demonstrative, dramatic, spontaneous, and theatrical, schizoids are unanimated, robotic, and lacking in energy and vitality. Whereas histrionics demand the center of attention, schizoids are socially disinterested. Whereas histrionics are hypersexualized, schizoids have little or no interest in such matters. Whereas histrionics are cognitively scattered and unable to focus, schizoids either focus intensely and creatively or, in their more severe form, become so withdrawn that they lack any motivation for sustained concentration. Whereas histrionics employ massive repression as their principal defense mechanism, schizoids either intellectualize or have so few conflicts and drives that there is little to repress.

Because schizoids are socially detached, they are often perceived as insensitive, cold, and humorless. Schizoids are indeed insensitive but in the same way that a scale might not display your weight correctly. They are not harsh or callous by nature. Normal persons manage their interpersonal presentation automatically at a level below conscious awareness. Social perception and reaction are so routine that social encounters run smoothly. Such abilities normally begin to develop at birth, with the attachment between mother and infant, and continue to grow in sophistication over most of the life span.

In contrast, schizoids lack internal models by which to represent interpersonal behavior. They may fail to reciprocate even smiles or nods, for example. Their appraisals about the intent, goals, and feelings of others are likely to be wrong much of the time or informed by factors that most of us would consider tangential or irrelevant, especially where communications have some subtle aspect or convey information related to feelings of conflict or irony. Leonard, for example, is confused by questions with emotional nuance. Whereas every normal person understands what it is like to be pulled in two different directions at once, the famous approach-approach conflict, such communications are far too complex for most schizoids. In more severe cases, the scope of understanding may not extend to even the coarsest categories of emotional experience—those basic emotions that primate theorists view as being hardwired into human nature, such as joy, surprise, disgust, anger, and fear. For this reason, Benjamin (1996, p. 349) refers to the schizoid as "an interpersonal 'black hole'—signals disappear forever without leaving a trace."

Because schizoids fail to attach to others, they cannot enjoy the warmth and support of an intimate relationship or develop a friendship that rests on a history of shared experiences—the "thick and thin"—or enjoy being part of a family. Hillary, as we have seen, found that she and her boyfriend simply had no foundation for relatedness. For the most part, schizoids meander along unobtrusively on the edge of social life as a benign and curious presence involved with their internal preoccupations, oblivious to others, and indifferent to either praise or criticism. When they do engage others, their speech tends to be slow and monotonous, emotionally vacant, and peppered with obscurities that signify either lack of attention or a failure to grasp the intent or internal emotional state of others. Movement is lethargic and lacking in gestural expressiveness. The meaning of events that might provoke anger, bring joy, or evoke sadness in normal persons is simply lost on them. Like Leonard, they are indifferent to criticism because they do not understand what it is like for others to feel frustrated.

Instead, schizoids seem complacent and satisfied with their lives and choose to remain aloof from the aspirations and competitiveness they see in others. Because their internal working models of the interpersonal world are so impoverished, their communications often seem peculiar or irrational, but not intentionally so. More often, communications are dry, impersonal, and unelaborated, perhaps with a touch of the formal and pedantically precise, like the compulsive. Life is described in an impersonal, abstract, mechanical manner.

Many schizoids are instrumentally competent and are capable of understanding the basic chores of life or formal demands of a basic job. Some are capable of functioning in more complex roles but do so without color or character. If pressured into social circumstances, schizoids simply become unresponsive and withdraw further into themselves. Leonard provided the first example, preferring the stacks to book checkout; Hillary provided a second example, preferring solitary study to socializing with classmates. Now consider the case of Doris (see Case 11.3).

For most people, including Doris, a job is a job. She doesn't understand what all the fuss is about. Technically, she has done everything asked of her and done it flawlessly, be it food preparation or other chores. However, Doris's responsibilities also include childcare, and that presents a problem. Her employer wants a caretaker for two 3-year-olds and wants Doris to interact with them and show sensitivity to the children's emotional needs. To Doris, this is confusing because the logic, purpose, and incentive of familial bonding escape her. Even more, the fine details of interpersonal relationships are beyond her. Instead, Doris has a lifetime pattern of solitary activities such as sewing her own clothes and spending her evenings alone. Her own life experiences include giving up a 2-month-old child for adoption because of the consequential infringement on her personal time. Doris has no interest in sexual activities and denies any emotional relationship with the baby's father. In fact, she shows no need to have close relationships at all and not "much use" for others.

How does the schizoid personality develop from an interpersonal perspective? No one is really sure, but clinical intuition suggests that schizoids probably possess interpersonal deficits from the very beginning of life. Whereas most infants develop one of several styles of attachment to caretakers, future schizoids are only weakly attached, if at all. Infant behaviors that normally reinforce caretaking, such as coos, smiles, and giggles, are infrequent or absent, leading to a sense of disappointment in the new parents. Inevitably, caretakers themselves withdraw from the child, caught in their own sense of loss and grief about a child who cannot respond to them and further narrowing the range of social inputs and human models. Benjamin (1996, p. 339) notes, "Life in the home would probably be colorless." Relationships between parent and child would probably be distant, cold, or perhaps formal and intellectualized. Strong displays of emotion would

CASE 11.3

After two weeks of work, Doris's employer suggested she seek counseling. Her duties include various household chores, such as light cooking and the care of two 3-year-old children. The concern was that she could not identity adequately with the children's emotional needs, and therefore could not function adequately in the role of caretaker. "My children might feel uncomfortable around her because she's, well . . . weird, and does not understand them," her employer asserted.

Although Doris appeared for the appointment neatly dressed, she nevertheless seems shy and withdrawn. Her soft voice is difficult to hear at times. When asked if she understands the reason for the referral, she replies that she does not, for her job responsibilities have been performed flawlessly.[1] She is not indignant, but does ← ②
state that the food she cooks "tastes good," that she never leaves the kitchen a mess, and that after her chores are performed, she spends most of her time alone in her room, and never disturbs any- ← ①
one. When asked if she feels bonded to the family, she answers, "I guess so," but only after a long, puzzled pause. She becomes more confused when asked which of the children is her favorite and why. Finally, she states, "I love them all equally." Though her words have ← ⑦
a hollow quality, she is not deliberately insincere.

Other areas of Doris's life show similar difficulties. At age 17, Doris had her first child, a baby girl, as a result of sexual activities with a teenage male who lived next door. She denies that he was ever her ← ③
boyfriend, says that that was the first and only time she ever had sex, that she "felt nothing," and has no interest in such matters. When asked about the experience, she recalls only the facts of her ← ⑦
pregnancy and her child's birthweight. She reports that she did not enjoy nursing the child and felt overstimulated by its constant demands on her time. After two months, she decided to give the child ← ②
up for adoption.

Doris spends most of her evenings sewing and makes her own ← ①
clothes. She notes, "I don't have much use for other people. When I'm working, I got to be with them because it's my job." Due to her less than adequate reading skills, a picture vocabulary test is used to assess her intellectual level. She scores within the normal range. Based on both the observations made and the information gathered in the clinical interview, it is recommended that Doris be placed in a position that does not require childcare. Her lack of emotion, preference for solitary activity, and inability to empathize with the emotional states and interpersonal needs of others, prerequisites to nurturance, make her a poor candidate for a caretaking role.

[1] Numbers mark aspects of the case most consistent with *DSM* criteria, and do not necessarily indicate that the case "meets" diagnostic criteria in this respect.

Schizoid Personality Disorder *DSM-IV* Criteria

A. A pervasive pattern of detachment from social relationships and a restricted range of expression of emotions in interpersonal settings, beginning by early adulthood and present in a variety of contexts, as indicated by four (or more) of the following:

(1) neither desires nor enjoys close relationships, including being part of a family

(2) almost always chooses solitary activities

(3) has little, if any, interest in having sexual experiences with another person

(4) takes pleasure in few, if any, activities

(5) lacks close friends or confidants other than first-degree relatives

(6) appears indifferent to the praise or criticism of others

(7) shows emotional coldness, detachment, or flattened affectivity

B. Does not occur exclusively during the course of Schizophrenia, a Mood Disorder with Psychotic Features, or another Psychotic Disorder, and is not due to the direct physiological effects of a general medical condition.

Note: If criteria are met prior to the onset of Schizophrenia, add "Premorbid," e.g. "Paranoid Personality Disorder (Premorbid)."

be greatly discouraged. Through childhood, future schizoids would fail to make friends and seldom join in peer group activities, preferring instead to remain alone. At school, they would probably be regarded as shy but intellectually normal. For schizoid children, restricted interpersonal experiences might produce a kind of self-imposed mental retardation, a lack of interest in the social world leading to broadly generalized skill and communication deficits. Other children might perceive them as odd or strange and subject them to merciless teasing, evoking the residuals of anxiety or anger, further contributing to their social alienation.

The Cognitive Perspective

The cognitive style of schizoid personalities closely supports their interpersonal behavior and defensive functioning. Of the deficits that schizoids possess, perhaps the most tragic is a failure to develop an intimate relationship with the self. More normal individuals with schizoid traits may become constructively self-absorbed, distancing themselves from the noise of the external world to better understand the internal harmonies wrought by their own semi-autistic originality. Isolative mathematicians, for example, may be comfortable functioning in a swirl of symbols found unfathomable to others. Rather than attach to persons, they attach to mathematical squiggles that are meaningful only to a small minority of human beings. Other schizoids may become philosophers or pursue some form of pure scientific research, thus allowing the free expression of their cognitive abilities while remaining detached from the omnipresent social world. Still others might become artists or sculptors, though it is more likely that such sensitivities are seen in conjunction with avoidant traits.

Although the preceding examples present schizoids at their most adaptive, any could include hints of the cognitive eccentricity normally associated with the schizotypal as well. For example, a schizoid mathematician might believe that math possesses some transcendent, almost magical quality by virtue of being the language through which the physical universe is organized. For some, high native intelligence seems to create an insatiable autistic curiosity about the formal relationships of things, which then becomes an organizing force for the entire personality. Without it, many would eventually collapse into psychosis. Though not apparently intellectually gifted, a shade of the schizotypal is perhaps seen in Leonard in his difficulty understanding the emotional dimension of language, his lack of coordination of emotions and facial expressions, and his slow, almost automatic movements. All these make Leonard seem odd, a usual depiction of a schizotypal person.

Normal-range individuals with strong schizoid traits often indulge themselves in isolative hobbies or develop a substantial fantasy life. Imagination compensates for perceived inadequacies or simply expresses a natural tendency to direct attention inward and develop a hypertrophied mental life. Only the latter tends toward the purely schizoid. Where withdrawal has an arrogant or oppositional quality, fantasy in a schizoid-like person sometimes betrays the presence of a secret grandiose self that longs for respect and recognition while offsetting fears that the person is really an outcast. These individuals combine aspects of the compensating narcissist with the autistic isolation of the schizoid, while lacking the asocial and anhedonic qualities of the pure prototype. Alternatively, where the individual also possesses avoidant traits, fantasy may compensate for exaggerated social fears. Whatever secondary personality characteristics are present, *any fantasy at all is a good prognostic sign:* Fantasies have themes, and themes signal an attachment to some emotion or idealized self-image that the therapist can draw out for discussion. For example, good rapport could be stimulated by focusing on Leonard's interest in model airplanes, Doris's interest in sewing, and Hillary's interest in geology.

The more isolated schizoids become, the more underdeveloped their inner self becomes. Such introversion gives way to an incapacitation of emotional depth that stifles spontaneity of expression, a sense of anticipation or surprise, and deep feelings of attachment, intimacy, or community. Consequently, the potential for a fully nurtured and developed self is squelched, and an impoverished and barren self remains. Some higher functioning schizoids are able to associate certain behaviors with emotions. However, their attempts at empathy may be perceived as tinny and unnatural. Other schizoids do possess vague remnants of feelings and are perplexed when they occasionally perceive these shadows of emotion. These individuals confuse the intellectual awareness of an appropriate emotion with the emotion itself, as if to say, "Here others would feel what they call 'sad'; therefore, I must be feeling 'sad' as well." Such a statement elucidates the early object-relations theory describing the emotional mimicry of the schizoid in terms of the as-if personality. Like a stranger in a strange land, schizoids possess logic, reason, and intelligence but cannot genuinely feel and, therefore, cannot understand the deep connectedness of normal human life, as with Hillary and her boyfriend.

The plight of the schizoid self is easily understood. The self is not a substance or a soul but a mental construct, and like any other construct, its contents can be either highly defined or poorly articulated. Identity develops over time as a result of interpersonal experience. Or, as social interactionism would say, the self consists of the reflected appraisals of others. Relatedness is fundamental, and individual identity develops out of social interactions. In time, our cognitive capacities mature to the point that we can reflect on our own experiences and preferences and draw conclusions about our own unique nature. Even extreme introverts, who shy away from social interaction, may nevertheless develop a highly articulated sense of identity. Despite their introversion, their capacity for emotion and interpersonal relatedness is preserved, and their fantasies contain interpersonal themes, even though their lives may not.

In contrast, detached from self as well as others, schizoids often show little awareness of their internal world. They are impoverished socially and lack any curiosity about their own nature, so they have only vague notions about who they are, where they are going, or what their goals might be. Doris and Leonard, for example, have a vaguely infantile quality. When asked what they are like as a person, their descriptions are brief and superficial. Their lack of clarity is neither elusive nor protective, but simply indicates the facts as they know them. Severe schizoids do not normally interact with others and do not understand the few interpersonal interactions they do have. Accordingly, they have few reflected appraisals to internalize, no motivation to elaborate on them, and, therefore, no sharply boundaried self that might be immediately accessible to conscious awareness about which to report.

Individuals with strong schizoid traits may enjoy introspection as intrinsic to the joy of mentation, but severe schizoids lose this capacity. They are not insightful, perceptive, discerning, intuitive, or perspicacious. Detached from self and others, the structure of the inner world suffers a scarcity of connections, as if the light of their being were forever on the edge of winking out completely, leaving only, as Kretschmer and other analysts have noted, a soulless void. To the observer, the severely schizoid mind is unchallenged and, therefore, unproductive. Withdrawn from life, the categories through which life experiences might be articulated tend to be gross and undifferentiated. They blur differences together or miss them entirely, homogenizing experience until the ability to articulate separate elements simply disappears, leaving them with nothing to talk about. With no involvement in life at large, they are usually deficient in broad areas of practical and cultural knowledge. As such, they should do poorly on tests that assume cultural immersion.

Writing from the perspective of cognitive therapy in Beck et al. (1990), Ottaviani argues that schizoids view themselves as observers of the world around them, not as participants. Detached from self or others and lacking in emotion, schizoids have only "a paucity of automatic thoughts" (p. 127) that might be identified as a basis for intervention. Moreover, schizoids do not obsess over negative feedback from others, the way an avoidant or compulsive might, for example. Instead, Ottaviani suggests that many schizoids see themselves as social misfits, but such appraisals lack any real negative impact. Because schizoids value detachment and isolation, the notion that they might be interpersonally awkward assumes the status of an incidental or offhand mental note, not a pressing concern. As such, schizoids may lack curiosity about why they are different or assume that nothing should be done about it. Consequently, they are not motivated to pursue therapeutic change. Finally, Ottaviani identifies various attitudes and assumptions associated with the schizoid personality, including, "Life is less complicated without other people," "I am empty inside," "Life is bland and unfulfilling," and "People are replaceable objects."

The Evolutionary-Neurodevelopmental Perspective

In the natural sciences, knowledge grows through a rigorous interplay of theoretical speculation and empirical research. The phenomena of the more loosely boundaried social sciences, however, are not nearly as accessible to controlled experiments. Instead, the social sciences develop multiple perspectives that offer different angles of looking at and explaining the same phenomenon. Each perspective captures some essential aspect, but no single point of view exhausts the total phenomenon with which the science is concerned. Personality provides the supreme example. Personality and its disorders are accessible through each of the classical and contemporary perspectives described previously, none of which really offers any possibility of falsifying the others. Because personality is concerned with the entire matrix of the person, some theoretical basis is required through which these multiple perspectives can be integrated, thus allowing comparisons and contrasts among the various personality disorders as total constructs.

The evolutionary theory of personality (Millon, 1990; Millon & Davis, 1996) generates three pleasure-deficient personality disorders: the schizoid, avoidant, and depressive personalities. The schizoid exhibits broad emotional, motivational, cognitive, and interpersonal deficits. Emotionally, schizoids tend to be insensitive to both pleasure and pain. They not only are unmotivated to pursue enjoyment or to feel enthusiastic or happy but also experience few distressing feelings such as sadness, anxiety, and anger. Consequently, schizoids have little motivation to either seek rewards or distance themselves from discomfort. Instead, they passively adapt to what life offers, only rarely taking the initiative to change their own circumstances. Lacking much capacity for emotional experience, schizoids fail to become involved in interpersonal relationships, turning neither to themselves nor others for reinforcements. Thus, they often exhibit broad cognitive deficiencies, including an impoverished knowledge base and globalized appraisal processes. In terms of the evolutionary model, the total schizoid personality is best referred to as the **passive-detached pattern.** A summary of its expression across eight clinical domains is given in Table 11.1.

In contrast to other models, the evolutionary theory also recognizes that diverse developmental influences interact reciprocally across all domains of personality. That is, because personality is concerned with the entire matrix of the person, causality interacts across all domains simultaneously. Accordingly, any single domain might be made the starting point from which to develop an explanation of the development of the schizoid personality. Beginning with biology, we might first assert that schizoids possess an inborn constitutional deficit for emotional experience. Such infants would attach themselves only weakly to caretakers in early infancy and thereby fail to internalize object

TABLE 11.1   The Schizoid Personality: Functional and Structural Domains

Functional Domains			*Structural Domains*		
	Impassive			***Complacent***	
Expressive Behavior	Appears to be in an inert emotional state, lifeless, undemonstrative, lacking in energy and vitality; is unmoved, boring unanimated, robotic, phlegmatic, displaying deficits in activation, motoric expressiveness, and spontaneity.		**Self-Image**	Reveals minimal introspection and awareness of self; seems impervious to the emotional and personal implications of everyday social life, appearing indifferent to the praise or criticism of others.	
	Unengaged			***Meager***	
Interpersonal Conduct	Seems indifferent and remote, rarely responsive to the actions or feelings of others, chooses solitary activities, possesses minimal "human" interests; fades into the background, is aloof or unobtrusive, neither desires nor enjoys close relationships, prefers a peripheral role in social, work, and family settings.		**Object-Representations**	Internalized representations are few in number and minimally articulated, largely devoid of the manifold percepts and memories of relationships with others, possessing little of the dynamic interplay among drives and conflicts that typify well-adjusted persons.	
	Impoverished			***Undifferentiated***	
Cognitive Style	Seems deficient across broad spheres of human knowledge and evidences vague and obscure thought processes, particularly about social matters; communication with others is often unfocused, loses its purpose or intention, or is conveyed via a loose or circuitous logic.		**Morphologic Organization**	Given an inner barrenness, a feeble drive to fulfill needs, and minimal pressures either to defend against or resolve internal conflicts or cope with external demands, internal morphologic structures may best be characterized by their limited framework and sterile pattern.	
	Intellectualization			***Apathetic***	
Regulatory Mechanism	Describes interpersonal and affective experiences in a matter-of-fact, abstract, impersonal, or mechanical manner; pays primary attention to formal and objective aspects of social and emotional events.		**Mood/ Temperament**	Is emotionally unexcitable, exhibiting an intrinsic unfeeling, cold, and stark quality; reports weak affectionate or erotic needs, rarely displaying warm or intense feelings, and apparently unable to experience most affects—pleasure, sadness, or anger—in any depth.	

Note: Shaded domains are the most salient for this personality prototype.

relationships—the images of self and other that normally provide the foundation for the development of a solid sense of identity and normal empathy. As a consequence, caretakers would react with disappointment and dismay, and eventually the affectionate cuddling of the child tapers off. Hence, the blueprints of the future schizoid are mapped out by the continued deprivation and lack of exposure to models of warmth and appropriateness. The cognitive consequences would be lack of self-complexity, an impoverished fund of information about the larger culture, and the ability to make only global appraisals and inferences about the internal emotional states of others.

Family styles of communicating in which ideas are aborted or are transmitted in circumstantial, disjunctive, or amorphous ways are likely to shape the growing child's own manner of communication; in short, the child's pattern of relating to others assumes the vague and circumstantial style of his or her home. Moreover, exposed to disrupted, unfocused, and murky patterns of thought, the child learns, both by imitation and by the need to follow the illogic that surrounds him or her, to attend to peripheral or tangential aspects of human communication, that is, to signs and cues that most people would view as irrelevant and distracting. This way of attending to, thinking about, and reacting to events, if extended beyond the family setting, will give rise to perplexity and confusion on the part of others. As a consequence, a vicious circle of disjointed and meaningless transactions may come to characterize the interpersonal relations, leading the child into further isolation and social distance. Together, these events foster increased cognitive obscurities and emotional insensitivities, traits that characterize the schizoid pattern.

Children learn to imitate the pattern of interpersonal relationships to which they repeatedly are exposed. Learning to be stolid, reticent, and undemonstrative can be an incidental product of observing the everyday relationships within the family setting. Families characterized by interpersonal reserve, superficiality, and formality or possessing a bleak and cold atmosphere in which members relate to each other in an aloof, remote, or disaffiliated way are likely breeding grounds for schizoid children, who evidence deeply ingrained habits of social ineptness or insensitivity.

Other pathways to the schizoid personality might be imagined beginning in the early experiential domain. First, a child with a normal capacity for attachment and reinforcement might experience profound neglect. Here, nothing exists to which the child might become attached, except perhaps inanimate objects, such as a blanket or a pillow. Extended over many years, children with only minimal opportunity for human interaction likewise suffer permanent deficits in the ability to relate meaningfully to others, becoming "cultural schizoids," in much the same way that some children suffer permanent intellectual loss, "cultural retardation," when early intellectual stimulation is lacking. Cold, overly formal, reserved, remote, or simply uninterested parents all fail to contribute to the development of interpersonal sophistication and a rich inner life that well-adjusted children possess. Instead, cultural schizoids are left with an impoverished sense of identity and only scant knowledge about the world at large. Aimless, awkward, and emotionally disengaged, they would expect few reinforcements from others, typically receive few in return, and become only peripherally integrated into the larger society.

In the psychodynamic tradition, the same child might develop a "false face" to satisfy caretaker demands to conform to some artificial standard of behavior. Here, natural personal and emotional development is constantly devalued as the child is forced down contrived developmental pathways, the explicit purpose of which is to stunt and eventually overgrow any genuine identity the child might possess. As a result, the potential for a genuine identity atrophies until, eventually, no real self remains. Given such extended brainwashing, the young adult may be left with only a superficial sense of identity, one experienced as inauthentic to self and others. Sometimes, seeds of the forgotten identity may be recovered through therapy and sometimes not. Such individuals are considered in the biopsychosocial-evolutionary model as schizoid, not because they fail to learn to attend to interpersonal cues, but because the cues to which they attend have replaced those that might be considered genuinely reinforcing had the child developed within normal interpersonal relationships. The false self does not experience real pleasures.

CONTRAST WITH OTHER PERSONALITIES

Schizoids share a variety of surface traits with other personality disorders. In each case, the key to distinguishing the schizoid lies in identifying a generalized absence

---

FOCUS ON DEVELOPMENT

Schizoid Personality Disorder in Childhood

Evidence of Developing Personality Patterns in Childhood

Freud wrote that the child is the father of the man. Although this research literature is still in its infancy, numerous points of continuity have been found between adult disorders and early manifestations of similar problems in childhood (Fennig & Carlson, 1995). The first account of schizoid personality in childhood was given by Ssucharewa in 1926 (Wolff, 1996). Symptoms included solitariness, odd thinking, flatness and superficiality of emotions, a tendency toward automatisms, impulsive behavior, inappropriate social behavior (clowning, rhyming, stereotypic neologisms), obsessive-compulsive behavior, heightened suggestibility, and various motor impairments, including clumsiness, awkwardness, abruptness of movement, and many superfluous movements. Contemporary thinking is that autism, Asperger's syndrome, and schizoid personality of childhood (Wolff, 1998) form a group of related disorders, a "schizoid spectrum." Although usually not as impaired as schizophrenic children, kids in these categories all show impaired social relations, developmental abnormalities, and delays of varying severity.

Wolff (1998) suggests that schizoid children are more impaired than autistic and Asperger's children on "theory of mind" tasks, which test a capacity to imagine what other people feel or think. Indeed, "lack of empathy" is a cardinal feature of the diagnosis. Other core characteristics noted were "solitariness (the children were 'loners') . . . increased sensitivity, at times with paranoid ideation; rigidity of mental set, especially the single-minded pursuit of special interests (such as electronics, architectural drawings, antiques, astronomy, dinosaurs, politics); and unusual styles of communicating such as odd use of metaphor, over- or undertalkativeness" (p. 124). In contrast to high-functioning autistic and Asperger's children, on follow-up the schizoid children showed better psychosocial adjustment as adults, not significantly different from the adjustment of their clinic-matched controls. However, they were not as able to reach their expected level of occupation or to as easily sustain an intimate sexual relationship, both characteristics of the adult schizoid personality.

of emotion and lack of desire for interpersonal contact. Both schizoids and schizotypals are relatively asocial, withdrawing from the company of others, but for different reasons. Schizotypals often feel a sense of social anxiety when in the company of others, perhaps reinforced by paranoid concerns, such as ideas of reference. Schizotypals may believe that others are referring to them in some way. When two people on the street are seen whispering to each other, a schizotypal may believe that he or she is the subject of the conversation. In contrast, schizoids are socially disinterested; the topics of others' conversations are of no concern to them. Moreover, whereas schizoids seem simply colorless and dull, schizotypals are notable for their broad cognitive eccentricities. These include magical thinking, for example, the notion that they can read the thoughts of others or have some sixth sense about the future, unusual perceptual experiences, and peculiarities of speech. In short, the schizotypal personality bears more of a resemblance to a subthreshold schizophrenic.

Likewise, both the schizoid and avoidant often seem socially hesitant and unresponsive, both withdraw interpersonally, and both may present as anxious if forced to endure some significant social encounter. The two personalities may be especially difficult to distinguish during a diagnostic interview, where the avoidant is too fearful or ashamed to be forthcoming and the schizoid simply has nothing to say. The crucial differences lie in the capacity for emotional feeling and the wish for social companionship. Avoidants have a rich emotional life but flee from contact with others out of fear of embarrassment, shame, or humiliation. Fearing condemnation or ridicule, they are acutely sensitive to the emotions of those around them and constantly evaluate the words and manners of others for cues of acceptance or rejection. Avoidants constantly scan their environment for potential threats. On the contrary, schizoids are considered insensitive, aloof, cold, and detached. They are not arrogant or callous, but simply lack a basic capacity for emotion and intimacy, even with their closest friends. Avoidants, however, have ample capacity for warmth and intimacy if trust can just be established. Finally, schizoids suffer little conflict, ambivalence, or disillusionment. In contrast, avoidants constantly feel trapped between the desire to seek social acceptance and the desire to withdraw into a private world of shame. Their disillusionment is deep and existential.

Both schizoids and depressives share an incapacity to experience joy or pleasure, appearing flat, colorless, solemn, and socially unresponsive. Both may exhibit evidence of psychomotor retardation, performing tasks slowly and methodologically, without evidence of any personal investment. Depressives, however, experience profound pain, feeling depleted, discouraged, and worthless. They not only are pessimistic about the future but also ruminate about what could have been and feel horribly guilty about possible misdeeds. They perceive their self-proclaimed inadequacies as contemptible, deserving of criticism and punishment. In contrast, schizoids lack emotional depth on almost every dimension and are incapable of the self-accusatory introspection of the depressive. Finally, the concerns of the depressive invariably have interpersonal overtones, whereas schizoids are socially disinterested and would never center their lives on the problems of interpersonal relationships.

Both schizoids and compulsives share a lack of emotional expressiveness, a tendency to intellectualize, and sometimes gravitate to similar occupations, though for different reasons. Moreover, compulsives' reliance on rules and regulations, their devotion to work at the expense of family life, and their need for the structure of the workplace all color their behavior with a detachment and passivity that superficially resemble the detachment of the schizoid, and the schizoid sometimes has idiosyncratic ideas that seem to possess a compulsive quality. Schizoids, however, prefer occupations that minimize interpersonal involvements and disregard or fail to appreciate social conventions. They are content to work away, day after day, in some isolated workplace cubicle, with few interruptions or social demands. Work that others find boring, the schizoid finds comforting. Compulsives, in contrast, overconform to social conventions and flourish in work that demands precision and detail, checking and cross-checking. Within their solemn exterior, the capacity for emotional expressiveness is intact, though it is seldom expressed. Accordingly, compulsives are best described as emotionally constricted, whereas schizoids are best seen as emotionally vacant. Moreover, schizoids are indifferent to interpersonal involvements, and their insensitivity to emotion prevents such intimidation.

PATHWAYS TO SYMPTOM EXPRESSION

Because schizoids exist with minimal emotions and a paucity of relationships, they seldom develop Axis I disorders. Instead, they cope by removing themselves from difficult situations. When the going gets tough, the schizoid gets going. From the perspective of normality, such a lifestyle lacks the richness of what it means to be human; from a schizoid perspective, however, it also lacks many of the problems. As always, it is important to remember that there is a logic that connects the personality pattern with its associated Axis I syndromes. As you read the following paragraphs, try to identify the connection between personality and symptom.

Anxiety Disorders

Although all personality patterns experience anxiety, schizoids normally do not experience deep emotional feelings, and schizoid features are absent in neurotic subjects (Tyrer, Casey, & Seivewright, 1986). Their flat, colorless style tends to immunize them against anxiety and mood disorders, a feature that stretches across each of our three cases. Nevertheless, schizoids sometimes develop anxiety disorders in response to overstimulation or understimulation. Given no safe route back to the safety of an asocial environment, some schizoids explode when cornered by unusual persistent social demands or heavy responsibility. Obsessions or compulsions related to fears of returning to the social world may sometimes develop during periods of extended isolation, particularly if the individual has a history of being stressed by extended or traumatic social contact. Imagine what might happen if Leonard, the librarian, was forced to work in customer relations, for example.

Dissociative Disorders

The cognitive architecture of the schizoid mind creates a vulnerability to distortions of consciousness. In normal individuals, a well-developed sense of identity functions as ballast, keeping the organism stable during periods of anxiety and stress. In contrast, schizoids have only a poorly cohesive, patchwork self, and readily experience altered perceptions of identity, estrangement from self, severe emptiness (Kumin, 1978), or depersonalization. Given their emotional impoverishment, they may also feel mechanical or even disembodied. Schizoid traits and dissociative experiences may also coexist in subjects who have experienced severe childhood abuse (Swett & Halpert, 1993), though borderline traits are probably more common.

Schizophrenic and Psychotic Disorders

Many of the characteristics of the schizoid personality resemble the so-called negative, or deficit, symptoms of schizophrenic syndromes. Schizoids have little capacity for emotional experience. Likewise, schizophrenics experience a flattening in the range and intensity of emotion. Schizoids are often directionless, drifting aimlessly through life. Likewise, schizophrenics suffer diminished goal-directed activity. Schizoids fail to relate interpersonally and are indifferent to praise and criticism. Likewise, schizophrenics may become reclusive to avoid social anxiety and overstimulation. Schizoids are anhedonic, rarely experiencing pleasure; so are many schizophrenics. Schizoids are rarely spontaneous, lack emotional and interpersonal investments, and thus find little of substance that might be communicated to others. Likewise, schizophrenics suffer decreases in the production and fluency of speech.

Not all schizoids go on to develop schizophrenic syndromes, and not all schizophrenic syndromes are preceded by a personality disorder. Nevertheless, the similarities noted previously argue that schizoid personality disorder is in many cases prodromal to a schizophrenic syndrome (Millon, 1981). Further, schizoids do sometimes experience brief psychotic episodes under conditions of stress. Schizoids who develop psychotic or schizophrenic symptoms tend to exaggerate their premorbid pattern. They exhibit profound lethargy and indifference to their surroundings, possibly appearing stuporous and moving only listlessly, if at all. Speech is slow and sometimes inaudible. They resist efforts to be involved in interpersonal activities and may report that events and things around them seem unreal or strange. Their characteristic emotional impoverishment may be compounded by a dreamy detachment and feelings of depersonalization. Disorganized and catatonic subtypes are probably more common than the paranoid variety, as the latter reflects feelings of social anxiety that schizoids would normally lack unless repeatedly subjected to social stressors. The disorganized subtype may be seen as a deterioration of the basic schizoid pattern, and the catatonic type may reflect an effort to fortress the self against threats of environmental overstimulation.

Therapy

The prognosis for the schizoid personality is not promising. Because schizoids have no desire for interpersonal relationships and little emotional capacity, they develop only a limited transference relationship, fail to see anything in therapy that will benefit them, and are indifferent to the praise or criticism of the therapist. For example, we can imagine Leonard, the librarian, and the therapist sitting in their respective chairs, not knowing what to say to each other. After Leonard managed to force out a few sentences, the hour would be over. On the other hand, not all schizoids are prototypal cases. Some exhibit only mild characteristics of the disorder and may maintain good vocational and social adjustment with persistence and patience. Without intrinsic motivators, the presence of external structure becomes immensely important.

THERAPEUTIC TRAPS

Probably the single most important trap in therapy with the schizoid subject is expecting too much. Neither Leonard, Doris, nor Hillary will ever become a social butterfly. Given their inability to infer the emotional states of others, they are likely to experience the therapeutic relationship as curious or perplexing. With few recorded autobiographical memories and only a limited ability to see connections between the actions of others and their own internal world, schizoids cannot be regarded as psychologically minded and are unlikely to respond to forms of insight therapy. Accordingly, the sophistication of any discussion with the subject must be keyed to the subject's level of understanding. This cannot be judged from their overall intellectual level, for schizoids may be intellectually bright yet socially unaware or naïve.

Another trap is that the therapist may feel frustrated and defeated and simply give up. Such a reaction is normal and only recaptures the frustration of many individuals who may have had dreams for the subject in the past, including parents, siblings, and teachers. Not everyone can be "reached," even with perfect empathy. Beginning therapists should be aware of this fact when working with patients who have schizoid traits. Even those who make substantial progress are at constant risk for resuming an isolative lifestyle of passive detachment, especially those who must return to settings that offer the opportunity for a solitary existence. Booster sessions to prevent such regressions are especially wise following termination.

THERAPEUTIC STRATEGIES

When subjects possess predominantly schizoid traits, therapy has three overarching goals. First, something should be found that the subject somewhat associates with pleasure. Second, contact with the interpersonal world should be increased, where social anxiety permits. Third, the individual should be involved vocationally or educationally, if possible.

From an interpersonal perspective, the therapist should determine who is now actively involved in the daily life of the subject. Because most schizoids rarely date or marry, couples therapy is usually not relevant. Nevertheless, if some significant other exists, he or she should probably be brought into the therapeutic process. After all, the schizoid is unlikely to portray the relationship accurately and may not understand the extent to which his or her own indifference and lack of emotional support and understanding have already put the relationship in jeopardy. We know Hillary's appraisal that she and her boyfriend had "nothing to say to each other," but it would be interesting to hear his side of the story. Because the companion is likely to possess more adaptive traits than the schizoid, this relationship may be important to preserve.

If the subject resides with the family, attitudes toward relationships can be explored in therapy with the eventual goal of conferencing with family members. Mutual indifference is probably not uncommon: Neither may be hostile, but the schizoid passively ignores the family, and the family actively ignores the schizoid. Parents may feel exhausted, defeated, or disappointed. These feelings can be explored, and their expectations can be replaced with more modest goals that allow the subject to be praised on a daily basis. Otherwise, to the extent that the subject feels anything at all, it is likely to be rejection, a vague global sense of having fallen short of expectations without really knowing why, as Leonard feels when he says of his boss, "I guess he thought I'd do better by now."

Because individuals with schizoid traits value their time alone, they can be indulged with absolute solitude following a period of participation with family members, who keep a diary of their interactions and note anything the subject seems to find enjoyable or rewarding. Subjects can examine their interactions and attitudes toward family life in individual therapy: Is the family experienced as controlling, punishing, intrusive, supportive, or none of the above? If the subject says that no feelings come to mind, an adjective rating scale can be completed on the family and examined for salient themes, which then become the point of departure for discussion. Moreover, in the overall strategic plan, a supportive family provides the background structure through which the individual may be introduced into other contexts, such as job or school.

Two other interpersonal assessments should be made. First, even subjects with a predominance of schizoid traits sometimes experience a degree of social anxiety, perhaps related to interpersonal failures or a sense of awkwardness. Because social anxiety can be defeated through known techniques, its presence indicates some preservation of affect, possibly a good prognostic sign. Here, schizoid traits may cloak aspects of an avoidant personality, which can be coaxed toward greater sociability. In addition, some assessment should be made of the extent to which schizoid traits might serve as an extreme form of defense, a numbing of self against a hostile world. Reports of an abusive childhood environment offer support for, but do not confirm, such a hypothesis.

Second, an effort should be made to explore the content of the subject's fantasies. Fantasy is usually regarded as maladaptive for withdrawn subjects, yet fantasies compensate for unfulfilled needs or perceived flaws in the self and, as such, provide rich material for therapy. Any fantasy at all indicates that the schizoid has some need or desire, which can be used by the therapist as a portal to the subject's private world. A superhero fantasy, for example, obviously indicates a perception that the self is weak and powerless. Any intervention that increases competency should also produce a more competent self-image, possibly leading to increased social desire, more rewarding and realistic social encounters, and so on. Accordingly, schizoids who report no fantasies might be encouraged to develop some, as this at least provides some information about what they find to be reinforcing. Eventually, the functional role that isolation plays in the individual's life can be examined in therapy and connected to the fantasy material.

Working from a cognitive perspective, Ottaviani in Beck et al. (1990) suggest setting up a hierarchy of social interaction goals that the patient may want to accomplish. A daily diary can be used to keep track of automatic thoughts, especially those immediately preceding and following any social encounter. The act of identifying thoughts and emotions can be therapeutic in itself, for schizoids tend to be broadly impoverished as to mental content. Further, schizoids can be asked to identify and discuss the mental states of others. With practice, the ability to respond accurately and empathetically should increase the reinforcement value of social situations. Role playing and in vivo exposure can then be used to practice social skills. Audio and video feedback should be constructive in helping subject and therapist identify problem areas; audio feedback can be used to provide an emotional range to the voice, and videotaping can be used to give subjects perspective on how others perceive them and help them become more animated while remaining socially appropriate.

Because schizoids often appraise their experiences globally, Ottaviani states, they may miss aspects of experience that are genuinely rewarding. Questions that draw attention to positive specifics help the individual learn what he or she prefers and why. These activities can then be repeated to make life more rewarding. Finally, cognitive and interpersonal approaches can be combined in group therapy, where schizoids can be encouraged to develop more constructive social skills and attitudes. In the beginning, most will approach with an attitude of disinterest and decline to participate extensively. Some feel socially anxious; others find the group process curious or confusing. Nevertheless, within an accepting group, many individuals can eventually be drawn toward gradual disclosure and participation while obtaining genuine feedback about how they are viewed by others. This feedback can provide insight into the severity of schizoid traits or whether a true avoidant personality has been cloaked by said traits. Either way, the distinguishing feature of a pure schizoid, disinterest and apathy toward interpersonal relationships, can be measured against the individual's reaction to positive feedback from others. As such, the prognosis can be amended to more accurately reflect the therapeutic outcome.

Summary

The schizoid is the personality disorder that lacks a personality. Schizoids prefer isolation because relationships seem to hold no rewards for them. They are often described as detached and emotionally flat, but in general, they are rarely noticed by anyone because they are so quiet and unobtrusive. The *DSM-IV* criteria for the schizoid focuses solely on what schizoids are lacking: any sense of being emotional, sexual, or interpersonal. Put on a continuum, the more normal variant of the schizoid is seen as an introvert who may have more developed emotional capacities and, though still preferring a solitary life, has a richly developed fantasy life. In the realm of normal personality, Oldham and Morris describe the solitary style: one who feels the most free when alone in a calm, self-contained, and self-sufficient lifestyle. Millon describes the retiring style as one who is capable of relating to others when necessary but truly prefers to be alone. On the opposite end, the most severe schizoids may seem to develop a kind of schizophrenic syndrome.

Several variations of the schizoid personality have been proposed. The languid schizoid blends schizoid tendencies with depressive characteristics. Remote schizoids have withdrawn so completely that they lost their innate capacity to feel and relate to others. The depersonalized schizoid is viewed as dreamy, distant, and cognitively absent. The affectless schizoid shares with the compulsive the desire for structured settings but not the compulsive's conflict of autonomy versus obedience.

Biological explanations of the schizoid remain speculative, but the arguments become more compelling as the schizoid moves into the realm of the more severely disordered. Schizoids are seen as chronically underactive or underaroused, which could be explained by a biological deficit in normal functioning. There is some preliminary genetic evidence for schizoid personality that is linked with schizophrenia, but other possibilities exist, such as focal brain abnormalities in the limbic system or in the reticular activating system.

Classical psychoanalysis has limited power to describe the schizoid personality primarily because psychodynamics are based on the premise that the person presents one view of self to the outside world but has deep inner struggles and conflicts that are hidden on the inside. The schizoid seems to be void on the inside. One exception to this thinking is Fairbairn, who traced the schizoid's lack of affection to the child who, at an early age, learns that love (represented by the breast) implies death and thus withdraws to protect the self. The object relationists, who focus on early interpersonal attachments, have more to offer, defining schizoids by their lack of early attachments.

It may seem counterintuitive to have an interpersonal perspective on a disorder that appears to have no interpersonal relationships, but living in a social world forces schizoids to have a pattern for interacting with others and it is their intrinsic lack of desire to do so that warrants interpersonal analysis. Kiesler describes this pattern as escapist-unresponsive because they ignore others and become hermetic. Although they are detached and not socially sensitive, schizoids are not callous or harsh toward other people. Their communication style tends to be dry and impersonal, and because they fail to attach to others, they never experience the pleasure of being part of a family or being loved by a friend or mate.

Cognitively, more normal schizoids may give free reign to their intellectual endeavors, becoming mathematicians or philosophers, but more severe schizoids appear to develop some cognitive eccentricities akin to the schizotypal. The more isolated the schizoid becomes, the more unlikely he or she is to have a coherent and rich sense of self. Schizoids are often unaware of any goals or drives that motivate them and, in the most severe cases, are incapable of introspection. Beck and Freeman describe schizoids as observers of life, not participants.

The evolutionary neurodevelopmental perspective describes the schizoid as one of the pleasure-deficient personalities, insensitive to both pleasure and pain. They passively accommodate to life's circumstances and rarely take the initiative to change things. This perspective also espouses multiple pathways to development of the schizoid personality, as all domains (biological, interpersonal, dynamic) interact to form the whole person.

Although the schizoid may appear to share some surface qualities with other disorders, such as avoidant, depressive, and compulsive, schizoids are identifiable by their lack of emotion or desire for human interaction. Schizoids appear relatively immune to anxiety and mood disorders but may be vulnerable to developing dissociative disorders, schizophrenic symptoms, and psychotic disorders.

The therapeutic outlook for the schizoid is fairly bleak. It is important to not expect too much change and to not get frustrated and give up too early on the schizoid. Some change can be effected by finding something the schizoid enjoys or derives pleasure from, increasing interpersonal contact, and engaging in a vocation or education. These goals can be achieved through interpersonal means as well as cognitive modalities focusing on a hierarchy of social interaction goals. Group therapy can be instrumental in affecting a substantiated differential diagnosis, thereby determining a more realistic prognosis. Role playing and in vivo exposure can help ensure that the changes extend beyond the walls of the clinic or hospital and help schizoids learn to broaden their interpersonal experiences.

Chapter 12

The Schizotypal Personality

Objectives

- What are the *DSM-IV* criteria for the schizotypal personality?
- Explain what is meant by *structurally defective personalities.*
- Are there childhood behaviors that are precursors of the schizotypal personality?
- The idiosyncratic personality is a normal variant of the schizotypal. Describe its characteristics and relate them to the more disordered criteria of the *DSM-IV.*
- Explain how different personality styles combine to form each of the subtypes of the schizotypal personality.
- Explain the significance of the terms *latent schizophrenia, pseudoneurotic schizophrenia,* and *ambulatory schizophrenics.*
- Explain Meehl's theory of schizotaxia. Is there any evidence supporting it?
- Do the findings on neuroanatomical and neurotransmitter research on schizophrenia apply to schizotypal subjects also?
- What is the viral hypothesis for schizophrenia?
- How does the psychodynamic perspective explain the schizotypal personality?
- What factors sustain the eccentric and odd interpersonal behavior of the schizotypal?
- Explain the meaning of the term *emotional reasoning.*
- Schizotypals share characteristics with other personality disorders. List these other disorders and explain the distinction between each and the schizotypal.
- List therapeutic goals for the schizotypal personality.

Others see them as eccentric, different, weird, odd, or strange. Excessively anxious around others, they keep themselves separated and isolated, even from those they have known for long periods of time. Some seem absorbed in stimulation that derives from their own internal world and may have difficulty expressing their thoughts and feelings coherently. When engaged interpersonally, they may seem distracted or unable to focus or even ramble from subject to subject. Emotions may have a constricted range or be completely inappropriate to objective events. They may have odd beliefs unsubstantiated by science; for example, they can communicate telepathically or somehow read the future. Some have perceptions that are equally odd; for example, they may think about long dead relatives, then suddenly get the feeling that these spirits are hovering in the room near them. Often, they are extraordinarily suspicious of the motives of others.

Such individuals are called **schizotypal personalities,** or schizotypals for the sake of convenience in this chapter. Given the preceding characteristics, it is not surprising that most researchers now believe that the schizotypal personality lies on a continuum with schizophrenia. As such, both schizotypals and schizophrenics are often referred to as **schizotypes.** The continuum that links the two disorders is called **schizotypy.** In line with schizophrenia research, schizotypal symptoms that suggest a surplus or exaggeration of normal functioning, such as delusions, hallucinations, and ideas of reference, are usually referred to as **positive symptoms,** and those that refer to interpersonal and motivational deficits are often referred to as **negative symptoms.**

Consider the case of Neal (see Case 12.1), a victim of unfortunate circumstances, who was arrested for possession of cocaine but later released on probation when urine tests prove negative for any illegal substance. Like many schizotypals, Neal experiences what are called **ideas of references,** meaning that he believes that other persons are referring to him or that he is somehow at the center of interpersonal events (see criterion 1). Rather than dismiss these happenings as bad luck, however, Neal instead concludes that he has been "set up." Moreover, he "knows" that the police officers are talking about him, simply because they keep looking at him and trying to hide it, as least from his perspective. Neal's referential ideas are probably related to the social anxiety reported by the police. Neal is uncomfortable around everyone, even though it appears he has no cause to be (see criterion 9). The more uncomfortable he feels, the more vigilant he becomes and the more likely he is to construe events so that they revolve around him.

Other unusual characteristics emerge during the clinical interview. Although Neal is asked simple biographical questions, the style and content of his responses are strange. He cannot connect with the purpose of the interview or the intent of the interviewer and is puzzled by basic questions, as if he and the interviewer were not sharing the same consensual social reality. Seemingly unambiguous inquiries lead to disconnected and somewhat tangential responses (see criterion 4), as if the main purpose of the question were lost, then recovered, then lost again. Whereas meaning and emotion are tightly coupled in the speech of most people, they are only loosely coordinated for Neal (see criterion 6). Sometimes, they are completely inappropriate to objective events, as if interpersonal interactions were being interpreted through frames of reference that are either wrongly applied or somehow emphasize trivial aspects of the interaction at the expense of those that are important or central.

Neal also reports unusual perceptual experiences reminiscent of schizophrenia. When he states that the true purpose of the interview has been "told to him," he is not speaking metaphorically. Instead, Neal is asserting that he has privileged access to information outside the realm of normal human experience (see criterion 2). He also reports unusual perceptual experiences that resemble hallucinations (see criterion 3). When Neal says that he has glimpsed the future, he literally believes that he has somehow looked ahead in time. When he claims that he can see what is happening in other

Neal was mandated to six months' mental health treatment as a condition of his probation.[1] He had been found in possession of a small quantity of crack cocaine when the house he rents a room in was raided. After testing negative for drugs, he was released, given probation, and sent for counseling. "I've thought for some time they wanted to set me up," he noted. "They kept looking at me from outside the cell, although they tried to hide it, so I know they were talking about me." Police report that his neighbors state that Neal has no friends and that he seems frightened of people. No one came to bail Neal out of jail.

Neal is 32 years old and has a tall, almost emaciated frame. His eyes are deeply set, and he rarely meets the gaze of others. There is a disjointed quality to his movements, as though his body is not solely within his own control. From the start of the interview, he seemed incapable of responding to the simplest questions. Only after a long silence could some answer be produced, and even these were often rambling and only tangentially related to the inquiry, as if he were free-associating midway through his own responses. Moreover, his emotions seem at odds with the substance of his words, sometimes smiling at a sad story. He claims to know the "true purpose" of the interview; it was "told to him," and he has "glimpsed the future." Further inquiries designed to determine whether his responses might only seem pathological because of poor word choice or phrasing show instead that Neal is being literal: He believes that he can occasionally see the future in a visual form. He also claims that he can sometimes see what is going on in other places and what might happen if he were to go there.

Getting an accurate and full history from Neal is difficult. According to a neighbor, Neal was born when his mother was in her mid- to late-40s. The identity of his father is unknown, and, to the neighbor's knowledge, no male has ever come around their home. His mother's whereabouts are unknown, but a neighbor believes she may live somewhere in the city. She abandoned Neal at age 12. The neighbor states that he did well in school, at least before his mother left. Nevertheless, "Neal was never normal," she says. "After his mother left, he became stranger, twisting his body up into knots and having conversations with himself." No information is available concerning whether he received treatment for these behaviors. Also unclear is how Neal supports himself currently. He claims to have worked as a window washer for downtown shop owners until his bizarre hair and unkempt appearance began to frighten customers. Currently, Neal is fixated on his run-in with police, occasionally mumbling something under his breath about "busting heads." Therapy will be difficult, even if he finds it possible to keep a schedule.

---

[1]Numbers mark aspects of the case most consistent with *DSM* criteria, and do not necessarily indicate that the case "meets" diagnostic criteria in this respect.

Schizotypal Personality Disorder
DSM-IV Criteria

A pervasive pattern of social and interpersonal deficits marked by acute discomfort with, and reduced capacity for, close relationships as well as by cognitive or perceptual distortions and eccentricities of behavior, beginning by early adulthood and present in a variety of contexts, as indicated by five (or more) of the following:

(1) ideas of reference (excluding delusions of reference)

(2) odd beliefs or magical thinking that influences behavior and is inconsistent with subcultural norms (e.g., superstitiousness, belief in clairvoyance, telepathy, or "sixth sense"; in children and adolescents, bizarre fantasies or preoccupations)

(3) unusual perceptual experiences, including bodily illusions

(4) odd thinking and speech (e.g., vague, circumstantial, metaphorical, overelaborate, or stereotyped)

(5) suspiciousness or paranoid ideation

(6) inappropriate or constricted affect

(7) behavior or appearance that is odd, eccentric, or peculiar

(8) lack of close friends or confidants other than first-degree relatives

(9) excessive social anxiety that does not diminish with familiarity and tends to be associated with paranoid fears rather than negative judgments about self

places and what might happen should he go there, he is speaking perceptually, not inferentially. Interestingly, Neal's revelations and extrasensory information seem to serve a protective function, making him suspicious but also making it possible to keep himself safe. When Neal becomes socially anxious and construes events so that they somehow point to him, he at least has a means of guarding himself. That's why they have become a basis for action in the course of his everyday life. And because Neal's fears are mostly fictions anyway, his countermeasures always seem to work, thus reinforcing superstitious beliefs and exotic cognitive modes.

Finally, like many schizotypals, Neal exhibits behaviors that seem odd or peculiar (see criterion 7). His next-door neighbor reports that he has been known to twist his body up in knots and have conversations with himself. Likewise, Neal claims to have worked as a window washer until his appearance and bizarre behaviors began to frighten customers. Perhaps they also frightened Neal. Given his social anxiety and the unusual cognitive methods through which he protects himself, it is not surprising that Neal has no close friends (see criterion 8). Instead, he is pretty much on his own, pursuing a minimalist existence at the margins of society.

Given the portrayal of Neal, we are now in a position to consider other issues. Personality can be likened to an office building. The workers have their own jobs, and the building complements their activities. Internal traffic is not shunted down convoluted pathways, for example, or turned out into the street. All workers and visitors find their destination easily, without wasted effort or frustration. The entire structure, in fact, just naturally encourages efficient functioning. Each person naturally integrates with the others so that, ideally, the entire complex functions as a single harmonious whole.

In the schizotypal, borderline, and paranoid personalities, however, structural defects prevent the whole from operating smoothly. For the paranoid, the building is too rigid and constrictive, so much so that anyone who enters must conform to its specific, predetermined rules or be ejected. In the borderline, the building is structured so loosely that its insides hardly seem separated into rooms. Instead, contents spill from one compartment to the next, so the entire structure seems labile and vulnerable to splitting or heaving unpredictably. In the schizotypal, the overall design possesses an eccentric and indecipherable logic, by which the bizarre is made normal and the normal made bizarre.

These three are the structurally defective personalities. Personality *style* expresses a way of functioning in the world; personality *structure* refers to the actual substrates that undergird functioning. A hand, for example, is made to write, grasp, and manipulate. That's what it does. Structurally, however, a hand is formed of bone, muscle, nerve, and tendon; without these, no hand can function. In the same way, structural domains of personality support its functional aspects, thus forming the architecture of the mind. Cognitive schemata, for example, provide structural support for the expression of cognitive styles. Self-image provides yet another structural component to personality, one that influences interpersonal ways of relating, as well as the operation of defense mechanisms, which support and protect self-esteem. Thus, compulsives see themselves as conscientious and conform scrupulously to external standards to make absolutely sure this image is confirmed; minor errors are magnified into major mistakes, leading to self-condemnation. As this example shows, structural elements of personality are so deeply imprinted that they actively transform the nature of objective events. No matter how successful the compulsive may be at fending off error, a deep fear that something has slipped by remains. Every interpersonal interaction takes place under a black, solemn cloud.

Through their rigidity, lability, and eccentricity, the structurally defective group is set apart from other personality disorders. Temporary periods dominated by bizarre behavior, irrational impulses, and semidelusional thoughts are common. Such individuals may drift in and out of contact with consensual social reality, as if caught up in a momentary dream. Unable to grasp the illusory character of these inner stimuli, they may be driven to engage in erratic and hostile actions or embark on wild and chaotic sprees they may only vaguely recall later. Every so often, their intrapsychic world erupts and overwhelms them, blurring their awareness and releasing bizarre impulses, thoughts, and actions. Most have a checkered and erratic history of relationships, school, and work performance, as with Neal. Lack of judgment and foresight and failures to

FOCUS ON DEVELOPMENT

Childhood Precursors of Schizotypal Personality Disorder

When Do Positive and Negative Symptoms Begin to Emerge?

Researchers have traditionally divided the symptoms of the schizophrenic syndromes into two types. First are the positive symptoms, mainly perceptual-cognitive in nature, which represent a surplus or exaggeration of normal functioning. These include suspiciousness, ideas of reference, odd beliefs, magical thinking, unusual perceptual experiences, and circumstantial and tangential speech. Second are the negative symptoms, mainly social-interpersonal in nature, which represent deficits in normal functioning. These include constricted or inappropriate affect, speech problems (i.e., poverty of speech, stilted speech), social indifference, social isolation, flatness of emotion, and odd behavior or appearance.

Because some children show schizoid-like behavior from early childhood, there has been some interest in determining if early behavioral manifestations of either the positive or negative symptoms might develop into full-fledged disorders later in life. S. Olin et al. (1997) studied teachers' ratings of adolescents who were subsequently diagnosed as schizotypal personalities and compared them with several groups, including a group of normal adolescents whose parents were both normal. They found that childhood analogs of adult schizotypal symptoms were evident as early as late childhood and early adolescence. When compared with children who later became healthy adults, children who later were diagnosed as schizotypal were more passive, more socially unengaged, more sensitive to criticism, and reacted more nervously. However, they were not rated as more anxious by their teachers. The preschizotypal children differed from children who later became schizophrenic, who were more disruptive and hyperexcitable. The results support a continuity of the negative symptoms from late childhood on into adulthood.

Unfortunately, no studies have yet addressed the positive symptoms of the schizotypal personality. Because it is developmentally normal for young children to believe in magic and to make attributions accordingly (Rosengren, Kalish, Hickling, & Gelman, 1994; Vikan & Clausen, 1993), it would be instructive to look at the development of these symptoms in schizotypal children. Perhaps a reluctance or inability to relinquish early magical thinking, which is developmentally normal and generally manifested by all children, may doom a child to some serious psychopathology later in life.

capitalize on native talents are common. Flashes of promise or achievement seldom endure without a highly tolerant and supportive social environment. Whereas other personality disorders often find a secure niche to match their habit systems, the structurally defective personalities repeat setbacks again and again. Nevertheless, most eventually manage to pull themselves together and gain enough of a foothold to prevent themselves from slipping into more serious, decompensated states.

With the portrait of Neal as an example, we now approach additional issues that form the plan of this chapter. First, we compare normality and abnormality; then we move on to variations on the basic schizotypal theme. After that, biological, psychodynamic, interpersonal, and cognitive perspectives on the schizotypal personality are described. These sections form the core of what is scientific in personality. By seeking to explain what we observe in character sketches like Neal's, the goal is to move beyond literary anecdote and enter the domain of theory. As always, we present history and description side by side, noting the contributions of past thinkers, each of whom tends to bring into focus a different aspect of the disorder. Developmental hypotheses are also reviewed but are tentative for all personality disorders. Next, the section "Evolutionary Neurodevelopmental Perspective" shows how the existence of the personality disorder follows from the laws of evolution. Also included are a comparison between the schizotypal and other theory-derived constructs and a discussion of how schizotypal personalities tend to develop Axis I disorders. Finally, we survey how the disorder might be treated through psychotherapy, again organizing our material mostly in terms of classical approaches to the field: the biological, interpersonal, cognitive, and psychodynamic perspectives. Along the way, we anchor abstract points in the text to case studies to provide concrete examples.

From Normality to Abnormality

Although the schizotypal personality is considered a severe personality disorder, some readers will find isolated schizotypal traits reflected in their own personalities. The more such characteristics possessed, the more the whole picture becomes "different." Oldham and Morris (1995) refer to the idiosyncratic style, a different drummer nourished by a unique belief system that contributes to an unconventional or even eccentric lifestyle. Such persons require few intimate relationships and are instead independent seekers of what is interesting and unusual, often being drawn to the extrasensory, supernatural, occult, or mystical. They are highly open to new experiences and novel interpretations of conventional ideas and are curious about alternative abstract formulations of the old and common. Often, they are highly aware of the reactions of others but nevertheless draw inspiration from internal sources. As such, consensual social reality is not the basis of their self-esteem. Instead, the subjective world of their own unique experiences is what they believe and value. If experience supports the existence of the supernatural or ESP, then objective, scientific proof is not required. Many are experimentalists who seek the limits of knowledge and of emotional and spiritual experience.

A less abnormal variant of the schizotypal personality can also be constructed by normalizing the diagnostic criteria of *DSM-IV* (see Sperry, 1995), paraphrased for that purpose here. Whereas the disordered individual has ideas of reference, interpreting events as if they held some special meaning specifically intended for the person (see criterion 1), those with a schizotypal style simply draw inspiration from their own internal world, leading them toward unusual interpretations and conclusions in which the individual plays a special role. Whereas the disordered may engage in magical thinking or hold odd beliefs, perhaps believing they are clairvoyant or telepathic (see criterion 2), those with the style may also hold certain unusual ideas or superstitions but are able to temporarily set these aside and adapt to what consensual social reality requires. Whereas the disordered may have strange perceptual experiences (see criterion 3), those with the style are interested in experiencing realities beyond our own, including the supernatural, mystical, or occult, but do not turn exclusively to these as a source of truth or inspiration. Whereas the disordered may be vague, get lost in tangential thoughts, or overelaborate ideas (see criterion 4), those with the style are simply drawn toward what is novel and abstract.

For each of the preceding applicable contrasts, Neal falls more toward the pathological side. He believes, for example, that the individuals outside his cell are talking about him. Moreover, he believes that he is clairvoyant and that this unusual ability extends into the future. Far from being able to set these strange beliefs aside, they instead become a foundation for future action. Neal "knows" what is going on in other places, and he believes that he can see what might happen if he were to go there. Rather than being inclined toward the novel and abstract, Neal's words seem vague and tangled. He rambles on as if the current contents of thought, whatever they might be, were somehow interfering with the overall plan of his discourse.

The remaining diagnostic criteria can also be put on a continuum (see Sperry, 1995). Whereas the disordered tend to lack close friends (see criterion 8) to the point of being suspicious and paranoid (see criterion 5), those with the style are nourished by an internal belief system and do not require that this system be validated by others. Whereas the disordered exhibit a constricted or inappropriate affect (see criterion 6), those with the style have some awareness of the responses that society is most likely to require or reward. Whereas the disordered may look or act in ways that are peculiar, odd, or exceedingly strange (see criterion 7), those with the style are simply unconventional because of their disregard of social standards. Finally, whereas the disordered exhibit excessive social anxiety that is not extinguished as familiarity increases (see criterion 9), those with the style are simply very observant and aware of the actions and feelings of others.

Again, when compared to the preceding contrasts, Neal comes out on the pathological side of the continuum. Far from being nourished by his own belief system, he suspects that the police have set him up. Far from observing what response social situations are most likely to require, Neal's emotions are inappropriate to the content of his speech, apparently disengaged from both his own control and the immediate expectations of others. Beyond being merely circumspect around others, Neal is a loner with no close friends. Exceeding what is merely unconventional, his odd, unkempt appearance impacts his vocational life, now nonexistent, and he has exhibited episodes of bizarre behavior, such as twisting his body up in knots. Collectively, these characteristics point to a diagnosis of schizotypal personality disorder.

Variations of the Schizotypal Personality

The evolutionary model (Millon, 1990) holds that the schizoid and avoidant shade gently into the schizotypal; thus, these personalities naturally form structural subtypes for this pattern (see Figure 12.1). Actual cases may or may not fall into one of these combinations.

THE INSIPID SCHIZOTYPAL

The **insipid** schizotypals represent a structural exaggeration of the passive-detached pattern. Like the schizoid, they are notably insensitive to feelings, seem indifferent to the external world, and appear drab, unmotivated, apathetic, inexpressive, sluggish, and joyless. Insipid schizotypals, however, exaggerate even this. Being detached, they have no connection to the external world. Being passive, they generate nothing inside themselves that might give substance to their identity.

Instead, they exist with form but no content. Some experience their mind and body as separate or decoupled. Others experience occasional existential crises—episodes of terror during which they feel hollow, dead, or nonexistent—and may grasp at anything to confirm their existence and avoid nothingness. Others see themselves as automatons without meaning or purpose. Their consciousness may seem to float, unconnected to the physical world, and lost in some dimension between being and nonbeing. Cognitive processes seem obscure, vague, and tangential. Symptoms of depersonalization are common. Social communications are responded to minimally or with inappropriate affect or peculiar ideas or in a circumstantial and confused manner. Speech

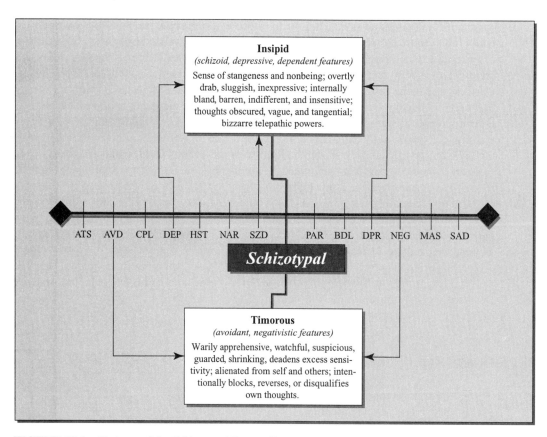

FIGURE 12.1   Variants of the Schizotypal Personality.

is monotonous, listless, or even inaudible. In some cases, depressive and dependent features may also be present.

Developmentally, insipid schizotypals are likely to have had family atmospheres of excessive indifference, impassivity, or formality. The family provides an important model for lifelong patterns of social reticence, interpersonal insensitivity, and discomfort with personal affection and closeness. Styles of fragmented and amorphous communication, complicated by disjointed, vague, confusing, and pointless interactions, are probably also a factor, leading to unfocused and irrelevant interpersonal relations. Given emotional deficits that flatten otherwise rich experiences and cognitive obscurities that further blur important distinctions, the opportunity for having satisfying interpersonal experiences is lost. Unable to communicate with either affect or clarity, they likely were shunned, overlooked, and invited to share few of the more interesting experiences to which others were drawn. Failing to interchange ideas and feelings with others, they remain fixed and undeveloped, continuing, therefore, in their disjointed, amorphous, and affectless state. Restricted in their social experiences, they acquire few social skills, find it increasingly difficult to relate socially, and perpetuate a vicious circle that fosters their isolation and accentuates their social inadequacies and cognitive deficiencies.

THE TIMOROUS SCHIZOTYPAL

Timorous schizotypals represent a structural exaggeration of the active-detached pattern. Like the avoidant, they are restrained, isolated, apprehensive, guarded, and socially shrinking. In contrast to the insipid variant, apathy and indifference are used protectively to damp down their sensitivities, feelings, and desires. Some develop exaggerations of avoidant scanning and hypervigilance, becoming drawn to strange signs and omens through which protective guidance can be obtained and malicious events controlled or averted. They may focus on irrelevant details or those that would escape the ordinary person and develop superstitious behaviors or rituals. Many devalue the self so completely that they deliberately confuse their own cognitive processes as a means of avoiding what is presumably rational and objective. Others turn the fantasy life cultivated by some avoidants into perceptions that are normally beyond the five senses. In effect, they create a new inner world populated by magical fantasies, illusions, telepathic relationships, and other odd thoughts that provide them with an existence more significant and rewarding than that found in reality. Others seek to jettison the self completely, voiding their identity and following a path similar to that of their insipid counterparts. Timorous schizotypals are excessively apprehensive, particularly in social encounters, exhibiting agitation and an anxious watchfulness. Most exhibit a distrust of others and a suspiciousness about their motives that rarely recede despite growing familiarity.

Developmentally, timorous schizotypals were likely exposed to belittlement, rejection, and humiliation. As a result, they have low self-esteem, feelings of incompetence, and a marked distrust of others. As a result of such harsh treatment, they protectively keep their distance from others, wall off from society, and insulate their feelings. Eventually, they avoid interacting with others at all, fearing that any amount of contact might lead to some negative appraisal. So convinced are they of their lack of worth that many come to denigrate themselves. Of the two subtypes, Neal more closely resembles the timorous schizotypal.

Early Historical Forerunners

Some of the personality disorders were apparently known to the ancients, but the schizotypal personality is a relatively new construct. Its history begins with its relation to schizophrenia and progresses through efforts to say exactly where the two syndromes begin and end. In Chapter 1, we noted that the social sciences are fundamentally different from the hard sciences, their phenomena are intrinsically loosely boundaried, and, therefore, many symptoms and characteristics seem loosely related and almost impossible to capture adequately within a single diagnostic term.

Difficulties in classifying schizophrenics predate even the origin of the term. In the fifth edition of his text, Kraepelin (1896) concluded that catatonia and hebephrenia, as well as certain paranoid disturbances, were all variations of dementia *praecox*—Latin for "premature mental deterioration"—and displayed a common theme of early onset and incurability. Kraepelin thus brought order and simplicity to what had previously been diagnostic confusion. In line with the traditions of German psychiatry, he assumed that some biophysical defect must underlie this new coordinating syndrome. Among the major signs that he considered central, in addition to the progressive and inevitable decline, were discrepancies between thought and emotion, negativism and stereotyped behaviors, wandering or unconnected ideas, hallucinations, delusions, and a general mental deterioration. His solution was to be challenged and modified by Eugen Bleuler in Switzerland and Adolf Meyer in the United States.

After observing hundreds of dementia praecox patients in the early 1900s, Bleuler concluded that the complex, and often highly creative, reactions and thoughts of his subjects contrasted markedly with the simple and meandering thinking that Kraepelin had observed. Furthermore, not only did many of his patients display their illness for the first time in adulthood rather than in adolescence, but a significant proportion evidenced no progressive deterioration, both of which Kraepelin considered defining features of the syndrome. For Bleuler, dementia praecox assumed an age of onset and developmental course not supported by the evidence. Instead, the primary symptoms, he maintained, were disturbances in the associative links between thoughts, a breach between affect and intellect, ambivalence toward the same objects, and an autistic detachment from reality.

The diversity of cases displaying a fragmentation of thought, feeling, and action led Bleuler, in 1911, to coin the term **schizophrenia,** literally a schism in the phrenos, or mind, commonly misunderstood as "split personality." Although he referred to "the group of schizophrenias," he retained the Kraepelinian view that these disorders were caused by a single physiological disease process, a neurological ailment that produced their common primary symptoms. Secondary symptoms, such as hallucinations and delusions, were attributed to the distinctive life experiences of his subjects and to their efforts to adapt to their basic disease. He believed that although psychological factors could shape the particular character of the schizophrenic impairment, life experiences alone could not produce schizophrenia.

Bleuler further expanded on Kraepelin by recognizing both nondeteriorating and intermediary cases, a position that Kraepelin (1919) accepted in his later years when writing of "autistic personalities" and those whose dementia is "brought to a standstill short of its full clinical course" (p. 237). Bleuler (1911) termed these cases *latent* schizophrenia, which he regarded as being far more frequent than the psychotic form, though such subjects were seldom seen in treatment. Schizophrenia was thus conceptualized dimensionally, existing on a continuum with normality, with symptoms that might be expressed "within normal limits" (Bleuler, 1924, p. 437). Both Bleuler and his contemporaries noted that latent schizophrenia often occurred in the families of more severe schizophrenics, evidence supporting a common biological link.

After Bleuler's revisions, other writers advanced terminology recognizing a partially expressed form of the disease. Zilboorg (1941) referred to *ambulatory* schizophrenics, a designation that he believed captured the presence of a basic disease process while asserting its continuity with more severe cases. According to Zilboorg:

These patients seldom reach the point at which hospitalization appears necessary either to the relatives or to the psychiatrist, and appear "to walk about life" like any other "normal" person—although they remain inefficient, peregrinatory, casual in their ties to things and to people. Such individuals remain more or less on the loose in the actual or figurative sense, outwardly and inwardly. (p. 154)

Delusions, hallucinations, and flatness of affect were to be regarded as only the "terminal phenomena" of the schizophrenic process, affecting the unfortunate few in which the full process was expressed. Other authors wrote about a *pseudoneurotic* schizophrenia (P. H. Hoch & Polatin, 1949), in which neurotic symptoms were superimposed over a latent, but stable, variant of schizophrenia that sometimes precipitated into psychosis but usually retained its "ambulatory" status.

The specific term **schizotype** was coined by Rado (1956) as an abbreviation of schizophrenic phenotype. The name stuck. Schizotypes, according to Rado, possess an inherited potential to develop the observable symptoms of the disease, though this may never occur. The defect experienced by the schizotype is a fundamental deficiency in the ability to feel pleasurable emotions—including joy, affection, love, and pride—but no similar reduction in the negative emotions, the only emotions they are capable of feeling with any intensity. The net effect is to reduce motivation by reducing their ability to enjoy life activities, reduce the capacity for satisfying interpersonal relationships, reduce self-confidence and sense of security, attenuate sexual functioning, and even diminish the capacity for self-awareness.

Rado did not see the course of the schizotypal pattern as inevitably fixed, however, as did Kraepelin with dementia praecox, but instead as moving forward and backward among a compensated state, a decompensated state, a disintegrated state, and a deteriorated state. With luck, compensated schizotypes would go through life without ever experiencing a psychotic break. Decompensated schizotypes have become overtly schizophrenic, exhibiting the characteristic thought disorder that reduces the individual to functional incompetence, according to Rado, but might return to a compensated state given appropriate treatment.

Attracted to Rado's formulation, Meehl (1962, 1990b) constructed a brilliant, speculative theoretical model, ushering in the contemporary era of schizophrenic research. According to Meehl, a single dominant gene produces a basic cognitive and cognitive-emotional "slippage" by altering some function of the synapse at all points in the nervous system, but in an extremely subtle way. Meehl called this hypokrisia, meaning "insufficiency of separation, differentiation, or discrimination" (1990b, p. 15). The presence of the schizotaxic gene, however, does not mean that its owner will develop a schizophrenia. Only a minority, those unfortunate in possessing other genes such as those activating social introversion, dispositionally high levels of anxiety or low capacity for pleasurable experience, for example, or persons exposed to unfortunate trauma or repeated insult actually develop schizophrenia.

Because the gene is "silent" in most cases, its owners cannot be identified on the basis of hallucinations or delusions. Meehl was thus led to develop a new methodology called taxometrics, the purpose of which was to classify subjects on the basis of characteristics associated with schizophrenia but not necessarily specific to schizophrenic or even associated with it in an obvious way. Whereas the diagnostic categories of the *DSM* are defined through the consensus of experts in the field, taxometrics represents a mathematical means of identifying categories of mental disorder. Although the methodology has not yet been widely applied, researchers have now identified a schizotypy taxon and replicated their results (Korfine & Lenzenweger, 1995; Lenzenweger & Korfine, 1992).

A number of studies looking for subtle schizophrenic signs in the family members of schizophrenics followed. The most important were the Danish adoption studies, begun in 1963 by Kety, Rosenthal, Wender, and Schulsinger (1968) designed to separate the influence of genetic and environmental variables. Both schizophrenia and latent schizophrenia were found more often in the biological relatives of schizophrenic adoptees than in other subjects, also adopted, of the same age, gender, social class, and length of time with biological mother. These results strongly supported the hypothesis of a schizophrenic spectrum.

The borderline schizophrenic subgroup, closest to the contemporary schizotypal, was described as exhibiting a history of chronic maladaptation, including:

1. Cognitive difficulties, such as vague, illogical, unrealistic thoughts.
2. Affective abnormalities, namely anhedonia, defined as an incapacity to experience pleasurable feelings.
3. Interpersonal difficulties, including a deep ambivalence toward intimate relationships with others or intense dependent involvements.
4. The presence of psychopathology characterized by multiple neurotic features such as obsessions, phobias, psychosomatic concerns, generalized anxiety, and micropsychotic episodes.

Despite these liabilities, such individuals were believed to persist without decompensating into a florid schizophrenic syndrome.

By the time work began on the *DSM-III* in 1980, a borderline schizophrenic syndrome was still regarded as somewhat ambiguous. The term borderline was widely used to refer not only to compensated schizotypes but also to the neurotic components of character disorder, the borderline personality organization of the psychodynamic perspective. To further clarify its boundaries with the psychoses and personality disorders, Spitzer, Endicott, and Gibbon (1979) developed provisional diagnostic criteria based on the results of the Danish adoption studies and their own literature review. A large sample of psychiatrists was then asked to rate each criterion in terms of how well it discriminated schizophrenia-like patients from those with an unstable, borderline condition or psychosis. On the basis of this study, the schizotypal personality disorder was officially born.

The Biological Perspective

As amply illustrated, the history of the schizotypal personality disorder has been strongly influenced by a belief in its biological underpinnings and its linkage with schizophrenia. Further studies have now firmly established that some genetic relationship links the two disorders (Kendler et al., 1993), though its exact nature, the specific gene or genes, and their chromosomal location remain unclear. Presumably, research profiting from the Human Genome Project, intended to produce a complete genetic map for Homo sapiens, will eventually aid the search. For now, researchers can only say, for example, that when one family member carries a schizophrenia or schizotypal personality disorder, the risk that others do also is increased, and the positive and negative symptoms are independently heritable (Kendler & Walsh, 1995). Presumably, some forms of schizophrenia may involve a single dominant gene, as Meehl's model predicts, and other forms may involve multiple genes. The two are not mutually exclusive.

Whatever the case, the emerging view, foreshadowed by Rado and Meehl, is that the schizotype is really the fundamental disorder. In contrast, schizophrenia is simply the terminal point of a genetic predisposition, arising in conjunction with persistent environmental stress or trauma. Schizophrenia is the special case; the schizotypal personality is the general case and, therefore, the proper focus of investigation (Raine & Lencz, 1995). Accordingly, researchers have now begun to extend the classic findings of schizophrenia research downward into the range of the schizotypal personality. Although thousands of studies on schizophrenics have been published, surprisingly little is known with certainty. The hope is that the study of the schizotypal personality will clarify and extend a great many tentative findings. The most straightforward hypothesis, which need not be supported for every line of research, is simply that every schizophrenic pathology should have a less pathological parallel in the schizotypal personality.

An important research tradition focuses on structural abnormalities in the schizophrenic brain, using recently developed technologies such as computerized tomography, which passes X-rays through sections of brain tissue, and magnetic resonance imagery (MRI), which takes more precise pictures of the brain using intense magnetic fields. Findings show that the ventricles, cavities in the brain between the hemispheres that contain cerebrospinal fluid, are enlarged in many schizophrenics, suggesting either some pathology in the development of the brain or perhaps an atrophy of brain tissue as a result of the disorder. Buchsbaum, Yang, and colleagues (1997) compared the ventricular volume of schizophrenic subjects, schizotypal personality subjects, and normals. Findings suggest decreased volume of the left frontal lobe. More important, however, the degree of ventricular enlargement was not as great for schizotypals as for schizophrenics and is not found in other personality disorders (Siever, Rotter, Losonczy, & Guo, 1995).

In addition to its large-scale structural features, the brain is composed of individual neurons that communicate with one another across the synapse via chemical messengers, called neurotransmitters. Without these, the billions of neurons of the brain would be isolated, unable to do anything. Thought itself would be impossible. Because cognitive distortions are so basic to the schizotypal personality, the study of neurotransmitters has become a natural route of investigation. Like schizophrenics, schizotypal subjects possess ideas of reference, thought disorder, perceptual aberrations, and paranoid symptoms, the so-called positive symptoms, which respond to antipsychotic medications (Joseph, 1997), though schizotypals require lower doses than do schizophrenics. Such a similar response to similar medication again argues for continuity between the two syndromes.

Precisely which neurotransmitters are involved, however? Antipsychotics work by blocking receptor sites for dopamine. Now more than 30 years old, the "dopamine hypothesis" holds simply that too much dopamine leads to the positive symptoms of schizophrenia. Indeed, any excess of dopamine should produce schizophrenic symptoms. This is exactly what occurs. Parkinson's disease, for example, is associated with a deficiency of dopamine. However, when Parkinson's patients are given drugs to increase dopamine levels, some develop positive symptoms (Celesia & Barr, 1970). Likewise, the psychosis induced by amphetamine abuse is produced through dopaminergic channels. Given such connections, it is hardly surprising that dopamine plays a role in the schizotypal personality. Research now shows that increases in the levels of chemicals in the blood that mark dopamine activity in the brain correlate with the positive symptoms of schizotypal personality disorder (Siever et al., 1993).

Combining the findings of anatomical and neurotransmitter research described previously, current thinking (Siever, 1995) is that structural brain defects account for negative symptoms in schizotypal personality disorder, and increased dopamine activity in areas of the limbic system account for the positive symptoms. Whether this reflects some hypersensitivity in the receptors or perhaps simply too many receptor sites is not yet known. Several kinds of dopamine receptors have now been identified, and their number and relative proportions are likely to become a central focus of future studies.

Another classic line of research focuses on neurovirology, an emerging subdiscipline, with the theory that at least some schizophrenics are afflicted with a viral infection of the brain during fetal development. The virus assimilates itself into the DNA and then lies dormant until somehow reactivated during puberty or early adulthood, ages when the risk for schizophrenia abruptly rises. Various studies support the viral theory. More schizophrenics are conceived in the winter months, the cold and flu season, than in summer months, for example. Machón, Huttenen, Mednick, and LaFosse (1995) compared schizophrenics born during an influenza epidemic in Finland in 1957 to control subjects born in 1955 and 1956, a relatively low influenza period. Subjects exposed to influenza during the second trimester of pregnancy were shown to be higher than controls on the cognitive-perceptual symptoms of schizotypy, with a trend toward interpersonal deficits as well. Other studies have shown that metabolites of clozapine, a relatively recently developed drug used to treat schizophrenia, inhibit the replication of human immunodeficiency virus (HIV-1), further strengthening the link between schizotypy and viral infection (Jones-Brando, Buthod, Holland, Yolken, & Torrey, 1997). Moreover, the viral hypothesis is not inconsistent with the high concordance rate of schizophrenia among identical twins, who share fetal circulation (Davis & Phelps, 1995).

Other miscellaneous but interesting findings have been reported. For example, subjects with high schizotypy scores tend to be shorter than normals (Wellman, Williams, Geaney, & Cowen, 1996). Like schizophrenics, normal subjects with high scores on schizotypy do not discriminate smells as well as normals (Park & Schoppe, 1997). Scores on cognitive measures of schizotypy predict vulnerability to nightmares (Claridge, Clark, & Davis, 1997). Different aspects of schizotypal personality disorder may be associated with either early or late puberty (Gruzelier & Kaiser, 1996). Schizophrenic subjects were less likely than their nonschizophrenic siblings to be breast-fed and exhibited more schizoid and schizotypal traits in childhood (McCreadie, 1997).

The Psychodynamic Perspective

The *DSM* and the psychodynamic perspective model psychopathology in profoundly different ways. The intention of the *DSM-III,* adopted in 1980, was to purge psychopathology of all theoretical assumption, return to description as the foundation of the classification system, and build from there, in the hope that with time and research, description would give way to explanation—the goal of science. In doing so, however, the *DSM-III* implicitly made certain assumptions of its own, notably that all psychopathologies should, and could, be diagnosed as categories and that the boundaries between various categorical entities are correct, even though the disease processes responsible for pathology in any one category are for the most part unknown. Each syndrome is thus treated as a discrete entity, potentially unrelated to any other.

In contrast, the psychodynamic perspective asserts that threads of continuity unify many psychopathologies that are only superficially different. As we have seen, the hysterical character is usually regarded as a more mature form of the histrionic, which is more infantile and pathological. Here, differences of degree masquerade as differences of kind. From a psychodynamic perspective, the *DSM* mutilates this continuum by presenting only a histrionic personality, forcing everything into a single category. The same is true of the schizotypal personality. Despite the *DSM*'s emphasis on the categorical and discrete, most analysts have historically viewed today's schizoids, avoidants, and schizotypals as existing at the nonpsychotic end of a continuum anchored at the psychotic extreme by schizophrenia (McWilliams, 1994).

Most mainstream clinicians would consider the metapsychological constructs of classical psychoanalysis to be far too remote from the particular person to be clinically useful. According to the classical view, schizophrenics react to a particularly harsh, cold, or withholding world by regressing back to a stage of development that existed before the ego was formed. Because the primary function of the ego is to coordinate the internal demands of the id, the prohibitions of the superego, and the constraints of external reality, almost everything we think of as distinctly human is thereby voided.

As the reality principle gives way to the fluidity of primary process thinking, behavior shifts abruptly as the id switches unpredictably from one drive state to another. Sense of time is absent or distorted. The boundary between internal and external worlds dissolves. Identity fragments. No superordinate motive synthesizes smaller goals into some superordinate action plan designed to fulfill some ultimate purpose. Loss of reality testing may be so complete that self and not-self are no longer strictly distinguishable. The individual may temporarily fuse with others or even with inanimate objects. Still more primitive levels of regression feature complete withdrawal into autistic or catatonic states, perhaps a protective retreat designed to shut others out, minimize all external stimulation, and thereby reinforce or preserve what little solidity the self might still possess. Neal has a degree of this, perhaps, but the description seems too severe.

By extension, the same logic would apply to the schizotypal. Rather than regress to some stage of development that preexists the ego, however, schizotypals would regress to some stable, but primitive, ego state characterized by temporary psychotic episodes. Again, normality provides an important reference point. Normal persons possess a coherent, integrated sense of self that provides a sense of continuity to experience and moderates the expression of impulses and feelings. Without this solid sense of self, we would be at the mercy of our drives and emotions, flung back and forth, like the borderline personality, from anger to tears, depending on the situation and the nature of our own personal associations. Like the borderline's, the internal world of the schizotypal is highly unintegrated, but for reasons that are primarily cognitive, not neurotic. In the borderline, waves of intense emotion wash over, swamp, and disrupt the formation of incipient self-structures that, given a friendly developmental environment, might otherwise form and contain these same emotions.

In the schizotypal, however, a basic neural capacity to consolidate a coherent sense of self, world, and others is somehow lacking. As a result, their internal representations are a jumbled mix of unassimilated and often contradictory memories, perceptions, impulses, and feelings. Any one of these can seize executive control and guide behavior temporarily before giving way to some other association. The desirable aspects of a particular stimulus object thus lead first to some positive emotion but just as easily call unintegrated negative aspects of the same stimulus object to consciousness, thus giving way to some negative emotion and vice versa. Consequently, schizotypals often seem affectively labile or neurotic, like the borderline. Borderlines, however, experience micropsychotic episodes mainly when overwhelmed by strong negative emotions, centering especially on anger and abandonment concerns. In contrast, schizotypals seem forever lost in the fog. They become mired in personal irrelevancies and tangential asides that seem vague, digressive, or even autistic.

Lack of integration at the basic level of internal self and other object-representations is a very important part of why the schizotypal is considered a structurally defective personality disorder. Moreover, it is important in creating a vulnerability to decompensation under even modest degrees of stress. Lacking a well-developed, coordinating ego, schizotypals discharge their emotions in haphazard ways, sometimes in a sequence of apparently unrelated actions. Often, they are easily overwhelmed by excess stimulation and must either seek retreat or suffer a psychoticlike disorganization. When social demands and expectations press hard against their uninvolved or withdrawn state, they may use their tendency to disorganize defensively by blanking out or seeming to drift off into another world. Undue encroachments may lead them to disconnect socially for prolonged periods, during which they may become confused and aimless, display inappropriate affect and paranoid thinking, and communicate in odd, circumstantial, and metaphorical ways.

Consider Neal again. Like most schizotypals, Neal is excessively anxious in social situations. Unable to separate tangential aspects of the consensual social world from those that are truly meaningful, his subjective world is a mixture of the relevant and irrelevant. Accidental aspects of reality are given as much heed as those that are planned or intended and become connected in ways that others find unfathomable. Obviously, Neal has trouble organizing his thoughts as it is. When forced into social encounters, he speaks slowly because, first, he finds it difficult to understand what others are requiring of him; second, he finds it difficult to coordinate his thoughts toward a single objective; and third, what concentration he does have becomes more brittle when he becomes more anxious. Unfortunately, during particularly stressful times, he sometimes becomes tangled up in his own mythologies. His social anxiety leads to ideas of reference, which lead him to rely on coping mechanisms that have a mystical flavor. For some schizotypals, the fear of total disintegration of self may lead to a frantic search for some safe harbor where the impending threat of existential annihilation can be weathered. Likewise, Neal's goal is simply to retreat. The inability to consolidate internal representations of self and others leads to alienation from others and, ultimately, to an alienation from self.

Many schizotypals possess superego residuals that are brought to bear unpredictably on their behavior and impulses, often leading to extraordinary guilt feelings. The word *residuals* is key, because the superego consists of the internalized prohibitions of caretakers, that is, the internalized objects of individuals central to early life experience, often called introjects. The normal superego expresses both the conscience and ego ideal, the prohibitions and prescriptions of life. In a crude sense, the conscience keeps you out of trouble, and the ego ideal gives you direction and value. The ego synthesizes the goals of the superego with ongoing behavior, so that actions are principled and goal-directed, rather than purely egocentric and gratification seeking.

In the schizotypal, however, images of introjects are as fragmented as the image of self. Bizarre mannerisms and idiosyncratic thoughts often reflect a retraction or reversal of forbidden acts or ideas, allowing repentance or nullification of perceived misdeeds, a defense mechanism known as undoing. Because schizotypals live in a subjective world populated by omens, a sixth sense, extrasensory information, and synchronicity, unforeseen connections among obscure metaphysical aspects of their world easily lead to unanticipated missteps that must be corrected through some equally magical means. Odd beliefs and ritualistic behaviors may be seen as superstitious means of undoing evil thoughts and actions that have "offended the spirits," essentially a process of atonement that attempts to put the individual right with the universe's own record keeping or correct some mistake by appeasing the powers that be. Because these actions serve to diminish the individual's inchoate moral anxiety, they further contribute to the construction of self-made, idiosyncratic realities composed of suspicion, illusion, and superstition rather than objective fact.

The Interpersonal Perspective

For the schizotypal, interpersonal behavior and cognitive style are closely tied and work together to perpetuate the disorder. The disorder mixes social communication with personal irrelevancies. Nonproductive daydreaming contributes to magical thinking and irrational suspicion, further obscuring the line between reality and fantasy. Paired with an absence of social interaction that might provide the corrective feedback of normal human relationships, the schizotypal can exhibit only socially gauche habits and peculiar mannerisms. In turn, this estrangement from self and others contributes to experiences of depersonalization, derealization, and dissociation. A preference for privacy and isolation drives schizotypals toward secretive activities and peripheral roles. As such, they often lack any awareness that their actions are inappropriate, and they may not understand why their actions are inappropriate even when the reasons are explained to them. Unable to grasp the everyday elements of human behavior, they misconstrue interpersonal communications and impose personalized frames of references, circumstantial speech, and metaphorical asides.

Although schizotypals often seem content to remain socially eccentric or odd, in fact, many are simply oblivious to implicit codes of conduct and subtle behavioral norms. Socially savvy individuals have a broad awareness of social scripts. Normal persons are aware of the internal emotional states of others and work to smooth over the rough edges of interpersonal encounters, an attribute called poise. Even relatively unpoised individuals, however, universally engage in impression management to optimize outcomes. In contrast, schizotypals do not understand implicit social codes and behavioral norms. The value of appearing composed and competent during a job interview may be lost on them, for example. Their social categories and scripts are simply coarse and incomplete. Knowledge of the nuances of everyday social interaction, the ability to read the intentions of others accurately and respond appropriately, and an awareness of the biasing effects of mood on cognition—all things that the social savant assumes—are either deficient, fraught with gaps, or simply absent.

Instead, schizotypals miss signals and social cues, chronically misdiagnose social situations, commit terrible gaffes that make others feel awkward, and even inadvertently insult those who might control their destiny. They not only impute wrong motives to others but also gear their own interpersonal responses to these misunderstandings. Thus, conversations meander unpredictably; get lost in vague, abstract metaphors; fail to rise above the concrete; are polluted by irrelevant intrusions; or seem burdened by a baggage of unintended connotations. No wonder, then, that schizotypals are experienced by others as being strange or weird.

The most unfortunate consequences, however, derive from the vicious circles such behavior creates. By responding to consensual social reality in nonconsensual ways, schizotypals lose the ability to drive social encounters in directions that are constructive or satisfying for either party. Recall from Chapter 2 that in the ideal interpersonal interaction, each person seeks to pull responses that validate his or her self-image. In effect, interpersonal communication confirms us to ourselves. Schizotypals do not invalidate others; they simply fail to validate them. As a result, others feel confused and awkward. Therapists know that they must function as a secondary ego for their schizotypal patients, bringing the conversation back to what is appropriate, allowing the schizotypal to test reality through the clinician, and so on.

For the average person, however, the schizotypal is surprising and confusing. Normals eventually get lost in the convoluted mass of digressions and lose track of the conversation. They may have no idea what the schizotypal is talking about or why. Eventually, normals either terminate the encounter abruptly or simply ignore what cannot be understood. The implicit message is either dismissiveness or disgust: "You are a nonentity, and I will ignore you," or "I don't like you. You make me feel strange. There is something wrong with you." A long history of such encounters may explain why schizotypals find interpersonal interactions vaguely punishing and exhibit such intense social anxiety. Most deeply wish to be left alone.

The existential consequence of this vicious circle is the deconstruction of a coherent self. As emphasized by symbolic interactionists and social psychologists, the self is a construct like any other construct but finds its content through interaction with others. Given their cognitive aberrations, schizotypals are likely to be as ineffective at relating to and understanding their own needs as they are oblivious to those of others. That is, the same kinds of cognitive errors that lead to mistakes in decoding the significance of events in the external world probably apply to the internal world as well. When schizotypals communicate with themselves through introspection or reflection, their self-talk suffers the same kinds of errors and distortions as when communicating with anyone else.

As a result, schizotypals never achieve the solid sense of identity associated with normal development. Their tendency to intrude tangentialities and irrelevant associations and to become inappropriately metaphorical or concrete makes the schizotypal self a particularly porous construct riddled with the products of these distorted reflections. Their intuition of self—their understanding of the essence of who they are—probably seems strange, foreign, even alien, in ways that normal persons cannot comprehend. For most of us, the intuition of our identity is so immediate that the self is an almost physical, vibrant presence, not a construct at all (hence Western dualism and the mind-body problem). For the schizotypal, however, the very processes that guide self-insight are distorted, and the content of the self is distorted as well. When combined with internalized feelings of self-neglect that the dismissiveness of others engenders, many schizotypals are left with a profound head start toward depersonalization and self-estrangement, even feelings of existential terror produced by feelings that the self might simply dissolve.

Consider the case of Matthew, the night watchman (see Case 12.2). Like many schizotypals, he seems to expect criticism and negativity, chronically misreads the motives of others, misdiagnoses social situations, and imbues interactions with malevolent intents. Nevertheless, Matthew has found a niche for himself that compensates for the social anxiety and suspiciousness that plague the schizotypal mind. He states frankly, "People make me nervous," and says that his night watchman job spares him the crowds and noise of the daytime. His only real human contact is with his brother, whom he sees sometimes over the holidays. Drifting over time into increasingly peripheral vocations, he has also worked as a janitor and a driver. The immediate problem, however, is his bizarre behavior: Matthew has been observed "skulking" around corners, muttering to himself, and cutting the back of his hand. After extensive probing, he admits that he sometimes feels dead and nonexistent. The cutting serves a functional role in his life, providing a strong, concrete counterpoint to the emptiness of his own identity. By reminding himself that he is real, Matthew is able to pull back from the brink of self-diffusion.

A developmental account of the schizotypal from an interpersonal perspective has been presented by Benjamin (1996). All children eventually develop their own autonomy, an important part of developing an identity that exists as separate from the caretaker. However, the parents of future schizotypals, according to Benjamin, send contradictory, illogical messages by punishing their children for taking autonomy while taking autonomy themselves in the very same way. She gives the example of the father who is rarely home but beats his child for not being home. Because such parents fear autonomy in their children, they imply that they somehow have access to information that exceeds what is empirically possible, perhaps a sixth sense about what the child might be doing wrong, for example. The parent might say, "You know that if you do that, I can see you. I'll know what you've done." Magical, detached observation from afar thus substitutes for real caring and parenting, modeling both magical thinking for the future schizotypal as well as how the schizotypal should care for others.

As adults, these individuals gravitate toward marginalized professions that assume privileged access to other modes of information or experience, perhaps fortune telling or astrology, for example. As they divine their special knowledge, they present it to their clients with a detachment modeled by their own parents: "Do what you will, the tea leaves say such and such." At the same time, Benjamin states, the parents controlled the child in bizarre ways that held the power of life or death over the destiny of the caretaker. Perhaps the mother or father would die unless certain household tasks were performed. The result, Benjamin states, is that behavior beyond what would be developmentally appropriate was required for the child to contain his or her own incredible power of destruction. This further distorts the basic experience of relating to others and eventually gives rise to superstitious beliefs and rituals about the power of the self and how it can be used, channeled, and controlled.

Although weird behavior necessarily requires a weird explanation, Benjamin (1996) explains the paranoid and socially withdrawn aspects of the schizotypal straightforwardly. Many schizotypals, she states, can be expected to have a long history of abuse. Paranoid symptoms develop in response to the intense experience of attack that this abuse generates. Fears of engulfment arise because schizotypals repeatedly experience themselves as having been invaded and co-opted. Retreat into time spent alone becomes

Matthew, age 37, works the night shift for a large security firm. Although he has guarded the same large food warehouse night after night for 13 years, he seldom interacts with other employees, preferring instead to spend time alone. Recently, however, his coworkers have been complaining of his strange behavior.[1] Matthew has been muttering incoherently and "skulking" around corners. After Matthew was seen cutting the skin on the back of his hand with a pocketknife, his supervisor made arrangements for a psychological evaluation. ⟵(7)

During the clinical interview, Matthew answered questions with ⟵(4) either one-word responses or very short phrases, usually waiting to be asked a second time before responding and refusing to make eye contact with the examiner. His answers were short and bizarre ⟵(4) and gave insight into a life devoid of any human connectedness. In fact, his only real personal contact is his older brother, whom ⟵(8) he sometimes sees during the holidays. His only significant relationship, he states, was with a girl in high school. "We graduated and I didn't see her any more," he says, beginning with almost no emotion and then trailing off into silence, with an occasional misplaced giggle. ⟵(6)

When asked why he likes his work, Matthew replies that the night shift spared him the crowds and noise of daytime. Moreover, he can ⟵(9) be by himself during his patrols and is not required to talk with anyone else. "People make me nervous," he states, smiling. When asked about past employment, he notes that he has worked as a janitor and a driver but has been homeless for a period of time, though it did not appear to worry him. Throughout the interview, he shows neither understanding nor curiosity about the events that led ⟵(4) to the evaluation, instead answering questions mostly in monotone. He seems impervious to the world around him.

After extensive probing and rephrasing, Matthew discloses that he sometimes fears that he is dead or nonexistent, that he feels more ⟵(3) like a thing than a person. Accompanying this revelation is his first genuine emotion of the interview. "I get terrified," he states. When these feelings occur, he quiets the dread by cutting himself. If he truly did not exist, "the cuts would not hurt, and he would not bleed." He is also helped by "mind messages." He calls out to the ⟵(2) "protective spirits," who answer his call, thus reaffirming his existence. Matthew seems undisturbed by the peculiarity of his statements or by his idiosyncratic lifestyle. Although his self-mutilation obviously requires treatment, in his view, it is a positive force that contributes to his comfort.

---

[1]Numbers mark aspects of the case most consistent with *DSM* criteria, and do not necessarily indicate that the case "meets" diagnostic criteria in this respect.

Schizotypal Personality Disorder
DSM-IV Criteria

A pervasive pattern of social and interpersonal deficits marked by acute discomfort with, and reduced capacity for, close relationships as well as by cognitive or perceptual distortions and eccentricities of behavior, beginning by early adulthood and present in a variety of contexts, as indicated by five (or more) of the following:

(1) ideas of reference (excluding delusions of reference)

(2) odd beliefs or magical thinking that influences behavior and is inconsistent with subcultural norms (e.g., superstitiousness, belief in clairvoyance, telepathy, or "sixth sense"; in children and adolescents, bizarre fantasies or preoccupations)

(3) unusual perceptual experiences, including bodily illusions

(4) odd thinking and speech (e.g., vague, circumstantial, metaphorical, overelaborate, or stereotyped)

(5) suspiciousness or paranoid ideation

(6) inappropriate or constricted affect

(7) behavior or appearance that is odd, eccentric, or peculiar

(8) lack of close friends or confidants other than first-degree relatives

(9) excessive social anxiety that does not diminish with familiarity and tends to be associated with paranoid fears rather than negative judgments about self

the most adaptive strategy. In the final analysis, Benjamin's model seems consistent with the famous double-bind theories of schizophrenia that evolved from Sullivan's original contributions, first put forward by Bateson and colleagues (1956). However, Benjamin's model offers additional specificity through the principles of interpersonal communication encoded in her SASB model.

The Cognitive Perspective

Although biology may somehow underlie the schizotypal personality, the salient manifestations of this biology are cognitive. First, schizotypals often seem unable to organize their thoughts. Histrionics may seem distractible or flighty, but these cognitive characteristics serve a function: They are stylistic, working in conjunction with massive repression to prevent anything from being considered too deeply. The neural architecture is fundamentally sound, but its operation is distorted from the top down, transformed by the needs of the total histrionic personality.

In the schizotypal, however, cognition seems distorted from the bottom up, as if the associative glue that binds smaller ideas into larger ones was somehow defective (Bleuler, 1911; Meehl, 1962). Cognitive psychologists often talk about neural networks and the notion of spreading activation. According to this model, every concept is like a node connected to many others in a huge conceptual network. When a particular concept is activated, some of its activation spreads out to adjacent nodes. When the activation of two or more different concepts intersects on a third, its activation reaches a threshold, and the concept is bumped up into conscious awareness. Free association works in essentially this way. Christmas, for example, naturally makes you think of Santa Claus, and Thanksgiving conjures thoughts of a turkey dinner. In the schizotypal, however, the idea of Christmas might produce an immediate association to reindeer noses because Rudolph's nose is red. The association to Rudolph is understandable, but somehow, the general and specific get confused, and the entire class concept of reindeer noses becomes activated.

Although its discussion here oversimplifies matters, a malfunctioning neural network can nevertheless serve as an important touchstone for understanding schizotypal cognition. Disordered language and communication are considered core to the disorder. In the schizotypal, spreading activation seems to travel down pathways other than those relevant to the immediate purpose of cognition. We saw that in Neal, for example, with his rambling answers that seemed to free-associate off themselves in midstream. At the lower ends of severity, this cognitive irregularity may be present through the unusual or idiosyncratic use of words, as if they held some meaning or nuance known mainly to the schizotypal. When asked to list words beginning with A or F, for example, even normal subjects with higher scores on a Magical Ideation Scale tended to generate rare words (Duchene, Graves, & Brugger, 1998). Even normal subjects with high schizotypy scores show less effective linguistic processing (Kravetz, Faust, & Edelman, 1998). In schizotypals, these effects are magnified. Cognition may sometimes seem almost autistic, as if following some internal logic not known to anyone else. At a somewhat more severe level, irrelevancies get drawn into the cognitive process, sidetracking the stream of consciousness into alleyways that lead to other alleyways that lead to still other alleyways.

For the same reason, schizotypals tend to be distractible (Hall & Habbits, 1996). Attention may shift topics abruptly as it meanders about in its own associative maze.

When these alleyways eventually lead back to the subject at hand, speech is said to be circumstantial, meaning that schizotypals seem to talk around the subject, temporarily losing their focus but eventually recovering at the end. Frank schizophrenics, in contrast, are derailed by their thought disorder. After associating through several coincidental connections, they never return to the main theme of the conversation. Nevertheless, schizotypals seem incapable of sustained, purposeful cognition, in which thought is deliberately and intensely focused toward achieving some goal or toward understanding a particular point or a sequence of steps in a complex logical argument. They make poor philosophers, for example, because they fail to contemplate coherently. Not surprisingly, both schizotypals and schizophrenics perform poorly in tasks of sustained attention, a finding that argues for continuity of these syndromes and appears to distinguish them from other personality disorders (Roitman, Cornblatt, Bergman, & Obuchowski, 1997).

Alternatively, some schizotypals seem to exhibit a disorder in the productivity of speech. In effect, nothing strikes them one way or the other, and nothing is worthy of remark. Matthew, whose answers are short and bizarre, comes closer to this than Neal. Such individuals usually have a schizoid quality, and their near mutism reflects an incapacity to experience pleasurable emotions and a constricted range of affect. They literally have nothing to say because nothing motivates them. As noted in the case, Matthew seldom makes eye contact with the interviewer. In fact, his life is almost devoid of human connectedness. Without some capacity for emotional experience, there is nothing to organize and motivate cognition. For example, Matthew has no interest in exploring the implications of a particular concept or developing a line of argument. Instead, his thought processes seem inherently diffuse. Although such schizotypals appear turned radically inward, alienated from society, it is more likely that their inner voices are just as silent, taking no more interest in the inherent joy of mentation than in anything in the external world. Cognitively, they are best described as vacant, a description that fits with Matthew's fear that he does not exist.

Other aspects of schizotypal cognition also seem partially schizophrenic but are more difficult to understand as "loose associative glue" or some inferential abnormality. As noted in *DSM-IV*, schizotypals often have strange beliefs that deviate significantly from subcultural norms yet nevertheless influence behavior. We have already discussed their interpersonal and psychodynamic aspects and now develop a cognitive interpretation.

Stone (1993), for example, reports the case of a schizotypal client who claimed to be able to see right through his head and read the titles from the bookcase behind him. Others may believe that they can view faraway places remotely (clairvoyance) or perhaps project themselves to the astral plane and observe the happenings of our own world from another dimension. Or they may believe that they can read minds or transmit their thoughts over great distances, see the future, or receive communications from animals. To generalize, we might say that schizotypals often claim access to information outside what would normally be available to the five senses, perhaps through magical, mystical, or occult powers. Neal and Matthew would both qualify. Also, schizotypals sometimes experience bodily illusions, perhaps feeling that they are outside their bodies or are somehow detached from the physical self, free-floating in space. Or they might feel that parts of their bodies have become uncoupled at the joints or that one part on the right side is disproportionally larger than the same part on the left. Such symptoms certainly make a sharp boundary with schizophrenia difficult to justify and strongly suggest continuity between the two disorders.

Lacking insight into their own eccentricity, schizotypals often act on the information that they receive from their strange sources. Writing in Beck et al. (1990), Ottaviani suggests that schizotypals present an especially exaggerated example of what is called emotional reasoning, whereby the individual assumes, for example, that a negative emotion automatically entails some negative external cause that can be identified. For example, schizotypals might confront a spouse or lover because their sixth sense tells them that the spouse or lover has been unfaithful, commingling fear and reality. Or they might conclude that noises in the house are evidence of evil spirits and sell the house on this basis. Or they might accept a dinner invitation from an acquaintance who drives a white car, symbolizing purity and goodness, but decline a similar invitation from an acquaintance who drives a black car. We can easily see Neal and Matthew caught up in such odd logics.

Although the beliefs and actions of schizotypals seem odd to outside observers, they may not be strange at all when coupled with their unusual experiences; the way schizotypals reason is different, in part, because their experiences are different. A long tradition in psychology asserts that every individual operates somewhat like a naïve scientist who needs to make sense of the world. Likewise, disciplines as fundamental as anthropology and existentialism assert that we are meaning-making creatures. When an unusual event occurs, we cannot resist developing a theory about its causes. Even if incorrect, the explanation gives comfort by assuring us that the world is predictable rather than random. Far from being irrational, then, schizotypals may simply construct the world on the basis of a different empiricism—one based on their own subjective reality, the only reality that anyone can ever experience anyway. In an intriguing experiment, Zimbardo, Andersen, and Kabat (1981) showed that subjects given the suggestion that they would become partially deaf, but not remember the suggestion, develop paranoid explanations of their experience. When asked why they could not hear, they explained that the researchers were whispering about them, for example. Perhaps, then, the inferences of schizotypals are appropriate given the evidence, and it is the evidence itself that is bizarre.

The Evolutionary-Neurodevelopmental Perspective

Perspectives, by definition, yield only limited insight. The evolutionary theory of personality (Millon, 1990; Millon & Davis, 1996) maintains that the schizotypal exists on a continuum of severity with the passively detached schizoid and actively detached avoidant personalities, both of which gradually merge into the social detachment characteristic of normal introversion (see Figure 12.2). The distinction between the schizoid and avoidant as personality disorders thus appears at the threshold of normality and gradually becomes sharper as severity increases.

Thus, the schizoid appears behaviorally inert, interpersonally unengaged, remote, indifferent, cognitively impoverished or even vacant, and temperamentally unexcitable. The avoidant appears behaviorally fretful and hesitant, interpersonally fearful, cognitively distracted, and temperamentally anguished and tense. Because the disorders are really conceptual dimensions rather than discrete categories, as represented in the *DSM,* particular individuals may be located anywhere on the schizoid-avoidant continuum, thus sharing traits with either disorder. Some individuals, therefore, lack the fear of social humiliation that characterizes the avoidant, possess a measure of intact emotional

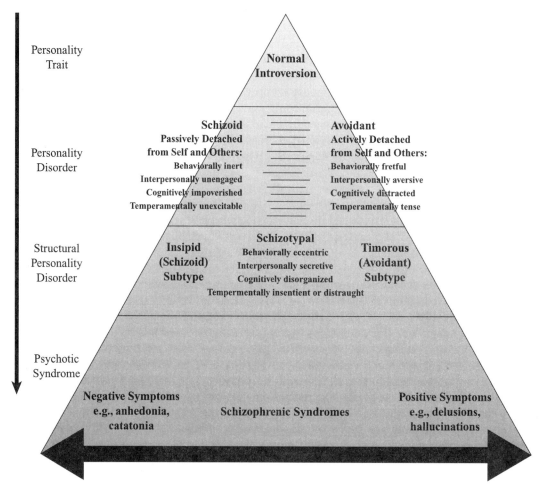

FIGURE 12.2 The Schizoid, Avoidant, and Schizotypal Personalities and Their Relationship to Schizophrenia.

capacity characteristic of the avoidant, and enjoy a well-developed fantasy life but nevertheless prefer the solitary lifestyle of the schizoid. At moderate levels of pathology, the structural matrix of the personality is fundamentally sound, and its expressed traits are integrated into the needs and functioning of the total personality.

As the level of pathology increases, however, defects in the very structural matrix that supports psychological functioning begin to amplify, distort, and transform underlying personality traits. For most subjects, these defects will have a biological-genetic foundation but be expressed and perpetuated cognitively and interpersonally. According to the evolutionary theory, the negative symptoms of the schizotypal capture and exaggerate the social apathy of the more intact schizoid, and the positive symptoms capture and exaggerate the more intact avoidant (see Figure 12.2).

Alienated from others and marginal members of society, schizoid-based schizotypals turn increasingly to solitary thoughts. Over time, shared social behaviors become fully subordinate to private fantasy. Their thoughts are left to wander unchecked by the logic and control of reciprocal social communication and activity. What they find within themselves is hardly rewarding—a barren, colorless void that offers no basis for joyful fantasy. Their inner personal world proves to be as dead and ungratifying as objective reality. They have no choice, so it seems, but to turn to unreal fantasies. These, at least, might fill in the void and give their existence some substance. Interest moves toward the mystical and magical, to needed illusions and ideation that enables the person to become a central, rather than a peripheral and insignificant, figure.

In an effort to minimize their awareness of external discomfort, avoidant-based schizotypals turn inward to fantasy and rumination, but this also proves to be self-defeating. Not only are their inner conflicts intense, but they spend much of their reflective time reliving and duplicating the painful events of the past. Their protective efforts only reinforce their distress. Moreover, given their low self-esteem, their inner reflections often take the form of self-reproval. They not only fail to gain solace from themselves but also find that they cannot readily escape from their own thoughts of self-derogation, from feelings of personal worthlessness and the futility of being themselves. In an effort to counter these oppressive inner thoughts, they may seek to block and destroy their cognitive clarity, that is, to interfere with the anguish of their discordant inner emotions and ideas. This maneuver not only proves self-defeating, in that it diminishes their ability to deal with events rationally, but further estranges them from communicating effectively with others. Even more destructive self-reproval and cognitive interference alienate them from their own existence. Having no place to go, they begin to create a new, inner world—one populated by magical fantasies, illusions, telepathic relationships, and other odd thoughts that provide them with not only an existence but one that is more significant and potentially rewarding than that found in reality.

Feelings of being hollow, empty, decaying, or dead inside, for example, caricature the depersonalized passive-detachment of the schizoid pattern. Lacking energy and initiative, these individuals neither engage others nor generate anything to fill their own internal void, like Matthew. Eventually, they exist only as living absence. Likewise, individuals who claim access to special modes of information and privileged dimensions of reality caricature the active-detachment of the avoidant, for whom hypervigilance and the construction of a withdrawn fantasy life are core traits. As the structural defect becomes more profound, it finally destroys integration itself as the defining characteristic of personality. Only the negative and positive symptoms of schizophrenia remain, residuals of the passive and active detachment of the schizoid and avoidant personalities (see Figure 12.2). Table 12.1 summarizes the total schizotypal pattern in terms of eight clinical domains.

CONTRAST WITH OTHER PERSONALITIES

The schizotypal is necessarily similar to the schizoid and avoidant but shares surface characteristics with the other structurally defective personalities, the paranoid and borderline. Both schizotypal and paranoid experience ideas of reference, are deeply suspicious of others, and prefer social isolation, though for different reasons. In the schizotypal, ideas of reference include signs and omens specially intended to guide or benefit the person. What the normal person would consider an interesting coincidence, the schizotypal may consider a revelation. As these are part and parcel of cognition, they can occur in conjunction with mystical states, are not necessarily troubling, and may be welcomed.

TABLE 12.1   The Schizotypal Personality: Functional and Structural Domains

Functional Domains		*Structural Domains*	
	Eccentric	Self-Image	***Estranged***
Expressive Behavior	Exhibits socially gauche and peculiar mannerisms; perceived by others as aberrant; disposed to behave in an unobtrusively odd, aloof, curious, or bizarre manner.		Exhibits recurrent social perplexities and illusions as well as experiences of depersonalization derealization and dissociation; sees self as forlorn, with repetitive thoughts of life's emptiness and meaninglessness.
	Secretive	**Object-Representations**	***Chaotic***
Interpersonal Conduct	Prefers privacy and isolation, with few, highly tentative attachments and personal obligations; has drifted over time into increasingly peripheral vocational roles and clandestine social activities.		Internalized representations consist of a piecemeal jumble of early relationships and affects, random drives and impulses, and uncoordinated channels of regulation that are only fitfully competent for binding tensions, accommodating needs, and mediating conflicts.
	Autistic	**Morphologic Organization**	***Fragmented***
Cognitive Style	Capacity to "read" thoughts and feelings of others is markedly dysfunctional; mixes social communications with personal irrelevancies, circumstantial speech, ideas of reference, and metaphorical asides; often ruminative, appearing self-absorbed and lost in daydreams with occasional magical thinking, bodily illusions, obscure suspicions, odd beliefs, and a blurring of reality and fantasy.		Possesses permeable ego-boundaries; coping and defensive operations are haphazardly ordered in a loose assemblage of morphologic structures, leading to desultory actions in which primitive thoughts and affects are discharged directly, with few reality-based sublimations, and significant further disintegrations into a psychotic structural level, likely under even modest stress.
	Undoing	**Mood/ Temperament**	***Distraught or Insentient***
Regulatory Mechanism	Bizarre mannerisms and idiosyncratic thoughts appear to reflect a retraction or reversal of previous acts or ideas that have stirred feelings of anxiety, conflict, or guilt; ritualistic or magical behaviors serve to repent for or nullify assumed misdeeds or "evil" thoughts.		Excessively apprehensive and ill at ease, particularly in social encounters; agitated and anxiously watchful, evincing distrust of others and suspicion of their motives that persists despite growing familiarity; or manifests drab, apathetic, sluggish, joyless, and spiritless appearance; reveals marked deficiencies in face-to-face rapport and emotional expression.

Note: Shaded domains are the most salient for this personality prototype.

In contrast, ideas of reference in the paranoid are usually associated with a fierce defense of autonomy, namely, the fear that others are somehow spying on the person. Thus, knowledge is extracted for the schizotypal but from the paranoid. Moreover, schizotypals may believe they can use their special insights to control others, whereas paranoids believe that others are attempting to control them.

Not surprisingly, both schizotypals and paranoids are often socially isolated. However, schizotypals seek social isolation because of repeated, hostile demands that they reform cognitively or face marginalization for being weird or strange. In contrast, paranoids directly destroy friendly associations by attributing hostile motives to others, for example, by repeated accusations. Schizotypals cannot reform cognitively, feel a sense of separateness, and choose to reject the world (Benjamin, 1996), whereas paranoids are rejected by the world. Finally, the paranoid is usually perceived as being cold, stubborn, and rigidly autonomous, whereas the schizotypal is open to experience to the point of cognitive disintegration.

Because the schizotypal and borderline personalities were originally carved from the same diagnostic rock, their overlap is of particular concern. Both experience emotional difficulties and temporary psychotic episodes, though for different reasons. Schizotypals are emotionally constricted or inappropriate, whereas borderlines are emotionally labile. Emotions in schizotypals mirror their idiosyncratic construction of reality. Because their interpretations are cognitively eccentric, their affect is subjectively appropriate but objectively inappropriate. In contrast, emotions in the borderline are driven interpersonally through their dichotomous appraisals of themselves and their relationships. Borderlines shift suddenly from all good to all bad, all loving to all hating, with few intermediate shades of gray. Although the speed with which the borderlines vacillate and their totalistic appraisals suggest a cognitive disorder, these symptoms are a consequence of their early attachments, not a neurocognitive deficit. The most discriminating feature, however, is likely to be their response to social isolation. Schizotypals seek separateness from the world; borderlines crave intimacy and desperately avoid abandonment.

PATHWAYS TO SYMPTOM EXPRESSION

The structurally defective personalities, particularly the schizotypal with its demonstrated relationship to schizophrenia, push the boundaries of the multiaxial system. Although personality is, by definition, the patterning of variables across the entire matrix of the person, the causal factors involved in creating and perpetuating the structurally defective patterns seem broader and more intricate than the syndromes of Axis I, which rests on the disease model, yet more narrow than those of Axis II. What we would normally think of as symptoms, then, seem closer to the core of the personality, caught somewhere between a consequence and a characteristic. The depersonalization of the insipid schizotypal, for example, is so logically connected to an exaggerated schizoid pattern that its separation as a symptom would diminish the subtype. Such distinctions have an artificial feel and remind us, as noted in the introductory chapters, that all taxonomies are limited social constructions. As you read the following paragraphs, try to identify the connection between personality and symptom.

Dissociative Episodes

Many individuals experience moments of detachment in which things seem strange or unreal, yet such estrangement and depersonalization are common in schizotypals. Observers of the passing scene, such persons remain uninvolved, sometimes even to the point of watching the course of events unfold from outside their physical bodies. In part, such feelings derive from a fundamental lack of affect, which promotes social detachment and prevents them from connecting meaningfully with others or from developing goals that might give meaning to their lives.

However, depersonalization may also reflect an attempt at self-desertion, an attempt to leave shameful and humiliating realities behind by fleeing existence itself. Alternatively, some schizotypals may seem to lose their personal identity in oceanic mystical states; these experiences are usually considered pleasurable, rather than terrifying.

Particularly for timorous schizotypals, recurrent illusions, magical thinking, and ideas of reference may be seen as an effort to supply some kind of content to the existential void, to anchor themselves to something substantial, to keep their boat afloat, even if that content is self-generated.

Psychotic Syndromes

As noted throughout this chapter, schizotypal personality disorder is believed to exist on a continuum with the schizophrenic syndromes. Although they exist on different axes, the difference appears to be one of degree rather than kind. Accordingly, the boundary between schizotypal personality and the schizophrenic syndromes is probably more arbitrary than objective. As a personality disorder, however, the schizotypal naturally assumes the presence of characteristics that stretch back to early adulthood.

In the absence of stress, then, during which many traits become more exaggerated or intense, schizotypals should be able to maintain their level of functioning. Should difficulties mount, however, or their coping efforts meet with failure, schizotypals may abandon their efforts to mobilize their resources or maintain reality contact and deteriorate into a psychotic disorder. In these severe states, they fail to discriminate between subjective experience and external reality; they become unable to carry out normal responsibilities or to behave in accord with conventional social expectations. Rational thinking disappears, previously controlled emotions erupt, and a disintegration and demoralization of self takes hold. For this reason, the *DSM-IV* stresses that the personality disorder can be diagnosed where it preexists the onset of a brief psychotic disorder, schizophreniform disorder, delusional disorder, or schizophrenia and reasserts itself once the psychotic symptoms of these disorders have remitted.

Depression

Many schizotypals, those without substantial schizoid characteristics, retain the capacity to feel some measure of emotion. Unfortunately, that emotion is often depression. Many are also biologically anhedonic, unable to experience more than a minimum of pleasurable feeling. In consequence, they either do not enjoy relating to others or find such relationships painful. In the end, they are usually dismissed contemptuously by others as weird or strange and drift aimlessly at the edge of society. Schizotypals have little capacity for experiencing reinforcement and develop few opportunities to acquire reinforcers. Schizotypals have no life plan, no sense of accomplishment, no ongoing interests, and no cherished relationships.

Therapy

The schizotypal is perhaps one of the easiest personality disorders to identify but one of the most difficult to treat with psychotherapy. The thought disorder and accompanying paranoid ideation work to distort communication between therapist and client and inhibit the formation of a trusting therapeutic alliance. Moreover, because schizotypals are inherently isolative and nonrelational, the therapist may sometimes be experienced as an intrusive presence. Because the alliance is the very foundation of therapy, medication is often needed before lasting progress can be made, especially with subjects who express the disorder severely.

THERAPEUTIC TRAPS

The expectations of the therapist and their influence on therapy are particularly important and may require careful monitoring. Most schizotypals initially see the therapist as attacking or humiliating (Benjamin, 1996). As anxiety increases, they may retreat further behind a curtain of disordered communication as a means of shielding themselves and confusing the intruder. Occasional retreats are universal. Therapists who become vexed when greeted with silence and emotional distancing only create an atmosphere that justifies such a reaction.

Instead, the need for distance must be respected, without conveying feelings of disapproval or inducing guilt, to which many subjects are especially sensitive. Not pushing too hard or too fast can prevent severe anxiety and paranoid reactions. Extraordinary patience may be required because schizotypals repeatedly misperceive aspects of the therapeutic relationship and then act on these misperceptions. Subjects who believe they have privileged access to information beyond the five senses sometimes apply their extrasensory powers to therapy and the therapist, believing that they can read the therapist's mind or arrive at conclusions about what the therapist secretly desires on the basis of tangential or irrelevant cues.

Accordingly, communication should be simple, straightforward, shorn of psychological jargon, and require a minimum of inference. Schizotypals find it difficult enough to bring order to their own thoughts, much less penetrate ambiguities and double messages carelessly introduced by others. The concrete is to be preferred over the poetic because the latter is naturally rich in connotations, which play havoc with schizotypal cognition. Special attention to the countertransference is in order, for unconscious feelings emitted by the therapist bring an unknown complexity to communication and are especially likely to be misconstrued by subjects.

STRATEGIES AND TECHNIQUES

What can be done in therapy often depends on the extent to which the thought disorder intrinsic to the syndrome can be controlled. Otherwise, every aspect of therapy becomes more complicated. Further, the appropriate goals and strategies for any particular subject depend on whether his or her symptoms most resemble an exaggerated schizoid pattern, an exaggerated avoidant pattern, or a mixture of the two. Strategies and techniques appropriate for the dominant underlying personality disorder can be used to supplement the primary goals of treating the schizotypal pattern (refer to the appropriate chapter).

Establishing a more normal pattern of interpersonal relationships is a primary goal of therapy. Social isolation intensifies cognitive deficits and allows social skills to atrophy. Contact with a therapist can prevent further deterioration. Because patterns of disordered family communication typify the early developmental environment of these subjects, therapy offers the chance for a novel, corrective interpersonal relationship through steady support and authenticity.

Accordingly, as emphasized by Benjamin (1996), the basic skills of humanistic therapy, including accurate empathy, mirroring, and unconditional positive regard, become particularly important. Benjamin states that the therapeutic alliance may represent a chance to experience a "nonexploitive protectiveness," one that eventually permits the schizotypal to give up management of the universe by magical means (p. 360). After an alliance has been established, subjects can be encouraged to voice distortions of reality as they occur, and these can be discussed in the context of the therapeutic relationship.

Benjamin (1996) further stresses that many schizotypals are likely to believe that harm may come to the therapist through their association. As such ideas are voiced, they can be tested realistically and tactfully refuted. In general, interpersonal therapy should enhance subjects' sense of self-worth and encourage the realization of positive attributes, an important step in defeating detachment, rebuilding motivation, and providing confidence necessary to take the first steps toward constructive social encounters outside therapy. Because schizotypals have difficulty sorting the relevant and irrelevant in interpersonal relationships, therapists may find that much of their time is spent helping the schizotypal test interpersonal reality and gain perspective on which behaviors might be appropriate in whatever situations are current in the subject's life. Repeated discussions of essentially similar situations may be necessary, as many schizotypals fail to realize that these are but variations on a theme. Basic social skills training is often helpful. Modeling behaviors provides an example that even concrete subjects can imitate. The ability to appraise interpersonal realities appropriately is an important step in decreasing social anxiety and accompanying paranoid symptoms while creating a capacity for appropriate affect and a sense of reward.

From a cognitive perspective, psychotherapy must adapt to the schizotypal's limited attentional resources and tendency to intrude tangential factors. Because many schizotypals are either overly concrete or overly abstract, learning may be generalized to other settings and situations only with great difficulty. Simplicity and structure help prevent the lessons of therapy from being obscured by the discombobulating effects of thought disorder. Furthermore, cognitive techniques allow the content of thought to be identified and eventually modified. This suggests that the combination of medication and cognitive therapy should be particularly effective.

Writing in Beck et al. (1990), Ottaviani indicates that the first step is to identity characteristic automatic thoughts, such as, "I am a nonbeing," as well as patterns of emotional reasoning and personalization, reviewed previously. Moreover, she suggests that assumptions underlying social interaction present an especially profitable avenue for change, as schizotypals usually believe that others dislike them. Subjects must be taught to act as naïve scientists and test their thoughts against the evidence. Feelings do not make facts; instead, each cognition is a hypothesis and should be disregarded if found inconsistent with the objective evidence. Even bizarre thoughts can be dealt with in this way. The thought, "I am leaving my body," for example, can be countered with prepared countercognitions: "There I go again. Even though I'm thinking this thought, it doesn't mean that it's true" (p. 141).

Because an effective grasp of objective reality is the Catch-22 of the cognitive approach, Ottaviani further suggests that schizotypals also be taught methods for gathering contrary evidence. Subjects can list evidence inconsistent with their predictions, for example. Going beyond content, cognitive style interventions can also be made. Rambling can be countered by requests for summary statements, and global statements can be countered by asking for elaboration. Finally, where subjects are not too paranoid or bizarre, group settings can be used to practice social functioning and provide feedback about distorted cognitions.

Because classical psychodynamic therapy is inherently unstructured, its use is probably not advised. As noted by Stone (1985), the purpose of psychodynamic therapy should be to internalize the therapeutic alliance. Because the early home environment of most schizotypals is likely to feature fragmented and chaotic communications, the ego boundaries of the schizotypal subject are only poorly developed. The interpretation of conflict not only disregards their desire for distance but also plays into their fear of engulfment. Accordingly, silence should be accepted as a legitimate part of the personality (Gabbard, 1994). Once this acceptance is felt, the subject may then begin to reveal hidden aspects of the self that can be adaptively integrated. Analytic procedures such as free association, the neutral attitude of the therapist, and the focus on dreams may foster an increase in autistic reveries and social withdrawal.

Probably the most useful analytic suggestion comes from Rado (1959), who suggests that identifying and capitalizing on some source of pleasure, however small, is a superordinate therapeutic goal. Motivation develops from the capacity for pleasure, and ultimately, only this can balance the painful emotions, attach the schizotypal to the real world, and prevent the dissolution of the self and cognitive disintegration that results from autistic withdrawal.

Summary

Schizotypals are often described as odd and eccentric and seemingly engrossed in their own world. Most researchers believe that the schizotypal personality lies on a continuum with schizophrenia called schizotypy. Schizotypals, like schizophrenics, experience both positive and negative symptoms. As one of the three structurally defective personalities (the paranoid and the borderline are the other two), schizotypals are set apart from other personalities in that they rarely find a comfortable niche in society and repeat the same setbacks again and again. However, most schizotypals are able to pull themselves together enough to prevent slipping into more serious decompensated states.

Despite the severe nature of this personality disorder, there are normal variants in society. Oldham and Morris (1995) describe the idiosyncratic style that "marches to a different drummer" and is highly open to new experiences and often attracted to the occult and supernatural. Normalizing the *DSM-IV* criteria also provides a more normal variant of schizotypals that draws inspiration from their own internal world and may hold certain superstitious beliefs but is able to suspend them to function effectively in society.

Some variations on the schizotypal personality are proposed by Millon (1990). The insipid schizotypal exaggerates the schizoid, passively detached pattern in addition to schizotypal features and is likely to have had a family background of indifference and formality. The timorous schizotypal shares the more actively detached style of the avoidant and is likely to have been belittled and rejected while growing up.

The schizotypal personality is a relatively new construct that has its origins in both the writings of Kraepelin and Bleuler, who studied dementia praecox patients and noticed how diverse their symptoms were. Bleuler conceptualized these patients on a continuum with schizophrenics at the most severe end and with schizotypals closer to normal because they could often appear to "walk about life" like any "normal" person. In 1956, Rado coined the term schizotype as an abbreviation for schizophrenic phenotype. He believed that schizotypals were not destined to decompensate into schizophrenia but could fluctuate between compensated and decompensated states and perhaps even live a normal life. Later family and genetic studies have supported this idea of a spectrum of schizophrenia.

The emerging viewpoint, stemming from biological research, is that schizotype is the fundamental disorder with schizophrenia being a special case and schizotypal personality being the general case. Brain studies that have been conducted with schizophrenics are currently being explored as to their applicability to schizotypal personality and to see if new light can be shed on this research with the perspective that schizotype is the fundamental disorder. This research shows a promising line of thought that involves not only brain anatomy and neurotransmitters but also neurovirology.

Psychodynamic theory would predict that schizotypals would regress to a stable, but primitive, ego state with temporary psychotic episodes. They lack a basic integration of the self and other object-representations; thus they are considered a structurally defective personality. The interpersonal perspective gives another slant on the schizotypal personality that highlights their tendency to obscure fact from fantasy and their isolation that prevents them from experiencing a corrective feedback. Schizotypals seem to lack an understanding of basic social codes and norms and often miss social cues that cause them to chronically misinterpret social situations. Benjamin presents a developmental account through an interpersonal understanding that focuses on parents sending illogical or contradictory messages about the child's learning to be autonomous.

Schizotypals seem unable to organize their thoughts; this disorganization seems to be from the bottom up. A possible explanation of this disorganization is a malfunctioning in their neural network. Schizotypals also are easily distracted, and many develop disorders in the productivity of speech. From a biopsychosocial perspective, the schizotypal personality lies on the continuum between the schizoid and the avoidant and usually develops symptoms more closely aligned with one of these disorders. As the level of pathology increases, the structural matrix seems to disintegrate.

The schizotypal shares traits with not only the schizoid and avoidant but also the paranoid and borderline personalities. They are vulnerable to developing dissociative episodes, psychotic symptoms, and depression. Therapy is extremely difficult with the schizotypal because of their thought disorder as well as their paranoid ideation, and success depends heavily on the severity of the thought disturbances. Their therapeutic goals depend on whether there are more avoidant or more schizoidal traits. Developing a strong therapeutic alliance is critical before distortions of reality can be confronted. Cognitive interventions must take into account schizotypals' limited attention span as well as address their automatic thoughts. Overall, cognitive therapy combined with medication will likely prove to be the most effective treatment for the schizotypal personality.

Chapter 13

The Paranoid Personality

Objectives

- What are the *DSM-IV* criteria for the paranoid personality?
- The vigilant personality is a normal variant of the paranoid. Describe its characteristics and relate them to the more disordered criteria of the *DSM-IV.*
- Explain how different personality styles combine to form each of the subtypes of the paranoid personality.
- Is there a genetic connection among paranoid personality, delusional disorder, and schizophrenia?
- Explain Freud's contention that paranoia is a defense against unconscious homosexual urges?
- How does *splitting* work in paranoid functioning according to object-relations theorists?
- Explain how megalomania and omnipotence relate to the paranoid's extremely low self-esteem.
- How does early abuse lead to the development of paranoid tendencies?
- Explain why the central cognitive problem of the paranoid is not perceptual but interpretive.
- How can signal detection theory help us understand paranoid thinking?
- What are the core beliefs of the paranoid?
- Lack of trust is the hallmark of the paranoid's thinking. Explain how that lack of trust affects their interpersonal world.
- Paranoids share characteristics with other personality disorders. List these other disorders and explain the distinction between each and the paranoid.
- Are paranoids prone to substance abuse?

- Therapy is very threatening to paranoids and equally difficult for the therapist. List some of the major pitfalls that the therapist must avoid.
- List therapeutic goals for the paranoid personality.

Undoubtedly, you have encountered people who question the integrity of *everything* said to them. Often, they are fearful that they will be taken advantage of and have no qualms expressing this fear. Distrust fills their lives to the extent that even family members and others who may be considered closest to them (if they have allowed any) are not excluded from this equation. Yet trust and self-determination are fundamental to existence. We trust others to have our best interest at heart, to come to our assistance in time of need, to provide helpful advice, to anticipate dire outcomes that might escape us, to inform us tactfully when our judgment is wrong, and to help keep our lives running smoothly. We may, at times, argue vehemently with our family and close friends, but when the chips are down, there is an understanding that those we love will "be there" to protect us and fight by our side, at a moment's notice, if necessary.

Among **paranoid personalities,** the focus of this chapter, the basic capacity for trust has somehow been destroyed. Most people see some fundamental goodness in human nature. Paranoids, however, usually view sincerity as a danger sign, a "Trojan Horse" sent to conceal evil schemes and nefarious intentions. Others are the enemy, waiting to rush in, strip them of their already-questionable safety and security, expose their precious vulnerabilities, and ultimately devour them with sadistic delight. For protection, paranoids wall themselves in to keep others out. Never letting their guard down, they watch vigilantly for any sign of impending onslaught from the deep recesses of their fortress. Nothing must escape their scrutiny. From the perspective of others, they are guarded, hostile, self-righteous, rigid, black-and-white thinkers, unwilling to consider the objective evidence and draw rational conclusions. Instead, they misread consensual social reality, attribute hidden motives to others, and even accuse lifelong friends of heinous betrayals. Standing alone against the world at the very precipice of destruction, paranoids bandage themselves with righteous indignation and self-pity, further fueling their anger.

To protect themselves against hidden assaults, paranoids search for information that corroborates their suspicions. Even the most incidental fact may become a huge brush stroke and subsequently be used to support sweeping conclusions. Gradually, unconnected facts are drawn together into a fabric that reveals the outcroppings of a dark conspiracy. Eventually, paranoids fabricate a "pseudocommunity" (Cameron, 1963) in which the objective attributes and intentions of real people have been lost, replaced instead by sinister traits and motives imposed by the paranoid mind. By creating a reality that confirms their fears, their anxious desperation grows ever more intense, fueling circles ever more vicious, leading to retreat behind ever stronger and higher walls, still greater vigilance, and finally, the discovery of new layers of intrigue, which function to keep the cycle going.

Reflect on the case of Ron (Case 13.1). Ron has been forced to seek counseling by the court, and he is not at all happy about it. Defensiveness and a thinly concealed aggression are part and parcel of the paranoid personality. Ron crosses his arms and never breaks eye contact. He is invested in letting others know that he is on his guard, he "knows" what is happening, and he is tired of what he regards as a thin façade of social propriety, when others really just want to exploit him. He refuses to share anything

CASE 13.1

Forced to seek counseling by the court, Ron was resistant from the very start, even though assured that confidentiality is an important part of the therapeutic relationship.[1] He postures himself defensively, crosses his arms tightly across his chest, taps his foot furiously in endless circles, and glares at the interviewer, never breaking eye contact. An aggressive stance is firmly in place. ← ③

For almost a year now, Ron has refused to pay child support to his former wife. Although he states openly that his position is "deplorable," he nevertheless answers specific questions only reluctantly. Sometimes, he challenges the therapist by asking, "Why would you need to know that? I just don't see the relevance." Otherwise, he deflects questions or gives only marginally useful information. When asked why he is evasive, he pauses, makes piercing eye contact, and says, "Because you never know when something might come back to haunt you." Obviously, he suspects that the therapist and the court have ulterior motives. What he does answer paints him in the role of the victim. ← ③

Eventually, he states that his wife has been unfaithful to him, and that he suspects even his children, ages 7 and 12, are not his own. ← ⑦ He becomes more defensive when asked why he believes his wife has been unfaithful. He offers no direct substantiation, but believes that she and his former best friend have been carrying on an affair. "I can see it in their eyes when we're together," he says. Apparently, the belief itself suffices for proof. Although he admits his children do resemble him, he also asserts indignantly that both his children and his friend have brown hair. The fact that his wife has brown hair is unimportant. He maintains that he should not be ordered to support a woman who has betrayed him and made his life intolerable.

Ron is also having trouble at work. He notes that his coworkers ← ② have been manipulating the time clock so that he is cheated out of pay, while adding it to their own checks. "I can't prove it yet, but I know they'll slip up. I'm keeping my eyes wide open for them. They're trying to humiliate me in front of society by making it impossible for me to provide for a family. They want to tarnish my good name before the community." ← ⑥ He admits that the family is having problems with money, which he attributes to his coworkers.

When asked why he believes these things, Ron becomes very agitated, ← ④ interpreting a simple request for information as blatant and insulting skepticism. Each subsequent gesture and inflection is viewed with suspicion. He continues with a fusillade of remarks that malign his wife, and now, the motivations of the therapist and ← ① the court. He states that he believes that he is the victim of a well-conceived plan. Even his putative children are perhaps coconspirators with all those involved. Moreover, he asserts, "I'll never forgive ← ⑤ the injustices that have been done to me, and I'll never forget them, either. My memory is long, and I'll see that those who have wronged me are made to pay. You can count on that." He glares at the interviewer one last time before leaving.

[1] Numbers mark aspects of the case most consistent with *DSM* criteria, and do not necessarily indicate that the case "meets" diagnostic criteria in this respect.

Paranoid Personality Disorder
DSM-IV Criteria

A. A pervasive distrust and suspiciousness of others such that their motives are interpreted as malevolent, beginning by early adulthood and present in a variety of contexts, as indicated by four (or more) of the following:

(1) suspects, without sufficient basis, that others are exploiting, harming, or deceiving him or her

(2) is preoccupied with unjustified doubts about the loyalty or trustworthiness of friends or associates

(3) is reluctant to confide in others because of unwarranted fear that the information will be used maliciously against him or her

(4) reads hidden demeaning or threatening meanings into benign remarks or events

(5) persistently bears grudges, i.e., is unforgiving of insults, injuries, or slights

(6) perceives attacks on his or her character or reputation that are not apparent to others and is quick to react angrily or to counterattack

(7) has recurrent suspicions, without justification, regarding fidelity of spouse or sexual partner

B. Does not occur exclusively during the course of Schizophrenia, a Mood Disorder with Psychotic Features, or another Psychotic Disorder and is not due to the direct physiological effects of a general medical condition.

Note: If criteria are met prior to the onset of Schizophrenia, add "Premorbid," e.g. "Paranoid Personality Disorder (Premorbid)."

substantial with the therapist because he "knows" that such information might be used against him. For Ron, others are on a need-to-know basis, and even then, he is reluctant to reveal much of anything (see criterion 3).

Ron has his reasons. Because trust and loyalty are such fundamental issues for paranoids, many become obsessed with the notion that their spouse or lover has been unfaithful. Ron has accused his wife of cheating, though he has no solid evidence, and even suspects that his children are not his own, although their ages would require an ongoing affair stretching 12 years into the past (see criterion 7). Strangely, Ron is tormented by the fact that both his children and his best friend have brown hair, even though his wife also has brown hair. He neglects the obvious in favor of data that support his own misinterpretation of reality. Moreover, he deeply fears and resents the possibility that he might be forced by the legal system to supply funds that will be used to raise someone else's children, and he is determined not to let this happen. Ironically, the more he is pushed to take responsibility for his children, the more aggressively certain he will become that they are not his at all.

Like other paranoid personalities, Ron's concern with deceit is easily generalized beyond a single forum or relationship. He could reconstruct reality in any number of ways, but he has chosen a path in which he is the victim and others are the beneficiaries. For example, he believes that his coworkers are manipulating the time clock (see criterion 2). He suspects that they not only cheat him out of pay but also add that money to their own checks, thus allowing them to enjoy the fruits of Ron's toil behind his back. Therefore, his indignation is doubly justified: His deficit is their surplus; his agony, their joy. The case does not elaborate, but we can easily imagine Ron lying awake at night, recycling the injustices done to him again and again, becoming angrier and angrier and more and more determined to avenge himself or at least catch them in the act. Like other paranoids, Ron holds grudges and seldom forgives an injury (see criterion 5). He can't, because he is always reconstructing reality so that others have self-consciously exploited or attacked him. Nothing is accidental.

Moreover, the putative attacks on Ron made through the time clock go beyond simple exploitation. Instead, they are attacks on his character (see criterion 6). If successful, they will prove something to the world: Ron is a person of low moral quality, and he is unable to provide for a family, apparently a characteristic essential to his self-respect and one he believes is essential to the respect of others. Thus, in addition to deceiving Ron, his enemies are now waging war on another, even more malicious front: They are attempting to deceive the public about him. Of the two forms of attack, Ron may fear the second even more than the first. He can potentially thwart attacks against his person, but he cannot as easily control the perceptions of others. Such distortions of reality could give way to further, more severe paranoid developments—perhaps the notion that others are talking about failures and inadequacies behind his back even though they may have no foundation in truth. In Ron's mind, others might be saying, "Yeah, I heard his take-home pay was so embarrassing his wife couldn't take it anymore and started screwing his best friend."

Given the portrait of Ron, we are now in a position to approach additional issues that form the plan of this chapter. First, we compare normality and abnormality; then we move on to variations on the basic paranoid pattern. After that, biological, psychodynamic, interpersonal, and cognitive perspectives on the paranoid personality are described. These sections form the core of what is scientific in personality. By seeking to explain what we observe in character sketches like Ron's, the goal is to move beyond literary anecdote and enter the domain of theory. As always, we present history and description side by side, noting the contributions of past thinkers, each of whom tends to bring into focus a different aspect of the disorder. Developmental hypotheses are also reviewed but are tentative for all personality disorders. Next, the Evolutionary Neurodevelopmental Perspective section presents a theory of how the existence of this personality pattern follows from the laws of evolution. Also included are a comparison between the paranoid and other theory-derived constructs and a discussion of how paranoid personalities tend to develop Axis I disorders. Finally, we survey how the disorder might be treated through psychotherapy, again organizing our material in terms of classical approaches to the field: the interpersonal, cognitive, and psychodynamic perspectives.

From Normality to Abnormality

It may again be time to assuage your medical student syndrome. From the preceding descriptions, you may have identified aspects of yourself that match with the paranoid pattern. However, paranoid-style thinking, when appropriate to the realistic demands of your environment, is healthy. In this form, you may think of these as your system of defenses, without which you would most certainly be very vulnerable to the random whims of potentially harmful events and interactions. Most readers will agree that the world is sometimes a dangerous place and that mistrust, when not carried to extremes, has definite survival value. In fact, there is a period of mistrust that is a vital part of human development. Young children go through a genetically programmed stage of stranger anxiety, during which they become anxious when confronted with unknown others and seek the comfort of familiar faces. Stranger anxiety thus functions as a means of keeping children close to the tribe, or at least to caretakers, and away from those that might do them harm, perhaps members of other tribes competing for scarce territory or food resources in the same area. Nature has provided a way of keeping children safe before they can understand or be told what they should do or not do.

Stranger anxiety is only a single example. In general, evolution favors those who can more easily recognize danger over those who cannot. On the whole, individuals who were alert to threat left more offspring than those who were oblivious to such matters, that is, the gullible and naïve (either extreme of trust is maladaptive). Moreover, the threats were not only physical but also social and economic, requiring an alertness to anyone who would lie or deceive to steal or control precious resources or gain some other advantage, all of which influence the number of offspring and their total evolutionary fitness, perhaps for generations. Paranoid mechanisms, then, are a natural part of our psychoevolutionary matrix, an adaptive and necessary extension of our most basic instinct of survival. Consequently, a tendency or vulnerability to paranoid thinking should be present in most human beings. When amplified beyond what is socially adaptive, the result is a paranoid personality disorder, of which Ron is but one example.

Oldham and Morris (1995) have proposed a "normal" variant of the paranoid: the **vigilant** style. Vigilant persons are highly independent, value their freedom, and are sensitive to issues of power, authority, and domination. They are cautious and reserved in dealing with others and enter relationships only after careful consideration. According to these authors, they not only listen to what others say but also pick up subtle meanings and expectations at multiple levels. When under attack, they quickly defend

FOCUS ON CULTURE

When Paranoids Become Spies

Can a Disordered Personality Take on the Nemesis Role?

Although paranoids are notorious for believing that they are being spied on, sometimes they succeed in becoming spies themselves. Such was the case with J. Edgar Hoover, part of a fascinating study on the paranoid personality completed by Hampton and Burnham (1990).

As noted by these authors, paranoids often have rigid, compulsive traits, especially perfectionism and a sense of earnestness. Hoover was no exception. A bright and hard-working student, he chose to walk six miles to attend the best high school, took some of the toughest courses, and finished with the highest honors. He turned down a scholarship to the University of Virginia, took a job at the Library of Congress, and graduated from the night program at George Washington University with a degree in law.

Hoover's career might have been unremarkable except for an unusual turn of events that would determine the character of his life. After obtaining his law degree, Hoover went to work for the Justice Department as a clerk. At the time, World War I had just begun, and German secret agents were at work in the United States subverting attempts to export arms to the allied powers. Moreover, the Russian Revolution was still fresh, and the specter of revolutionary communism loomed over the world. As his career took off, Hoover was tapped again and again to rout the forces of evil. Communists were rounded up and deported. Even the terrorism of the Ku Klux Klan was held at bay, though Hoover had to disobey orders to do it.

In 1924, he became head of the FBI. Like any good paranoid, however, Hoover accepted the position conditionally. He had to be able to draw up harsh rules, be separated from outside political influence, and be allowed to grow the agency according to his own high moral principles. Hoover demanded absolute control. And he got it, establishing rigorous standards of efficiency and merit, ridding the agency of corruption, and requiring the utmost secrecy concerning all its activities.

Hoover's story is that of a paranoid who succeeded in harnessing his idealism and dogmatic righteousness for the best purposes of the country. Continuing to track communist agents, Hoover would eventually identify and expose a variety of subversives. Hoover knew that the Manhattan Project discoveries were being reported to the Russians. Hoover knew about the activities of Ethel and Julius Rosenberg, Alger Hiss, and many others in high positions of government, but again and again Congress refused to act. Not surprisingly, only another paranoid, Senator Joe McCarthy, was eager to investigate his claims. When Hoover died in his sleep in 1972 during the Nixon administration, his moral dogmatism and natural suspicion had protected the country under 10 presidents. See Hampton and Burnham (1990) for greater detail on Hoover's interesting life.

themselves and are not shy about doing so. Further, they are touchy where criticism is concerned but not easily intimidated, and they readily defend what they see as inalienable rights. Fidelity and loyalty are among their highest values, and they thrive when communication is direct and nonthreatening. Many such individuals find a valued niche somewhere in society, where their keen nose for conspiracy serves them well (see "Focus on Culture: When Paranoids Become Spies").

Another way of developing a normal variant of the paranoid is by examining the *DSM-IV* criteria of an Axis-II disorder and noting how more adaptive intensities of these criteria may be adaptive (see Sperry, 1995). Whereas the disordered individual believes, without adequate foundation, that others are attempting to harm, exploit, or deceive him or her (see criterion 1), those with the style simply prefer to remain somewhat distant until others can be carefully appraised. Whereas the disordered individual suspects, with no adequate foundation, that close friends or associates have been disloyal (see criterion 2), an individual with the style places a premium on fidelity, frankness, openness, and honesty; is more open to the evidence; and does not alienate others on the basis of suspicion alone. Whereas disordered individuals are reserved about sharing confidential information with others for fear that it will be used against them (see criterion 3), those with the style have several trusted lieutenants or friends but nevertheless play their cards closely with those who are only acquaintances.

For each of the preceding applicable contrasts, Ron emerges more toward the pathological side. At the end of the interview, he appears to be building an argument that the therapist, the court, his coworkers, and perhaps even his children are conspiring against him. Whenever he encounters resistance, especially in the form of someone who might help him test reality, he becomes more adamant. He doubts the loyalty of his friends; his best friend, who is supposedly sleeping with his wife; and his coworkers, who are supposedly rigging the time clock to cheat him out of money. Far from having a few trusted friends, Ron cannot even bring himself to share information with his therapist. Instead, he prefers to keep his world closed to others. He puts up walls as a defensive strategy. "Knowledge is power," Ron would probably argue, and if others are given knowledge, their power over him can only increase.

Other diagnostic criteria can be put on a continuum with normality (see Sperry, 1995). Whereas the disordered individual interprets benign communications as containing hidden threats or demeaning messages (see criterion 4), the individual expressing the style is simply attuned to the subtleties and nuances of communication at many different levels. A disordered person nurses grudges and rarely forgives an insult (see criterion 5), while a more balanced individual would be perturbed by constructive criticism but would give it serious consideration without feeling unduly attacked. Whereas the disordered individual perceives attacks where none are intended and responds almost reflexively with angry counterattacks (see criterion 6), a more regulated personality would not invest in discovering hidden messages but would respond to negative comments assertively and with adequate restraint. Finally, whereas the disordered person suspects, again with no adequate basis, that a significant other has been sexually unfaithful (see criterion 7), the person demonstrating the style simply regards loyalty, trust, and fidelity as high virtues and has great respect for those who honor them.

Ron demonstrates the more pathological side of most of these contrasts. More than just being sensitive to messages across multiple levels, Ron tends to distort the communications of others in preconceived ways. For example, he is reluctant to share information with the therapist, even when assured of confidentiality, and interprets a request for information as a belittling skepticism. Neither can Ron respond in a nondefensive manner to criticism or give it constructive consideration. Because he believes that others are attempting to harm him without reason, he asserts that his memory is long and that he will never forget the injustices done to him. Moreover, he tends to perceive insults where none exist and holds grudges based on his misperceptions. Rather than exercising constructive restraint by speaking with his supervisor about his coworkers and the time clock, he instead fabricates their actions into a more generalized plot to socially humiliate him. Finally, far beyond valuing trust, loyalty, and fidelity and recognizing it in others, he forges his reality to say that his wife is cheating on him.

Variations of the Paranoid Personality

Although the paranoid personality is a tightly knit syndrome, its features nevertheless combine with those of several other personalities, producing variations of the core prototype, described in the following paragraphs and summarized in Figure 13.1. Actual cases may or may not fall into one of these combinations.

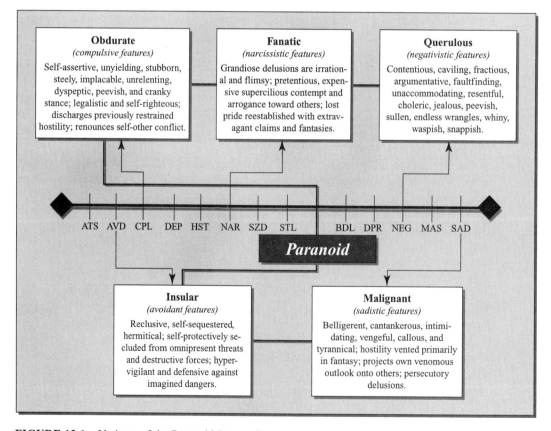

FIGURE 13.1   Variants of the Paranoid Personality.

THE FANATIC PARANOID

The **fanatic** paranoid pattern often resembles its less troubled cousin, the narcissistic personality, as this variant is an interweaving of both paranoid and narcissistic traits. Like the narcissist, the fanatic variant of the paranoid pattern comes across as arrogant, pretentious, and expansive and maintains an air of contempt toward others. A major difference is that narcissists often achieve some success, whereas fanatic paranoids have run hard into reality, their narcissism profoundly wounded. Thus fallen from grace, their self-image of perfection shattered, fanatic paranoids seek to reestablish lost pride through extravagant claims and intricate fantasies. By endowing themselves with illusory powers, they become superheroes or demigods, ready to prevail against an evil universe.

Eventually, delusions of grandeur become their primary coping mechanism. By assuming a grandiose identity, fanatic paranoids offset the collapse of self-esteem produced by objective reality. They may present themselves as a holy saint, inspired leader, or talented genius. Elaborate schemes may be devised by which to deliver the world from sin, lead the planet to world peace, solve long-standing scientific problems, or create utopian societies. Often, their plans are sufficiently detailed to draw at least passing interest. When their ideas are eventually dismissed by others, they are likely to attribute interference to intangible powers, perhaps secret government agencies that have conspired to preserve the status quo. Projection, righteous indignation, and a sense of omnipotence combine to create a defensive armor in this subtype.

Developmentally, fanatic paranoids are similar to compensating narcissists. Overindulged and unrestrained by their parents, their imagination of what they might become in life was given free reign and encouraged by caretakers, perhaps as a means of compensating for poor family status. Once beyond the protective confines of the household, however, their image of superiority was quickly and unmercifully destroyed by the outside world. Completely defeated, saddled with a crushed sensed of self-worth, and unwilling to face reality, they retreat deeper inside their private world of fantasy, creating a compensatory universe in which they can assume their former station, fulfill previous ambitions, and salvage their existence (see "Focus on Culture: Paranoid Conditions and Cult Leaders").

THE MALIGNANT PARANOID

Malignant paranoids combine aspects of the paranoid and sadistic personalities. Such individuals have built expectations that they will be on the receiving end of others' aggressions. Highly sensitive to power issues, their strategy is to dominate you before you can dominate them. Intimidating and belligerent, they possess a ruthless desire to avenge past wrongs and triumph over others. Even when they are alone, the long list of perceived wrongs done to them constantly rises into awareness, thus keeping a potential for aggression close to the surface. However, many have found that their actual efforts at abusing and terrorizing others routinely backfire, which leads them to seek retribution more through fantasy than action. These setbacks are wrought by their own hand, as their chip-on-the-shoulder attitude toward others provokes abundant antagonism.

As they become more isolated, left to ruminate over this self-created perpetual cycle of interpersonal hostility, fanatic paranoids begin to cogitate on the perceived malicious nature of their hostile environment, complete with the venomous individuals who inhabit it. Via the intrapsychic mechanism of projection, they begin to attribute their own acrimony to others, ascribing to them all of the enmity they feel within themselves. As the line between objective antagonism and imagined hostility grows thin, the belief that others are intentionally persecuting them may take on almost delusional proportions.

The need to protect their autonomy against any and all outside influence is a defining feature of this variant because nothing is so valuable and so vulnerable to them as their sense of self-worth. This is particularly evident in the content of their persecutory delusions. The malevolence they perceive emanating from others is neither casual nor random but designed to intimidate, offend, undermine their self-esteem, control their thoughts, and weaken their will. They are ever alert against their darkest fears: Others will make them soft and yielding, forced to submit to authority, or worse, tricked into surrendering their self-determination.

THE OBDURATE PARANOID

Obdurate paranoids combine aspects of the paranoid and compulsive personalities, but like all paranoid patterns, they are more unstable and pathological than their compulsive counterparts. Like the compulsive, they are rigid, perfectionistic, grim, humorless, tense, overcontrolled, small-minded, peevish, legalistic, and self-righteous. However, whereas compulsives temper their angst with the belief that success and happiness can be achieved by conforming to the dictates of authority, obdurate paranoids renounce this dependency, taking on a posture of unabashed self-assertion. They actively rebel against any and all external constraints in a maladaptive effort to regain their sense of perceived control and overturn injustices previously doled out on them.

While they do continue to seek clarity from imposed rules and regulations, they are now the imposers of a system that is used to attack others, usually through either legal action or the setting of impossible rules that cannot realistically be followed. Those in this paranoid personality's wake are despised for their weakness, their sloppiness and lack of regard for disciplined behavior, their failure to live an organized life, and their hypocrisy.

Despite these assertions of nonconformity and dominance, however, obdurate paranoids are not likely to eschew deep-seated feelings of guilt and fear of retribution. Further, they may appear to function normally much of the time but possess tightly compartmentalized persecutory delusions. These tendencies go largely unnoticed, but the individual's hypersensitive antennae are perpetually in alert mode, noticing any unusual twitch, remark, or facial expression emanating from nearby others. It is not unusual for this paranoid pattern to project their anger onto others—thereby creating the perception of hostile intent from innocuous or absent signals. In fact, what we now think of as "classical paranoia," that is, compartmentalized beliefs separate and apart from a patient's usual thought process, usually emanates from those of the obdurate variant because of their tightly controlled, segmented belief structure: When a sensitive nerve is touched, their otherwise normal functioning is impaired and the hidden beliefs become manifest.

THE QUERULOUS PARANOID

The **querulous** paranoid combines aspects of the paranoid with negativistic patterns, with the latter contributing characteristics such as discontentment, pessimism, stubbornness, vacillation, and vengefulness. When combined with paranoid projection, these traits are amplified into overt hostility and forthright delusions. This result manifests in tones of faultfinding, sullenness, resentfulness, contentiousness, jealousy, and insistence on being forever wronged or cheated. It is rare to find these individuals in sustained, healthy relationships. Instead, these persons tend to give up their quests for affection and move to a contrived stance of autonomy and self-determination, renouncing their social needs yet harboring a cloaked sense of dejection. While they state their newfound independence with vengeful fury, the querulous variant remains deeply troubled by interpersonal discontentedness and feelings of indecisiveness, with hidden feelings vacillating between desiring the company of others and feeling repulsed by them.

As envy mounts, they often complain that the achievements of others reflect unfair advantages or preferential treatment. Grumbling turns to anger and spite as their fantasies of being taken advantage of accrete ever more injustices. Legal action against those who have wronged them is common, as are erotic delusions because the querulous paranoid does still seek affection even while refusing it. This is done via the intrapsychic projection mechanism, whereby the individual comes to believe that the feelings of the self are actually emanating from others. Thus, by projecting their own desires onto others, it becomes "them" who make lewd remarks or otherwise suggest sexual intentions. Accusations of infidelity, deceit, and betrayal are often made against innocent relatives and friends, a further synthesis of the negativistic and paranoid patterns.

THE INSULAR PARANOID

The **insular** paranoid combines aspects of the paranoid and avoidant personalities. Such individuals are often moody, apprehensive, and hypersensitive to criticism, especially where their worth and achievements are concerned. Extremely vulnerable, many insular paranoids seek solace in self-focused ways. For example, they may engage in abstruse intellectual activities to enhance their self-esteem or indulge in drugs and alcohol to calm their fears. Especially fearful of shame and humiliation, insular paranoids seek to defend themselves against both real and imagined dangers. More than most, they seek to protect themselves from a world both threatening and destructive. As such, they may isolate themselves for long periods of time, a means of keeping the inevitable judgments of others out of their lives.

Insular paranoids also have an unusually strong fear of being controlled. They not only seek to prevent external influence but also desire to rely solely on their own conclusions and beliefs. Unwilling to check their thoughts against consensual reality, they grow more and more out of touch with the surrounding world, eventually losing the ability to distinguish fantasy from reality. Fears of shame and humiliation, an important component of both the paranoid and avoidant patterns, easily inflate to full-blown conspiracies. Eventually, their thoughts may become so painful and terrifying that they begin intentionally to interrupt the continuity and focus of their perceptions, distracting themselves from their own thoughts. By deserting themselves, their inner world becomes a chaotic mélange of distorted, incidental, and unconnected notions, the threshold of a decompensated paranoid state.

Early Historical Forerunners

Mention of paranoid conditions predates even the writings of Hippocrates more than 2,000 years ago. Translated literally from its Greek origin, the term means "out of one's mind" and was used in ancient times as a general designation for madness. Stone (1997) suggests that it is possible that certain religious prophets of the Old Testament exhibited paranoid characteristics, though he notes that this is perhaps better left undetermined. Certainly, Yahweh's injunction in the first commandment, "Thou shalt have no other Gods before me," appears appropriate at a point in history when tribal cohesion was a prerequisite for cultural survival and suggests that paranoid ideologies are more likely to arise whenever the collective identity of the group is threatened.

The notion that God is a jealous God and that those who follow other belief systems will burn in Hell forever for disobeying the Almighty smacks of righteous indignation and the lack of good humor typical of paranoid patterns. Paradoxically, it would seem that divine omnipotence and narcissistic injury go hand in hand, at least where God is concerned. What an insult it is when those you have created no longer wish to worship you. In contemporary times, such spiritual artifacts have a kind of desperate in-group versus out-group flavor reminiscent of the loyalty and fidelity that paranoids demand, something strangely misplaced in an era of multiculturalism and religious tolerance. Such points, of course, are highly controversial. At least where religion is concerned, one person's paranoid is another's prophet or god (see "Focus on Culture: Paranoid Conditions and Cult Leaders").

Medical references to paranoid conditions disappeared in the second century, only to resurface in the 1700s. Following the proposals of Kahlbaum (1882), Kraepelin narrowed the meaning of the term **paranoia** in 1896 by restricting it to highly systematized and well-contained delusions in subjects without other personality deterioration. He believed that perhaps 40% of those with paranoid delusions ultimately deteriorated to dementia praecox, most of the remainder decompensated to a "paraphrenic" level of bizarre thoughts and perceptual hallucinations, and only a very small proportion did not deteriorate at all. For the early Kraepelin, the paranoid personality was simply one station on the road to dementia praecox. Such individuals were thus classified together with all other deteriorated syndromes.

Not until the eighth edition of his famous text did Kraepelin address the premorbid character of persons disposed to paranoid conditions, now explicitly termed paranoid personalities. Kraepelin (1921) noted classic characteristics such as mistrust; continuous feelings of being treated unjustly, of being interfered with and oppressed, and of secret coalitions working against the person; keen interest in secret motives and intrigues; an emotional irritability and discontented mood; faultfinding; and an excessive valuation of the self—all characteristics found in our case of Ron. Nevertheless, Kraepelin continued to regard the paranoid personality as existing on a continuum with more severe paranoid psychoses. Over three-quarters of a century later, the empirical research on this question is still equivocal.

In the first several decades of the twentieth century, other theorists formulated constructs similar to our contemporary paranoid personality. Birnbaum (1909) spoke of paranoids as possessing overvalued ideas heavily charged with emotion. Bleuler (1906) asserted that individuals with a paranoid constitution would fall short of a delusional system. Others, who do not misinterpret life events more than normal persons, he maintained, instead exhibit a resistance to change leading to a rigidification in their beliefs and, ultimately, a paranoid delusional system. Like Bleuler, Meyer (1908) held that paranoids do not adjust their beliefs to the facts. However, he also noted their inclination to isolate themselves and their resistance to the efforts of others to influence their misinterpretations. Schneider (1923/1950) spoke of two types of the fanatic psychopath. The

FOCUS ON CULTURE

Paranoid Conditions and Cult Leaders

Paranoid Personality, Charisma, and Interpersonal Influence

In a study of the paranoid personality, Hampton and Burnham (1990) explore the character of the Reverend Jim Jones, the cult leader famous for the 1978 mass suicide in Jonestown, Guyana, where more than 900 people died, including almost 300 children, most by drinking cyanide-laced Kool-Aid.

As noted by these authors, Jones showed signs of pathology from early in life. As a 6-year-old, he often greeted his next-door neighbor, a university professor, by saying, "Good morning, you son-of-a-bitch." His mother was a factory worker; his father, a member of the Ku Klux Klan. He graduated from college in 1961 and was ordained in 1964. He bought churches in Los Angeles and San Francisco, building a congregation dazzled by oratory and religious claims. He worked hard at instilling terror into his congregation, describing his divinely inspired vision of the coming nuclear holocaust. Claiming sometimes to be the spirit of Christ and sometimes that of Lenin, he preached the virtues of socialism and persuaded his flock to empty their pockets into the coffers of the People's Temple.

Yet, Jones also did good things, such as establishing soup kitchens and social programs and adopting seven children. Such ostensibly altruistic acts allowed Jones to present an extraordinary face to the world. Eventually, he was awarded the title "Humanitarian of the Year" by the *Los Angeles Herald.*

As his paranoia began to amplify, Jones decided to relocate his command center to Guyana. Almost 1,000 members of his church followed him, and together they founded Jonestown, a safe haven from nuclear holocaust and the persecution of groups back in the United States. Far from creating a heaven on earth, Jones stripped his followers of all autonomy, imposing "a regimen of terror, physical punishment, beatings, exhaustion, emotional dependency, and tyranny" (Hampton & Burnham, 1990, p. 79). Eventually, Jones became convinced that he was being persecuted by unseen forces, particularly the CIA. Those who disagreed with him, he said, would be killed.

The paranoid personality traits of Jones are easy to identify. From an early age, Jones was secretly grandiose. In the era of his Los Angeles and San Francisco churches, for example, he identified himself with the spirit of Christ. Later, he claimed privileged access to special knowledge, his visions of a nuclear war. Entangled with his grandiosity was a lust for power, a deep suspiciousness of those "on the outside," demands for absolute loyalty, severe punishments for breaking this loyalty, and the elevation of his own need for loyalty to the level of religious dogma. The smallest disagreement was treason. To sustain his appetite for domination, Jones worked hard to create strong in-group/out-group feelings in his flock, especially a sense that the end was always near. This he followed up with techniques of mind control, sleep-depriving his followers, and working them to exhaustion. Given his grandiosity, Jones appears as a mix of the paranoid and narcissistic personality disorders, an especially powerful combination for the aspiring charismatic cult leader.

combative type is expansive, aggressive, and actively quarrelsome. They complain bitterly about past injustices and may seek retribution through litigation. In contrast, the eccentric type is quietly suspicious, makes hidden assumptions about the motives of others, and is supposedly drawn to the beliefs of secretive sects. Ron would appear to combine aspects of both of Schneider's types.

The Biological Perspective

Given the irritability and aggressiveness of the paranoid, many observers have wondered whether these syndromes might have some basis in temperament. As the personality disorders go, paranoids struggle under enormous pressures and appear to generate tremendous amounts of energy. They rarely relax. Instead, they are perpetually on defensive high alert, their sympathetic nervous system tuned to a fault, literally mobilized for fight or flight. Most appear tense and guarded, eyes focused sharply on whatever comes under intense scrutiny. Some may make quick movements or may remain frozen, as if waiting for some sign of the enemy presence. For example, Ron appears poised to leap from his seat while talking to the therapist. Whether faced with danger or not, paranoids maintain a high level of preparedness, bracing for the impending emergency. Even when alone, their favorite list of grudges and injustices may be replayed repeatedly until they seethe with hostility and vengefulness. Logically, some biophysically derived fund of energy would seem necessary to keep the fires burning.

Although some temperamental foundation might be linked to the paranoid personality, it is unlikely that there exists a specific *paranoid temperament.* As we have emphasized throughout the book, temperament may constitute part of the basic soil of personality, but it is certainly not the whole garden. Instead, temperament directs certain developmental pathways by channeling the child toward one road, rather than others. A child with an irritable and aggressive temperament may develop paranoid, sadistic, antisocial, or borderline patterns (and possibly some combination). Other factors in his or her early environment, particularly reciprocal interactions with caretakers, certainly influence the particular coping patterns and affective receptivity the child develops. An infant who seems chronically difficult to soothe and withholding of affection, for example, produces feelings of anger and resentment in most parents. If these feelings are not well tolerated, it is possible that caretakers might begin to withdraw their own affection and begin to regard the child as a burden, paving the way for sadistic abuse and thus the formation of hostile, attacking internal objects that are later projected as part of an adult paranoid personality.

An as-yet unsettled issue concerns the relationship among paranoid personality, delusional disorder, and paranoid schizophrenia. Essentially, this is the same question that concerned early theorists, including Kraepelin, as noted previously. Perhaps, then, the paranoid personality is part of the schizophrenic spectrum, with delusional disorder located at an intermediate point of severity. A small body of research has examined the genetic relationship among these three disorders. As reviewed by Bernstein, Useda, and Siever (1995), only two of five studies have found a significant relationship between the paranoid personality and schizophrenia. Kendler and Gruenberg (1982), for example, studied both the biological and adoptive relatives of adoptees who developed schizophrenic syndromes. Their findings showed that paranoid personality disorder was more common in the biological relatives of adoptees, suggesting a genetic relationship.

In contrast, other studies suggest minimal to no relationship between the disorders of this spectrum. For example, Maier, Lichtermann, Minges, and Heun (1994) found that paranoid personality disorder was more common in relatives of unipolar depressives than in the relatives of schizophrenia, schizoaffective, or schizophreniform disorder subjects. Similarly, studies by Kendler, Masterson, and Davis (1985) suggest a stronger genetic association between paranoid personality disorder and delusional disorder than between these and schizophrenia. Because delusions may be systematized to different depths, they are often difficult to distinguish from the cognitive distortions of the paranoid personality. Accordingly, the difference between delusional disorder, persecutory type, and the paranoid personality may be one of degree rather than kind. Though it is often said that delusional individuals lack the capacity to doubt their delusion, and paranoid personalities can admit that their beliefs are possibly untrue, at least in principle, it is probable that for some persons, the capacity to doubt fluctuates with emotional state. Some individuals will not be able to admit doubt when extremely angry or anxious.

The Psychodynamic Perspective

Freud believed, from his very earliest studies, that projection (the assignment of one's own undesirable traits or emotions onto others) was a central mechanism of paranoid thinking. In one of his most famous analyses, Freud considered the case of Schreber. Formerly an eminent physician and presiding judge in the highest court in Saxony, Schreber wrote detailed memoirs of his paranoid psychotic experiences. He believed, for example, that he was a victim of soul murder perpetrated by his doctor and that his body was slowly being transformed by God.

Apparently, Freud never saw Schreber personally, and his analysis appears to be based solely on the memoirs (Bowlby, 1973). With a sample size of only one, Freud arrived at a startling conclusion: Paranoia was a defense against unconscious homosexual urges! In a series of circuitous transformations, the original impulse ("I love him"), considered too repugnant for conscious awareness, is denied, then reversed by reaction formation ("I do not love him, I hate him"), resulting in aggressive feelings and overwhelming guilt, which must be projected outward ("I do not hate him, he hates me!"). Finally, the sequence ends with rationalization ("I hate him because of his hatred for me"). Paranoid delusions were explained as developing as a consequence of a withdrawal of libido from the homosexual object, followed by regression to a narcissistic stage of libidinal development. Here, primary process thinking dominates, with the result that the energy can be reconstructed and returned to the outside world through projection (Bak, 1946). Although ingenious, Freud's account seems fantastic by contemporary standards.

Whatever the merits of his contribution, Freud analyzed only paranoia, a singular symptom, and not the more contextual character type of paranoid personality consisting of an entire constellation of traits. After the psychosexual theory of character development fell into place, the concept of a paranoid character developed, rooted in anal-sadism (Ferenczi, 1919). The idea of an anal character is strongly associated with the compulsive personality, individuals who responded to caretaker control by developing ambivalence between guilty obedience and an angry defiance (Rado, 1959), but who eventually conformed vehemently to parental demands for perfection through reaction formation.

In contrast, paranoids react strongly against attempts to control their defecation. As caretakers become more and more frustrated, the child, who might defecate at any point, begins to develop suspicion about their motives whenever they are found hovering nearby (Menninger, 1940). Thus, preservation of autonomy becomes the major theme associated with toilet training, and the future paranoid learns that authority functions to undermine self-determination and free will. Coercion results in resentment, enduring grudges, and increased resistance. We certainly see this in Ron, who is extremely resistant to being controlled by the courts through the inevitability of making child support payments.

As psychoanalysis matured, instinct psychology was rethought in terms of ego psychology and object-relations theory. It became apparent that sexual and aggressive instincts, as conceptualized by Freud, were always experienced in context with the "representations" of persons formed in the mind of the developing infant, called objects. Actual people come and go, but the representations of early caretakers remain as a template for all future relationships. Object-representations are thus empowered to influence behavior across the life span. As a result, psychoanalysis simultaneously became both more interpersonal and cognitive.

According to object-relations theory, early stages of development are characterized by splitting. The primitive ego is not yet able to comprehend that aspects of self and others are composed of integrated, multilayered positive and negative aspects woven into a single, complex image. The normal adult mind, on the other hand, generally easily recognizes that most everything is possessed of these multiple aspects. Some are good and some are bad, to different degrees and in different ways. Maturity thus means coming to grips with ambivalence and the ability to tolerate and accept ambiguity and conflicting information. In contrast, the primitive ego, as yet unable to fuse disparate components, knows only all-good and all-bad representations of itself and others. The "good mother" and the "bad mother," for example, are very much separate entities, just like the "good self" and the "bad self." Splitting thus resembles dichotomous thinking, in that the objects that are split are completely polarized into what is experienced as good and pleasurable versus what is experienced as bad and unpleasurable.

Object-relations theorists maintain that the paranoid personality operates at a borderline level of personality organization (Kernberg, 1979), which is, by definition, dominated by splitting. Representations of self and others are highly polarized in all good and all bad, so that persons functioning at the borderline level often shift suddenly in their emotions. At one moment, they seem totally loving, trusting, and idealizing; frustrate them, however, and they shift suddenly to total hatred, condemnation, and rage. In the paranoid, the all-good images remain inside the self, and the all-bad images are projected outward. The external world thus becomes the source of all unpleasurable feelings, and the source of everything that is desirable and good remains inside the self, protected from contamination. Projection is thus doubly reinforcing; first, the bad aspects of yourself and others are neutralized and controlled by being disowned; second, the good or desirable parts that are left behind now become that much better, more pristine, virtuous, and innocent—important traits of the paranoid's self-image.

Projection, then, according to the psychodynamic paradigm, cleanses the self of whatever is undesirable but does so at a tremendous cost: The genuine negative feelings that exist inside the self are experienced as coming from outside the self. Because whatever is bad or undesirable originates internally, it seems to follow the subject around. In a sense, paranoids just cannot get away from themselves, and persecution seems ubiquitous. As such, paranoids are vulnerable to self-referential constructions of reality, namely, ideas of reference and overgeneralized conspiracies. In effect, they are haunted and confronted by their own projected contents, eerie specters that shadow and persecute an innocent, all-good victim. They can run, but they can't hide. Whenever and wherever the paranoid feels vulnerable, for example, it is because others are somehow acting to make him or her feel that way. What others see, however, is someone who is perpetually irascible, perhaps even explosive, without adequate cause, perhaps without any apparent reason. Naturally, others react with irritation themselves, providing substantive support for what before were irrational fears. Eventually, projection may thus acquire a basis in reality.

We certainly see this in Ron. When the therapist asks for information, Ron becomes incensed and interprets the request as a display of skepticism. Thereafter, he projects his own aggression onto the therapist, who now belongs to the ranks of those who would attack and conspire against him. In this way, Ron turns his own phantom fears into reality. Almost anyone would be irritated with him. His coworkers probably feel the same way, only more so because they are chronically exposed to him. If they whisper among themselves about his strange reactions, they have good reason. From Ron's perspective, their whispers are not reality-based complaints about his behavior but instead covert machinations designed to bring him down.

Secondary defense mechanisms also arise in response to the vicious circles that paranoids create. As noted by Stone (1993), paranoids put psychological and geographical distance between themselves and others. Isolation serves as a means of resisting both invasion and external influence. Moreover, retreat from social life quells somewhat the agony of self-referential ideas, which are amplified when others are physically present. Paranoids also make use of fantasy and righteous indignation. Through revenge fantasies, they exact vengeance on their persecutors and reestablish their autonomy. Whereas before, the weak paranoid was at the mercy of the world, now the world is at his or her mercy. The paranoid swells with righteous indignation, glorified by the moral authority of a suddenly empowered, long-suffering victim, as Ron paints himself. Omnipotence and indignation further serve as means of cohering a self-representation perilously close to diffusion, much like the function of the grandiose self in the narcissistic personality (Stone, 1993). Keeping the self coherent forestalls or prevents psychotic disintegration. The internal and external worlds are distorted, but at least the self is preserved. Finally, rationalization and displacement are also commonly observed.

Many writers have noted the megalomania, that is, extreme overvaluation of the self, that exists among paranoids and its associated omnipotence. Both of these phenomena are related to pathologically low self-esteem. Grandiosity compensates for deep feelings of inferiority, and omnipotence compensates for the sense that the individual is completely ineffective or has no power in the world. According to McWilliams (1994), the relationship between the paranoid personality and the omnipotence of primitive narcissism betrays immense concerns with shame, guilt, and envy. All three call the perfection of the narcissistic self into question, and all three are projected onto others. Shame, for example, derives from feeling that the individual is somehow defective, inferior, or ugly in the sight of others and that these others are acutely aware of such shortcomings.

In fact, the hazy fear that their shameful acts have been exposed underlies the development of many ideas of reference. If you take a moment to think about your own shameful secrets, the worst-case scenario is easily envisioned: Not only have you been found out but others are secretly discussing you, eagerly gossiping about your shameful acts but without letting you know that they know. To rid themselves of such intolerable notions, paranoids project shame and then naturally conclude that it is others who are actively trying to shame or humiliate them. Perhaps Ron, for example, feels that he should be much further along in his career, or perhaps he simply feels ashamed that the family is having money problems and thus needs to construct a scenario in which his coworkers are conspiring to exploit him. His suspicions distort reality, but they at least salvage what little self-esteem he has. The experiences of guilt and envy are essentially dealt with the same way. Where paranoids might feel guilty, it is others who have wronged them. Where others have characteristics that paranoids envy, it is others who envy them.

Now consider the case of Stephen, the child genius (see Case 13.2). Stephen is obviously highly intelligent, having obtained his doctorate in physics at the age of 23. We can imagine how proud his parents must have been, as both lacked a formal college education. We can also speculate that Stephen must have felt enormous pressure to stand out just as much among his colleagues as he did among his fellow students. Unfortunately, his own megalomania keeps getting in the way of his progress, creating conflicts with supervisors who feel that he spends too much time on his own "secret schemes" and not enough on company projects.

Despite his objective intellectual gifts, it appears that Stephen has a fragile self to defend. Evidence of a crushingly low self-esteem is found not only in his grandiosity, but also in his condescending reaction to constructive criticism and in his need to conceal his own projects. To defend himself, Stephen has chosen a path already trod by his own father, probably because he knows it to be an excuse to which his parents will resonate: Not only was the father too brilliant for those around him, but the son is, as well. Accordingly, Stephen is convinced that his coworkers and supervisors are trying to undo him by stealing his ideas, by not paying him what he is worth, and by appraising his work as "absurd schemes." Such misread signals and unwillingness to consider the evidence are part of the paranoid pattern. Stephen's solution is to counterattack by spending even more time on a scheme that would not only "revolutionize the industry" but also vindicate and avenge him against his critics. Unfortunately, the reverse proves true. Stephen's plan is rejected for overlooking certain simple facts of logic and efficiency. Faced with objective evidence of failure not easily denied, Stephen withdraws to his home and begins drinking to excess. After a series of similar rejections, he is finally faced with two choices: either crumble under self-condemnation or retreat into a world of complete fantasy. Stephen chose the latter.

Akhtar (1992, pp. 167–168) describes overt and covert aspects of the paranoid personality, closely paraphrased here. In the area of self-concept, paranoids overtly seem arrogant, self-righteous, and easily enraged. Covertly, however, they feel timid and inferior and are plagued by doubt and guilt. In the area of interpersonal relations, they overtly seem mistrustful, humorless, accusing, and cold. Covertly, however, they are exquisitely sensitive, naïve, frightened of power and authority, vengeful, and grudge holding. Overtly and covertly, Stephen fits this profile. He is definitely arrogant and self-righteous, as evidenced through his reaction to constructive criticism of his pet projects, also evidence of his sensitivity and self-doubt. Had Stephen been blessed with a greater sense of self-worth, he would have been able to make use of such criticism in the spirit in which it was intended and perhaps even get his associates excited about his ideas, which he instead safeguards jealously as his own private property. Moreover, as the child genius prematurely pushed forward by the momentum of his own intellect, Stephen is easily seen as being frightened of power and authority.

CASE 13.2

The shy only child of informally educated parents, Stephen was considered a "child genius" in his early school years. Having always been pushed by his parents to succeed, he received his doctorate in physics at 23 and was a celebrated student in his department. Subsequently, however, things turned sour. He held several middle-level positions as a research physicist in a number of industrial firms, going from one to another following a series of disputes, claiming that others were trying to steal his ideas.[1] ← 1

Stephen's father also had considerable difficulty in his career. Although uneducated in a formal sense, he understood a great deal of technical information, consulting with several companies who sought someone with his detailed knowledge and inventive mind. But these positions did not long endure. In less than a year, two at most, Stephen's father would alienate almost all of his colleagues, accusing them of trying to steal his ideas and of not paying him what he was worth. Stephen recalled quite vividly the dinner table conversations when his father would be furious because he was being "fired again" because he was "too smart for the fools around him."

In a similar pattern, Stephen's own arrogance and egocentricity were now creating conflicts with his supervisors, who felt Stephen ← 3 spent too much time on his own "secret schemes" and not enough on company work. Anyone who commented on his projects, even in a constructive manner, was subsequently greeted with condescension. ← 4 sion. Eventually, Stephen was assigned less important jobs that made him feel that both his supervisors and subordinates were ← 6 "making fun of him" by not taking him seriously.

Almost as revenge, Stephen began to work on a scheme that would "revolutionize the industry," a new thermodynamic principle that, ← 5 when applied to his company's major product, would prove extremely efficient and economical. He worked in private as long as possible, refusing to share any of his ideas with his "turncoat col- ← 2 leagues." After several months of what was conceded by others as "brilliant thinking," he presented his plans to the company president. Brilliant though it was, the plan overlooked certain obvious simple facts of logic and economy.

Upon learning that his plan had been rejected, Stephen withdrew to his home and established a habit of drinking to excess. Thereafter, he became obsessed with "new ideas," proposing them in intricate schematics and formulas to a number of government officials and industrialists. New rebuffs followed, which led to further efforts at self-inflation. Not long thereafter, he lost all semblance of reality and control. For a brief period, he convinced himself that he was Niels Bohr, a famous quantum physicist. Whether such grandiose delusions could be attributed to his drinking problem and personality problems, or were better conceived as an outgrowth of his paranoid personality pattern alone, was a major question for clinical assessment.

[1] Numbers mark aspects of the case most consistent with *DSM* criteria, and do not necessarily indicate that the case "meets" diagnostic criteria in this respect.

Paranoid Personality Disorder *DSM-IV* Criteria

A. A pervasive distrust and suspiciousness of others such that their motives are interpreted as malevolent, beginning by early adulthood and present in a variety of contexts, as indicated by four (or more) of the following:

(1) suspects, without sufficient basis, that others are exploiting, harming, or deceiving him or her

(2) is preoccupied with unjustified doubts about the loyalty or trustworthiness of friends or associates

(3) is reluctant to confide in others because of unwarranted fear that the information will be used maliciously against him or her

(4) reads hidden demeaning or threatening meanings into benign remarks or events

(5) persistently bears grudges, i.e., is unforgiving of insults, injuries, or slights

(6) perceives attacks on his or her character or reputation that are not apparent to others and is quick to react angrily or to counterattack

(7) has recurrent suspicions, without justification, regarding fidelity of spouse or sexual partner

B. Does not occur exclusively during the course of Schizophrenia, a Mood Disorder with Psychotic Features, or another Psychotic Disorder and is not due to the direct physiological effects of a general medical condition.

Note: If criteria are met prior to the onset of Schizophrenia, add "Premorbid," e.g. "Paranoid Personality Disorder (Premorbid)."

In the area of social adaptation, Akhtar states that paranoids are industrious, driven, and successful when working on their own. Covertly, however, they have frequent interpersonal problems, carry personal issues into the workplace, work poorly as part of a team, and are oblivious to aesthetic appreciation. In the area of love and sexuality, they are overtly unromantic and averse to sexual humor and gossip. Covertly, however, they doubt their sexual ability and may have sadomasochistic tendencies. In the area of ethics and ideals, they overtly value the intellectual but seem moralistic and religiously fundamental. Covertly, however, they are morally idiosyncratic, sometimes with sociopathic tendencies. Of these, Stephen is definitely not a team player. The remaining descriptors seem to apply more to Ron, who is certainly moralistic and obviously not much of a romantic.

Contemporary psychodynamic developmental accounts of the paranoid personality emphasize the importance of early abuse. Whereas normal persons learn a basic sense of trust during early development, the paranoid learns basic mistrust. Such concerns are often symbolically expressed as a fear of being eaten up or devoured, which might be referred to as boundary loss or a fear of engulfment. McWilliams (1994) stresses the presence of criticism and ridicule in the families of future paranoids and the possibility that the child may have been scapegoated for attributes that the family would like to disown. As noted by Blum (1980, 1981), Freud anticipated the modern view through his paper on the Wolf Man, which links paranoia and sadomasochism. Such elements appear in the case of Schreber, whose father invented and published methods of child-rearing that featured cruel exercises and harnesses, through which even the posture of a child could be controlled, ostensibly to prevent poor circulation and eventual paralysis. Apparently, the young Schreber had been a prime benefactor of his father's "wisdom" throughout his childhood. As a result of such evidence, Freud's original hypothesis has been generalized: Paranoids do not possess latent homosexual wishes but nevertheless long for comfort from the same-sex parent, their abuser, most often the father, which may be mistaken as a homosexual wish.

Other developmental facets of the paranoid personality often reflect variations on the theme of early sadistic abuse or readily follow as an understandable consequence of early abuse. Searles (1956) stresses the desire for revenge that is often found in paranoids. Cameron (1963) emphasizes that as a result of such treatment, children become supersensitive to subtle hints of hostility, contempt, criticism, and accusation. Hypervigilance provides a means of protection against deception and sudden attack. Because paranoids do not discriminate in their projections, their entire world becomes a "pseudo-community" populated by persecutory others. Grandiosity may be seen as a compensation for abuse as well as a means of reinforcing the boundaries of the self against dissolution (Bursten, 1973; Kernberg, 1982). Auchincloss and Weiss (1994) regard the paranoid character as needing a magical connection to caretakers, an intolerance of indifference. Better to suffer and be connected than to be ignored.

In the case of Stephen, none of these developmental hypotheses are easily sustained based on the evidence presented, because abuse does not appear in the case write-up. Nevertheless, certain facts stand out. For one, Stephen has many aspects of the narcissistic personality and thus somewhat resembles the description of the fanatical paranoid, described previously. We note further that Stephen's parents pushed him forward, certainly not as a means of gratifying his own needs, but as a means of gratifying theirs, a compensation for poor family status. We can imagine Stephen as the perfect little genius, celebrated by his parents but also carrying a great responsibility. The implicit message was: "We, your parents, wanted to be so much more than we are. Now, you must succeed where we have not. Otherwise, the verdict of the world on your family becomes reality. Save us. If you are brilliant, you are loved." Accordingly, Stephen's grandiosity defends not only his own self-worth but also the worth of the family. Given such high expectations, shortcomings were probably inevitable. Because these are intolerable to his narcissistic need for perfection, they must be externalized. The ultimate result is a paranoid personality that decompensates into a paranoid psychosis.

The Interpersonal Perspective

The interpersonal perspective is concerned with how human beings interact and how these interactions support, invalidate, and elaborate the self-image. Sullivan is considered the father of this approach, reacting against the classical psychoanalysis of Freud, whereby pathology was always a property of the person. Instead, Sullivan saw psychopathology as emerging from an individual's relationships and patterns of communication.

According to Sullivan (1956, p. 145), there are two requirements for the development of a paranoid "slant" on life. The first is an intense insecurity related to some kind of inferiority, whether real or perceived. So intense is this insecurity that it constantly intrudes on awareness, producing considerable anxiety. Because future paranoids believe that the inferiority is easily observed by others and cannot be disguised, it becomes a deficiency in the self that is beyond repair, producing chronic feelings of insecurity, shame, and humiliation, felt most acutely in the presence of others.

The second requirement is a transfer of blame, away from themselves and onto others, whereby, "It is not that I have something wrong with me, but that he does something to me" (Sullivan, 1956, p. 146). All of us, according to Sullivan, have at some point been unfairly blamed by significant others and left with a lingering bad feeling, only to conclude, "I wouldn't have this sense of discomfort if other people didn't treat me unfairly" (p. 147). Faced with chronic feelings of insecurity, the paranoid apparently takes the additional step and concludes that humiliation is not the by-product of social relationships, but their purpose. Thus released from psychosexual bondage, early abuse and intense feelings of inferiority or insecurity, whatever their origin, can be seen as an essential part of the development of the paranoid personality. Sullivan's explanation accounts for how someone as brilliant as Stephen, who is not an abuse victim, nevertheless develops a paranoid personality disorder despite his objective gifts.

The old saying that all relationships are based on trust is trite but true. We trust our friends and parents to be well intentioned, to have our best interests at heart. We trust that our significant others will be loyal and faithful. We trust that teachers will present the issues in an interesting and illuminating way, though we know that this is often wishful thinking. Whatever the relationship, the foundation is a mutual respect for each other as human beings, an I-thou relationship. Paranoids respect others, but only in terms of their potential for harm, as invaders or infidels. Only the strong survive. Everyone is best regarded as a treacherous psychopath, ready to cheat and deceive with sadistic joy. Others can only be trusted to pretend to be trustworthy. When the drawbridge is lowered, the enemy will march in nonchalantly, seize the element of surprise, and wreak havoc. Attack could come from any direction, at any time. This is the ultimate implication of Sullivan's (1956): "He does something to me."

By reacting as if everyone were the enemy, paranoids seek to secure their safety and autonomy and protect themselves against outside influence. To make the world safe for themselves, paranoids develop interpersonal characteristics designed to forestall attack, secure protection, and establish formal channels for relating to others but also prevent attachment and dependence, noxious signs of weakness. Autonomy, rationality, and control form the keystones of their strategy, with many manifestations both subtle and gross. Paranoid delusions, in particular, may be seen as rationality run amok, reconstructions of social reality famous for their internal consistency, a hallmark of a good scientific theory but infamous for being completely wrong, as we will see in the cognitive section, next.

Autonomy is so important that paranoids sometimes imagine themselves as being, ideally, something like a fascist state: totally self-sufficient, yet fearsome enough to intimidate aggressors on their borders. No person is an island, but paranoids nevertheless require total control over what happens in their own life. Marcus provides the arch example of this, ruling his classroom with an iron fist and keeping careful records of all his activities as an educator. No one is going to surprise Marcus with something unanticipated. Toward the normal range, paranoids may flourish in relatively isolated venues where they make the rules and call the shots and control whom they interact with and who interacts with them. By making social contacts from the safety of their own turf, they control who enters their world and to what extent, choose the fronts on which they are willing to risk vulnerability, and moderate their degree of exposure. Many small business owners, for example, succeed because paranoid traits are adaptive in such settings. Paranoid styles can function competently on their own, then, but need to do so from great interpersonal distance and on their own terms.

When thrust into social settings, paranoids become acutely aware of issues of social rank and status. Weakness is despised as inconsistent with a self-image of strength and invulnerability. At times, they may harp on the faults of others as a means of projecting dissatisfaction with their own shortcomings. Preoccupied with their own insecurities, they are notoriously sensitive to perceived slights, which indicate that others are on the attack, expect them to submit to external control, or consider them inferior. Like compulsives, they tend to have little or no sense of humor, perhaps because levity might be an invitation to let down their guard. Moreover, a precariously low self-esteem makes it impossible for paranoids to laugh at themselves. Ambiguous communications may be interpreted as veiled insults, proof positive that others wish to attack them. By responding angrily with their own insults and threats, paranoids establish a reputation for being abrasive, contentious, and "dug-in."

Although paranoids function best on their own, they do sometimes surround themselves with those considered tirelessly loyal. Such trustworthy souls function as the eyes and ears of the paranoid. As the interpersonal parallel of a buffer state, loyal persons function to insulate paranoids from the anxiety associated with interaction with the surrounding world, which tends to increase their reality distortions and systematized delusional content. Nevertheless, paranoids usually believe that loyalty is extremely fragile. When the moment of truth arrives, they expect their associates to break ranks, leaving them alone and defenseless. Ron, for example, eventually trusts the interviewer enough to share some of his issues, only to have that trust collapse quickly later in the same session. Paranoids believe that loyalty is nonexistent or easily bought and sold. Interpersonal relationships are thus infected with ambivalence; paranoids want to trust but are deeply fearful of harm or betrayal.

As their fearfulness grows, paranoids feel the need to control those around them. They must know the whereabouts of others at all times and know what they are working on and why. In effect, paranoids seek the security of omniscience by monitoring the activities of their associates or family members, sometimes almost to the point of obsessive checking. In this way, the all-seeing eye keeps suspiciousness under rein. Because everything is known, there is nothing to fear. At the same time, however, paranoids impress others as being intensely private, volunteering almost nothing about their emotional life or their activities beyond what business immediately requires. No one should know the paranoid's business, but he or she must know everyone else's. By putting others on a need-to-know basis, paranoids protect themselves against the plots of others. Knowledge is power, and there is no reason to give that power away. Loyalty to paranoids thus means submitting to their need to control while making others' own life an open book.

As the severity of the disorder increases, the need for control gives way to an active, searching suspicion. When others resist the subject's all-seeing eye by walling off, the paranoid assumes they have something to hide. As a result, the need to know and control becomes more intense. The scrutiny of others grows more as paranoids seek to reassure themselves that no threat exists. False accusations may sometimes be used deliberately to test the loyalty of confidants, a necessary evil designed to provoke others so they can judge others' reactions.

Exasperated by constant observation and mistrust, otherwise friendly souls may break off their relationship with the subject without explanation. The inner circle of trusted confidants naturally becomes smaller and smaller as tired and frustrated friends end their relationships. Former associates may be seen as having defected to the enemy camp, carrying with them secret information that might be used to develop even more nefarious plans. Some individuals become obsessed that a mole lurks somewhere in their midst, taking mental notes on their activities and passing information back to an unseen coalition. Paralyzed with fear, paranoids in positions of power may launch witch-hunts that divide and demoralize their own organization, as has sometimes happened in spy agencies. By this point, submission and openness are no longer enough to allay their fears. Events that fail to confirm their suspicions only prove how deceitful others can be.

As their relationships become increasingly strained, they also become more affectively intense. Rationality gives way to increasingly distorted reconstructions of social reality. By projecting the negative aspects of themselves onto others, paranoids are confronted by the very things that they find intolerable. What the public sees is a crazy person who seems certain that he or she is being persecuted and who seems bent on exposing conspiracies that do not exist or exacting vengeance for evil deeds never committed. Anger, resentment, and hostility invade these paranoids' communications. Becoming even more hypersensitive, they may feel unforgivably wronged by casual acquaintances who have no role in their life beyond delivering the morning newspaper, for example. Such sensitivities create numerous long-standing grudges. They may assert that others have exploited them, taken credit for their ideas, stolen promotions, or undermined their reputation, as the case of Stephen shows. Ostensibly pleasant social engagements are particularly suspect, a diversion intended to lull the paranoid into a false sense of security.

Another important barrier to normal interpersonal relationships is the paranoid's attitude toward feelings of attachment and dependence. Paranoids defend their autonomy not only against hidden threats but also against tender emotions, which signal vulnerability.

In effect, control of others becomes a substitution for attachment. In the personality style range, paranoids are fiercely loyal to those who are certain to be loyal to them. At the level of disorder, however, tender emotions are associated with weakness; intimacy is threatening. This could be a factor for Ron, who chronically doubts both his wife and his best friend. A skeptical and stubborn person thus gives way to someone who is irascible, cynical, and, possibly, dangerous.

When feelings of attraction are projected, paranoids begin to believe that others are deliberately creating in them a desire for closeness or dependency. In response, they keep their distance. By hardening themselves against a need for love, they purge themselves of susceptibility to deceit or subjugation. Spouses may report that the paranoid is cold and rational, reluctant to share emotions, intolerant of intimacy, secretive without good reason, overcontrolling, insecure, mistrustful of family and close friends, hypersensitive to criticism, unwilling to negotiate conflicts, prone to develop grudges that are held for years, quick to make harsh judgments, convinced that others are working against him or her, and incredibly jealous. Suspicions that sexual partners have been unfaithful are an important diagnostic criterion.

The interpersonal development of the paranoid personality has been described in detail by Benjamin (1996) using her SASB model. First, future paranoids tend to have parents who are "sadistic, degrading, and controlling" (p. 314). Although loyalty to the family is expected, harsh punishment is delivered with a cold, serious attitude and the implicit message that the child is so inherently bad or evil that cruelty is justified. Future paranoids, she states, thus learn to expect attack and abuse and come to identify with abusive caretakers. Second, the parents of future paranoids expect autonomy and punish emotional dependency. If the child gets into a fight, the parents' response may be, "What did you do to set it off?" (p. 315). Alternatively, tears might be greeted with contempt or with threats of further discipline. The result is a mistrustful, isolated adult who fights back neediness, detests dependency, and never asks for help.

Benjamin (1996) further states that future paranoids were often scapegoated and compared unfavorably with other family members, basically continuing the earlier notion that the child is fundamentally bad and, therefore, deserves punishment. The child was accused, not of stupidity or laziness, but of being arrogant, hostile, stubborn, or excessively dominant or independent. Parents might adopt an obvious double standard, preferring certain children while blaming, disciplining, and holding grudges against the paranoid for events that were clearly beyond his or her control. To humiliate the child, the parents might discuss him or her with others in a negative light, even with the child present. The result is an adult highly sensitive to issues of power and status while being overly concerned with whether rewards and punishments have been meted out equally.

Finally, according to Benjamin (1996), future paranoids were rewarded for competence in some area that the caretakers approved, particularly a parenting role. Because high performance was expected, the accomplishments or contributions of the subject were not much appreciated, contributing to increasing levels of resentment over the years. The result is an adult who functions well when left on his or her own but creates and exacerbates conflict through demands for acknowledgment of his or her contributions.

The Cognitive Perspective

Cognitively, paranoids have much in common with the compulsive personality. Both are keen observers, with an outstanding attention to detail motivated by fear. Compulsives, however, sublimate their interpersonal conflicts in an effort to satisfy their internalized objects, their condemning parents, who have taken up residence in a carping superego. In contrast, paranoids are perpetually under attack from their internalized objects but project these attacks, which are then experienced as coming from external sources. After having been pushed all his life to satisfy the expectations of his parents, for example, we can imagine the self-condemnation that Stephen must feel.

Furthermore, both the compulsive and the paranoid have superego pathologies that take the joy out of life. Compulsives, however, become "hyperadjusted," whereas paranoids become keen observers who are extremely suspicious of the motives of others. A constant fear that danger might go undetected compels them toward scrutiny of the smallest details of their interactions. All communications are analyzed for nuance, double meaning, and their implications for power, status, and threat to autonomy. Because the abstract is inherently slippery, everything must be concretized. Ambiguity becomes intolerable.

As noted by Shapiro (1965), suspiciousness goes beyond a contextual trait to an active mode of cognition—not just a consequence but also a cause, a "preoccupying expectation" (p. 56), of which hypervigilance is an important part. Suspiciousness is not the detached curiosity of the scientist. Instead, it is energy invested with a bias toward discovering anything that confirms the original suspicion. Paranoids do not seek to test reality; they seek an empirical foundation that validates self-referential constructions that they are being conspired against and influenced, for example. From the very beginning, their mission is one of discovery, not hypothesis testing. Ron is not interested in proving whether his coworkers are cheating him out of his pay; rather, he is interested only in proving that they are cheating him.

The central cognitive problem of the paranoid, then, is not perceptual but interpretive. The same basic stimulus inputs are received fine, but the information is processed with the explicit goal of identifying plots, persecutions, slights, and criticisms. Stephen, for example, is not interested in discovering the limitations of his ideas and how they might be better adapted to their purpose. When faced with constructive criticism, he sees only the "criticism" and never the "constructive." Suspicion is thus a central mechanism in perpetuating the disorder. Every discovery of additional evidence simultaneously fuels anxiety, indignation, and resentment, which justifies the need for ongoing scrutiny in turn.

Because paranoid thinking is different from normal thinking, it has its own criteria for success. We all bring our own filter to the facts, but we nevertheless do test reality with some degree of scientific detachment. When inconsistencies arise, they become the object of intense interest. Eventually, they are approached logically and either solved or tolerated as not yet explainable. Most of us would agree that few things are either one way or the other and that a tolerance for ambiguity and complexity is necessary in contemporary life.

Paranoid thinking, however, is neither disinterestedly inductive nor logically deductive. Instead, it is a search process, and its success depends on its ability to see through external appearances and uncover concealed truths. Unless surface realities are somehow penetrated, paranoids remain convinced that the truth is concealed—they are in the dark while others are aware. For this reason, paranoids cannot let themselves be swayed by the interpretations of others, who would only deceive them or feed them misinformation. Instead, they are self-contained, impervious to external influence or correction.

As noted by Shapiro (1965, p. 64), the paranoid style ultimately ends in a "loss of reality" similar to that experienced by the compulsive, but much more severe. By this, Shapiro does not mean that suspicion as a mode of cognition necessarily eventuates in a psychotic break, but instead, that the wholeness of social reality, its fabric and feel, is simply lost. The search for clues is guided by an attention that magnifies every small detail, as if paranoids were asking again and again, "Is this all? Is this all? Here's something, there must be more." Each tiny feature must be compulsively put under a microscope.

Shapiro (1965) uses the difference between hearing and listening as an example. A sound technician, he notes, hears the technical aspects of the audio, not the music. The same is true for the paranoid. By zeroing in on the tiniest detail, the ability to make holistic appraisals is lost. The pleasant atmosphere of a party, the ambiance of a nice restaurant—such things are simply not appreciated. As noted by Akhtar (1992), discussed previously, even aesthetic appreciation becomes impossible. Unable to understand the overall tone of a social engagement, for example, paranoids lack the sense of proportion necessary to appraise the details of interpersonal interactions. The eventual outcome is a strange autism of detail, a new world fabricated completely from decontextualized detail. Shorn of context, the paranoid is now free to entertain hypotheses of dubious probability and to imbue these details with idiosyncratic meanings that are consistent with their dark suspicions. This accounts for the paradoxical fact that both a paranoid and a normal person can agree on the objective course of events but not on their interpretation.

Elaborating on Shapiro, there is yet another important reason that paranoids are always groping for clues: The evidence that might conclusively prove their case simply does not exist. Undoubtedly, paranoids do discover coincidences that are strange and convincing, at least to them. However, their construction of the world is simply wrong. There is no proof because there is no proof. Perhaps this explains why paranoids feel that things are kept from them, others are hiding something, and surface appearances conceal dark secrets. Once such a conviction develops, objective support must seem strangely inaccessible. Ever searching for insight into an illusory level of reality, paranoid cognition disintegrates into indicators and frequencies. Anything that occurs too often is suspect, as is anything that does not occur often enough or otherwise seems out of the ordinary. And because life is rich with thousands of elements that might be monitored, some of them will inevitably be found to be out of bounds. These fabricated clues keep the search going.

Consider the case of Marcus, the paranoid professor (see Case 13.3). Marcus has taught chemistry for more than 20 years. Just as molecules can be broken down into atoms, Marcus is used to looking at the world in an analytic way. He has a history lacking in close, personal relationships, in part due to frequent family moves but also due to his strict, regimented childhood. With his parents now dead and minimal contact with his brother, he has made sure that no one will get close enough to gather information that might be used against him. Presenting problems reflect his increasing preoccupation with the idea that students, fellow faculty, and the department chair are plotting against him. For evidence, Marcus has managed to tie together the animosity of his fellow faculty with the complaints of the students that he is rude and rigid.

From the holistic perspective of everyday life, that is, what people value and how they really behave, Marcus's assertion is absurd. For one thing, it requires some hidden mechanism whereby bad and good students can be secretly divided up and the bad ones exclusively shunted to Marcus. When the slackers run into the strong headwind of taskmaster Marcus, he makes sure they quickly learn that they cannot take advantage of him by

CASE 13.3

Marcus, a professor at the university, has taught chemistry for over 20 years. Never an overly friendly man, in recent years he has become increasingly alienated from his colleagues.[1] Students now regularly complain about his rude behavior during office hours. He has been known to pause during lectures, look at the class, and say, "I know what you're doing." After gentle suggestions from the department chair that he seek therapy were ignored, a firmer recommendation was made in writing. Several appointments were made and then cancelled, until Marcus finally learned that he would otherwise be taken off the teaching schedule.

Marcus refers to himself as a "military brat." His family moved 11 times by his eighteenth year. His parents are now deceased, and he has little contact with his older brother. He describes his early years as an extension of military life. He and his brother were expected to follow the rules of the home without discussion or emotion. As a slight, thin child, Marcus was an easy target for bullies at each new school. He learned to fend off attacks by keeping his distance, excelling in school, and becoming vigilant.

At the beginning of the session, Marcus maintains that there is nothing wrong with him. "The system allows mediocrity," he states, "but I will not allow it in *my* classroom. The students think they can just breeze through my classes without working. By the end of the first week, they know they are mistaken." At this, Marcus pauses and seems to smile to himself.

As the interview continues, Marcus maintains that the student's complaints are part of a larger plot involving other instructors and even the department chair. To upset their plans, he has resolved to rule his classes "with an iron fist." He lays traps for the cheaters, and states that several have now been caught and brought up on charges of academic dishonesty. "I have no use for the other faculty," he states boldly. "They are jealous of my intelligence. They want me out of the department because I make them look bad. They had their chance, and now, we are at an impasse, and I will never give in or trust them again." He concedes that it is possible that he is wrong, but "highly unlikely." "The faculty make sure that every semester I get the bad students," he continues. "That way, when they complain about their low grades, it looks like I'm a lousy teacher."

Marcus is firm in his beliefs. He states that he has always done things his way, and that he has always been right in the past. He has known for some time that he would need to fight for his position at the university. In anticipation of a court battle, he has kept careful records of all his activities as an educator. He seems to relish the coming battle. "There is not a single blemish on my record," he says proudly. "I have followed the rules to the letter, and I have the goods on those who haven't." He concludes by saying that he will comply with the order to continue therapy, because he knows that he was referred because the department is looking for an excuse for his dismissal.

[1] Numbers mark aspects of the case most consistent with *DSM* criteria, and do not necessarily indicate that the case "meets" diagnostic criteria in this respect.

Paranoid Personality Disorder
DSM-IV Criteria

A. A pervasive distrust and suspiciousness of others such that their motives are interpreted as malevolent, beginning by early adulthood and present in a variety of contexts, as indicated by four (or more) of the following:

(1) suspects, without sufficient basis, that others are exploiting, harming, or deceiving him or her

(2) is preoccupied with unjustified doubts about the loyalty or trustworthiness of friends or associates

(3) is reluctant to confide in others because of unwarranted fear that the information will be used maliciously against him or her

(4) reads hidden demeaning or threatening meanings into benign remarks or events

(5) persistently bears grudges, i.e., is unforgiving of insults, injuries, or slights

(6) perceives attacks on his or her character or reputation that are not apparent to others and is quick to react angrily or to counterattack

(7) has recurrent suspicions, without justification, regarding fidelity of spouse or sexual partner

B. Does not occur exclusively during the course of Schizophrenia, a Mood Disorder with Psychotic Features, or another Psychotic Disorder and is not due to the direct physiological effects of a general medical condition.

Note: If criteria are met prior to the onset of Schizophrenia, add "Premorbid," e.g. "Paranoid Personality Disorder (Premorbid)."

breezing through his class. However, they also complain to the department, and it is these complaints that Marcus knows will be used as evidence to dismiss him. Marcus has lost perspective on the situation. Convinced of an inevitable court battle with the university over his faculty position, he has gone to great lengths to document his unblemished record. At many levels, Marcus is convinced he is under attack. To defend himself, he lays traps for cheaters and brings them up on charges of academic dishonesty.

Signal detection theory provides another way of understanding paranoid thinking. A signal is detected on the basis of an indicator, a blip on a radar screen, for example. Some blips are real, and some are not. Those that are real are said to be true positives: positive because the indicator detects a signal or signature; true because the signature reflects objective reality. Conversely, when a signature is detected that turns out wrong, it is said to be a false positive: The signal was detected, but it does not correspond to objective reality. A true negative refers to the absence of a signature when no signal is present. A false negative refers to failure to detect a signature when something in fact exists that should produce a signal; the indicator reads negatively, but falsely so.

In warfare, survival often depends on the ability to detect an enemy, even if many false positives are generated as a result. In this sense, the life of the paranoid resembles submarine warfare. If an enemy submarine can seize the element of surprise, it launches torpedoes. The other sub is often sunk before it even had a chance to react. Paranoids are caught in a kind of submarine warfare because survival depends on never allowing a false negative, that is, never missing the presence of a threat, even if a large number of false positives are generated thereby. Paranoids by definition distort reality, so they never really know which positives are false positives and which positives are true positives. Paranoids never know exactly where the truth lies. The enemy is there; this they believe with certainty, but how close and how deeply infiltrated are impossible to answer.

Struggling to unravel the threads of plots that do not exist, paranoids push themselves into a chronic state of emergency. With the barbarians at the gate, their apocalyptic visions of engulfment verge on realization. Because the cost of a false negative is checkmate, no cloaked sub must ever go undetected, no matter how many phantoms are created in the process. When a single false negative means annihilation, a thousand false positives have survival value, no matter how frightening. Trust leads only to a "Trojan Horse" scenario, and everyone becomes the enemy. Worse, because the enemy often seems to escape the best detection efforts, they must be very stealthy and highly intelligent and, therefore, all the more dangerous. The only protection is total fear of everyone. Obviously, the natural tendency is toward delusional generalization into a worldwide conspiracy.

Consider Ron again, who is convinced that his coworkers are skimming his paycheck. Ron hasn't yet found the evidence he needs as proof. He never will, because no one is skimming him (although he may discover something that he can misconstrue as proof). As convinced as he is, objective support must seem strangely inaccessible. Ron cannot question his own hypothesis, however, because he began with certainty, and his self-esteem will not support an iota of self-doubt. Ron's therapist asked him why he believes these things about his coworkers. He reads this request for information as apparent skepticism, and his radar immediately engages into a mode of hypersensitivity. Now, the therapist is suddenly a threat and, as such, has joined the coalition against him. Better to assume such, than to trust someone who would pass confidential information on to your enemies. In his position, Ron can't afford the risk.

The paranoid personality has also been analyzed within the cognitive therapy movement. Not unlike paranoids themselves, cognitive theorists hold that traits are only surface realities. Traits refer to consistencies in behavior, and behind every behavioral consistency lies a cognitive consistency. Whether explicitly articulated or not, every personality trait expresses a belief, and it is beliefs that determine behavior. Core beliefs, which may be either conscious or unconscious, are held to be true regardless of time, place, or circumstance. Conditional beliefs express the interactive role between person and situation: If such-and-such occurs, then such-and-such will result. In turn, conditional beliefs feed into instrumental beliefs, which concern what the person can or cannot do to affect the surrounding world.

According to Beck et al. (1990), paranoids carry a posture of mistrust beyond what is adaptive. They see themselves as righteous and mistreated and view others as devious, deceptive, and secretly manipulative. To counteract the threat of being controlled or demeaned under a guise of innocence, he states, they become guarded, hypervigilant, and suspicious. Beck et al. (p. 48) note a number of core beliefs, paraphrased here as, "I am vulnerable," and "Others cannot be trusted." Conditional beliefs include variations of, "I must be careful not to let others take advantage of me," and "If a person is friendly, he or she must be out to use you." Instrumental beliefs include, "I must always be on my guard," and "I must be alert to hidden motives."

In addition to these, many other beliefs can be generated (see Table 13.1). Almost any trait, especially an interpersonal trait, can be turned into a statement of belief. For example, cynicism might be cast as, "The universe is an unfair place," and hypervigilance might be portrayed as, "I need to be aware of everything that goes on around me if I am not to get hurt." Similarly, hypersensitivity to perceived slights might be cast as, "I must defend myself strongly against the slightest attack." The traits of being convicted and of dichotomous thinking might be portrayed as, "I must not let others influence my views in the slightest," and "Things become clearer when viewed in their purest form."

The Evolutionary-Neurodevelopmental Perspective

Although perspectives on personality offer a particular point of view, they do not tell the whole story. From an evolutionary standpoint, paranoid traits are danger detectors, expressing an intense fear of imminent attack or impending predation, especially when associated with deceit and duplicity. The hypervigilance of paranoids, their constant mobilization for fight or flight, and their constant questioning of the obvious are not unlike an organism that senses something not quite right and fears that a camouflaged predator lurks nearby, ready to pounce at any moment, bringing sudden death from out of the darkness.

In this scenario, the game played out between hunter and hunted is concerned with the real versus the unreal, the ability to detect unusually fine discrepancies of a devouring chameleon against a background specifically chosen to seem ordinary, if not mundane. Successful predators do not announce nonchalantly, "I am here to eat you!" but instead crouch down, blend in, make keen observations at a distance, move silently, pick their moment, close in, and finally, seize the element of surprise. The cheetah springs, the gazelle dies, and the world goes on.

Although such scenarios depict evolution at work, they are also a powerful metaphor for understanding why paranoid traits should exist at all. In the preceding example, such characteristics are intrinsically associated with the possibility of immediate threats to survival. But more, they are deeply and intrinsically concerned with perceptual and

TABLE 13.1   **Traits Associated with the Paranoid Personality**

Mistrustful	Reluctant to presume others' goodwill.
Suspicious	Scrutinizes the actions of others for any hint of malevolent or selfish motive.
Vigilant	Actively scans surroundings and inspects interactions for signs of danger.
Cynical	Believes positive expectations will be spoiled, that human nature is inherently selfish, and that the universe is unjust.
Rivalrous	Actively engages in social comparison.
Wronged	Views self as innocent victim of injustice. Sees self at short end of social comparisons.
Jealous	Questions the loyalty of intimate associates, including spouse.
Thin-Skinned	Hypersensitive to perceived slights. Easily enraged by narcissistic injury.
Seething	Recounts past wrongs while boiling with anger.
Revengeful	Determined to "balance the books," through own action, if necessary.
Guarded	Maintains self-protective posture. Indiscriminately secretive and evasive.
Convicted	Impervious to correction by new information or information inconsistent with previous views.
Humorless	Takes everything seriously. Especially unable to laugh at self. Brittle.
Dichotomous	Polarizes perceptions in terms of good versus evil, just versus unjust, "me versus everyone else."
Self-Contained	Impervious to correction based on the advice of others.
Self-Important	Believes own experience has special significance. Personalizes neutral events. Constructs world with self at center.
Self-Righteous	Certain of own superior virtue or clearer understanding. Arrogant and indignant.
Self-Justifying	Views own transgressions as either a defensive necessity or as "payback" for the malevolence or wrongs of others.

epistemological riddles, that is, with what is real and what is not and what is true and what is a lie. Specifically, the camouflaged predator analogy predicts that paranoia should be concerned with the disambiguation of threats that exist at the very threshold of perception.

The potential for paranoid fear, then, is probably as basic to evolution as evolution is to life, at least wherever evolution implies predation. Paranoid fear thus emerges as a disorder of epistemology wrought by overactive danger detectors. The conclusion is that wherever life exists in the universe, thou shalt find paranoids. Moreover, wherever intelligent life exists, thou shalt find the potential for a caricatured rationality, self-perpetuating disorders of the personal construct system that have their beginning as an attempt to identify danger by pushing beyond the obvious but end by pushing beyond the plausible. Such ontological attributions of the unknown, otherwise known as delusions, thrive on fear. Where the normal person hears a sound in the woods and dismisses it as the wind, the delusional mind finds a hidden agency. For paranoids, there is much more to nothing than we are led to believe: The truth is out there.

Paranoid traits have great survival value when moderately expressed. Organisms that sense threat and run away live to reproduce another day. Paranoid traits such as suspiciousness, vigilance, and a fear of novelty, then, should be expressed widely in any gene pool confronted with predatory threat or competition for resources. All members of the species should, therefore, exhibit some low level of paranoid potential, which can be provoked to paranoid states given persistent objective threats, perhaps traumatic stress, for example. Other members of the species will obtain relatively more paranoid potential through natural recombinant processes. Such "natural paranoids" express high vigilance and a low threshold for suspicion.

Finally, because paranoia is as ubiquitous as danger, we would expect its symptoms to arise in association with a wide range of mental disorders, especially the personality disorders, where vicious circles are the rule. In these mixed cases, the paranoid dimension is often an insidious and secondary development, fusing slowly into the fabric of an earlier pattern. Paranoid symptoms are likely to occur in disorders for which fusion is the theme, such as the dependent, who seems instrumentally helpless to resist almost any threat, whatever its magnitude. In contrast, paranoid traits become integral components of only a few personalities, notably the narcissistic, avoidant, compulsive, sadistic, and negativistic, each of which naturally faces profound confrontations between the self and the social world. These are considered in a following section. The paranoid personality pattern's structural and functional domains are summarized in Table 13.2.

A number of the roots by which certain milder personality styles eventuate in a paranoid pattern are described briefly in the following paragraphs.

The fanatic subtype is likely to have been overvalued and indulged by their parents, given the impression that their mere existence was of sufficient worth in itself. Few developed a sense of interpersonal responsibility, failing to learn how to cooperate, to share, or to think of the interests of others. Unrestrained by their parents and unjustly confident in their self-worth, their fantasies had few boundaries, allowing them to create fanciful images of their power and achievements. The social insensitivity and exploitiveness of these future paranoids led inevitably to interpersonal difficulties. Once beyond the protective home setting, they ran hard against objective reality. Their illusion of omnipotence was challenged, and their self-centeredness and ungiving attitudes were attacked. In time, their image of eminence and perfection was shattered. Rather than face or adapt to reality or build up their competencies to match their high self-esteem, they turned increasingly to the refuge of fantasy. Rationalizing their defects and lost in their imaginary gratifications, they retreated and become further alienated from others.

The characteristic experiential history of the malignant paranoids suggests that they were subjected to parental antagonism and harassment. Many served as scapegoats for displaced parental aggression. Instead of responding with anxiety as a consequence of this mistreatment, they acquired the feeling that they had "to be contended with" and that they could cause trouble and "get a rise" out of others through their unyielding and provocative behaviors. Mistrustful of others and confident of their powers, they rejected parental controls and values and supplanted them with their own. Rebellious of parental authority, they developed few inner controls, often failing to learn to restrain impulses or to avoid temptations.

These paranoids are characterized best by their power orientation, their mistrust and resentment of others, and by their belligerent and intimidating manner. There is a ruthless desire to triumph over others, to vindicate themselves for past wrongs by cunning revenge or callous force, if necessary. In contrast to their nonparanoid counterpart, these personalities have found that their efforts to outwit and frustrate others have only

TABLE 13.2   The Paranoid Personality: Functional and Structural Domains

Functional Domains		*Structural Domains*	
	Defensive	Self-Image	*Inviolable*
Expressive Behavior	Is vigilantly guarded, alert to anticipate and ward off expected derogation, malice, and deception; is tenacious and firmly resistant to sources of external influence and control.	Self-Image	Has persistent ideas of self-importance and self-reference, perceiving attacks on own character not apparent to others, asserting as personally derogatory and scurrilous, if not libelous, entirely innocuous actions and events; is pridefully independent, reluctant to confide in others, highly insular, experiencing intense fears, however, of losing identity, status, and powers of self-determination.
	Provocative	Object-Representations	*Unalterable*
Interpersonal Conduct	Not only bears grudges and is unforgiving of those of the past, but displays a quarrelsome, fractious, and abrasive attitude with recent acquaintances; precipitates exasperation and anger by a testing of loyalties and an intrusive and searching preoccupation with hidden motives.	Object-Representations	Internalized representations of significant early relationships are a fixed and implacable configuration of deeply held beliefs and attitudes, as well as driven by unyielding convictions that, in turn, are aligned in an idiosyncratic manner with a fixed hierarchy of tenaciously held but unwarranted assumptions, fears, and conjectures.
	Suspicious	Morphologic Organization	*Inelastic*
Cognitive Style	Is unwarrantedly skeptical, cynical, and mistrustful of the motives of others, including relatives, friends, and associates, construing innocuous events as signifying hidden or conspiratorial intent; reveals tendency to read hidden meanings into benign matters and to magnify tangential or minor difficulties into proofs or duplicity and treachery, especially concerning the fidelity and trustworthiness of a spouse or intimate friend.	Morphologic Organization	Systemic constriction and inflexibility of undergirding morphologic structures, as well as rigidly fixed channels of defensive coping, conflict mediation, and need gratification, create an overstrung and taut frame that is so uncompromising in its accommodation to changing circumstances that unanticipated stressors are likely to precipitate either explosive outbursts or inner shatterings.
	Projection	Mood/ Temperament	*Irascible*
Regulatory Mechanism	Actively disowns undesirable personal traits and motives and attributes them to others; remains blind to own unattractive behaviors and characteristics, yet is overalert to and hypercritical of similar features in others.	Mood/ Temperament	Displays a cold, sullen, churlish, and humorless demeanor; attempts to appear unemotional and objective, but is edgy, envious, jealous, quick to take personal offense and react angrily.

Note: Shaded domains are the most salient for this personality prototype.

prompted the others to inflict more of the harsh punishment and rejection to which they were previously subjected. Their strategy of arrogance and brutalization has backfired, and they seek retribution, no longer as much through direct action as through fantasy.

The obdurate subtype stems from a conflation of paranoid and compulsive personality features. These persons have a background of parental overcontrol through contingent punishment. Most have striven to meet parental demands and to avoid errors and transgressions, thereby minimizing punitive treatment and the threat of abandonment.

In early life, they sought to model themselves after authority figures, foregoing their independence and following the rules with utmost precision. As a consequence of their rigid conformity, they lack spontaneity and initiative, are unable to form deep and genuine relationships, and are indecisive and fearful of the unknown. For various reasons, differing from case to case, the security these paranoids sought to achieve through submission and propriety was not attained. Lacking guidance and support from others, intolerant of suspense, and dreading punishment lest repressed anger erupt, they drew into themselves, turned away from their dependent conformity, and sought solace, if they could, in their own thoughts. Although renouncing their dependency, obdurate paranoids cannot relinquish their lifelong habits. Thus, feelings of guilt and fear become acute as they begin to assert themselves. Anticipating punishment for their nonconforming behaviors and feeling that such actions deserve condemnation, they project these self-judgments on others and now view them to be hostile and persecutory.

Although they assert their newfound independence with prideful self-assurance, querulous paranoids remain irritable, dissatisfied, and troubled by discontent and ambivalence. They cannot forget their resentments and their feeling of having been mistreated and exploited. They often perceive the achievements of others as unfair advantages, preferential treatments that are undeserved and have been denied to them. Disgruntlement and complaints mount. Fantasies expand and weave into irrational envy. Their grumbling comments turn to overt anger and hostility. Each of these may feed into a theme of unjust misfortune. If unchecked, they are whipped, bit by bit, into a psychotic delusion of resentful jealousy. In similar fashion, erotic delusions may evolve among these patients. Although they consciously repudiate their need for others, these paranoids still seek affection from them. Rather than admit these desires, however, they will defensively project them, interpreting the casual remarks and actions of others as subtle signs of amorous intent. However, they are unable to tolerate these "attentions" because they dread further betrayal and exploitation. As a consequence, querulous paranoids insist that they must be "protected" against erotic seduction by others. Innocent victims may be accused of committing indignities, of making lewd suggestions, or of molesting them.

The insular paranoids are the most likely of the paranoid personalities to be precipitated into a frank psychotic disorder when confronted with painful humiliation and derogation from others. Although they have sought by active withdrawal and isolation to minimize their social contacts, this coping defense is not impenetrable.

Struggling feverishly to control their surging anger, they may turn their feelings inward and impose on themselves harsh judgments and punitive actions. These efforts may not succeed, however. Accusations of their own unworthiness are but mild rebukes for the suspicion and fury they feel. Self-mutilation and suicide, symbolic acts of self-desertion, or brutal attacks against others, a direct expression of their rage, may become the only punishments that "fit the crime."

CONTRAST WITH RELATED PERSONALITIES

Given the ubiquity of paranoid fear and its survival value in moderate degrees, it is not surprising that the paranoid personality shares characteristics with many other personalities.

All severe personality syndromes—the paranoid, schizotypal, and borderline—experience transient psychotic episodes. Those of schizotypals tend to be eccentric, superstitious, or magical in nature; those of borderlines are grossly irrational, scattered, and unsystematic. In contrast, paranoids are skillful at developing internally consistent belief systems that seem distantly plausible, were the world only more perfidious. Moreover, paranoids are deeply concerned with self-determination. Faced with the loss of external recognition and power, they frequently revert to internal sources of supply, creating an enhanced self-image through fantasy that is deserving and strong. The reversible psychotic states of paranoid personalities thus contain elements of grandiosity and righteous indignation, strategies that compensate, or cohere, a fragile self-construct while expressing the deep desire to be left alone, to exist in utter autonomy. In contrast, borderlines tend to diffuse under stress, becoming frantic in response to possible abandonments.

Both avoidants and paranoids are chronically tense and mistrustful and share a hyperalertness to possible interpersonal threats. Moreover, both are suspicious and fearful of being shamed, humiliated, or embarrassed; both can be intensely secretive; and both use fantasy as an important means of coping with their inadequacies. Avoidants, however, see themselves as being woefully inadequate or defective. Paranoids share such concerns at a more unconscious level but transform weakness into compensatory illusions of strength through projection and reaction formation. Thus, avoidants usually shrink from conflict, whereas paranoids readily vent their dissatisfaction.

Both personalities are reluctant to confide in others. Avoidants, however, are reluctant to share information because they fear it will confirm their negative self-image, whereas paranoids fear that such information will be used against them. Both personalities have few friends or confidants. Avoidants, however, acknowledge a desperate loneliness, whereas paranoids view relationships as a source of vulnerability. Finally, paranoids tend to be aloof, humorless, and aesthetically blunt, whereas avoidants show sensitivity, a good sense of humor, and often, a well-developed artistic capacity. However, avoidants whose self-esteem is near collapse may acquire traits of the paranoid personality.

Both the narcissistic and paranoid personalities can be grandiose, and neither tolerates conscious awareness of imperfections of the self. Moreover, both are cold to those they dislike and bear long-lasting grudges. Paranoids, however, are slow to warm up, whereas narcissists are vulnerable to flattery, something that only arouses suspicion in the paranoid. Nevertheless, paranoids are capable of intense devotion and can enjoy equitable relationships with loyal individuals who apparently share their values. In contrast, narcissists exploit almost everyone around them. Finally, narcissists expect others to cater to their needs, exhibit a cool sense of superiority, expect things to turn out for the better, and can be socially engaging. In contrast, paranoids expect others to frustrate their needs, seem tense, expect to be attacked at any moment, and are socially abrasive. Narcissists who suffer chronic deflation of the self, however, may develop paranoid defenses, by asserting that envious others have sabotaged their success or the realization of their ingenious ideas, for example, as a means of explaining repeated setbacks or objective and public failures.

The sadistic and paranoid personalities share similarities at the level of observable behavior. Both are rigid and dogmatic, both tend to see the world in black-and-white terms, both shun the tender emotions as evidence of weakness, and usually both experienced considerable abuse during development. Paranoids, however, project their aggressive impulses. Literally stalked by their projected objects, they see their own behavior as a normal reaction to an insufferably cruel world. Other persons naturally experience them not as victims ever on the defensive but as abrasive instigators whose actions are often positively sadistic. To the casual observer, a paranoid striking back against those who have been disloyal or persecutory is easily confused with a sadistic personality.

Nevertheless, the two personalities exhibit profound differences. Future sadistic personalities are likely to have identified with their aggressor during development. As adults, they delight in indulging feelings of anger and hostility, victimizing others as part of their ego ideal. Sadistic personalities sometimes build complex internal working models of others to maximize the suffering they can inflict. In contrast, paranoids see the world rather simplistically, as me versus everyone else. Sadistic personalities, however, sometimes develop paranoid traits in response to intense, chronic fears of retribution or payback for their vicious abuses of others.

Both paranoid and antisocial personalities are cold, jealous guardians of their autonomy, but for different reasons. As we noted in Chapter 5, the antisocial personality is poorly named; the label "antisocial" suggests more an effect than a cause and does precious little to explain the process behind the product. As such, the category mixes widely differing characteristics. A better term would be the *aggressive personality,* individuals who defend their autonomy as an intrinsic part of their overall psychological makeup, untransformed by psychodynamic factors. Such persons are naturally dominant and territorial, actively shedding or breaking restraints on their free action, and seem grossly lacking in conscience. If others are damaged, that is not their concern.

In contrast, paranoids see themselves as vigorously and righteously defending their boundaries against the encroachment of attackers. Stalked by projected, vicious objects, they see the entire world as composed of antisocials and psychopaths, individuals who destroy without a sense of guilt. Paranoids are capable of relating as peers to others who share their values and have considerable conscience where these relationships are concerned. In contrast, aggressive personalities are bent on dominating everyone.

Finally, paranoid and compulsive personalities value rationality, rigidly controlling themselves while overcontrolling and blaming others (Benjamin, 1996) but for different reasons. Moreover, both can be dogmatic moralists, and their rigidity distorts attentional and cognitive processing (Shapiro, 1965), but again, for different reasons. Compulsives deeply fear making a mistake. As children, they identified with cold, formalistic caretakers, were encouraged to follow the straight and narrow path, and were harshly punished whenever perfection was not attained. As such, they tend to be cold, rigidly conforming, and emotionally unavailable. Their introjects, that is, the contents of the superego, constantly harp about poor performance. To compensate, their attention zeroes in on detail, so much so that they may drown in indecisiveness in a quixotic attempt to explore all possible solutions to a problem or gather all relevant information before making a decision.

In contrast, paranoids were attacked as children, regardless of their performance. So sadistic and cruel are their introjects that any undesirable aspect of the self must be spit out, projected onto others, and replaced by a purified or innocent self-image, not the frequently wrong or disobedient self-image of the compulsive. Such developmental differences lead compulsives to overconform and subordinate their identity, whereas paranoids rebel, seeing all authority as a source of attack, and vigorously defend their self-determination. The attention of the paranoid narrows as a means of anticipating potential avenues of attack and shoring up defenses before the attack occurs. The mistake they fear is some defensive oversight, perhaps disloyalty within the ranks.

PATHWAYS TO SYMPTOM EXPRESSION

Although different individuals vary in terms of their specific characteristics and thus develop different disorders, there exists some logic connecting the personality disorder and the ensuing syndrome. Reversible paranoid conditions sometimes develop in connection with temporary medical conditions. Paranoid reactions may also occur because of loss of sensory or cognitive functioning; for example, paranoid trends may develop in connection with the progression of Alzheimer's disease. Interestingly, when the personality of afflicted individuals is rated by their spouses, those who develop paranoid delusions are usually found to have been more hostile from the beginning (Chatterjee, Strauss, Smyth, & Whitehouse, 1992). Paranoid reactions may also occur as a result of acquired deafness, a phenomenon that can be generated experimentally by assessing subjects after the hypnotic suggestion that they become deaf, without knowing why (Zimbardo et al., 1981). As you read the following paragraphs, try to identify the connection between personality and symptom.

Delusional Disorder

As previously noted, there is some genetic evidence to suggest an association between the paranoid personality and delusional disorder. This is not surprising, as the *DSM-IV* gives delusional disorder several subtypes that parallel concerns of the paranoid personality. Thus, the jealous subtype believes that a significant other has been unfaithful; the grandiose subtype believes that he or she has some tremendous talent or has made some monumental discovery; and the persecutory subtype believes that he or she is being conspired against, poisoned, secretly harassed or observed, and so on. Because conviction and the systematization of beliefs must always be a matter of degree, the paranoid personality and delusional disorder would appear to lie on a continuum. The diagnosis of one disorder does not preclude the diagnosis of the other; however, both can be assigned. Stephen, who convinced himself that he was Niels Bohr, constitutes an example of such a case.

Anxiety Disorders

Guardedness, hypervigilance, and mobilization of the fight-flight system suggest an association between the paranoid personality and the anxiety disorders. Less severe examples of the paranoid personality often exhibit chronic and diffuse worry and complaints of fatigue and difficulty concentrating, suggesting generalized anxiety. Paranoids who suddenly feel themselves unable to distinguish safe versus unsafe situations may experience panic attacks related to feelings of impending attack or collapse of self-esteem. Symptoms include a suddenly racing heart, sweating, trembling, derealization, and fear of losing control. In a preliminary study, J. Reich and Braginsky (1994) found paranoid personality in over half of panic disorder patients diagnosed in the anxiety clinic of a community mental health center. Obsessive-compulsive disorders are also sometimes seen in paranoid personalities. The content of obsessions is probably focused on perceived slights or insults or other matters of rank or status, played repeatedly in the mind.

Mood Disorders

As noted by psychodynamic thinkers, the paranoid personality may be viewed as a compensated state that defends against a precariously low self-esteem. Rather than implode, the person attributes his or her pathetic condition to the external world and eventually develops paranoid traits, which contribute to the coherence of the self-representation and cover the depression. Beyond this, we might also speculate that depression is a natural reaction to a world in which others are aligned against the individual without sufficient cause, in which his or her spouse has been unfaithful, in which loyal friends defect to the enemy, and others are consistently insulting and demeaning. As for bipolar disorder, associations with the Cluster A personality disorders are frequent. Paranoids who exhibit such symptoms will probably possess strong narcissistic trends. Fanatic paranoids in particular are noted for their self-importance and self-righteous buoyancy.

Somatization Disorders

Many personality disorders exhibit physical symptoms, referred to in *DSM-IV* as somatoform disorders. The common thread to each is the presence of physical symptoms not adequately explained by a medical condition or actual physical illness. Physical symptoms are an ideal candidate for a hidden psychological purpose; medicine is not an exact science, all medical tests have some degree of error, and physical perceptions are largely subjective. Where both a somatization disorder and a personality disorder exist, avoidant and paranoid patterns have been found to be frequent (Rost et al., 1992). Perhaps this is not surprising, as both personalities withdraw socially under fears of shame and humiliation.

For the paranoid, somatic symptoms may be seen as part of a broader effort to withdraw and wall off the outside world. As a variation on the same theme, physical symptoms may be used to shed the shame associated with not being able to engage the world effectively. One can hardly be expected to engage others if physical circumstances do not permit it. Alternatively, physical symptoms may counter efforts by family members to blame the subject for a general lack of accomplishment or to elicit sympathy from scapegoating family members. Such disorders might present in conjunction with delusional disorder, somatic type, perhaps as the conviction that one has or has been deliberately infected with some insidious disease, for example. Finally, tentative research suggests that paranoid, avoidant, and compulsive personalities are apparently commonly associated with body dysmorphic disorder (Veale et al., 1996).

Substance Abuse

Wherever there are chronic feelings of anxiety, there is also a potential for self-medication. Paranoids abuse a variety of substances, including alcohol, opiates, cocaine (Kranzler, Satel, & Apter, 1994), and amphetamines. Alcohol, in particular, may be used to provide some relief for feelings of anxiety, hypervigilance, guardedness, and self-referential ideas. However, alcohol may also have the effect of liberating aggression from normal controls, thereby producing a potential for violence. Alcoholic murderers tend to be asocial psychopaths; nonalcoholic individuals who are drunk at the time they commit murder are often found to be paranoid personalities (Vuckovic, Misic-Pavkov, & Doroski, 1997). Other researchers have found that when the paranoid personality is linked to alcoholism, it is usually linked to more severe symptomatology (Morgenstern et al., 1997). Finally, in one study, paranoid personality disorder was found to be more than twice as prevalent as antisocial personality disorder in a sample of sober outpatients enrolled in an alcoholism treatment program (Nurnberg, Rifkin, & Doddi, 1993).

Therapy

The paranoid personality is a challenging psychotherapy case. Most paranoids resist serious delusions; they come into contact with psychological services only at the request of others, as in two of the case studies in this chapter. A spouse may insist on either therapy or divorce, or a boss may insist on either therapy or termination. Most paranoids are regarded as suspicious, testy, and emotionally closed. The greatest improvement is likely to occur in subjects who are fairly high functioning, where the expectation of sadistic treatment is not so deeply ingrained and the notions of persecution are more open to reality testing and falsification. In more severe cases, therapy may make particularly troublesome periods infrequent but cannot revamp the entire personality system.

As noted by Turkat (1990) and as with most pathological personality patterns, paranoids do not present stating, "I need help, I am paranoid," but instead present seeking symptom relief from the fallout of their own hostile vicious circles. One subject may complain of an inability to relax, another may want to become more assertive because others are so antagonizing, and another may complain of being passed over for a promotion. Because symptom-focused treatment misses the real problem, therapists should be sensitive to the possibility that these symptoms are driven by an underlying personality disorder and ask, "Why is this person having these problems?" (p. 47). Questions must be offered in a supportive context, however, for paranoids are naturally secretive and do not readily lay themselves open to scrutiny by others.

THERAPEUTIC TRAPS

Perhaps more than with any other personality disorder, therapy with the paranoid subject is a battle to avoid numerous traps. Many ways to go wrong exist. Without a doubt, the most lethal is direct confrontation of semidelusional notions. Paranoid systems are not scientific hypotheses and cannot be disproved through supposedly objective evidence. First, paranoids' beliefs that others are attacking them are an empirical fact from their developmental history, one carried into inappropriate contexts in adulthood. Such beliefs are so core to the identity of the paranoid that success means a falsification of the self. Confrontation thus implies that something is wrong with who the subject is and, therefore, becomes just another attack. Even the most well-intentioned therapist may thus become the object of suspicion.

Just beginning therapy is highly stressful to most paranoids. Because fears of attack and blame drive the disorder, trust and the therapeutic alliance become a critical priority. Many therapists push for progress faster than trust can be established. Others may directly assert that they can be trusted, an effort that paranoids usually perceive as devious. Once an alliance is established, it remains fragile; one ambiguous slip can be interpreted as condescending and hurtful, destroying whatever foundation has been laid, and set therapy back months. Stone (1993) distinguishes between paranoids whose parents were abusive and those whose parents were both abusive and deceitful. The latter, he suggests, constantly fear that others are lying to them and sometimes require many months or years just to trust the therapist.

Moreover, because intimacy makes paranoids feel exposed and vulnerable, they often react against perceptions of closeness and warmth by retreating into the safe shell of emotional isolation. Some may even quit therapy. Unconditional warmth is a new experience for individuals perpetually mobilized for unexpected, vicious onslaughts. Overeager efforts to draw the paranoid back into the open usually intensify feelings of discomfort. During such times, patience is a virtue. Therapists should not require greater comfort in the transference than what the paranoid can give. Accordingly, time, consistency, and an "I'm okay, you're okay" attitude that respects the need for distance are probably the best course. Distance at least gives control back to the paranoid; any other path requires the subject to submit to someone not yet trusted, a contradiction.

Because paranoids are often blaming and abrasive, they naturally provoke the same countertransference reactions. Seldom are they the most rewarding clients. Nevertheless, progress requires that no defensiveness and counterhostility seep into the therapist's communications. Therapists must contain their own defensive and hostile feelings. Otherwise, a realistic basis for feelings of attack and vulnerability is created, and therapy just replays the same vicious circle that paranoids experience in real life. In response to provocation, some therapists naturally become more directive and take control of the session. This humiliates the paranoid, who senses the loss of control and feels that the therapist is trying to expose him or her to vulnerability and attack. Accordingly, directive interventions should be closely inspected for their underlying motives, especially when the therapist is male or has competitive issues or issues with authority.

Finally, offering interpretations and comments to paranoids is a fine art that develops only over time. Given their hypersensitivity to slights and their tendency to oversimplify, the most well-intentioned comment can be transformed into slander, laying the foundation for a grudge that sabotages further work. Some paranoids are sincere in their misperceptions; others enjoy the power of making the therapist squirm under the illusion of having offended them. During such tests, the subject is exquisitely interested in the therapist's reaction: Will the therapist blame the subject or simply set matters straight without the need to blame anyone? By containing his or her own negative counterreaction, the therapist passes the test and sets the groundwork for a very different kind of relationship. Therapy with paranoids always requires tact, the ability to phrase comments so that alternative, hostile interpretations are disallowed.

THERAPEUTIC STRATEGIES AND TECHNIQUES

Writing from an interpersonal perspective, Benjamin (1996) suggests that paranoids naturally see the therapist as critical and judgmental and that when trust is finally established, treatment is already well underway. Because paranoids were taught to be loyal to the family, they are usually reluctant to explore connections between the developmental past and their behavior in the present. Confiding in the therapist amounts to betraying family secrets to a stranger.

Given their history, paranoids require what Benjamin (1996, p. 332) calls "noncoercive holding," basically, soothing empathy and affirmation as an antidote to early abuse. In addition, paranoids should eventually realize that their own feelings of vulnerability do not automatically mean that they have been attacked and that the expectation of attack follows directly from their experiences with caretakers. By realizing that their own hostility implicitly puts them in the role of their abusers, paranoids may find the will to explore alternative roles. By separating emotionally from caretakers, paranoids can purge themselves of vicious introjects that keep attacking night and day and must be projected, thus absolving themselves of hostility. Benjamin also suggests that countertransference feelings are best admitted honestly and constructively. This offsets a major childhood factor for most paranoids: the implicit attitude of condemnation felt from their families.

Writing in Beck et al. (1990), Pretzer notes that the paranoid personality is perpetuated by core beliefs that others cannot be trusted and will intentionally inflict hurt where possible. Interventions should modify this assumption, without being perceived as a personal attack. Because paranoids require safety, they are unable to relax their vigilance and defensiveness, core factors in perpetuating the disorder. Accordingly, a heightened sense of self-efficacy should function to reassure subjects that problems will not be overwhelming but can be handled effectively as they arise. Eventually, self-efficacy should lead to a measure of relaxation, thus making the paranoid accessible to traditional cognitive methods, such as the exploration of automatic thoughts. However, such techniques require disclosure, which makes the secretive paranoid uncomfortable.

Accordingly, Pretzer suggests therapy should begin behaviorally, by focusing on goals set by the subject and approaching the least threatening goals first. Because these problems are a consequence of the total personality system, issues that the therapist might select as a point of intervention are inevitably brought into play. There are two principal ways that self-efficacy can be increased. First, paranoids often overestimate the intensity of objective threats or underestimate their ability to solve the problem. Here, more realistic assessments lead to an improved sense of efficacy. Second, if skills appropriate to the situation are lacking, intervention can focus on teaching coping skills that might reduce the subject's sense of threat and anxiety.

Finally, Pretzer notes that cognitive style interventions can address the paranoid's black-and-white thinking and tendency to overgeneralize. Subjects can be asked to rate the extent to which others have followed through on particular requests, for example, or to rate their own competency in particular areas. Focusing on specifics breaks down totalizing cognitions, puts persons and events in a more realistic light, and brings a measure of complexity to a dichotomous worldview. By generalizing from the therapy session to real life, paranoids are able to assess situations more competently and with greater objectivity, defusing their need for projection. New perspectives on others can be gained by monitoring interpersonal experiences and the cognitions and emotions that accompany them. By gathering more information, paranoids fill in the gaps that exist in their fund of knowledge about the motives of others. Alternative explanations can then be explored.

From a behavioral perspective, Turkat (1990) discusses a variety of techniques that can be useful with paranoid personalities. Hypersensitivity to criticism produces anxiety and should, therefore, be accessible to behavioral techniques of anxiety reduction. Essentially, the subject first learns some antianxiety response, perhaps progressive muscle relaxation or cognitive modification. Next, a hierarchy of anxiety-provoking situations is constructed. As the subject moves upward, each situation in the hierarchy is paired with the antianxiety response. With repeated trials, subjects gradually learn to control the intensity of their anxiety, and the anxiety itself begins to be extinguished and is replaced by a relaxing alternative.

Because anxiety is only a surface manifestation of the disorder, however, Turkat (1990) recommends that the social behavior of the paranoid be modified. First, the breadth of social attention should be examined, perhaps by having subject and therapist watch videotapes of human interaction, perhaps a soap opera. Because paranoids miss a variety of social cues, the clinician can easily evaluate how their attention is distorted and provide corrective feedback that permits them a more realistic picture of human relationships. Social information processing can be modified by teaching the paranoid the correct interpretation of social cues, accomplished through role playing, videotaped feedback, and direct instruction. The hope is that subjects will eventually learn to take the observer role and become self-correcting.

The psychodynamic perspective emphasizes many aspects of these approaches but also draws on the theory of bipolar self-representations—that paranoid grandiosity compensates for underlying feelings of depression, including low self-esteem, vulnerability, inadequacy, powerlessness, and a sense of defectiveness or worthlessness. According to Kleinian object-relations theory, the paranoid-schizoid position is a primitive stage of development, during which the synthetic functions of the ego do not permit the good and bad characteristics of self and others to be integrated. In the paranoid personality, the "good me" and "bad me" are separate entities, with the "bad me" being projected out of the self and onto others, who become attackers and persecutors. Because the paranoid-schizoid position resolves into the depressive position, treatments that can convert paranoid thinking into an acknowledged depression are more likely to be successful.

At this more advanced stage of object-relations development, ambivalent feelings and disappointments are tolerated and contained and, therefore, become amenable to conscious reflection. Moreover, by moving from paranoid projection to depression, the subject can be treated by more traditional methods. As stressed by Gabbard (1994), the ultimate purpose of therapy is an attributional shift, whereby paranoids come to see their problems as deriving from internal causes, not the external environment. Psychodynamic thinkers also stress the value of empathizing with the paranoid view of the world and of relationships, while also suggesting alternative interpretations. Therapists should acknowledge the possibility that some negative interpretation is correct but nevertheless seek to shift the weight of probability to a more adaptive or realistic hypothesis (Stone, 1993).

Summary

Among paranoid personalities, the capacity for trust has been destroyed. While it is part of our normal, human development to have some mistrust of others, especially when we are young (stranger anxiety) or if we live in life-threatening situations, a persistent and extreme mistrust of others is maladaptive. Within the normal range of personality styles that include paranoid characteristics are Oldham and Morris's (1995) vigilant style, who are highly independent and valuing of their independence. Normal paranoid styles can also be viewed as simply normalizing the *DSM-IV* criteria, such as valuing honesty and fidelity without alienating friends and family instead of suspecting close friends of being disloyal without evidence.

Several variants exist of the paranoid personality that combine paranoid traits with other personalities. The fanatical paranoid is a mix with the narcissistic personality who has had a serious narcissistic wound. The malignant paranoid combines the paranoid with the sadistic personality and is hypersensitive to issues of power and domination. The obdurate paranoid shares traits with the compulsive personality and may function more normally in society than most paranoids. The querulous paranoid is a paranoid with negativistic traits who feels perpetually as though he or she has been cheated in life. Last, the insular paranoid shares characteristics with the avoidant personality, tending to be the most isolated of the paranoids.

While biologically, there does not appear to be a paranoid temperament, most likely the same irritable and aggressive temperament that may also lead to antisocial, sadistic, or borderline personality plays a role in the paranoid, with early environmental factors playing a great role in determining the ultimate path of development. Limited empirical research conducted on the heritability of a paranoid personality has been inconclusive as have been studies that try to link paranoid personality to schizophrenia and delusional disorder.

The classical psychodynamic perspective offers an interesting insight into the paranoid, namely their overdependence on the defense mechanism of projection. Strict Freudian interpretation of the paranoid personality holds that the paranoia is a defense against homosexual urges that are unacceptable to the individual. Later in the century, object-representationalists began to see the paranoid as polarizing life into categories of all good and all bad. By using projection to eliminate any of the bad in the self, they become all good; hence anything external becomes all bad. Because the negative thoughts are within the paranoid, they follow the paranoid wherever they go in life. Later dynamicists proposed secondary defense mechanisms such as using isolation, indignation, and megalomania or extreme overvaluation of the self as well as early abuse in the development of the paranoid personality.

Paranoids closely resemble compulsives in their cognitive style. Both are keen observers, attending to every detail and nuance of a situation; and both are intolerant of ambiguity. For the paranoid, suspiciousness becomes the entire mode of thinking where all of their energy is spent discovering not if people are cheating them, but how they are cheating them. Their self-statements may include, "I must always be on my guard," and "I must be alert to hidden motives."

Interpersonally, Sullivan proposed that paranoids not only have an extreme insecurity related to a feeling of inferiority but also blame others instead of themselves for these perceived shortcomings. Paranoids treat others as the enemy, which precludes the development of any attachments. Occasionally, paranoids surround themselves with loyal persons who can act as the eyes and ears of the paranoid, routing out evil plots being planned against them. Developmentally, Benjamin describes an environment of harsh punishment in childhood that leads the paranoid to expect that the world is going to attack. The paranoid might have also been used as a scapegoat for the family.

The biopsychosocial evolutionary perspective adds yet another angle to understanding the paranoid personality. Paranoid traits act as "danger detectors" from impending attacks and serve a useful purpose of saving the life of the individual. Thus, the potential for paranoid fear is probably an inevitable outcome of evolution and, expressed in moderation, is highly beneficial to the organism.

Paranoid traits are expressed by all of the severe personality disorders but also in avoidants, narcissists, sadists, antisocials, and compulsives. They also often overlap with delusional disorder; anxiety disorders; mood disorders, particularly depression and perhaps bipolar disorder; somatization disorders in an effort to escape the shame of not being able to engage the world effectively; and substance abuse, especially when the paranoid is experiencing symptoms of anxiety.

Therapy seems to be most successful with paranoids closer to normal on the spectrum. Numerous traps must be avoided when working with the paranoid. The most dangerous is directly confronting the paranoid's semidelusional notions, which will be construed by the client as proof of another attack. Benjamin proposes a soothing empathy as an antidote to earlier abuse to increase the intimacy between the client and therapist. Cognitive techniques should focus on modifying the assumption that others are not to be trusted and improving their sense of self-efficacy. Behaviorally, coping skills training may be effective, as well as anxiety-reducing exercises such as gradual exposure to an anxiety hierarchy paired with a cognitive relaxation method. Object-relations therapy may also be useful as a first step to get paranoids to convert their paranoid symptoms into an acknowledged depression; then they can be treated with traditional methods.

Chapter 14

The Borderline Personality

Objectives

- What are the *DSM-IV* criteria for the borderline personality?
- The mercurial personality is a normal variant of the borderline. Describe its characteristics and relate them to the more disordered criteria of the *DSM-IV.*
- Explain how different personality styles combine to form each of the subtypes of the borderline personality.
- How does HIV status relate to the borderline personality?
- Borderlines show intense moodiness and rapidly shifting emotions. What, if any, is the connection to affective and manic-depressive disorders?
- Explain the psychoanalytic origin of the term *borderline group of neuroses.*
- Explain Kernberg's notion of levels of organization as characteristic of the borderline personality.
- What causes a failure of object constancy in the borderline?
- Explain why Masterson and Adler both believed that it is the mother who is ultimately responsible for creating borderline pathology.
- Explain the dynamics of self-injurious behavior in the borderline.
- Describe the interpersonal dynamics of the borderline personality.
- What are the factors that Benjamin considers important in the development of the borderline personality?
- What is the relationship between childhood sexual abuse and borderline pathology?
- Why are borderlines so cognitively dependent on external structures?
- What is the meaning of the term *PTSD/borderline,* coined by Kroll?
- What are the core beliefs of the borderline?
- Borderlines share characteristics with other personality disorders. List these other disorders and explain the distinction between each and the borderline.

- Why are borderlines such difficult patients in therapy? Why should therapists guard against issues of countertransference when working with borderlines?
- List therapeutic goals for the borderline personality.

To live a life analogous to a soap opera is to live the life of a **borderline personality.** Wrought with emotional ups and downs, these individuals are known to be unstable and especially angry. What fuels the chaos are intense interpersonal needs and sudden shifts of opinion about others, who may be painted as loving, sensitive, and intelligent one minute and accused of neglect and betrayal the next. When left alone, even for short periods, borderline personalities feel intolerably lonely and empty. With romantic relations typically stormy and intense, they spend most of their time either making up or breaking up. They make frantic attempts to avoid abandonment, including suicidal gestures. In addition, they fail to realize that their clinginess via dramatic and drastic measures drives others away. Plagued by feelings of anxiety, depression, guilt, and inferiority, many engage in self-destructive behaviors, indulging themselves impulsively in drugs or promiscuous sexual activity. Some even mutilate their own bodies by cutting or burning. Lacking a mature sense of self-identity, they flip-flop on goals and values, suddenly change jobs on impulse, and reverse previous opinions with indifference. During stressful periods, this incohesiveness makes them susceptible to temporary psychotic states and dissociative episodes. The borderline personality is peppered with many aspects of other personality disorders. Throughout this chapter, we embark on the roller coaster ride that so aptly depicts this personality.

For the sake of convenience in this text, borderline personalities will be referred to simply as borderlines. Consider the case of Jenny (see Case 14.1). What is immediately striking about Jenny, and about many borderlines, is a specific kind of instability in their relationships. Jenny swings from loving people to hating them and back again, as if she knew only two modes of appraisal: either complete idealization as the best person on earth or devaluation as a demon from Hell (see criterion 2). The immediate recipient of these alternating attitudes is her stepmother, Vera, who is understandably bewildered by such sudden and never-ending shifts of attitude. Later, we find out that Jenny refers to Vera as the "wicked witch" and describes her boyfriend as "evil." Shades of the same are perhaps seen when she talks about her father, who taught her "not to rely on people, 'cause one minute they're here and the next they're gone," as if loyalty could consist only of dichotomous extremes.

What Jenny seems to need most is magical fusion with a loving caretaker. Indeed, feelings of abandonment seem to underlie the intense anger she feels toward her father. Apparently, Jenny sees Vera as replacing not only her real mother but also Jenny herself. A hunger strike, locking herself in her room, and demanding that her father divorce Vera are all frantic efforts to avoid abandonment and recapture the past (see criterion 1). She has also threatened suicide, run away from home, and been arrested for drug possession (see criterion 5).

Moreover, Jenny seems devoid of life goals or consistent values. Whereas normals develop a solid sense of identity that defines the person and gives direction to life, Jenny lacks a stable identity that might anchor her (see criterion 3) against the influence of intense, transient impulses that threaten to seriously damage her life (see criterion 4).

Jenny, age 25, was brought for evaluation by her stepmother, Vera.[1] "Sometimes she seems to adore me, and sometimes she hates my guts," Vera said, bewildered. "She knows we love her, but she just goes on and on like this. Sometimes, when it gets real bad, she accuses us of planning behind her back to hurt her." Jenny's efforts to restrain her emotions are obvious. Initial moments of decorum give way suddenly as Jenny bursts forth with an erratic stream of anger, accusation, and feelings of betrayal. The meaning of her words and emotions is difficult to track.

(2) *(9)* *(6)*

Jenny is no stranger to psychotherapy. According to her stepmother, Jenny was hospitalized in her teens and has been in therapy twice before, each time for about a year. She has an episodic history of substance abuse, including marijuana, alcohol, amphetamines, "ecstasy," LSD, and most recently, cocaine. She has been sexually active since her first intercourse with an older cousin at age 12 and hates to be without a boyfriend. Jenny's mother died of cancer when Jenny was 9. Her father married Vera two years later. Vera's two sons and Jenny's older brother got along well from the start.

(4)

Jenny, however, responded to her mother's death and her father's subsequent marriage to Vera with a mixture of withdrawal, anger, and increasingly outrageous behavior. After a suicide attempt, running away from home, and arrests for drug possession, she was deemed unmanageable by the family and sent to a strict boarding school at age 14. She still threatens suicide from time to time, and seems to have no life goals or real values.

(5) *(3)*

Her anger seems total and indiscriminate. She is angry at the circumstances that brought her here. She has just been released from the hospital, where she was recovering from minor internal injuries sustained after jumping out of her boyfriend's Jeep while on the way to a concert, something she has done before. She insists she did it because they were arguing and she was high and just wanted to get away, describing him as "evil." She obviously despises Vera, referring to her as the "wicked witch" several times during the interview.

(8) *(4)*

Her most intense anger, however, is reserved for her father, who "never gave a damn," abandoning her and the memory of her mother by marrying Vera. The worst thing is not his abandonment, she says, but that he doesn't even know he did it. "The only good he ever did was teach me not to rely on people, 'cause one minute they're here and the next they're gone," she continues. She has even gone on a hunger strike and locked herself in her room and demanded her father and Vera divorce.

Jenny believes that he sent her away because she both looked and behaved like her mother, and that her father couldn't handle having a young version of his dead wife in his new life. The death of her mother and alienation from her father have left her feeling "hollow inside," she states. "Sometimes life is like moving in slow motion and I seem like an observer, looking at everything from the outside, numb." Sometimes during these periods she cuts herself with a razor blade, "'cause it hurts, but I end up feeling better afterwards. It shakes me up inside and pulls me back to reality."

(9)

[1] Numbers mark aspects of the case most consistent with *DSM* criteria, and do not necessarily indicate that the case "meets" diagnostic criteria in this respect.

Borderline Personality Disorder
DSM-IV Criteria

A pervasive pattern of instability of interpersonal relationships, self-image, and affects, and marked impulsivity beginning by early adulthood and present in a variety of contexts, as indicated by five (or more) of the following:

(1) frantic efforts to avoid real or imagined abandonment. **Note:** Do not include suicidal or self-mutilating behavior covered in Criterion 5.

(2) a pattern of unstable and intense interpersonal relationships characterized by alternating between extremes of idealization and devaluation

(3) identity disturbance: markedly and persistently unstable self-image or sense of self

(4) impulsivity in at least two areas that are potentially self-damaging (e.g., spending, sex, substance abuse, reckless driving, binge eating). **Note:** Do not include suicidal or self-mutilating behavior covered in Criterion 5.

(5) recurrent suicidal behavior, gestures, or threats, or self-mutilating behavior

(6) affective instability due to a marked reactivity of mood (e.g., intense episodic dysphoria, irritability or anxiety usually lasting a few hours and only rarely more than a few days)

(7) chronic feelings of emptiness

(8) inappropriate, intense anger or difficulty controlling anger (e.g., frequent displays of temper, constant anger, recurrent physical fights)

(9) transient, stress-related paranoid ideation or severe dissociative symptoms

These include polysubstance abuse and the habit of leaping from moving vehicles to get away from her "evil" boyfriend.

Further, Jenny seems swept up in intense, rapidly changing emotions (see criterion 6), especially anger (see criterion 8). At the beginning of the interview, she makes an attempt at impression management, but finally her anger bursts forth into a stream of accusations. In fact, Jenny seems angry at just about everything all the time. She despises Vera and argues with her "evil" boyfriend. She is angry with her father for marrying Vera and abandoning her and her mother, even though he is unaware of his "crimes" against her. Sometimes, her anger is so intense that she accuses Vera and her father of planning to hurt her (see criterion 9). Perhaps she cannot imagine how life could become so dissatisfying, believing that the course of events would need to be helped along by some evil agency to be so effective in its misery.

Obviously, Jenny feels misunderstood, alienated, and alone. Although everyone feels this way at some time, Jenny reports constantly feeling "hollow inside," apparent evidence of feelings of emptiness (see criterion 7), but probably more closely related to dissociation (see criterion 9). Jenny notes, for example, that life sometimes seems to be "moving in slow motion" and that she is "like an observer" watching things "from the outside," evidence of breakdown in the normally integrated functions of consciousness. To pull herself back from these twilight states, she engages in "cutting," using the undeniable reality of intense pain as a reference point that shocks her back to the real world.

Although subjects like Jenny are well known to many therapists, the borderline construct has proven remarkably controversial. Indeed, the very label borderline presages problems of definition. Logically, anything known primarily for bordering something else obviously cannot be its own entity. Accordingly, it is not surprising that the borderline personality has been reformulated again and again. Zanarini and Frankenburg (1997) note six main historical conceptions:

1. The psychodynamic perspective, which views the borderline as a level of personality organization (Kernberg, 1967) subsuming a variety of character pathologies between neurosis and psychosis.

2. Reflects the influence of the neo-Kraepelinian idea that mental disorders are biological in origin and, therefore, should be diagnosed as discrete categories, as reflected in the work of Gunderson (1984). Though the term borderline clearly contradicts a categorical conception, this approach is nevertheless endorsed by the *DSM*.

3. Reflects a tendency to experience temporary psychotic states and regards the borderline as existing on a continuum with schizophrenia.

4. Reflects a sudden shifting of emotions, irritability, and chronic depressive states and views the borderline as existing on a continuum with the affective disorders (Akiskal, 1981).

5. Reflects an inability to delay gratification and views the borderline as an impulse control disorder related to substance abuse and the antisocial personality (Zanarini, 1993).

6. Reflects the belief that many borderlines have a sexual abuse history and suggests that the syndrome has much in common with posttraumatic stress disorder (Herman & van der Kolk, 1987; Kroll, 1993).

Each of these threads in the history of the borderline personality has produced its own literature, in some cases amounting to hundreds of articles. In fact, more has been written on the borderline than on any other personality disorder—far too much for comprehensive review and integration. Given its limitations of space, this chapter has two primary goals: first, to review the contemporary and historical issues involved in efforts to define the syndrome, grouped mainly within the biological and psychodynamic perspectives; and second, to provide a discussion of borderline symptoms and traits, thereby giving you a feel for the borderline person, even though controversies and compromises have left the syndrome an admittedly heterogeneous entity.

Given the portrait of Jenny, we now approach additional issues that form the plan of this chapter. First, we compare normality and abnormality; then we move on to variations on the basic borderline theme. Next, biological, psychodynamic, interpersonal, and cognitive perspectives on the borderline personality are described. These sections form the core of what is scientific in personality. By seeking to explain what we observe in character sketches like Jenny's, the goal is to move beyond literary anecdote and enter the domain of theory. As always, we present history and description side by side, noting the contributions of past thinkers, each of whom tends to bring into focus a different aspect of the disorder. Developmental hypotheses are also reviewed but are tentative for all personality disorders. Next, the section "Evolutionary Neurodevelopmental Perspective" shows how the existence of the personality disorder follows from the laws of evolution. Also included are a comparison between the borderline and other theory-derived constructs and a short discussion of how borderline personalities tend to develop Axis I disorders. Finally, we survey how the disorder might be treated through psychotherapy, again organizing our material in terms of classical approaches to the field: the interpersonal, cognitive, and psychodynamic perspectives.

From Normality to Abnormality

Although its symptoms are obviously severe, the borderline personality can nevertheless be viewed as existing on a continuum with normality. The **mercurial style** (Oldham & Morris, 1995) is described as living a roller coaster life. Frequent ups and downs are the rule, and attachment is the central theme in all relationships. Echoing the borderline's frantic attempts to avoid abandonment is a desire always to be involved in a passionate romantic relationship. Such individuals, these authors state, process experience emotionally rather than logically, showing their feelings with spontaneity and creativity. Socially, they are lively and engaging, with an open mind toward experimenting with various roles and value systems. Exhibiting aspects of the dependent and histrionic personalities, they urgently seek closeness with their partners, like a merging of souls but even more intensely. They expect the same from others and quickly become hurt whenever the same desire is not forthcoming. Anger and resentment follow. Most of the preceding applies to Jenny but is not sufficiently severe to capture her level of pathology.

Another way of developing a normal variant of the borderline is by creating more adaptable parallels to the borderline personality disorder criteria listed in *DSM-IV* (see Sperry, 1995). Whereas the disordered individual will do almost anything to avoid perceived abandonment, those with the borderline style simply are sensitive to anything that might impact the quality of attachment in their relationships. Whereas the borderline personality disorder exhibits unstable relationships that alternate rapidly between idealization and devaluation, those with the style may read more into behaviors and events than is warranted but can take a more realistic and complex perspective on their relationships. Whereas the disordered feature a disturbance of identity and an unstable self-image, those with the style diminish self-uncertainty by being more experimental and curious about alternative lifestyles, roles, and value systems. Whereas the disordered tend to be impulsive in self-damaging ways, those with the style are simply somewhat sensation-seeking, but in ways that primarily add to the richness of experience rather than subtract from it.

For each of the preceding applicable contrasts, Jenny, our angry stepdaughter, falls convincingly toward the pathological side. Far from being simply concerned with the quality of her attachments, her behavior reflects intense, pervasive abandonment themes focused especially on the connection between her father and her stepmother. Jenny obviously feels replaced and probably fears that her stepmother is more important to her father than is she. Far from reading more into events than is warranted, Jenny's feelings about others, especially Vera, swing from loving to hating. Far from being simply experimental and curious in a way that builds self-identity, Jenny seems too consumed with emotional upheavals to allow for life goals or real values to develop. Finally, Jenny is not simply sensation-seeking in ways that add to the richness of life; instead, she is impulsive in harmful ways, including substance abuse and leaping from her boyfriend's Jeep.

Other diagnostic criteria for the borderline personality can be placed on a continuum with normality (see Sperry, 1995). Whereas the disordered tend to be affectively unstable and make suicidal gestures or engage in self-mutilation, the borderline style tends to be spontaneous and emotionally intense and only occasionally overreacts or over-dramatizes. Chronic feelings of emptiness plague those with the disorder, yet those with the style actively pursue social venues and creative pursuits that help make life entertaining. Whereas the disordered exhibit intense displays of anger that are difficult to control, those with the style tend to be more emotionally intense but nevertheless able to step back and see the effects of their moods on others. Whereas the disordered exhibit temporary paranoid ideation or dissociative symptoms under stressful conditions, those with the style are not vulnerable to such symptoms.

The aforementioned characteristics of a borderline are presented in Jenny's case, though hers are more toward the pathological side of the applicable contrasts. Far from being merely more emotionally intense or spontaneous than average, she is emotionally labile, as seen most readily at the beginning of the clinical interview and again in the intense argument with her boyfriend. Moreover, her emotions are so intense that they contribute to a dissociative dysphoria that Jenny "treats" by cutting herself with a razor blade. Finally, she experiences periods of intense anger that she controls only with great difficulty, as evidenced by a rapid erosion of decorum that gives way to an erratic stream of hatred and accusation directed at Vera near the beginning of the interview. As Bockian (2002) succinctly explains, people with the disorder may struggle throughout their lives to gain a sense of identity while managing feelings of inadequacy, impulsiveness, self-destructive behavior, and even suicidal ideations.

Variations of the Borderline Personality

In general, personality disorders alone are difficult to diagnose, and more than most, borderlines are those frequently misdiagnosed (Bockian, 2002). Both theory and research argue that the *DSM* borderline pattern overlaps nearly every other personality disorder, with some exceptions. Because most subjects diagnosed as borderline are female by a ratio of 2 to 1 or even higher, subjects with dependent, histrionic, avoidant, depressive, and negativistic features are common, though for different reasons. In general, any personality pattern that makes others the center of life is at risk to develop a borderline personality. The desire to magically fuse with others who will support you emotionally and meet your every need is evidence of both ego weakness and identity disturbance, leading to instability in interpersonal relationships and feelings of emptiness and desperation when others seem to separate. In contrast, a *DSM* borderline diagnosis is probably less likely for male compulsive, sadistic, paranoid, and some narcissistic personalities, for whom dogmatism, righteous indignation, or grandiosity artificially boost the coherence of the self, giving it rigid boundaries inconsistent with those of the more permeable borderline. A summary of the borderline subtypes is given in Figure 14.1. Actual cases may or may not fall into one of the combinations described in the following sections.

THE DISCOURAGED BORDERLINE

The **discouraged** borderline is mixed with the dependent or avoidant patterns. Such individuals pursue a strategy of submissive attachment to just one or two significant others.

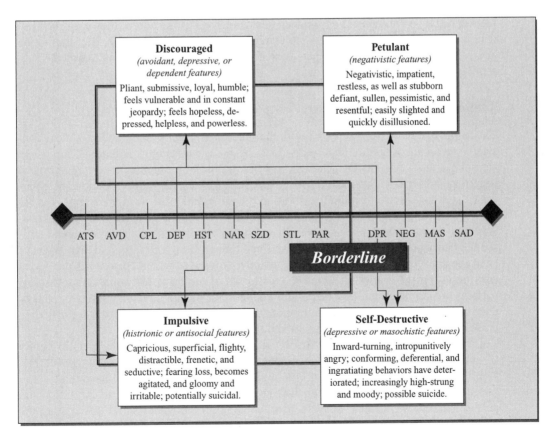

FIGURE 14.1   Variants of the Borderline Personality.

Prominent personality traits include not only avoidance of competition, loyalty, and humility but also masochistic subordination and a parasitic clinginess.

By exclusively relying on a single someone, discouraged borderlines "put all their eggs in one basket." Always fearing that their lifeline is threatened, their world is chronically destabilized. Consequently, they are ever preoccupied with their lack of security, mainly their own helplessness, self-doubt, and lack of self-sufficiency. To reinforce their relationships, they cling tenaciously to whoever is available, merging their own identity into that of their partner. Given such profound needs, they are easily panicked by a sense of isolation or aloneness and easily feel depressed and powerless. Simple responsibilities seem monumental, everything is a burden, and life is empty and heavy. Should their sense of futility intensify, they may regress to a state of marked depression or infantile dependency, requiring others to tend to them as if they were infants.

Other discouraged borderlines mix characteristics of the depressive personality. Such individuals have been taught to be conscientious and proper. They respect authority, tend to be grim and humorless, and expect rewards contingent on compliance and submission. Borderline characteristics begin to develop when the individual senses that this interpersonal pact has been violated too often—that others have selfishly failed to supply promised rewards of affection. Resentful and angry, they no longer believe that conformity will forestall desertion. Instead, they feel coerced into submission and betrayed—emotions that periodically break through normal controls. Because anger is not only inconsistent with their self-image but also alienates or provokes those on whom they depend, intense negative feelings are experienced as dangerous. In response, they may swing to the opposite pole, becoming excessively preoccupied with self-reproach. Self-mutilation and suicidal attempts, symbolic acts of self-desertion, may be used to control their resentment or as punishment for anger.

THE IMPULSIVE BORDERLINE

The **impulsive** borderline is mixed with the histrionic or antisocial pattern. Unless constantly receiving attention, such individuals become increasingly seductive, impulsive, capricious, and irresponsible. Though most borderlines are famous for dysregulation of negative emotions, subjects with histrionic traits become even more behaviorally hyperactive and cognitively scattered, exhibiting a dysregulation of positive affects that includes frenetic gaiety, frantic gregariousness, and irrational and superficial excitement. At times, they lose all sense of propriety and judgment. Individuals with a stronger antisocial history become even more impulsive and thoughtless, both failing to plan ahead or heed the consequences of their actions as they struggle to free themselves from social constraints. At the borderline level, the strategies of the basic histrionic and antisocial patterns are simply much less successful than before. As such, they are likely to experience many disappointments, to go for extended periods of time without the security they crave, and to succumb to hopelessness and depression.

The impulsive borderline is especially likely to have experienced the chaotic family (Linehan, 1993) or soap opera environment (Benjamin, 1996), which encourages drama, a desire for stimulus variety, and an intolerance of boredom. Many will have felt a sense of security and attachment only when their parents acknowledged some exhibitionistic performance or when their misbehavior was intense enough to stand out against the background noise of chaos and discord. Many were exposed to exhibitionistic parental

FOCUS ON RISK FACTORS

HIV and Personality Disorders

High-Risk Behavior and Disease Susceptibility

Personality disorders are more common among those infected with Human Immunodeficiency Virus (HIV), with borderline personality being one of the most frequent. For example, Perkins, Davidson, Leserman, Liao, and Evans (1993) found a higher prevalence of personality disorder among HIV-positive than HIV-negative subjects, with borderline the principal diagnosis. Later studies have supported this finding. In a longitudinal study, Jacobsberg, Frances, and Perry (1995) discovered that almost two-fifths of subjects who tested seropositive could be diagnosed with a personality disorder. Among subjects who did not know their HIV status, significantly more HIV-positive than HIV-negative subjects could be diagnosed as borderlines. Others have found that personality disorders and other serious mental conditions may impair self-assessment of risk and reduce the effectiveness of educational programs (Knox, Boaz, Friedrich, & Dow, 1994).

Why would HIV and personality disorder go together? Personality disorders are often linked to impulsivity, and impulsivity is linked to high-risk behaviors. By definition, impulsive individuals fail to think through the consequences of their actions. Borderlines, for example, are famous for sudden shifts of emotion and impulsive actions, including spending sprees and heavy alcohol and substance abuse. Moreover, impulsivity is linked to unprotected sex and multiple sexual partners, a principal way through which HIV is spread. Likewise, a significantly greater proportion of subjects with antisocial personality disorder engage in needle sharing than those without antisocial personality disorder.

Further research will be necessary to test additional hypotheses linking the personality disorders with HIV infection. For example, it is possible that some narcissistic personalities feel a special sense of invulnerability or that they are "above" using a condom. Dependent personalities might be reluctant to refuse a partner who desires unprotected sex. Individuals with sadistic traits might deliberately infect others. Antisocials might lie about their sexual history or HIV status. Because casual sex is common in our society, those who practice it are obliged to size up their partners for traits that might be linked to high-risk behaviors.

models and learned to depend on sex-role stereotypic compliments—physical attractiveness for histrionics and manliness for antisocials—as the basis for their self-esteem. In general, they are especially sensitive to external sources of reward and move impulsively and capriciously from one engaging item to the next. Thus oriented to the external world, they fail to develop a solid self-identity that might anchor them during periods of stress. As a consequence, they are always on unsure footing, constantly on edge, never quite sure who will provide the attention and stimulation they desperately require. Periods of brooding, dejection, and hopelessness alternate with simulated euphoria as they shift from acknowledging to denying their condition.

THE PETULANT BORDERLINE

The **petulant** borderline is mixed with the negativistic (passive-aggressive) personality. When even more dyscontrol is added to the active-ambivalence of the negativist, the result is someone who is even more unpredictable, restless, irritable, impatient, complaining, disgruntled, stubborn, sullen, pessimistic, resentful, and envious of the happiness and success of others. They resent those on whom they depend and hate those to whom they must plead for love. In contrast to other borderline subtypes, most petulants have seldom had their needs satisfied on a regular basis and have never felt secure in their relationships. Stubborn and demanding, they openly register their disappointments.

Unable to find comfort with others, they may become increasingly bitter and discontent, caught between two pathological extremes. At times, they express feelings of worthlessness and futility, become highly agitated or deeply depressed, express self-condemnation, and develop delusions of guilt. At other times, their habitual negativism becomes completely irrational, driving them into rages in which they distort reality, make excessive demands of others, and viciously attack those they see as having trapped them and forced them into intolerable conflicts. Their moods become a way of threatening others that further trouble is coming unless something is done. However, following these wild outbursts, petulants turn their hostility inward and become remorseful, plead for forgiveness, and promise to behave and make up for their transgressions. Alternatively, they may express fatigue and somatic disorders as a means of milking others' attention while burdening them at the same time. As children, they are likely to have felt mishandled and cheated, perhaps caught in a power struggle between caretakers who used the child as a pawn. For them, affection was never free of conflictful feelings.

Consider the case of Georgia (see Case 14.2). Elizabeth, who has come to the university counseling center seeking help and advice on coping with a problem parent, describes her mother, Georgia. Georgia synthesizes many of the characteristics of the borderline and negativistic personalities. For example, she vacillates between blaming Elizabeth and smothering her, an example of the borderline traits, devaluation and idealization. Consistent with the tendency of the negativist to try to recapture ideal love, Georgia adored Harold, her husband, early in their marriage but later became disenchanted, asserting that everything he did for her was never right or never enough. Indeed, in her more petulant moments, Georgia will tell you that no one has ever appreciated her—another characteristic of the negativistic personality but here synthesized with the unstable relationships characteristic of the borderline. Her social contact with the surrounding neighborhood, throwing tantrums and alienating others, provides even more evidence. Moreover, Georgia's vocational history is typical of the negativist, in that some minor problem that apparently stands as a symbol of her mistreatment gets blown out of proportion, leading to indignation and loss of employment. However, her anger and inability to find a meaningful direction in life are also characteristic of the identity disturbance, unstable affect, and sudden inappropriate anger of the borderline. In fact, intense expressed anger, more anger than would ordinarily be attributed to a passive-aggressive person, is one of the defining characteristics of the case.

Given her history, Georgia appears caught in an unresolvable conflict that prevents finding a single, stable course of action. She desperately wants affection and approval from the significant others in her life, yet she seems unsure how to ask for them. Moreover, she is deeply resentful but fears asserting her anger. As a result, Georgia finds herself in a constant state of turmoil. First, she tries to be ingratiating and acquiescent,

Elizabeth, age 21, presented at the university counseling center seeking professional help related to problems at home. Her mother, Georgia, has a long history of psychological problems, and is now going through a difficult period.[1]

Georgia believes that she has never been appreciated by anyone, including her own mother, husband, children, and employers. Georgia was the middle child in a family of moderate means. The second daughter of three children, she was always compared unfavorably to her older sister, an excellent student and now a prominent attorney. In contrast, Georgia was an average student, although her teachers felt she could do much better. In fact, Georgia was the "black sheep" of the family, who never lived up to her mother's expectations. She recalls her mother saying over and over again during their many arguments, "I should have abandoned you when I realized what a lousy kid you were."

Georgia married Elizabeth's father, Harold, whom she apparently adored, the summer after their high school graduation. In the early years, Harold did everything for Georgia, but somehow, it was never right or never enough, and her attitude toward him changed. Harold, a solid individual by Elizabeth's account, sees Georgia as a troubled soul who "can't get her life together." Elizabeth and her younger brother avoid their mother as much as possible. "Sometimes she shifts, like between blaming you one minute and smothering you with love the next," Elizabeth says. "She can't make up her mind whether to love you or hate you. It's ridiculous." **2**

Georgia's erratic behavior has had a similar outcome both socially and vocationally. She makes a good first impression, but her numerous part-time jobs always end the same way, with Georgia seizing on some minor problem and voicing an angry indignance over the way she was treated. Social contacts had the same course. **6** "She alienated everyone in our neighborhood," Elizabeth stated. **8** "Some people she'd piss off, others felt smothered by her neediness, and some got both. Over and over again, she'd make friends, then throw a tantrum, and call them and cuss them. Whenever she's excluded from community activities, she gets mad because **9** she swears they're talking about how to keep her out."

Presently, Georgia is being seen twice a week for treatment of depression. According to Elizabeth, her history includes threats of **5** suicide, though she has never actually gone further. Currently, she is very angry that Harold refuses to use part of the children's college fund to finance a month-long stay at a Caribbean resort, and **8** says she will no longer speak to him. In response, Harold is simply exasperated. **4**

[1] Numbers mark aspects of the case most consistent with *DSM* criteria, and do not necessarily indicate that the case "meets" diagnostic criteria in this respect.

Borderline Personality Disorder
DSM-IV Criteria

A pervasive pattern of instability of interpersonal relationships, self-image, and affects, and marked impulsivity beginning by early adulthood and present in a variety of contexts, as indicated by five (or more) of the following:

(1) frantic efforts to avoid real or imagined abandonment. **Note:** Do not include suicidal or self-mutilating behavior covered in Criterion 5.

(2) a pattern of unstable and intense interpersonal relationships characterized by alternating between extremes of idealization and devaluation

(3) identity disturbance: markedly and persistently unstable self-image or sense of self

(4) impulsivity in at least two areas that are potentially self-damaging (e.g., spending, sex, substance abuse, reckless driving, binge eating). **Note:** Do not include suicidal or self-mutilating behavior covered in Criterion 5.

(5) recurrent suicidal behavior, gestures, or threats, or self-mutilating behavior

(6) affective instability due to a marked reactivity of mood (e.g., intense episodic dysphoria, irritability or anxiety usually lasting a few hours and only rarely more than a few days)

(7) chronic feelings of emptiness

(8) inappropriate, intense anger or difficulty controlling anger (e.g., frequent displays of temper, constant anger, recurrent physical fights)

(9) transient, stress-related paranoid ideation or severe dissociative symptoms

but when this fails, she explodes with accusations that she is unloved and unappreciated. With her hopes dashed, Georgia quickly becomes increasingly hostile. Her resentments are then turned inward, creating guilt and a sense of worthlessness.

THE SELF-DESTRUCTIVE BORDERLINE

All borderlines are at times self-destructive, perhaps to the point of self-mutilation. In the **self-destructive** borderline subtype, however, self-destruction serves the needs of a comorbid masochistic pattern. Like the petulant borderline, the self-destructive type is unable to find a comfortable niche with others. Unlike the petulant type, self-destructive borderlines do not become increasingly testy and bitter over time. Instead, their masochistic traits cause them to turn inward, where destructive feelings can be expressed upon the self. In the past, these individuals presented a veneer of sociability and conformity. Underneath, however, were both a desire for independence and a genuine fear of autonomy. As a result, their social propriety cloaked a deeply conflictful submission to the expectations of others. To control these oppositional tendencies, they struggled to present a façade of self-restraint and self-sacrifice. Ever deferential and ingratiating, most have bent over backwards to impress their superiors with their conformity, all the while denying their dependencies and becoming even more conflicted.

At times, these antagonisms have given rise to public displays and bitter complaints about being treated unfairly, of expecting to be disillusioned and disapproved by others, and of no longer being appreciated for their diligence, submissiveness, and self-sacrifice. With the persistence of ambivalent feelings, self-destructive borderlines often begin to voice growing distress about a wide range of physical symptoms. As more subtle means of discharging negative feelings prove self-defeating, tension and depression mount beyond tolerable limits. They may accuse others of despising them, seeking to destroy their worth, and plotting to abandon them. Inordinate demands for attention and reassurance may be made. They may threaten to commit suicide and thereby save others the energy of destroying them slowly. The self-destructive and discouraged borderline subtypes perpetuate their pathology by deliberately putting themselves in positions of excessive vulnerability, making themselves so dependent and clingy that others could only become exasperated.

The Biological Perspective

More than anything else, the intense moodiness and rapidly shifting emotions of the borderline personality have caused observers to wonder whether some biological abnormality might underlie the disorder or at least create a predisposition that favors its development. Some biological basis seems necessary to fuel the intense emotional reactivity of the borderline, as seen in Jenny and Georgia. After all, anger is an intensely arousing emotion, as Jenny shows us consistently throughout her case study. Alternatively, we might suppose that reactivity itself has some biological basis. Perhaps some people simply react more intensely than others given any negative stimulus, and borderlines fall at the extreme upper end of such a distribution.

Because borderlines not only act out frantically but also frequently feel depressed, the early history of the borderline construct is confounded with the history of manic-depressive illness. From the earliest times, writers recognized persons with intense and changeable moods. Homer, Hippocrates, and Aretaeus vividly described impulsive anger, intense activity, irritability, and depression, noting both the vacillation among these "spells" and the personalities in which they are embodied. As with most medical and scientific knowledge, these early writings were suppressed in medieval times, to be discovered again with the beginning of the Renaissance. During this time, some writers emphasized emotional instability as the essence of the syndrome; others focused on shifts from excitement to depression. The putative relationship between the borderline personality and the affective disorders remains controversial even today.

Famous for their descriptive acumen, Kraepelin (1921), Kretschmer (1925), and Schneider (1923/1950) all noted symptoms we would now recognize as borderline, though mainly in connection with manic-depressive illness. Kraepelin identified four associated temperaments, one of which, the excitable personality, resembles our contemporary borderline. Such individuals could display "great fluctuations in emotional equilibrium," "fall into outbursts of boundless fury," "shed tears without a cause, give expression to thoughts of suicide, [and] bring forward hypochondriacal complaints" (pp. 130–131). Kretschmer ascribed to such individuals a "hostile attitude toward the world," with "a sharpness, nervousness, and jerky restless moodiness" (p. 140). Closest to our contemporary conception of the borderline, however, is Schneider's labile personality, characterized by "abrupt and rapid changes of mood," so that "sometimes the small stimulus is sufficient to arouse a violent reaction" (p. 116). For Kraepelin, such symptoms were produced by a metabolic anomaly. For Kretschmer, they were an extreme manifestation of a temperamental continuum spanning the borderline and schizoid. For Schneider, the difficulty was primarily constitutional, an outgrowth of the subject's own organic matrix. Whatever their cause, the resemblance of the descriptions to Georgia and Jenny is striking.

The hypothesis that borderlines begin life with strong temperamental characteristics has great intuitive appeal. Certain cardinal characteristics of the borderline—namely, impulsivity, irritability, hypersensitivity to stimulation, emotional lability, reactivity, and intensity—have all been associated with a biological foundation. An individual, however, rarely begins life as a borderline personality though the presence of extreme characteristics early on is undoubtedly correlated with extreme outcomes. A predisposition to high emotional reactivity, for example, helps lay the foundation for intense relationships throughout life, beginning with intense, and possibly aversive, interactions between mother and child. Possession of any one of these characteristics would require careful parenting, but taken collectively in the context of the chaotic and often equally intense borderline family, future borderlines are not likely to internalize standards of behavior that might moderate their emotions or inhibit their expression, leaving biology to determine behavior.

The leading contemporary exponent of the temperament hypothesis is Akiskal (1981), who argues that borderlines and their family members frequently share characteristics of a cyclothymic temperament, a view reminiscent of Kraepelin. Such persons experience mood swings that resemble manic depression. To the outside observer, their emotions seem arbitrary and unstable, completely unconnected to external events. Viewed in this way, the emotional instability represents something of a trait, with the borderline as the beginning point of a continuum of instability running from Axis II to relatively less intense changes of cyclothymia and on to the exaggerated cycles of manic-depressive illness.

Other researchers have studied the link between the borderline personality and respective neurotransmitters. Siever and Davis (1991) associate the disorder with abnormalities in impulse action in which serotonin is diminished and norepinephrine is overactive, producing activation without behavioral inhibition. Serotonin has been linked to impulsive aggression, a cardinal trait of the syndrome, as well as to self-directed aggression such as suicide and suicide risk (Van Praag, 1991) and self-mutilation. In fact, personality disorder subjects with the greatest serotonergic abnormalities are at the highest risk for self-directed aggression (New, Trestman, Mitropoulou, & Benishay, 1997).

The Psychodynamic Perspective

Early analysts recognized three levels of functioning: normal, neurotic, and psychotic. Although everyone was expected to function at one of these levels, it eventually became apparent that some subjects did not fit neatly into this threefold scheme. Given a libido withdrawn totally into the self, psychotic subjects, according to Freud, would not respond to psychoanalysis; he considered their degree of withdrawal inaccessible given the usual analytic tools. His new science was a science of the whole mind, but as a therapy, it could be applied only to neurotics. Any subject who showed good reality contact was not psychotic by definition and, therefore, was analyzable, at least in principle.

Eventually, however, early analysts began to notice a more troubled group of subjects who could not be called psychotic, but who failed to benefit from standard psychoanalytic therapy. Georgia and Jenny would probably fall into this group. Because reality testing was preserved, their very existence required explanation. Seeking to define such individuals, Stern (1938) used the phrase borderline group of neuroses, regarded as neurotic but resistant to the couch. He listed and discussed 10 characteristics for these first borderlines, including classics such as a quickness to anger; depression or anxiety in response to interpretive probes about self-esteem; the use of projection to attribute internal anger to hostile sources in the environment; and "difficulties in reality testing," that is, nonpsychotic deficits in judgment and empathic accuracy. With Stern's contribution, the term borderline was on its way to becoming an informal fixture in psychodynamic discussions.

During the 1940s and 1950s, many writers made contributions that would eventually be incorporated into the contemporary view (Stone, 1986). Just after World War II, the term borderline began to appear in the formal analytic literature. Schmideberg (1947, 1959, p. 399) presaged themes still relevant today. The borderline was "not just quantitatively halfway between the neuroses and psychoses," she stated. Instead, "the blending and combination of these modes of reaction produce something qualitatively different." Borderlines are "stable in [their] instability," she argued (or, as Elizabeth quotes her father, Georgia is a troubled soul who "can't get her life together"). All borderlines experience "disturbances affecting almost every area of their personality and life, in particular, personal relations and depth of feeling" (1959, p. 399). Other writers influenced the borderline construct without using the term. For example, Erikson (1956) contributed indirectly to the borderline construct through his discussions of ego identity and early identity formation, an antecedent of the DSM criterion of identity disturbance.

The early 1950s represent an important turning point in the history of the construct (Stone, 1986). Previously, the term borderline was associated with the schizophrenic syndromes. With Knight (1953), however, the construct took a much more analytic cast, allowing it to advance substantially in popularity and take on a more contemporary cast. Knight brought to the foreground the importance of ego weakness and its connection to psychotic episodes, stating that the "normal ego functions of secondary-process think-ing, integration, realistic planning, adaptation to the environment, maintenance of object relations, and defenses against primitive unconscious impulses are severely weakened" (p. 165). The ego of the borderline, according to Knight, is "laboring badly" under the stress of traumatic events and pathological relationships. "Integration, concept forma-tion, judgment, realistic planning, and defending against eruption into conscious think-ing of id impulses and their fantasy elaborations" are severely impaired, "while other ego functions, such as conventional (but superficial) adaptation to the environment and su-perficial maintenance of object relationships may exhibit varying degrees of intactness" (Knight, 1953, p. 165). As many writers have noted, borderlines often look much more adaptive or competent than they really are. Georgia, for example, makes good enough of a first impression to get hired but then can't keep her job.

The most important contribution to contemporary psychodynamic conceptions, how-ever, is Kernberg's (1967) idea of levels of organization in personality. Unlike the idea of borderline states or conditions, the idea of a borderline level of organization draws attention to a quality of integration of intrapsychic elements that is stable over time, yet falls midway on the continuum from neurosis to psychosis. All the personality disor-ders, as well as many psychodynamic character types, can be put on this continuum. Conceived as a level of personality organization, the borderline is thus much broader than the borderline personality described by the *DSM*. For example, Kernberg puts the schizoid personality at a lower level of borderline functioning. Yet, the socially removed style of schizoids is inconsistent with the intense interpersonal need of *DSM* border-lines, specifically, their frantic attempts to avoid abandonment, listed as the first diag-nostic criterion. What then, does borderline mean as a level of personality organization?

The borderline level is probably best understood in contrast to normality, which helps us better determine where the borderline is deficient. As Kernberg (1994) writes, normals exhibit an integrated concept of self and others, called **ego identity,** which not only gives coherence to the self but also provides a foundation for a healthy self-esteem and a sense of self-identity that endures across time and situation and gives direction to life goals. Most of us know who we are, our likes and dislikes, our core values, ways we are similar to and yet different from others, and where we're going in life. More-over, a well-integrated ego identity provides ego strength, the ability to resist pressure or stress, just as a ballast allows a ship to weather a storm. Additionally, Kernberg notes that normals possess a mature, internalized value system, the superego, permitting adaptive adult capacities such as personal responsibility and appropriate self-criticism.

The neurotic level is somewhat similar to normality. A well-developed ego identity supports a deep capacity for interpersonal intimacy and sexual love, with sufficient ego strength to tolerate anxiety, control impulses, and function effectively and creatively in work (Kernberg, 1994). Although neurosis is a form of psychopathology, it is by no means disabling. The distinction between normal and neurotic, according to Kernberg, lies primarily in the presence of unconscious feelings of sexual guilt. Pathologies of aggression are reserved for lower levels of personality organization. In Kernberg's schema, the obsessive-compulsive, depressive-masochistic, and hysterical personalities all function at the neurotic level. Given their intense anger and hostility, neither Georgia nor Jenny can be said to function at this level.

In contrast to the ego identity and cohesiveness of the normal and the neurotic, the psychotic level is characterized by a nearly complete fragmentation or diffusion of identity. Nearly everything we usually think of as personality is lost at this level. The capacity to test reality, to distinguish between self and others, for example, ebbs and flows. The constructs that represent the self and particular persons in the individual's life are not understood as integrated wholes. Instead, aspects of the self may temporarily fuse with aspects of others, resulting in a kind of object-relational kaleidoscope that has little relation to external reality. By definition, the psychotic level is characterized by an absence of ego strength and, therefore, an inability to inhibit even minor impulses from actively intruding into ongoing affairs. Moreover, without an integrated ego, the individual cannot develop a coherent plan of action that allows goals to be profitably pursued, much less balance the inhibitions of the superego with the random eruption of id impulses, which might be triggered by internal stimulation from his or her own stream of consciousness or through actual environmental events. The psychotic level seems too severe for Georgia and Jenny, who exhibit reality contact and a nonfragmented, somewhat fluid, sense of identity.

The borderline level of organization exists between the neurotic and psychotic and, as such, has characteristics of both. Kernberg (1994) refers to a triad of identity diffusion, primitive emotional displays of great intensity, and problems with impulse control. Like the neurotic, the borderline retains the capacity to test reality. In fact, many borderlines function at a high level indistinguishable from neurosis much of the time. However, the neurotic is capable of an array of mature defenses, whereas those at the borderline level are comparatively primitive variants of "splitting." Good and bad images of objects are actively separated. Thoughts such as, "Mommy has some good things about her and some bad things about her," are simply not possible.

In Kernberg's view, these good and bad images form two separate identification systems, either of which may be projected onto the self or outside world. Thus, subjects may switch rapidly between idealizing others (a projection of the good image) and completely devaluing them (a projection of the bad image). Thus, Georgia can't seem to make up her mind whether to blame Elizabeth or smother her with love, and Jenny sometimes adores Vera and sometimes hates her.

Understanding the relationship of splitting to the wider constellation of borderline symptoms requires an understanding of its role in normal development. According to Kernberg, borderlines are fixated at Mahler's separation-individuation phase (Mahler et al., 1975), specifically, in the rapprochement subphase, which runs from about 16 to 30 months of age. But the names and timings are technically unimportant. What is important is that separation-individuation precedes object constancy; the future borderline cannot distinguish between self and other before an image of the nurturing figure as a permanent presence is internalized. As the saying goes: Out of sight, out of mind. The fear is that when Mommy leaves, she will be gone forever, never to return.

The adult borderline persistently reexperiences this same overwhelming separation anxiety. Thus, borderlines often seem dependent and clingy and are unable to tolerate being alone for long periods of time. Like Mommy, a spouse or lover might never be seen again. In Jenny, this primitive separation anxiety is recaptured in her relationship with her father. Jenny has no internalized, stable image of her father, therefore, no appreciation of a love that might endure across time and circumstance. As such, she cannot comprehend his ability to simultaneously possess two different kinds of love: the love for Vera and the love for his daughter. Accordingly, Vera is viewed as a substitution rather than an addition to the family, thereby supplanting Jenny. Thus, Vera is hated and hated totally, the extreme of devaluation. Lack of stable internalized images of attachment figures creates considerable anxiety and the concomitant possibility of regression to more primitive ego states, especially for borderlines facing developmental milestones that require separation, such as leaving home for college or enduring a period of occupational training away from their spouse.

What causes a failure of object constancy? According to Kernberg, borderlines have a surplus of aggression, either constitutionally or because of frustration of their early needs by insensitive caretakers. As such, the integration of "identification systems of opposite quality" (Kernberg, 1985a, p. 69) becomes extremely threatening. Were integration to occur, the intensity of rage and hatred directed at the bad image would likely destroy the good image. Even if borderlines were to achieve an integrated conception of their significant others, this image would receive so much rage that the composite would be destroyed or alienated and the good object, the good Mommy, along with it. The situation is not unlike pouring a bucket of black paint and a bucket of white paint together; the black dominates.

As such, borderlines linger in the separation-individuation phase long beyond the development of cognitive abilities that might allow for more sophisticated appraisals, using splitting defensively as a means of keeping good and bad objects apart. Splitting thereby explains the identity diffusion of borderlines and their tendency to suddenly switch from profoundly positive to profoundly negative affects, features that lay the foundation for chaotic relationships, lack of commitment to life goals, lack of insight into the core values that might define personal existence, and an inability to inhibit the expression of strong affects and impulses, including those related to promiscuity and substance abuse. Everything that the ego does as the executive agency of the personality is considerably weakened. As Kernberg (1985a, p. 121) states, such individuals may also exhibit sexual pathologies, and all "evince nonspecific manifestations of ego weakness, that is, lack of anxiety tolerance, of impulsive control, and of sublimatory functioning in terms of an incapacity for consistency, persistence, and creativity in work." All of these characteristics are found in Georgia and Jenny, though in different ways.

Because the borderline, by this argument, defines a level of organization among intrapsychic structures, there is naturally a question of its relation to the character styles of classical psychoanalysis as well as to the *DSM* personality disorders. Rather than dump all of these into a single level called borderline, Kernberg (1994) provides additional differentiation by subdividing the borderline into two sublevels, one of which has more in common with psychosis and the other with neurosis. The more neurotic-like borderline organization includes the sadomasochistic, cyclothymic, dependent, histrionic, and those narcissistic personalities compensated by grandiosity. The lower level includes the paranoid, hypochondriacal, schizotypal, hypomanic, and antisocial personalities, as well as what Kernberg calls "malignant narcissism." All the personalities at the higher and lower levels express the borderline personality organization but in different ways, depending on the particulars of their character or personality style. In contrast, no stylistic variations exist in the *DSM* borderline, conceptualized simply as another personality disorder existing alongside the others.

Although Kernberg has been the most influential, other object-relations thinkers have emphasized the related themes of attachment and separation-individuation. Although every child begins life absolutely dependent on caretakers, eventually each child must grow into a separate person. According to Masterson and Rinsley (1975), the growing autonomy of the future borderline challenges the caretaker's desire to maintain closeness. In response, the child develops an intense ambivalence toward the caretaker, usually the mother, sometimes giving in to coercive clinging and sometimes reacting with a negativistic withdrawal. The conflict between wishing to retain the nurturance of the caretaker and developing as a unique individual prevents the child from integrating good and bad images of the mother. Nor can the child, caught in the conflict, consolidate his or her own identity.

Stressing that the caretaker may be borderline as well, Masterson (1972, 1976) sees the mother as encouraging the child to continue his or her symbiotic clinging. At the same time, the mother threatens to withdraw love should the child strive toward autonomy. This sets up a profound fear of abandonment played out across life, in which dependence brings reward and independence is equated with loss of love. The child is thereby caught in a lose-lose ambivalence between assertiveness and abandonment, creating a foundation for classic borderline symptoms such as unstable relationships, a tendency to search for idealized or romanticized fusions, as well as states of emptiness and depression. According to Masterson, then, it is the mother who is ultimately responsible for creating the borderline pathology, not the constitution of the subject.

Still another twist on the object-relations view is represented in Adler (1985), who sees the borderline as suffering from a failure in object constancy caused by insensitive or inadequate mothering. In other words, borderlines fail to internalize a representation of a caretaker that provides reassurance, a "holding-soothing object," to carry them through times when the caretaker cannot be physically present. What Adler calls an insufficiency theory would appear to explain a number of cardinal symptoms. First, without a caretaker with whom to have meaningful, empathic interactions, the future borderline cannot develop a stable sense of self-identity able to withstand stressful times. Regression to a more primitive ego state is, therefore, a perpetual risk. Second, because the developing self cannot organize itself around positive interactions with the caretaker, it is instead left only with feelings of profound emptiness caused by the absence of positive introjects and a chronic dysphoria (reminiscent of the classic analytic view that depression is caused by object loss). Third, the absence of object constancy explains why borderlines frantically avoid abandonment and require the actual physical presence of their significant other. In effect, they are searching for the holding-soothing object that early development would not provide. We know nothing of Jenny's mother, but we do know that Georgia was regarded as the "black sheep" of the family and compared unfavorably to her older sister, now a prominent attorney. According to Adler, Georgia is searching for a holding-soothing object to love and appreciate her.

The conception of the borderline as a discrete diagnostic entity also has its foundations in the psychodynamic tradition. The first systematic empirical study of a borderline sample was undertaken by Grinker, Werble, and Drye (1968). Using cluster analytic methods, these researchers found four groups, unified by several common characteristics, namely, "anger as the main or only affect, defect in affectional relationships, absence of indications of self-identity and depressive loneliness" (p. 176). The so-called core borderline group exhibited "vacillating involvement with others," "overt or acting-out expressions of anger," pervasive depression, and "absence of indications of consistent self identity" (p. 87).

The most highly developed research program, however, has been developed by Gunderson and colleagues (Gunderson, 1977, 1979; Gunderson, Carpenter, & Strauss, 1975; Gunderson & Singer, 1975). These authors viewed the borderline as a diagnostic entity clearly distinguishable from schizophrenic syndromes and neurotic conditions. Beginning with a thorough review of prior work (Gunderson & Singer, 1975) and opportunities to carry out a series of empirical studies, Gunderson and colleagues developed the

Diagnostic Interview for Borderlines (DIB) "to achieve diagnostic reliability specifically for borderline patients" (Gunderson, Kolb, & Austin, 1981, p. 896) on the basis of Gunderson and Singer's (1975) literature review of borderline conditions.

One of the best ways to study a construct is by examining the content of established instruments. Where the focus is on a single construct, interrelationships among its various content aspects are readily apparent. The DIB has been revised to increase its specificity and to "refine its format, phrasing, and scoring system" (Zanarini et al., 1989). By surveying these topic areas, clinicians quickly gain an appreciation for how traits of the larger personality pattern hang together. The revised DIB uses 97 items, grouped into 22 summary statements, to assess functioning in four broad areas: affect, cognition, impulse action patterns, and interpersonal relationships. As a significant extension, Zanarini (1993) has suggested that the borderline personality might best be considered an "impulse spectrum disorder" rather than a variant of the affective disorder spectrum. The *DSM* definition of the borderline personality largely represents a synthesis of Kernberg and Gunderson's contributions. The 22 summary statements of the DIB-R are presented in Table 14.1.

The Interpersonal Perspective

Although borderlines have a reputation for being angry, difficult, impulsive, and erratic, they can function with stability for long time periods under certain conditions. They perform well if given structure and much more poorly without it. Finding a significant other who provides a stable and accepting environment has proven most beneficial to the harmony of a borderline's interpersonal relations. In such cases, structure within the relationship is sustained through well-defined and easily met expectations. Often, however, potential for interpersonal stability is derailed as borderlines lapse into stereotypical misinterpretations of their current mate's intentions or behaviors. Again, the onus of abatement usually rests on the caring and tolerant individuals in their lives who have a knack for anticipating misinterpretations, choosing their words carefully, and diffusing trouble as it occurs by centering the subject on the authentic and healthy realities of current relationships. In effect, they insulate the subject when necessary but usually provide reassurance and supplement the reality testing of the borderline person during periods of incipient chaos. Georgia and Harold provide an example, though Georgia's negativistic traits make Harold's job almost impossible at times.

Moreover, similar to most personality disorders, the borderline diagnosis is but a matter of degree. The needs and pathologies of some individuals are more profound than others. Those with a less cohesive sense of self, with greater emotional dysregulation and more identity disturbance, will find few individuals outside the therapy office willing to create the "holding environment" necessary to assuage their pathologies. Conversely, those with a more cohesive sense of self, with less emotional dysregulation and less identity disturbance, are more easily tolerated during the bad periods because the relationship is reinforcing for both parties at least some of the time. Such subjects often have redeeming qualities that make the trying times "worth it" in the eyes of their spouse or lover. In the context of a stabilizing relationship, the borderline person might seem outgoing, highly intelligent, and blessed with a good sense of humor, for example. Alternatively, the significant other may simply have complementary traits that the subject, for whatever reason, finds calming to a certain degree.

TABLE 14.1   Summary Statements from the Revised Diagnostic Interview for Borderlines

Affect Section (The person . . .)
. . . Has had a chronic low-grade depression or experienced one or more major depressive episodes.
. . . Has had sustained feelings of helplessness, hopelessness, worthlessness, or guilt.
. . . Has chronically felt very angry or frequently acted in an angry manner
      (i.e., has often been sarcastic, argumentative, or quick-tempered).
. . . Has chronically felt very anxious or suffered from frequent physical symptoms of anxiety.
. . . Has experienced chronic feelings of loneliness, boredom, or emptiness.

Cognition Section (The person . . .)
. . . Has been prone to odd thinking or unusual perceptual experiences
      (e.g., magical thinking, recurrent illusions, depersonalization).
. . . Has frequently had transcient, nondelusional paranoid experiences
      (i.e., undue suspiciousness, ideas of reference, other paranoid ideation).
. . . Has repeatedly had "quasi" delusions or hallucinations.

Impulse Action Patterns Section (The person . . .)
. . . Has had a pattern of serious substance abuse.
. . . Has had a pattern of sexual deviance (i.e., promiscuity or paraphilia).
. . . Has had a pattern of physical self-mutilation.
. . . Has had a pattern of manipulative suicide threats, gestures, or attempts
      (i.e., the suicidal efforts were mainly designed to elicit a "saving" response).
. . . Has had another pattern of impulsive behavior.

Interpersonal Relationships Section (The person . . .)
. . . Has typically tried to avoid being alone or felt extremely dysphoric when alone.
. . . Has repeatedly experienced fears of abandonment, engulfment, or annihilation.
. . . Has been strongly counterdependent or seriously conflicted about giving and receiving care.
. . . Has tended to have intense, unstable close relationships.
. . . Has had recurrent problems with dependency or masochism in close relationships.
. . . Has had recurrent problems with devaluation, manipulation, or sadism in close relationships.
. . . Has had recurrent problems with demandingness or entitlement in close relationships.
. . . Has undergone a clear-cut behavioral regression during the course of psychotherapy
      or psychiatric hospitalization.
. . . Has been the focus of a notable countertransference reaction on an inpatient unit or in psychotherapy,
      or formed a "special" relationship with a mental health professional.

Adapted from Gunderson and Zanarini (1992).

Nevertheless, the stormy interpersonal life of the borderline personality, where action flows freely from mood, is legendary. Although everyone wants a special someone, many borderlines hunger for that one relationship to validate their very existence, a powerful or nurturing figure who can make them feel secure. At the beginning, they feel magically involved, idealizing their partner, putting him or her on a pedestal as the greatest thing the world has ever seen. Because their partner is so special, borderlines are special, too, for it is they who are the recipient of the love and affection of this perfect person. Distance is intolerable and separation unthinkable. At one time, Jenny probably felt exactly this way about her boyfriend.

As a consequence of their concentrated need to be intensely emotionally connected with someone, borderlines have tremendous abandonment fears. These have already been discussed in a psychodynamic context, but the interpersonal perspective adds a sense of immediacy and context somewhat neglected in psychodynamic formulations,

FOCUS ON BEHAVIOR

Borderlines and Self-Injury

Is There a Rationale for Self-Injury?

Most researchers make a distinction between self-injurious behavior and self-mutilation (Herpertz, 1995). Self-injurious refers to moderate forms of self-inflicted bodily injury such as cutting, carving, and burning of the skin, as well as manipulative suicidal behavior. Such moderate forms of harm to self are characteristic of the borderline personality. Self-mutilation is generally considered to be a wider category that includes self-injurious behavior and other forms of more severe self-harm, such as enucleation, castration, and amputation of body parts. These more severe forms are generally associated with schizophrenic disorders and, on occasion, psychotic breakdowns of transsexual subjects.

Although self-mutilating borderlines usually show more serious suicidal ideation and have more recent suicide attempts than nonmutilators (Soloff, Lis, Kelly, Cornelius, & Ulrich, 1994), self-injurious borderlines generally deny suicidal intent, and the wounds they inflict on themselves are not life threatening. Research (Herpertz, 1995) suggests what may be a consistent set of characteristics. Self-injurious behavior occurs mostly in women, starting in early adulthood and peaking between the ages of 18 and 24. Frustrating external events and a buildup of overwhelming emotions—dysphoria, anger, despair, and anxiety—usually precede an episode of self-injurious behavior. The episode itself seems impulsive in nature and is usually followed by a quick release of tension; it is especially motivating in that most patients report a marked reduction in pain during the episode. In fact, some researchers (Liebenluft, Gardner, & Cowdry, 1987) have found that half of self-injurious borderlines typically report feeling no pain during the episode. These "analgesic" patients appear to constitute a separate subcategory of self-injurious individuals who reinterpret painful sensations and are more prone to dissociative disorders (Russ et al., 1996).

What developmental factors might increase the likelihood of self-injurious behaviors? Parental sexual abuse and emotional neglect during childhood, also related to the genesis of the borderline personality, are significantly related to self-injurious behaviors (Dubo, Zanarini, Lewis, & Williams, 1997). Moreover, self-injurious behavior seems to abate with age, just as borderlines tend to burn out with age. Sadly, for some subjects, self-injurious behavior remains a lifelong practice. At an advanced age, it may include the same self-injurious behaviors along with sabotage of treatment, starvation, and polypharmacy (Wijeratne, Stern, & Howard, 1996).

with their emphasis on internal psychic structures. For most borderlines, being attached to someone rises to the level of a pseudo-biological need, like water or air, as it does for Jenny. Even when securely involved in a relationship, fears of abandonment impose themselves on reality to an almost delusional degree, as if their self-cohesiveness or self-identity might dissolve if the relationship were to end. They may feel, for example, that they are nothing without a certain person, life would be empty without him or her, and their very existence depends on preserving the relationship. To compensate these fears, significant others should nurture, love, and protect the borderline, always be physically available, and never leave. Although Jenny adores Vera at times, she would probably like nothing better than for Vera to simply disappear.

Fears of abandonment are not confined to fantasy, but instead distort borderlines' perception of the communications and actions of others as part of everyday life. They are easily provoked by things that others would never notice. Innocent or irrelevant events or comments may be construed as implying criticism or condemnation. Other events are perceived as their loved one's waning affections or others have refused to consider their feelings or simply no longer care. Even efforts to establish simple boundaries may signify total rejection, the borderline's worst fear. The statement, "I'll be needing the car today at noon," for example, might be taken as implying, "And you won't be coming with me." As a result, minor events are regularly given unintended significance and blown completely out of proportion, producing major interpersonal catastrophes. From the perspective of borderlines, they will soon be cast aside, left lost and alone, with no one to care. The feeling that someone important to the subject is actively distancing may provoke an emergency reaction, punctuated by a tearful, helpless paralysis and a near-manic hyperactive display of anger.

The distortions produced by abandonment fears work to amplify the pathology, producing vicious circles. Significant others cannot be allowed to simply walk away. To secure their attachments, borderlines make frantic attempts to avoid separation. In the normal person, reasonable attempts at reconciliation include taking time out to gain perspective on the issues, suggesting alternatives that might be satisfactory to both sides, or even a mutually agreed cooling-off period. Separation fears, however, leave the borderline with the characteristic mix of panic and rage that usually wears down even the most tolerant individuals. Thus, Jenny goes on a hunger strike, locks herself in her room, and demands that her father and Vera divorce.

In effect, borderlines create the vicious circles they fear most. A mate unable to tolerate such intensity, for example, naturally entertains thoughts of getting out of the relationship. Eventually, fears of abandonment, which originally existed only in imagination, begin to become real. We cannot, for example, imagine that Jenny's boyfriend will want to continue in the relationship when he is described as evil and has to put up with her anger and instability. Inevitably, such thoughts are reflected in the quality of the relationship itself, perhaps through emotional distancing or omissions of nurturance. Borderlines sense these and become angry enough to drive the relationship to the breaking point. Sometimes, they switch to a posture of helplessness and contrition that begs for reconciliation. Alternatively, both parties may be so enmeshed that chaos and conflict become the soul of the relationship. They break up, move out, reconcile, move back, fight once more, and finally break up again, with suicidal gestures and self-destructive, impulsive acting out all the way through.

Consider the case of Elsa (see Case 14.3). Elsa is about to divorce for the third time and is feeling desperate and depressed. Though Elsa and her husband were living apart, there was still hope for the relationship until Elsa began calling her husband four or five times a day, her version of the frantic efforts to avoid abandonment for which borderlines are famous. In response, her husband seems to have realized that the only way out of the vicious circle that was their marriage is to drop Elsa altogether. So he changed his number and moved, and she has no idea of his whereabouts. The pathological source in the relationship becomes apparent when Elsa notes that the marriage gave her "someone to be." The terms of the divorce are generous, but without a solid

A polished and attractive woman of 47, Elsa entered therapy because "I'm just not feeling up to par, and never have." Feelings of depression and despair increased substantially after this, her third, marriage began to dissolve.[1] Not yet divorced, but living apart from her husband, she reports extreme anger and feelings of worthlessness at being left helplessly alone. She states that she cannot deal with the situation, and instead spends her time shopping, buying what she cannot afford, drinking too much, and looking for someone to take the place of her husband. "Marital therapy failed," she states, and "after I began phoning him four or five times a day, he has changed his number and moved away. I have no idea where he is." ⑧ ④ ①

Elsa seems to have two sides to her. In some ways, she is immersed in the existential angst appropriate to a teenager, still trying to discover "who Elsa really is." In other ways, she seems hard, calculating, and embittered. The anger she feels toward her husband seems inappropriate given that the terms of the divorce are quite generous. Though admittedly not a particularly good relationship, the marriage nevertheless gave Elsa "someone to be." Sometimes her husband is described as "the most loving person," and sometimes as "the asshole." ③ ⑧ ②

Instability runs through Elsa's history. She has lost contact with her oldest brother. Her mother's numerous marriages have left her with a combination of half-sisters, half-brothers, and ex-stepsiblings. Family infighting has taken the place of genuine communication. Certain parts of the extended family are divided into factions that no longer speak to each other. Elsa states that she always received the "short end of the stick" when her mother remarried. Because each marriage required a move, Elsa was unable to make lasting friends as a child, and her schoolwork suffered. Her mother didn't care about her grades, and Elsa found it convenient to adopt this apathetic attitude rather than make a real effort in her studies.

Elsa states that although she never really loved any of her husbands, she "completely lost it" when each marriage failed. Probing further, she discloses that she has been hospitalized three times, twice following suicide attempts, once for substance abuse. She received follow-up therapy after each hospitalization, and is being seen by a different therapist at the current time. Initially, she thought very highly of her latest therapist, feeling sure that he would finally get to the root of the problem. More recently, she is disappointed and angry that he is not more readily accessible to her and is unable to see her more than twice a week. Although her visit today seems designed to secure additional nurturance, Elsa will be referred back to the therapist she is currently seeing. ⑥ ⑤ ②

[1] Numbers mark aspects of the case most consistent with *DSM* criteria, and do not necessarily indicate that the case "meets" diagnostic criteria in this respect.

Borderline Personality Disorder
DSM-IV Criteria

A pervasive pattern of instability of interpersonal relationships, self-image, and affects, and marked impulsivity beginning by early adulthood and present in a variety of contexts, as indicated by five (or more) of the following:

(1) frantic efforts to avoid real or imagined abandonment. **Note:** Do not include suicidal or self-mutilating behavior covered in Criterion 5.

(2) a pattern of unstable and intense interpersonal relationships characterized by alternating between extremes of idealization and devaluation

(3) identity disturbance: markedly and persistently unstable self-image or sense of self

(4) impulsivity in at least two areas that are potentially self-damaging (e.g., spending, sex, substance abuse, reckless driving, binge eating). **Note:** Do not include suicidal or self-mutilating behavior covered in Criterion 5.

(5) recurrent suicidal behavior, gestures, or threats, or self-mutilating behavior

(6) affective instability due to a marked reactivity of mood (e.g., intense episodic dysphoria, irritability or anxiety usually lasting a few hours and only rarely more than a few days)

(7) chronic feelings of emptiness

(8) inappropriate, intense anger or difficulty controlling anger (e.g., frequent displays of temper, constant anger, recurrent physical fights)

(9) transient, stress-related paranoid ideation or severe dissociative symptoms

identity of her own, what Elsa has lost is herself. In a way, she is like the dependent personality, caught up in a magical fusion with the significant other, only to be devastated when this defining relationship ends. For Elsa, this is a pattern that repeats again and again, and each time she "completely lost it," with attempted suicide seemingly part of the picture. Looking for the next fusion, Elsa has devalued her previous therapist, who is trying to put the brakes on the number of sessions she demands per week. She wants someone new and nurturing.

A second feedback loop relates the consequences of perceived abandonment to self-image. Borderlines frequently feel worthless and empty. Because we tend to regard ourselves as others regard us and because borderlines perceive others as likely to abandon them, they eventually begin to wonder whether abandonment is all they are worth. The tumult created by intense relationships, often in conjunction with a chronic history of physical abuse for sons and sexual abuse for daughters (Stone, 1993), naturally leads to feelings of being empty and worthless, supported by cognitions such as, "I am disposable, and no one will love me," "I am worthy only of being abandoned," and "I exist to satisfy the temporary pleasure of others, not to be loved for myself." We find exactly this in Elsa, for whom depression, despair, and feelings of worthlessness are part of everyday life.

These beliefs are exacerbated by the continuing chaos of interpersonal relationships. Depression is the natural outgrowth of such dynamics, as the case of Elsa shows, as well as suicidal ideation and actual suicide attempts, for which she had been hospitalized. Both can be used manipulatively to coerce nurturance or simply to express anger and resentment. Depression frustrates those who have "failed" the subject or "demanded too much," and suicidal gestures heap guilt onto those who might blame themselves were the attempt successful. Self-damaging impulsive behavior, including classic self-mutilations such as cutting and burning, are both a consequence of the borderline's self-image and a means of shocking or controlling others. One response to feeling abandoned is to abandon yourself.

However, not all borderlines solely desire fusion with a nurturing figure. Fusion brings a powerful intimacy that banishes feelings of emptiness and worthlessness (at least someone thinks enough of the subject to want to merge their two souls together as one), while conferring the equally powerful feeling of being protected against harm. However, fusion also leads to a fear of engulfment. When borderlines do not sabotage their relationships by creating endless cycles of chaos, they may have equally powerful fears of losing their identity in the relationship or of being capsized by the reality of their helpless dependency. The emptiness of not being attached to fantasies of fusion, usually idealization of a magical romantic figure, leads in turn to fears of total dependence on someone else for a sense of self-worth and self-esteem. Greater intimacy exaggerates fears of being vulnerable and exposed, leading back to desires for separation but also to chronic feelings of emptiness, worthlessness, and depression. The answer to this paradox is to never let any relationship become too stable. Here, chaos is not just a pathological outcome but also an instrumental strategy. When relationships become too normal or things are going too well, stability must be sabotaged. By keeping others frustrated and exasperated, the borderline creates a soap opera that keeps each side of the dilemma just barely tolerable. Of the cases discussed, Georgia would be most likely to be caught in this dynamic. On the one hand, she wants to be attached to others, but getting too close makes her feel vulnerable and afraid.

The borderline personality has been examined from the perspective of the SASB by Benjamin (1996). Like other authors, she emphasizes that borderlines fear abandonment and wish to be nurtured. The caretaker secretly wants the subject to be needy, the borderline believes and, therefore, engages a strategy of friendly dependency while undermining his or her own chances for happiness or success. Friendly dependency creates the need for a rescuer, who is quickly idealized. As boundaries between the two are suspended, the subject confides in the rescuer in great detail and begins to make large demands of time. When not enough love is delivered, the borderline devalues the caretaker, now fallen from grace, and switches to a strategy of hostile control, dependency with a vengeance, essentially an effort to milk nurturance from his or her insensitive counterpart.

Benjamin (1996) lists four features in the development of the borderline personality. First is family chaos, which includes factors such as "fights, affairs, abortions, infidelity, drunken acting out, suicide attempts, murders, imprisonment, disowning, and illicit births" (p. 118). Any of these events might be considered tragic, but they contribute to a sense of drama in the borderline family that keeps life safe from boredom. The future borderline often plays some central or pivotal role. The lability of the family, its rapid change of configuration and cohesiveness, models the intense and shifting emotions seen in the adult borderline. We see an example of this in Elsa, the unstable spouse. Her family is split into warring factions that no longer talk to each other; her mother remarried repeatedly, contributing to ongoing instability in the family constellation; and she is no longer in contact with her oldest brother.

Family chaos is accompanied by a second factor: traumatic abandonment. The child, Benjamin (1996) states, is left alone without nurturance, without adequate protection and, importantly, without knowing when the caretakers will return. The implicit message is that the child is abandoned for being bad. During these periods, many children are sexually abused by powerful others, thus laying the foundation for dissociative episodes. Some children "numb out"; for other children, physical pain becomes associated with erotic pleasure. The latter provides one pathway to the later development of self-mutilation. As Benjamin notes, however, not all borderlines are sexual abuse victims.

The third factor Benjamin (1996) discusses seems intended to rein in constructive drives that might allow the future borderline to overcome the past and escape the grip of pathology. The family regards autonomy as bad and "dependency and sympathetic misery with the family" as good (p. 121). Any reason the child finds to believe that he or she is special is met with demeaning punishment, putting the subject back into his or her role as a defective member of a miserable family. The same holds for pride of accomplishment, perhaps even for simple displays of happiness. Genuine joy or constructive striving is simply disloyal. Because we usually treat ourselves as others treat us, future borderlines learn to sabotage themselves whenever anything in life, including psychotherapy, is going too well. The internalized images of early caretakers must be appeased with failure or even self-mutilation. The internal dialogue reads: "If you want me to feel pain, know that I do. I affirm and agree that I deserve punishment and suffering. Here is the evidence. Now you must know how much I love you, and you must love me too" (p. 122). Self-attack thus represents a "gift of love" (p. 122) intended to satisfy vicious introjects. Only when the borderline is totally miserable will those who have been critical and withholding offer nurturance, Benjamin's fourth and final factor.

FOCUS ON DEVELOPMENT

Borderline Personality and Sexual Trauma

Connections between Trauma and Safe Attachments

Although the conceptualization of the borderline personality and its causes remain unclear (Paris, 1994a, 1994b; Zanarini & Frankenburg, 1997), most empirical research shows a marked relationship between childhood trauma and borderline symptoms. Risk factors that differentiate borderline patients usually include loss, histories of sexual and physical abuse, severe neglect or emotional abuse, being witness to domestic violence, and parental substance abuse or criminality (Guzder, Paris, Zelkowitz, & Marchessault, 1996; Laporte & Guttman, 1996; Zanarini et al., 1997).

Of these, many studies suggest an especially significant relationship between childhood sexual abuse and the development of the borderline personality (see Paris, 1994b; Sabo, 1997; Zanarini & Frankenburg, 1997). To unravel factors that might contribute to abuse, Silk, Lee, Hill, and Lohr (1995) constructed an index of the severity. Cases were coded in terms of who abused the subject, how long the subject was abused, and whether penetration occurred. Results showed that ongoing sexual abuse in childhood was the best predictor of the severity of borderline symptoms, including parasuicide, chronic hopelessness and worthlessness, transient paranoia, regression in therapy, and an intolerance of being alone.

The authors speculate that severe, continuous sexual abuse affects the child's capacity to form satisfying, safe attachments. Children come to believe that others are "unsafe and interested only in their own gratification," leading to "a belief in a malevolent object world" (p. 1062). Sadly, Michael Stone's (1981) words still ring true today, almost two decades later:

> I suspect there is another and purely psychogenic factor contributing to the excess of females among groups of borderline patients . . . the occurrence of incestuous experiences during childhood or adolescence. . . . Chronic victimization of this sort, by a father or an uncle, cannot help but have damaging effects upon the psychic development of a young girl. These effects will generally consist of impaired relationships with men, mistrust of men, inordinate preoccupation with sexual themes, impulsivity in the area of sex, and often enough, depression. (p. 14)

The Cognitive Perspective

The cognitive style of borderlines may be viewed as the direct result of the split architecture of their object-representations. Regression is evident in their tendency to function well under structured conditions in the presence of a constant object, but to deteriorate to more primitive levels of functioning without structure and without the ensured presence of others. That is, when the presence of significant others is ensured, borderlines often seem to have a more firm hold on reality.

When relationships are threatened, however, their level of ego functioning begins to slip. Secondary process thinking, based on the reality principle, begins to give way to primary process thinking, based on wishes, fantasies, and direct drive discharge. The ability to weigh facts, to consider situations from the viewpoints of everyone involved, to develop a plan adaptive in both the short term and long term, and to keep id impulses from overriding conscious controls begins to give way as the ego functions weaken or are suspended entirely over the course of temporary psychotic episodes. At this level, splitting and its associated mechanisms, such as projective identification, dominate the clinical picture. Such individuals exhibit their needs transparently, appearing clinging, demanding, or rageful, for example, or all three in succession. The tendency to regress to lower levels of ego function has inspired some to term such subjects the psychotic character (Frosch, 1960, 1964, 1970).

The level of borderline cognition is also dependent on the degree of structure in the external environment. Clinicians have long known that borderlines look healthier on structured tests, such as pencil-and-paper personality tests, but less healthy on projective instruments, such as the Rorschach Inkblot Test or Thematic Apperception Test, where the subject invents stories based on pictures. In any projective situation, subjects appeal to their own internal structure to bring order to the interpretation of an ambiguous stimulus. Most human behavior involves the interaction between individual characteristics and situational constraints. Almost everyone stops at a red light; in such highly scripted situations—the social equivalent of a structured test—borderlines are often able to behave in accordance with social expectations. As a result, they often look more competent or healthy than they really are. Because borderlines have little internal structure to bring to unscripted situations, however, they can only project fluidity onto ambiguity. In effect, borderlines borrow the structure of the environment to organize themselves. Without such structure, they can quickly regress to more primitive ego states.

All personality disorders have a certain cognitive style. In the compulsive personality, excessive rigidity is enforced by a preponderance of "should statements." Compulsives must perform to perfection, and anything less is horribly flawed and condemned. Narcissists deserve the endless loyalty and service of others because they are all good and all knowing by definition. The histrionic is excessively impressionistic; nothing is processed in depth. The borderline, however, is distinguished by a fluidity of thought and emotion, and the degree of fluidity is dependent on the quality of relationships and on the amount of structure inherent in task demands. Even the integrated judgments of the more neurotic borderlines are fragile and cannot be sustained under the weight of the intense affect characteristic of regressed periods. Jenny, for example, does not jump from her boyfriend's Jeep when they're getting along; likewise, Elsa's spending spree takes place in the context of marital difficulties. Solid attachments, therefore, foster better judgment.

Other cognitive characteristics of the borderline personality can be deduced from the idea of split object-representations. Many statements or actions that would create intense cognitive dissonance in individuals with an integrated sense of identity do not cause dissonance for the borderline person. Split object-representations are effectively two opposite ways of viewing self, other, and world, any of which may be in effect at any time, depending on the circumstances. Assume, for example, that the actions of a friend summon up images of a controlling and verbally abusive caretaker; the borderline would undeniably lash out in anger. A few moments later, this same friend may somehow be redeemed as the world's greatest friend, depending on the subject's stream of consciousness. By definition, such separate images are deliberately kept apart so that they cannot conflict; accordingly, they cannot cause the subject cognitive dissonance.

When attention is called to such reversals of opinion and action, borderlines usually dismiss these discrepancies with shallow rationalizations and nonchalance. Borderlines cannot be bothered with their own paradoxical behavior.

Another observation of the borderline personality that intersects the cognitive perspective comes from Kroll (1993), who noted that borderlines often appear to be at the mercy of their own stream of consciousness. The identity diffusion of borderlines suggests that they are particularly vulnerable to intrusive thoughts and images, including flashbacks and nightmares. Borderlines do seem to associate from one unpleasant thought to the next, evoking a succession of intense affective states connected only by the private experiences of the person. For example, a new acquaintance might be looked at admiringly until it is discovered that he or she has a particular mannerism that resembles someone in the past with whom the borderline has unresolved issues. Awareness of this similarity may bring to mind morbid memories so intense that the acquaintance becomes a lightning rod for the negative emotions that he or she has unwittingly evoked. To the outside observer, the sequence of emotions seems discontinuous and irrational. In fact, the stream of consciousness simply flows with its own logic, derived from the unique life history of the individual.

For this reason, Kroll (1993) argues that the borderline personality is essentially similar to posttraumatic stress disorder (PTSD), in that most borderlines have a history of early traumatic experiences. Thus, Kroll speaks of the PTSD/borderline, a hybrid entity consisting of individuals whose abuse history has led to cognitive disturbances characteristic of those of posttraumatic stress. He writes that such persons suffer "first and foremost from a disorder of the stream of consciousness" that "has become its own enemy" and cannot be turned off (p. xv). As with PTSD, the cognitive apparatus of the PTSD/borderline has been changed so that the individual is condemned to reexperience the original trauma. Actual images and memories may come flooding back to consciousness at unpredictable moments in whole, fragmented, or distorted forms. In addition, the stream of consciousness consists of "unwelcome somatic sensations, negative self-commentaries running like a tickertape through the mind, fantasied and feared elaborations from childhood of the abuse experiences, and concomitant strongly dysphoric moods of anxiety and anger" (p. xv). Other characteristics, such as unstable identity, intolerance of aloneness, and self-destructiveness, may also be linked to past abusive experiences. From this perspective, the psychodynamic approach is seriously deficient because it emphasizes objects, that is, fantasied projections, rather than the importance of real experiences of abuse.

Writing in Beck et al. (1990), Pretzer regards dichotomous thinking, the chronic use of mutually exclusive categories, as the central cognitive distortion of the borderline personality. By construing the world in either/or terms, borderlines are forced into extreme interpretations that disqualify adaptive responses proportional to situational needs; there are few intermediate responses, few shades of gray, and few qualitatively complex appraisals following a period of detached deliberation. Opinions of self, world, and future tend to be either completely positive or completely negative. As noted by Pretzer (quoted in Beck et al., 1990, p. 186), beliefs formed in this context include, "The world is dangerous and malevolent," "I am powerless and vulnerable," and "I am inherently unacceptable."

By thinking in dichotomous terms, borderlines have little opportunity to make subtle revisions or to elaborate aspects of past opinions in one way or another without completely discarding the original appraisal. This creates a considerable conundrum in living, namely: How do you change your mind? For the borderline, the solution is to switch rapidly from one extreme to its diametrical opposite. Moreover, because affect and cognition are closely connected, borderlines cannot easily vary the intensity of their emotions. Instead, they tend to be intense all the time, but in opposite ways, what observers witness as a succession of intense, random, and irrational emotional states. All of the cases presented in this chapter exemplify such "rigid fluidity."

The Evolutionary-Neurodevelopmental Perspective

In terms of the evolutionary model that unifies this text, borderlines fail to attach themselves strongly to any single polarity. This is signified by their intense ambivalence and inconstancy, emotional lability, behavioral unpredictability, identity diffusion, and tendency to swing from one position or opinion to its opposite. Many readers will assert that, because a personality consists of traits that endure across time and situation, the borderline's lack of consistent traits across time and situation nullifies its classification as a personality disorder. Moreover, it might be argued that because the *DSM* borderline is defined as much by its symptoms (i.e., self-mutilation) as by its personality traits, as well as containing diagnostic criteria that resonate highly with other personality disorders, it is rarely diagnosed as a personality disorder standing on its own. Finally, they might point out that from the psychodynamic perspective, where the construct was born, the borderline is only a level of personality organization (Kernberg, 1967, 1984, 1985a) that explicitly requires one or more other personality diagnoses for its content. Accordingly in their view, the term borderline makes more sense as a modifier that distinguishes, for example, a well-integrated, neurotic-level histrionic personality (which psychodynamic clinicians would refer to as a hysteric character) from the more emotionally labile infantile histrionic.

We can, however, venture a broader conception, one that argues that the borderline is necessary to the taxonomy of personality disorders, without committing a part-whole fallacy of deriving the construct from a single perspective on personality or simply grafting it to the classification system because it seems pragmatic. Although the preceding criticisms have merit, the integration of personality is only an abstract, academic, idealized conception. Just as individuals differ in terms of the extent to which they resemble a single personality prototype, they differ in the extent to which the elements of their personality are tightly or loosely interwoven. Because the normal personality is well integrated by definition, its elements function harmoniously together. Here, the very notion of personality domains, such as cognition or defense, destroys the whole by reducing the person to parts and making the parts the primary focus of attention.

We have previously argued that valid taxonomies of personality cannot be derived from any single perspective exactly for this reason: A part is no substitute for the whole and cannot function in place of the whole. We may talk about personality from the perspective of cognitive styles or object relations or biology, but we do so with the understanding that every perspective starts with assumptions that both reveal and conceal. The assumptions giveth, and the assumptions taketh away. Eventually, it becomes necessary to return to a more holistic conception or lose something ineffable, the total organization of behavior that is personality. And this is what is lost in the borderline.

By this reasoning, the borderline emerges as a pathology in the level of personality integration, but one not confined to psychodynamic conceptions. In Chapter 1, we noted that in an idealized causal model of personality, every domain of personality influences every other domain, lending the whole the emergent tenacity that makes personality both more than the sum of its parts and personality disorders notoriously difficult to treat. Psychodynamic defenses, interpersonal interactions, cognitive styles, and biological variables interact to form a single, interwoven, dynamic system. Otherwise, it would not be possible to speak about personality at all. By this reasoning, the borderline is, necessarily, characterized by looseness and fluidity, by moments when one part of the personality, or some particular concern, seems to seize control of the whole and then is suddenly usurped by another. The consequence is rapidly shifting emotions and a chain of impulsive behaviors that appears poorly orchestrated or even arbitrary.

As a pathology of the total integration of personality, the borderline construct might be applied to almost any personality disorder. Clinical experience suggests, however, that dependent, histrionic, narcissistic, antisocial, and negativistic personalities are more frequently found in conjunction with a borderline diagnosis. Whatever the actual content, such individuals follow one of two developmental pathways. In the first, the personality develops a significant level of integration but breaks down under conditions of persistent environmental stress. In the second, no significant level of integration develops. Those following the first pathway are best referred to as borderline histrionics, for example, letting borderline modify histrionic; and those following the second pathway might be referred to as dependent borderlines, indicating that the consequences of a lack of integration swamp the contribution of personality traits to organized behavior. Whatever the case, the common feature across borderline personalities is a looseness of organization or looseness of internal regulation and lack of coordination of behavior to environmental exigencies, most easily observed in impulsive action, rapidly changing emotions, and suddenly shifting appraisals. This conception should be distinguished from the *DSM* borderline, the primary focus of this chapter. A summary of the borderline personality in terms of the eight clinical domains is given in Table 14.2. The following brief summary of the developmental experiences of the subvariants of the defectively structured borderline personality may be supplemented by reference to prior chapter discussions of their more basic personality styles.

Self-destructive and discouraged borderline types perpetuate their plight by abdicating self-responsibility and clinging tenaciously to others. This places them in a most vulnerable position since they are increasingly devoid of capacities for autonomy, and they find themselves viewed with exasperation by those on whom they depend. Failure to achieve support from others may lead either to marked self-disparagement or to frenetic efforts to solicit attention and approval. These erratic behaviors and mood swings foster increased inner disharmony and maladaption, resulting in the loss of intrapsychic control and consequent brief psychotic episodes.

The skillful seductiveness of the impulsive (histrionic) borderline may not only foster new difficulties but also falter as an instrumental strategy. These personalities not only are shallow and capricious but give little in return for their subtle though excessive demands on others; as a result, they are unable to establish enduring close relationships. Furthermore, because of their exteroceptive orientation and their intrapsychic repressions, they fail to acquire inner resources from which they can draw sustenance. As a consequence, they are always on unsure footing, constantly on edge and never quite sure that they will secure the attention and esteem they require from others. Anxious lest they be cut adrift and left on their own, they proceed through cyclical swings of simulated

TABLE 14.2   The Borderline Personality: Functional and Structural Domains

Functional Domains		Structural Domains	
	Spasmodic	**Self-Image**	**Uncertain**
Expressive Behavior	Displays a desultory energy level with sudden, unexpected, and impulsive outbursts; abrupt, endogenous shifts in drive state and inhibitory controls; not only places activation and emotional equilibrium in constant jeopardy, but engages in recurrent suicidal or self-mutilating behaviors.		Experiences the confusions of an immature, nebulous, or wavering sense of identity, often with underlying feelings of emptiness; seeks to redeem precipitate actions and changing self-presentations with expressions of contrition and self-punitive behaviors.
	Paradoxical	**Object-Representations**	**Incompatible**
Interpersonal Conduct	Although needing attention and affection, is unpredictably contrary, manipulative, and volatile, frequently eliciting rejection rather than support; frantically reacts to fears of abandonment and isolation, but often in angry, mercurial, and self-damaging ways.		Internalized representations comprise rudimentary and extemporaneously devised, but repetitively aborted learnings, resulting in conflicting memories, discordant attitudes, contradictory needs, antithetical emotions, erratic impulses, and clashing strategies for conflict reduction.
	Capricious	**Morphologic Organization**	**Split**
Cognitive Style	Experiences rapidly changing, fluctuation, and antithetical perceptions or thoughts concerning passing events, as well as contrasting emotions and conflicting thoughts toward self and others, notably love, rage, and guilt; vacillating and contradictory reactions are evoked in others by virtue of behaviors, creating, in turn, conflicting and confusing social feedback.		Inner structures exist in a sharply segmented and conflictual configuration in which a marked lack of consistency and congruency is seen among elements; levels of consciousness often shift and result in rapid movements across boundaries that usually separate contrasting percepts, memories, and affects, all of which lead to periodic schisms in what limited psychic order and cohesion may otherwise be present, often resulting intransient, stress-related psychotic episodes.
	Regression	**Mood/Temperament**	**Labile**
Regulatory Mechanism	Retreats under stress to developmentally earlier levels of anxiety tolerance, impulse control, and social adaptation; among adolescents, is unable to cope with adult demands and conflicts, as evident in immature, if not increasingly infantile, behaviors.		Fails to accord unstable mood level with external reality; has either marked shifts from normality to depression to excitement, or has periods of dejection and apathy, interspersed with episodes of inappropriate and intense anger, as well as brief spells of anxiety or euphoria.

Note: Shaded domains are the most salient for this personality prototype.

euphoria in which they seek to solicit the attention they need and periods of brooding dejection, hopelessness, and self-depreciation. When their dread of desertion reaches monumental proportions, they lose all control and are swept either into a chaotic and manic cry for help or into a deep and intransigent gloom.

Petulant borderlines themselves create inconsistency by their own vacillations, unpredictability, unreasonableness, sullenness, and revengeful nature. Because they have learned to anticipate disappointment, they often jump the gun, alienating others before being subjected to alienation. Moreover, their tensions keep churning close to the surface, leading them to act petulantly, impulsively, and precipitously. Their lack of controls results in endless wrangles with others and precludes their achieving the affections they so desperately seek. Dejected, angry, and pessimistic, they may periodically become violent, exploding with bitter complaints and recriminations against the world or, conversely, turn against themselves, become self-sacrificing, plead forgiveness and contrition, and reproach and derogate their self-worth.

Broad and pervasive sociocultural forces may also play a significant role in the development of all of the borderline personality patterns. This is likely to be found where a society's values and practices are fluid and inconsistent, such as appears increasingly prominent in current Western societies, notably the United States.

An amorphous cultural state, so characteristic of our modern times, is clearly mirrored in the interpersonal vacillations and affective instabilities that characterize the borderline personality. Central to our recent culture have been the increased pace of social change and the growing pervasiveness of ambiguous and discordant customs to which children are expected to subscribe. Under the cumulative impact of rapid industrialization, immigration, mobility, technology, and mass communication, there has been a steady erosion of traditional values and standards. Instead of a simple and coherent body of practices and beliefs, children find themselves confronted with constantly shifting styles and increasingly questioned norms whose durability is uncertain and precarious (Millon, 1987). And yet, because the borderline personality is so clinically common, yet so clinically problematic and complex in its understandings, it is not surprising that biosocial models of the borderline personality are perhaps better developed than for any other personality disorder. Linehan (1993) sees the disorder primarily as a problem of emotional regulation, which involves both emotional vulnerability and the inability to regulate emotional states. Borderlines not only are sensitive to a broad range of emotional stimulation but also react quickly and intensely and take a long time to cool down, meaning that they are easily provoked again. Intense emotional states thus become chronic and self-perpetuating. What is at issue, however, is what developmental factors promote these adult characteristics. As Linehan explains, the regulation of emotion requires that the individual first learn to accurately label emotional states and then deal with the emotional associations these states bring to mind.

Perpetually wrought with the implicit dissonance of dueling forces, the adult borderline represents what happens when the "difficult temperament" (Thomas & Chess, 1977) meets an "invalidating environment," described in detail by Linehan (1993):

Rather than mirror and validate the child's personal experience of the world, the invalidating environment punishes and trivializes. First, it tells the individual that she is wrong in both her description and her analyses of her own experiences, particularly in her views of what is causing her own emotions, beliefs and actions. Second, it attributes her experiences to socially unacceptable characteristics or personality traits. (p. 49)

Rather than recognize and validate personal experience, the environment projects its own emotions, motives, and characteristics onto the future borderline. Linehan (p. 50) gives the examples, "You are angry, but you just won't admit it," and "When she says no, she means yes." At the same time, actual negative emotions are long-standing negative dispositions, such as overreactivity or hypersensitivity. Again, it is the individual who is wrong. Finally, failure is also attributed to negative traits, such as lack of discipline or laziness. To sum up Linehan's view, the developmental environment not only emits erratic and random communications that fail to understand the borderline as a unique individual with genuine potentials but also concurrently dispenses the unending message, "You are bad." Some of this is seen when Georgia, the borderline mom, recalls her own mother saying repeatedly, "I should have abandoned you when I realized what a lousy kid you were."

The consequences of this development pattern are severe. Without adequate mirroring and validation, subjects cannot learn to label their private and emotional experiences accurately, they cannot develop realistic life goals, they cannot develop expectations about what normal interactions might be like, and they cannot learn to interpret their own reactions as valid. Moreover, because their invalidating environment cannot tolerate the expression of negative emotions, borderlines learn that intense displays are necessary if any response is to occur. Family types that engender a borderline personality include the chaotic family, riddled with substance abuse, parental absence and neglect, and a general soap opera lifestyle (Benjamin, 1996), as well as the perfect family, which cannot tolerate negative emotional displays and cannot understand why children cannot simply control their feelings. See Linehan (1993) for a discussion of broader biosocial factors that indirectly contribute to the development of the borderline personality, including sexual abuse and the role of cultural ideals in the lives of women.

Although the family forms the proximal environment in which temperament and the forces of socialization interact, other authors have recognized the sociocultural environment as a powerful but indirect influence on personal development. As noted by Paris (1994b), society varies in terms of its level of integration over time. Individuals who grow up in an integrated society are protected somewhat from developing borderline traits. In contrast, those who grow up in the context of a disintegrating society are more frequently led down pathways that encourage borderline behavior. Our own society, he argues, expects the individual to function independently even while levels of social support and efforts to contain deviant behavior are decreasing. The net effect is an increase in impulsiveness, substance abuse, and, ultimately, other behaviors characteristic of the borderline, such as self-mutilation and suicidal gestures.

Similarly, Millon (1987) holds that traditional societies provide experiences with other persons and institutions that offer some protection against the influence of early abuse within the family. Today, however, the extended family is less coherent, and children have less contact with aunts, uncles, and grandparents—thus diminishing the opportunity of a second chance to develop healthy attachments that might supplant or heal wounds at the hands of parents or siblings. Similarly, the role of traditional institutions, such as church and school where concepts of beliefs, values, and proper conduct are emphasized in conjunction with academic lessons, has decreased. The result is a society as diffusive and fluid as the borderline personalities it creates.

CONTRAST WITH RELATED PERSONALITIES

Given its history, it is not surprising that the *DSM* borderline overlaps a variety of other personality disorders. The first diagnostic criterion, frantic efforts to avoid abandonment, resonates with the dependent and histrionic personalities. The dependent desperately needs an instrumental surrogate, without which feelings of panic quickly rise to the surface. Histrionics need an instrumental surrogate as well, but they also need to feel physically attractive, to be the center of attention, and to believe that they themselves are idealized by their companions. Abandonment is thus double jeopardy for histrionics, being both a separation and a commentary on the insufficiency of their attractive power. The avoidant could be included here because avoidants need a mate who is willing to face a world where they feel shamed, defective, and incapable.

As to the second diagnostic criterion, dependents, histrionics, narcissistics, and negativists are particularly prone to idealize romantic encounters, and narcissists are particularly likely to devalue those who are no longer admiring, who withhold "narcissistic supplies" for any reason. The dependent and histrionic are likely to have a poorly developed sense of self, and the histrionic, narcissistic, and negativistic personalities are beset with a highly unstable sense of self, the third borderline criterion. Narcissistic, histrionic, and negativistic personalities are particularly prone as well to emotional extremes, including anger. More pathological narcissistic and histrionic personalities are also likely to experience chronic feelings of emptiness. Finally, borderline, schizotypal, and paranoid personalities exhibit paranoid fears, and borderline and histrionic personalities are prone to dissociative episodes. The highest overlap may be with the *DSM-III-R* self-defeating personality (Gunderson, Zanarini, & Kisiel, 1995), perhaps because their interpersonal chaos and self-destructive behavior certainly have the quality of setting borderlines up for painful experiences and failure.

However, contrasts can also be created with many of these same constructs. The regressive thought disorder of the borderline often resembles the schizotypal personality, but the borderline is famous for its unstable mood and its association with depression; the schizotypal is not. Moreover, the borderline disorganizes in connection with interpersonal themes, whereas schizotypal thought may seem eccentric about almost anything. Transient psychotic episodes in the borderline are thus more reactive to the character of external events. Both borderlines and histrionics are emotionally labile and attention seeking. Both may sexualize their relationships, but the borderline more easily gives way to anger and more readily experiences feelings of emptiness and loneliness, which is typically repressed in the histrionic. Both borderline and paranoid personalities exhibit paranoid fears, but the paranoid makes a rigid impression and wants to be left alone. In contrast, the borderline seems labile and fluid and fears being left alone. Moreover, borderlines are often overtly self-destructive and sometimes self-accusing, whereas the paranoid accuses others. Both borderlines and antisocials can be impulsive in self-damaging ways. However, antisocials typically lack remorse for their actions and pursue impulsive gratification as an end in itself. In contrast, impulsivity in the borderline personality is more often used to assuage feelings of emptiness and worthlessness. Finally, both borderlines and dependents fear abandonment. However, dependents react to threats of separation by becoming more submissive and pleasing, whereas the borderline reacts with angry demands intended to coerce nurturance.

PATHWAYS TO SYMPTOM EXPRESSION

Each personality disorder exhibits a pattern of Axis I vulnerabilities that grows out of the logic of the construct itself. Because the *DSM* borderline personality has been defined by symptoms as much as by traits, much of its relationship with Axis I has already been implicitly discussed. Because borderlines both habitually distort the meaning of interpersonal events and regularly plunge their relationships into chaos and discord, borderlines often live with ongoing, diffuse anxiety. The perception of loss of support or abandonment sometimes leads to episodes of panic, perhaps accompanied by dissociative symptoms or paranoid ideation. When borderlines can reassure themselves that their attachments are somewhat secured, their symptoms are likely to abate. Dissociative symptoms may be especially prominent in females with a severe abuse history (Galletly, 1997). As you read the following sections, try to identify the connection between personality and symptom.

Depression

Depression and the borderline personality are so strongly associated that many see depression as more than just a lifestyle consequence, arguing instead that borderlines possess a biophysical disposition to depressive episodes, putting the disorder on the affective spectrum (Akiskal, 1981). Whatever the merit of this hypothesis, borderlines often present with a composite of depression, irritability, and hostility, accompanied by a variety of physical complaints. Moreover, they experience a crushingly low self-esteem, intensified by a pervasive sense of the self as bad and worthless, along with global feelings of inefficacy and helplessness. Intense guilt and self-condemnation may be felt at having driven others out of their lives, usually after efforts to control others with hostility. In a pathological attempt to secure shaken relationships, self-mutilation may be used as a means of appeasing vicious introjects (Benjamin, 1996), though it is also apparently used as an antidote to impending dissociation, a means of proving that "something is real."

Other Disorders

Other Axis I disorders may accompany the borderline personality. Individuals with prominent dependent and histrionic traits are especially likely to exhibit somatic symptoms. These establish an objective claim to long wished-for nurturance, thus bonding caretakers more closely to the borderline while reducing threats of abandonment and demands for competent performance. The chaotic families of borderlines often provide models for substance abuse (Feldman, Zelkowitz, Weiss, & Vogel, 1995), and parental substance abuse is a risk factor for the development of borderline pathology in children (Guzder et al., 1996). Any number of substances may be used recreationally with peers or as a means of self-medication in the face of persistent anxiety or depression. Abuse becomes more likely for individuals who carry antisocial traits. Moreover, the presence of substance abuse predicts a higher level of borderline pathology, increased self-destructive and suicidal thoughts and behavior, and poorer clinical course (Links, Heslegrave, Mitton, & van Reekum, 1995). Finally, borderline personality disorder is often diagnosed in subjects with eating disorders (Kernberg, 1995; Steiger, Jabalpurwala, & Champagne, 1996), linked to specific features of family dysfunction (Waller, 1994), and found to predict weight preoccupation (Claridge, Davis, Bellhouse, & Kaptein, 1998).

Therapy

Borderlines are notoriously difficult patients. Most experienced therapists are likely to have several stories to share about borderline personalities who caused no end of problems. Because borderlines often appear at first glance healthier than they really are, therapy often focuses on some apparently simple issue, only to become increasingly complex over time. In fact, simply establishing an alliance can prove extraordinarily difficult. A large proportion just quit therapy, citing problems with the therapist, who is then devalued just like many others. Those who do continue may require repeated hospitalization as indicated by the strength of the impulse for self-mutilation or suicide. Nevertheless, it is also true that borderline pathology is a matter of degree, and treatment with less severe patients is often highly gratifying. Many borderlines have a range of highly developed social skills, along with an intrinsic motivation to restrain contrary and troublesome impulses. Therapeutic gains can lead to extended periods of productive functioning and interpersonal harmony, which provide the therapist with an unusual opportunity to see therapeutic goals realized.

THERAPEUTIC TRAPS

One of the fundamental principles of therapy holds that interpersonal pathologies are recaptured in the therapeutic relationship itself. For the borderline personality, this means high expectations for nurturance from the therapist, inevitably followed by distorted perceptions of the therapeutic relationship and periods of intense anger and manipulation. Borderlines not only idealize and then devalue the therapist but also bring into therapy threats of suicide and, sometimes, frequent and repeated self-mutilation, dramatic physical evidence of psychopathology. Clinicians who treat borderlines should carefully monitor their own countertransference feelings to maintain a healthy level of detachment from the emotional lability and intensity to which every session is susceptible. In fact, many clinicians find it necessary to limit the number of borderline patients in their caseload. Otherwise, they risk therapeutic burnout, dreading sessions with their borderline patients and even finding that their countertransference feelings overflow into other subsequent therapy sessions. Another common trap is failure to maintain personal boundaries, creating a vicious circle of chronic giving-in to the borderline's demands for increased attention and nurturance (Benjamin, 1996).

Another potential problem lies in neglecting the importance of comorbid personality disorders. In the *DSM,* the borderline personality disorder is a heterogeneous collection defined by both symptoms and personality traits. Subjects often present as a more severe variant of some other personality disorder, particularly the negativistic, depressive, histrionic, and avoidant. Because the borderline personality can be considered a level of personality organization, for any given individual, the meaning of his of her particular symptoms and Axis I disorders is often decipherable only in the context of comorbid personality disorders. In other words, self-mutilation in a borderline client with dependent and masochistic features may have a different meaning than self-mutilation in a borderline client with histrionic features. Because the borderline category is less homogeneous than other personality disorders, treatment cannot as easily proceed on the basis of a borderline diagnosis alone.

Many therapists worry that depression and explosive hostility, which often signify acute breaks with reality, can lead to a more permanent decompensatory process. Among the early signs of a growing breakdown are marked periods of discouragement and persistent dejection. At this phase, therapists are advised to shift into a more supportive mode, while maintaining boundaries and avoiding blatant manipulations. Because many therapists feel burdened and frustrated by their borderline subjects, they may be tempted to react dismissively, with the implicit message to "just snap out of it." Such reactions represent a snapshot of the borderline's history and current interpersonal relationships, where demands are made to function, whatever the individual's mental state (Linehan, 1993). If the therapist is perceived in the same way, regression may accelerate. A consistent and appropriate level

FOCUS ON THERAPY

Marsha Linehan and Dialectical Behavior Therapy

Leading Models of Personality Disorder Treatment

Developed by Marsha M. Linehan, Dialectical Behavior Therapy (DBT; 1993) is a therapeutic approach specifically designed for the treatment of Borderline Personality Disorder
and suicidal behaviors and is currently the field's leading model in treating one of the most
difficult of personality disorders. It uses both cognitive and behavioral techniques, such as
problem solving, exposure techniques, skills training, contingency management, and cognitive modification, to effect a hierarchy of treatment goals. Potential outcomes of DBT
intervention may include successfully teaching skills that will allow borderlines to regulate
emotions, tolerate distress, and effectively interact with others. However, for such coveted
abilities to be attained, the distinguishing aspects of DBT must be adhered to: accept and
validate current behaviors, acknowledge and treat the behaviors that pose disruption to the
therapeutic process, perceive the therapeutic relationship as indispensable to treatment,
and accentuate the dialectical processes. The most notable and fundamental dialectical
strategy is the process of accepting the individual's behavior while simultaneously guiding
them to change. Concurrent are the underlying challenges inherent in maintaining dialectical thinking while targeting a patient's cognitive inflexibility. While the therapist is challenged with reframing the patient's view of past suicidal behaviors, for example, from
self-destructive dysfunction to learning and problem-solving experiences, he or she must
also validate the individual's emotions and feelings. Such paradox is not only the core
component of the dialectical model but also essential to its efficacy.

of concern, together with a strong alliance that helps anchor borderlines to realistic interpretations of their stormy relationships, often forestalls increasing feelings of emptiness and depression. Subjects in crisis should be evaluated tactfully for the possibility of
suicide and hospitalized when necessary.

THERAPEUTIC STRATEGIES AND TECHNIQUES

An important goal is to bring calm to the borderline's chaotic relationships. According
to Benjamin (1996), the borderline is in a Catch-22 that sabotages therapy, whether
there is progress or no progress. Although therapy usually has a good beginning, eventually the subject realizes that the therapist is not an infinite fountain of nurturance and
begins to enact extreme behaviors, such as overdoses, self-mutilation, and suicidal gestures. As Benjamin explains, this causes the therapist to begin a subtle withdrawal, perhaps just a reluctance to schedule extra appointments or receive phone calls.

Sensing the increased distance, Benjamin (1996) states, the borderline becomes critical and accuses the therapist of not caring enough and quits therapy in some dramatic
fashion. Later, the borderline phones wanting to continue, and the therapist agrees, fearing legal consequences or the borderline's self-destructive actions. Obviously, this vicious
circle does not require that the borderline quit therapy, but only that the therapist surrender the desired emotional supplies as a consequence of the subject's manipulations. As

long as the therapist seems to hold out, the borderline continues to exacerbate and regress. Alternatively, the subject may genuinely improve but then suddenly regress as termination approaches. To arrive at a healthy state implies the need to end the client-therapist relationship, which then leaves the subject feeling abandoned and fearful. Again, pathology is the solution, at least from the subject's perspective.

The best way to stop these cycles is to prevent them from starting. Whereas the borderline believes the problem is not enough love and attention, the therapist should offer an agreement in "strength-building" (Benjamin, 1996, p. 134). Limits should be set and maintained. Refusals to meet classic borderline manipulations can be excluded in advance by putting them into the overall mission of therapy, the road to health, as a larger context. For example, the therapist might say, "You're right that I won't be willing to talk with you whenever you call. . . . The reason is that . . . your pattern now is to be very needy . . . if I were to do what you want in the way you want, you would become weaker, not stronger" (p. 134). This approach establishes boundaries while affirming the subject, thus the borderline cannot feel ignored or abandoned.

As therapy progresses, phone calls and extra sessions must be limited. The focus must be on the subject's strengths and how these strengths can be brought to bear in the given situation. Self-consciously keeping this goal in mind helps therapist and subject remain focused on the pathology as the enemy and keeps therapy from degenerating into the chaos of the borderline's other relationships. Once maladaptive patterns are recognized, therapy can block their perpetuation. For example, Benjamin (1996, p. 136) holds that borderlines give up their self-destructive behaviors if they can "divorce" their "internalized abusive attachment figures." Fantasies can be examined to determine who is appeased by injury to the self. Next, the link between the present and past can be weakened with penetrating questions, such as, "Do you love this person enough to give him or her your self-destruction?" Alternatively, a dislike of the internalized image can be fostered or an attachment to someone else can be fostered to replace its influence.

Writing in Beck et al. (1990), Pretzer suggests that although borderlines exhibit many cognitive distortions, dichotomous thinking is especially prominent. An attachment figure may be seen as either totally accepting or completely condemning, for example. Because emotion and thought are so closely linked, such black-and-white appraisals lead to proportionately intense emotional reactions, throwing borderlines' lives into desperate panic and their interpersonal relationships into turmoil. The first time the subject feels ignored, his or her appraisal changes, and the attachment figure is saturated with absolute evil. Likewise, borderlines cannot feel somewhat guilty, only totally bad and worthless. Because no shades of gray exist, more adaptable reactions simply are not available. As such, a strong therapeutic alliance is particularly important, for the therapist is easily classified as completely malevolent or untrustworthy as well.

With this foundation, the therapist can help the subject test reality in areas where dichotomous thinking dominates. For example, the individual can be asked to define the elements that go into being trustworthy and untrustworthy. Once an adequately complex definition is achieved, actual persons in the subject's life can be evaluated and shown to occupy a position somewhere between these polar opposites. With practice, borderlines can learn to identify automatic thoughts that caricature the interpersonal world, thus paving the way toward a new and more realistic way of experiencing others: Not everyone will criticize, hurt, or abandon you. If successful, existing relationships should settle down somewhat, and new relationships get a more realistic beginning. The same holds for the borderline's self-image. By refuting dichotomous images of themselves, borderlines learn that they are not absolutely unredeemable but instead have a variety of both good and bad qualities, and the bad can be segregated out and worked on in therapy. In turn, these changes feed into decreases in emotional intensity. Anger, for example, can be expressed to a moderate degree and in constructive ways. Where necessary, role playing and social skills training can be used to provide the borderline with experience in interpersonal interactions of moderate intensity.

Although the focus on dichotomous thinking is straightforward, several characteristics of the borderline complicate cognitive therapy (Beck et al., 1990). Many borderlines begin from a position of basic mistrust, making any therapeutic alliance tenuous at best. With the therapist explicitly acknowledging difficulties; taking special care to communicate clearly, assertively, and honestly; and especially maintaining congruence between verbal and nonverbal cues, an alliance should develop over time. In addition, a lack of basic trust feeds into a discomfort with intimacy. Many borderlines become anxious if their boundaries are overstepped. Subjects can be asked how therapy can be made more comfortable and should be allowed input into the pace of therapy and topics discussed. Finally, Pretzer notes that concrete behavioral approaches can be valuable in serving several important purposes. Without a clear identity, most borderlines find it difficult to set goals and maintain priorities from week to week. With concrete, specified goals, progress is more tangible and easier to measure. Moreover, subjects are not required to reveal deeply personal thoughts and feelings before trust is established, and the initial success can provide motivation to continue in therapy. Goals should be discussed frequently to keep subjects focused.

Psychodynamic thinkers are agreed that modifications of the classical technique are necessary to prevent the borderline from regressing in the unstructured environment of the couch. However, they are divided on whether to advocate supportive or expressive therapy. Because the borderline suffers from ego weakness and the therapist acts as an auxiliary ego for the subject, supportive therapy seems logical. However, Kernberg (1985a) argues that supportive therapy may perpetuate pathology by allowing borderlines unlimited gratification of pathological needs, specifically, a need to express anger at early caretakers, now symbolized by the therapist. The borderline personality is not a pathology of ego weakness, but a pathology of object relations. Instead, Kernberg proposes that confrontation can be therapeutic when addressed to borderlines' tendency to alternate between idealization and devaluation. Confrontation does not connote hostility, but simply an effort by the therapist to draw attention to the long list of discrepant statements made by borderlines in therapy and their lack of concern in making them.

Thus, if the subject asserts that an abusive lover is perfect, the therapist might say, "I'm confused. You just told me that your lover physically abused you. Does that sound like the perfect boyfriend?" In confrontive activities, the therapist functions as a mature, self-observing ego that strives for a consistency of impressions and behavior. Posing such questions not only lays a foundation for insight but also requires the subject to integrate split object-representations of self and others into more realistic composites, establishing more solid boundaries between borderlines and their significant others, bringing additional cohesion to the self, thereby decreasing identity diffusion. By addressing problems in the transference early, the way is set for a more realistic perception of the therapy later; thus a genuine alliance, one not based on fantasied objects, can be established.

Other thinkers argue that early confrontation and interpretation simply incite the borderline, who then quits therapy. From Adler's (1985) perspective, for example, the borderline suffers from an absence of soothing-holding introjects. Given the distortions to which they are subject, borderlines are unable to appreciate the therapist as a separate individual authentically interested in their welfare. Because, at this stage, the borderline can relate only to his or her projections, no real alliance is yet possible. By providing consistent support, the subject is able to internalize the soothing-holding qualities of the therapeutic relationship. Thereafter, the borderline is in a better position to grasp the therapist as a real person. Ironically, the available data (Wallerstein, 1986) seem to suggest that confrontation and supportive therapy represent dichotomous extremes. As such, each works for different patients, and both are likely to be required with the same patient at different times.

Many therapists have found credence in resorting to alternative forms of therapy when dealing with borderline personality disorder. For example, Bockian (2002) has used relaxation training, expressive arts therapy, and music therapy as supplemental therapeutic strategies when treating borderline personality disorder. These therapeutic alternatives are effective in assuaging the depressive and anxious symptomatology. Relaxation techniques can be used to allow the individual a sense of calm and control in managing daily life. Whether encouraging autogenic training or guided imagery, the goal is to strengthen the borderline's relaxation skills, thereby tempering anxiety states. The desired result of expressive arts therapy—dance, music, art therapy, or psychodrama—is to minimize feelings of self-consciousness, encourage self-exploration, strengthen alternative modes of self-expression, and heighten self-awareness. Music therapy, according to the American Music Therapy Association (AMTA), is suitable for the treatment of symptoms associated with sexual abuse, posttraumatic stress disorder, and substance abuse—experiences often linked with a borderline personality (Bockian, 2002).

Summary

Borderlines are characterized by their unstable relationships and emotional reactions. Everything about them seems frantic, chaotic, and impulsive. They swing rapidly from adoration to hatred within minutes and seemingly without provocation. The very construct and term borderline personality has remained controversial throughout the years and has produced an extensive literature with each new incarnation.

Given the severity of this disorder, it is difficult to imagine a normal variant of the borderline, but indeed there is such a thing. Oldham and Morris (1995) describe the mercurial style, who always need to be in a passionate relationship, possess an urgency to their closeness, and have a roller coaster kind of life, usually processing life emotionally rather than logically. Normalizing DSM-IV criteria also gives us a more normal variant that may be very sensitive to anything that may impact their relationships or sensation seeking, but in a way that enriches their life, not destroys it.

The borderline overlaps with many other personality styles and has some interesting variations. The discouraged borderline is mixed with aspects of the dependent or avoidant personality, who attaches to usually just one or two significant others. The impulsive borderline is a mixture of histrionic or antisocial traits and often becomes extraordinarily behaviorally hyperactive. The petulant borderline is a blend of negativistic features and may never get their needs met or feel insecure in their attachments. The self-destructive borderline is peppered with masochistic traits that cause them to turn their destructive feelings inwards on themselves.

Intuitively, it seems logical that the borderline must possess some fundamental temperament of high emotional reactivity that disposes them to the intense and volatile relationships that later develop. A "cyclothymic temperament" has been suggested as a possible biological predisposition to developing the borderline personality. Other researchers have been exploring a link between borderline personality and certain neurotransmitters.

Freud identified patients who were not psychotic but were resistant to his type of therapy. Stern later characterized these types as a "borderline group of neuroses." These patients often projected internal anger to sources in the environment. Later analysts believed borderline personality was more than a blending of neuroses and psychoses. In the 1950s, the term borderline began to be applied to people whose normal ego functions were severely weakened by traumatic events and pathological relationships. As a result, aspects of the self may fuse with aspects of others. Borderlines develop a split between good and bad images of things, forming two separate identification systems, hence facilitating a rapid fluctuation between adoration and hatred toward the same object. Since this formulation, the object relationists have dominated the discussion of borderline personality in dynamically oriented circles, including Masterson and Adler.

Interpersonally, borderlines are characterized by their stormy relationships with others. They are famous for their adoration of and intense emotional connection with a partner and then rapidly changing to hatred and resentment. They seem to sabotage their relationships with the chaos they bring to every relationship. Their intense fear of abandonment distorts their perceptions of the actions and communications of others. Depression, suicide ideation, and suicide attempts are a natural outgrowth of the kinds of dynamics that play out for the borderline. Benjamin's SASB model cites four features that lead to the development of borderline personality: family chaos; traumatic abandonment; family values that thwart autonomy, expressions of happiness, and accomplishment and encourage dependency and misery; and a family that offers nurturance only when the individual is miserable.

Cognitively, borderlines can be described as fluid. The degree of fluidity usually depends on the quality of their relationships and with the amount of structure in the task to be performed (i.e., solid attachments make for better judgment). Their cognitions may also be characterized by their split object-representations, often leading to their seemingly paradoxical behaviors. Dichotomous thinking also seems to be present in the borderline, which may help account for much of the rapid change in behaviors and affective expression. Other cognitive characteristics of the borderline have led some to assert a connection between PTSD and the borderline personality.

An evolutionary neurodevelopmental synthesis provides a well-developed theory of the borderline. Linehan sees borderlines as primarily a problem of emotion regulation that leaves them vulnerable not only to be quickly aroused but also slow to cool down. Developmentally, Linehan believes that the child with a "difficult temperament" meets an "invalidating environment" that punishes and trivializes the child for his or her emotions; thus, the child fails to learn to label experiences accurately and trust his or her feelings. Millon argues that the structure of modern society fails to provide opportunities for children to have a "second chance" to develop healthy attachments if their parents fail to provide this necessary element. Borderlines fail to attach to any polarity, signifying their profound ambivalence and lability. From this perspective, it has been argued that the borderline personality is pathological with respect to the level of personality integration.

Although many borderline patients first present as relatively healthy individuals, they promptly become difficult and complex to treat. Often revealed in the course of therapy is their inherent inclination to developing depressive symptoms as well as somatic symptoms, substance abuse, and eating disorders. They often recreate their chaotic patterns in interpersonal relationships with the therapist and constantly try to overrun the therapist's personal boundaries. The therapist must also be aware of comorbid personality disorders and be savvy of the borderline's attempts at manipulation. One of the most critical goals in therapy is to bring calm to the borderline's chaotic relationships. Their dichotomous thinking must also be addressed but is complicated by their position of general mistrust. It is generally believed that supportive therapy only serves to perpetuate the pathology and that a more confrontive therapy should be more effective. However, this often incites the borderline to quit therapy. Hence, some combination of providing consistent support to build a therapeutic relationship and a gentle and thoughtful confronting will provide the best results.

Chapter 15

Personality Disorders from the Appendices of DSM-III-R and DSM-IV

Objectives

- What are the two personality disorders listed in the appendix of the *DSM-III-R* that are excluded from the *DSM-IV?*
- What are the *DSM-III-R* criteria for the self-defeating (masochistic) personality?
- The self-sacrificing and yielding personalities are normal variants of the masochistic. Describe their characteristics and relate them to the more disordered criteria offered by the *DSM-III-R.*
- Explain how different personality styles combine to form each of the subtypes of the masochistic personality.
- Could the masochistic personality be considered a maladaptive adjustment to extreme social inadequacy?
- Masochists share characteristics with other personality disorders. List these other disorders and explain the distinction between each and the masochist.
- What are the *DSM-III-R* criteria for the sadistic personality?
- The controlling personality is a normal variant of the sadistic personality. Describe and relate it to the more disordered criteria offered by the *DSM-III-R.*
- Explain how different personality styles combine to form each of the subtypes of the sadistic personality.
- Sadistic personalities share characteristics with other personality disorders. List these other disorders and explain the distinction between each and the sadist.
- What are the two personality disorders listed in the appendix of the *DSM-IV?*
- What are the *DSM-IV* criteria for the depressive personality?

- Could there be a normal variant to the depressive personality?
- Explain how different personality styles combine to form each of the subtypes of the depressive personality.
- Are depression and dysthymia the same disorder?
- Depressives share characteristics with other personality disorders. List these other disorders and explain the distinction between each and depressives.
- How are compulsives and negativists similar? How do they differ?
- What are the *DSM-IV* criteria for the passive-aggressive personality?
- Could there be a normal variant to the negativistic personality?
- Explain how different personality styles combine to form each of the subtypes of the negativistic personality.
- Negativists share characteristics with other personality disorders. List these other disorders and explain the distinction between each and negativists.

Each *DSM* contains an appendix, a place where disorders warranting additional study can be placed apart from those described in the main body of the text. Ideally, as empirical evidence accumulates, the status of these provisional disorders is revised on the basis of scientific findings alone. Such disorders either graduate to the level of accepted clinical currency or are dismissed from the *DSM* altogether.

This chapter includes four personality disorders; two, though present in the appendix of the third revised version of the *DSM* (APA, 1987), were dropped from *DSM-IV*, though more for political than scientific reasons. Despite their controversial nature, they are, nevertheless, widely known among clinicians and describe aspects of human nature that have no equivalent in the remaining constructs. Moreover, their existence is predicted by the evolutionary theory.

The Self-Defeating (Masochistic) Personality

Life is tough enough without making things even more difficult. Some people, however, deliberately put obstacles in their own way, seem to court suffering, and need to fail. Such individuals are called **masochistic personalities,** though they were termed "self-defeating" personalities in the *DSM-III-R*. Cursed with an uncanny sense for defeating themselves, they routinely set sail for stormy weather and call down setback, loss, frustration, and grief on themselves. When they do experience good fortune, they react with confusion or displeasure and secretly frown at the joy that others might feel for them. Real accomplishments they attribute to luck, specifically to avoid a sense of pride. Paradoxically, they may willingly contribute to the achievements of others, while subtly undermining progress toward their own goals. In love, they often discard genuinely caring persons as tiresome or boring, turn otherwise ordinary mates into persecutors, and seem subtly attracted to those who are insensitive or even sadistic (see Case 15.1).

The self-defeating or masochist is thus fundamentally different from the other personality disorders, who want to succeed, however subjectively success is defined, but

Theresa entered the therapist's office with downcast eyes, slumped shoulders, and a blotchy face, as if she had been crying recently.[1] She had come at her husband's suggestion. While arranging the appointment, he mentioned that she might be depressed, but followed up with a curious statement: "She torments herself . . . she's been this way for as long as I've known her . . . she seems to live for it. I hope you can help her, but even if you do, she'll probably find a way to turn it around." "Don't let her enjoy herself too much," he added sarcastically, "or you might make her suicidal."

Theresa looks younger than her 21 years. Her expression and posture are that of a young child about to be punished for doing something wrong. Although she could be quite attractive, this is overshadowed by her self-effacing mannerisms and takes some time to notice. She begins by apologizing in advance, "I shouldn't be taking up your time when you could be helping other people." She notes further, "Nothing can be done for me, I was meant to suffer."

Theresa is the older of two girls raised by their mother. Her father abandoned the family before they were old enough to remember him. Her mother was loving, but so busy working two jobs that the girls saw her only a few minutes each day. Nevertheless, the family was stable until, as an adolescent, Theresa developed recurrent infections that required repeated hospitalizations. Because her mother was the sole source of income, the family was usually broke trying to pay the bills. Now, her mother has no money saved for retirement, and neither child has a college fund. Theresa accepts full responsibility and feels unbearably guilty. "My mom basically worked her life away trying to keep me healthy," she says through the tears.

Though she has worked very hard, things somehow never work out for Theresa. She goes to school, works a full-time job, and takes care of the house, but sees herself as incompetent regardless of the effort put forth. "Everything I touch falls apart." she says. Her performance at work is excellent, but she "forgets" to ask for a lighter load during midterms and has to call in sick, angering her coworkers. Then, her hard-fought grades sag because she allows herself to be scheduled for overtime during finals week. Sometimes, she takes classes that are too hard without the necessary prerequisites and has to give up and withdraw, forfeiting her effort completely. When her husband volunteers to find her a tutor and do the housework, she refuses, saying she doesn't want to burden him with responsibilities that are rightfully hers. Yet, despite her work, she always finds time to send birthday and holiday cards and even volunteers at church, but complains that no one follows up on her offers of friendship because she is always depressed.

If something does go right, Theresa refuses to celebrate, or else celebrates, but refuses to have a good time, and works extra hard for the next few weeks. "Christmas and birthdays are the worst," her husband states. "It's terrible watching her try to get out from under the burden of all the gifts, most of which she returns. One time I got pissed off, and all I could think of was telling her she won the lottery."

[1] Numbers mark aspects of the case most consistent with *DSM* criteria, and do not necessarily indicate that the case "meets" diagnostic criteria in this respect.

Self-Defeating Personality Disorder
DSM-III-R Criteria

A. A pervasive pattern of self-defeating behavior, beginning by early adulthood and present in a variety of contexts. The person may often avoid or undermine pleasurable experiences, be drawn to situations or relationships in which he or she will suffer, and prevent others from helping him or her, as indicated by at least five of the following:

(1) chooses people and situations that lead to disappointment, failure, or mistreatment even when better options are clearly available

(2) rejects or renders ineffective the attempts of others to help him or her

(3) following positive personal events (e.g., new achievement), responds with depression, guilt, or a behavior that produces pain (e.g., an accident)

(4) incites angry or rejecting responses from others and then feels hurt, defeated, or humiliated (e.g., makes fun of spouse in public, provoking an angry retort, then feels devastated)

(5) rejects opportunities for pleasure, or is reluctant to acknowledge enjoying himself or herself (despite having adequate social skills and the capacity for pleasure)

(6) fails to accomplish tasks crucial to his or her personal objectives despite demonstrated ability to do so, e.g., helps fellow students write papers, but is unable to write his or her own

(7) is uninterested in or rejects people who consistently treat him or her well, e.g., is unattracted to caring sexual partners

(8) engages in excessive self-sacrifice that is unsolicited by the intended recipients of the sacrifice

B. The behaviors in A do not occur exclusively in response to, or in anticipation of, being physically, sexually, or psychologically abused.

C. The behaviors in A do not occur only when the person is depressed.

find themselves tripped up again and again by their traits. Masochists trip themselves up, often at the very edge of success, and are willing to work hard at it, if necessary. In a perverse elaboration on Descartes, the masochist's motto is, "I hurt, therefore I am" (Shainess, 1987).

The meaning and acceptance of masochism have waxed and waned over time. As a term, it is a recent invention, having been coined in 1896 by German neurologist Krafft-Ebing as a sexual perversion to describe males who were impotent unless subjected to abuse or humiliation. The concept of a class of persons who seem to enjoy suffering as an orientation to life, however, has been around for centuries. The meaning of the term has since broadened to fit the concept so that most contemporary clinicians, especially those who are psychodynamic, are as familiar with the masochistic personality as they are with any other diagnostic entity. In 1987, it was provisionally described in the appendix of the revised third edition of the *DSM* as the self-defeating personality.

True to its name, the disorder ran into difficulties almost immediately. Despite its origin, masochism has historically been thought of as an extension of the feminine and submissive. The classical psychodynamic notion is that masochistic personalities unconsciously encourage and enjoy the abuse they receive. The empirical fact is that most cases of domestic violence are perpetrated by males. When these two are brought together, the result is a political powder keg. At least partially for this reason, the disorder was dropped from the *DSM-IV.* Nevertheless, it continues to enjoy widespread currency among clinicians as a construct that explains a great many facets of human behavior. Moreover, a number of studies suggest that the disorder is common (Kass, 1987; J. Reich, 1987), and its existence is predicted by the evolutionary model.

As an example of a masochistic personality, consider the case of Theresa. Her husband's comments set up the diagnosis, made even more dramatic by the fact that they are volunteered. Thus, we learn that Theresa torments herself, it's the pattern of her life, and "she seems to live for it" (see criterion 1). She even takes classes that are too difficult, without having the necessary prerequisites, forcing her to give up, withdraw, and waste her time and effort. Like most masochistic personalities, Theresa rejects the assistance that others offer (see criterion 2). When she gets herself in trouble in her classes, her husband offers to find a tutor for her, but she refuses under the thin excuse of not wanting to burden him, thus ensuring a bad outcome. When good things happen to her, she finds a way to undermine their effects (see criterion 3). For example, she refuses to celebrate the good or celebrates but refuses to enjoy it. She even returns most of her Christmas gifts to the store. Her husband even warns the therapist not to "let her enjoy herself too much, or you might make her suicidal." Although he is being sarcastic, the meaning of his words is clear. Theresa also punishes herself by failing to accomplish her personal goals (see criterion 6). "Everything I touch falls apart," she states. In fact, she uses work to impose on her school performance, and she uses school to impose on her work performance. Like most masochists, she is also excessively self-sacrificing (see criterion 8). She always finds time to send cards on important events and volunteers for church and then complains that no one seems to want her as a friend.

Given the portrait of Theresa, we are now in a position to approach additional issues that form the plan of this section. First, we compare normality and abnormality; then we move on to variations on the basic masochistic theme. These sections form the core of what is scientific in personality. By seeking to explain what we observe in character sketches like Theresa's, the goal is to move beyond literary anecdote. As always, we present history and description side by side, giving special attention to the several subtypes of each of the disorders discussed in the sections. Next, the section "Evolutionary Neurodevelopmental Perspective" shows how the existence of the personality disorder follows from the laws of evolution. Also included are a contrast between the masochistic and other theory-derived constructs and a discussion of how masochistic personalities tend to develop Axis I disorders.

FROM NORMALITY TO ABNORMALITY

Although such persons would seem extremely rare, masochistic traits are as ubiquitous as guilt and, therefore, are easily found on a continuum with normality. In their normal expression, they can be considered adaptive, idealized, and, perhaps, almost saintly. The **self-sacrificing** style (Oldham & Morris, 1995) live to serve and to be helpful to others. When they are allowed to give selflessly of themselves, everything is right with the world. Forever putting others above themselves, they have a reputation for being kind, considerate, and charitable. Always forgiving, they believe that people should be accepted and appreciated for who and what they are, not judged harshly by some extrinsic or legalistic standard. Although they willingly shoulder the burdens of life for those they love, they feel uncomfortable when their good deeds are singled out for praise, honestly believing that no thanks or recognition is necessary.

Moving closer toward pathology, Millon et al. (1994) describe the **yielding** style, individuals who usually possess abilities far in excess of what they lay claim to but nevertheless prefer to remain deferential and unassuming. They avoid displaying their real talents and abilities and instead place themselves in an inferior light to avoid any hint of competition. Sometimes, they seem to encourage others to take advantage of them. Although such traits have historically been associated with women, in fact, they are just as likely to be found in males (Stone, 1993).

Another way of creating a more normal masochistic personality style is by normalizing the diagnostic criteria of the *DSM-III-R*. Whereas individuals with the disorder seem to seek out disappointment, failure, or mistreatment (see criterion 1), those with the style do not. Whereas the disordered individual rejects or undoes the assistance of others (see criterion 2), the style tends to focus on the welfare of others before self. Whereas the disordered responds with negative emotions after positive personal events (see criterion 3), the style prefers to remain humble and resists taking public credit for accomplishments. Whereas the disordered sometimes deliberately provokes anger or rejection from others (see criterion 4), the style is charitable and deferential, sometimes to the point of indulging misbehavior. Whereas the disordered refuses pleasurable activities (see criterion 5), the style enjoys activities that fall short of self-serving hedonism. Whereas the disordered fails to accumulate personal accomplishments despite adequate ability (see criterion 6), the style prefers to work behind the scenes in devotion to the achievements of others. Whereas the disordered rejects legitimate sources of nurturance (see criterion 7), the style is sometimes too indulgent in trying to bring out the positive in others. Whereas the disordered is excessively self-sacrificing (see criterion 9), the style is fulfilled by putting others before self, but not pathologically so. For each of the preceding applicable contrasts, Theresa falls more toward the pathological side.

VARIATIONS OF THE MASOCHISTIC PERSONALITY

Not every masochistic personality is like our guilty wife. In fact, although Theresa does not exhibit all the diagnostic criteria of the masochistic personality, she is, nevertheless, more of a pure type, meaning that she does not combine characteristics of any other disorders with her basic masochistic pattern. Masochists often exhibit features of other personality disorders, however. The resulting moods and actions that these individuals manifest give a different coloration to the basic masochistic pattern that makes them similar to, yet different from, pure cases like Theresa's. Variants of the masochistic personality are summarized in Figure 15.1. Actual cases may or may not fall into one of these combinations.

The Self-Undoing Masochist

Classical psychoanalysis views the masochist as actively and repetitively searching for circumstances that lead to suffering or even destruction. From the outside, such persons seem gratified by misfortune, failure, or humiliation, preferring instead to be disgraced, victimized, or even ruined. Driven by a "success neurosis," they experience favorable outcomes as producing anxiety and guilt, not pleasure and happiness.

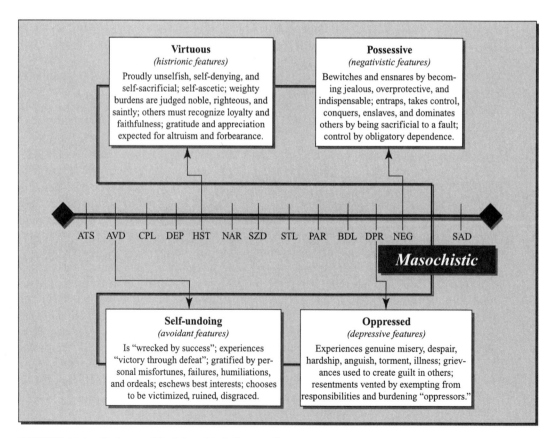

FIGURE 15.1 Variants of the Masochistic Personality.

Rather than suffer success, **self-undoing** masochists search out failure or punishment, subtly reversing their good fortune. Seemingly striving hard for accomplishment, they either stop just short of its attainment or manufacture some means of proving themselves unable to follow through. Covertly, they are gratified by their own defeat (Schneider, 1923/1950). Fearing things will suddenly turn sour, they would rather be pitied as an unfortunate victim of circumstance than as someone who had striven hard but failed. Failure may bring on a sense of relief that they must no longer live up to some standard. As such, they combine aspects of the masochistic and avoidant personalities.

The Possessive Masochist

Like other masochists, **possessive** masochists give constantly of themselves. However, they are unable to let go of their attachments. Instead, they become so indispensable and self-sacrificing that others are unable to withdraw from them without feeling incredibly cruel. Others become entrapped and dominated by a dependency driven by the fulfillment of their every need. Through ostentatious sacrifices, possessive masochists intrude into the daily affairs of their children, spouses, friends, and peers, meddling in activities, romance, occupation, and anywhere else they can obtain a foothold. Ostensibly altruistic acts create grounds for inducing guilt in others, which may be used to prevent them from distancing or ending the relationship. Mates are overprotected and jealously guarded, bribed for love, and controlled through guilt. In effect, they become self-sacrificing vampires whose kindness bleeds their victims dry.

The Oppressed Masochist

As a combination of the depressed (see later in this chapter) and masochistic personalities, **oppressed** masochists mope around complaining of their terrible condition but end by saying, "But don't let my suffering make you worry about me; do what is best for you." In one voice, they disavow any need for assistance and explain that they do not want to burden others, yet present themselves as having suffered the slings and arrows of outrageous misfortune. Anyone who comes to their aid eventually feels emotionally drained and guilty, made to feel as if moving on with his or her own life was an abandonment. Hypochondriacal manipulations may come to the fore when no other method of gaining love and dependence seems available. Becoming a sorrowful invalid is a rather pathetic solution, a genuine but self-created suffering that forces others to be caring and nurturing. Oppressed masochists do not necessarily enjoy their suffering; their discomforts are merely an instrumentality designed to secure pity and assistance.

The Virtuous Masochist

As a combination of the histrionic and masochistic personalities, **virtuous** masochists are proudly unselfish and self-sacrificial. Self-denial, asceticism, and stoic tolerance of adversity are seen as noble and righteous, a sign of purity and saintliness, the glorification of misery. Rather than accept the inferior status of other masochists, they assert their specialness by sacrificing themselves completely to others or for some meritorious cause, all the while manipulating circumstances so that their good deeds are open to public view.

If others withdraw their attention or distance their emotional bond, the masochist may complain that they are ungrateful and thoughtless and should remember that the masochist has been faithful and giving. Superficial altruism may occasionally give way

FOCUS ON VICTIM BEHAVIOR

Psychopathology of Victims of Aggression

Does Passivity Lead to Victimization?

Self-defeating personality disorder (called the masochistic personality in this text) was dropped from the *DSM-IV* as a diagnostic category. The decision came after considerable debate over the viability and clinical utility of the construct (Fiester, 1991). Many authors, in fact, have argued that the disorder was dropped for essentially political reasons.

In spite of the decision by the Axis II committee, the masochistic personality has a long clinical tradition useful in describing the behavior of certain patients. Although passivity under conditions of threat may be an adaptive response and, therefore, should not be pathologized, some individuals seem to manifest vulnerabilities that incite aggression from others. In the interpersonal perspective, for example, the principle of complementarity holds that submission elicits dominance from others. Rather than eliminate the masochist from *DSM-IV,* it would have been wiser to have retained it in the appendix as a provisional disorder in need of further study.

How might such vulnerabilities arise? One possibility is child abuse (Chabrol et al., 1995). The literature on childhood victimization suggests that children chronically victimized by their peers suffer from deficits in self-esteem. Perhaps children with low self-esteem are unable to fight back for some reason or more readily become the focus of teasing or scapegoating. In fact, chronic victimization by peers during the school years is associated with a variety of adjustment problems (Egan & Perry, 1998). Studies have found that submissiveness and physical weakness, for example, may lead to increased victimization over time (Hodges, Malone, & Perry, 1997; Schwartz, Dodge, & Coie, 1993).

Egan and Perry (1998) tested two hypotheses: First, low self-regard promotes victimization by peers over time, and second, a child's level of self-regard modulates the impact of victimization. Results suggest that low self-regard, particularly when assessed as a child's self-perceived social competence within the peer group, contributes to victimization. Moreover, a sense of social failure and inadequacy among an individual's peers leads to increases in victimization over time. However, a sense of self-efficacy, measured as confidence in an individual's standing in the peer group, serves to protect at-risk children from being victimized.

From this perspective, masochistic behavior in adults could be seen as being on a continuum with low self-regard within the peer group. As perceived competence within the peer group decreases and self-regard declines, the individual at first becomes the object of minor levels of victimization. With further declines, however, victimization grows, until finally a sort of identification with the aggressor takes place. Instead of trying to escape punishment, victims see themselves as being so contemptible that such treatment is their due. Masochism, then, could be seen as a maladaptive adjustment to extreme social inadequacy.

to self-congratulatory pride, and past good deeds may be used to justify a sense of being entitled to emotional support from others. Even when they get their way, however, a low sense of self-worth continues to lurk just below the surface, a consciousness that the appreciation of others is manipulated rather than genuine. At times, they may also exhibit features of the dependent personality.

EVOLUTIONARY NEURODEVELOPMENTAL PERSPECTIVE

Psychodynamically, the masochistic seems to run counter to the pleasure principle. Freud went through multiple conceptualizations of the masochist in his lifetime, and later analysts have expanded his work in many directions. Object relations suggests many pathways of possible development for the masochist and that there is no one, single masochistic personality. Interpersonally, masochists assume that others will try to beat them down, so they come to relationships already beaten down waving a white flag and presenting no challenge. Cognitively, masochists find themselves caught between hope and fear and tend to completely reinterpret past events. They also tend to use self-pity as a way of comforting themselves when others don't appreciate their suffering. The evolutionary approach incorporates all of these perspectives; more specifically, masochistic personalities are conceived as being reversed on the pleasure-pain polarity, thus signifying that the individual experiences what is emotionally painful as a means of fulfilling his or her survival aims. Discomfort and abuse may be sought for many different reasons.

The danger of being totally abandoned in a punitive world generates greater anxiety than to be attached to another when such negative consequences are being experienced. Unable to understand the source of the noxious experience, the infant has learned to feel more secure when it is close to or clings onto an attachment object, albeit a frequently rejecting and hostile one. Such patterns are likely to be intensified when the punitive parent is inconsistent in its ministrations. At times, parents such as these are likely to be frustrating, depriving, or rejecting and, at other times, guiltily oversolicitous and possessively nurturing. The grounds for developing these masochistic inclinations are only further strengthened by this form of vacillatory behavior.

Parental support and encouragement may not be forthcoming for achievements and autonomy. For example, children who receive nonambivalent parental affection and support *only* when they are ill, injured, or deficient are likely to conclude that they not only are defective and incompetent but also are loved and encouraged only when things are problematic or go wrong. Further, they learn that they can deflect otherwise hostile and critical parents by enacting deficiencies or illnesses on their own. Hence, if parents exhibit affection and attention only when the child is suffering or handicapped, that child will learn willingly to appear disadvantaged or ill as an instrumentally effective style of behavior, an attitudinal orientation that sets the seeds for what ultimately takes the shape of masochistic behaviors.

In its extreme form, such children may actually harm themselves—banging their body against hard objects, burning themselves, intentionally falling down stairs or off porches—enacting anything that intensifies their public pain and suffering. Such acts serve to ward off further physical punishment, but they also give these children what little power they can gain for themselves, even if only to take charge over their own hurtful experiences. In this perverse way, these children find some small sphere with which they can undo their parents' domination. Finding this niche of self-control may provide the basis of the future masochist's "pleasurable" self-abusive behaviors. In the following sections, we contrast the masochist with related personalities and explore pathways to symptom expression. Table 15.1 presents a review of the total masochist.

Contrast with Related Personalities

Masochists share numerous traits with other personality disorders. Both depressives and masochists live under a heavy burden of oppressive guilt, suffering from an overly

TABLE 15.1   The Masochistic Personality: Functional and Structural Domains

Functional Domains		*Structural Domains*	
	Abstinent		***Undeserving***
Expressive Behavior	Presents self as nonindulgent, frugal, and chaste; is reluctant to seek pleasurable experiences, refraining from exhibiting signs of enjoying life; acts in an unpresuming and self-effacing manner, preferring to place self in an inferior light or abject position.	**Self-Image**	Is self-abasing, focusing on the very worst personal features, asserting thereby that self is worthy of being shamed, humbled, and debased; feels that self has failed to live up to the expectations of others and, hence, deserves to suffer painful consequences.
	Deferential		***Discredited***
Interpersonal Conduct	Distances from those who are consistently supportive, relating to others when self can be sacrificing, servile, and obsequious, allowing, if not encouraging, them to exploit, mistreat, or take advantage; renders ineffectual attempts of others to be helpful and solicits condemnation by accepting undeserved blame and courting unjust criticism.	**Object-Representations**	Object-representations are composed of failed past relationships and disparaged personal achievements, of positive feelings and erotic drives transposed into their least attractive opposites, of internal conflicts intentionally aggravated, of mechanisms for reducing dysphoria being subverted by processes that intensify discomfort.
	Diffident		***Inverted***
Cognitive Style	Hesitant to interpret observations positively for fear that, in doing so, they may not take problematic forms or achieve troublesome and self-denigrating outcomes; as a result, there is a habit of repeatedly expressing attitudes and anticipations contrary to favorable beliefs and feelings.	**Morphologic Organization**	Because of a significant reversal of the pain-pleasure polarity, morphologic structures have contrasting and dual qualities—one more or less conventional, the other its obverse—resulting in a repetitive undoing of affect and intention, of a transposing of channels of need gratification with those leading to frustration, and of engaging in actions that produce antithetical, if not self-sabotaging, consequences.
	Exaggeration		***Dysphoric***
Regulatory Mechanism	Repetitively recalls past injustices and anticipates future disappointments as a means of raising distress to homeostatic levels; undermines personal objectives and sabotages good fortunes so as to enhance or maintain accustomed level of suffering and pain.	**Mood/Temperament**	Experiences a complex mix of emotions, at times anxiously apprehensive; at others, forlorn and mournful, to feeling anguished and tormented; intentionally displays a plaintive and wistful appearance, frequently to induce guilt and discomfort in others.

Note: Shaded domains are the most salient for this personality prototype.

self-critical conscience. Depressives, however, feel overwhelmed by their troubles, are resigned to their suffering, and are often satisfied to ruminate alone. In contrast, the masochist requires a partner, a persecutor, and will create one when necessary by exaggerating ordinary human conflicts, investing others with hidden motives, and then reacting with either indignation, a feature shared with the paranoid (McWilliams, 1994), or massive self-pity. Moreover, masochism often hides a sadistic purpose that the depressive lacks: The persecutor must be persecuted for being the persecutor. Acting out their conflicts gives masochists a greater sense of energy than is possessed by the lethargic depressive.

Comparisons and contrasts can also be made with the dependent, compulsive, and borderline personalities. Both the masochist and dependent are submissive, overtly noncompetitive, and bond parasitically to their partner. Dependents, however, return affection with affection and give of themselves to further strengthen their enmeshments. In contrast, masochists give their all to put their dedication on public view, capitalize on their own self-pity, cast the recipients of their kindnesses in the role of being insufficiently appreciative, or else achieve a super-enmeshment that cannot be denied. Both masochists and compulsives have strong underlying guilt feelings. The masochist, however, elicits punishment, whereas the compulsive greatly fears it. Finally, both masochists and borderlines sometimes share a tendency toward self-mutilation. Masochists, however, mutilate to undo their own guilt, whereas borderlines mutilate more to confirm their existence and forestall identity diffusion. Moreover, borderlines react frantically to the possibility of abandonment, whereas masochists sometimes use abandonment either to confirm their low self-worth and evoke self-pity or to display further evidence of their misfortune to others.

Pathways to Symptom Expression

Masochistic personalities are vulnerable to a number of Axis I disorders. As always, it is important to remember that there is a logic that connects the personality pattern with its associated Axis I syndromes. As with depressives, masochists frequently experience the chronic gloom of dysthymia. Following rejection, these feelings may escalate into a major depression and then seem to subside again into the slow torment characteristic of the personality.

In part, depression may be used instrumentally to elicit sympathy from others, particularly where it can be attributed to dashed hopes and tragic self-sacrifice. Even the virtuous masochist, whose reaction formation trades suffering for the mantle of righteousness, sometimes deflates under the worldview that life's punishments are intrinsically cruel and unusual. A diffuse anxiety may be mixed with these depressive feelings.

Like the dependent and depressive, the masochist is highly vulnerable to fears of loss and abandonment. Particularly where they have made themselves exclusively dependent on a mate or caretaker for basic survival, they are likely to fear that desperate self-sacrificial efforts are not sufficient to protect them against personal loss. States of panic may also emerge under these conditions, especially when the attachments needed to maintain their stability are in serious jeopardy.

Finally, physical symptoms and illnesses that lack adequate medical foundation may be used to evoke sympathy from others, solidify unstable attachments, reduce criticism and hostility from others, exact sadistic revenge by further burdening unhappy caretakers, or even placate their own guilty feelings as a symbolic self-flagellation.

The Sadistic Personality

When most of us think of sadism, we think of either the violent psychopath or the use of dominance and pain to accentuate sexual pleasure. But there is a difference between sadistic behavior and a **sadistic personality.** Although psychopaths can be instrumentally aggressive and hostile to the point of murder, only when the knowledge that others are suffering gives the individual pleasure does behavior become sadistic. And only when the inflicting of psychological or physical pain becomes the organizing principle for life does the individual become a sadistic personality. Assault committed during robbery, for example, is one thing; torturing someone for no apparent reason is quite another. Intentionality is thus core to the definition of the construct.

As with masochism, the acceptance of a sadistic personality has waxed and waned over time. The term **sadism** was coined by Krafft-Ebing (1867, 1937) in response to the works of the famous French author, the Marquis de Sade, who derived sexual pleasure by dominating others and causing them pain. Krafft-Ebing defined sadism as "the experience of sexual, pleasurable sensations (including orgasm) produced by acts of cruelty, bodily punishment, afflicted on one's own person or when witnessed in others, be they animals or human beings" (1937, p. 80). Furthermore, he held that the "innate desire to humiliate and hurt" (p. 82) was characteristic of all humans. In claiming that the origins of sadism extend beyond the merely sexual, Krafft-Ebing was only recognizing what human beings have known for centuries: There exists a certain class of persons for whom the ability to aggressively inflict psychological and physical suffering is not a means to an end, but an end in itself.

Though well known to history and contemporary society, the sadistic personality nevertheless appears only in the appendix of the third revised edition of the *DSM,* published in 1987, as a provisional personality disorder requiring further study. The intent was to describe a long-standing, maladaptive pattern of cruel, demeaning, and aggressive behavior, usually seen in forensic settings and distinct from other personality disorders (Fiester & Gay, 1991), particularly the antisocial. Unfortunately, the disorder was not continued in *DSM-IV.* In part, it was dropped because of scientific concerns, such as the relatively low prevalence rate of the disorder in many settings. However, there were also political reasons. Physically abusive, sadistic personalities are most often male, and it was felt that any such diagnosis might have the paradoxical effect of legally excusing cruel behavior.

As an introduction to the sadistic personality, consider the case of Chuck (see Case 15.2). Like many sadistic personalities, Chuck has found a niche for himself in a job that naturally allows him to make life difficult for others. If he gets to inflict some gratuitous suffering along the way, Chuck will tell you that that's just part of his job. Indeed, he is good at what he does, a fact that no doubt won him his supervisory role in the first place. But that's the problem. Everyone would like work to be fun, but Chuck finds his job gratifying in pathological ways (see criterion 4). He gets a rush from intimidating others into handing over their money, almost as if he had a personal score to settle (see criterion 6). Like other sadistic personalities, he intimidates others into doing what he wants. For example, he sometimes "pays visits" to customers who aren't sufficiently respectful. Worse, he lies about the legal limits of his role (see criterion 5), frightening people by claiming that he can take away their home if they don't pay. If they don't give in, he keeps calling back and counts down the days to keep the pressure on. Once, he

Chuck is a middle-level supervisor for a debt-collection agency. He is good at what he does, and he enjoys his work. He is here because of a bad evaluation, one Chuck believes was rigged by his own supervisor to prevent Chuck from taking his job, a feat in which Chuck feels confident in succeeding.[1] The evaluation claims that Chuck is too hard on his subordinates, specifically, that he disciplines them publicly, and does so deliberately to humiliate them. ← ②

With great zeal, Chuck pronounces himself a fair supervisor, but emphasizes that no one is going to slack off on his watch. He expects a full day from everyone, with no chatter, no down time, no small talk, no coming in late, and no excuses for not getting assigned work done. "I don't work with problem employees. I pressure them until they work, and if they don't have the good sense to quit, then I find reason to fire them!" he says, smirking. "Not everyone can do this kind of work," Chuck says, almost glowing, "but it's made for me. I love making people do their job, but I get the biggest rush from collecting debt. I collect more debt than anyone." Though his job is usually done on the phone, he confided that has in fact "paid visits" to customers who are not sufficiently respectful of his efforts. ← ③ ← ⑥ ← ④ ← ⑥

Chuck was born in South Boston to a fiercely religious Italian family, the fifth of six children. He notes proudly that his family "had no goddamn idea what to do with me." His four sisters are described as "virgins that should be in a nunnery." His only brother has always been actively involved with the church, and considered joining the seminary, but decided to teach instead. "I had no such ambitions," Chuck states, "and the family always looked down on me." He notes sarcastically that "there was so damn much saintliness in our family that God must have decided to throw in a devil, me, to test their faith." He smiles at that idea, and goes on to describe himself as a "tough little fucker" who was first a problem in school, then a problem because he was never in school, then a juvenile delinquent with a talent for fighting. "My smart mouth got me in a lot of trouble when I was young. That's the reason I'm so damn good at my job." He still studies weapons, and collects books on war. ← ⑧

Chuck's relationship with his family is distant. He has never married but boasts about the several girlfriends he "services." His life seems centered on his work, where manipulative aggressiveness is not only approved, but rewarded. Chuck sees himself as an "enforcer of the law" and is somehow righteously empowered by this egotistical interpretation. Chuck described one case with great satisfaction where he so completely intimidated a debtor that she fled completely across the country. "Sometimes, I tell them we can put a lien on their home and take it away, even though there's no such thing," he boasts. "Then I keep calling them back and count down the days." He does not perceive his behavior to be a problem. ← ⑥ ← ⑤

[1] Numbers mark aspects of the case most consistent with *DSM* criteria, and do not necessarily indicate that the case "meets" diagnostic criteria in this respect.

Sadistic Personality Disorder *DSM-III-R* Criteria

A. A pervasive pattern of cruel, demeaning, and aggressive behavior, beginning by early adulthood, as indicated by the repeated occurrence of at least four of the following:

(1) has used physical cruelty or violence for the purpose of establishing dominance in a relationship (not merely to achieve some noninterpersonal goal, such as striking someone in order to rob him or her)

(2) humiliates or demeans people in the presence of others

(3) has treated or disciplined someone under his or her control unusually harshly, e.g., a child, student, prisoner, or patient

(4) is amused by, or takes pleasure in, the psychological or physical suffering of others (including animals)

(5) has lied for the purpose of harming or inflicting pain on others (not merely to achieve some other goal)

(6) gets other people to do what he or she wants by frightening them (through intimidation or even terror)

(7) restricts the autonomy of people with whom he or she has a close relationship, e.g., will not let spouse leave the house unaccompanied or permit teen-age daughter to attend social functions

(8) is fascinated by violence, weapons, martial arts, injury, or torture

B. The behavior in A has not been directed toward only one person (e.g., spouse, one child) and has not been solely for the purpose of sexual arousal (as in Sexual Sadism).

intimidated a woman so thoroughly that she fled across the country to get away from him, a story he recounts with great satisfaction.

Aggressive domination seems to be Chuck's only interpersonal strategy. He is a physically threatening person, and in his own way, he is very successful, though his approach has begun to backfire in the office. Just as he pressures the debtors, he pressures his subordinates. If someone slips out from under his thumb, he doesn't call that person aside into the privacy of his office and explain why his or her behavior is in error. Instead, he makes a public spectacle of intimidating, humiliating, and demeaning the person in front of the other workers (see criterion 2). Everyone must know that he is the boss—he sets down the rules. No one slacks off around Chuck, because he doesn't tolerate it. He imposes harsh discipline (see criterion 3) and weeds out supposed slackers by finding an excuse to fire them. Aggression is so much a part of Chuck that he even enjoys studying the instruments of aggression and books about war (see criterion 8).

Given the portrayal of Chuck, we are now in a position to approach additional issues that form the plan of this section. First, we compare normality and abnormality; then we move on to variations on the basic sadistic theme. Developmental hypotheses are also reviewed but are tentative for all personality disorders. Next, the section "Evolutionary Neurodevelopmental Perspective" shows how the existence of the personality disorder follows from the laws of evolution. Also included are a contrast between the sadistic and other personality disorders and a discussion of how sadistic personalities tend to develop Axis I disorders.

FROM NORMALITY TO ABNORMALITY

As a vampire who feeds on the suffering of others, the sadist is only rarely encountered in the course of everyday life. Nevertheless, sadistic traits and behaviors are common. Teasing, for example, travels under the guise of good-natured fun but is often intended to embarrass, shame, and ridicule. Sadistic traits have also been observed to covary within the normal range. For example, Millon et al. (1994) describe the **controlling** style—individuals who enjoy the power to direct and intimidate, to evoke obedience and respect. Tough and unsentimental, they make effective leaders by assigning tasks and coercing performance from subordinates. They also gain satisfaction by dictating and manipulating the lives of those around them.

Where cruelty is expressed more through emotional than physical abuse, many sadistic personalities are able to rationalize their actions and thus put themselves in a favorable light. Although others see them as impulsively aggressive and stubborn, for example, sadists may think of themselves as energetic, assertive, and realistic. What is dominating and callous to others is competitive and not overly sentimental to the sadist, who views kindness as weakness. By normalizing their pathological characteristics, sadistic personalities enhance their self-image of strength, power, and forthrightness.

Many do find a niche for themselves in roles where hardheadedness is required. Sadistic stereotypes that often cross the boundary between normality and pathology include the disciplinarian stepparent, whose strictness oppresses and suffocates; the puritanical preacher, whose hellfire sermons are deliberately designed to force the flock onto the straight and narrow; the authoritarian police officer, who gloats from behind the badge while writing your ticket; the petty bureaucrat, whose regulatory maze and eye for detail induce suicidal ideation; and the harping mother, who delights in making her children feel guilty about the sacrifices she has made (Leary, 1957). In every case, there is something about making someone else feel bad, powerless, or ashamed that gives the subject a perverse satisfaction.

Though the name is almost a contradiction, a sadistic personality style can also be developed by normalizing the diagnostic criteria of the *DSM-III-R*. Whereas the personality disorder establishes dominance through physical cruelty or violence (see criterion 1), the style does not, but instead uses an imposing physical presence as a means of pulling for respect in interpersonal transactions. Whereas the disordered individual humiliates and demeans others publicly (see criterion 2), those with the style simply enjoy an image of strength and hold this as part of their self-image. Whereas the disordered discipline those within their control unusually harshly (see criterion 3), the style is authoritative, not authoritarian. Whereas the disordered finds pleasure in the suffering of others (see criterion 4) for its own sake, those with the style feel gratified only where punishment was administered and justice was served. Whereas the disordered lies to inflict pain or harm (see criterion 5), those with the style do not, but they may not hesitate to smile when others become snared in their own deception. Whereas the disordered forces others to action through intimidation (see criterion 6), those with the style use their position of power for the greater good. Whereas the disordered restrict the freedom of those within their sphere of influence (see criterion 7), those with the style create rules and expect them to be followed, though within reasonable limits. Whereas the disordered are fascinated by the instruments or results of aggression, those with the style simply admire the potential of strength and its various symbols to evoke respect. For each of the contrasts applicable to Chuck, he falls more toward the pathological end.

VARIATIONS OF THE SADISTIC PERSONALITY

Not every sadistic personality is like Chuck, the debt collector. Most of the diagnostic criteria of the sadistic personality apply to Chuck, but not all. Other sadists combine the criteria in different ways, in different settings, and with a different history. Many have secondary personality characteristics that synthesize with the major pattern. Some of these are described in Figure 15.2. Actual cases may or may not fall into one of these combinations.

The Explosive Sadist

Most persons tend to become aggressive or hostile by degrees. In contrast, **explosive sadists** are distinguished for sudden eruptions of uncontrollable rage, frequently vented against members of their own family as safe targets. Explosive sadists appear to be coping competently until some unknown threshold is reached, after which they react instantaneously with abusive defiance and possibly physical violence. In contrast to other sadists, their displays of aggression are not used instrumentally to dominate others, but instead release pent-up feelings of frustration or humiliation. Neither do they conduct themselves in a surly and truculent manner. Many are hypersensitive to feelings of betrayal, or they may be deeply frustrated by the futility and hopelessness of life. Physical assaults are often the product of a verbally unskilled individual unable to express a reaction, who feels helpless to respond in any other way. Periodically under control, but lacking in psychic cohesion and, therefore, vulnerable to impulsive discharge, the explosive sadist represents a combination of the sadistic and borderline personalities.

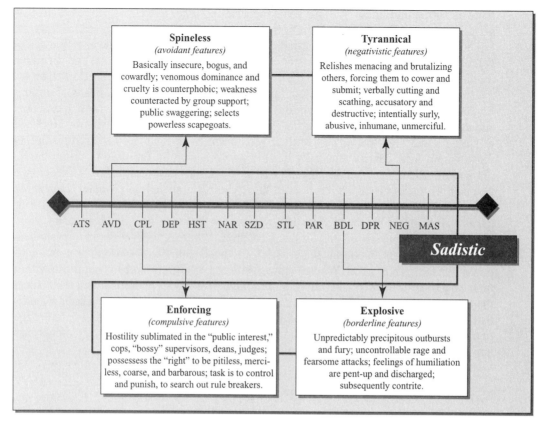

FIGURE 15.2 Variants of the Sadistic Personality.

The Tyrannical Sadist

The **tyrannical** sadist and the malevolent antisocial are perhaps the most frightening and cruel of the personality disorder subtypes. Some are physically assaultive, whereas others overwhelm their victims by unrelenting criticism, forceful anger, and vulgar and bitter tirades. Tyrannical sadists seem to relish the act of menacing and brutalizing others in the most unmerciful and inhumane ways. More than any other personality, they derive a deep satisfaction from creating suffering, observing its effects, and reflecting on their actions. Violence may be employed intentionally to inspire terror and intimidation. Resistance only seems to stimulate them more. Often calculating and cool, tyrannical sadists are selective in their choice of victims, identifying scapegoats who are easily intimidated and unlikely to react with violence in return. Frequently, their goal is not only to inflict terror but also to impress the audience with their total, unrestrained power. Most intentionally dramatize their surly behavior. Although these individuals are in many respects the purest form of the psychopathic sadist, they also exhibit characteristics of the negativistic or paranoid personalities.

The Enforcing Sadist

Every society charges certain agents with the power to enforce its rules to protect the common good. At their best, such individuals recognize the weight of their mission and balance social and individual needs, consider extenuating circumstances, and dispassionately judge intentions and effects before rendering a final verdict. In contrast, the **enforcing** sadist is society's sadistic superego, vested in punishment for its own sake, unable to be appeased. Military sergeants, certain cops, university deans, and the harsh judge all feel that they have the right to control and punish others. Cloaked within socially sanctioned roles, they mete out condemnation in the name of justice with such extraordinary force that their deeper motives are clear. Ever seeking to make themselves seem important, these sticklers for rules search out those guilty of some minor trespass, make them cower before the power of their position, and then punish them with a righteous indignation that reeks of repressed anger and personal malice. Despite their responsibility to be fair and balanced, such individuals are unable to put limits on the emotions that drive their vicious behaviors. Though not as troublesome, many minor bureaucrats also possess such traits. The enforcing sadist represents a combination of the sadistic and compulsive personalities.

The Spineless Sadist

Not all sadists are intrinsically dominant, cruel, and vicious like the tyrannical and enforcing subtypes. Some are deeply insecure, even cowardly. **Spineless** sadists are a combination of the avoidant and sadistic personalities; their private world is peopled by aggressive and powerful enemies. Attack can only be forestalled by creating an image of strength, a sense of mutual ensured destruction. For spineless sadists, aggressive hostility is a counterphobic act, designed to master their own inner fearfulness, while sending a message of strength to the public that they will not be intimidated. Displays of courage serve to divert and impress the audience with a façade of potency that says, "I will not be pushed around." Neither naturally mean-spirited nor intrinsically violent, the spineless sadist caricatures the swaggering tough-guy or petty tyrant. Having been repeatedly subject to physical brutality and intimidation, these individuals have learned to employ aggression instrumentally against others who seem threatening and abusive. Fearful of real danger, they strike first, hoping to induce a measure of fearfulness that forestalls further antagonisms. Many spineless sadists join groups that search for a shared scapegoat, a people or ethnic population set aside by the majority culture as a receptacle for hate and prejudice.

EVOLUTIONARY NEURODEVELOPMENTAL PERSPECTIVE

When Freudian theory had only one drive, it was difficult to explain the sadist. However, when he theorized the instinct of thanatos, sadism was readily explained. Later analysts extended the psychosexual model to include a form of aggressive sadism at each stage. Ego psychologists later argued that instead of being a part of sexual drive, sadistic acts give the sadist a feeling of superiority and omnipotence. They often use isolation, projection, rationalization, and displacement as defense mechanisms. Interpersonally, sadists regularly violate the rights of others, ridicule and taunt others, and generally try to control others. Cognitively, they are acutely sensitive to the psychological states of others even if they ignore their own vulnerabilities and sensitivities. They use this awareness to exploit people as effectively and cruelly as possible. Biologically, the sadist most likely shares features with the antisocial and paranoid personalities, such as low activation of aggressive energy and a hostile temperament. From an evolutionary perspective, the sadist, like the masochist, is more than the sum of its parts, so no one perspective has causal priority; instead, each integrates with, and reinforces, the others. Like the masochist, the sadistic personality is reversed on the pleasure-pain polarity. The sadist, however, expresses this reversal actively through malevolent intentions and outright violence, a hostile enmeshment that exists to create pain in relationships. The early environment of the sadist produces a sense of helplessness that is dealt with by taking omnipotent control of others in ways that lead to vicious circles in which hostility is expected and evoked. The sadist can also be thought of as a more pathological version of the negativistic personality, one in whom resentment at being controlled has given way to a desire to control in turn.

Although sadistic characteristics may be traced in part to biogenic dispositions, psychogenic factors will shape the content and direction of these dispositions; moreover, psychogenic influences often are sufficient in themselves to prompt these behaviors. The following hypotheses focus on the role of experience and learning, but remember that, as far as personality patterns are concerned, biogenic and psychogenic factors interrelate in a sequence of complex interactions.

Infants, who for constitutional reasons are cold, sullen, testy, or otherwise difficult to manage, are likely to provoke negative and rejecting reactions from their parents. It does not take long before a child with this disposition is stereotyped as a "miserable, ill-tempered, and disagreeable little beast." Once categorized in this fashion, momentum builds up, and we may see a lifelong cycle of parent-child feuding.

Parental hostilities may stem from sources other than the child's initial disposition; for example, children often are convenient scapegoats for displacing angers that have been generated elsewhere. Thus, in many cases, a vicious circle of parent-child conflict may have its roots in a parent's occupational, marital, or social frustrations. Whatever its initial source, a major cause for the development of a sadistic personality pattern is exposure to parental cruelty and domination.

Hostility breeds hostility, not only in generating intense feelings of anger and resentment on the part of the recipient but, perhaps more importantly, in establishing a model for vicarious learning and imitation. It appears to make little difference as to whether a child desires consciously to copy parental hostility; mere exposure to these behaviors, especially in childhood when alternatives have not been observed, serves as an implicit guide as to how people feel and relate to one another. Thus, impulsive or physically brutal parents arouse and release strong counter feelings of hostility in their children; moreover, they demonstrate in their roughshod and inconsiderate behavior both a model for imitation and an implicit sanction for similar behaviors to be exhibited whenever the child feels anger or frustration.

Sadists go out of their way to denigrate any values that represent what they themselves did not receive in childhood. In its stead, the future sadist asserts that the only true philosophy of life is one guided by living for the moment, discharging one's hostile feelings, and distrusting the so-called goodwill of others.

Although warmth and sensitivity are usual parts of most intimate encounters, nascent sadists view such encounters as likely preludes to later humiliations and the ultimate control by another. Hence, whatever its possibilities may have been, this usually reinforces the future sadist's suspiciousness and wish to maintain control over new relationships.

Table 15.2 summarizes the sadistic personality in terms of eight clinical domains. Contrasts with other personality constructs are examined in the following section, followed by a sketch of its Axis I vulnerabilities.

TABLE 15.2   The Sadistic Personality: Functional and Structural Domains

Functional Domains		*Structural Domains*	
	Precipitate	**Self-Image**	***Combative***
Expressive Behavior	Is disposed to react in sudden abrupt outbursts of an unexpected and unwarranted nature; recklessly reactive and daring, attracted to challenge, risk, and harm, as well as unflinching, undeterred by pain, and undaunted by danger and punishment.		Is proud to characterize self as assertively competitive, as well as vigorously energetic and militantly hardheaded; values aspects of self that present pugnacious, domineering, and power-oriented image.
	Abrasive	**Object-Representations**	***Pernicious***
Interpersonal Conduct	Reveals satisfaction in intimidating, coercing, and humiliating others; regularly expresses verbally abusive and derisive social commentary, as well as exhibiting vicious, if not physically brutal, behavior.		Internalized representations of the past are distinguished by early relationships that have generated strongly driven aggressive energies and malicious attitudes, as well as by a contrasting paucity of sentimental memories, tender affects, internal conflicts, shame, or guilt feelings.
	Dogmatic	**Morphologic Organization**	***Eruptive***
Cognitive Style	Is strongly opinionated and close-minded, as well as unbending and obstinate in holding to preconceptions; exhibits a broad-ranging authoritarianism, social intolerance, and prejudice.		Despite a generally cohesive morphologic structure composed of routinely adequate modulating controls, defenses and expressive channels, surging powerful and explosive energies of an aggressive and sexual nature threaten to produce precipitous outbursts that periodically overwhelm and overrun otherwise competent restraints.
	Isolation	**Mood/Temperament**	***Hostile***
Regulatory Mechanism	Can be cold-blooded and remarkably detached from an awareness of the impact of own destructive acts; views objects of violation impersonally, as symbols of devalued group devoid of human sensibilities.		Has an excitable and irritable temper that flares readily into contentious argument and physical belligerence; is cruel, mean-spirited and fractious, willing to do harm, even persecute others to get own way.

Note: Shaded domains are the most salient for this personality prototype.

Contrast with Related Personalities

The sadistic personality shares major traits with a number of other personality disorders. Negativistic and sadistic personalities share strong resentment and anger that often lead to overt hostility. They never forget past wrongs done them. Moreover, negativists often seem covertly sadistic in the way they frustrate and obstruct others.

In contrast to the sadist, however, negativists are deeply ambivalent about issues of love and loyalty. They seek fusion with others and become aggressive as a response to disappointment, sensing that their precious offering of themselves has been taken for granted or, worse, thrown away for another. Nevertheless, negativists still have a shaken faith that life can be turned around, and a rewarding existence is not impossible. If love could be ensured, all would be forgiven. For this reason, they vacillate between covert aggression and genuine helpfulness, often making them seem emotionally erratic. In contrast, sadists are hell-bent on inflicting pain on others, on spoiling their lives, and on making them kneel down under absolute control. Their mantra is: Dominate or be dominated. Negativists react to a sense of loss for what could have been; sadists feel that others' pain is their gain.

Sadistic and antisocial personalities are indifferent to the rights of others and often use aggression instrumentally, but for different reasons. The sadist uses aggression to secure dominance and is concerned that others be intimidated and know that it is the sadist who is the source of their suffering. In contrast, antisocials may be greedy and grasping, but their joy lies in the having. Aggression is a means to an end, not an end in itself, as with the sadist. Moreover, many antisocials are able to delay gratification, for example, in the service of swindling others out of their money. Sadists are generally more direct. Their joy is that others know that they are controlled and finally resign themselves to a position of weakness.

The sadistic personality also shares important traits with a number of other patterns. For example, both sadistic and paranoid personalities expect hostility from the social environment, so much so that they sometimes seethe with a hostility that seems barely contained. Further, both project their own aggressive impulses and interpret ambiguous messages as being belligerent or insulting, and both place a premium on autonomy and realism, even though the paranoid's worldview is highly distorted. However, whereas sadists wish to go forth and subdue, paranoids are walled off. Their hostility is reactive to slights and injustices for which they believe others are responsible. The narcissistic and sadistic personalities often share a sense of omnipotence, but for different reasons. Narcissists are grandiose about their own talent and brilliance. Other persons are often exploited in a way that seems sadistic to the observer. However, narcissists expect others to service their needs and consider such special treatment justified by their superior ability. Here, a sense of omnipotence is derived primarily through observation of the self. In contrast, sadists use their control of others to signify omnipotence to both themselves and others. Everyone should know who is in control.

Pathways to Symptom Expression

Sadistic personalities are vulnerable to a number of Axis I disorders. As always, it is important to remember that there is a logic that connects the personality pattern with its associated Axis I syndromes. Symptoms are particularly likely to arise when the effectiveness of sadists' aggression or their position of dominance is threatened. Anxiety disorders may reflect fears of retribution or revenge, legal or otherwise. Because sadists monitor the helplessness of others as an indicator of omnipotence, they may experience feelings of worthlessness and depression as the formerly oppressed become empowered to resist their cruelty. They are also vulnerable to substance abuse, usually as a means of heightening their self-confidence, retrieving a sense of energy, or relieving a nagging sense of self-doubt. Explosive sadists may abuse alcohol as a means of dealing with feelings of guilt.

Because sadists see aggression as the fundamental human motive and so anticipate hostile counterattacks from others, they sometimes develop clinically significant paranoid fears that wax and wane, depending on their confidence and circumstances. Chuck, for example, believes that his lousy review is a setup to prevent him from taking his supervisor's job. Finally, sadists who are forced to withdraw socially, those whose power and authority are suddenly overturned, perhaps, sometimes develop delusional ideas, usually with a paranoid or persecutory flavor.

The Depressive Personality

Almost imperceptibly at first, then more and more, you begin to feel sad, empty, or irritable. Gradually, things that used to fascinate you are no longer interesting. Hobbies, favorite recreations, and spending time with the ones you love are no longer pleasurable and may even seem burdensome. The day becomes dominated by feelings of lethargy, being tired, run down, or overwhelmed by life. Your movements and mental processes may seem to move in slow motion, thoughts crawling like molasses. Concentration can be difficult. Problems that used to be solved quickly are no longer as easily thought through. You may spend hours worried about whether life will ever return to normal. You may have problems going to sleep at night or with waking up too early the next morning. You might even seem to sleep all the time. You might gain weight or be so caught up in brooding that you forget to eat. You might feel worthless or guilty far in excess of what the circumstances should warrant. These symptoms are all associated with major depression, an Axis I disorder.

In contrast, there are people for whom "depressiveness" is more than a symptom. Although they do indeed feel sad and guilty, their emotional state emerges as an expectable consequence of an entire matrix of pervasive, long-standing characteristics. Always in a dejected and gloomy mood, they see themselves as inadequate and worthless. They submerge themselves in criticism for even minor shortcomings and tend to blame themselves when things go wrong. A pervasive pessimism leads them to anticipate the worst—to expect that life will always go wrong and never improve. Their days are spent brooding and worrying, ignoring the good and dwelling on the bad. Saturated with guilt, they wish that life could be different, but instead of taking the initiative, they berate themselves for missed opportunities and feel powerless to change their destiny. Such individuals may indeed be depressed, but their depression emerges from a way of thinking, feeling, and perceiving—a **depressive personality.**

Consider Evan, our next case study (see Case 15.3). Evan is making an attempt at therapy, but he's not the most optimistic person in the world. In fact, Evan doesn't know why he bothers anymore. His comment about five previous attempts is a way of setting expectations for his current effort, evidence of a pessimism that colors his whole outlook (see criterion 6). In one voice, he accuses his past therapists of not caring, but then he turns it around on himself by saying, "If I were someone else, I wouldn't like me either." Anyone else would recognize that the odds of getting five therapists in a row who didn't "care" are vanishingly small. Evan, however, first exaggerates the negative, then follows up with a globalized attribution in a one-two punch against the self (see criterion 3). Instead of focusing realistically on what is good and bad about himself, he seems to assert that he is all bad and, implicitly, that he will never be liked and no one will care about him. Later, he states that he knows his life is not right, and it is his fault. Not surprisingly, Evan has no enthusiasm for work, and it shows.

Pessimism and an inadequate, worthless self-image are only two of what for Evan are a matrix of personality problems. At night, he broods instead of sleeps, recycling his problems repeatedly in his mind (see criterion 4). His usual mood is determined by the words he uses to convey his outlook on life (see criterion 1). Things are "depressing,"

CASE 15.3

"I don't know why I bother," Evan says. "I've tried therapy five times before, but it never works out. Nothing ever works outs. I wasn't getting any better and the therapists don't really care. I don't really blame them, I guess. If I were someone else, I wouldn't like me either."[1] He called at the suggestion of a coworker at the video store, where he works part-time. His manager complains that he works slowly and shows no enthusiasm for customer relations. "Even the other guys are starting to avoid me," he says.

Evan seems focused on some inner wound. He is overweight and his skin looks pasty. He looks tired and complains of hours each night spent brooding instead of sleeping. His speaks slowly and uses words such as depressing, futile, and hopeless. The overall impression he creates is that this could well be the last time he may be able to muster up some hope for change.

Evan has almost no social support. He acknowledges a few acquaintances at the store where he works, but says that they cannot really be considered friends. When asked why this is, he maintains that he is fundamentally different from other people. For others, the world is an adventure, he states, but for him it is threatening, lonely, and disappointing. He believes others are frightened away because "they can sense, even smell, that I am not right, that I've fallen so far short of what could have been."

His words are forced out with great guilt. "I know it is my fault if my life is not right, but I just can't seem to do anything about it, I'm a worthless human being. I'm at my best when I'm zoned out in front of the TV," he continues. "That way, I can distract myself from the misery of who I am."

In addition to his job at the video store, Evan has been taking classes at the local community college off and on for the past 10 years. Nevertheless, he is still six credits short of an associate's degree. His C– average is attributed to difficulty concentrating, which makes reading a chore. "A single chapter seems like an eternity," he says. Worse, Evan states, "I have fallen so far short of what I wanted to do and be in life." He states again, "I can never make up for that lost time, I can never repair the damage, and the clock just keeps ticking. Sometimes, it's all I can think about."

Evan is the youngest of four children. All his siblings are older by at least nine years. "We don't have anything in common," he laments. "They're from a different generation, they don't understand me. I don't think they'd even miss me. They were a complete family before I got here, and they'll be a complete family if I was gone. That will never change." His father is a pilot for a major airline who never bonded with his son. His mother had a successful real estate career, "but she says she had to give that up for me." He is currently "disconnected" from his family, although they all live in the area. "They were not the family I was supposed to have," he observes. "I tried to keep in touch. When I first became depressed, things got a little better, but everyone seems to avoid me now."

[1] Numbers mark aspects of the case most consistent with *DSM* criteria, and do not necessarily indicate that the case "meets" diagnostic criteria in this respect.

Depressive Personality Disorder
DSM-IV Criteria

A. A pervasive pattern of depressive cognitions and behaviors beginning by early adulthood and present in a variety of contexts, as indicated by five (or more) of the following:

(1) usual mood is dominated by dejection, gloominess, cheerlessness, joylessness, unhappiness

(2) self-concept centers around beliefs of inadequacy, worthlessness, and low self-esteem

(3) is critical, blaming, and derogatory toward self

(4) is brooding and given to worry

(5) is negativistic, critical, and judgmental toward others

(6) is pessimistic

(7) is prone to feeling guilty or remorseful

B. Does not occur exclusively during Major Depressive Episodes and is not better accounted for by Dysthymic Disorder.

"futile," and "hopeless." Worse, Evan has almost no social support; he has acquaintances but no friends. For others, "the world is an adventure," but for Evan, it is "threatening, lonely, and disappointing." People are frightened away, he states, because "they can sense, even smell, that I am not right, that I've fallen so far short of what I could have been." More likely, Evan closes himself off because he feels guilty about not living up to expectations and becomes excessively self-conscious about his perceived shortcomings when he is around others. Because his presentation is accompanied by excessive guilt (see criterion 7), he may also feel too pathetic to deserve friends and feel that his loneliness and hopelessness are a just fate.

Given the portrait of Evan, we now approach additional issues that form the plan of this section. First, we compare normality and abnormality; then we move on to clinical variations on the basic depressive personality. Next, the section "Evolutionary Neurodevelopmental Perspective" shows how the existence of the personality disorder follows from the laws of evolution. Also included are a comparison between the depressive and other personality constructs and a discussion of how depressive personalities tend to develop Axis I disorders.

FROM NORMALITY TO ABNORMALITY

Characteristics of a normal-range depressive personality style can be developed by creating less extreme parallels to the diagnostic criteria described in the *DSM-IV.* Whereas the usual mood of the depressive personality disorder is typically gloomy or dejected (see criterion 1), the personality style is more reflective of the negative aspects of self and situation but is not so overcome by them that joy becomes an impossibility. Whereas the disordered individual has a self-image of incompetence, worthlessness, or inadequacy (see criterion 2), individuals with the style are simply more self-conscious of their standing relative to similar others but are able to take constructive initiative when necessary. Whereas the disordered is overly self-critical (see criterion 3), the style is aware of both positive and negative aspects of the self but tends to focus on the negative. Whereas the disordered broods and worries (see criterion 4), the style takes time to think things through from a realistic perspective. Whereas the disordered is sometimes overly critical and negativistic toward others (see criterion 5), those with the style are perturbed by those who need to exaggerate the good at the expense of what is realistic or tend to neglect to consider the effects of their behavior on others. Whereas the disordered is pessimistic (see criterion 6), the style is realistic, giving the negative its due. Whereas the disordered is excessively guilty and remorseful (see criterion 7), those with the style have a low threshold for apologizing for their conduct but are not obsessed by perceived shortcomings or failings. Evan falls more toward the pathological end.

VARIATIONS OF THE DEPRESSIVE PERSONALITY

Not every depressive personality is like Evan. The depressive often exhibits features of other personality disorders. The resulting moods and actions that these individuals manifest give a different coloration to the basic depressive pattern that makes them similar to, yet different from, cases like Evan. Such subtypes of the depressive personality are summarized in Figure 15.3. Actual cases may or may not fall into one of these combinations.

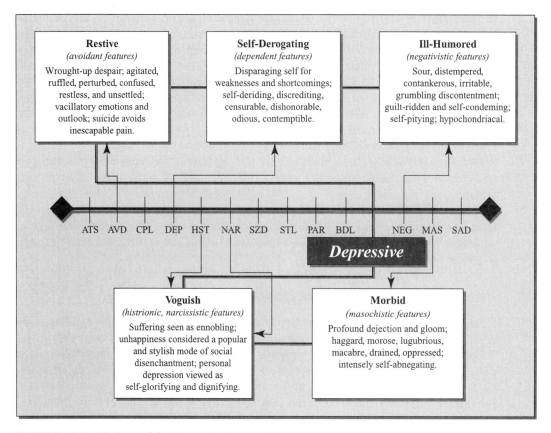

FIGURE 15.3 Variants of the Depressive Personality.

The Ill-Humored Depressive

As a combination of the depressive and negativistic personalities, the **ill-humored** subtype presents with grumbling discontent, endless complaints, and chronic irritability. Fears of bodily disease and illness are common. Such individuals act out their conflicts and ambivalent feelings, displaying bitterness and resentment alternating with periods of self-accusation and guilt. They find contentment in nothing and vacillate between tormenting themselves and turning their negativism against others, demanding that their complaints be heard. When others react by insisting that they give up their moody despair, the ill-humored are likely to become more forthright in oppressing others with their own bad feeling. For limited periods of time, they may become agitated, wring their hands, and pace about. In some cases, they exhibit hostile depressive complaints, bemoaning their sorry state and demanding attention to their manifold physical illnesses, pains, and incapacities. As Kretschmer (1925) has described them, they appear cold and selfish, irritable, and critical; they rejoice in the failures of others; and they never wish others the rewards and achievements of life.

The Voguish Depressive

As a mix of the depressive and histrionic or narcissistic patterns, the **voguish** depressive sees suffering as something noble. Both Schneider (1923/1950) and Kraepelin (1921) found that certain depressives display vanity and voguishness. This subtype asserts that only those gifted with special sensitivities have the capacity to feel with such depth and self-consciousness. By making pain the subject of contemplation, they find a philosophical refuge that affords them a status other depressives lack. Some display an aesthetic preoccupation, a way of dressing and living that gives stature to their unhappy moods. Using fashionable language and reading avant-garde authors, they create a perception of acute suffering and awareness that draws attention and evokes admiration from others. Popular modes of disenchantment are adopted as a means of attracting the interest of a certain fringe element for whom alienation from the mainstream is always the recurrent theme. If Evan were to develop a fascination with existentialism and wax philosophically about the futility of life, he would take on characteristics of this subtype.

The Self-Derogating Depressive

The **self-derogating** variant of the depressive personality resembles the depressive-masochistic character (Kernberg, 1988). Such individuals exhibit extraordinary guilt that lurks just below the surface, together with a need to discharge this guilt through various forms of self-punishment. When conflicts with others arise, they anticipate abandonment, leading them to admit weaknesses and condemn themselves to deflect further criticism and secure help and support.

Actual loss of an instrumental surrogate or significant attachment figure almost invariably prompts severe dejection. Feelings of resentment and hostility, which might provoke actual abandonment, are turned inward and thereby transformed into expressions of self-criticism or reacted against as verbalizations of remorse. Such maneuvers decrease the individual's sense of self-worth, but at least temper the anger of others and prompt them to react in ways that make the subject feel worthy and loved. Hostile feelings and resentments are thus disguised because acts of self-derogation shift to others the responsibility to respond and induce guilt in others.

The Morbid Depressive

As a combination of the masochistic and dependent patterns, the **morbid** depressive exhibits a deep depressive paralysis that frequently blends into an Axis I clinical depression. Morbid depressives exhibit deep feelings of gloom and profound dejection. They slump down, turn their gaze away from others, and hold their heads like a heavy millstone. They may lose weight and look haggard and drained or awaken several hours too early, their mind filled with oppressive thoughts and a growing dread of the new day.

A vague dread of impending doom, an utter helplessness, a pervasive sense of guilt, and resignation to their hopeless fate are common. Such reports are a by-product of the belief that they are incapable of coping with their problems, a consequence of their dependent features. When not lost in deep gloom, morbid depressives engage in a withering self-contempt, demeaning everything about themselves and seeing only the worst of what they have done in life. Plagued with a relentless and obsessive pessimism, they assert that things will always get worse and never get better. They are outcasts, doomed to suffer forever as victims of fate and their own helplessness. Evan, our video clerk, has many of these qualities.

The Restive Depressive

As a mix of the depressive and avoidant personalities, **restive** depressives exhibit anguish and agitation. Thoughts about the problems others have caused them produce a perturbed discontent that rarely shows itself in overt behavior. Instead, restive depressives restrain their irritability by turning it inward, manifesting despondency and disaffection with themselves. They are nervous, fretful, and distracted, and their emotional life consists of a sequence of brittle moods, usually short-lived and intense. Unable to get a firm hold on their feelings, they may commit self-destructive acts, expressed either directly through violent suicide or indirectly through severe alcohol or drug abuse. Despairing that anything in life will ever be rewarding, they feel obligated to do something to express a deeply pessimistic view of both life and themselves. Feeling defeated and helpless, seeing no way to restore their participation in the good life, many of these restive types conclude that they must rid themselves of the inescapable suffering of their painful existence. Suicide becomes the final act that demonstrates that they can indeed control their lives.

FOCUS ON RESEARCH

Depressive Personality or Dysthymia?

Are Dysthymia and Depressive Personality Synonymous?

In the *DSM-IV,* the depressive personality is not classified with the other Axis II disorders, but instead is listed in the appendix as a disorder requiring further research. The depressive is controversial, in part, because its proper location in the multiaxial system is uncertain. Some suggest that it should be considered a characterological variant of depression. Here, pessimism and a temperamental disposition to negative affective states would create a vulnerability to depression as a mood disorder. Others argue that the depressive personality is redundant—that it merely reflects the influence of a background depression so long-standing and pervasive that its symptoms have become crystallized as trait-like features. The usual objections involve the perceived overlap between depressive personality and dysthymia and the clinical utility of the new construct (Sherman, 1995).

The results of the Mood Disorders Field Trials (M. Keller, Hanks, & Klein, 1996) go a long way in clarifying this controversy. Although there was substantial overlap between subjects diagnosed as dysthymic and those diagnosed as having a depressive personality, many dysthymics did not meet criteria for depressive personality. Thus, the overlap was not complete. In fact, the proportion of those with depressive personality disorder who had never met criteria for dysthymia was high (Shea & Hirschfeld, 1996), providing strong support that the depressive personality describes a domain of functioning that cannot be accounted for by dysthymia alone.

Furthermore, a personality dimension described as negative affectivity (Tellegen, 1985; D. Watson & Tellegen, 1985) captures many of the experiences of those diagnosed as depressive personalities. Also called neuroticism, negative affectivity refers to a persistent proneness to negative experiences, namely moodiness, nervousness, stress, a low threshold for becoming annoyed or irritated, excessive worry, and difficulty concentrating. High scores on this dimension contribute negatively to subjective well-being (DeNeve & Cooper, 1998). Taken together, the Field Trials, along with research using measures of negative affectivity and neuroticism, point to a crucial taxonomic distinction: The disposition to experience negative emotional states must be separated from the emotional states themselves. The first is an Axis II disorder; the second belongs to Axis I.

EVOLUTIONARY NEURODEVELOPMENTAL PERSPECTIVE

From a biological perspective, it is likely that there are genetic factors and inherited neurotransmitter profiles that play a role in the development and maintenance of the depressive personality although more research needs to be done before we understand the complex ways in which these interact with life experiences. The psychodynamic perspective offers the notion that there is an impoverishment of ego that leads to melancholia. These individuals represent themselves as worthless, incapable of achievement, and deserving to be cast out and punished. Object relations theorists emphasize the themes of self-criticism and vulnerability to object loss for the depressive. Bowlby's well-known attachment literature (e.g., Bowlby, 1969) has also shed significant light on how the depressive develops. The interpersonal perspective argues that they correctly perceive that they are being rejected by others but do not recognize how their behavior causes others to withdraw. Depressives' interpersonal style leads to and perpetuates their feelings of being inadequate and unworthy. Cognitively, depressives are pessimistic across every domain of their lives. Beck et al. (1990) propose that hopelessness and helplessness lie at the heart of the depressive personality and color not only the perceiving of new stimuli but also the retrieval of the memories.

In the evolutionary model (Millon, 1990; Millon & Davis, 1996), the depressive personality is referred to as the **passive-pain pattern.** Characteristics include glumness, pessimism, an inability to experience pleasure, and psychomotor retardation. In conjunction with a history of significant losses, there is a sense of having given up, of accepting despair, of resigning himself or herself to an anguished destiny fraught with misery and self-criticism, one in which personal fulfillment is no longer possible.

The inclination to experience a troubled life with depressive symptomatology is not necessarily maladaptive in all of its aspects. Such inclinations signify an ability to communicate helplessness and dependency that elicits nurturing attention and care. Hence, the disposition to become depressed may have been selectively reinforced to serve an important function in the course of evolution. Problematic in certain regards, this temperamental disposition may have enhanced the likelihood that those who deeply suffer the slings and arrows of life will likely elicit protective care to a greater extent than those who are incapable of expressing such feelings. In sum, depressiveness may not only stem from a fusion of biogenic and psychogenic sources but also reflect qualities that increase individual survival.

Contemporary studies suggest that genetic and neurochemical factors play a distinct though modest role in various depressive personality subtypes. Work in population and family studies, specifically those focused on twins and adoptees, suggest several biological markers of a depressogenic inclination. However, evidence gathered in numerous family studies indicates that there is considerable heterogeneity among depressive disorders, be they exhibited in a clinical syndrome or a personality disorder. This work suggests that there are numerous heterogeneous subtypes that may not differ genotypically; on the other hand, there may be genotypically distinct types that do not differ phenotypically.

It appears that depressive affect may be grounded at a very early stage in development. It is at this time that the child acquires experiences, through parental feeling and behavior, that its environment is receptive and caring or indifferent and distant. The child learns at this time to discriminate experiences of a pleasurable character from those more painful in nature. Fundamental feelings of security and attachment result from an adequate level of sensory gratification and nurturance. However, a failure to experience clear and unequivocal signs of warmth and acceptance at the sensory level may create fundamental feelings of insecurity, emotional detachment, and isolation.

A distinction should be made between the experiences of the depressively prone and the avoidantly prone child. In the depressive, we see parental distancing or indifference; in the avoidant, we see rejection and devaluation. The depressive infant lacks experiences of warmth and closeness; the avoidant does experience parental interaction, but it is of a deprecating and belittling nature. The depressive child learns to give up, since its efforts to bring forth the deficient warmth are unsuccessful.

The origins of depressive withdrawal are found not only in extraordinary circumstances such as those associated with total parental disengagement or death but also in lesser form among infants who lack important experiences of warmth and parental responsiveness. This may be seen in the less problematic parent-child relationships reported in the work of Bowlby (1969) and Mahler et al. (1975). Both recount circumstances in which the child is unable to experience the affection and consistent support of a significant maternal-like person. Bowlby's work describes studies of children and lower animals faced with troublesome separations from parental-like figures. Following initial protests and efforts to search for and retrieve the lost objects, the child gives up and withdraws into what Bowlby describes as despair and disorganization. Withdrawn and inactive, such children learn to make few demands on their environment, become emotionally detached rather than attached, conserve their energies, develop a generalized sense of hopelessness and, because of their limited capacities and immaturity, feelings of helplessness.

Given the preceding as a base, youngsters who are prone to depression approach adolescence with serious doubts concerning their potential appeal as a member of their gender. Anticipating disinterest or derogation from their peers, these youngsters cannot retreat to their homes seeking acceptance and understanding. Devaluing themselves and expecting to be further devalued by all segments of their social world, they turn inward to minister and pamper themselves, disinclined to venture forth to be further alienated and derided in peer-group relationships. Their lack of confidence in themselves and in what they will elicit interpersonally further reinforces the belief that they are unattractive persons who will be further humiliated by others.

Depressively prone youngsters not only allow themselves little pleasure but also are self-punitive and self-sadistic. Increasingly distressing though it may be to look into themselves, they continue to find the reality of self to be despicable and condemnable. Wherever they go, the despised self is inherent, an ever-present and condemned existence. The result of such introspection disrupts their cohesion and uncovers a fragile psychic state that produces a chronic series of depressogenic feelings, experiences, and relationships.

Unlike the avoidant, who desperately seeks to avoid painful feelings of shame and humiliation, depressives passively accept what they view as no longer avoidable. As with the masochistic personality, depressives seem to desire suffering, perhaps more suffering than their history, circumstances, or actual personal failures would warrant. They exaggerate their misery, magnify imperfections, and accuse themselves in order to deepen and wallow in their own misery, all while eliciting the sympathy of others. Gradually, life dwindles into nothingness. A comparison and contrast with similar personality constructs follows. Table 15.3 presents a review of the total depressive pattern.

TABLE 15.3   The Depressive Personality: Functional and Structural Domains

Functional Domains		Structural Domains	
	Disconsolate	**Self-Image**	**Worthless**
Expressive Behavior	Appearance and posture convey an irrelievably forlorn, somber, heavyhearted, woebegone, if not grief-stricken quality; irremediably dispirited and discouraged, portraying a sense of permanent hopelessness and wretchedness.		Judges self of no account, valueless to self or others, inadequate and unsuccessful in all aspirations; barren, sterile, impotent; sees self as inconsequential and reproachable, if not contemptible, a person who should be criticized and derogated, as well as feel guilty for possessing no praiseworthy traits or achievements.
	Defenseless	**Object-Representations**	**Forsaken**
Interpersonal Conduct	Because of feeling vulnerable, assailable, and unshielded, will beseech others to be nurturant and protective; fearing abandonment and desertion, will not only act in an endangered manner, but seek, if not demand, assurances of affection, steadfastness, and devotion.		Internalized representations of the past appear jettisoned, as if life's early experiences have been depleted or devitalized, either drained of their richness and joyful elements or withdrawn from memory, leaving him or her to feel abandoned, bereft, and discarded, cast off, and deserted.
	Pessimistic	**Morphologic Organization**	**Depleted**
Cognitive Style	Possesses defeatist and fatalistic attitudes about almost all matters; sees things in their blackest form and invariably expects the worst; feeling weighed down, discouraged, and bleak, gives the gloomiest interpretation of current events, despairing as well that things will never improve in the future.		The scaffold for morphologic structures is markedly weakened, with coping methods enervated and defensive strategies impoverished, emptied and devoid of their vigor and focus, resulting in a diminished, if not exhausted, capacity to initiate action and regulate affect, impulse, and conflict.
	Asceticism	**Mood/Temperament**	**Melancholic**
Regulatory Mechanism	Engages in acts of self-denial, self-punishment, and self-tormenting, believing that he or she should exhibit penance and be deprived of life's bounties; there is not only a repudiation of pleasures, but also harsh self-judgments as well as self-destructive acts.		Is typically woeful, gloomy, tearful, joyless, and morose; characteristically worrisome and brooding; low spirits and dysphoric state rarely remit.

Note: Shaded domains are the most salient for this personality.

Contrast with Related Personalities

The depressive shares major traits with several other patterns. The schizoid, avoidant, and depressive personalities seem socially withdrawn and unable to find pleasure in life. Schizoids, however, lack a basic capacity to experience emotions of any kind with any intensity. Accordingly, they appear withdrawn because they lack affectionate feelings necessary for social bonding. In contrast, depressives feel deeply anguished. Obviously unhappy, depressives nevertheless understand the concept of happiness, whereas the schizoid cannot. Moreover, though depressives may withdraw from the social world, they are socially attached, meaning that certain relationships are valuable, have been valuable, or could be valuable to them.

Both avoidants and depressives often feel a sense of shame, fixate on their failures, and sometimes close themselves off from the world. Avoidants, however, desperately want to join socially but take the perspective of others in viewing themselves as intrinsically defective. In contrast, depressives just give up and accept their pathetic state as inevitable and irreversible. They withdraw because they lack the energy for social interactions or because they want to be alone in their misery.

The depressive also shares traits with the masochistic, negativistic, and borderline personalities. The depressive and masochistic are so similar that some authors view them as a single constellation, the depressive-masochistic character (Kernberg, 1988). Both share an obvious discontent. Nevertheless, depressives are best distinguished by their hopelessness and social withdrawal, whereas masochists, though evidently unhappy, participate in their social surrounds and create situations of setback or failure that compound their own misery.

Both the depressive and negativistic share an abiding pessimism, a feeling of personal misfortune, and a sense of being misunderstood and devalued, but for different reasons. Negativists feel that others overcontrol, depersonalize, and take advantage of them. Their pessimism and discontent are a direct reaction to the feeling that authority is improperly vested. In contrast, the pessimism and discontent of the depressive are far more broadly generalized. Moreover, the negativist fights back passive-aggressively, whereas the defeated depressive has no fight left.

The borderline personality is frequently dysphoric and depressed and, therefore, appears on the surface similar to the depressive personality. However, borderlines are intensely labile; their emotions may suddenly shift from love to hatred, for example. In contrast, the depressive is steadily and passively gloomy.

Pathways to Symptom Expression

As always, it is important to remember that there is a logic that connects the personality pattern with its associated Axis I syndromes. Depression and dysthymia should be the most common comorbid Axis I syndromes for the depressive personality. As noted previously, individuals with more depressive personality features should be more disposed to the development of major depressive episodes. Logically, the depressive personality is nothing if not a disposition toward being depressed. Because depression has numerous vegetative aspects, some individuals should exhibit a variety of vague somatic complaints, evidence of a preoccupation with bodily symptoms. Depressives who are especially prone to brooding may also show evidence of an anxiety disorder. The interpersonal perspective argues that symptoms should subside somewhat at the formation of new relationships and then increase as rejection mounts. As this occurs, self-esteem should decrease and feelings of worthlessness increase.

The Negativistic (Passive-Aggressive) Personality

Some people just seem unsure of which way to turn in life. Ever ambivalent, they vacillate between uneasy feelings of dependence and an equally uneasy desire for self-assertion. Simultaneously needy and independent, they agree to conform to requests for performance, but nevertheless have strong issues with authority and resent external control. Inevitably, they feel misunderstood, unappreciated, and disillusioned. As their discontent deepens, they begin to find fault with the way others treat them and engage in indirect or passive forms of behavioral and emotional protest. On the surface, they agree to follow through but then sabotage the expectations of others through procrastination, intentional inefficiency, shoddy workmanship, and subtle obstruction. Stubborn, uncooperative, contrary, nitpicking, sulking, pouting, and pessimistic, they dampen the spirits of those around them. Though they sometimes make genuine confessions of remorse, eventually they become sullen and oppositional once more. All despise and defy authority and seek to avenge their disillusionment by undermining anyone who would require something from them.

Such individuals are often called **passive-aggressive** personalities. In this chapter, **negativistic** is the preferred designation, a newer label that captures the broader elements of the total pattern. The pattern is perhaps best understood as being both similar and opposite to the compulsive. In terms of the evolutionary model, both are ambivalent patterns that struggle mightily with issues of obedience and defiance (Rado, 1959). The negativistic pattern, however, is actively ambivalent, whereas the compulsive is passively ambivalent. As such, compulsives follow a strategy of containment, suppressing their conflicts to appear self-controlled, perfectionistic, orderly, and morally scrupulous. In contrast, negativists work out their resentments on the surrounding world, but only in indirect ways, thus symbolizing their inability to break free of ambivalence and pursue a strategy of overt opposition.

Consider the case of Kim (see Case 15.4). Because Kim is presenting for therapy of her own free will, you would think that she wants to get the most out of the experience. But her personality keeps getting in the way (see criterion 1). Her first strategy is to transfer responsibility for therapy totally to the therapist. Asked what she would most like to change, she replies, "You're the doctor; how would I know what's going on?"; her aim is to create a lose-lose situation in which any further inquiry effectively calls the therapist's credentials into doubt. Essentially, Kim is implying, "As a doctor, you should know what the problem is, and if you don't, how can you call yourself a doctor?" If the therapist buys into this, no information can be gathered and therapy cannot proceed. If the therapist doesn't buy into this, the therapist is unworthy of his or her degree. The correct response would be some variant of, "Perhaps as more information comes to light, you and I can work collaboratively on the issues that emerge."

As the interview moves on, Kim adopts a new strategy: She overelaborates what she believes is irrelevant and underelaborates the relevant. She technically conforms to the requirements of the interview, but in the wrong way. Moreover, whenever the therapist offers some interpretation, Kim is now more than happy to produce relevant biographical information that refutes the hypothesis. Eventually, she concludes by saying, "I guess you don't know me any better than anyone else," an invitation to reduce the interview to an argument by provoking, "How could I, you won't tell me a damn thing!" from the interviewer. All of the previous in itself, however, is valuable diagnostic data— much more valuable than Kim would like it to be.

The subtle confrontation that Kim desires begins to subside only when the interviewer touches on deeper issues by asking if she has been coerced into coming (see criterion 4). Further diagnostic evidence now comes into view. Her complaint that the doctor doesn't understand her converges with a similar complaint about her husband, who "doesn't appreciate me, doesn't understand me," and just wants her to "fake nice" (see criterion 2). She states that she has come to therapy to "make amends for being

CASE 15.4

At the beginning of the clinical interview, it was obvious that Kim, age 23, was dissatisfied with her life.[1] When asked what she would most like to change, Kim exclaimed, "You're the doctor, how would I know what's going on!" As the interview wore on, a basic pattern became clear. Kim would overelaborate anything irrelevant to the treatment process, and underelaborate anything relevant.

Her claim of ignorance about her problems eventually proved to be a setup. As soon as the doctor would offer an interpretation of her problem, Kim would argue that that could not possibly be the case, or produce contradictory biographical information that had been previously withheld, all while blaming the doctor. "I guess you don't understand me any better than anyone else," she sighed. Sometimes her expression was more obviously sullen; sometimes her oppositionalism was concealed with a smile.

Because Kim obviously felt ambivalent about therapy, it was important to determine if she had been somehow "coerced" into coming. At this point, her manner abruptly changed. She acknowledged that she was not too happy at present and supposed she wanted therapy, to "make amends for being a such a bitch." As Kim gained some control over her emotions and allowed her resistance to subside somewhat, she stated that the first order of business would be fixing her relationship with her husband. She claimed that she needed more emotional space. "I must drive him crazy, but that's me," she said. "He's so damn controlling. He's such an idiot and he doesn't even know it and I resent it. He doesn't appreciate me, and he doesn't understand me, he just wants me to fake nice," she continued, obviously hostile. "I'm like everyone else would be if they didn't feel tied to social protocol and bogus civility. And he seemed so perfect and lovable at first!"

When asked directly about her family relationships, Kim noted that these had always been a problem, except when she was very young. As a little girl, she was regarded as adorable and cute. At family gatherings, her mother and father showed her off, referring to her as "our pride and joy." But at age 10, life changed. Her mother became pregnant, and announced that because Kim was becoming a woman, she would have to pull her weight in the household, sharing the washing, ironing, cooking, and dishwashing. If she neglected her chores, harsh punishment followed. "I supposed they did what they thought was right for me," Kim reflected, "but what they felt was right turned me into a slave, while they treated my sister like a goddess. She got away with everything. I got them back, though. I knew just where to make a mistake."

Apparently, Kim has no insight into the connection between her early development and current problems in her marriage. In fact, she quickly becomes resistant and defensive whenever anything is asked of her, even where it furthers her own larger plan. Toward the end, the session degenerated into a "gripe session," with Kim refusing to "own" any of her difficulties. Others were overly controlling, she was only reacting to the injustices forced upon her. At the end of the interview, she asks in a covertly accusing tone, "I'm supposed to feel better, right?

---

[1] Numbers mark aspects of the case most consistent with *DSM* criteria, and do not necessarily indicate that the case "meets" diagnostic criteria in this respect.

Negativistic Personality Disorder
DSM-IV Criteria

A. A pervasive pattern of negativistic attitudes and passive resistance to demands for adequate performance, beginning by early adulthood and present in a variety of contexts, as indicated by four (or more) of the following:

(1) passively resists fulfilling routine social and occupational tasks

(2) complains of being misunderstood and unappreciated by others

(3) is sullen and argumentative

(4) unreasonably criticizes and scorns authority

(5) expresses envy and resentment toward those apparently more fortunate

(6) voices exaggerated and persistent complaints of personal misfortune

(7) alternates between hostile defiance and contrition

B. Does not occur exclusively during Major Depressive Episodes and is not better accounted for by Dysthymic Disorder.

such a bitch," yet whenever anything is asked of her, she immediately becomes defensive, resistant, and argumentative. Toward the end, the interview has degenerated into a gripe session (see criterion 3). A resentment of authority (see criterion 4) is indirectly present through a resentment of the therapist's control, the instrument of authority, and a resentment of whatever power her husband might have presumed for himself in their relationship. Moreover, Kim's resistance at the beginning of the interview was probably created because the therapist's credentials create an aura of prestige that, for her, is symbolic of authority. The origins of her resentment are made clear when she notes that when her parents demanded that she pull her own weight in the household, "What they felt was right turned me into a slave." Like most negativists, Kim resents those who have been more fortunate than she (see criterion 5), as evidenced by her attitude toward her sister, whom her parents "treated like a goddess." Finally, Kim shows that a considerable fund of guilt underlies her resentment (see criterion 7) when she supposes she wants therapy to "make amends for being such a bitch" to her husband.

Given the portrait of Kim, we are now in a position to approach additional issues that form the plan of this section. First, we compare normality and abnormality; then we move on to variations on the basic negativistic theme. The section "Evolutionary Neurodevelopmental Perspective" shows how the existence of the personality disorder follows from the laws of evolution. Also included are a comparison between the negativistic and other personality constructs and a discussion of how negativistic personalities tend to develop Axis I disorders.

FROM NORMALITY TO ABNORMALITY

Although the negativistic personality is obviously pathological in its full expression, negativistic traits and behaviors are frequently found in the course of everyday life. Almost everyone knows what it feels like to be overcontrolled and how that experience summons thoughts of getting revenge in some indirect way or at least making life a little more difficult for the controlling person. Most people have such thoughts around tax time, for example, when the government is experienced as autocratic, unfair, and exacting. Fuming with anger underneath the burden of meeting a deadline just to give away their hard-earned money to an entity that shows them no appreciation, most individuals experience daydreams of getting inside the system and causing trouble or even secretly bringing about its downfall. Such thoughts are normal, but they represent what negativists feel most of the time. To them, every request or expectation feels like a willful imposition. Meeting requests or honoring expectations feels like submission, and meeting demands feels like humiliation.

Another way of creating a negativistic personality style is to normalize the diagnostic criteria for the negativistic personality disorder found in *DSM-IV* (see Sperry, 1995). Whereas individuals with the personality disorder resist fulfilling social and occupational duties (see criterion 1), those with the personality style conform to expectations but would like to put their own personal stamp on their productions. Whereas the disordered complains of being misunderstood and unappreciated (see criterion 2), the style makes substantial contributions but enjoys receiving due credit. Whereas the disordered is sullen and argumentative (see criterion 3), the style is able to get along with others, becoming resistant only when sensing a sense of entitlement from others. Whereas the disordered unreasonably criticizes and scorns authority (see criterion 4), the style is able to use protest constructively without exaggerating faults. Whereas the disordered is envious of those more fortunate (see criterion 5), those with the style do not begrudge others their good fortune but may become quickly disappointed if their own efforts are not appropriately rewarded. Whereas the disordered complains about personal misfortune (see criterion 6), those with the style are simply more conscious of the distribution of rewards in life but are nevertheless able to take initiative to better their own situation. Finally, whereas the disordered vacillates between defiance and expressions of remorse (see criterion 7), the style does not act out so extremely that such expressions are necessary. For each of these application contrasts, Kim falls more toward the pathological side.

VARIATIONS OF THE NEGATIVISTIC PERSONALITY

Figure 15.4 presents a summary of the subtypes of this pattern. Actual cases may or may not fall into one of these combinations.

The Circuitous Negativist

In the first *DSM* (1952), the passive-aggressive was grouped together with the passive-dependent. The **circuitous** negativist reflects the wisdom of this early alliance, a combination of the negativistic and dependent personalities. Indirect resistance to the expectations of others is an almost defining feature, especially where such expectations

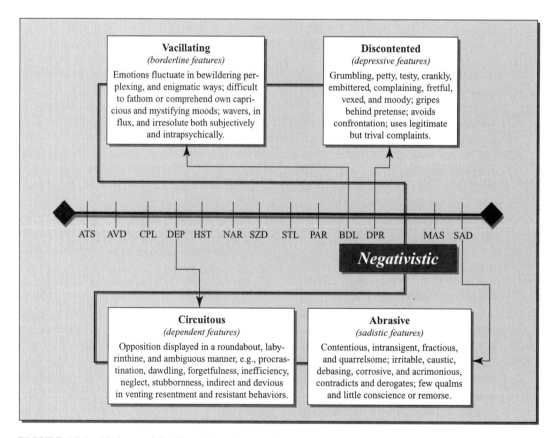

Vacillating
(borderline features)
Emotions fluctuate in bewildering perplexing, and enigmatic ways; difficult to fathom or comprehend own capricious and mystifying moods; wavers, in flux, and irresolute both subjectively and intrapsychically.

Discontented
(depressive features)
Grumbling, petty, testy, crankly, embittered, complaining, fretful, vexed, and moody; gripes behind pretense; avoids confrontation; uses legitimate but trival complaints.

ATS   AVD   CPL   DEP   HST   NAR   SZD   STL   PAR   BDL   DPR   MAS   SAD

Negativistic

Circuitous
(dependent features)
Opposition displayed in a roundabout, labyrinthine, and ambiguous manner, e.g., procrastination, dawdling, forgetfulness, inefficiency, neglect, stubbornness, indirect and devious in venting resentment and resistant behaviors.

Abrasive
(sadistic features)
Contentious, intransigent, fractious, and quarrelsome; irritable, caustic, debasing, corrosive, and acrimonious, contradicts and derogates; few qualms and little conscience or remorse.

FIGURE 15.4   Variants of the Negativistic Personality.

assume compliance and thus value the individual as a means to an end, not as a unique human being. As the name suggests, these persons avenge themselves mainly in roundabout and covert ways that undercut and frustrate anyone who would take them for granted or demand a certain level of performance.

Their exact methods vary but include procrastination, dawdling, stubbornness, forgetfulness, and intentional inefficiency. Fearful of expressing resentments directly, the circuitous negativist fulfills obligations with foot-dragging slowness and inconsistent performance. Depending on the prominence of dependent features, feigned incompetence or exhausting requests for help may be used to frustrate others. Given a looming deadline or the need to perform at unusually high levels, somatic complaints may be used passive-aggressively as a means of excusing them from work, thus increasing the level of tension for everyone else.

The Abrasive Negativist

Whereas circuitous negativists struggle with their internal resentments, **abrasive** negativists remain caught in the conflict between their own agenda and a loyalty to others but have become more overtly and intentionally contentious and quarrelsome nonetheless. Such individuals, in fact, feel so torn by conflict that every request or expectation feels like a major burden, an opportunity to incur contempt. Past experience has shown them that even their most conscientious performances are likely to be evaluated with disappointment and derision. Abrasive negativists are so tired and jaded that they have deep doubts about whether life will work out or whether happiness is even possible at all.

The abrasive negativist fears that loyalty and the tender emotions are only a sad illusion created to conceal the perverse cruelty of human nature. Many were subjected as children to "damned if you do and damned if you don't" situations by their attachment figures. As such, minor frictions tend to exacerbate into major confrontations and power struggles. Some take special joy in spotting inconsistencies in the behaviors or ethical standards of anyone who would require something from them. They construct arguments that amplify observed contradictions and shove these squarely in the face of their antagonists, just for the sadistic pleasure of undermining their self-confidence and watching them squirm.

Aware of the sadistic power of the superego, many take the moral high ground and dogmatically insist that others are either hypocritical or mentally defective. When pressed, even such indirect oppositionality may give way to contemptuous faultfinding and outright insults. During such periods, anyone who crosses their path may become an object of scorn and derision. Abrasive negativists represent a blend of the negativistic and sadistic personalities.

The Discontented Negativist

As a combination of the negativistic and depressive personalities, **discontented** negativists are the consummate gripers. In contrast to circuitous negativists, who sabotage through covert action or inaction any satisfaction others might receive from accomplishing their goals, the discontented negativist attacks emotionally through annoying complaints, thinly cloaked criticisms, and unsubtle digs. Whereas the abrasive negativist can be brutal, the discontented negativist fights a war of attrition, actually a series of small battles designed to wear down the enemy.

Constantly disapproving, they seek some thin rationale by which to be negative and faultfinding. They point out imperfections, pick at old wounds, work others into a state of irritation, and then complain further that their concerns have not been properly addressed. Often, their assertions have some basis in fact but represent trivial concerns in the context of the larger plan. Some represent themselves as persons of goodwill who are exasperated with the problem at hand, perhaps struggling with the inefficiency or ineptitude of those around them, especially those who give the orders. By getting attention for their complaints, some may cultivate the image of being more competent than their managers, whose recognized status and authority they deeply resent.

The Vacillating Negativist

Representing a combination of the negativistic and borderline patterns, the **vacillating** variant is distinguished by unstable and rapidly fluctuating emotions and attitudes. They may, for example, present themselves as affectionate, predictable, interesting, even charming, but then suddenly become irritable, oppositional, and disagreeable. Or they may appear self-assured, decisive, and competent, only to abruptly regress to a clinging dependency. Or they may be pleased with themselves one moment, only to become angry and depressed the next. Torn by conflict, the thoughts of vacillating negativists seem to flow freely in almost any direction, putting them at the mercy of rapidly changing emotions. Emotions are expressed directly and primitively, untransformed by a cohesive self-structure that might give direction to behavior. Tantrums are common. Unable to fathom the source of such shifts, others find them aversive, if only because their emotional maelstroms are difficult to understand.

EVOLUTIONARY NEURODEVELOPMENTAL PERSPECTIVE

The psychodynamics of the negativist can be traced to either a satisfying first stage of the oral phase where basic trust is established with the second half of the oral phase where sadistic biting develops or to the anal stage where issues of autonomy versus external control are confronted. Cognitively, the negativist is skeptical and cynical, extremely rigid, controlled by "I should not" statements, and suffers from black-and-white thinking. Interpersonally, negativists are excessively concerned with the distribution of rewards and become bitterly jealous. In work situations, negativists assume that they will be exploited by others and promise to complete tasks on which they do not deliver.

The evolutionary interpretation stresses the interplay of factors across all domains of personality. In this model, negativists are portrayed as being actively ambivalent, conflicted between putting their own needs first versus deferring to the agenda of others. Compulsives are also conflicted but are portrayed as passively ambivalent. Thus, compulsives react against feelings of rebellion to become impressively conscientious. They overconform to rules, while worrying that authority figures might still find some reason to disapprove of them. The mechanism of reaction formation produces excessive self-control, leaving their emotional expression constricted.

In contrast, negativists are impressively frustrating. Conflicted on the self and other polarities, they eventually find either alternative distasteful. Being without a consistent or single-minded direction in life, they often shift erratically back and forth, manifesting fluctuating attitudes and unpredictable behaviors. If they move toward the fulfillment of what others desire, they become irritated and annoyed with themselves for doing so, quickly shifting their thoughts and feelings in favor of doing their own thing. In so doing, however, they jeopardize the security and support they need from others, leading them quickly to become contrite and to reverse their position again. They either agree to perform but fail to follow through or engage a reverse conscientiousness, anticipating what others want but perverting the meaning of the task or rendering their performance useless in the big picture. Their emotions ride close to the surface, making them appear immature or childish at times. Nevertheless, their resentments are not expressed openly against others but instead are displaced onto safer targets, usually by putting obstacles between others and their desires.

Infants whose behaviors and moods vary unpredictably may develop rather normal and stable patterns as they mature. The possibility arises, however, that a disproportionately high number of such "difficult to schedule" infants will continue to exhibit a "biologically erratic" pattern throughout their lives, thereby disposing them to develop the features of the negativistic.

Fretful and nervous youngsters are good candidates for the negativistic pattern also because they are likely to provoke bewilderment, confusion, and vacillation in parental training methods. Such irregular children may set into motion erratic and contradictory reactions from their parents, which then serve, in circular fashion, to reinforce their initial tendency to be spasmodic and variable.

The central role of inconsistent parental attitudes and contradictory training methods in the development of the negativistic personality has been referred to repeatedly in our discussions. Although every child experiences some degree of parental inconstancy, negativistic youngsters are likely to have been exposed to appreciably more than their share. Their parents may have swayed from hostility and rejection at one time to affection and love another; this erratic pattern has probably been capricious, frequent, pronounced, and lifelong.

As a consequence, these children may develop a variety of pervasive and deeply ingrained conflicts such as trust versus mistrust, competence versus doubt, and initiative versus guilt and fear. Their self-concept will be composed of contradictory appraisals; every judgment they make of themselves will be matched by an opposing one. Am I good or am I bad; am I competent or am I incompetent? Every course of behavior will have its positive and its negative side. Thus, no matter what they do or think, they will experience a contrary inclination or value by which to judge it.

Their internal ambivalence is paralleled by their inability to gauge what they can expect from their environment. How can they be sure that things are going well? Have they not experienced capricious hostility and criticism in the past when things appeared to be going well? Their plight is terribly bewildering. Unlike the avoidant and histrionic personalities, who can predict their fate, who "know" they will consistently experience humiliation or hostility, negativistics are unable to predict what the future will bring. At any moment, and for no apparent reason, they may receive the kindness and support they crave; equally possible, and for equally unfathomable reasons, they may be the recipient of hostility and rejection. They are in a bind; they have no way of knowing which course of action on their part will bring relief; they have not learned how to predict whether hostility or compliance will prove instrumentally more effective. They vacillate, feeling hostility, guilt, compliance, assertion, and so on, shifting erratically and impulsively from one futile action to another.

Paradoxical and contradictory parental behaviors often are found in "schismatic" families, that is, in families where the parents are manifestly in conflict with each other. Here, there is constant bickering and an undermining of one parent by the other through disqualifying and contradicting statements. Children raised in this setting not only suffer the constant threat of family dissolution but also are often forced to serve as mediator to moderate tensions generated by their parents. They constantly switch sides and divide their loyalties; they cannot be "themselves," for they must shift their attitudes and emotions to satisfy changing and antagonistic parental desires and expectations. The different roles they must assume to placate their parents and to salvage a measure of family stability are markedly divergent; as long as the parents remain at odds, these children must persist with behavior and thoughts that are intrinsically irreconcilable.

Whether the negativistic personality expresses more passive-aggressive or more vacillating behaviors depends on the relative strength of the polarities that compose the construct. Those who are more ambivalent than active are likely to remain bound by existing power structures. As such, they express their dissatisfaction in indirect ways, the subtle sabotage of procrastination, intentional inefficiency, shoddy workmanship, as well as sulking, pouting, and pessimistic attitudes that wring the joy out of those around them. Contained by external constraints, these individuals are passive and aggressive simultaneously. In contrast, those who are more active than ambivalent more readily express their conflicts in their environment, shifting from one moment to the next in their behaviors, thoughts, and feelings. They tend to cycle from one pole of their ambivalence to the other, generating a state of perpetual discontent and dysphoria that superficially resembles the borderline personality. Table 15.4 presents a review of the total negativistic personality.

Contrast with Related Personalities

Anger, resentment, and oppositionality cut across a variety of personality patterns. Both the paranoid and the negativist feel that they have been mistreated or injured by others; both rarely own blame; both seem complaining, hostile, and lacking in tender feelings; and both deeply resent feeling controlled. Paranoids, however, insulate themselves from others and seek the safety of their castle walls. For the most part, their complaints revolve around fears and suspicions that others are talking about them or trying to influence them and undermine their autonomy.

In contrast, negativists react against feelings of being unappreciated and taken for granted in the course of being controlled. They may be suspicious, but they are more overt in voicing their complaints. Given consistent praise, loyalty, love, and a measure of independence, their attachment to authority figures is more remediable, and an eventual willingness to contribute as part of a team can be created. Negativists must feel that they belong, not that they are being used. Moreover, negativists do experience periods of conscious guilt and contrition. Paranoids fight off or project such feelings, asserting that others are trying to make them feel guilty.

Both the narcissist and the negativist are hypersensitive to perceived slights, both find it difficult to be genuinely happy for others, and both may seem to exhibit a sense of entitlement, but for different reasons. Narcissists are unable to appreciate the joy of others because they are lacking in empathy, whereas negativists begrudge others their joy and success because of a deep discontent at the way life has treated them. Moreover, narcissists are hypersensitive because their ego inflation compensates for deep feelings of inferiority, whereas negativists are hypersensitive because they feel others are not adequately sympathetic to the cosmic injustices they have suffered. Narcissists are entitled because of their supposed intrinsic superiority; negativists are entitled to good fortune or at least a reprieve from bad fortune. Finally, narcissists need to feel admired, whereas negativists need to feel appreciated. Narcissists can be bitching and complaining when such supplies are not forthcoming, but for the most part, they relate to others

TABLE 15.4 The Negativistic Personality: Functional and Structural Domains

	Functional Domains			Structural Domains	
	Resentful			**Discontented**	
Expressive Behavior	Resists fulfilling expectancies of others, frequently exhibiting procrastination, inefficiency, and obstinate as well as contrary and irksome behaviors; reveals gratification in demoralizing and undermining the pleasures and aspirations of others.		**Self-Image**	Sees self as misunderstood, luckless, unappreciated, jinxed, and demeaned by others; recognizes being characteristically embittered, disgruntled, and disillusioned with life.	
	Contrary			**Vacillating**	
Interpersonal Conduct	Assumes conflicting and changing roles in social relationships, particularly dependent and contrite acquiescence and assertive and hostile independence; conveys envy and pique toward those more fortunate, as well as actively concurrent or sequentially obstructive and intolerant of others, expressing either negative or incompatible attitudes.		**Object-Representations**	Internalized representations of the past constitute a complex of countervailing relationships, setting in motion contradictory feelings, conflicting inclinations, and incompatible memories that are driven by the desire to degrade the achievements and pleasures of others, without necessarily appearing so.	
	Skeptical			**Divergent**	
Cognitive Style	Is cynical, doubting, and untrusting, approaching positive events with disbelief and future possibilities with pessimism, anger, and trepidation; has a misanthropic view of life, is whining and grumbling, voicing disdain and caustic comments toward those experiencing good fortune.		**Morphologic Organization**	There is a clear division in the pattern of morphologic structures such that coping and defensive maneuvers are often directed toward incompatible goals, leaving major conflicts unresolved and full psychic cohesion often impossible by virtue of the fact that fulfillment of one drive or need inevitably nullifies or reverses another.	
	Displacement			**Irritable**	
Regulatory Mechanism	Discharges anger and other troublesome emotions either precipitously or by employing unconscious maneuvers to shift them from their instigator to settings or persons of lesser significance; vents disapproval by substitute or passive means, such as acting inept or perplexed, or behaving in a forgetful or indolent manner.		**Mood/Temperament**	Frequently touchy, temperamental, and peevish, followed in turn by sullen and moody withdrawal; is often petulant and impatient, unreasonably scorns those in authority and reports being annoyed easily or frustrated by many.	

Note: Shaded domains are the most salient for this personality prototype.

from a baseline of insouciance, the belief that everything will turn out okay; the negativist relates to others from a baseline of discontentment.

On the surface, the negativist is also similar to several other personalities. The erratic attitudes and emotions of some negativists—especially anger, resentment, and a tendency to be easily frustrated—resemble the borderline personality, especially its emotional lability. Negativists vacillate in response to a dual orientation, the conflict between following the agenda of others and putting their own needs and desires first.

In contrast, the lability of the borderline stems from a basic lack of cohesiveness in the self-construct. Negativists are usually capable of regulating their drives and conflicts but do not know which way to turn. The borderline lacks such a capacity. The negativistic and sadistic personalities are obviously similar in acting against others, but sadists are direct and usually want others to know the source of their suffering, whereas the negativist fears authority and acts covertly and passive-aggressively. Negativistic and antisocial personalities are often quick-tempered and contrary, and both may feel they have received a raw deal from life. However, antisocials are self-concerned, possess a deficient conscience, and therefore go through life remarkably free of guilt and anxiety. In contrast, the negativist has superego introjects but rebels and suffers horribly from guilt and anxiety. Negativists, masochistic, and depressive personalities are all discontent, but depressives blame themselves, whereas masochists need to be blamed by others.

Pathways to Symptom Expression

As always, it is important to remember that there is a logic that connects the personality pattern with its associated Axis I syndromes. Because ambivalence is felt subjectively as anxiety, moodiness, and discontent, negativists are likely to experience anxiety disorders, often tinged with depressive complaints. Such feelings crystallize and vent their tensions and provide a subtle means of expressing anger and resentment. To an extent, anxiety is instrumental. Usually, tension is discharged in brief episodes of passive-aggressive behavior or through verbal channels. When this is not possible, however, panic attacks or generalized anxiety can develop. Phobic symptoms may be used for secondary gain by giving negativists a reason not to meet the expectations of others or to excuse themselves from task demands.

Other disorders can also occur. Depressive episodes are common, ranging from occasional severe depressive episodes to a more subtle but pervasive dysthymia. Negativistic personalities most frequently display an agitated dysphoria, vacillating between anxious futility, despair, and self-deprecation on the one hand and a bitter discontent and demanding irritability on the other. Such sour moods and complaints also ruin things for others and give the negativist compensatory feelings of retribution. Somatoform disorders are not unusual in situations of unresolvable conflict, but they usually have an added, passive-aggressive benefit that makes them especially burdensome to others. Finally, negativists share with the paranoid a deep concern about autonomy and external control, suggesting that paranoid decompensation could occur in some cases.

Summary

Although the term masochistic was coined in reference to a specific male sexual perversion, it quickly became associated with the feminine and submissive. Hence, it has become a politically charged construct that has been dropped from the *DSM-IV*. The masochistic personality also has several normal variants that are often described as saintly. For example, Oldham and Morris's (1995) self-sacrificing style lives to serve others. Millon's yielding style is moving closer toward the pathological end of the spectrum in that this style tends to remain deferential to others despite possessing superior abilities.

Several variants of the masochist blend with other personality traits. The self-undoing masochist blends traits with the avoidant personality where failure brings some kind of relief from anxiety. Possessive masochists blend with negativistic traits and tend to try to guilt others into staying with them. Oppressed masochists combine depressive traits with the masochistic ones and tend to complain about their terrible lives although they do not necessarily enjoy their sufferings. Virtuous masochists are a blend with histrionic traits as well as dependent ones and are stoic in their suffering, while continually manipulating others with their generous giving.

Masochists share many traits with other personalities, including the depressive, dependent, compulsive, and borderline personalities. They are also vulnerable to developing dysthymia, panic disorders, and somatoform disorders.

Like the term masochism, sadism has become a politicized construct. Originally coined in response to the Marquis de Sade, who derived sexual pleasure by causing others to suffer, it quickly came to describe other, nonsexual behaviors. Also like masochism, sadism has been dropped from the *DSM-IV,* although it was only in the appendix of the *DSM-III-R.* While true sadists are only seldom encountered in everyday life, sadistic traits and behaviors are all around us. Millon's controlling style is an example of normal variants of the sadistic personality who enjoy using their power to direct and intimidate others.

Some combinations with other personality traits are possible. Explosive sadists possess borderline traits and seem to use their aggression as an outlet for emotions rather than like other sadists who use it to gain control. The tyrannical sadist possesses features of the negativistic or paranoid and is particularly frightening and cruel. The enforcing sadist has many compulsive traits and acts like society's sadistic superego. The spineless sadist is combined with avoidant traits where hostility is a kind of a counterphobic act. The sadist also shares many traits with negativists, antisocials, paranoids, and narcissists. They are also vulnerable to certain Axis I disorders such as anxiety disorders, substance abuse, and paranoid fears.

For depressive personalities, being depressed is more than a symptom. Like a person suffering from depression, depressive personalities feel sad and guilty, but their emotional state is indicative of an entire matrix of pervasive and long-standing characteristics of feeling worthless and inadequate. On the continuum toward normality, people with depressive traits may be reflective of negative aspects but are not overcome by them and are self-conscious of their standing but able to take criticism constructively.

There are several variations of the depressive personality that mix with other personality traits. The ill-humored depressive is a mixture with the negativistic personality that complains endlessly and is chronically irritable. The voguish depressive is a mixture with histrionic or narcissistic features that sees suffering as noble. Self-derogating depressives possess some dependent features where they feel guilt and must discharge it though self-punishment. The morbid depressive shares features with the masochistic personality and frequently blends into an Axis I clinical depression. The restive depressive has avoidant features, expressing anguish and agitation. Depressives may share many traits also with the schizoid, compulsive, and borderline personalities. They are also often diagnosed with dysthymia, major depressive episodes, as well as with anxiety syndromes.

Negativists vacillate between feelings of dependence and a need for self-assertion, usually feel misunderstood, and act out their frustrations in indirect ways. Normal traits of this personality may be seen when people feel overcontrolled by someone and have fantasies about ways to make the overcontrolling person suffer. More normal variants may possess the same basic tendencies but are able to function in society and get along with others socially.

Several variations on the negativistic personality exist. The circuitous negativist is a mixture with dependent traits that covertly undercuts others. The abrasive negativist shares traits with the sadistic personality and is more overtly hostile and vile to others. The discontented negativist is a combination of the negativist with depressive traits, a person that constantly gripes. Vacillating negativists are mixed with borderline traits and experience rapid changes in their emotions and attitudes.

The negativist shares many qualities with other personality types, including the paranoid, narcissistic, antisocial, and masochistic. Anxiety, phobias, depressive episodes, and paranoid decompensation are but some of the Axis I types of disorders to which the negativist is vulnerable.

References

Abraham, K. (1927a). Character formation on the genital level of the libido. In *Selected papers on psychoanalysis*. London: Hogarth. (Original work published 1924)

Abraham, K. (1927b). Contributions to the theory of the anal character. In *Selected papers on psychoanalysis*. London: Hogarth. (Original work published 1921)

Abraham, K. (1927c). The influence of oral eroticism on character formation. In *Selected papers on psychoanalysis*. London: Hogarth. (Original work published 1924)

Adler, G. (1985). *Borderline psychopathology and its treatment*. Northvale, NJ: Aronson.

Ainsworth, M. D. S. (1969). Object relations, dependency, and attachment: A theoretical review of the infant-mother relationship. *Child Development, 40*, 969–1027.

Ainsworth, M. D. S. (1972). Attachment and dependency: A comparison. In J. L. Gewirtz (Ed.), *Attachment and dependency* (pp. 97–137). New York: Wiley.

Akhtar, S. (1992). *Broken structures*. Northvale, NJ: Aronson.

Akhtar, S., & Thomson, J. A., Jr. (1982). Overview: Narcissistic personality disorder. *American Journal of Psychiatry, 139*, 12–20.

Akiskal, H. S. (1981). Subaffective disorders: Dysthymic, cyclothymic and bipolar II disorders in the "borderline" realm. *Psychiatric Clinics of North America, 4*, 25–46.

Alarcon, R., Foulks, E., & Vakkur, M. (in press). *Personality and culture: Clinical interactions between personality, personality disorders, and culture*. New York: Wiley.

Alexander, F. (1930). The neurotic character. *International Journal of Psychoanalysis, 11*, 292–313.

Allport, G. W. (1937). *Personality: A psychological interpretation*. New York: Holt.

Allport, G. W., & Odbert, H. S. (1936). Trait-names: A psycho-lexical study. *Psychological Monographs, 47*(No. 211).

Almagor, M., Tellegen, A., & Waller, N. G. (1995). The Big Seven Model: A cross-cultural replication and further exploration of the basic dimensions of natural language trait descriptors. *Journal of Personality and Social Psychology, 69*, 300–307.

Alneas, R., & Torgersen, S. (1997). Personality and personality disorders predict development and relapses of major depression. *Acta Psychiatrica Scandinavica, 95*(4), 336–342.

American Psychiatric Association. (1952). *Diagnostic and statistical manual of mental disorders*. Washington, DC: Author.

American Psychiatric Association. (1980). *Diagnostic and statistical manual of mental disorders* (3rd ed.). Washington, DC: Author.

American Psychiatric Association. (1987). *Diagnostic and statistical manual of mental disorders* (3rd ed., rev.). Washington, DC: Author.

American Psychiatric Association. (1994). *Diagnostic and statistical manual of mental disorders* (4th ed.). Washington, DC: Author.

American Psychiatric Association. (2000). *Diagnostic and statistical manual of mental disorders* (4th ed., text rev.). Washington, DC: Author.

Apt, C., & Hurlbert, D. (1994). The sexual attitudes, behavior, and relationships of women with histrionic personality disorder. *Journal of Sex and Marital Therapy, 20*(2), 125–133.

Arieti, S. (1955). *Interpretation of schizophrenia*. New York: Brunner/Mazel.

Auchincloss, E. L., & Weiss, R. W. (1994). Paranoid character and intolerance of indifference. In J. M. Oldham & S. Bone (Eds.), *Paranoia: New psychoanalytic perspectives* (pp. 27–48). Guilford, CT: International Universities Press.

Bak, R. C. (1946). Masochism in paranoia. *Psychoanalytic Quarterly, 15*, 285–301.

Balthazar, M. L., & Cook, R. J. (1984). An analysis of the factors related to the rate of violent crimes committed by incarcerated female delinquents. *Journal of Offender Counseling, Services, and Rehabilitation, 19*, 103–118.

Bartlett, F. C. (1932). *Remembering*. Cambridge, England: Cambridge University Press.

Bates, J. E. (1980). The concept of difficult temperament. *Merrill-Palmer Quarterly, 26*, 299–319.

Bates, J. E. (1987). Temperament in infancy. In J. D. Osofsky (Ed.), *Handbook of infancy* (2nd ed., pp. 1101–1149). New York: Wiley.

Bateson, G., Jackson, D. D., Haley, J., & Weakland, J. (1956). Toward a theory of schizophrenia. *Behavioral Science, 1*, 251–256.

Bateson, G., & Ruesch, J. (1951). *Communication, the social matrix of psychiatry.* New York: Norton.

Baumrind, D. (1967). Child care practices anteceding three patterns of preschool behavior. *Genetic Psychology Monographs, 75,* 43–83.

Baumrind, D. (1971). Current patterns of parental authority. *Developmental Psychology Monograph, 4*(Parts 1, 2).

Baumrind, D. (1980). New directions in socialization research. *American Psychologist, 35,* 639–652.

Beck, A. T. (1963). Thinking and depression: Idiosyncratic content and cognitive distortions. *Archives of General Psychiatry, 9,* 324–344.

Beck, A. T. (1976). *Cognitive therapy and the emotional disorders.* New York: International Universities Press.

Beck, A. T., Freeman, A. F., & Associates. (1990). *Cognitive therapy of personality disorders.* New York: Guilford Press.

Beck, A. T., Rush, A. J., Shaw, B. F., & Emory, G. (1979). *Cognitive therapy of depression.* New York: Guilford Press.

Belsky, J., & Rovine, M. (1987). Temperament and attachment security in the strange situation: An empirical rapprochement. *Child Development, 58,* 787–795.

Benedict, R. (1934). *Patterns of culture.* New York: Houghton Mifflin.

Benjamin, L. S. (1974). Structured analysis of social behavior. *Psychological Review, 81,* 392–425.

Benjamin, L. S. (1986). Adding social and intrapsychic descriptors to Axis I of *DSM-III.* In T. Millon & G. L. Klerman (Eds.), *Contemporary directions in psychopathology: Toward the DSM-IV* (pp. 599–638). New York: Guilford Press.

Benjamin, L. S. (1996). *Interpersonal diagnosis and treatment of personality disorders.* New York: Guilford Press.

Berman, S. M. W., & McCann, J. T. (1995). Defense mechanisms and personality disorders: An empirical test of Millon's theory. *Journal of Personality Assessment, 64*(1), 132–144.

Bernstein, D. P., Useda, D., & Siever, L. J. (1995). Paranoid personality disorder. In W. J. Livesley (Ed.), *The DSM-IV personality disorders* (pp. 45–57). New York: Guilford Press.

Beutler, L. E. (1986). Systematic eclectic psychotherapy. In J. Norcross (Ed.), *Handbook of eclectic psychotherapy* (pp. 74–131). New York: Brunner/Mazel.

Beutler, L. E., & Clarkin, J. F. (1990). *Systematic treatment selection.* New York: Brunner/Mazel.

Bibring, E. (1953). The mechanism of depression. In P. Greenacre (Ed.), *Affective disorders.* New York: International Universities Press.

Billings, A. G., & Moos, R. H. (1982). Psychosocial theory and research on depression: An integrative framework and review. *Clinical Psychology Review, 2,* 213–237.

Birnbaum, K. (1909). *Die psychopathischen Verbrecker.* Leipzig, Germany: Thieme.

Black, D. W., & Noyes, R. (1997). Obsessive-compulsive disorder and Axis II. *International Review of Psychiatry, 9*(1), 111–118.

Blacker, K., & Tubin, J. (1991). Hysteria and hysterical structures: Developmental and social theories. In M. J. Horowitz (Ed.), *Hysterical personality* (pp. 95–142). New York: Aronson.

Blair, R. J. R. (1995). A cognitive developmental approach to morality: Investigating the psychopath. *Cognition, 57,* 1–29.

Blair, R. J. R., Jones, L., Clark, F., & Smith, M. (1995). Is the psychopath morally insane? *Personality and Individual Differences, 19,* 741–752.

Blair, R. J. R., Jones, L., Clark, F., & Smith, M. (1997). The psychopathic individual: A lack of responsiveness to distress cues? *Psychophysiology, 34,* 192–198.

Blais, M. A., Hilsenroth, M. J., & Castlebury, F. D. (1997). Content validity of the *DSM-IV* borderline and narcissistic personality disorder criteria sets. *Comprehensive Psychiatry, 38*(1), 31–37.

Blatt, S. J. (1974). Levels of object representation in anaclitic and introjective depression. *Psychoanalytic Study of the Child, 29,* 107–157.

Bleuler, E. (1906). *Affectivitat, suggestibilitat, paranoia.* Halle, Germany: Marhold.

Bleuler, E. (1922). Die probleme der schizoidie und der syntonie. ZeitschriJ fucr die gesamte. *Nurologie und Psychiatrie, 78,* 373–388.

Bleuler, E. (1924). *Textbook of psychiatry.* New York: Macmillan.

Bleuler, E. (1929). Syntonie–schizoidie–schizophrenie. *Neurologie und Psychopathologie, 38,* 47–64.

Bleuler, E. (1950). *Dementia praecox or the group of schizophrenias* (J. Zinkin, Trans.). New York: International Universities Press. (Original work published 1911)

Bloom, B. L. (1992). *Planned short-term psychotherapy: A clinical handbook.* Boston: Allyn & Bacon.

Blum, H. (1980). Paranoia and beating fantasy: Psychoanalytic theory of paranoia. *Journal of the American Psychoanalytic Association, 28,* 331–361.

Blum, H. (1981). Object inconstancy and paranoid conspiracy. *Journal of the American Psychoanalytic Association, 29,* 789–813.

Bockian, N. R. (2002). *New Hope for People With Borderline Personality Disorder.* Roseville, CA: Prima Publishing.

Bornstein, R. F. (1993). *The dependent personality.* New York: Guilford Press.

Bornstein, R. F. (2001). A meta-analysis of the dependency-eating-disorders relationship: Strength, specificity, and temporal stability. *Journal of Psychopathology and Behavioral Assessment, 23,* 151–162.

Bornstein, R. F., Rossner, S. C., Hill, E. L., & Stepanian, M. L. (1994). Face validity and fakability of objective and projective measures of dependency. *Journal of Personality Assessment, 63,* 363–386.

Bouchard, T. J., Lykken, D. T., McGue, M., Segal, N. L., & Tellegen, A. (1990). Sources of human psychological differences: The Minnesota study of twins reared apart. *Science, 250,* 223–228.

Bowlby, J. (1969). *Attachment and loss: Volume I. Attachment.* New York: Basic Books.

Bowlby, J. (1973). *Attachment and loss: Volume II. Separation: Anxiety and anger.* New York: Basic Books.

Breuer, J., & Freud, S. (1895). *Studies on hysteria.* Leipzig: F. Deuticke.

Briquet, P. (1859). *Traite clinique et therapeutique a l'hysterie.* Paris: J. B. Balliere & Fils.

Brown, L. S. (1992). A feminist critique of the personality disorders. In L. S. Brown & M. Ballou (Eds.), *Personality and psychopathology: Feminist reappraisals* (pp. 206–228). New York: Guilford Press.

Buchsbaum, M. S., Yang, S., Hazlett, E., Siegel, B. V., Jr., Germans, M., Haznedar, M., et al. (1997). Ventricular volume and asymmetry in schizotypal personality disorder and schizophrenia assessed with magnetic resonance imaging. *Schizophrenia Research, 27*(1), 45–53.

Budman, S. H. (1981). Looking toward the future. In S. H. Budman (Ed.), *Forms of brief therapy* (pp. 461–467). New York: Guilford Press.

Budman, S. H., & Gurman, A. S. (1988). *Theory and practice of brief therapy.* New York: Guilford Press.

Bursten, B. (1972). The manipulative personality. *Archives of General Psychiatry, 26,* 318–321.

Bursten, B. (1973). Some narcissistic personality types. *International Journal of Psychoanalysis, 54,* 287–300.

Buss, A. H., & Plomin, R. (1984). *Temperament: Early developing personality traits.* Hillsdale, NJ: Erlbaum.

Buss, D. M., & Shackelford, T. K. (1997). Susceptibility to infidelity in the first year of marriage. *Journal of Research in Personality, 31,* 193–221.

Butcher, J. N., Dahlstrom, W. G., Graham, J. R., Tellegen, A., & Kaemmer, B. (1989). *Minnesota Multiphasic Personality Inventory-2 (MMPI-2). Manual for administration and scoring.* Minneapolis, MN: University of Minnesota Press.

Butcher, J. N., Williams, C. L., Graham, J. R., Archer, R. P., Tellegen, A., Ben-Porath, Y. S., et al. (1992). *MMPI-A (Minnesota Multiphasic Personality Inventory-Adolescent): Manual for administration, scoring, and interpretation.* Minneapolis, MN: University of Minnesota Press.

Cadoret, R. J., Troughton, E., Bagford, J., & Woodworth, G. (1990). Genetic and environmental factors in adoptee antisocial personality. *European Archives of Psychiatric Neurologic Science, 239,* 231–240.

Cale, E. M., & Lilienfeld, S. O. (2002). Histrionic personality manifestations of psychopathy? *Journal of Personality Disorders, 16*(1), 52–72.

Calsyn, D. A., Fleming, C., Wells, E. A., & Saxon, A. J. (1996). Personality disorder subtypes among opiate addicts in methadone maintenance. *Psychology of Addictive Behaviors, 10*(1), 3–8.

Cameron, N. (1947). *The psychology of the behavior disorders.* Boston: Houghton-Mifflin.

Cameron, N. (1963). *Personality development and psychopathology.* Boston: Houghton Mifflin.

Cameron, N., & Margaret, A. (1951). *Behavior pathology.* Boston: Houghton Mifflin.

Campbell, S. B. (1973). Mother-infant interaction in reflective, impulsive, and hyperactive children. *Developmental Psychology, 8,* 341–349.

Caplan, P. J. (1991). How do they decide who is normal? The bizarre, but true, tale of the *DSM* process. *Canadian Psychology, 32,* 162–170.

Carson, R. C. (1969). *Interaction concepts of personality.* Chicago: Aldine.

Cattell, R. B. (1971). *Abilities: Their structure, growth, and action.* New York: Harcourt Brace and Jovanovich.

Cattell, R. B. (1982). *The inheritance of personality and ability.* New York: Academic Press.

Celesia, G. G., & Barr, A. N. (1970). Psychosis and other psychiatric manifestations of levodopa therapy. *Archives of Neurology, 23.*

Chabrol, H., Telmon, N., Peresson, G., Alengrin, D., Bras, P., Rouge, D., et al. (1995). Psychopathology of victims of aggression. *Medicine and Law, 14,* 631–633.

Charcot, J. (1875). *Leóns sur les maladies du système nerveux* (2nd ed.). Paris: Delahaye.

Chatterjee, A., Strauss, M. E., Smyth, K. A., & Whitehouse, P. J. (1992). Personality changes in Alzheimer's disease. *Archives of Neurology, 49*(5), 486–491.

Chess, S., & Thomas, A. (1984). *Origins and evolution of behavior disorders.* New York: Brunner/Mazel.

Chomsky, N. (1959). A review of C. F. Skinner's "Verbal Behavior." *Language, 35,* 26–58.

Cicchetti, D., & Beeghly, M. (1987). Symbolic development in maltreated youngsters: An organizational perspective. In D. Cicchetti & M. Beeghly (Eds.), *Atypical symbolic development* (pp. 47–68). San Francisco: Jossey-Bass.

Cicchetti, D., & Carlson, V. (Eds.). (1989). *Child maltreatment: Theory and research on the causes and consequences of child abuse and neglect.* New York: Cambridge University Press.

Circirelli, V. G. (1982). Sibling influence throughout the lifespan. In M. E. Lamb & B. Sutton-Smith (Eds.), *Sibling relationships* (pp. 267–284). Hillsdale, NJ: Erlbaum.

Claridge, G., Clark, K., & Davis, C. (1997). Nightmares, dreams, and schizotypy. *British Journal of Clinical Psychology, 36*(3), 377–386.

Claridge, G., Davis, C., Bellhouse, M., & Kaptein, S. (1998). Borderline personality, nightmares, and adverse life events in the risk for eating disorders. *Personality & Individual Differences, 25*(2), 339–351.

Clark, L. A. (1990). Toward a consensual set of symptom clusters for assessment of personality disorder. In J. N. Butcher & C. D. Spielberger (Eds.), *Advances in personality assessment* (Vol. 8, pp. 243–266). Hillsdale, NJ: Erlbaum.

Clark, L. A., McEwen, J. L., Collard, L. M., & Hickok, L. G. (1993). Symptoms and traits of personality disorder: Two new methods for their assessment. *Psychological Assessment, 5*(1), 81–91.

Clausen, J. (1966). *Ability structure and subgroups in mental retardation.* Oxford, England: Spartan Books.

Cleckley, H. (1941). *The mask of sanity.* St. Louis, MO: Mosby.

Cleckley, H. (1950). *The mask of sanity* (2nd ed.). St. Louis, MO: Mosby.

Cleckley, H. (1964). *The mask of sanity* (4th ed.). St. Louis, MO: Mosby.

Cleckley, H. (1988). *The mask of sanity: An attempt to clarify some issues about the so-called psychopathic personality.* (Rev. ed.). St. Louis, MO: Mosby.

Cloninger, C. R. (1978). The link between hysteria and sociopathy: An integrative model of pathogenesis based on clinical, genetic, and neurophysiological observations. In H. S. Akiskal & W. L. Webb (Eds.), *Psychiatric diagnosis: Explorations of biological predictors* (pp. 189–218). New York: Spectrum.

Cloninger, C. R. (1986). A unified biosocial theory of personality and its role in the development of anxiety states. *Psychiatric Developments, 3,* 167–226.

Cloninger, C. R. (1987a). Neurogenetic adaptive mechanisms in alcoholism. *Science, 236,* 410–416.

Cloninger, C. R. (1987b). A systematic method for clinical description and classification of personality variants. *Archives of General Psychiatry, 44,* 573–588.

Cloninger, C. R., & Guze, S. B. (1975). Hysteria and parental psychiatric illness. *Psychological Medicine, 5,* 27–31.

Cloninger, C. R., Przybeck, T. R., & Svrakic, D. M. (1991). The tridimensional personality questionnaire: U.S. normative data. *Psychological Reports, 69,* 1047–1057.

Cloninger, C. R., Reich, T., & Guze, S. B. (1978). Genetic-environmental interactions and antisocial behavior. In R. D. Hare & D. Schalling (Eds.), *Psychopathic behavior: Approaches to research.* Chichester, England: Wiley.

Colligan, R. C., Morey, L. C., & Offord, K. P. (1994). The MMPI/MMPI-2 personality disorder scales: Contemporary norms for adults and adolescents. *Journal of Clinical Psychology, 50*(2), 168–200.

Coolidge, F. L., & Merwin, M. M. (1992). Reliability and validity of the Coolidge Axis II Inventory: A new inventory for the assessment of personality disorders. *Journal of Personality Assessment, 59*(2), 223–238.

Coolidge, J. C., & Brodie, R. D. (1974). Observations of mothers of 49 school phobic children. *Journal of the American Academy of Child Psychiatry, 13,* 275–285.

Cornell, D. G., Warren, J., Hawk, G., & Stafford, E. (1996). Psychopathy in instrumental and reactive violent offenders. *Journal of Consulting and Clinical Psychology, 64*(4), 783–790.

Costa, P. T., Jr., & McCrae, R. R. (1989). *The NEO-PI/NEO-FFI manual supplement.* Odessa, FL: Psychological Assessment Resources.

Costa, P. T., Jr., & McCrae, R. R. (1992). *The NEO-PI-R manual.* Odessa, FL: Psychological Assessment Resources.

Crick, N. R. (1995). Relational aggression: The role of intent attributions, feelings of distress, and provocation type. *Development and Psychopathology, 7,* 313–322.

Crick, N. R., & Bigbee, M. A. (1998). Relational and overt forms of peer victimization: A multiinformant approach. *Journal of Consulting and Clinical Psychology, 66,* 337–347.

Crick, N. R., & Grotpeter, J. K. (1995). Relational aggression, gender, and social-psychological adjustment. *Child Development, 66,* 710–722.

Crittenden, P. M. (1990). Internal representation models of attachment relationships. *Infant Mental Health Journal, 11,* 259–277.

Crockenberg, S. (1985). Toddler's reaction to maternal anger. *Merrill-Palmer Quarterly, 31,* 361–373.

Cronbach, L. J., & Meehl, P. E. (1955). Construct validity in psychological tests. *Psychological Bulletin, 52,* 281–302.

Crosby, R. M., & Hall, M. J. (1992). Psychiatric evaluation of self-referred and non-self-referred active duty military members. *Military Medicine, 157,* 224–229.

Cummings, J. S., Pellegrini, D. S., Notarius, C. I., & Cummings, E. M. (1989). Children's responses to angry adults as a function of marital distress and history of interparent hostility. *Child Development, 60,* 1035–1043.

Dabbs, J. M., Hopper, C. H., & Jurkovic, G. J. (1990). Testosterone and personality among college students and military veterans. *Personality and Individual Differences, 11*(12), 1263–1269.

Dabbs, J. M., & Morris, R. (1990). Testosterone, social class, and antisocial behavior in a sample of 4,462 men. *Psychological Science, 1*(3), 209–211.

Dahl, A. A. (1996). The relationship between social phobia and avoidant personality disorder: Workshop report 3. *International Clinical Psychopharmacology, 11*(Suppl. 3), 109–112.

Davanloo, H. (Ed.). (1980). *Short-term dynamic psychotherapy.* Northvale, NJ: Aronson.

Davidson, E. H. (1986). *Gene activity in early development.* Orlando, FL: Academic Press.

Davis, J. O., & Phelps, J. A. (1995). Twins with schizophrenia: Genes or germs? *Schizophrenia Bulletin, 21*(1), 13–18.

Deckel, A. W., Hesselbrock, V. M., & Bauer, L. (1996). Antisocial personality disorder, childhood delinquency, and frontal brain functioning: EEG and neuropsychological findings. *Journal of Clinical Psychology, 52*(6), 639–650.

DeNeve, K., & Cooper, H. (1998). The happy personality: A meta-analysis of 137 personality traits and subjective well-being. *Psychological Bulletin, 124*(2), 197–229.

Derlega, V. J., Winstead, B. A., & Jones, W. H. (1991). *Personality: Contemporary theory and research.* Chicago: Nelson-Hall.

Deutsch, H. (1942). Some forms of emotional disturbance and their relationship to schizophrenia. *Psychoanalytic Quarterly, 11,* 301–321.

Dodge, K., Murphy, R., & Buchsbaum, K. C. (1984). The assessment of intention-cue detection skills in children: Implications for developmental psychopathology. *Child Development, 55,* 163–173.

Dohrenwend, B. P., & Dohrenwend, B. S. (1976). Sex differences and psychiatric disorders. *American Journal of Sociology, 81,* 1447–1454.

Dornbusch, S. M., Ritter, P. L., Leiderman, P. H., & Roberts, D. F. (1987). The relation of parenting style to adolescent school performance. *Child Development, 58,* 1244–1257.

Dorr, A. (1985). Contexts for experience with emotion, with special attention to television. In M. Lewis & C. Saarni (Eds.), *The socialization of emotions* (pp. 55–85). New York: Plenum Press.

Dubo, E., Zanarini, M., Lewis, R., & Williams, A. (1997). Childhood antecedents of self-destructiveness in borderline personality disorder. *Canadian Journal of Psychiatry, 42,* 63–69.

Duchene, A., Graves, R. E., & Brugger, P. (1998). Schizotypal thinking and associative processing: A response commonality analysis of verbal fluency. *Journal of Psychiatry and Neuroscience, 23*(1), 56–60.

Dunn, J., & Kendrick, C. (1981). Interaction between young siblings: Associations with the interactions between mothers and first-born. *Developmental Psychology, 17,* 336–343.

Easser, B. R., & Lesser, S. R. (1965). Hysterical personality: A reevaluation. *Psychoanalytic Quarterly, 34,* 389–405.

Egan, S., & Perry, D. (1998). Does low self-regard invite victimization? *Developmental Psychology, 34*(2), 299–309.

Ellason, J. W., Ross, C. A., & Fuchs, D. L. (1995). Assessment of dissociative identity disorder with the Millon Clinical Multiaxial Inventory–II. *Psychological Reports, 76,* 895–905.

Ellason, J. W., Ross, C. A., & Fuchs, D. L. (1996). Lifetime Axis I and II comorbidity and childhood trauma history in dissociative identity disorder. *Psychiatry: Interpersonal and Biological Processes, 59*(3), 255–266.

Elliott, C., & Gillett, G. (1992). Moral insanity and practical reason. *Philosophical Psychology, 5*(1), 53–67.

El Sheikh, M., Cummings, E. M., & Goetsch, V. (1989). Coping with adult's angry behavior: Behavioral, physiological, and verbal responses in preschoolers. *Developmental Psychology, 25,* 490–498.

Emde, R. N. (1979). Positive emotions for psychoanalytic theory: Surprises from infancy research and new directions. *Journal of the American Psychoanalytic Association, 39,* 5–44.

Emde, R. N. (1989). The infant's relationship experience: Developmental and affective aspects. In A. Sameroff & R. N. Emde (Eds.), *Relationship disturbances in early childhood: A developmental approach* (pp. 33–51). New York: Basic Books.

Emery, R. E. (1982). Interparental conflict and the children of discord and divorce. *Psychological Bulletin, 92,* 310–330.

Erikson, E. H. (1956). The problem of ego identity. *Journal of the American Psychoanalytic Association, 4,* 66–81.

Erikson, E. H. (1959). *Identity and the life cycle.* New York: International Universities Press.

Escalona, S. (1968). *Roots of individuality.* Chicago: Aldine.

Escalona, S., & Heider, G. (1959). *Prediction and outcome.* New York: Basic Books.

Escalona, S., & Leitch, M. (1953). *Early phases of personality development.* Champaign, IL: Child Development.

Escovar, L. A. (1997). The Millon inventories: Sociocultural considerations. In T. Millon (Ed.), *The Millon inventories: Clinical and personality assessment* (pp. 264–285). New York: Guilford Press.

Eysenck, H. J. (1964). *Crime and personality.* Boston: Houghton Mifflin.

Eysenck, H. J. (1967). *The biological basis of personality.* Springfield. IL: Thomas.

Fahlen, T. (1997). Personality traits in social phobia: I. Comparisons with healthy controls. *Journal of Clinical Psychiatry, 56*(12), 560–568.

Fairbairn, W. R. D. (1940). *An object-relations theory of the personality.* New York: Basic Books.

Farrington, D. P. (1977). The effects of public labeling. *British Journal of Criminology, 17,* 112–125.

Feinstein, A. R. (1977). A critical overview of diagnosis in psychiatry. In V. M. Rakoff, H. C. Stancer, & H. B. Kedward (Eds.), *Psychiatric diagnosis* (pp. 186–206). New York: Brunner/Mazel.

Feldman, R. B., Zelkowitz, P., Weiss, M., & Vogel, J. (1995). A comparison of the families of mothers with borderline and nonborderline personality disorders. *Comprehensive Psychiatry, 36,* 157–163.

Fenichel, O. (1945). *The psychoanalytic theory of neurosis.* New York: Norton.

Fennig, S., & Carlson, G. (1995). The importance of childhood psychopathology in the assessment of adult psychopathology. *Psychiatric Annals, 25*(4), 201–211.

Ferenczi, S. (1919). Sonntagsneurosen. *International Journal for Psychoanalysis, 5,* 46–48.

Ferenczi, S. (1980). Stages in the development of a sense of reality. In *First contributions to psychoanalysis* (pp. 213–239). New York: Brunner/Mazel. (Original work published 1913)

Fergusson, D. M., Horwood, L. J., & Lynskey, M. T. (1993). Prevalence and comorbidity of *DSM-III-R* diagnoses in a birth cohort of 15-year-olds. *Journal of the American Academy of Child and Adolescent Psychiatry, 32,* 1127–1134.

Ferrari, J. R. (1995). Perfectionism cognitions with nonclinical and clinical samples. *Journal of Social Behavior and Personality, 10*(1), 143–156.

Ferri, E. (1976). *Growing up in a one-parent family.* Slough, England: NFER.

Ferster, C. B. (1973). A functional analysis of depression. *American Psychologist, 28,* 857–871.

Feske, U., Perry, K. J., Chambless, D. L., Renneberg, B., & Goldstein, A. J. (1996). Avoidant personality disorder as a predictor for treatment outcome among generalized social phobics. *Journal of Personality Disorders, 10*(2), 174–184.

Field, T. M. (1985). Affective responses to separation. In T. B. Brazelton & M. W. Yogman (Eds.), *Affective development in infancy.* Norwood, NJ: Ablex.

Fiester, S. J. (1991). Self-defeating personality disorder: A review of data and recommendations for *DSM-IV. Journal of Personality Disorders, 5*(2), 194–209.

Fiester, S. J., & Gay, M. (1991). Sadistic personality disorder: A review of data and recommendations for *DSM-IV. Journal of Personality Disorders, 5,* 376–385.

First, M. B., Gibbon, M., Spitzer, R. L., Williams, J. B. W., & Benjamin, L. S. (1997). *User's guide for the structured clinical interview for DSM-IV Axis II personality disorders.* Washington, DC: American Psychiatric Press.

Fleming, B. (1990). Dependent personality disorder. In A. T. Beck & A. Freeman (Eds.), *Cognitive therapy of personality disorders* (pp. 283–308). New York: Guilford Press.

Ford, M. R., & Widiger, T. A. (1989). Sex bias in the diagnosis of histrionic and antisocial personality disorders. *Journal of Consulting and Clinical Psychology, 57,* 301–304.

Frances, A. (1985). Validating schizotypal personality disorder: Problems with the schizophrenia connection. *Schizophrenia Bulletin, 11,* 595–597.

Frank, J. D. (1961). *Persuasion and healing.* Baltimore: Johns Hopkins University Press.

Frank, L. K. (1936). *Projective methods.* Springfield, IL: Thomas.

Freedman, M. B., Leary, T., Ossorio, A. G., & Coffey, H. S. (1951). The interpersonal dimension of personality. *Journal of Personality, 20,* 143–161.

Freud, S. (1924). The economic problem of masochism. In J. Strachey (Ed. & Trans.), *The standard edition of the works of Sigmund Freud* (Vol. 19, pp. 159–170). New York: Norton.

Freud, S. (1925a). Character and anal eroticism. In J. Strachey (Ed. & Trans.), *The standard edition of the works of Sigmund Freud* (Vol. 9, pp. 169–175). New York: Norton. (Original work published 1908)

Freud, S. (1925b). On narcissism: An introduction. In *Collected papers* (Vol. 4). London: Hogarth. (Original work published 1914)

Freud, S. (1925c). Some character types met with in psychoanalytic work. In J. Strachey (Ed. & Trans.), *The standard edition of the works of Sigmund Freud* (Vol. 14, pp. 310–333). London: Hogarth. (Original work published 1916)

Freud, S. (1950). Libidinal types. In *Collected papers* (Vol. 5). London: Hogarth. (Original work published 1931)

Frick, P. J., & Loney, B. R. (1999). Outcomes of children and adolescents with oppositional defiant disorder and conduct disorder. In H. C. Quay & A. E. Hogan (Eds.), *Handbook of disruptive behavior disorders* (pp. 507–524). Boston, MA: Plenum Press.

Friedlander, K. (1945). Formation of the antisocial character. *Psychoanalytic Study of the Child, 1,* 189–203.

Fromm, E. (1947). *Man for himself.* New York: Holt, Rinehart and Winston.

Fromm, E. (1955). *The sane society.* New York: Holt, Rinehart and Winston.

Frosch, J. (1960). Psychotic character. *Journal of the American Psychoanalytic Association, 8,* 544–555.

Frosch, J. (1964). The psychotic character. *Psychiatric Quarterly, 38,* 81–96.

Frosch, J. (1970). Psychoanalytic considerations of the psychotic character. *Journal of the American Psychoanalytic Association, 18,* 24–50.

Gabbard, O. G. (1994). *Psychodynamic psychiatry in clinical practice.* Washington, DC: American Psychiatric Press.

Galletly, C. (1997). Borderline-dissociation comorbidity. *American Journal of Psychiatry, 154,* 1629.

Gardner, H. (1985). *The mind's new science: A history of the cognitive revolution.* New York: Basic Books.

Garfield, S. L. (1957). *Introducing clinical psychology.* New York: Macmillan.

Garmezy, N. (1986). Developmental aspects of children's responses to the stress of separation and loss. In M. Rutter, C. E. Izard, & P. B. Read (Eds.), *Depression in young people: Developmental and clinical perspectives* (pp. 297–323). New York: Guilford Press.

Gay, P. (1988). *Freud: A life for our time.* New York: Norton.

Gibbs, N. A., & Oltmanns, T. F. (1995). The relation between obsessive-compulsive personality traits and subtypes of compulsive behavior. *Journal of Anxiety Disorders, 9*(5), 397–410.

Gilligan, C. (1981). *In a different voice.* Cambridge, MA: Harvard University Press.

Gillstrom, B. J., & Hare, R. D. (1988). Language-related hand gestures in psychopaths. *Journal of Personality Disorders, 2*(1), 21–27.

Gittelman, R., Mannuzza, S., Shenker, R., & Bonagura, N. (1985). Hyperactive boys almost grown up: I. Psychiatric status. *Archives of General Psychiatry, 42,* 937–947.

Glickhauf-Hughes, C., & Wells, M. (1995). Narcissistic characters with obsessive features: Diagnostic and treatment considerations. *American Journal of Psychoanalysis, 55*(2), 129–143.

Glidewell, J. C. (Ed.). (1961). *Parental attitudes and child behavior.* Oxford, England: Charles C Thomas.

Goldsmith, H. H., & Gottesman, I. I. (1981). Origins of variation in behavioral style: A longitudinal study of temperament in young twins. *Child Development, 52,* 91–103.

Gosling, S. D., John, O. P., Craik, K. H., & Robins, R. W. (1998). Do people know how they behave? Self-reported act frequencies compared with online codings by observers. *Journal of Personality and Social Psychology, 74*(5), 1337–1349.

Gottman, J. M., & Katz, L. F. (1989). Effects of marital discord on young children's peer interaction and health. *Developmental Psychology, 25,* 373–381.

Graham, J. R. (1990). *MMPI-2: Assessing personality and psychopathology.* New York: Oxford University Press.

Gray, J. A. (1987). *The psychology of fear and stress* (2nd ed.). Cambridge, England: Cambridge University Press.

Greenberg, J. R., & Mitchell, S. A. (1983). *Object relations in psychoanalytic theory.* Cambridge, MA: Harvard University Press.

Griesinger, W. (1867). *Mental pathology and therapeutics.* London: New Syndenham Society. (Original work published 1845)

Griesinger, W. (1868). A little recognized psychopathic state. *Archiv fuer Psychiatric und Neurologie, 1,* 626–631.

Grinker, R. R., Werble, B., & Drye, R. C. (1968). *The borderline syndrome.* New York: Basic Books.

Grove, W. M., Eckert, E. D., & Heston, L. (1990). Heritability of substance abuse and antisocial behavior: A study of monozygotic twins reared apart. *Biological Psychiatry, 27*(12), 1293–1304.

Gruzelier, J. H., & Kaiser, J. (1996). Syndromes of schizotypy and timing of puberty. *Schizophrenia Research, 21*(3), 183–194.

Gunderson, J. G. (1977). Characteristics of borderlines. In P. Hartcoills (Ed.), *Borderline personality disorders* (pp. 173–192). New York: International Universities Press.

Gunderson, J. G. (1979). The relatedness of borderline to schizophrenic disorders. *Schizophrenia Bulletin, 5,* 17–23.

Gunderson, J. G. (1984). *Borderline personality disorder.* Washington, DC: American Psychiatric Press.

Gunderson, J. G., Carpenter, W., & Strauss, J. S. (1975). Borderline and schizophrenic patients: A comparative study. *American Journal of Psychiatry, 132,* 1257–1264.

Gunderson, J. G., Kolb, J. E., & Austin, V. (1981). The diagnostic interview for borderline patients. *American Journal of Psychiatry, 138,* 896–903.

Gunderson, J. G., Phillips, K. A., Triebwasser, J., & Hirschfeld, R. M. A. (1994). The diagnostic interview for depressive personality. *American Journal of Psychiatry, 151*(9), 1300–1304.

Gunderson, J. G., & Ronningstam, E. (1990). *Diagnostic interview for narcissism* (2nd ed.). Belmont, MA: McLean Hospital.

Gunderson, J. G., Ronningstam, E., & Bodkin, A. (1990). The diagnostic interview for narcissistic patients. *Archives of General Psychiatry, 47*(7), 676–680.

Gunderson, J. G., & Singer, M. T. (1975). Defining borderline patients: An overview. *American Journal of Psychiatry, 132,* 1–10.

Gunderson, J. G., Zanarini, M. C., & Kisiel, C. L. (1995). Borderline personality disorder. In W. J. Livesley (Ed.), *The DSM-IV personality disorders* (pp. 141–157). New York: Guilford Press.

Guntrip, H. (1952). A study of Fairbairn's theory of schizoid reactions. *British Journal of Medical Psychology, 25,* 86–104.

Guzder, J., Paris, J., Zelkowitz, P., & Marchessault, K. (1996). Risk factors for borderline pathology in children. *Journal of the American Academy of Child and Adolescent Psychiatry, 35*(1), 26–33.

Hall, G., & Habbits, P. (1996). Shadowing on the basis of contextual information in individuals with schizotypal personality. *British Journal of Clinical Psychology, 35*(4), 595–604.

Hamburger, M. E., Lilienfeld, S. O., & Hogben, M. (1996). Psychopathy, gender, and gender roles: Implications for antisocial and histrionic personality disorders. *Journal of Personality Disorders, 10*(1), 41–55.

Hampton, W. H., & Burnham, V. S. (1990). *The two-edged sword: A study of the paranoid personality in action.* Santa Fe, NM: Sunstone Press.

Hare, R. D. (1978). Electrodermal and cardiovascular correlates of psychopathy. In R. D. Hare & D. Schalling (Eds.), *Psychopathic behavior: Approaches to research* (pp. 107–143). New York: Wiley.

Hare, R. D. (1991). *The Hare psychopathy checklist–revised manual.* Toronto, Ontario, Canada: Multi-Health Systems.

Hare, R. D. (1993). *Without conscience: The disturbing world of the psychopaths among us.* New York: Pocket Books.

Hare, R. D., Harpur, T. J., Haskstian, A. R., Forth, A. E., Hart, S. D., & Newman, J. P. (1990). The revised psychopathy checklist: Reliability and factor structure. *Psychological Assessment, 2,* 338–341.

Hare, R. D., & McPherson, L. M. (1984). Psychopathy and perceptual asymmetry during verbal dichotic listening. *Journal of Abnormal Psychology, 71,* 223–235.

Harkness, A. R., & McNulty, J. L. (1994). The personality psychopathology five (PSY-5): Issues from the pages of a diagnostic manual instead of a dictionary. In S. Strack & M. Lorr (Eds.), *Differentiating normal and abnormal personality* (pp. 291–315). New York: Springer.

Harris, G. T., Rice, M. E., & Cormier, C. A. (1991). Psychopathy and violent recidivism. *Law and Human Behavior, 15,* 625–637.

Hartmann, H. (1958). *Ego psychology and the problem of adaptation.* New York: International Universities Press.

Hartung, C. M., & Widiger, T. A. (1998). Gender differences in the diagnosis of mental disorders: Conclusions and controversies of the *DSM-IV. Psychological Bulletin, 123,* 260–278.

Herman, J. L., & van der Kolk, B. A. (1987). Traumatic antecedents of borderline personality disorder. In B. A. van der Kolk (Ed.), *Psychological trauma* (pp. 111–126). Washington, DC: American Psychiatric Press.

Herpertz, S. (1995). Self-injurious behavior: Psychological and nosological characteristics in subtypes of self-injurers. *Acta Psychiatrica Scandinavica, 91*(1), 57–68.

Hesselbrock, V. M., Meyer, R. E., & Keener, J. J. (1985). Psychopathology in hospitalized alcoholics. *Archives of General Psychiatry, 42,* 1050–1055.

Hetherington, E. M. (1972). Effects of paternal absence on personality development in adolescent daughters. *Developmental Psychology, 7,* 313–326.

Hetherington, E. M., Cox, M., & Cox, C. R. (1982). Effects of divorce on parents and children. In M. Lamb (Ed.), *Nontraditional families* (pp. 223–288). Hillsdale, NJ: Erlbaum.

Hinshaw, S. P., Lahey, B. B., & Hart, E. L. (1993). Issues of taxonomy and comorbidity in the development of conduct disorder. *Development and Psychopathology, 5,* 31–49.

Hirschfeld, R. M. A., Klerman, G. L., Gough, H. G., Barrett, J., Korchin, S. J., & Chodoff, P. (1977). A measure of interpersonal dependency. *Journal of Personality Assessment, 41,* 610–618.

Hoch, A. (1910). Constitutional factors in the dementia praecox group. *Review of Neurology and Psychiatry, 8,* 463–475.

Hoch, P. H., & Polatin, P. (1949). Pseudoneurotic form of schizophrenia. *Psychiatric Quarterly, 23,* 248–276.

Hodges, E. V. E., Malone, M. J., & Perry, D. G. (1997). Individual risk and social risk as interacting determinants of victimization in the peer group. *Developmental Psychology, 33,* 1032–1039.

Hoffart, A., & Hedley, L. M. (1997). Personality traits among panic disorder with agoraphobia patients before and after symptom-focused treatment. *Journal of Anxiety Disorders, 11,* 77–87.

Holdcraft, L. C., Iacono, W. G., & McGue, M. K. (1998). Antisocial personality disorder and depression in relation to alcoholism: A community-based sample. *Journal of Studies on Alcohol, 59*(2), 222–226.

Horney, K. (1937). *The neurotic personality of our time.* New York: Norton.

Horney, K. (1939). *New ways in psychoanalysis.* New York: Norton.

Horowitz, M., Marmar, C., Krupnick, J., Wilner, N., Kaltreider, N., & Wallerstein, R. (1984). *Personality styles and brief psychotherapy.* New York: Basic Books.

Hueston, W. J., Mainous, A. G., & Schilling, R. (1996). Patients with personality disorders: Functional status, health care utilization, and satisfaction with care. *Journal of Family Practice, 42,* 54–60.

Hurlbert, D., & Apt, C. (1991). Sexual narcissism and the abusive male. *Journal of Sex and Marital Therapy, 17,* 279–292.

Hurley, D. A., & Sovner, R. (1995). Six cases of patients with mental retardation who have antisocial personality disorder. *Psychiatric Services, 46*(8), 828–831.

Hyler, S. E., & Rieder, R. O. (1987). *PDQ-R: Personality diagnostic questionnaire-revised.* New York: New York State Psychiatric Institute.

Intrator, J., Hare, R., Stritzke, P., & Brichtswein, K. (1997). A brain imaging (single photon emission computerized tomography) study of semantic and affective processing in psychopaths. *Biological Psychiatry, 42*(2), 96–103.

Jacobsberg, L., Frances, A., & Perry, S. (1995). Axis II diagnoses among volunteers for HIV testing and counseling. *American Journal of Psychiatry, 152*(8), 1222–1224.

Johnson, B. (1995). Narcissistic personality as a mediating variable in manifestations of posttraumatic stress disorder. *Military Medicine, 160,* 40–41.

Johnson, M. R., & Lydiard, R. B. (1995). Personality disorders in social phobia. *Psychiatric Annals, 25*(9), 554–563.

Jones, S. S., & Raag, T. (1989). Smile production in older infants: The importance of a social recipient for the facial signal. *Child Development, 13,* 147–165.

Jones-Brando, L. V., Buthod, J. L., Holland, L. E., Yolken, R. H., & Torrey, E. F. (1997). Metabolites of the antipsychotic agent clozapine inhibit the replication of human immunodeficiency virus type 1. *Schizophrenia Research, 25*(1), 63–70.

Joseph, S. (1997). *Personality disorders: New symptom-focused drug therapy.* New York: Haworth Medical Press.

Joubert, C. E. (1998). Narcissism, need for power and social interest. *Psychological Reports, 82*(2), 701–702.

Jung, C. G. (1921). Psychological types. Zurich: Rasher Verlag.

Kagan, J. (1989). Temperamental contribution to social behavior. *American Psychologist, 44,* 668–674.

Kagan, J., Reznick, J. S., & Snidman, N. (1988). Biological bases of childhood shyness. *Science, 240*(4849), 167–171.

Kagan, J., Reznick, J. S., & Snidman, N. (1989). Issues in the study of temperament. In G. A. Kohnstamm, J. E. Bates, & M. K. Rothbart (Eds.), *Temperament in childhood.* New York: Wiley.

Kahlbaum, K. L. (1882). *Uber zyklisches irresein, irrenfreund.* Berlin, Germany: Springer.

Kaplan, M. (1983). A woman's view of the *DSM-III. American Psychologist, 38,* 786–792.

Kardiner, A. (1939). *The psychological frontiers of society.* New York: Columbia University Press.

Karen, R. M. (1994). Negative psychometric outcomes: Self-report measures and a follow-up telephone survey: Comment. *Journal of Traumatic Stress, 7*(1), 135–140.

Kass, F. (1987). Self-defeating personality disorder: An empirical study. *Journal of Personality Disorders, 1,* 168–173.

Kass, F., Spitzer, R. L., & Williams, J. B. W. (1983). An empirical study of the issue of sex bias in the diagnostic criteria of *DSM-III* Axis II personality disorders. *American Psychologist, 38,* 799–801.

Keller, L. E. (1996). Invisible victims: Battered women in psychiatric and medical emergency rooms. *Bulletin of the Menninger Clinic, 60*(1), 1–21.

Keller, M., Hanks, D., & Klein, D. (1996). Summary of the *DSM-IV* mood disorders field trial and issue overview. *Psychiatric Clinics of North America, 19*(1), 1–28.

Kelly, G. A. (1955). *The psychology of personal constructs* (Vols. 1 & 2). New York: Norton.

Kendler, K. S., & Gruenberg, A. M. (1982). Genetic relationship between paranoid personality disorder and the "schizophrenic spectrum" disorders. *American Journal of Psychiatry, 139*(9), 1185–1186.

Kendler, K. S., Masterson, C. C., & Davis, K. L. (1985). Psychiatric illness in first-degree relatives of patients with paranoid psychosis, schizophrenia, and medical illness. *British Journal of Psychiatry, 139,* 1185–1186.

Kendler, K. S., McGuire, M., Gruenberg, A. M., O'Hare, A., Spellman, M., & Walsh, D. (1993). The Roscommon family study: III. Schizophrenia-related personality disorders in relatives. *Archives of General Psychiatry, 50,* 781–788.

Kendler, K. S., & Walsh, D. (1995). Schizotypal personality disorder in parents and the risk for schizophrenia in siblings. *Schizophrenia Bulletin, 21*(1), 47–52.

Kernberg, O. F. (1967). Borderline personality organization. *Journal of the American Psychoanalytic Association, 15,* 641–685.

Kernberg, O. F. (1975). *Borderline conditions and pathological narcissism.* New York: Aronson.

Kernberg, O. F. (1979). Two reviews of the literature on borderlines: An assessment. *Schizophrenia Bulletin, 5,* 53–58.

Kernberg, O. F. (1982). *Paranoid regression, sadistic control and dishonesty in the transference.* Unpublished manuscript.

Kernberg, O. F. (1983, September). *Clinical aspects of narcissism.* Paper presented at Grand Round Cornell Medical Center, Cornell University, New York.

Kernberg, O. F. (1984). *Severe personality disorders: Psychotherapeutic strategies.* New Haven, CT: Yale University Press.

Kernberg, O. F. (1985a). *Borderline conditions and pathological narcissism.* Northvale, NJ: Aronson.

Kernberg, O. F. (1985b, August). *Clinical diagnosis and treatment of narcissistic personality disorder.*

Paper presented at Swedish Association for Mental Health, Stockholm.

Kernberg, O. F. (1988). Clinical dimensions of masochism. *Journal of the American Psychoanalytic Association, 36,* 1005–1029.

Kernberg, O. F. (1989a). An ego psychology object relations theory of the structure and treatment of pathologic narcissism: An overview. *Psychiatric Clinics of North America, 12,* 723–729.

Kernberg, O. F. (1989b). Narcissistic personality disorder in childhood. *Psychiatric Clinics of North America, 12,* 671–694.

Kernberg, O. F. (1989c). The narcissistic personality disorder and the differential diagnosis of antisocial behavior. In O. F. Kernberg (Ed.), *Narcissistic personality disorder.* Psychiatric Clinics of North America, 12, 553–570.

Kernberg, O. F. (1992). *Aggression in personality disorders and perversions.* New Haven, CT: Yale University Press.

Kernberg, O. F. (1995). Technical approach to eating disorders in patients with borderline personality organization. *Annual of Psychoanalysis, 23,* 33–48.

Kernberg, O. F. (1996). A psychoanalytic theory of personality disorders. In J. F. Clarkin & M. F. Lenzenweger (Eds.), *Major theories of personality disorder* (pp. 106–140). New York: Guilford Press.

Kety, S. S., Rosenthal, D., Wender, P. H., & Schulsinger, F. (1968). Mental illness in the biological and adoptive families of adopted schizophrenics. In D. Rosenthal & S. S. Kety (Eds.), *Transmission of schizophrenia* (pp. 345–362). Oxford, England: Pergamon Press.

Kiesler, D. J. (1983). The 1982 Interpersonal Circle: A taxonomy for complementarity in human transactions. *Psychological Review, 90,* 185–214.

Kiesler, D. J. (1986). The 1982 Interpersonal Circle: An analysis of *DSM-III* personality disorders. In T. Millon & G. L. Klerman (Eds.), *Contemporary directions in psychopathology: Toward the* DSM-IV (pp. 571–597). New York: Guilford Press.

Kiesler, D. J. (1996). *Contemporary interpersonal theory and research: Personality, psychopathology, and psychotherapy.* New York: Wiley.

Klein, D. F. (1970). Psychotropic drugs and the regulation of behavior at activation in psychiatric illness. In W. L. Smith (Ed.), *Drugs and cerebral function.* Springfield, IL: Thomas.

Klein, M. H., Benjamin, L. S., Rosenfeld, R., Treece, C., Husted, J., & Greist, J. H. (1993). The Wisconsin personality disorders inventory: Development, reliability, and validity. *Journal of Personality Disorders, 7,* 285–303.

Kleiner, L., & Marshall, W. L. (1985). Relationship difficulties and agoraphobia. *Clinical Psychology Review, 5,* 581–595.

Klose, D. A. (1995). M. Scott Peck's analysis of human evil: A critical review. *Journal of Humanistic Psychology, 35*(3), 37–66.

Knight, R. P. (1953). Borderline states. *Bulletin of the Menninger Clinic, 17,* 1–12.

Knox, M., Boaz, T., Friedrich, M., & Dow, M. (1994). HIV risk factors for persons with serious mental illness. *Community Mental Health Journal, 30*(6), 551–563.

Koch, J. L. (1891). *Die psychopathischen minderwer-tigkeiten.* Ravensburg, Germany: Maier.

Kohut, H. (1968). The psychoanalytic treatment of narcissistic personality disorders. *Psychoanalytic Study of the Child, 23,* 86–113.

Kohut, H. (1971). *The analysis of the self: A systematic approach to the psychoanalytic treatment of narcissistic personality disorders.* New York: International Universities Press.

Kohut, H. (1977). *The restoration of the self.* New York: International Universities Press.

Korfine, L., & Lenzenweger, M. F. (1995). The taxonicity of schizotypy: A replication. *Journal of Abnormal Psychology, 104*(1), 26–31.

Kraepelin, E. (1896). *Psychiatrie: Ein lehrbuch* (5th ed.). Leipzig, Germany: Barth.

Kraepelin, E. (1904). *Lectures on clinical psychiatry.* New York: Wood.

Kraepelin, E. (1913). *Psychiatrie: Ein lehrbuch* (8th ed., Vol. 3). Leipzig, Germany: Barth.

Kraepelin, E. (1919). *Dementia praecox and paraphrenia.* Edinburgh, Scotland: Churchill Livingstone.

Kraepelin, E. (1921). *Manic-depressive insanity and paranoia.* Edinburgh, Scotland: Churchill Livingstone.

Krafft-Ebing, R. (1867). *Moral insanity: Its recognition and forensic assessment.* Berlin, Germany: Erlangn.

Krafft-Ebing, R. (1937). *Psychopathia sexualis.* New York: Physicians and Surgeons Book. (Original work published 1882)

Kranzler, H. R., Satel, S., & Apter, A. (1994). Personality disorders and associated features in cocaine-dependent inpatients. *Comprehensive Psychiatry, 35*(5), 335–340.

Kravetz, S., Faust, M., & Edelman, A. (1998). Dimensions of schizotypy and lexical decision in the two hemispheres. *Personality and Individual Differences, 25*(5), 857–871.

Kretschmer, E. (1918). *Der sensitive beziehvngswahn.* Berlin, Germany: Springer Verlag.

Kretschmer, E. (1921). *Körperbau und Charakter* [Body build and character]. Berlin, Germany: Springer Verlag.

Kretschmer, E. (1925). *Körperbau und Charakter* [Body build and character] (2nd ed.). Berlin, Germany: Springer Verlag.

Kretschmer, E. (1926). *Hysteria.* New York: Nervous and Mental Disease.

Kroll, J. (1993). *PTSD/borderlines in therapy.* New York: Norton.

Kumin, I. M. (1978). Emptiness and its relation to schizoid ego structure. *International Review of Psycho-Analysis, 5*(2), 207–216.

Ladd, E. R., Welsh, M. C., Vitulli, W. F., & Labbe, E. E. (1997). Narcissism and causal attribution. *Psychological Reports, 80*(1), 171–178.

Lahey, B. B., & Loeber, R. (1997). Attention-deficit/hyperactivity disorder, oppositional defiant disorder, conduct disorder, and adult antisocial behavior: A life span perspective. In D. A. Stoff, J. Breiling, & J. D. Maser (Eds.), *Handbook of antisocial behavior* (pp. 51–59). New York: Wiley.

Laing, R. D. (1960). *The divided self.* Chicago: Quadrangle.

Lam, D. H., Green, B., Power, M. J., & Checkley, S. A. (1996). Dependency, matching adversities, length of survival and relapse in major depression. *Journal of Affective Disorders, 37*(2/3), 81–90.

Lambert, N. M. (1988). Adolescent outcomes for hyperactive children: Perspectives on general and specific patterns of childhood risk for adolescent educational, social, and mental health problems. *America Psychologist, 43,* 786–799.

Landrine, H. (1987). On the politics of madness: A preliminary analysis of the relationship between social roles and psychopathology. *Psychology Monographs, 113,* 341–406.

Landrine, H. (1989). The politics of personality disorder. *Psychology of Women Quarterly, 13,* 325–339.

Lang, P. J. (1968). Fear reduction and fear behavior: Problems in treating a construct. In J. M. Schlien (Ed.), *Research in psychotherapy* (Vol. 3, pp. 90–102). Washington, DC: American Psychiatric Association.

Laporte, L., & Guttman, H. (1996). Traumatic childhood experiences as risk factors for borderline and other personality disorders. *Journal of Personality Disorders, 10*(3), 247–259.

Lasch, C. (1978). *The culture of narcissism.* New York: Norton.

Lazarus, A. A. (1968). Learning theory and the treatment of depression. *Behavior Research and Therapy, 6,* 83–89.

Lazarus, A. A. (1973). Multimodal behavior therapy: Treating the BASIC ID. *Journal of Nervous and Mental Diseases, 156,* 404–411.

Lazarus, A. A. (1976). *Multimodal behavior therapy.* New York: Springer.

Lazarus, A. A. (1981). *The practice of multimodal therapy.* New York: McGraw-Hill.

Leary, T. (1957). *Interpersonal diagnosis of personality.* New York: Ronald.

Lenzenweger, M. F., & Korfine, L. (1992). Confirming the latent structure and base rate of schizotypy: A taxometric approach. *Journal of Abnormal Psychology, 101,* 567–571.

Lewinsohn, P. M. (1974). A behavioral approach to depression. In R. J. Friedman & M. M. Katz (Eds.), *The psychology of depression: Contemporary theory and research.* Washington, DC: V. H. Winston.

Lewis, C. C. (1981). The effects of parental firm control: A reinterpretation of findings. *Psychological Bulletin, 90,* 547–563.

Lewis, M., & Saarni, C. (Eds.). (1985). *The socialization of emotions.* New York: Plenum Press.

Lidz, T., Cornelison, A., Terry, D., & Fleck, S. (1958). Intrafamilial environment of the schizophrenic patient: VI. The transmission of irrationality. *Archives of Neurology and Psychiatry, 79,* 305–316.

Liebenluft, E., Gardner, D., & Cowdry, R. (1987). The inner experience of the borderline self-mutilator. *Journal of Personality Disorders, 1,* 317–324.

Lilienfeld, S. O., Van Valkenburg, C., Larntz, K., & Akiskal, H. S. (1986). The relationship of histrionic personality disorder to antisocial personality and somatization disorder. *American Journal of Psychiatry, 143,* 718–722.

Linehan, M. M. (1993). *Cognitive-behavioral therapy of borderline personality disorder.* New York: Guilford Press.

Links, P. S., Heslegrave, R. J., Mitton, J. E., & van Reekum, R. (1995). Borderline personality disorder and substance abuse: Consequences of comorbidity. *Canadian Journal of Psychiatry, 40*(1), 9–14.

Livesley, W. J. (1987). Theoretical and empirical issues in the selection of criteria to diagnose personality disorders. *Journal of Personality Disorders, 1,* 88–94.

Livesley, W. J., Jackson, D. N., & Schroeder, M. L. (1989). A study of the factorial structure of personality pathology. *Journal of Personality Disorders, 3,* 292–306.

Livesley, W. J., Jackson, D. N., & Schroeder, M. L. (1992). Factorial structure of traits delineating personality disorders in clinical and general population samples. *Journal of Abnormal Psychology, 101*(3), 432–440.

Livesley, W. J., Jang, K. L., Jackson, D. N., & Vernon, P. A. (1993). Genetic and environmental contributions to dimensions of personality disorder. *American Journal of Psychiatry, 150*(12), 1826–1831.

Livesley, W. J., Jang, K. L., & Vernon, P. A. (2003). Genetic basis of personality structure. In T. Millon & M. Lerner (Eds.), *Handbook of psychology: Volume 5. Personality and social psychology* (pp. 59–85). New York: Wiley.

Livesley, W. J., & Schroeder, M. L. (1990). Dimensions of personality disorder: The *DSM-III-R* cluster A diagnoses. *Journal of Nervous and Mental Diseases, 178*(10), 627–635.

Livesley, W. J., Schroeder, M. L., & Jackson, D. N. (1990). Dependent personality disorder and attachment problems. *Journal of Personality Disorders, 4,* 131–140.

Loeb, J., & Mednick, S. (1977). A prospective study of predictors of criminality: 3 electrodermal response patterns. In S. Mednick & K. Christiansen (Eds.), *Biosocial bases of criminal behavior.* New York: Gardner.

Loeber, R. (1988). Behavioral precursors and accelerators of delinquency. In W. Buikhuisen & S. A. Mednick (Eds.), *Explaining criminal behavior* (pp. 51–67). Leiden, Holland: Brill.

Loeber, R. (1991). Antisocial behavior: More enduring than changeable? *Journal of the American Academy of Child and Adolescent Psychiatry, 30,* 393–397.

Loeber, R., Burke, J. D., Lahey, B. B., Winters, A., & Zera, M. (2000). Oppositional defiant disorder and conduct disorder: A review of the past 10 years, part I. *Journal of the American Academy of Child and Adolescent Psychiatry, 39,* 1468–1484.

Loeber, R., & Stouthamer-Loeber, M. (1986). Family factors as correlates and predictors of juvenile conduct problems and delinquency. In M. Toury

& N. Morris (Eds.), *Crime and justice* (Vol. 7). Chicago: University of Chicago Press.

Lombroso, C. (1887). *L'Uomo deUnquente.* Bocca: Totina.

Lombroso, C., & Ferrero, W. (1916). *The female offender.* New York: Philosophical Society.

Loranger, A. W., Sartori, N., Andreoli, S., Berger, P., Bucheim, P., Channabasavanna, S. M., et al. (1994). The international personality disorder examination. *Archives of General Psychiatry, 51,* 215–224.

Louth, S. M., Williamson, S., Alpert, M., Pouget, E. R., & Hare, R. D. (1998). Acoustic distinctions in the speech of male psychopaths. *Journal of Psycholinguistic Research, 27*(3), 375–384.

Lu, Y. C. (1962). Contradictory parental expectations in schizophrenia: Dependence and responsibility. *Archives of General Psychiatry, 6,* 219–234.

Luisada, P. V., Peele, R., & Pittard, E. A. (1974). The hysterical personality in men. *American Journal of Psychiatry, 131,* 518–521.

Lykken, D. T. (1957). A study of anxiety in the sociopathic personality. *Journal of Abnormal and Social Psychology, 55,* 6–10.

Lykken, D. T. (1995). *The antisocial personalities.* Hillsdale, NJ: Erlbaum.

Maccoby, E., & Martin, J. (1983). Socialization in the context of the family: Parent-child interaction. In In P. H. Mussen (Series Ed.) & E. M. Hetherington (Vol. Ed.), *Handbook of child psychology: Vol. 4. Socialization, personality, and social development* (4th ed., pp. 1–101).

Maccoby, E. E., & Jacklin, C. N. (1974). *The psychology of sex differences.* Stanford, CA: Stanford University Press.

Machón, R. A., Huttenen, M. O., Mednick, S. A., & LaFosse, J. (1995). Schizotypal personality disorder characteristics associated with second-trimester disturbance of neural development. In A. R. Raine, T. Lencz, & S. A. Mednick (Eds.), *Schizotypal personality* (pp. 56–78). Cambridge, England: Cambridge University Press.

MacKinnon, R. A., & Michels, R. (1971). *The psychiatric interview in clinical practice.* Philadelphia: Saunders.

Magnusson, D., & Bergman, L. R. (1990). A pattern approach to the study of pathways from childhood to adulthood. In L. Robins & M. Rutter (Eds.), *Straight and devious pathways from childhood to adulthood* (pp. 101–115). Cambridge, England: Cambridge University Press.

Mahler, M. S., Pine, F., & Bergman, A. (1975). *The psychological birth of the human infant: Symbiosis and individuation.* New York: Basic Books.

Maier, W., Lichtermann, D., Minges, J., & Heun, R. (1994). Personality disorders among the relatives of schizophrenia patients. *Schizophrenia Bulletin, 20*(3), 481–493.

Malan, D. H. (1976). *The frontier of brief psychotherapy: An example of the convergence of research and clinical practice.* New York: Plenum Medical Book.

Manicavasagar, V., Silove, D., & Curtis, J. (1997). Separation anxiety in adulthood: A phenomenological investigation. *Comprehensive Psychiatry, 38*(5), 274–282.

Mannuzza, S., Klein, R. G., Bonagura, N., Malloy, P., Giampino, T. L., & Addalli, K. A. (1991). Hyperactive boys almost grown up: Replication of psychiatric status. *Archives of General Psychiatry, 48,* 77–83.

Marlowe, D. B., Husband, S. D., Lamb, R. J., & Kirby, K. C. (1995). Psychiatric comorbidity in cocaine dependence: Diverging trends, Axis II spectrum, and gender differentials. *American Journal on Addictions, 4*(1), 70–81.

Marmor, J. (1953). Orality in the hysterical personality. *Journal of the American Psychoanalytic Association, 1,* 656–671.

Marshall, J. R. (1996). Comorbidity and its effects on panic disorder. *Bulletin of the Menninger Clinic, 60*(2, Suppl. A), A39–A54.

Mash, E. J., & Johnston, C. (1982). A comparison of the mother-child interactions of younger and older hyperactive and normal children. *Child Development, 53,* 1371–1381.

Maslow, A. (1968). *Toward a psychology of being* (2nd ed.). New York: D. Van Nostrand.

Masterson, J. F. (1972). *Treatment of the borderline adolescent: A developmental approach.* New York: Wiley.

Masterson, J. F. (1976). *Psychotherapy of the borderline adult: A developmental approach.* New York: Brunner/Mazel.

Masterson, J. F., & Rinsley, D. (1975). The borderline syndrome: The role of the mother in the genesis and psychic structure of the borderline personality. *International Journal of Psychoanalysis, 56,* 163–177.

Maudsley, H. (1874). *Responsibility in mental disease.* London: King.

McBurnett, K., Lahey, B. B., Rathouz, P. J., & Loeber, R. (2000). Low salivary control and persistent aggression in boys referred for disruptive behavior. *Archives of General Psychiatry, 57,* 38–43.

McCreadie, R. G. (1997). The Nithsdale schizophrenia surveys 16: Breast-feeding and schizophrenia: Preliminary results and hypotheses. *British Journal of Psychiatry, 170*(4), 334–337.

McKay, D., Neziroglu, F., Todaro, J., & Yaryura-Tobias, J. A. (1996). Changes in personality disorders following behavior therapy for obsessive-compulsive disorder. *Journal of Anxiety Disorders, 10*(1), 47–57.

McMahon, R. C., Malow, R. M., & Penedo, F. J. (1998). Substance abuse problems, psychiatric severity, and HIV risk in Millon clinical multiaxial inventory–II personality subgroups. *Psychology of Addictive Behaviors, 12*(1), 3–13.

McMahon, R. C., & Richards, S. K. (1996). Profile patterns, consistency and change in the Millon clinical multiaxial inventory–II in cocaine abusers. *Journal of Clinical Psychology, 52*(1), 75–79.

McWilliams, N. (1994). *Psychoanalytic diagnosis.* New York: Guilford Press.

Mead, M. (1928). *Coming of age in Samoa.* New York: Blue Ribbon Press.

Meehl, P. E. (1962). Schizotaxia, schizotypy, schizophrenia. *American Psychologist, 17*(12), 827–838.

Meehl, P. E. (1990a). Schizotaxia as an open concept. In A. I. Rabin, R. Zucker, R. Emmons, & S. Frank (Eds.), *Studying persons and lives* (pp. 248–303). New York: Springer.

Meehl, P. E. (1990b). Toward an integrated theory of schizotaxia, schizotypy, and schizophrenia. *Journal of Personality Disorders, 4,* 1–99.

Meloy, J. R. (1996). Pseudonecrophilia following spousal homicide. *Journal of Forensic Sciences, 41,* 706–708.

Menninger, K. (1930). *The human mind.* New York: Alfred Knopf.

Menninger, K. (1940). Character disorders. In J. F. Brown (Ed.), *The psychodynamics of abnormal behavior* (pp. 384–403). New York: McGraw-Hill.

Meyer, A. (1908). The problem of mental reaction-types, mental causes and diseases. *Psychological Bulletin, 5,* 245–261.

Michelsson, K., Rinne, A., & Paajanen, S. (1990). Crying, feeding and sleeping patterns in 1- to 12-month-old infants. *Child Care, Health, and Development, 16,* 99–111.

Miliora, M. T. (1995). The dialectics of historical fantasy: The ideology of George Lincoln Rockwell. *Psychohistory Review, 23*(3), 259–281.

Miller, B. L., Darby, A., Benson, D. F., & Cummings, J. L. (1997). Aggressive, socially disruptive and antisocial behavior associated with fronto-temporal dementia. *British Journal of Psychiatry, 170*(2), 150–155.

Millon, T. (1969). *Modern psychopathology: A biosocial approach to maladaptive learning and functioning.* Philadelphia: Saunders.

Millon, T. (1981). *Disorders of personality: DSM-III Axis II.* New York: Wiley.

Millon, T. (1987). On the genesis and prevalence of the borderline personality disorder: A social learning thesis. *Journal of Personality Disorders, 1,* 354–372.

Millon, T. (1990). *Toward a new personology: An evolutionary model.* New York: Wiley.

Millon, T. (1993). *Millon Adolescent Clinical Inventory (MACI) Manual.* Minneapolis, MN: National Computer Systems.

Millon, T. (1997). *The Millon inventories.* New York: Guilford Press.

Millon, T. (with Grossman, S., Meagher, S., Millon, C., & Everly, G.). (1999). *Personality-guided therapy.* New York: Wiley.

Millon, T. (2003). It's time to rework the blueprints: Building a science for clinical psychology. *American Psychologist, 58,* 949–961.

Millon, T., Blaney, P. H., & Davis, R. D. (Eds.). (1999). *Oxford textbook of psychology.* New York: Oxford University Press.

Millon, T., & Davis, R. D. (1996). *Disorders of personality: DSM-IV and beyond* (2nd ed.). New York: Wiley.

Millon, T., Davis, R. D., & Millon, C. (1996). *The Millon clinical multiaxial inventory–III manual.* Minneapolis, MN: National Computer System.

Millon, T., Simonsen, E., Birkit-Smith, M., & Davis, R. D. (Eds.). (1999). *Psychopathy: Antisocial, criminal, and violent behavior.* New York: Guilford Press.

Millon, T., Tringone, R., Millon, C., & Grossman, S. (in press). *Millon Pre-Adolescent Clinical Inventory (M-PACI) manual.* Minneapolis, MN: NCS Pearson Assessments.

Millon, T., Weiss, L., Millon, C., & Davis, R. (1994). *MIPS: Millon index of personality styles manual.* San Antonio, TX: Psychological Corporation.

Mischel, W. (1970). Sex-typing and socialization. In P. H. Mussen (Ed.), *Carmichael's manual of child psychology* (3rd ed., pp. 3–72). New York: Wiley.

Moffitt, T. E. (1993). Adolescence-limited and life-course-persistent antisocial behavior: A developmental taxonomy. *Psychological Review, 100,* 674–701.

Morey, L. (1992). *The personality assessment inventory.* Odessa, FL: Psychological Assessment Resources.

Morey, L. C., Waugh, M. H., & Blashfield, R. K. (1985). MMPI scales for *DSM-III* personality disorders: Their derivation and correlates. *Journal of Personality Assessment, 49*(3), 245–251.

Morgenstern, J., Langenbucher, J., Labouvie, E. W., & Miller, K. J. (1997). The comorbidity of alcoholism and personality disorders in a clinical population: Prevalence rates and relation to alcohol typology variables. *Journal of Abnormal Psychology, 106,* 74–84.

Morrison, A. P. (1986). Introduction. In A. P. Morrison (Ed.), *Essential papers on narcissism* (pp. 1–12). New York: New York University Press.

Morrison, J. R. (1980). Adult psychiatric disorders in parents of hyperactive children. *American Journal of Psychiatry, 137,* 825–827.

Moss, H. B., Yao, J. K., & Panzak, G. L. (1990). Serotonergic responsivity and behavioral dimensions in antisocial personality disorder with substance abuse. *Biological Psychiatry, 28*(4), 325–338.

Mueller, E., & Silverman, N. (1989). Peer relations in maltreated children. In D. Cicchetti & V. Carlson (Eds.), *Child maltreatment: Theory and research on the causes and consequences of child abuse and neglect* (pp. 529–578). New York: Cambridge University Press.

Mulder, R. T., Wells, J. E., Joyce, P. R., & Bushnell, J. A. (1994). Antisocial women. *Journal of Personality Disorders, 8,* 279–287.

Murphy, L. B. (Ed.). (1962). *The widening world of childhood.* New York: Basic Books.

Murphy, L. B., & Moriarty, A. E. (1976). *Vulnerability, coping, and growth.* New Haven, CT: Yale University Press.

Murray, H. A. (Ed.). (1938). *Explorations in personality.* New York: Oxford University Press.

Nelsen, J. (1995). Varieties of narcissistically vulnerable couples: Dynamics and practice implications. *Clinical Social Work Journal, 23*(1), 59–70.

Nestadt, G., Romanoski, A. J., Samuels, J. F., Folstein, M. F., & McHugh, P. R. (1992). The relationship between personality and *DSM-III* Axis I disorders in the population: Results from an epidemiological survey. *American Journal of Psychiatry, 149*(9), 1228–1233.

New, A. S., Trestman, R. L., Mitropoulou, V., & Benishay, D. S. (1997). Serotonergic function and self-injurious behavior in personality disorder patients. *Psychiatry Research, 69*(1), 17–26.

Neziroglu, F., McKay, D., Todaro, J., & Yaryura-Tobias, J. A. (1996). Effect of cognitive behavior therapy on persons with body dysmorphic disorder and comorbid Axis II diagnosis. *Behavior Therapy, 27*(1), 67–77.

Nigg, J. T., & Goldsmith, H. H. (1994). Genetics of personality disorders: Perspectives from personality and psychopathology research. *Psychological Bulletin, 115*(3), 346–380.

Nurnberg, H. G., Rifkin, A., & Doddi, S. (1993). A systematic assessment of the comorbidity of *DSM-III-R* personality disorders in alcoholic outpatients. *Comprehensive Psychiatry, 34*(6), 447–454.

Okonogi, K. (1996). Ajase complex and Japanese mentality. *Journal of Clinical Geropsychology, 2*(2), 93–101.

Oldham, J. M., & Morris, L. B. (1990). *The personality self-portrait.* New York: Bantam Books.

Oldham, J. M., & Morris, L. B. (1995). *The new personality self-portrait: Why You Think, Work, Love and Act the Way You Do.* New York: Bantam Books.

Olin, J. T., Schneider, L. S., & Kaser-Boyd, N. (1996). Associating personality pathology with emotional distress in caregivers of patients with Alzheimer's disease. *Journal of Clinical Geropsychology, 2*(2), 93–101.

Olin, S., Raine, A., Cannon, T., Parnas, J., Schulsinger, F., & Mednick, S. (1997). Childhood behavior precursors of schizotypal personality disorder. *Schizophrenia Bulletin, 23*(1), 93–103.

Ono, Y., Yoshimura, K., Sueoka, R., Yamauchi, K., Mizushima, H., Momose, T., et al. (1996). Avoidant personality disorder and taijin kyoufu: Sociocultural implications of the WHO/ADAMHA international study of personality disorder in Japan. *Acta Psychiatrica Scandinavica, 93,* 172–176.

Osofsky, J. D., & Danzger, B. (1974). Relationships between neonatal characteristics and mother-infant interaction. *Developmental Psychology, 10,* 124–130.

Overholser, J. C. (1991). Categorical assessment of the dependent personality disorder in depressed inpatients. *Journal of Personality Disorders, 5,* 243–255.

Pajer, K. A. (1998). What happens to "bad" girls: A review of the adult outcomes of antisocial adolescent girls. *American Journal of Psychiatry, 155,* 862–870.

Pajer, K., Gardner, W., Rubin, R. T., Perel, J., & Neal, S. (2001). Decreased cortisol levels in adolescent girls with conduct disorder. *Archives of General Psychiatry, 58,* 297–302.

Pantony, K. L., & Caplan, P. (1991). Delusional dominating personality disorder: A modest proposal for identifying some consequences of rigid masculine socialization. *Canadian Psychology, 32,* 120–133.

Papousek, H., & Papousek, M. (1975). Cognitive aspects of preverbal social interaction between human infants and adults. In R. Porter & M. O'Conner (Eds.), *Parent-infant interaction* (pp. 241–260). Amsterdam: Elsevier.

Paris, J. (1994a). *Borderline personality disorder: A multidimensional approach.* Washington, DC: American Psychiatric Press.

Paris, J. (1994b). The etiology of borderline personality disorder: A biopsychosocial approach. *Psychiatry: Interpersonal and Biological Processes, 57*(4), 316–325.

Park, S., & Schoppe, S. (1997). Olfactory identification deficit in relation to schizotypy. *Schizophrenia Research, 26*(2/3), 191–197.

Parker, G. (1983). *Parental overprotection: A risk factor in psychosocial development.* New York: Grune & Stratton.

Patterson, G. R. (1977). Accelerating stimuli for two classes of coercive behaviors. *Journal of Abnormal Child Psychology, 5,* 335–350.

Patterson, G. R. (1982). *Coercive family process.* Eugene, OR: Castalia.

Peck, M. S. (1983). *People of the lie: The hope for healing human evil.* New York: Simon & Schuster.

Perkins, D., Davidson, E., Leserman, J., Liao, D., & Evans, D. (1993). Personality disorder in patients infected with HIV: A controlled study with implications for clinical care. *American Journal of Psychiatry, 150*(2), 309–315.

Pfohl, B., Blum, N., & Zimmerman, M. (1997). *Structured interview for* DSM-IV *personality (SIDP-IV).* Washington, DC: American Psychiatric Press.

Piaget, J. (1926). *The language and thought of the child.* New York: Harcourt Brace.

Piaget, J. (1954). *The construction of reality in the child.* New York: Basic Books.

Pinel, P. (1801). *Traite medico-philosophique sur l'alienation mentale.* Paris: Richard, Cailleet Ravier.

Pinel, P. (1806). *A treatise on insanity* (D. Davis, Trans.). New York: Hafner.

Plomin, R. (1990). The role of inheritance in behavior. *Science, 248,* 183–188.

Plomin, R., DeFries, J. C., & McClearn, G. E. (1990). *Behavioral genetics: A primer* (2nd ed.). New York: Freeman.

Plomin, R., & Dunn, J. (Eds.). (1986). *The study of temperament: Changes, continuities, and challenge.* Hillsdale, NJ: Erlbaum.

Pretzer, J. L., & Beck, A. T. (1996). A cognitive theory of personality disorders. In J. F. Clarkin & M. F. Lenzenweger (Eds.), *Major theories of personality disorder* (pp. 36–105). New York: Guilford Press.

Prichard, J. C. (1835). *A treatise on insanity.* London: Sherwood, Gilbert and Piper.

Pulver, S. (1970). Narcissism: The term and the concept. *Journal of the American Psychoanalytic Association, 18,* 319–341.

Purves, D., & Lichtman, J. W. (1985). *Principles of neural development.* Sunderland, MA: Sinauer.

Quay, H. C. (1965). Psychopathic personality as pathological stimulus seeking. *American Journal of Psychiatry, 122,* 180–183.

Rado, S. (1956). Schizotypal organization: Preliminary report on a clinical study of schizophrenia. In S. Rado & G. E. Eaniels (Eds.), *Changing concepts of psychoanalytic medicine* (pp. 225–236). New York: Grune & Stratton.

Rado, S. (1959). Obsessive behavior. In S. Arieti (Ed.), *American handbook of psychiatry* (Vol. 1). New York: Basic Books.

Rado, S. (1969). *Adaptational psychodynamics.* New York: Science House.

Raine, A., & Lencz, T. (1995). Conceptual and theoretical issues in schizotypal personality research. In A. Raine, T. Lencz, & S. A. Mednick (Eds.), *Schizotypal personality* (pp. 1–18). Cambridge, England: Cambridge University Press.

Ramsey, A., Watson, P. J., Biderman, M. D., & Reeves, A. L. (1996). Self-reported narcissism and perceived parental permissiveness and authoritarianism. *Journal of Genetic Psychology, 157*(2), 227–238.

Reich, A. (1960). Pathologic forms of self-esteem regulation. *Psychoanalytic Study of the Child, 15,* 215–232.

Reich, J. (1987). Prevalence of *DSM-III-R* self-defeating (masochistic) personality disorder in normal and outpatient populations. *Journal of Nervous and Mental Diseases, 175,* 52–54.

Reich, J. (2000). The relationship of social phobia to avoidant personality disorder: A proposal to reclassify avoidant personality disorder based on clinical empirical findings. *European Psychiatry, 15,* 151–159.

Reich, J., & Braginsky, Y. (1994). Paranoid personality traits in a panic disorder population: A pilot study. *Comprehensive Psychiatry, 35*(4), 260–264.

Reich, J., Noyes, R., Coryell, W., & Gorman, T. W. (1986). The effect of state anxiety on personality measurement. *American Journal of Psychiatry, 143,* 760–763.

Reich, W. (1949). *Character analysis* (3rd ed.). New York: Farrar, Straus and Giroux.

Reid, J. B., Patterson, G. R., & Loeber, R. (1982). The abused child: Victim, instigator, or innocent bystander. In D. Bernstein (Ed.), *Response, structure and organization.* Lincoln: University of Nebraska Press.

Reisman, D. (1950). Authority and liberty in Freud's thought. *University of Chicago Round Table, 638,* 20–32.

Reiss, D. (1981). *The families' construction of reality.* Cambridge, MA: Harvard University Press.

Rettew, D. C. (2000). Avoidant personality disorder, generalized social phobia, and shyness: Putting the personality back into personality disorders. *Harvard Review of Psychiatry, 8,* 283–297.

Ribot, T. (1890). *Psychologie des sentiments.* Paris: Delahaye and Lecrosnier.

Rienzi, B. M., Forquera, J., & Hitchcock, D. L. (1995). Gender stereotypes for proposed *DSM-IV* negativistic, depressive, narcissistic, and dependent personality disorders. *Journal of Personality Disorders, 9*(1), 49–55.

Rienzi, B. M., & Scrams, D. J. (1991). Gender stereotypes for paranoid, antisocial, compulsive, dependent, and histrionic personality disorders. *Psychological Reports, 69,* 976–978.

Robins, L., & Rutter, M. (Eds.). (1990). *Straight and devious pathways from childhood to adulthood.* New York: Cambridge University Press.

Robins, L. N. (1986). The consequence of conduct disorder in girls. In D. Olweus, J. Block, & M. Radke-Yarrow (Eds.), *Development of antisocial and prosocial behavior: Research, theories, and issues* (pp. 382–414). Orlando, FL: Academic.

Rodrigues, T. A., & Del Porto, J. A. (1995). Comorbidity of obsessive-compulsive disorder and personality disorders: A Brazilian controlled study. *Psychopathology, 28*(6), 322–329.

Roitman, S. E. L., Cornblatt, B. A., Bergman, A., & Obuchowski, M. (1997). Attentional functioning in schizotypal personality disorder. *American Journal of Psychiatry, 154*(5), 655–660.

Roland, A. (1992). *In search of the self in India and Japan: Toward a cross-cultural psychology.* Delhi, India: Ajanta.

Ronningstam, E. (1996). Pathological narcissism and narcissistic personality disorder in Axis I disorders. *Harvard Review of Psychiatry, 3,* 326–340.

Ronningstam, E., Gunderson, J., & Lyons, M. (1995). Changes in pathological narcissism. *American Journal of Psychiatry, 152*(2), 253–257.

Rosen, K. V., & Tallis, F. (1995). Investigation into the relationship between personality traits and OCD. *Behavior Research and Therapy, 33*(4), 445–450.

Rosenfeld, H. (1964). On the psychopathology of narcissism. *International Journal of Psychoanalysis, 45,* 332–337.

Rosengren, K., Kalish, C., Hickling, A., & Gelman, S. (1994). Exploring the relation between preschool children's magical beliefs and causal thinking. *British Journal of Developmental Psychology, 12*(1), 69–82.

Rost, K. M., Akins, R. N., Brown, F. W., & Smith, G. R. (1992). The comorbidity of *DSM-III-R* personality disorders in somatization disorder. *General Hospital Psychiatry, 14*(5), 322–326.

Roth, R. M., & Baribeau, J. (1997). Gender and schizotypal personality features. *Personality and Individual Difference, 22,* 411–416.

Rothschild, B., Dimson, C., Storaasli, R., & Clapp, L. (1997). Personality profiles of veterans entering treatment for domestic violence. *Journal of Personality Disorders, 12*(3), 259–274.

Rushton, J. P. (1985). Differential K theory: The sociobiology of individual and group differences. *Personality and Individual Differences, 6,* 441–452.

Russ, M., Clark, W., Cross, L., Kemperman, I., Kakuma, T., & Harrison, K. (1996). Pain and self-injury in borderline patients: Sensory decision theory, coping strategies, and locus of control. *Psychiatry Research, 63*(1), 57–65.

Rutter, M., & Giller, H. (1983). *Juvenile delinquency: Trends and perspectives.* Hammondsworth, England: Penguin.

Sabo, A. (1997). Etiological significance of associations between childhood trauma and borderline personality disorder: Conceptual and clinical implications. *Journal of Personality Disorders, 11*(1), 50–57.

Salzman, L. (1985). *Treatment of the obsessive personality.* New York: Aronson.

Sankowsky, D. (1995). The charismatic leader as narcissist: Understanding the abuse of power. *Organizational Dynamics, 23*(4), 57–71.

Schmideberg, M. (1947). The treatment of psychopaths and borderline patients. *American Journal of Psychotherapy, 1,* 45–55.

Schmideberg, M. (1959). The borderline patient. In S. Arieti (Ed.), *American handbook of psychiatry* (Vol. 1, pp. 398–416). New York: Basic Books.

Schneider, K. (1950). *Psychopathic personalities* (9th ed.). London: Cassell. (Original work published 1923)

Schroeder, M. L., Wormworth, J. A., & Livesley, W. J. (1992). Dimensions of personality disorder and their relationships to the Big Five dimensions of personality. *Psychological Assessment, 4*(1), 47–53.

Schwartz, D., Dodge, K. A., & Coie, J. D. (1993). The emergence of chronic peer victimization in boys' play groups. *Child Development, 64,* 1755–1772.

Searles, H. (1956). The psychodynamics of vengefulness. *Psychiatry, 19,* 31–39.

Sears, R. R. (1972). Attachment, dependency, and frustration. In J. L. Gerwirtz (Ed.), *Attachment and dependency* (pp. 1–27). New York: Wiley.

Sears, R. R., Maccoby, E. E, & Levin, H. (1957). *Patterns of child-rearing.* Evanston, IL: Row, Peterson.

Shaefer, E. S. (1965). Configurational analysis of children's reports of parent behavior. *Journal of Consulting Psychology, 29,* 552–557.

Shainess, N. (1987). Masochism or self-defeating personality? *Journal of Personality Disorders, 1*(2), 174–177.

Shapiro, D. (1965). *Neurotic styles.* New York: Basic Books.

Shapiro, D. (1981). *Autonomy and rigid character.* New York: Basic Books.

Shea, M., & Hirschfeld, R. (1996). Chronic mood disorder and depressive personality. *Psychiatric Clinics of North America, 19*(1), 103–120.

Sheldon, W. H. (with Stevens, S. S.). (1942). *The varieties of temperament: A psychologist of constitutional differences.* New York: Harper.

Sherman, Y. (1995). Depressive personality disorder. *Journal of Clinical Psychiatry, 56*(6), 266.

Siever, L. J. (1992). Schizophrenia spectrum personality disorders. In A. Tasman & M. B. Riba (Eds.), *Review of psychiatry* (Vol. 11, pp. 25–42). Washington, DC: American Psychiatric Press.

Siever, L. J. (1995). Brain structure/function and the dopamine system in schizotypal personality disorder. In A. R. Raine, T. Lencz, & S. A. Mednick (Eds.), *Schizotypal personality* (pp. 272–288). Cambridge, England: Cambridge University Press.

Siever, L. J., Amin, F., Coccaro, E. F., Trestman, R. L., Silverman, J. M., Horvath, T. B., et al. (1993). CSF homovanillic acid in schizotypal personality disorder. *American Journal of Psychiatry, 150*(1), 149–151.

Siever, L. J., & Davis, K. L. (1991). A psychobiological perspective on the personality disorders. *American Journal of Psychiatry, 148,* 1647–1658.

Siever, L. J., Klar, H., & Coccaro, E. (1985). Biological response styles: Clinic implications. In L. J. Siever & H. Klar (Eds.), *Psychobiological substrates of personality* (pp. 38–66). Washington, DC: American Psychiatric Press.

Siever, L. J., Rotter, M., Losonczy, M., & Guo, S. L. (1995). Lateral ventricular enlargement in schizotypal personality disorder. *Psychiatry Research, 57,* 109–118.

Siever, L. J., & Trestman, R. L. (1993). The serotonin system and aggressive personality disorder. *International Clinical Psychopharmacology, 8*(Suppl. 2), 33–39.

Sifneos, P. E. (1972). *Short-term psychotherapy and emotional crisis.* Cambridge, MA: Harvard University Press.

Silk, K., Lee, S., Hill, E., & Lohr, N. (1995). Borderline personality disorder symptoms and severity of sexual abuse. *American Journal of Psychiatry, 152*(7), 1059–1064.

Silverthorn, P., & Frick, P. J. (1999). Developmental pathways to antisocial behavior: The delayed-onset pathway in girls. *Development and Psychopathology, 11,* 101–126.

Simeon, D., Gross, S., Guralnik, O., & Stein, D. J. (1997). Feeling unreal: 0030 cases of *DSM-III-R* depersonalization disorder. *American Journal of Psychiatry, 154*(8), 1107–1113.

Singer, M. T., & Wynne, L. C. (1965). Thought disorder and family relations of schizophrenics, III: Methodology using projective techniques. *Archives of General Psychiatry, 12,* 187–212.

Skinner, B. F. (1957). *Verbal behavior.* New York: Apple-Century-Crofts.

Skodol, A. E., Oldham, J. M., Hyler, S. E., & Stein, D. J. (1995). Patterns of anxiety and personality disorder comorbidity. *Journal of Psychiatric Research, 9*(5), 361–374.

Smith, P. B., & Pederson, D. R. (1988). Maternal sensitivity and patterns of infant-mother attachment. *Child Development, 59,* 1097–1101.

Soloff, P., Lis, J., Kelly, T., Cornelius, J., & Ulrich, R. (1994). Self-mutilation and suicidal behavior in borderline personality disorder. *Journal of Personality Disorders, 8*(4), 257–267.

Sperling, M. (1973). Conversion hysteria and conversion symptoms: A revision of the classification and concepts. *Journal of the American Psychoanalytic Association, 21,* 745–771.

Sperry, L. (1995). *Handbook of diagnosis and treatment of the DSM-IV personality disorders.* New York: Brunner/Mazel.

Spitzer, R. L., Endicott, J., & Gibbon, M. (1979). Crossing the border into borderline personality and borderline schizophrenia. *Archives of General Psychiatry, 36,* 17–24.

Sprock, J. (2000). Gender-type behavioral examples of histrionic personality disorder. *Journal of Psychopathology and Behavioral Assessment, 22,* 107–122.

Sroufe, L. A., & Waters, E. (1976). The ontogenesis of smiling and laughter: A perspective on the organization of development in infancy. *Psychological Review, 83,* 173–189.

Staats, A. W. (1986). Behaviorism with a personality: The paradigmatic behavioral assessment approach. In R. O. Nelson & S. C. Hayes (Eds.), *Conceptual foundations of behavioral assessment* (pp. 242–296). New York: Guilford Press.

Starcevic, V. (1992). Comorbidity models of panic disorder/agoraphobia and personality disturbance. *Journal of Personality Disorders, 6,* 213–225.

Steiger, H., Jabalpurwala, S., & Champagne, J. (1996). Axis II comorbidity and developmental adversity in bulimia nervosa. *Journal of Nervous and Mental Diseases, 184*(9), 555–560.

Stein, D. J., Trestman, R., Mitropoulou, V., & Coccaro, E. (1996). Impulsivity and serotonergic function in compulsive personality disorder. *Journal of Neuropsychiatry and Clinical Neurosciences, 8*(4), 393–398.

Steinberg, L., Elmen, J. D., & Mounts, N. S. (1989). Authoritative parenting, psychosocial maturity, and academic success among adolescents. *Child Development, 60,* 1424–1436.

Stern, A. (1938). Psychoanalytic investigation of and therapy in the borderline group of neuroses. *Psychoanalytic Quarterly, 7,* 467–489.

Stone, M. H. (1981). Borderline syndromes: A consideration of subtypes and an overview, directions for research. *Psychiatric Clinics of North America, 4,* 3–24.

Stone, M. H. (1985). Disturbances in sex and love in borderline patients. In R. C. DeFries, B. Friedman, & R. Corn (Eds.), *Sexuality: New perspectives* (pp. 159–186). Westport, CT: Greenwood Press.

Stone, M. H. (1986). *Essential papers on borderline disorders.* New York: New York University Press.

Stone, M. H. (1993). *Abnormalities of personality: Within and beyond the realm of treatment.* New York: Norton.

Stone, M. H. (1997). *Healing the mind: A history of psychiatry from antiquity to the present.* New York: Norton.

Stormberg, D., Ronningstam, E., Gunderson, J., & Tohen, M. (1998). Pathological narcissism in bipolar disorder patients. *Journal of Personality Disorders, 12,* 179–185.

Sullivan, H. S. (1947). *Conceptions of modern psychiatry.* New York: Norton.

Sullivan, H. S. (1953). *The interpersonal theory of psychiatry.* New York: Norton.

Sullivan, H. S. (1956). *Clinical studies in psychiatry.* New York: Norton.

Summers, F. (1994). *Object relations theories and psychopathology: A comprehensive text.* Hillsdale, NJ: Analytic Press.

Swett, C., & Halpert, M. (1993). Reported history of physical and sexual abuse in relation to dissociation and other symptomatology in women psychiatric inpatients. *Journal of Interpersonal Violence, 8*(4), 545–555.

Tellegen, A. (1985). Structures of mood and personality and their relevance to assessing anxiety, with emphasis on self-report. In A. Tuma & J. Maser (Eds.), *Anxiety and anxiety disorders.* Hillsdale, NJ: Erlbaum.

Tellegen, A., & Waller, N. G. (1987, August). *Reexamining basic dimensions of natural language trait descriptors.* Paper presented at the 95th annual convention of the American Psychological Association, New York.

Thapar, A., & McGuffin, P. (1993). Is personality disorder inherited? An overview of the evidence. *Journal of Psychopathology and Behavioral Assessment, 15*(4), 325–345.

Thomas, A., & Chess, S. (1977). *Temperament and development.* New York: Brunner/Mazel.

Thomas, A., Chess, S., & Birch, H. G. (1963). *Behavioral individuality in early childhood.* New York: New York University Press.

Thomas, A., Chess, S., & Birch, H. G. (1968). *Temperament and behavior disorders in children.* New York: New York University Press.

Thomas, A., Chess, S., & Korn, S. J. (1982). The reality of difficult temperament. *Merrill-Palmer Quarterly, 28,* 1–20.

Tisdale, M. J., Pendeliton, L., & Marler, M. (1990). MCMI characteristics of *DSM-III-R* bulimics. *Journal of Personality Assessment, 55,* 477–483.

Tizard, B., & Hodges, J. (1978). The effect of early institutional rearing on the development of 8 year old children. *Journal of Child Psychology and Psychiatry, 19,* 99–118.

Triandis, H. C. (1994). Major cultural syndromes and emotion. In S. Kitayama & H. R. Markus (Eds.), *Emotion and culture: Empirical studies of mutual influence.* Washington, DC: American Psychological Association.

Triandis, H. C. (1995). *Individualism and collectivism.* Boulder, CO: Westview Press.

Tschanz, B. T., Morf, C. C., & Turner, C. W. (1998). Gender differences in the structure of narcissism: A multisample analysis of the narcissistic personality inventory. *Sex Roles, 38*(9/10), 863–870.

Turing, A. (1936). On computable numbers with an application to the Entscheidens problem. *Proceedings of the London Mathematical Society, 42,* 230–265.

Turkat, I. D. (1990). *The personality disorders.* New York: Pergamon Press.

Turkat, I. D., & Carlson, C. (1984). Data-based versus symptomatic formulation of treatment: The case of a dependent personality. *Journal of Behavior Therapy and Experimental Psychiatry, 15,* 153–160.

Turner, S. M., Beidel, D. C., Borden, J. W., & Stanley, M. A. (1991). Social phobia: Axis I and II correlates. *Journal of Abnormal Psychology, 100*(1), 102–106.

Tyrer, P., Casey, P. R., & Seivewright, N. (1986). Common personality features in neurotic disorder. *British Journal of Medical Psychology, 59*(3), 289–294.

Van Praag, H. M. (1991). Serotonergic dysfunction and aggression control. *Psychological Medicine, 21*(1), 15–19.

van Velzen, C. J. M., Emmelkamp, P. M. G., & Scholing, A. (2000). Generalized social phobia versus avoidant personality disorder: Differences in psychopathology, personality traits, and social and occupational functioning. *Journal of Anxiety Disorders, 14,* 395–411.

Veale, D., Boocock, A., Gournay, K., & Dryden, W. (1996). Body dysmorphic disorder: A survey of fifty cases. *British Journal of Psychiatry, 169*(2), 196–201.

Vikan, A., & Clausen, S. (1993). Freud, Piaget, or neither? Beliefs in controlling others by wishful thinking and magical behavior in young children. *Journal of Genetic Psychology, 154*(3), 297–314.

Virkkunen, M. (1985). Urinary free cortisol secretion in habitually violent offenders. *Acta Psychiatrica Scandinavica, 72,* 40–44.

Voeltz, L. M., & Evans, I. M. (1982). The assessment of behavioral interrelationships in child behavior therapy. *Behavioral Assessment, 4,* 131–165.

von Feuchtersleben, E. (1847). *Lehrbuch der arztlichen Seelenkunde.* Vienna: Gerold.

Vuckovic, N., Misic-Pavkov, G., & Doroski, M. (1997). Forensic-psychiatric characteristics of murder: Alcoholic aspect. *Psihijatrija Danas, 29,* 97–110.

Wachtel, P. L. (1983). Integration misunderstood. *British Journal of Clinical Psychology, 22,* 129–130.

Wagner, M. E., Schubert, H. J. P., & Schubert, D. S. P. (1979). Sibship-constellation effects on psychosocial development, creativity, and health. In H. W. Reese & L. P. Lipsitt (Eds.), *Advances in child development and behavior* (Vol. 14, pp. 58–148). New York: Academic Press.

Waldron, S., Shrier, D. K., Stone, B., & Tobin, F. (1975). School phobia and other childhood neuroses: A systematic study of the children and their families. *American Journal of Psychiatry, 132,* 802–808.

Walker, L. E. (1994). Are personality disorders gender biased. In S. A. Kirk & S. D. Einbinder (Eds.), *Controversial issues in mental health* (pp. 22–29). New York: Allyn & Bacon.

Waller, N. G. (1994). Borderline personality disorder and perceived family dysfunction in the eating disorders. *Journal of Nervous and Mental Diseases, 182,* 541–546.

Waller, N. G., Kojetin, B. A., Bouchard, T. J., Lykken, D. T., & Tellegen, A. (1990). Genetic and environmental influences on religious interests, attitudes, and values: A study of twins reared apart and together. *Psychological Science, 1*(2), 138–142.

Wallerstein, R. S. (1986). *Forty-two lives in treatment: A study of psychoanalysis and psychotherapy.* New York: Guilford Press.

Warren, M., & Capponi, A. (1995). The role of culture in the development of narcissistic personality disorders in America, Japan, and Denmark. *Journal of Applied Social Sciences, 20*(1), 77–82.

Watson, D., & Tellegen, A. (1985). Toward a consensual structure of mood. *Psychological Bulletin, 98,* 219–235.

Watson, P. J., Morris, R. J., & Miller, L. (1998). Narcissism and the self as continuum: Correlations with assertiveness and hypercompetitiveness. *Imagination, Cognition and Personality, 17*(3), 249–259.

Weissman, M. M., & Paykel, E. S. (1974). *The depressed woman: A study of social relationships.* Chicago: University of Chicago Press.

Wellman, N. A., Williams, J. H., Geaney, D. P., & Cowen, P. J. (1996). Schizotypy and height: Reduced height in high-schizotypal healthy men. *Personality and Individual Differences, 21*(5), 823–825.

Whorf, B. (1956). *Language, thought, and reality.* New York: Wiley.

Widiger, T. A. (1998). Invited essay: Sex biases in the diagnosis of personality disorders. *Journal of Personality Disorders, 12*(2), 95–118.

Widiger, T. A., Corbitt, E. M., & Funtowitz, M. N. (1994). No: Are personality disorders gender biased? In S. A. Kirk & S. D. Einbinder (Eds.), *Controversial issues in mental health* (pp. 32–38). Boston: Allyn & Bacon.

Widiger, T. A., & Costa, P. T. (1994). Personality and personality disorders. *Journal of Abnormal Psychology, 103*(1), 78–91.

Widiger, T. A., & Spitzer, R. L. (1991). Sex bias in the diagnosis of personality disorders: Conceptual and methodological issues. *Clinical Psychology Review, 11,* 1–22.

Widiger, T. A., Trull, T. J., Clarkin, J. F., Sanderson, C., & Costa, P. T. (1994). A description of the *DSM-III-R* and *DSM-IV* personality disorders with the Five-Factor model of personality. In P. T. Costa Jr. & T. A. Widiger (Eds.), *Personality disorders and the Five-Factor model of personality* (pp. 41–56). Washington, DC: American Psychological Association.

Wiggins, J. S. (1966). Substantive dimensions of self-report in the MMPI item pool. *Psychological Monographs, 80*(No. 630, Whole 22).

Wijeratne, C., Stern, J., & Howard, R. (1996). Self-mutilation in an elderly patient with personality disorder: Case report. *International Journal of Geriatric Psychiatry, 11,* 75–79.

Williams, R. J. (1973). The biological approach to the study of personality. In T. Millon (Ed.), *Theories of psychopathology and personality* (2nd ed., pp. 29–38). Philadelphia: Saunders.

Williamson, S., Harpur, T. J., & Hare, R. D. (1991). Abnormal processing of affective words by psychopaths. *Psychophysiology, 28,* 260–273.

Wilson, E. O. (1978). *On human nature.* Cambridge, MA: Harvard University Press.

Winnicott, D. W. (1956). On transference. *International Journal of Psychoanalysis, 37,* 382–395.

Winnicott, D. W. (1958). Primitive emotional development. In D. W. Winnicott (Ed.), *Collected papers.* London: Tavistock. (Original work published 1945)

Wolff, S. (1996). The first account of the syndrome Asperger described? *European Child and Adolescent Psychiatry, 5,* 119–132.

Wolff, S. (1998). Schizoid personality in childhood. In E. Schopler, G. B. Mesibov, & L. J. Kunce (Eds.), *Asperger syndrome or high-functioning autism?* New York: Plenum Press.

Wonderlich, S. A., Swift, W. J., Slotnick, H. B., & Goodman, S. (1990). *DSM-III-R* personality disorders in eating disorder subtypes. *International Journal of Eating Disorders, 9,* 607–616.

Yankelovich, D. (1981). New rules: Some implications for advertising. *Journal of Advertising Research, 22,* 9–16.

Zanarini, M. C. (1993). BPD as an impulse spectrum disorder. In J. Paris (Ed.), *Borderline personality disorder: Etiology and treatment* (pp. 67–85). Washington, DC: American Psychiatric Press.

Zanarini, M. C., & Frankenburg, F. R. (1997). Pathways to the development of borderline personality disorder. *Journal of Personality Disorders, 11*(1), 93–104.

Zanarini, M. C., Gunderson, J. G., Frankenburg, F. R., & Chauncey, D. L. (1989). The revised diagnostic interview for borderlines: Discriminating BPD from other Axis II disorders. *Journal of Personality Disorders, 3*(1), 10–18.

Zanarini, M. C., Williams, A., Lewis, R., Reich, R., Vera, S., Marino, M., et al. (1997). Reported pathological childhood experiences associated with the development of borderline personality disorder. *American Journal of Psychiatry, 154*(8), 1101–1106.

Zanolli, K., Saudargas, R., & Twardosz, S. (1990). Two-year-olds' responses to affectionate and caregiving teacher behavior. *Child Study Journal, 20,* 35–54.

Zetzel, E. R. (1968). The so-called good hysteric. *International Journal of Psychoanalysis, 49,* 256–260.

Zilboorg, G. (1941). Ambulatory schizophrenia. *Psychiatry, 4,* 149–155.

Zimbardo, P. G., Andersen, S. M., & Kabat, L. G. (1981). Induced hearing deficit generates experimental paranoia. *Science, 212*(4502), 1529–1531.

Author Index

Subject Index

110267

LINCOLN CHRISTIAN COLLEGE AND SEMINARY